1 9 9 5
Guide to Literary Agents

Edited by Kirsten C. Holm

WRITER'S DIGEST BOOKS

CINCINNATI, OHIO

Distributed in Canada by McGraw-Hill Ryerson,
300 Water Street, Whitby Ontario L1N 9B6.
Distributed in Australia by Kirby Books, Private Bag
No. 19, P.O. Alexandria NSW2015.

Managing Editor, Market Books Department:
Constance J. Achabal;
Supervisory Editor: Mark Garvey;
Production Editor: Richard D. Muskopf.

International Standard Serial Number
ISSN 1078-6945
International Standard Book Number
0-89879-680-6

Cover illustration by Tim Stout

Contents

Literary Agents

Script Agents

Resources

Indexes

From the Editor

Many times the author/agent relationship is likened to a marriage. A writer usually spends some time "playing the field," getting to know different agents and deciding what are desirable qualities in an agent. After some searching, one agent seems to be particularly attractive and reciprocates that feeling, and a courtship begins. If both agent and author think they've found what they're looking for, they get "hitched," and start their life together with a common goal. Sometimes that relationship stays strong throughout a writer's career. Sometimes it begins to fray as the parties grow apart, and is dissolved.

Working on this book is like planning the wedding. I start out with an overall idea of what I want to accomplish—and a specific date by which it all needs to come together. The invitations are sent out, and when the replies start coming in the book begins to take shape. Article topics and writers are matched together like bridesmaids and groomsmen. The deadline looms. Last minute problems are solved. The "to do" list gets shorter as items are crossed off, one by one. And finally, the day has arrived. For better or worse, the book is sent to the printer.

In some respects this edition represents a double ceremony. With art and photo representatives moved to *Artist's and Graphic Designer's Market* and *Photographer's Market*, script agents are more prominently featured, taking an equal place alongside literary agents. Articles written specifically for screenwriters, more detailed listings, and more accurate indexes of script subjects and formats make this edition an unparalleled resource for screenwriters.

Literary agents

The articles in the literary agent section this year follow the basic courtship pattern. We start out with a general guide to what to expect in *The Right Agent for You*. Two checklists, *Ask Not Only What Your Agent Can Do for You* . . . and *. . . But Also What You Can Do for Your Agent* help you narrow down what makes an agent attractive, and what you can do to make yourself attractive to an agent. In your search you will come up against the question of reading fees. We invited two members of Association of Authors' Representatives to make their cases for and against, in *On the Merits*. Arnold Goodman, Chairman of AAR's Ethics Committee discusses issues surrounding agents and professional ethics, with practical tips on how to make sure your agent is trustworthy. Jane Dystel discusses how she has put together a stable of clients in *Building a Client List*.

Once you have an agent, there are new issues to confront. The relationship with your agent may be intimate and friendly. It may be strictly business. But for it to work, the relationship must be based on mutual trust and respect. If your work is purchased by a publisher, then a third party, an editor, enters the picture. Agent Edward A. Novak III, writer Alan Steinberg and editor Jonathan Karp winningly present their different perspectives in a trio of articles illuminating the dark corners of this triangle.

How Things Work: Book Auctions presents the first in what will be a continuing series of short interviews with an agent explaining a technical topic. This year, agent Glen Hartley of Writers' Representatives explains how book auctions are structured.

Looking forward, Liza Landsman's article, *New Media and the Agent*, discusses changing roles for writer and agent in an increasingly computer-oriented industry. Electronic rights and interactive multimedia publishing present opportunities for writers, along with potential pitfalls. Ms. Landsman argues that a knowledgeable advocate is as necessary in this new world as in the old.

The agent listings this year contain a new feature, an idea borrowed from our other market books. Insider Reports present interviews with agents about recent sales. While the details are specific, the information is general, and adds to an understanding of how deals can be made.

Script agents

With this edition, script agents come into focus, and articles aimed directly at the screenwriter start off the new emphasis on this section. *The Ins and Outs of Working with Script Agents*, by Gary Salt of Paul Kohner, Inc., presents the basics of finding and working with script agents. David Dworski considers the author/agent relationship from his experience on both sides in *Myths, Magic and Misconceptions*. In *What an Agent Really Looks For*, Carolyn Hodges discusses the skills a writer needs to create a professional script that will attract an agent's attention. In *Pitching a Winner*, J. Michael Straczynski gives a basic introduction to what pitching is, who does it and where.

The script agent listings also are more clearly focused. Each agent was queried as to specific types of scripts they handle, from movies of the week to variety shows. More accurate script subjects are included. Agents find work for their clients rewriting others' work as well as writing their own. Under the "Recent Sales" heading we differentiate between scripts that were optioned or sold and scripting assignments.

Resources and Indexes

The Resources section, consisting of Professional Organizations, Books and Publications and the Glossary, all have significant additions, recognizing the increased presence of script agents.

The Indexes are considerably augmented as well. More agents indicated additional areas of interest, and the script subjects have been modified. Script formats are also indexed. A new Geographic Index quickly identifies literary and script agents in the vicinity.

Last minute details

So the day has come. The guests have arrived. The music is starting. The attendants are in line. A last minute check. Something old, something new, something borrowed, something . . . blue? (Oh well, skip that.) In a short while all the planning and preparation will be history. And this book will help in your search for the agent that's right for you. I hope each one of you catches the bouquet.

Wishing you the best of luck and a successful year,

kirsten campbell holm

How to Use Your *Guide to Literary Agents*

This book is exclusively for writers ready to work with a professional to find outlets for their work, whether that's a hardcover coffee table book, mass market paperback, half-hour sitcom or blockbuster movie. Your *Guide* is specifically designed to provide you with the information you need to find the most appropriate representative for your work and your career as a writer.

What's in the book

The book is divided into literary agents and script agents. Each section contains feature articles and listings. The temptation may be to go directly to the listings and start sending out your query letters. But if you've spent time writing and polishing your work until it's just right, you owe it to yourself to take the time to find the best agent.

Feature articles, written by agents and other industry professionals, provide perspectives on the author/agent relationship, as well as demystify just exactly what an agent does. The agents, editors and writers we've invited to write are all successful at what they do. Their insights come from years of experience and offer information you'll need to be successful. This year, for the first time, we present articles from several successful script agents, with tips on how to find an agent for your TV or movie scripts.

Each section opens with a brief introduction, with tips on approaching literary or script agents, and an explanation of the ranking system we use to designate openness to submissions. Next are the listings, full of specific information from the agencies themselves on what they are interested in seeing and how to present it for their best consideration. This year we've borrowed an idea from the other market books, and included several "Insider Reports," step-by-step examinations of how an agent made a specific deal happen for a book, a book with a movie, and a script.

Literary agents

Nonfee-charging literary agents earn income from commissions made on the sale of manuscripts. Their focus is selling books, and they do not edit manuscripts or promote books that have already been published. These agents tend to be more selective, often preferring to work with established writers and experts in specific fields. While most will accept queries from new writers, a few of them are not looking for new clients. Be sure to check the listing carefully to determine an agent's current needs.

Fee-charging literary agents charge writers for various services (e.g., reading, critiquing, editing, evaluation, consultation, marketing, etc.), in addition to a commission on sales. Since they are being compensated for additional services, they are generally more receptive to handling the work of new writers. Some agents charge a reading or handling fee only to cover the additional costs of this openness. Other agents offer services designed to improve your manuscript or script. However, in some cases reading and other fees can be extremely high, and payment rarely ensures that an agent will agree to take you on as a client.

Your best bet is to develop your novel, nonfiction book or script to the point at which it is saleable enough to attract an agent who makes all or most of her income through commissions. If you do approach a fee-charging agent, be sure to understand completely what the fee will cover. If you choose to pay for a critique or edit, request references and sample critiques. As with any financial transaction, make sure you know what you'll be getting before any money changes hands.

Script agents

Script agents are grouped in one section; those that charge fees are clearly indicated with an open box (□) symbol. Most agents listed are signatories to the Writers Guild of America's Artists' Manager Basic Agreement (copies of which are available from the WGA for $4). The WGA prohibits its signatories from charging reading fees to WGA members, but they are allowed to do so for non-members. Most signatories do not charge reading fees as an across-the-board policy. They are also allowed to charge for various other services, such as critiquing, editing or marketing a script.

Many agents who handle books also deal to some degree in scripts, and vice versa. Those agents handling at least 10-15% in another area, and in the case of fee-charging agents either report a sale or are a signatory of the WGA, have a cross-reference in the secondary section in addition to their full listing in their primary area of representation. Those agents handling less than 10 to 15 percent in the secondary area are listed in the Additional Agents at the end of each section.

Getting the most from the book

Once you've decided what type of agent to pursue, you can further narrow your search for the right agent in one of two ways: reading through the listings or using the Subject Index at the back of the book.

Reading through the listings gives a more comprehensive idea of who is out there and what they are looking for. It can give you an idea of relative practices from one agency to another. And if you're writing on a narrower area, that's the way to find your agent.

Another way to work is through the Subject Index. The index is divided into separate sections for nonfee-charging and fee-charging literary agents and script agents. Literary agents are further divided by fiction and nonfiction subject categories, i.e., horror fiction or military nonfiction. Subjects for scripts, such as biography or romantic comedy, are listed alphabetically.

Several special indexes in the back of the book will expedite your search. A Geographic Index has been added this year for those who would prefer dealing with an agent located in their own vicinity. The new Format Index for Script Agents will help in determining agencies interested in handling scripts for particular types of TV programs or movies. An Agents Index helps you locate individual agents who may be employed by large agencies.

Target submissions to make your queries count

With a list of the agents who handle the kind of work you create, read the listings to find the agencies that will be most interested in representing your work.

Check the number code after each listing to determine how receptive the agency is to submissions. Other areas to check are the types of work the agency handles; terms, including commission and contract information; and preferred method of submission, found under the "Handles" subhead.

Writing is not "one size fits all" when it comes to representation. Most agents are not likely to consider subjects outside their specific interests or needs, and can resent the time it takes to wade through inappropriate submissions. Consider only those agents whose interests correspond with your type of work. Study the terms to determine whether the commission and contract policies are acceptable to you. Recent sales information can also be helpful, as it provides clues to the quality of work and caliber of clients represented by a particular agency.

One reader's method

One reader devised her own successful scheme to find an agent. First, she went through the book carefully, particularly studying the categories of information given: subjects they were interested in; percentage of unpublished writers, sales, etc. She drew up a list of agents who dealt largely in nonfiction, which she was writing. She then made a chart and ranked those agents from a low of 1 to a high of 5. Agents who only took a small percentage of new writers received a 1, those who had been in business for a certain length of time received a 5, an agent that placed her type of nonfiction received a 5, and so on. When she was finished she totaled the points and ranked the agents accordingly. She queried them in that order, and signed with the sixth agent on her list.

When you are confident you have targeted the best agent for your work, submit it according to the procedures outlined in the listing. For more specific information on approaching agents, see The Right Agent for You in Literary Agents and The Ins and Outs of Working with Script Agents, as well as the introduction for each chapter.

Key to Symbols and Abbreviations

‡ *A listing new to this edition*
* *Agents who charge fees to previously unpublished writers only*
□ *Script agents who charge reading or other fees*
● *Comment from the editor of* Guide to Literary Agents
ms — manuscript; mss — manuscripts
SASE — self-addressed, stamped envelope
SAE — self-addressed envelope
IRC — International Reply Coupon, for use on reply mail in countries other than your own.
The Glossary contains definitions of words and expressions used throughout the book.
The Table of Acronyms translates acronyms of organizations connected with agenting or writing.

Listing Policy and Complaint Procedure

Listings in Guide to Literary Agents *are compiled from detailed questionnaires, phone interviews and information provided by agents. The industry is volatile and agencies change addresses, needs and policies frequently. We rely on our readers for information on their dealings with agents and changes in policies or fees that differ from what has been reported to the editor. Write to us if you have new information, questions about agents or if you have any problems dealing with the agencies listed or suggestions on how to improve our listings.*

Listings are published free of charge and are not *advertisements. Although the information is as accurate as possible, the listings are* not *endorsed or guaranteed by the editor or publisher of* Guide to Literary Agents. *If you feel you have not been treated fairly by an agent or representative listed in* Guide to Literary Agents *we advise you to take the following steps:*
● *First try to contact the listing. Sometimes one phone call or a letter can quickly clear up the matter.*
● *Document all your correspondence with the listing. When you write to us with a complaint, provide the name of your manuscript, the date of your first contact with the agency and the nature of your subsequent correspondence.*
● *We will write to the agency and ask them to resolve the problem. We will then enter your letter into our files.*
● *The number, frequency and severity of complaints will be considered in our decision whether or not to delete the listing from our upcoming edition.*

Guide to Literary Agents *reserves the right to exclude any listing for any reason.*

Literary Agents

The Right Agent for You: Where to Look and What to Do

by Kirsten Holm

Writers create manuscripts. Agents sell them. Publishers create books. Readers buy them. It's the "literary food chain." To survive, you either have to be a very big fish yourself, or have someone you trust who knows her way around the pond and can tell you who not to swim with and what not to swallow. That someone is your agent.

But even attracting an agent's attention can, at best, be difficult. At worst, it can leave you disillusioned, having spent more money than you can afford on services that won't help. For a new, previously unpublished writer, in particular, there can be more questions than answers. This article addresses the novice writer with basic information on how to approach an agent, preparing and presenting your work and what to expect in working with an agent.

Are you ready for an agent?

Before you start looking for an agent you must have a clear idea of what you want and expect from this relationship. Too many writers jump into the pool, uninformed and unwary. Taking the time to educate yourself *before* you get involved will make you feel less like a fish out of water. To have a successful relationship with an agent, you must be realistic about your writing and what an agent can do.

First, take a long look at your work. Is it appropriate for an agent to handle this material, or would it be more effective to market it yourself? Agents do not represent poetry, magazine articles or short stories. Most do not handle material suitable for academic or small presses. The commission earned could not justify the time spent submitting these works. Those who do take on such material generally represent authors on larger projects first, and will take on these smaller items only as a favor to their clients.

Do not look for an agent with only a good idea in your head or even a first draft in your hand. You are ready to look for an agent when you have a completed manuscript—edited, revised and rewritten—that you believe has a readily identifiable, accessible market of readers.

What is an agent?

An agent is your business representative, whose primary job is to sell a work to the publisher pledging to handle it most effectively. An agent should know which publishing houses handle particular subjects or types of work well, as well as individual editor's tastes and enthusiasms. An agent must keep up with the trends in an industry that has experienced seismic changes in the past few years.

That knowledge translates into access. An agent can get a quicker read for a manuscript because editors know each submission is backed by the agent's reputation, just as the recommendation of a friend who knows your interests will attract your attention over the praise of a stranger, however fulsome that stranger's praise may be.

However, agents are not magicians. An agent cannot sell an unsaleable property. He cannot solve your personal problems. He will not be your banker, CPA, social secretary or therapist. It is primarily a business relationship, dependent on your producing manuscripts he can sell. This is not to say that a personal friendship doesn't develop, it can and often does. But the agent is not doing you a favor, working with you out of charity. He expects to be paid from the profits of your complementary efforts.

Before you begin your search you need confidence in yourself as well as your work. You will, in all probability, encounter a lot of rejection before you meet with success. You must be able to take rejection without a word of explanation and keep writing.

In the same way, you must be ready to analyze encouragement and resist jumping at the first agent to respond favorably. It is all too common for a new writer, overwhelmed by the blandishments of a persuasive agent, to pay out hundreds, if not thousands of dollars, elated that someone has recognized at last the value of her book.

Take your writing seriously; it is the biggest factor in finding a representative. Spend the time you need to make your writing singular and appealing and it won't matter if you are writing your first work or your two hundred and first. Believe in it and yourself without going overboard. Touting yourself as "better than Grisham" or "bigger than Waller" sounds empty and boastful, and will turn an agent off before you get any further. Be prepared to work at finding the right agent, not just the first one. If you're willing to do all this, you're ready to look for an agent.

Learn before you look

Finding an agent can be as difficult as finding a publisher, if not more so. Start by reading all you can about agents and authors. The articles in this book, as well as in previous editions, illuminate different areas of the author/agent relationship. Organizations such as the Association of Authors' Representatives (AAR), the National Writers Union, and Poets & Writers Inc. all have informative materials on this topic, and are listed in the Resources section at the back of the book. *Publishers Weekly* covers publishing news affecting agents and others in the publishing industry in general, and discusses specific events in the "Hot Deals," "Rights" and "Behind the Bestsellers" columns.

There are a number of paths to take in finding an agent. Most agents find clients either through referrals or direct contact. Referrals can come from current clients or editors, recommending a writer to an agent's attention. If you have friends who have already secured agents, ask if they will refer you. Don't be offended if someone will not share the name of his agent. Some will, some won't without ascertaining that your work is appropriate for that agent, and some won't, period.

Many agents report that, surprisingly, their hobbies include reading for pleasure. Agents read numerous literary and consumer magazines and often directly contact a writer whose work they enjoy. Particularly if you are writing fiction, publication of your shorter work in the larger literary or genre-specific periodicals can attract the attention of an agent whose interests match yours.

Direct contact is often made through a query letter or proposal package. Agents agree to be listed in directories such as the *Guide to Literary Agents* so writers can learn what an agent wants to see, and how she wants to see it. By checking the Subject Index at the back of the book and studying the listings carefully, you can target those agents who specifically handle your type of work, saving yourself time and money by making each submission count.

You can also make contact in person. Agents often attend writers' conferences and seminars, looking to meet prospective clients. Usually time is set aside at the end of the conference for brief one-on-one discussions, which may result in an invitation to submit your work. We have included information on what conferences an agent attends under the heading "Writers' Conferences" in the agency listings. Even if you are not seeking representation at that time, the more you know about how agents work the easier your search will be when you are ready.

Another good way to find agents is through your own reading. If there is a published book similar to your own work, check the introduction. Writers often thank their agents (which also bodes well for a pleasant working relationship!). Another tack is to call the contracts department of the publisher and ask who the agent of record is for that title. They will have this information at hand since advances and royalties, almost without exception, go straight to the agent, who deducts her expenses and commission and sends the balance to the writer.

Making contact

Almost all agents are interested in new writers. Writers die, stop writing or leave one agent for another. In order to keep up, an agent must be on the lookout for new talent. An agent does not, however, want to be buried by complete manuscripts on topics they would not ever dream of handling. They can get very testy about this, I assure you.

Spend time learning what an agent is interested in handling. While many agents say what they basically look for is good writing, most have particular areas they enjoy. Pay attention to what they say they handle. If you've written a home improvement how-to, look for an agent who has handled this type of material before, one who has her network of editors and publishers interested in this subject already mapped out.

While some very reputable agents do not belong to any professional organizations, those who do are required to maintain certain professional and ethical standards. Members of the AAR and the Writers Guild of America (WGA) have agreed to abide by a code of ethics. We have noted these affiliations in the listings. AAR's code of ethics accompanies a list of its members and an explanatory pamphlet on literary agents, and is available for $5 and SAE with 52¢ postage. The WGA's Artists' Manager Basic Agreement is available for $4. Addresses for both organizations are in the Resources section at the back of the book.

Reading and critique fees

In deciding which agents to approach, the new writer will come face to face with the issue of reading and criticism fees. This issue is as controversial among agents as it is among writers.

Reading fee policy change

While AAR does not accept new members who charge reading fees, it permitted those members who charged fees prior to the October 1991 merger of SAR and ILAA to continue to do so until December 31, 1995. Effective January 1, 1996, all AAR members are prohibited from directly or indirectly charging such fees or receiving any financial benefit from the charging of such fees by any other party.

Reading fees are intended to cover the additional costs of extra readers that report on manuscripts to the agent. This can save the agent time and open the agency to a larger number of submissions. Reading fees vary from $25 up to $450. Often the fee is nonrefundable, although some agents will refund the fee if they decide to take you on as a client. Others will refund the fee if they sell the work. Some agents include a brief critique or report for the fee. Agents Ethan Ellenberg and Denise Marcil, both members of AAR, offer their differing perspectives on the question of reading fees in the articles *On the Merits: The Case Against* and *The Case for Reading Fees*.

The AAR and the WGA differ somewhat in their guidelines on reading fees. Effective January 1, 1996, all AAR members are prohibited from directly or indirectly charging a reading fee. Prior to that date, members who charged reading fees before the October 1991 merger of the Society of Authors Representatives and the Independent Literary Agents Association are allowed to continue, provided they comply with a number of requirements designed to protect the client. See Arnold Goodman's article *Write and Wrong: Literary Agents and Ethics* for a detailed discussion of the issue from the AAR's viewpoint.

The WGA's Artists' Manager Basic Agreement enjoins a WGA signatory agency from charging a reading fee *to WGA members*. If you are not a member, a signatory agency may charge you a reading fee. Many signatory agencies do not, as an across-the-board policy.

Criticism or editorial services are offered by a number of agents. Rarely does the payment of a critique fee ensure representation. It is up to you to determine the value of these services. The fees vary widely for these services, as do the quality and extent of the critiques. One important thing to keep in mind is that an agent who devotes a significant portion of his time to editing and critiquing manuscripts will have that much less time for actively marketing a work.

Sometimes an agent will say that a manuscript is interesting but needs work. While the agent does not offer editorial services herself, she can recommend a freelance editor or "book doctor" to you. Recently the WGA issued a rule that their signatories cannot do this. The WGA believes that, while an agent may have good intentions, it would be too difficult to differentiate those who are trying to help from those who may have a financial or professional interest in the editing relationship that develops at their suggestion. Again, you must investigate any potential editor's qualifications before you contract for his services.

Give them what they want

Once you've narrowed down who to send your work to, you'll need to put together your submission. Check an agent's guidelines and stick to them. Most agents accept unsolicited query letters. Many request a two- to five-page outline or chapter summary. Never send a complete manuscript until you are invited to do so. Send no more and no less than what an agent asks for. Anything else, no matter how politely introduced, will irritate the reader and delay any response you hope to receive.

If an agent asks for your manuscript, make sure it looks attractive and is easy to read. It should be crisp and clean, not dog-eared or smudged. The pages should be typed, double-spaced on one side of 8½ × 11 nonerasable paper and relatively free of typos and corrections. Make sure the type is dark and clear; computer printouts should be produced on at least a near-letter-quality printer.

Every submission should be accompanied by a self-addressed, stamped envelope (SASE). Some writers save money by sending a disposable copy of their outline or manuscript along with a self-addressed stamped postcard with various responses to be checked off. If you are submitting work to a script agent, a postcard can be used to acknowledge receipt of the work, but an SASE should also be sent since many script agents request a release form with complete manuscripts and will send you one if they are interested in seeing more.

Your query letter is extremely important. It must convey your abilities as a writer. It also must be short. It may be difficult to summarize a work you've become so close to, but you will lose your audience if you cannot hit the highlights and leave the agent wanting more.

A query letter should be a brief, one-page introduction to you and your work. Begin with stating your purpose—you have a manuscript and would like the agent to consider representing you. Include what type of manuscript it is—romance, psychology, computer how-to. Answer the agent's question: "What is it you want?"

In the next paragraph, tell why you are querying her. If you met the agent at a conference and were invited to submit your work, remind her. If you were referred by a client, say so. If you know of another author's work she represents that is similar to your own or that you particularly admired, mention it. Show that you've done a little research and know something about her interests. Answer the question: "Why *me*?"

Next, introduce the work. Tell the agent what she needs to know about your manuscript in one or two paragraphs. You *must* be able to boil it down to a bite-size summary that is informative, interesting and leaves her intrigued. Answer the question: "What have you written?"

Then, introduce yourself. Include personal information only if it pertains to your work. If you are the chef at a private supper club and have written a cookbook, or are a sex therapist who has developed a new approach that has revolutionized your patients' lives, announce those qualifications up front. Mention any previous publishing credits if you have them. If you haven't any, don't mention it. Don't apologize for the fact that you're a new writer. If the manuscript is good, it won't matter. If you haven't worked on it enough, the agent will know. Answer the questions: "Why did you write this? Why should I read what you've written?"

Close with an offer to send an outline and sample chapters or the complete manuscript. Some agents ask for a summary along with the query; some only want the query initially and will tell you what to send if they are interested.

Once your manuscript has been requested, give the agent enough time to read it. It will, in most cases, not be read immediately, but be placed at the bottom of a tall stack to be read in the evenings and weekends after the agent has taken care of business for her existing clients. Sometimes assistants are given the task of weeding out the possibles from the nevers and passing them on to the agent. It may seem unfair not to have the agent's full attention, but you will appreciate her focus on her clients once she is your representative.

If you have not heard back on your manuscript from an agent in six to eight weeks (check each agent's reporting time to be sure), a polite call asking when you can expect to hear is not out of order. Do not pre-suppose an antagonistic relationship and do not take it personally if your work has not been read yet. Agents are people, too. They have families, celebrate holidays, fall ill or have emergencies, just like you. Give it time. More than two to three months, however, and you should reevaluate whether this agent has the time to represent you adequately.

Evaluate an agent before you sign on

Once you've received an offer of representation, you must determine whether this is the right agent for you. There are no rules or regulations governing agents, no licensing or accreditation agencies. When it comes down to it, anyone with a phone and mail drop-off can call himself an agent. Before you agree to anything, determine if the agent is legitimate and has the experience, ability and contacts to sell your work. While you and your agent may not become intimate, a pleasant working relationship is important.

Remember you are entering into a business relationship: You are employing the agent. You have the right to ask for information to convince you she knows what she's doing. Ask for references or other information that will help you determine this. Most agents are happy to provide recent sales or editorial references. Call the contracts department of the publisher to ascertain that a sale actually was made by the agent claiming it. Call the editor and *briefly* state that you are considering this agent as your representative, and ask how the editor would characterize the agent's submissions.

Do not be won over by an impressive brochure or bullied by a dismissive attitude. Most agents are proud of their achievements and want to share them. Some agents feel this information is confidential, but may be willing to share it with writers they are offering representation to. You have the right to ask reasonable questions that will help you make a decision. Asking for recent sales is okay; asking for the average size of clients' advances is not. If you are polite in your requests for information and an agent responds with anger or contempt, that tells you something you need to know about how working together would be.

Talk to other writers about their experiences with agents. Computer services such as America Online often have writers' clubs, where you can post a request for any information about a particular agent. Writers' organizations such as the National Writers Association, National Writers Union and Poets & Writers, Inc. maintain files on agents their members have dealt with, and can share this by written request or through their membership newsletters.

One reader of the *Guide* believes that clues to an agent's personality can often show in articles written by that agent. She makes an effort to find this material, or asks if the agent has written anything she could read. An agent might even be flattered to know that you would like read *her* work. To help you with this, we've included notes in the listings directing you to articles written by an agent in both current and previous editions of this book.

Understand any contract *before* you sign

Some agents offer written contracts, while others do not. If your prospective agent does not, ask for at least a "memorandum of understanding" that details the basic arrangements of expenses and commissions. If your agent does offer a contract, be sure to read it carefully, and *keep a copy to refer to*.

The National Writers Union has drafted a Preferred Literary Agent Agreement and a pamphlet, *Understanding the Author-Agent Relationship*, which is available to members. (Membership is $75 and is open to all writers actively pursuing a writing career. See the Resources section.) They suggest clauses that delineate such issues as:

- the scope of representation (One work? One work with the right of refusal on the next? All work completed in the coming year? All work completed until the agreement is terminated?);
- the extension of authority to the agent to negotiate on behalf of the author;
- compensation for the agent, and any subagent, if used;
- manner and time frame for forwarding monies received by the agent on behalf of the client;
- termination of the agreement;
- the effect of termination on concluded agreements as well as ongoing negotiations;
- arbitration in the event of a dispute between agent and client.

What to expect when you're represented

Once you have become a client, you may have questions on what to expect. Your agent should be interested in your future as a writer. She will probably offer general editorial advice, but not all agents do. She will protect your business interests. She should keep in touch regarding the progress in selling your work. This doesn't mean notifying you of each rejection, but she should let you know on a regular basis where your manuscript has been and who has seen it.

When your agent receives a bid that's in the ballpark, she'll contact you and explain the offer. Ask her to explain anything you don't understand. She's your representative; working in synch will make everybody's role easier.

The publisher will send your advance and any subsequent royalty checks directly to the agent. Your agent will deduct her commission, usually 10 to 15 percent. Most agents charge a higher commission when using a subagent for foreign, dramatic or other specialized rights.

Your agent may also deduct some expenses, which may include postage, photocopying, long-distance calls and faxes and express mail or messenger services. You should discuss what expenses will be deducted before signing with an agency. Ask to be notified in advance of any large or unusual expenses.

An agent's job is not done when a sale is made. You can also call on your agent to handle disputes or problems that arise with your editor or publisher. Safeguarding an author's rights can be a very important part of the job. For example, agent Berenice Hoffman joined her client Judith Applebaum in a recent suit against HarperCollins over accounting and payment of subsidiary rights royalties that led the publisher to reform their subrights payment system. Edward Novak's article, *The Literary Agent: Savant, Savior or Svengali?*, gives some insights into the continuing relationship between an agent and author from an agent's point of view. Alan Steinberg's article, *Playing the Game: The Writer-Agent-Editor Relationship*, discusses these relationships from a writer's perspective. Jonathan Karp's article, *Sleazeballs, Titans or Impresarios? The Truth About Literary Agents*, presents the editor's point of view, from his position as editor at Random House.

When the party's over

Once you have an agent you may find she is not the right agent, for a variety of reasons. How do you get out of a bad relationship? First, check your written agreement to see if there are any specific procedures spelled out. If not, write a brief, businesslike letter, stating that you no longer think the relationship is advantageous and you wish to terminate it. Instruct the agent not to make any new submissions and give her a 30 or 60 day limit to continue as representative on submissions already under consideration. You can ask for a list of all publishers or production companies who have rejected any of your unsold work, as well as a list of those currently looking at your work. If the agent has made sales for you, she will continue to receive those monies from the publisher, deduct her commission and remit the balance to you. A statement and your share of the money should be sent to you within 30 days. You can also ask that all manuscripts in her possession be returned to you.

Additional information

For more information on working with agents, see the articles written by agents and other writing professionals in the Literary Agents section. The introduction to each section contains information pertaining to the agencies listed in that section and will help you understand more about the entries.

At the back of the book we've included a number of indexes. For literary agents, the Subject Index is broken down between nonfee-charging and fee-charging agents; script agents are grouped together. Subjects are listed for nonfiction and fiction categories for literary agents; for script agents the subjects are listed alphabetically. Agencies who have specified an interest in handling particular types of material are listed within each subject section.

We've also included an Agents Index, which will be helpful if you have heard about a good agent, but do not know the agency she works for. We asked the agencies to list their staff members, and then listed these names alphabetically with their agency affiliation in parentheses. The page number for the agency's listing is in the Listing Index.

Many agents are located in New York for books and Los Angeles for scripts. With computers, faxes and special phone services this is becoming less important. This year we've added a geographic index for those who would prefer to work with an agent closer to home.

To broaden the opportunities for your work, we've cross-referenced agents handling both books and scripts. Script agencies handling more than 10 to 15 percent book manuscripts also appear among the literary agents, and literary agents handling 10 to 15 percent scripts also appear among the script agents. The cross-reference contains contact information, breakdown of work currently handled and a note to check the full listing in the appropriate section. Fee-charging literary agents must report a sale or be a signatory of the WGA to be cross-referenced. Those agencies handling less than 10 to 15 percent in a secondary field continue to be listed in the Additional Agents at the end of each section.

Swimming in the deep end

Your relationship with your agent comes down to trust. In representing you, your agent trusts you are a professional, serious about your writing and able to fulfill the commitments you make. You must have confidence in her representation, in her advice, and in her handling of your book-related financial responsibilities for your relationship to be successful.

Ask Not Only What Your Agent Can Do for You . . .

AAR Checklist for Authors

Authors don't always know what questions to ask (or are too timid to ask) about the policies, practices, and services of agents. The Association of Authors' Representatives has developed a checklist of topics which can be used by authors seeking to enter into a professional relationship with an agent. It is the hope of the AAR that this will help to create a more comfortable relationship among authors and agents, demystify agent activities, and reduce misunderstandings.

1. Is your agency a sole proprietorship?
2. Are you a member of the Association of Authors' Representatives?
3. How long have you been in business as an agent?
4. How many people does your agency employ?
5. Of the total number of employees, how many are agents, as opposed to clerical workers?
6. Do you have specialists at your agency who handle movie and television rights? Foreign rights? Do you have sub-agents or corresponding agents overseas and in Hollywood?
7. Do you represent other authors in my area of interest?
8. Who in your agency will actually be handling my work? Will the other staff members be familiar with my work and the status of my business at your agency? Will you oversee or at least keep me apprised of the work that your agency is doing on my behalf?
9. Do you issue an agent-author contract? May I review a specimen copy? And may I review the language of the agency clause that appears in contracts you negotiate for your clients?
10. What is your approach to providing editorial input and career guidance for your clients or for me specifically?
11. How do you keep your clients informed of your activities on their behalf? Do you regularly send them copies of publishers' rejection letters? Do you provide them with submission lists and rejection letters on request? Do you regularly, or upon request, send out updated activity reports?
12. Do you consult with your clients on any and all offers?
13. Some agencies sign subsidiary contracts on behalf of their clients to expedite processing. Do you?
14. What are your commissions for: (1) basic sales to U.S. publishers; (2) sales of movie and television rights; (3) audio and multimedia rights; (4) British and foreign translation rights?
15. What are your procedures and time-frames for processing and disbursing

client funds? Do you keep separate bank accounts segregating author funds from agency revenue?

16. What are your policies about charging clients for expenses incurred by your agency? Will you list such expenses for me? Do you advance money for such expenses? Do you consult with your clients before advancing certain expenditures? Is there a ceiling on such expenses above which you feel you must consult with your clients?

17. How do you handle legal, accounting, public relations, or similar professional services that fall outside the normal range of a literary agency's functions?

18. Do you issue 1099 tax forms at the end of each year? Do you also furnish clients upon request with a detailed account of their financial activity, such as gross income, commissions and other deductions, and net income, for the past year?

19. In the event of your death or disability, or the death or disability of the principal person running the agency, what provisions exist for continuing operation of my account, for the processing of money due to me, and for the handling of my books and editorial needs?

20. If we should part company, what is your policy about handling any unsold subsidiary rights to my work that were reserved to me under the original publishing contracts?

21. What are your expectations of me as your client?

22. Do you have a list of Do's and Don'ts for your clients that will enable me to help you do your job better?

Reprinted by permission of the Association of Authors' Representatives.

. . . But Also What You Can Do for Your Agent

26 Guidelines for Working with an Agent

1. Don't expect your agent to do all your career-building for you. Continue making and using professional contacts, gathering information, seeking endorsements for your work, etc.
2. Be polite, straightforward, honest, and businesslike at all times.
3. Write or call your agent whenever you need to, but otherwise be patient and keep mum. With few exceptions, agents have neither the time nor the inclination for a friendly chat.
4. Your agent will write or call whenever there is news to report. If you have heard little or nothing from your agent, however, it is reasonable to call or write every four to six months to see what has happened.
5. Do not call your agent collect.
6. Once you have agreed to let an agent represent a project, provide him with the following information:
   a. The names, employing organizations, and addresses of any editors, producers, or directors who have asked to see your work.
   b. The names, employing organizations, and addresses of any editors, producers, or directors who have read and enjoyed your earlier work.
   c. The names of any editors, publishers, producers, directors or producing organizations that you do *not* want your work submitted to (if any).
   d. The names and employing organizations of any editors, producers, or directors who have already seen and rejected your project in its current (or very similar) form.
   e. Where, when, and by whom part or all of the project has been previously published or produced, if anywhere.
7. Be clear and explicit about what you want and need, especially when it comes to publishing and production contracts.
8. If there is a minimum amount of money that you must get for your project, or a specific amount you want your agent to ask for, let him know as soon as he has agreed to represent the manuscript.
9. Don't expect your agent to make decisions for you. Agents will bring you offers, answer your questions, and make suggestions, but only you can decide what to accept, what to turn down, when to ask for more, and how much more to ask for. Indeed, this is part of your responsibility as an agented author.
10. Let your agent know whether or not you would like to receive copies of rejection letters.
11. If your agent does not automatically send you a list of the people and organizations to which your project has been submitted, feel free to ask for it. Also feel free to ask for updates two or three times a year.
12. Allow your agent a reasonable amount of time to sell your work. Don't doubt the agent's effectiveness until a manuscript has received at least fifteen rejec-

tions. (If your agent gives up on a piece before it has received at least a dozen rejections, it hasn't been given a decent chance.)

13. If you are having trouble of any kind with a publisher or producing organization, let your agent know, especially if it involves money. It is your agent's job to try to straighten things out for you.

14. If you ever have a problem with your agent, write, or (preferably) call him to discuss the issue. Be honest, firm, forthright, calm, and concerned.

15. Remember that your agent has many other clients. Expect him to be responsive and helpful—but don't expect constant and immediate availability.

16. Don't let publishers or producers make an end run around your agent. If you are approached directly about a project your agent is representing, don't agree or even indicate what terms or how much money you want. Get the person's name, phone number, and employer, and pass on this information to your agent, who will take things from there. This is not only good business, it's your legal obligation. (You *may* answer questions that are not about money or rights—e.g., "When do you think you can have the project finished?")

17. If your agent is approached about a project of yours which he is not representing, he will refer the inquiry to you. He will not ask for, nor is he entitled to, a fee or commission for this referral.

18. It is not necessary to ask whether your agent would be interested in seeing further projects. Simply send each new project to your agent with a short cover letter. (But don't inundate the agent with your work—it's rude and unprofessional. Furthermore, most agents will handle no more than two or three projects by the same writer at once.)

19. When you send your agent a new project, expect a response in two to eight weeks. If necessary, make a polite but firm follow-up call after two months. After three months, unless the agent has been ill or on a long vacation, you have a problem: the agent isn't doing his job.

20. Your agent has the right to decline to represent any future project you send.

21. If you want to discuss an idea for a new project, have a business-related question, or need some professional advice, feel free to call or write your agent. Be reasonable, though: limit phone calls to 10 to 20 minutes, and don't badger your agent with constant questions and ideas.

22. Don't expect your agent to get excited about your work; from his point of view, it's just a commodity to be sold. If your agent does get excited, don't be surprised if the excitement disappears after the project is sold—or after it has been rejected a few times.

23. When an agent says, "I'm sure I can sell this project," never assume that they will—or that they won't. No one ever really knows what publishers and producers will buy—including the publishers and producers themselves.

24. If your agent asks to be reimbursed for reasonable expenses such as photocopying and overseas airmail costs, do so within three weeks. Do not ask to have these charges deducted from your future earnings.

25. If you expect to be out of town for more than two or three days, let your agent know when, where, and how to reach you.

26. If your agent drops you as a client after failing to sell one or more of your projects, don't be surprised or angry. Agents constantly take on new clients, then drop all but the most successful ones later.

From *The Writer's Book of Checklists*, by Scott Edelstein, published by Writer's Digest Books. Reprinted by permission of the publisher.

EDITOR'S NOTE: *The issue of reading fees is controversial for writers and agents, and particularly difficult for less-experienced novice writers. We invited two agents to present their arguments for and against reading fees so readers could hear both sides of the story. Knowing what a reasonable reading fee covers can help determine when a fee may be unreasonable.*

On the Merits: The Case for Reading Fees

by Denise Marcil

Do you charge a reading fee?

That's a tricky question these days for agents, publishers and writers' organizations. Why would an author choose to pay a reading fee to an agent, especially when many agents read for free? The answer is you usually get what you pay for.

The volume of unsolicited queries, phone calls, and manuscripts that agents receive is staggering. Every year, my small agency receives at least 2,000 letters, 1,000 cold calls, and hundreds of partial or complete manuscripts. I already represent 75 authors, yet more than 3,000 other writers approach me each year seeking my time, expertise and advice, and a promise of representation. They expect me to provide this gratis, while my own clients pay me. I read my clients' work and offer editorial comments and suggestions. They value my 20 years experience in the business and the service they receive, and are willing to compensate me for my time.

Yet, many criticize reading fees. Do authors without agents expect other professionals such as dentists, lawyers or decorators to work pro bono? I doubt it. The practice prevailing in our profession permits a lot of authors to take advantage of us, or at least to try to do so.

It is important for writers to understand the issue of compensation. Literary agencies work on small margins. Most agencies employ two to seven people, including the owner. Our office environments are generally hectic, and the agent spends most of the day on the phone. I don't know any agent who reads in the office. Rather, we read at home, on our own time — nights and weekends. I even read manuscripts while on vacation. Most agents I know work over 60 hours a week. It's difficult to make time for new writers.

Paying a reading fee should be considered simply a cost of pursuing representation. Writing is a business, and most writers expect to be paid for their craft. I've

Denise Marcil *is president of Denise Marcil Literary Agency, Inc., which she founded in 1977. Ms. Marcil represents a wide variety of commercial fiction and nonfiction, from romances to management books, specializing in commercial women's fiction. She has been featured in many publications including* The New York Times, The Los Angeles Times, Business Week, The New Yorker *and* Working Woman surveyed many agents about their practices with new authors. I've found that few nonfee agents actually respond positively to query letters. Most accept new clients from referrals, not queries. I've been told by many nonfee agents that, because of the time needed to read a manuscript or even a few chapters, they don't want the obligation to provide comments or criticism. They can read a few pages and stop at any point, obviating the need for a considered response.

Many new writers are frustrated by rejections with the comment, "Sorry, but it's not right for me." This is invariably the response of a nonfee agent. Writers cannot understand why they can't find an agent willing to read their work, to say nothing of selling it.

Agents, like other business people, are in business to earn money. We may, indeed, love our work, but we need to make a living from it. Certainly there are professionals who work pro bono and others who volunteer their services because they enjoy what they do and enjoy doing good. Some writers, musicians and artists are not compensated at all, or only minimally. However, all the agents I know work for a livelihood, to put food on the table.

New writers should expect to pay for at least some of the agent's or staff member's time spent in reading, criticism, analysis and encouragement, and the time it takes to type a response, file a copy and return the original. In fact, the modest fees that some agents charge do not come close to covering the actual cost of the agent's time and overhead. My current fee of $45 is only one-quarter of the cost I estimate for my time and overhead in reading and responding to three chapters and an outline. Imagine the costs associated in reading a complete manuscript.

Another option for serious new writers is "book doctors" or freelance editors. Their minimum fees are $30 per hour.

The trade-off for authors who don't wish to pay either an agent or freelance editor is that often their work can go unread.

The argument often given against reading fees is that they can lead to abuse. Some companies or individuals charge excessive reading fees, i.e., hundreds of dollars, with the promise of a critique and the implication of representation when there is no intention of representation. In other words, these people are not primarily literary agents and mislead authors.

Therefore, authors would be wise to question a fee-charging agent about what they can expect for the fee and if the agent reads material with the intention of representing it.

Here are some questions to ask:
- What critique will I get for this fee? How extensive is it?
- Who will read the manuscript? Who will write the critique?
- How long will it take for a response?
- How many manuscripts do you request each month, and from how many queries?
- How many clients do you take on each year?

If the new writer is informed, there should be no surprise as to what the fee covers. You can decide if it is worth paying for. It's your career.

On the Merits: The Case Against Reading Fees

by Ethan Ellenberg

I don't charge reading fees. I never have. Of all the dangers new writers face trying to enter professional publishing, reading fees is one of the trickiest. Rejection is par for the course; reading fees go beyond rejection and can be an actual tax, absorbing tens or hundreds or more of your hard earned money.

First, a definition. A reading fee is a fee charged by an agent to read your work. The reading fee is usually accompanied by a critique. I've seen fees advertised from $40 to $600. The theory behind the reading fee is relatively straightforward and simple. You're trying to sell your book. No professional writer, editor, agent or publisher has ever read or evaluated your work before. This is your chance to have a professional read and evaluate your work. In return, you pay a fee, just the way you would a lawyer or doctor who gave you a paid consultation.

It sounds fine, even wise. Why go through the long, laborious, ego-bruising process of sending out your manuscript before you have any sense of what it's worth or what's right or wrong with it?

Here's what's wrong with the whole reading fee scenario and why I object to it so vehemently.

First of all, who is the person reading your book? Is it really the agent or is it someone else? If it is the agent, is he really qualified to render an opinion? Does he sell at least a score of new books each year? Does he work in your genre or area of expertise? How long has he been in business and how much of his income is derived from reading fees? If "someone else" is reading, who is this person and what qualifies him to evaluate your work?

I read a lot of agent listings in all the major books. I examine the ads I see for new agencies. I listen to clients who talk about their first attempts at breaking into the business and writers I meet at conferences who tell me horror stories. Here it is, simply put: Some agents who charge reading fees are marginal agents, who at best are trying to learn the business at your expense. They may have no expertise, no qualifications, no credits and no insight into professional publishing. You might even be in danger of encountering some who are out and out crooks. You are not getting what you are paying for and you may be far better off joining a critique group or a writers' workshop at the local community college.

I'm not overly taken with even the best case scenario, which is as follows. The agent is a professional, with a strong publishing background, who sells a few dozen new projects each year. The agent is adept in the genre he is reading and personally reads your manuscript and writes a personal critique. This can work. It's possible that as long as the fee is modest, you could learn something important

Ethan Ellenberg *has led his own New York-based literary agency for more than a decade. The agency has more than 70 clients and specializes in commercial fiction, especially romance and thrillers, nonfiction books on health/spirituality, and children's books of all types.*

from this experience. What mitigates against it, even in this best-case scenario?

The agent is being paid and may well soften a real critique because of the fee. The critique is for someone who is not a client and has no standing with the agent; the easiest thing to do is to quickly put together a thoughtless analysis and get the work off your desk. A few obvious criticisms, a couple of bones of encouragement, and that's it. Editorial guidance is a hard thing to do well, and you may be getting third-rate work from a first-class agent. There is always a large subjective component to writing. The agent may simply not be the right person to be evaluating your work, whatever his skills.

I think the whole reading fee issue is an important one, on its merits and for another reason. It's important to me because I believe new writers shouldn't be exploited as they try to enter the business. The peripheral issue that it points to is the difficulty in obtaining professional advice, especially editorial advice in commercial publishing.

I don't have a good answer to that one; it's a major problem. I consider my editorial abilities one of the most important skills I bring to the table when I offer my services to a new client. I greatly regret that there are simply not enough professionals around, working in a viable system to do the serious editorial work that would help many writers. But that's the truth, and reading fees historically have not been an answer. Most agents good enough to really sell books are simply too busy to do critiques.

That's why my policy is no reading fees, ever. And no other fees of any kind to examine a work or to market it. Reading fees sometimes hide under other names, like "marketing fees" or "administrative fees." It's true that in return, we mainly use a form rejection and we cannot tell you why your work was not accepted by my agency. That's the bargain we make and I still feel it's the best one. We pay very close attention to our unsolicited manuscripts and still sign new writers from the unsolicited mail. I hope any writer contemplating paying a reading fee seriously evaluates whether they are really getting what they are paying for and whether or not it's worth it.

Write and Wrong: Literary Agents and Ethics

by Arnold Goodman

Unlike doctors, lawyers, accountants, engineers, plumbers, electricians, etc., literary agents need not be licensed. Anyone with a telephone, word processor and letterhead is free to call himself a literary agent. Neither references nor experience are required. No governmental agency keeps an eye on the manner in which agents conduct business. There are no rules or regulations. Provided one does not break any laws or commit a crime, virtually anything goes.

So how do you, as a writer, decide whether you should sign with a particular agent? After all, there's a lot at stake. When you turn your manuscript over to an agent, you are entrusting that individual with your writing career, your valuable proprietary rights and your money.

Evaluating an agent

Before signing on the dotted line, some questions will occur to you.

What kind of reputation does that agent have? What kind of relationships does she have in the publishing industry? Does she know the editors who might be receptive to reading (and acquiring) your material? How will your material be presented? Will your agent be accessible to you if you have questions? Will she keep you apprised about submissions and be candid in giving you editors' reactions to your manuscript? How skilled is she at negotiating publishing and other related rights contracts? How aggressive will that agent be in attempting to place film and television rights in your material, or in licensing translation rights to foreign publishers? When the publisher pays monies over to your agent, how soon thereafter will you receive your share? How will you know if you're being properly paid?

Many of these questions deal with the professional competence of an agent; others go to assessing an agent's integrity and honesty. Both areas, of course, are inextricably intertwined, and while it is important for a writer to get answers to all of these questions, I want to focus specifically on how a writer can evaluate the trustworthiness of an agent.

Is an agent trustworthy?

Unfortunately, there simply is no easy or straightforward way to make this kind of assessment.

Certainly, an agent will provide a prospective client with information about his professional background, commission rates, the kind of subject matter that interests him. In some instances, the agent will send a printed brochure or information sheet which addresses these subjects.

Arnold Goodman, *a former practicing lawyer in the publishing and entertainment industries, organized Goodman Associates in 1976. The agency represents adult trade fiction and nonfiction. He serves as the chairperson of the Ethics Committee of the Association of Author's Representatives.*

But very little of this is helpful in determining whether the agent is, in fact, reputable, honest, and a person of integrity.

Direct interrogation of an agent by a writer about this sensitive area is probably not a worthwhile pursuit. If you are a new writer, you'll probably be so ecstatic at having your work accepted for representation by an agent — any agent — that you won't want to upset the applecart by asking these kinds of questions.

The mere fact that an agent has been in business for a certain number of years is not, in itself, sufficient evidence of trustworthiness. Moreover, an agent is not likely to disclose in a conversation or a printed brochure that several of his (former) clients have lodged complaints about the agent's business practices, that he is *persona non grata* at several publishing houses, that he neglects to keep clients apprised about materials on submission, that he is not easily accessible, or — simply stated — that he just has a bad reputation!

Various lists and directories of agents can only go so far. Using a directory as a starting point, you need to research on your own before you commit yourself to any agent.

Researching an agent further

You may find help by contacting the Authors Guild, the American Society of Journalists and Authors (ASJA), the National Writers Union, Poets & Writers, or other writers' organizations of this kind. If you're not a member it's more difficult, but not impossible, to get assistance and the kind of hard information you are seeking. These organizations are staffed by individuals sympathetic to writers, and it's hard to imagine that your request for information will go unanswered — particularly if you are tactful and diplomatic in your approach.

Since the staffs of these organizations constantly field questions from their members about agents and the agency relationship, and deal with their members' grievances (real or imagined) about agents, they are in an excellent position to know the reputations of various agents. If there has been a history of complaints (rather than one or two isolated incidents) about the business practices of a particular agent, the staff would likely be aware of that. While this kind of information is not generally disseminated, it will be informally provided to any member who takes the trouble to ask.

Neither the ASJA, nor the Authors Guild nor the National Writers Union maintains lists of recommended agents. But ASJA does keep a list of the agents who represent its members. ASJA openly encourages its members to network with one another and share information about agents. In its newsletter, ASJA often alerts its members to specific kinds of problems or grievances which have arisen between its members and agents although specific names are rarely mentioned.

Poets & Writers publishes its own directory of agents. The organization is, however, essentially an information clearinghouse for writers. You can call the Information Center at Poets & Writers for answers to some of the questions writers have about agents. It is open from 11-3, Monday through Friday. If you have a question or complaint they cannot answer, they will refer you to people and organizations who can.

The National Writers Union urges its members to complete detailed questionnaires about the agency relationship. The NWU keeps these on file and permits its members to peruse them. Completed questionnaires are used as a resource in counselling members in this area.

The Authors Guild specifically encourages its members to deal with agents who are members of the Association of Authors' Representatives.

Association of Authors' Representatives (AAR)

AAR is a trade association comprised of more than 275 individual literary and dramatic agents. It is the only trade association in existence in the United States for literary agents. It holds periodic meetings at which common concerns and problems are addressed. Often, members are briefed by experts about developments and trends in the publishing industry. AAR publishes a newsletter circulated to the AAR membership as well as to the publishing community at large.

Membership in AAR is open to any literary and dramatic agent whose primary business is representing writers and dealing with rights in literary and dramatic material. There are, of course, reputable agents who are not members of AAR. However, to qualify for AAR membership, a certain level of experience must be demonstrated, which assures a degree of competence and professionalism.

AAR was formed in 1991 by the merger of the Society of Authors' Representatives (SAR) and the Independent Literary Agents Association (ILAA) two trade associations which had existed side-by-side for a number of years and which decided that one large powerful organization would be more effective than two smaller ones. All AAR agents must subscribe to and agree to be bound by the organization's Canon of Ethics.

AAR's Canon of Ethics

An examination of that Canon reveals what literary agents themselves believe are proper standards of professional behavior; it sheds light on what the agent members believe is the appropriate way to deal with their clients and to conduct their business.

Some basic principles emerge:

- Conflicts of interest are not permitted and are to be scrupulously avoided. An agent's allegiance is solely to his or her client.

Translated into practical terms, this means that an agent's compensation is derived exclusively from the writer-client. An agent cannot accept any form of compensation from a publishing company, or a film company, for example, in return for steering a particular manuscript to that company for a first look.

An agent cannot wear two hats. For example, he cannot act as an agent while at the same time negotiating with his own client to acquire rights in a client's material, and then act as a film or a television producer or as a book packager of that same material. (Book packagers are in the business of putting the various elements of a book together, and then selling the "package" to a publishing company in return for a royalty or profit participation in which the writer-client does not share.)

- Funds received by the agent which belong to the client are to be safeguarded by depositing them in a special bank account set up solely for that purpose. These funds may not be co-mingled with the agent's other business or personal funds. The client's share of these monies is to be paid over to the client within a specified (brief) period of time. The agent's financial records—insofar as they pertain to transactions involving the client—are open to the client for inspection.

To my knowledge there have not been many instances where an agent has run off with a client's funds, or where the client's funds (co-mingled with the agent's funds) have been attached by the agent's creditors, but it has occurred on occasion. It seems entirely prudent for a writer to have the added protection of having these funds in a special account, out of reach of the agent's creditors.

- If the agent seeks reimbursement from the client for certain expenses (photocopy-

ing, messengers, long distance phone calls, etc.), the client must specifically agree in advance to pay these charges; they cannot be billed (or deducted from the client's monies) as an afterthought.
● The agent is required to keep the client up to date regarding the status of submissions made on behalf of the client. If a writer requests additional information from the agent about her materials, contracts, etc., the agent is required to furnish it.
● The agent is pledged to keep financial and other information about the client confidential.

This is significant for a number of reasons. A writer should be able to rest easy when disclosing to an agent a book idea that has been germinating. There need not be a concern that the agent will reject the idea and then suggest the idea to another client.
● AAR agents are pledged to principles of honorable co-existence, directness and honesty in their relationships with other AAR members. They undertake not to mislead, deceive, dupe, defraud or victimize their clients, their agent colleagues and any other persons with whom they do business.

Practically speaking, AAR agents are required by the Canon to deal openly and honestly with their clients and with the publishers with whom they do business. For example, the Canon would preclude an agent from making misstatements of fact to an editor interested in acquiring rights to a manuscript. While it may seem like a useful sales tactic, the agent cannot tell an editor that he or she has another offer in hand when that is not the case. Dealing in an honest, open, straightforward manner facilitates and dignifies the entire submission and contract negotiating process. Moreover, in the publishing business, where it is commonplace for tens, if not hundreds of thousands of dollars to be committed in the course of a phone call, it's imperative to be able to rely on those with whom you are dealing.

Reading fees are discouraged

The difficult and complex reading fee issue is specifically addressed in the AAR Canon of Ethics. The practice of charging writers a fee to review their work is officially "discouraged," and after January 1, 1996, banned completely. The organization's take on this subject is that the practice too easily lends itself to abuse. From personal experience—first as the Chairperson of the ILAA Ethics Committee and now in a similar position for AAR—I received all too many letters from writers complaining that even though they had paid the fee (hundreds of dollars in many instances), they had not received a useful evaluation of their material. Many had paid the requested fee, received a report and were then invited to pay yet an additional fee for a more detailed analysis. Fortunately, very few of these complaints were directed against our own members but being made aware that this kind of dealing occurs with a degree of regularity was an eye-opening experience for me and my colleagues.

That is not to say that every agent who charges a reading fee is engaging in nefarious practices. There are some fee-charging agents who do render a valuable service to writers. The problem for a writer, of course, is in knowing how to separate the wheat from the chaff.

Nevertheless, AAR frowns on the practice and will not consider for new membership any agent who charges reading fees. It did permit those few members who charged such fees to continue to do so until January 1, 1996, provided they complied with specific regulations promulgated by the organization. After that time, no members of AAR are permitted to charge reading fees.

Know what you'll get for your money

AAR's regulations are helpful guidelines to any writer asked to pay a fee to have material reviewed, for they are designed to insure that the writer is aware of exactly what services will be rendered—and by whom.

AAR requires that any agent-member who charges a reading fee provide to the writer, *prior to the writer making any payment*, a written statement setting forth this information:

● description of the nature and extent of the services to be rendered including a statement as to whether the work will be read in whole or in part;

● whether a written report will be rendered and, if so, the nature and extent of that report;

● statement as to whether the services will be rendered by the agent personally and, if not, the professional background of the person who will render the services;

● a statement as to when the writer will receive the report;

● the amount of the fee, including not only the intial fee but any additional fees which may be requested for additional services;

● an explanation of how the fee is determined, i.e., hourly rate, length of manuscript to be reviewed, length of the report, etc.;

● a statement as to whether and under what circumstances all or any part of the fee is refundable, e.g., if the agent takes on the writer for representation.

Moreover, the agent is required to advise the writer up-front that payment of the reading fee neither guarantees that the agent will take on the writer as a client nor that the work will necessarily be made more saleable to publishers.

I think it's clear that the AAR position is that the writer must know exactly what she is getting into before writing a check.

AAR's Ethics Committee

The AAR bylaws provide for a permanent Ethics Committee charged with promoting observance of the Canon. The Committee investigates all complaints lodged against members and makes a determination as to whether a breach of the Canon has occurred. The Association's bylaws provide for punitive action to be taken against members found in violation, which may be in the form of a reprimand, censure, suspension or even expulsion from the organization. Fortunately, the Ethics Committee has had few occasions to meet—a testament to the professional manner in which the AAR members conduct their business.

A professional, and personal, relationship

While the focus of this article has been on the many things that can go wrong in the writer-agent relationship, the truth is that this kind of thing is the exception rather than the rule. The vast majority of literary agents are dedicated, hardworking professionals of high integrity who care about writers and books and are committed to representing their clients with vigor and enthusiasm. Moreover, clients, for the most part, care about and respect their agents; the relationship often transcends the solely professional to one of friendship.

Building a Client List

by Jane Dystel

Several years ago, when I first became a literary agent, an award-winning journalist from a major newspaper came to me for representation. He wanted to do a book on the merger of two tabloid newspapers. I very much wanted to work with this writer, but for the life of me, couldn't imagine who would buy a book on this subject, and I told him so.

A week later, he was back with another idea which *was* very interesting to me. He proceeded to write a book proposal and we sold it for a very good advance. That writer has gone on to publish four books, with a fifth currently in production. He is now simultaneously working on a major biography and a novel, both of them under contract with publishers.

This experience taught me to trust my instincts whenever possible and to be straightforward about my opinions. These are valuable tools which have served me well in my agenting career. This article is about how I built a client list and is meant to encourage authors in their writing endeavors and help them arrive at marketable book ideas.

Go with what you know

In setting the goals for creating a client list so many years ago, I knew I had to stick to what I knew. (This, incidentally, is a very important rule for all writers to follow as well—all the time. Obviously, it is a cliché, but an enormously useful one, nevertheless.)

Before I became an agent, I had been in publishing for 18 years; I had been an editor as well as a publisher. During these years I sold books to buyers at both the major book chains and the independent wholesalers. All of my experience was with nonfiction, and it was there that I decided to begin.

Over the years, I had edited a number of cookbooks and I was a fairly decent cook myself. In addition, I loved reading cookbooks and articles about food. When Rick Grausman, former U.S. representative to the Cordon Bleu, came to me with his idea to do a book, I jumped at it. Neither he nor I knew much about doing a book proposal, but he had a wonderful office kitchen, and so I invited editors to join us there for lunch prepared from recipes included in the book. Eventually, we sold his book to Workman Publishers.

Several cooking authors followed on topics ranging from chocolate to regional Italian and American cuisine. Two books, *The Splendid Table* by Lynne Rosetto Kasper and *Bobby Flay's Bold American Food*, were named best book of the year by the James Beard Foundation and the International Association of Culinary Professionals.

While none of these authors had ever written books before, they were all creative people who were extremely knowledgeable about their subjects. The rest

Jane Dystel *has been in the publishing business for 25 years. She has been an editor and publisher of the* World Almanac, *and is now the founder and president of Jane Dystel Literary Management. She lives in New York with her husband and two children.*

simply became a matter of finding the right agent and publisher.

Sometimes the idea comes first

Often agents generate ideas for books themselves, based on trends they see in publishing and the wider world. Sometimes these ideas come from personal experience, sometimes from general knowledge of popular culture.

When I became an agent, I was starting my own business for the first time. Needless to say, I was extremely nervous. This was in the mid-1980s, when entrepreneurship was coming into its own. One night I had dinner with David Liederman, founder of David's Cookies. I spent quite a while trying to convince David to write a book for young people starting out on their own, as I was obviously preoccupied with the subject. The result was *Running Through Walls*. Some years later, after David had lost a lot of weight following a food plan he developed himself, I sold his diet book for even more money. Here, again, was an example of someone who successfully wrote about what he knew.

Personal contact at writers' conferences

One of the things I love to do is speak at writers' conferences, and frequently I'm approached by a writer I wind up inviting to send me work.

Several years ago I was in Santa Barbara at a conference, when a former client approached me to say hello. We spent several hours together talking about some major changes she had made in her life. Elaine St. James had hit upon something that had made a real difference to her, and she wanted to write about it. Several months later we sold *Simplify Your Life: 100 Ways to Slow Down and Enjoy the Things That Really Matter*, which, to date, has sold over 100,000 copies. Elaine is currently working on her next book, *Inner Simplicity*, which promises to be even more successful. She had turned a personal choice into advice for her readers and, by doing so, she'd stepped right into a major lifestyle trend.

On the lookout for good ideas and great writers

Another way I've built my client list is by reading magazines and newspapers, both national and regional, as much as possible. By doing this, I can spot trends more easily while, at the same time, identifying good ideas and new writers. On top of all the magazine and proposal reading I do after work every day, I try to read at least three newspapers, including *The New York Times*, and one magazine. (I have found regional magazines such as *Chicago* and *The Washingtonian* very helpful in finding talented writers. National magazines such as *Vanity Fair*, *The New Yorker*, *GQ*, *Cosmopolitan* and *People*, meanwhile, are great for spotting trends.) Understandably, after all of this reading I often crawl into bed bleary-eyed.

Would-be authors do well to watch the news, I've found. This can help in both fiction and nonfiction writing. The more reading you do on current events, the better.

In the mid-1980s when law was "hot" — on television, in movies and in books — I worked with a talented Washington journalist on a book entitled *The Litigators*. John A. Jenkins went on to write a major biography of Marvin Mitchelson, the controversial lawyer who made palimony a household word. Other news stories which I developed into books with prestigious authors included the stock market dive in 1987, the trials and tribulations of Leona Helmsley, the separation of Mia Farrow and Woody Allen, and the bombing of Pan Am Flight 103 over Lockerbie, Scotland.

In the past ten years, the true crime genre — accounts of crimes that have actually occurred — has been very hot (although it has slowed down considerably of late). The entire area has become very competitive. Proposals and books must be completed almost overnight and, oftentimes, the advance money isn't huge, but it can be a good jumping off point for many new writers. Maria Eftimiades, a writer at *People*, sold *Lethal Lolita: The Amy Fisher Story* after I approached her with the idea. This was made into a major television movie, for which she received a substantial sum, and Maria has gone on to become a very successful author.

Several years ago, I started noticing that there seemed to be far more pregnant women around. Then, 18 years after my daughter was born, I, too, became pregnant and gave birth to a beautiful boy. So, for both personal and professional reasons I began to pay special attention to the parenting category, which has recently become quite profitable.

The first author who approached me in this area, Nancy Samalin, had already been published very successfully and ran a number of parenting workshops. Professional credentials such as these are very important in establishing authority on a nonfiction topic. Nancy's newest project deals with having more than one child — an idea with which a publisher approached her.

Since these two books were sold, I've worked with several different authors on various child guidance and parenting topics, from kids' nutrition to telling fairy tales. Though this market is also becoming somewhat crowded, I still look for unique ideas with a perspective different from other works on the same subject.

Contacting writers directly

Another way I have built my client list is by contacting the winners of various media awards when I read about them. Several years ago, I saw a list of Pulitzer Prize winners in *The New York Times* which included journalist Walt Bogdonich. Walt was a reporter at the *Wall Street Journal* and had been investigating the United States health care system for ten years. I sold his book for a large advance and we are currently working on another major investigative subject. I contacted Lou Kilzer after he won his second Pulitzer, and encouraged him to write about World War II. *Churchill's Deception* was published recently and we are working together again on his second book.

I also take note of newspaper series which I think will work as books. *South of Heaven: A Year In the Life of an American High School at the End of the Twentieth Century*, by Thomas French, is about a suburban high school during a single school year and is one very good example of this. It first appeared in *The St. Petersburg Times*. Doubleday purchased it and published it in 1993.

In addition, I pay special attention to personal memoirs with a broader message. Lorene Cary's *Black Ice* deals with her experiences in the early 1970s as a black student at the predominantly white St. Paul's Academy. Lorene is a magazine writer with obvious literary skill and I felt her time at St. Paul's was important to document. From the sales of her book, my hunch was right. Barack Obama, the first black president of the *Harvard Law Review*, came from a mixed family with a fascinating background and grew up in many exotic places. His memoir, *Journeys in Black and White*, has many universal themes and messages.

Fiction: readers, recommendations and referrals

Fiction, in many ways, is more difficult to succeed in for both agent and author. Finding fiction authors to fill out my client list has been a real challenge. Initially, because I had no novelists on my list, I could depend only on manuscripts that came to me on an unsolicited basis. (Because of the volume of manuscripts I currently handle, this is, for the most part, no longer possible.)

Before I take on a new novelist, I have a manuscript read three times. First I have a trusted outside reader review the manuscript and, if he recommends it, I have my inhouse (and very talented) editor review it. If she likes it, I read the novel and only then do I call the author and tell him that I want to represent it. My readers loved *Entries From a Hot Pink Notebook* by Todd Brown and, several months after we took it on, I sold it to an editor who had initially rejected it but just couldn't forget it. *Entries* is being published in June of 1995, and Todd is currently working on his second novel.

Recommendations by other clients and editors have brought me some very talented writers as well. Several years ago, I journeyed to Tulsa, Oklahoma for The Tulsa Night Writers Writers' Conference. There I met William Wood, a published author who was a speaker. Though Bill was already represented, we stayed in touch, and several months later he sent his friend Gus Lee, a major fiction talent to me. Gus has since published two very successful novels and is delivering the third to his publisher in a few months. Shortly after Gus became a client, Bill joined me as well, and we've now sold two of his novels, one of which is currently being made into a movie starring Tom Selleck.

What can you do?

The lessons I have learned in building a client list can easily, in my opinion, be used by writers to get their ideas published.

- Write about what you know. This is true in both fiction and nonfiction.
- Try to make your idea a little bit different than those already on the market. Remember, there are no new ideas, it's just the way they're presented. Be aware of trends and study bestseller lists very carefully.
- With nonfiction especially, establish your credentials. Credibility is very important in today's competitive market.
- If at all possible, attend writers' conferences. There is much to be learned there, and the people you meet can often be very helpful to you in your publishing efforts.
- Read as much as possible. This helps in your area of interest, but it also helps you to learn how to write better.
- Visit bookstores. Being aware of what's being published is very important

Finally, remember, much of getting published has to do with serendipity and good luck. You might meet ten agents you don't like or who don't want to take you on and, suddenly, you'll be introduced to one in an unexpected way who is a perfect fit. Or you can't quite get the right angle on your nonfiction idea, and the thirtieth publisher you or your agent approaches will have an editor who sees the perfect handle. Keep your eyes and ears open and never, never give up!

The Literary Agent: Savant, Savior or Svengali?

by Edward A. Novak III

Not too long ago, I found myself sitting in a conference room of a New York publisher, overlooking lower Fifth Avenue on a rather humid day during summer's last gasp. Seated at one end of a long table were an author, a client of mine, along with her closest friend and advisor, who I quickly realized probably hadn't read a book in 20 years. On the other end sat the book's editor, the company's publisher and its executive editor.

This interesting group was having a series of intense disagreements about the author's manuscript, which had been rushed to completion in order to make a very tight deadline. The editors were satisfied with the book and wanted to move ahead and publish it as is. The author, a perfectionist, was not yet happy with it and wanted to postpone publication in order to revise and rewrite the manuscript just one more time.

I was asked to sit in the middle and referee the dispute.

This task is one, as a literary agent, I loathe performing and was made more difficult because, in my opinion, my client was creating much of the disagreement. However, at the end of two hours of pleading, posing, debating, page-turning, occasional fist pounding and all sorts of other foolishness, we all were able to shake hands and walk away happy. The book will be published with minimal delay, the publisher will not lose any orders and the author will have the opportunity to make the requested changes.

I felt as though I had escaped with my scalp.

In a perfect world, every author receives a healthy advance for his or her book and writes quickly and professionally in lockstep with an editor who edits and markets the book quickly and professionally, knowing full well that the publisher will make a healthy profit, and everyone is a satisfied customer on the date of publication.

In reality, however, the vast majority of published authors do not make a living from their craft, most books lose money and rarely is a book written and published without harsh words exchanged at some point. And that's when the popular image of the literary agent, wheeling and dealing at breakneck speed on the speaker-phone and over expense-account lunches in tony Manhattan restaurants, is shattered by the reality that an agent performs a number of crucial, difficult and time-consuming functions in the publishing process that sometimes involve walking a very skinny and loose tightrope, with the author holding one end and the editor holding the other.

Edward A. Novak III is an independent agent based in Pennsylvania. He was formerly editorial director of the Acton and Dystel agency in New York and an editor with Charles Scribner's Sons and Macmillan Publishing Company. He holds degrees from Georgetown University and the University of Chicago.

Relationships from an agent's point of view

A number of questions emerge from this apparent confusion of images:
- We know authors write and editors edit, but what do literary agents do?
- What is an agent's relationship with his or her authors?
- What is an agent's relationship with editors?
- Do these relationships change through the course of the publishing process?

I have been both an editor and a literary agent, so I believe I understand the business from a couple of different perspectives. However, the purpose of this article is to answer these questions from the agent's perspective, so let's go from there.

The first thing to keep in mind is literary agents are, first and foremost, professionals in business for themselves. Most query letters from aspiring authors ask for some kind of indeterminate help to get published. When you ask a lawyer or a doctor for "help," it usually means trouble; when you ask a literary agent for "help," it involves opportunity. Let me define that kind of help: agents take risks, broker ideas and provide professional services and counseling. In exchange, we charge a commission.

Literary agents take risks, like other businesspeople searching for new clients. We do not wait for opportunities to waltz in through the door. In fact, a small minority of my clients solicited me with query letters; most of the authors with whom I work are people I sought out.

For example, about three years ago two journalists with hot ideas, one from Washington DC and the other from Los Angeles, came to my attention and I heavily wined and dined both of them without any commitment from either of them to me or even to the idea of writing a book. I won the battle with the writer who lived 3,000 miles away and lost the battle with the writer who lived 100 miles down the road. Taking those risks, which I do frequently, involved spending time away from my office and a lot of money out of my pocket.

In either event, the author soliciting an agent or the other way around, the agent risks time (which cannot be billed like a lawyer's time) and expense (telephone, mail, fax, travel) in the hope that each client's work will return the investment.

Brokering an idea doesn't just mean reading an aspiring author's manuscript and shipping it out to a publisher with a cover letter. Sometimes it means creating an idea for a book, finding an author to write the book and only then finding a publisher to take it on. Sometimes it means working with an editor to create an idea and then finding the right author for it. It *always* means taking this thing—this idea, which is nothing more than a notion, something less than air—and making it so attractive to some very smart and knowledgeable people that they are willing to pay the author money for it.

For most agents I know, this doesn't just involve slick talk and eating fancy French cuisine. It also means reading a lot—newspapers from cities around the country, magazines on a variety of subjects, books of every description—and thinking a lot: Is there the potential for a book in this magazine article? Does this writer display talent? Why does this book succeed while another like it fails?

Brokering also means knowing the marketplace and having some kind of knack for negotiating. It means knowing which publisher is up and which one is down. Knowing which editor has a keen understanding of crime fiction, for instance, and which one concentrates on journalism. Knowing who pays a lot of money and markets their books well and who is stingy. Knowing if your client's book has blockbuster appeal (and how to ask for blockbuster money) or genre appeal (and how not to kill a deal by asking for too much money). Knowing when to shake hands, sometimes via fax, and when to walk away from the bargaining table, even if it's by phone.

Professional service and counseling? Well, you've just read about one piece of service I gave a client. Earlier today, another client who writes novels called and we discussed plot elements for his next book for about half an hour. Two weeks ago, I had lunch with another client, who had just moved from Chicago to Washington DC and was looking for a new nonfiction subject that would enhance his career. Another author is considering writing in a different genre, using a pseudonym. And always, I consider how every decision may affect my client not just next month, but next year and perhaps even five years down the road.

Creative relationships and business relationships

My hope is that I have answered what an agent does, what his relationship is to his authors and what it is to editors, or at least placed it in context. The relationships between author, editor and agent are tricky because the publishing process involves both creative relationships and business relationships and, by nature, there is a tension between these two aspects of what we do.

Quite frankly, back in the "old days," when editors such as Maxwell Perkins dominated the publishing industry and influenced so heavily the course of American literature, a lot of the functions described previously in this article would have been handled by an author's editor. The pace and mission of American publishing have changed, however, and thrown most successful writers into the arms of their literary agents.

A lot of editors complain to me that publishing has become so market-driven and profit-oriented that much of the creativity has been taken out of their jobs. Ten years ago, there used to be dozens of first-rate publishing houses; after a glut of absorptions, mergers, acquisitions and other such leveraged buyouts, there are far fewer great publishing houses still standing on their own.

Publishers are now publicly owned, not family owned, and are operated with the same concern for profitability as General Electric. This means less job security for editors. The era of editors staying employed by the same company for a career is a faint memory, save for a very few. Editors switch jobs, get hired and fired at an alarming rate and, as a result, most publishing gossip focuses not on books, but jobs. The status quo, it is often joked, is the state of flux.

Writers and editors both depend on agents

The direct result of this activity is twofold. First, editors now focus on acquisition and marketing rather than the development of authors and ideas and have become dependent on agents for new book ideas. I learned part of this lesson the hard way back in my days as an editor. I found a journalist with a great idea and encouraged him to write a book; he was so convinced by my arguments that he took the idea to an agent who then sold it to another publisher.

The second result is that authors nowadays might work not with one or two editors in a career but a dozen or more and by necessity must rely on the one constant in their professional lives: their agent. That journalist made the right decision; with the threat of an imminent takeover hanging over the head of my employer, I took a job offer with another company six months later. Had he signed with me, he would have been abandoned by his editor.

An interesting dynamic has evolved, therefore, concerning the relationships between author and agent, editor and agent, author and editor. You might say that what happens between author and agent is proactive while that between authors and editors is reactive and editors and agents just stare at each other across the demilitarized zone from their trenches, venturing out for sorties at night. In other words, we are all business partners.

Market-driven publishing and its effect

The reasons for this state of affairs are not hard to understand. Editors are under a lot of pressure to make money with every book they acquire; the days of losing money with authors until their breakthrough book are over. The interests of editors are dictated by their employer and if the interests of the author and the publisher should happen to intersect, fine. If not, guess who has top priority?

Agents, on the other hand, find their interests and those of the author are almost always the same. The more money the author makes, the more money the agent makes. The longer an author's career, the more income the agent takes in. The more successful an agent's clients, the more referrals of new clients he gets.

If it is surprising that I am portraying this "gentleman's profession" rather crudely, it is because the bottom line has changed. Charles Scribner's Sons, the publisher of Hemingway and Fitzgerald, used to occupy the upper floors of a small, cozy building on Fifth Avenue in midtown Manhattan. Nowadays, the publisher is part of Viacom, a multi-mega-billion dollar conglomerate, and for some unfathomable reason, the publisher's name has been changed to Scribner. Books throughout the industry are often referred to as "product." Publishers, in fact, no longer "publish"; rather, they "exploit copyrights." And there is serious discussion about whether or not books will be replaced by CD-ROM.

The publisher, through its representative, the editor, tries to maximize profits. It seems that if it can pay an author no advance and no royalty for a book and secure all subsidiary rights in perpetuity, it will (though I've never heard of such a thing). That's called business. It seems that it is the agent's job, on the other hand, to convince the publisher to pay far too much advance for each of his or her client's books, so much money that the book can never hope to earn out the advance and the author will never have to hope for or rely on a royalty check. That's business, too.

It results in a primarily adversarial, albeit cordial, relationship between agents and editors. Adversarial because there is always, always, always bickering over money. Cordial because editors and agents are dependent on each other and must work together. I like most of the editors with whom I do business and am friendly with many others, and I hope they like me too. But we mostly rely on each other and keep an arm's length by necessity.

Put another way, my clients get presents at Christmas; the editors get cards.

Balancing writers' and editors' interests

Does this dynamic ever change? Sure—go back and read the opening paragraphs of this article. What happened in that conference room is unusual. For the most part, I took the side of the publisher against my client. Why? Two reasons.

First, editors are also professionals. The editor's job is to ensure my client's book is good and gets marketed well. In her I place my trust on these issues. Secondly, the issues under discussion had nothing to do with business, which is my primary concern; rather, we were arguing over the content of a manuscript. Ultimately, the publisher has and should have editorial control over a book. The editor is and should be the judge of what is acceptable and what is not and, when such a judgment is made in good faith, no agent in his or her right mind will disagree (at least not publicly). Remember, the publisher's name goes on the spine and title page of the book. It is not in the publisher's interest to publish bad books.

In this particular case, my client was unwittingly making a career decision. If agreement could not be reached, in my judgment, there would be no book. Ever. I am loathe, I mentioned, to intervene in such disagreements for two reasons: 1) because of the old saying about too many cooks; and 2) an agent injects a business presence into any discussion over the content of a book. As someone who loves books and has edited them, I also understand that business considerations can sometimes poison a book by altering the original vision of the author. And it serves no one's interest to publish anything other than a good book.

I agreed to sit between these warring groups because I wanted to save my author's career. My job that day, therefore, was not to express an opinion but to mediate, to seek a middle ground from which both sides could work without anyone thinking, "Well, he said that only because he's the agent." Try getting your parents or your children to agree with you on a definition of "good music"; then have your best friend try to settle the dispute in order to understand my position.

"Staying on the same page"

After describing all these difficult situations, who do I think is the good guy and who is the bad guy? From my perspective as the agent, no one is good or bad. Why? Because the one phrase I use with editors and authors the most is "let's make sure we stay on the same page." It means discussing things not in terms of who's right and who's wrong; it means just making sure the issues everyone is concerned about are the same and then seeking common ground. That's what successful partners in a creative business do.

The final question, then, becomes: Is there a point where harmony can be reached in the publishing process and between author, editor and agent?

No.

Precisely because we are partners in a creative business. Tensions will always exist.

Ask my friend "Bill," an agent who was struggling to get his foundling business off the ground. As far as one of the biggest publishers in town was concerned, he was a nobody until one of his clients wrote a bestseller. Instantly, the president of that publisher became best friends with Bill and photos of them hugging were seen in *Publishers Weekly*. Bill sold them the author's next book. How long do you think that "friendship" will last until the tension sets in? It all depends on how well Bill is able to keep everyone on the same page.

Playing the Game: The Writer-Agent-Editor Relationship

by Alan Steinberg

Back in college, when I first conjured myself as Famous Writer, I romanticized everything: basking, like Youngblood Hawke, in sexy notoriety; choosing luxuriously between solicitous Big Apple agents; spending weekends editing at the Hamptons cottage with my own personal Maxwell Perkins; feigning surprise when they track me to my yacht—in St. Tropez—to announce my first Pulitzer.

All these fantasies, by the way, have actually happened. They just haven't happened to me.

At least, not exactly. I did achieve notoriety for my 1990 bestseller, *Behind the Mask* (Viking), the autobiography of former baseball umpire Dave Pallone, who was fired for being gay. I did land a first-rate New York agent—though I solicited *him*. And I have experienced, if not Hamptons Nirvana with a Fitzgeraldean mentor, at least easy Lake Michigan breeziness with three exceptional editors at Morrow, Viking and Crown. The Pulitzer and yacht still elude, but they've never been goals. I'm just happy to be in the same ballpark every day with the other pros, suiting up with them to play the game.

One of the least-explored aspects of that game, however, is writer-agent-editor relationships. Where do you read about that? If not for regular exchanges with a fellow Chicago author friend, I would have no dialogue on these key confederations, no knowledge other than my own experience. Which prompts me now to offer some of those experiences to others with big time hopes, for whatever they're worth.

Agent loves writer loves agent . . .

Let's start with the agent-writer relationship.

The toughest part, of course, is getting one. It took me eight years from the day I sold my first national magazine article (a *People* bio). In 1983 I became a contributing writer on the new *Inside Sports* and started doing major profiles. In 1986, my editor told me that legendary hockey author Stan Fischler had been impressed with my portrait of former NHL superstar Don "Murder" Murdoch, the first NHL player suspended for substance abuse. So I phoned Fischler in New York and said I wanted to write books but needed an agent, and he graciously recommended his. I sent the agent copies of my best work. Amazingly, he took me on.

He's been my agent ever since.

To date, he's brought me four book projects: *Born to Referee* (Morrow), the autobiography of Jerry Markbreit, the NFL's most accomplished referee; *Behind*

Alan Steinberg is the author of four books, three screenplays, and over 100 magazine articles included in People, Penthouse, Saturday Evening Post, Inside Sports *and many more. He gives writing talks and workshops nationwide.*

the Mask; my most recent book, *Rebound: The Dennis Rodman Story* (Crown); and my next one, which I'll mention shortly. *Mask* was a *New York Times* bestseller — the author's Oscar, maybe a once-in-a-lifetime event. *Born* and *Mask* both earned paperbacks; *Mask* and *Rebound* turned movie options; all three were critically received. Point is, I think the measure of even small success in this business is part writer's talent and part agent's intelligence and skill in matching subject and writer.

Another interesting aspect: I said my agent got me four book deals. But he put me in position to have *six*. Two just didn't pan out. They did get underway, however, and both were potential blockbusters coveted by dozens of authors. One was with Joe Montana after his fourth Super Bowl win, making him the industry's darling-of-the-moment. (The high six-figure deal comprised the largest advance , to that time, in sports book history.) Another was with a legendary rock supergroup, a $100 million-a-year industry unto themselves. I spent a week working with Montana; six weeks with the rockers. Although the deals eventually jammed (through no fault of ours), my agent had *me* in the driver's seat.

How we work: I get two, you get one . . .

My agent and I conduct nearly all of our business by phone, though we have met numerous times in New York. We like and respect each other, but between projects we only talk about once a month. We rarely share mundane concerns, though if I have a pressing problem I can tell him. I've never been to his home in the Hamptons and he's never been to my flat near Wrigley Field. That's largely due to geography; I live in Chicago and he's in New York.

Literate and multi-tracked, his interests are varied (former lawyer and minor league baseball team owner, founder of "RBI," an inner city baseball league). So when he calls me, it's about business. But I can call him about anything. That access is crucial, especially since I recently decided to branch away from sports autobiographies. It was important that he agree and see the value, which he does. Thus, the next book he's secured for me is with Kareem Abdul-Jabbar, but it's called *Black Profiles in Courage*.

As a freelance, I rely heavily on my agent for book deals. After all, except when I'm on occasional magazine assignment, *he's* the one in regular contact with editors, athletes, celebrities, politicians, and their representatives. If something sounds right for me, he puts my name in the mix. Since we're in accord now on my new direction, the range of that mix has broadened considerably. Of three projects currently pending, one is with a world-famous athlete, another with an infamous TV and radio personality, and a third with a rock music legend. My agent pursued the rock legend book; I went after the other two.

That's another thing: young writers' expectations of what agents do is skewed. After workshops I give every year, would-be writers tell me they think that once you have an agent, you just wait for him to get you work. Fact is, a book agent's main job is not to hustle projects for clients, but to negotiate deals clients bring in. I remember my agent warning me after the Pallone book, "You've been lucky so far. I got you your first two books. But for the most part, *you'll* have to get the projects. I'll keep your name out there, but for every ten I go after you'll be lucky to get one." And though I've beaten those odds, that's how it really works for most of us.

Editors in the mix

In nine years, my agent and I have never had a major dispute. If something's bothering me, he addresses it and we move on. If I'm late with a manuscript, he doesn't hound me. He reminds me of the deadline—*once*—and leaves the rest to me and my editor. However, if I need him to serve as buffer between publisher/editor and me, he does so willingly.

Latest example. Last year, when I fell behind on *Rebound* . . . Uh, "behind" isn't accurate. Accurate is: two weeks to deadline with *zero* written. Up Crap Creek, *deep*. Naturally, I called my agent. "Talk to the editor," I wimped. "Explain what a nice guy I am." Comedian, ho-ho. Still, he called and said *something* right because it did buy me time. But credit also my one-in-a-million editor. He was like a favorite uncle: patient, sympathetic, witty, relentlessly supportive. Also ingenious. Because when I still didn't deliver, and deadline day approached and his boss was ticked off and said to tell me to *return the advance* (the one phrase that makes grown writers weep . . . or produce), he invented a way out.

To wit: "Send me two chapters—polished—within a week. If they're good, we won't say anything. If she doesn't ask about it, keep plugging away. When she does ask, I'll show her what amazing stuff we have and cross my fingers." Jesus, I thought. There *is* a God. "*But*," he finally exhorted, "it better *be* amazing stuff." Incentive! Pressure! Debtor's prison! Somehow, I deblocked and completed the book—19 chapters, plus intro and epilogue—in eight weeks flat. Spit-polished. (I surpassed myself; a nonfiction book normally takes me three to four months. *Mask* took six.)

Turned out his boss never asked about it again, my editor loved what I wrote, Crown accepted it, nice book; I'm still alive in the business.

Different editors, different styles

My relationships with two other editors were equally smooth. On my first book, about the football referee, I had a highly regarded veteran editor, a big-name pro. I felt intimidated; I knew I needed a hit in my first at-bat. Turned out, unexpectedly, to be a female . . . a football fanatic who knew more about the game than some of my male fantasy football pals. And a delightful human being, like my Crown editor; sweet-tempered, infinitely patient, sympathetic to writer's peculiarities. A perfect disposition to deal with a nervous rookie with a clean new bat.

After a couple introductory chats about the book's structure (which I'd naively assumed was determined by the editor), she said, "Oh, I trust your judgment" and left it to me. She never called for two straight months. Eventually, I raised the courage to send her Part One and my suggested approach to Part Two. The anxiety of awaiting my first professional verdict was worse than waiting to learn my draft number in college, which, after all, could've been a ticket to *death*. Finally, while I was out one day, she left a fateful message on my machine:

"Alan, it's 4:30, New York time, on Monday. I've just read the chapters. I think it's *terrific*. I think it's the way to go with Part One, and I think doing Part Two as various topics is an *excellent* idea. Uh, I don't have anything to say to you except that, if you want to talk to me, I'll be in on Tuesday, of course. But I think you're right on the money here and I would just keep doing what you're doing." (A pause, enthused) "It's very good. I really enjoyed reading it. Thanks. Bye-bye."

No, thank *you*. Because I never again doubted my ability to invent the right structure for a book. It boosted my confidence immensely, made me *feel* professional for the first time.

My *Behind the Mask* editor was high-strung, more hands-on, alert to every roadblock, openly concerned about office politics that might affect the book, which he, apparently alone in the industry, knew would be "hot" and controversial. He called constantly to check my progress. His main concern was accuracy because the book was loaded with explosive personal material, some potentially libelous. By working closely with me on my style as well as structure, he made me understand the importance of absolute accuracy in checking facts, and of keeping the emotional drama of experience *inside* the facts. I still recall vividly his calls to ask me, "So Alan, have you got your goddam facts straight yet?" It became a running joke. But because of his unblinking eye and drill sergeant guidance, *Mask* was the tightest manuscript of complex material I ever composed.

Obviously, it paid off, with a bestseller, my finest moment. His too, he admitted to me later. And it was only after the book hit the *Times* list, an unexpected surprise even to him, that he sent me a note revealing his emotions for the first time in six months: "Congratulations! You did a *terrific* job!" Of course, he meant both of us; working closely with an expert editor, as he knew, can be as much a collaboration as working with another writer. Strangely, as with my Morrow editor, I never met him face to face. I did, however, glimpse him in the audience in a videotape of Dave Pallone's appearance on the Donahue show to promote the book.

Since I only have dialogue with one other author, I have no idea if my experiences with agents and editors are common. I suspect I've been blessed: I've never had a major problem with either. Over the years, I've been casually solicited by three other agents to join with them. I've declined, though I like all three very much personally. I have a solid foundation and history with my current agent. I respect his ability to find me projects I cannot find myself, and I appreciate his understanding of my talents, potential and professional goals.

Besides, I'm still working an angle to get invited to his home in the Hamptons.

Sleazeballs? Titans? Impresarios? The Truth About Literary Agents

by Jonathan Karp

Let's assume, for the sake of argument, you are a beginning writer, unknown, unpaid and unconnected.

You've written a manuscript. It is *brilliant*, the best work you've ever done. If you can only get it into the hands of someone with an open mind, someone who isn't jaded or overwhelmed, you're sure your work will be appreciated as the classic it is.

You need an agent, of course, but you can't seem to get anyone to pay attention. No matter how carefully you craft your query letter, no matter what strategy you try—subtle self-confidence or shameless titillation—no one will give your manuscript the reading you deserve.

What do you do?

You could buy a New Age self-help book and chant your way to success. You could go to writers' conferences and woo every would-be literary broker in attendance. Or you could do the sensible thing: Find out the name of the literary agent who has represented the books you respect the most, and which are most similar to yours. The rights department of every publishing house will tell you each book's agent. A query letter to that person, eloquently praising the agent's superior taste and high standards, ought to guarantee you at least 15 minutes of quality reading time.

Congratulations! You have an agent

Let's assume the agent finishes your manuscript and agrees with you. *It's brilliant!* Now you have a new problem.

Who is this agent? Sleazeball? Titan? Impresario? Is this person really the right choice to represent your masterpiece? After all, a writer like you and a property like this only come around rarely. With the right wheeling and dealing, you could be on your way to a major book career, to say nothing of the movie possibilities. At worst, this thing is a three-part TV miniseries with Jaclyn Smith and Richard Chamberlain.

The truth is, all you can do is trust your judgment and hope. As you may have discerned, the literary industry is completely unregulated. Your agent may be a part-time aerobics instructor, dog-breeder or Wal-Mart manager. At least twice a week, I receive calls from literary agents I've never heard of hoping to sell me

Jonathan Karp *is an editor at Random House, where he has worked on* Municipal Bondage, *by Henry Alford;* The God in Flight, *by Laura Argiri;* Bombardiers, *by Po Bronson;* Thank You For Smoking, *by Christopher Buckley;* Need, *by Lawrence David;* Just Do It, *by Donald Katz; and* Stand Before Your God, *by Paul Watkins.*

next year's bestseller. This friendly cold caller, probing aimlessly in the nebulous realm of a conglomerate publisher, could be your hard-working agent.

The good news is that just about all of the agents who call me are intelligent, well-intentioned, professional and amiable. A few are boring, or represent some really cheesy books, but all in all, they're a pleasant lot. Let's face it; no one decided to become a literary agent out of greed, gluttony, pride or any other deadly sins. In fact, most of them seem to have gravitated to the business for understandable reasons—they value independence, initiative and creativity. To their amazement, they found the ideal way to exercise those yearnings, and have even formed their own verb to describe it—*agenting.*

Agents do not have it easy. They have to handle endless questions and requests, most of which are almost cosmically unanswerable: *Why did they reject it? Why doesn't anyone want to publish the paperback? Why won't they pay me more when they're shelling out six-figure advances to writers who don't possess half my talent?*

Then, they have to attempt to bond with editors like me, who, although perennially looking for new writers, can only take on a few each year. No matter how nice or charming or powerful an agent is, if the writer and subject don't intrigue us, no sales pitch, however artful or charismatic, is going to make a difference.

Whenever I meet with these agents and they ask me what I'm looking for, I'm often tempted to respond, *"You know what I'm looking for! The next John Irving! The next David Halberstam! The next Reinventing Government or Closing of the American Mind!"* Sure, it's helpful to know that an editor doesn't garden, cook, have a cat, or play golf, but really, most of us are looking for the same thing—intelligent, lively writers who have something fresh, important and interesting to tell us. Whenever I challenge agents about this, they usually acknowledge that they know when they've got a big book.

In other words, there's only so much an agent can do. If the idea is sound, the writer is good, and the agent persists, someone ought to buy it eventually. A resourceful agent can easily figure out which editor to call.

Congratulations! You have a publisher

When the agent does reel in an interested publisher, the author is presented with a new set of questions. Is this the best deal possible? Is the agent doing everything right?

Once again, all you can really do is trust your judgment and hope. In most cases, agents will not be flooded with dramatically different offers. Some publishing houses may pay bigger advances upfront, but other houses may publish the book so well that subsequent royalties will be more lucrative. Agents can make all sorts of demands about consultation, approval, and control of rights—negotiating the fine print for weeks or months—but if you and your publisher feel good about each other, none of this haggling matters. Most of us want to keep you happy, as long as you're making your best effort. After all, our interest *is* mutual: We all want to make our contribution to culture, and the bottom line.

If things do begin to deteriorate, then an agent can certainly speak up for your interests and occasionally advance them, but ultimately, the best action may be to move you to a house that will treat you as you like. If a publishing house doesn't believe in you, there's not much an agent can do.

So, to summarize:

If you've got a good idea and have executed it well, it doesn't really matter who is selling it.

If you're offered a book contract, it doesn't take a genius to negotiate it, and there aren't that many differences from contract to contract, anyway.

If things go awry at the publishing house, in most cases, on that particular book, you're screwed. Sometimes publishers can't achieve their projected advance sales to bookstores. When that happens, advertising and promotion budgets are cut, no matter who the agent is.

What then, do agents do that makes them worth ten to fifteen percent of your earnings?

• The good ones look after the long-term interests you may not be able to see.

• They guide you through your proposals and manuscripts so you maximize the commercial and literary potential.

• They keep you from pursuing bad ideas, and they have the guts to tell you to write another draft, even if it means losing you as a client.

• They save you the unsavory task of discussing money, restrain you from badgering your publisher, and say the aggressive, critical things you'd prefer to avoid saying.

• They are usually your most vocal supporters within the industry, praising your work to every editor, writer, critic and reader they think can help you.

• They make sure harried and distracted publishers are maximizing their marketing campaigns, advertising in the right places, sending the right message to bookstores.

• They help get your book sold in foreign countries (even when they don't control those rights).

• They suggest paperback and book club editors who might appreciate your sensibility.

• They are a sounding board and a confidence-booster in an insecure business.

All of this, in my view, is worth fifteen percent.

I've read the magazine clichés about agents — that they are sharks and dishonest opportunists, or potentates who set the agenda for the entire industry. The clichés aren't true.

In five years of publishing, I've never had an agent yell at me or make an unreasonable demand. Once, an agent hung up the phone in anger, but even he later apologized, and turned out to be a tremendously helpful advocate for his client.

The most dishonest thing an agent has done — once — is inflate the sales figures of a client's book. But most publishers regard sales figures provided by agents with skepticism anyway.

All in all, the worst things agents have done, on only a few occasions, is prolong lunch with excruciatingly dull anecdotes or bombard me with ridiculously inappropriate submissions. Both sins are pardonable, especially if the next manuscript is a masterpiece.

Perhaps it's even yours.

How Things Work:
Book Auctions

The book auction, unheard of a few decades ago, is very much a fixture in publishing today. From Kelsey Grammer's autobiography to Betty Eadie's account of her return from the dead, agents are selling manuscripts through competitive bidding in an attempt to claim as much money as possible for their clients. "It's the same as for any other kind of merchandise," says Glen Hartley of Writer's Representatives. "An auction is when a group of bidders escalates the price of a book."

The criteria for manuscripts sold at auction are various. It could be timely material or a work with universal appeal. "For the most part, when you're not talking about mega blockbuster things, you first send out the submissions. Usually you have a sense of how significant interest is, and how many parties are interested, and that will determine if you want to hold a formal auction. It's more of an intuitive feeling of how many, how much, and how high their interest will go."

Hartley feels that any book could be a candidate for an auction. "I think it really just depends upon how many copies people anticipate selling. It would be foolish of any agent to send out a book whose best prospects might be a minimal amount and expect to hold an auction. You could do it but it wouldn't gain that much money over a straightforward sale."

When Hartley decides that a manuscript is eliciting enough interest to warrant a formal auction, he sets the auction date. "You usually fax a list of basic terms that you are looking for, which includes the rights that are up for sale, say world rights or simply North American or world English rights, and the royalty terms you want, and the various other clauses you might want to see in the final contract, so everybody knows these are the basic elements you are working with. You might also set a minimum bid, under which you will not accept any offers. And then, throughout the auction, people can improve not only on the price, but even on the terms you've already specified. A formal auction is usually held in that way, with a specific time that bids are to begin."

Once all the bids are in from the interested parties, Hartley ranks them from lowest to highest, preparing for the second round. "Let's say you have a book you know everybody is ready to pay more than $100,000 for, and you've set that as a minimum bid. Then people will start calling that morning, and somebody offers 100, someone else offers 125, and others offer 110 and 150. You'd start the second round by calling the person who offered 100, the minimum amount, and you'd tell them that the high bid at this time is 150. Top it or not. They usually are ready to go ahead, or will have to confer for a few minutes, but they'll soon call back and say, 'Well, yes, we're offering 170.' Then they are the high bidder and you go to the next person on the list and inform them what the current high bid is and ask whether they want to go ahead or not."

Minimum bid vs. floor

The minimum bid is set by the agent; the "floor," however is different. A minimum bid is simply the dollar figure at which the auction begins. A floor is established when one publisher makes an early offer, that, if accepted, becomes the minimum for bidding by other publishers. Floors are usually a generous amount, and include the right to match the top bid and exceed it by a given amount, usually ten percent. "A floor is usually arrived at through negotiation with an agent, but is actually brought to the table by the publisher. With a floor, the agent is giving somebody the right to ultimately buy the book for at least that amount, and in the end, to top the highest bid by a certain amount. Sometimes a publisher will call and say, 'Will you take a $300,000 floor?' You can say 'Yes,' you can say 'No,' or you can say 'No, we'll take a floor for $400,000.' There is a process of negotiation there. But if you're willing to accept a floor, that means you also have to be prepared to sell that book to that particular publisher in the end, because what comes with a floor is the right to sit out the auction and come back in at the end and match the highest bid and top it.

"The person who holds the floor increases his chances of gaining the book in two ways. One, he's already shown that he's very serious, and everybody knows that a floorholder may well come back in and buy the book at the end. It can scare off some people from wanting to participate. Two, if the floor is set at a very high amount, it could actually amount to what's known as a preemptive bid. It's so high that nobody else will go higher, so the floorholder becomes the buyer."

What makes the best bid best?

However, it's not always the highest bid that wins the book. "It's up to the agent to accept the floor or not. If you haven't accepted a floor and don't make clear in the terms of your auction that you may not accept the highest bid, then you might well be forced to accept it no matter what. We usually try to include a phrase in every auction we've held where there is no accepted floor, that the author reserves the right to determine what is the best bid.

"If it's not a matter of the most money, you might not want to hold an auction to begin with. If you do hold one, if there is very little disparity in price range, or even if there is a great disparity, but an author has particularly liked one house's plans for the book, or one particular editor's sympathetic understanding of what he or she is doing, then at the end of the auction if the author is willing to forego more money for that opportunity, it's his or her choice to make. And I've seen that happen."

During the course of an auction, bidders can increase not only the amount of money, but also improve on the terms. "Let's say you had put into the terms you were looking for a hard/soft deal, that is, a commitment to publish the paperback as well, and you had put in a 7½ percent royalty rate on the trade paperback edition, with an escalator to 10 percent after a certain number of copies. Somebody might say, 'We'll not only offer this amount of money, but we're also offering you a 10 percent royalty straight on the paperback.'

"Often along the course of an auction, someone will say they'll guarantee a full page ad in the *New York Times Book Review*, or they guarantee a certain amount to be spent in advertising and a ten-city author tour. Those things enter into the negotiations. I think the amount of money paid to acquire a particular book usually determines what a publishing house will do to publicize it. The more money invested in a particular book, almost commits the publisher to spending more money to get it back."

Another factor under negotiation during an auction might be bestseller bonuses. If the book makes it to certain levels on the *New York Times Book Review* the author receives a certain amount of money for each week at that position.

"There's usually a cap on that, and the money is paid in addition to the advance. There are different things people can do with that, as well. They can pay you that money immediately. If it's truly bonus money, it shouldn't wait to be paid on the next royalty statement."

Safety in numbers

Hartley feels that multiple submissions have become a way of life in publishing. "If you aren't doing multiple submissions, only going to one publisher at a time, it can sometimes take months and months if you don't find the right person immediately. It doesn't usually make sense for an author or an agent to go through that protracted process. You might go to one house at a time if you know that there's one editor or one house that's really perfect for a book, but for the most part, multiple submissions are standard procedure. In fact, as much as people may complain about it, they sometimes like it, because they have the reassurance that other publishers feel the book is worthwhile also.

"In the same way, auctions can work to a publisher's benefit as well as an author's, in that they get to see what their colleagues and competitors will pay for a book. But auctions are really the exception, for the most part, to the number of books sold by any particular agent."

New Media and the Agent

by Liza Landsman

Every day we hear more about the coming "Information Age" and the "New Media" explosion. However, most people have only a vague sense of what all this emerging technology will mean in their everyday lives. New media is the marriage of computer and video technology, combining existing methods of communication and entertainment (including audio, video, art, music, photography, etc.), to extend the possibilities of both.

In addition to instant banking, faster data transmission and remote education, etc., new media is already having an impact in other areas. Arts and entertainment fields quickly embraced the new media. Film, television and video-gaming industries have capitalized eagerly on what new media brings, expanding the existing audience to new consumers eager for the products and services provided by the new technologies.

Publishing, however, was slow to jump on the new media bandwagon, feeling it might threaten print publishing as we know it. However, most publishers have come to realize that in a consumer-driven marketplace, you've got to go where the buyers are. And consumers were light years ahead of most publishers, accepting a new format for reference and literary material, and demanding increased speed and quality of information transmission. The industry reexamined its attitude, and realized that rather than replace print publishing, new media would provide new outlets for writers and print products. To take full advantage of this potential, writers and agents need to think about how new technology will affect their roles and how to make the changes pay off for them.

The relationship between content owners/creators and content exploiters is central, and publishers occupy a strong position going into the game. Early on, many major houses felt electronic rights to books they published had potential value. Although they were incapable of exploiting these rights themselves, publishers held onto these rights whenever possible. Some have, in essence, created a virtual warehouse of backlist rights, including classic titles for which the contracts were drafted pre-electronic age and whose language may be cloudy enough to allow the publisher to claim ownership.

Now, of course, most publishers in the U.S. have a new media division, and even small presses have joint ventures or work-for-hire relationships with software companies. Writers must recognize the need for a strong advocate when negotiating these complex terms. The sophisticated agenting community regards the battle over electronic rights as the gateway to the new frontier.

The new deal

Control of electronic and/or new media project rights can often make or break a multi-layered contract. A new branch of literary agenting has developed, encompassing electronic and new media rights. This may be the fastest growing and

Liza Landsman is Director of New Media at Writers House Inc., a literary agency in New York City.

most complex form of publishing. To move into the 21st Century, the publishing industry must reinvent itself. New media can present both entertainment and information in a variety of formats: CD-ROM, online services, books, computer games, film, television and endless combinations of all the media.

For example, many popular computer and CD-ROM games include characters and plot lines which can be developed in other ways. Once a game is successful, a novelization of the plot line or new stories featuring the characters can be published in print books. In addition, films can be produced using these same plot lines and characters. All of the products, based on one underlying concept, form a synergistic relationship generating many products and numerous licenses.

With the advent of new media, the agent's role changes in a couple of important ways. First, they must think of themselves as more than simply authors' representatives. There are many creative people involved in the development of interactive projects, many of whom could benefit from a relationship with an agent. These include content developers, software developers, game designers, software engineers, audio engineers, as well as writers and artists. These people may be familiar with their own specialized field but lack the broader perspective — and the connections — essential for survival in this competitive, evolving marketplace. Literary agents must start thinking of themselves as potential representatives of all content creators and contributors.

Second, today's literary agents must familiarize themselves with how electronic rights deals are structured. Projects involving multimedia development tend to be more collaborative than book projects. Rarely can one individual be singled out as the sole creative force behind a product. These products are most often the fruit of the combined efforts of writers, artists, technicians and designers. Someone must carefully orchestrate these marriages if there is to be any hope of a successful and competitive product emerging. Some publishers feel that this is their arena. However, as the race to buy content becomes more competitive, content creators (and their representatives) find they can assert more control over the process. The agent's role becomes more like that of a packager, working with a group of talented individuals and companies on a single project. The agent must not only be a strong negotiator, but also a capable consensus builder.

Deals are generated from a variety of sources. Sometimes, an author/creator conceives of a project which the agent sells as a whole unit to a publisher. Sometimes, however, the ideas flow from another direction. In one instance, a large, prominent software publisher approached me with an idea for an enormous project. They had envisioned the overall concept, a home management guide that could do everything from teaching you how to bake bread to balancing your checkbook. They needed creative people to flesh out the distinct areas. I was able to provide several writers and designers who not only brought form to their nebulous ideas but also added concepts which enhanced the final product immeasurably. Ultimately, it proved to be a highly successful marriage of technology and content, and resulted in a CD-ROM product with an online component, which will be distributed through bookstores, software outlets and various online services.

Bringing the pieces together

Selling a project, obviously, is just the beginning. Once an initial idea is licensed, the agent puts together an ensemble cast of creative talent to generate an entire package of new media products. The creator is paired with a developer and perhaps a graphic artist, as well as a print publisher and software company.

Not every company has access to all methods of presentation. For example, a computer company which produces CD-ROM games may not have a print publishing division. In that case, the agent works out a joint arrangement with the computer company and a print publisher. Even when a single buyer corporation has all the divisions necessary to produce a multimedia project, coordinating all the elements and working out contractual details can be complicated. This is why an agent is necessary for many new media projects. The work of the agent is longer, more complex and fraught with pitfalls. In return, though, the varieties of product lines are greater.

Keeping thoroughly up to date

In representing clients in new media, agents must have a firm grasp of the various technologies involved. This means learning about the means of production and various techniques involved, such as silicon graphic machines, full-motion video, image texturing, interface design, software engines, etc., and knowing which players perform which services, who is competent, who is pushing the envelope, and who is creating cutting edge technology. It means knowing each company's means of distribution: Are they strong in bookstores but weak in software outlets? Can they successfully identify the market, then capture an adequate share? Good distribution means the difference between life and death for a product, and it's even trickier when the products themselves are difficult to categorize.

To successfully represent a new media client, the agent must be comfortable with an industry that changes while the ink on the contract is drying and be willing to tackle and sift through an enormous amount of information every week, from the daily newspapers to the dozens of trade journals covering the topic. Players jump around a great deal, and an agent has to know who is where.

In addition, the range of possible content customers is expanding, from the traditional options of publishers and film and television companies, to include media, cable and phone companies. An unusual mix of enterprises populates the multimedia universe. A new media agent has to think fast and remain compatible with a flexible, almost technically promiscuous environment. New media agenting is not for the faint of heart!

There is a vast need for diverse talent and eclectic creativity, and agents play a part in answering it. In time, a broad range of entertainment and information products will be conceived as CD-ROMs, from technical and scholarly works offering an endless amount of information, to high concept entertainments providing sheer, unadulterated fun. Online services and web sites on the Internet will provide greater access to entertainment and educational material. Interactive television produced by film, television, cable, satellite and phone companies in conjunction with writers, designers and technical experts, will bring gaming, shopping and a new breed of entertainment programming into the home. Location-based entertainment centers will provide interactive film and gaming experiences created by writers and designers to a global audience.

However, there is a caveat! Material that is "book appropriate" doesn't necessarily translate into other media. Simply because "it can be done" does not mean that it *should* be. Prudent agents consider carefully whether there is "value added" by casting the material in another format. There has been something of a gold rush on the electronic frontier, and many writers (as well as publishers and agents) have felt the need to see their material re-purposed. However, many works are not improved upon by such transformation. Quality of idea, marketability, and ability to execute the concept is important in the selection of new media projects and clients. A good match can benefit both client and agent over the duration of their relationship.

A brave new world

This is an exciting and strange time for the publishing industry. New media technology will lead to new creative partnerships and result in fresh products. While the impact will be great, new media does not sound the death knell of print publishing. It will change its face, however, providing publishers with more areas of creative development and profit. It will force publishers to keep up with the changing market and evolve in ways that take advantage of those changes. But by doing so, publishers will create new markets and attract new consumers. Those companies and individuals who can meet these challenges will be able to creatively expand their products to an ever-wider, more technologically literate world.

Literary Agents: Nonfee-charging

Agents listed in this section generate from 98 to 100 percent of their income from commission on sales. They do not charge for reading, critiquing, editing, marketing or other services. They make their living solely from their contacts and experience, with time their most limited commodity.

For you as a writer looking for an agent, this can cut two ways. On one hand, it will cost you no more than postage to have your work considered by an agent with an imperative to find saleable manuscripts: Her income depends on her clients' incomes. Her job is to know the market, who is buying what and when. Effective agents generally know a large number of editors who specialize in a variety of work, and know how to present a work to producers and studios interested in TV and movie rights. They capitalize on that knowledge and devote their time to selling.

On the other hand, these agents must be more selective, offering representation to writers whose work is outstanding and requires minimal shaping and editing. They often prefer to work with established authors, celebrities or those with professional credentials in a particular field. These agents simply don't have the time to nurture a beginning writer through many stages of development before a work is saleable.

Standard operating procedures

Most agents open to submissions prefer to initially receive a query letter that briefly describes your work. Some agents (particularly those dealing largely in fiction) ask for an outline and a number of sample chapters, but you should send these only if you are requested to do so in an agent's listing. It takes time for the agents to answer the detailed questionnaires we use to compile the listings. If an agent specifies what to send her, follow it to the letter. She is telling you exactly what she needs to judge your abilities and extend an offer of representation.

Always send a self-addressed stamped envelope (SASE) or postcard for reply. If you have not heard back from an agent within the approximate reporting time given (allowing for holidays and summer vacations) a quick, polite call to ask when it will be reviewed would be in order. Never fax a query letter, outline or sample chapters to an agent without permission to do so. Due to the volume of material they receive, agents tend to take a long time to consider queries, so you may want to send queries to several different agents at a time. It is best, however, to have the complete manuscript considered by only one agent at a time.

Commissions range from 10 to 15 percent for domestic sales and usually are higher for foreign or dramatic sales, often 20 to 25 percent. The difference goes to the subagent who places the work.

Many agents in this section charge for ordinary business expenses in addition to the commission. Expenses can include foreign postage, fax charges, long distance phone calls, messenger and express mail services and photocopying. Some charge only for what they consider "extraordinary" expenses. Make sure you have a clear understanding of what these are before signing an agency agreement. Most agents will agree to discuss these expenses as they arise.

While most agents deduct expenses from the advance or royalties before passing them on to the author, a few agents included here charge a low ($50 or less) one-time only expense fee upfront. Sometimes these are called "marketing" or "handling" fees. Agents charging more than $50 in marketing fees are included in the Literary Agents: Fee-charging section.

Effective January 1, 1996, all members of the Association of Authors' Representatives (AAR) will be prohibited from charging reading or evaluation fees.

Special indexes and additional help

To help you with your search, we've included a number of special indexes in the back of the book. The Subject Index is divided into sections for nonfee-charging and fee-charging literary agents and script agents. Each of thse sections in the index is then divided by nonfiction and fiction subject categories. Some agencies indicated that they were open to all nonfiction or fiction topics. These have been grouped in the subject heading "open" in each section. This year we have added a number of new topics, including education, how-to, humor and popular culture in nonfiction, and horror in fiction. Many agents have indicated additional areas of interest in their listings this year.

We've included an Agent Index as well. Often you will read about an agent who is an employee of a larger agency and may not be able to locate her business phone or address. We asked agencies to list the agents on staff, then listed the names in alphabetical order along with the name of the agency they work for. Find the name of the person you would like to contact and then check the agency listing. You will find the page number for the agency's listing in the Listings Index.

A geographic index lists agents state by state for those who are looking for an agent close to home.

Many literary agents are also interested in scripts; many script agents will also consider book manuscripts. Nonfee-charging script agents who primarily sell scripts but also handle at least 10 to 15 percent book manuscripts appear among the listings in this section, with the contact information, breakdown of work currently handled and a note to check the full listing in the script section. Those nonfee-charging script agencies that sell scripts and less than 10 to 15 percent book manuscripts appear in "Additional Nonfee-charging Agents" at the end of this section. Complete listings for these agents appear in the Script Agent section.

Before contacting any agency, check the listing to make sure it is open to new clients. Those designated (V) are currently not interested in expanding their rosters.

For more information on approaching agents and the specifics of the listings, read *How to Use Your Guide to Literary Agents* and *The Right Literary Agent For You*. Also see the various articles at the beginning of the book for explorations of different aspects of the author/agent relationship.

We've ranked the agencies listed in this section according to their openness to submissions. Below is our ranking system:

   I   Newer agency actively seeking clients.
   II Agency seeking both new and established writers.
   III Agency prefers to work with established writers, mostly obtains new
       clients through referrals.
   IV Agency handling only certain types of work or work by writers under

certain circumstances.

V Agency not currently seeking new clients. We have included mention of agencies rated **V** to let you know they are currently not open to new clients. In addition to those ranked **V**, we have included a few well-known agencies' names who have declined the opportunity to receive full listings at this time. *Unless you have a strong recommendation from someone well respected in the field, our advice is to approach only those agents ranked I-IV.*

ACTON, LEONE, HANSON & JAFFE, INC. (II), (formerly Acton, Dystel, Leone & Jaffe, Inc.), 928 Broadway, Suite #303, New York NY 10010. (212)254-5800. Fax: (212)254-6140. Contact: M. Perkins. Estab. 1976. Member of AAR. Represents 200 clients. 30% of clients are new/previously unpublished writers. Specializes in commercial nonfiction and fiction; some category fiction; some literary fiction. Currently handles: 50% nonfiction books; 50% novels.
Handles: Nonfiction books, novels. Considers these nonfiction areas: animals; biography/autobiography; business; child guidance/parenting; current affairs; ethnic/cultural interests; gay/lesbian issues; government/politics/law; history; humor; military/war; money/finance/economics; music/dance/theater/film; nature/environment; New Age/metaphysics; popular culture; psychology; religious/inspirational; science/technology; self-help/personal improvement; sports; true crime/investigative; women's issues/women's studies. Considers these fiction areas: action/adventure; contemporary issues; detective/police/crime; erotica; ethnic; family saga; feminist; glitz; historical; literary; mainstream; mystery/suspense; romance; sports; thriller/espionage. Query. Reports in 2 weeks on queries; 1 month on fiction mss and 3 weeks on nonfiction mss.
Recent Sales: *The Edge*, by Mark Olshaker (Crown); *You Wouldn't Believe What My Grandchild Did*, by Lois Wyse (Simon & Schuster).
Terms: Agent receives 15% commission on domestic sales; 19% on foreign sales. Offers written contract. Charges for photocopying and express mail.
Tips: Obtains new clients through recommendations from others. Requires SASE for response.

ADLER & ROBIN BOOKS INC., (II), 3409 29th St., Suite 3, Washington DC 20008. (202)363-7410. Fax: (202)686-1804. Contact: Beth Pratt-Dewey. Estab. 1986. Represents 30 clients. 20% of clients are new/previously unpublished writers. Currently handles: 98% nonfiction books; 2% juvenile books. Member agents: Bill Adler, Jr., Beth Pratt-Dewey, Lisa Swayne.
Handles: Nonfiction books. Considers these nonfiction areas: animals; anthropology/archaelology; biography/autobiography; business; child guidance/parenting; computers/electronics; cooking/food/nutrition; current affairs; ethnic/cultural interests; gay/lesbian issues; government/politics/law; health/medicine; history; how-to; money/finance/economics; nature/environment; popular culture; religious/inspirational; science/technology; self-help/personal improvement; true crime/investigative; women's issues/women's studies. Considers these nonfiction areas: action/adventure; contemporary issues; detective/police/crime; historical; literary; mainstream; mystery/suspense; romance (contemporary, gothic, historical, regency); science fiction; thriller/espionage. Query with outline/proposal. Reports in 6 weeks on queries.
Recent Sales: *Tis the Season: Vegetarian Christmas*, by Nan Blanchard (Simon & Schuster); *The Network: Inside the Tight-Knit World of Black America's Self-Made Moguls, Athletes, Executives, Politicans, and Other Power Brokers*, by Elizabeth Lesly (McGraw Hill).
Terms: Agent receives 15% commission on domestic and foreign sales. Offers written contract.
Tips: Obtains new clients through recommendations.

AGENCY CHICAGO (I), P.O. Box 11200, Chicago IL 60611. Contact: Ernest Santucci. Estab. 1990. Represents 14 clients. 50% of clients are new/previously unpublished writers. Specializes in ghost writing. Currently handles: 40% nonfiction books; 20% scholarly books; 10% novels; 10% movie scripts; 20% TV scripts.
Handles: Nonfiction books, sports books. Considers these nonfiction areas: art/architecture/design; environment; fitness; gambling; sports; true crime. Considers these fiction areas: erotica;

The double dagger before a listing indicates the listing is new in this edition.

experimental; regional; westerns/frontier. Send outline/proposal, bio and SASE. Reports in 2 months.

Terms: Agent receives 10-15% commission on domestic sales; 15% on foreign sales. Offers written contract, binding for 1 year.

Writer's Conferences: Attends Midwest Writers Conference; International Writers and Translators Conference.

Tips: Obtains new clients through recommendations. "Do not send dot matrix printed manuscripts. Manuscripts should have a clean professional look, with correct grammar and punctuation." Include SASE. No phone calls.

AGENTS INC. FOR MEDICAL AND MENTAL HEALTH PROFESSIONALS (II), P.O. Box 4956, Fresno CA 93744-4956. Phone/fax: (303)751-5642. Director: Sydney H. Harriet, Ph.D. Estab. 1987. Member of APA. Represents 30 clients. 45% of clients are new/previously unpublished writers. Specializes in "writers who have education and experience in the medical and mental health professions. It is helpful if the writer is licensed, but not necessary. Prior book publication not necessary." Currently handles: 75% nonfiction books; 5% scholarly books; 20% novels.

Handles: Nonfiction books, novels, some scholarly books. Considers these nonfiction areas: business; child guidance/parenting; current affairs; health/medicine; how-to; nutrition; psychology; science fiction; science/technology; self-help/personal improvement; sociology; sports; sports medicine/psychology; mind-body healing; reference. Considers these fiction areas: contemporary issues; commercial and literary: detective/police/crime; horror; mystery/suspense; science fiction; thriller/espionage genres acceptable. Query with vita and SASE. Reports in 2 weeks on queries; 1 month on mss.

Recent Sales: *Grains for Better Health*, by Danielle Chase and Maureen Keane (Prima Publishing).

Terms: Agent receives 15% commission on domestic sales; 20% on foreign sales. Offers written contract, binding for 6-12 months. "After contract with a publisher is signed, office expenses are negotiated."

Writer's Conferences: Attends numerous Southwest and Rocky Mountain conferences. Also available for conferences by request.

Tips: "Now interested in receiving more novels and business-oriented proposals. Majority of our clients are referred. The rest are obtained from writers using this guide. Our specialty has been to help writers with their manuscripts. If the idea is unique, but the writing needs work, that's where we have done our best work. We rarely receive manuscripts that are contracted immediately. Unfortunately, we cannot respond to queries or proposals without receiving a return envelope and sufficient postage."

THE JOSEPH S. AJLOUNY AGENCY (II), 29205 Greening Blvd., Farmington Hills MI 48334-2945. (810)932-0090. Fax: (810)932-8763. Contact: Joe Ajlouny. Estab. 1987. Signatory of WGA. "Represents humor and comedy writers, humorous illustrators, cartoonists." Member agents: Joe Ajlouny (original humor, how-to); Elena Pantel (music, popular culture); Gwen Foss (general nonfiction).

Handles: "In addition to humor and titles concerning American popular culture, we will consider general nonfiction in the areas of 'how-to' books, history, health, cookbooks, self-help, social commentary, criticism, travel, biography and memoirs." Query first with SASE. Reports in 2-4 weeks.

Recent Sales: *No Chairs Make for Short Meetings*, by Richard Rybolt (NAL/Dutton); *Famous Peoples' Cats*, by Ronna Mogelon (St. Martin's Press).

Terms: Agent receives 15% commission on domestic sales. Charges for postage, photocopying and phone expenses. Foreign and subsidiary rights commission fees estalished on per-sale basis.

Writer's Conferences Attends ABA (Chicago); Mid-America Publishers Assoc. (Grand Rapids MI, Sept.) Book Fair (Frankfurt, Germany).

Tips: Obtains new clients "typically from referrals and by some advertising and public relations projects. We also frequently speak at seminars for writers on the process of being published. Just make sure your project is clever, marketable and professionally prepared. We see too much material that is limited in scope and appeal. It helps immeasurably to have credentials in the field or topic being written about."

LEE ALLAN AGENCY (II), P.O. Box 18617, Milwaukee WI 53218-0617. (414)357-7708. Fax: call for number. Contact: Lee Matthias. Estab. 1983. Signatory of WGA. Represents 25 clients. 50% of clients are new/previously unpublished writers. Specializes in suspense fiction. Currently handles: 15% nonfiction books; 75% novels; 5% movie scripts; 5% TV scripts. Member agents: Lee A. Matthias (all types of genre fiction and screenplays, nonfiction).

Handles: Nonfiction books, juvenile books, novels. Considers these nonfiction areas: child guidance/parenting; cooking/food/nutrition; health/medicine; music/dance/theater/film; nature/environment; popular culture; science/technology; self-help/personal improvement; true crime/investigative. Considers these fiction areas: action/adventure; detective/police/crime; fantasy; glitz; historical; horror; mystery/suspense; psychic/supernatural; romance (contemporary, historical); science fiction; thriller/espionage; westerns/frontier; young adult.

- This agency reports that it is closed to queries and submissions through 6/95.

Also Handles: Movie scripts (feature film), TV scripts (TV mow, episode drama). Considers these script subject areas: action/adventure; comedy; contemporary issues; detective/police/crime; horror; mystery/suspense; psychic/supernatural; romantic comedy and drama; science fiction; thriller; westerns/frontier.

Terms: Agent receives 15% commission on domestic sales; foreign higher. Offers written contract. Charges for photocopying, international telephone calls and/or excessive long-distance telephone calls."

Tips: Obtains new clients mainly through recommendations and solicitations. If interested in agency representation, "read agency listings carefully and query the most compatible. Always query by letter with SASE or IRC with envelope. A very brief, straightforward letter (one-two pages, maximum) introducing yourself, describing or summarizing your material will suffice. Avoid patronizing or 'cute' approaches. We *do not reply* to queries *without* SASE. Do not expect an agent to sell a manuscript which you know is not a likely sale if nonagented. Agents are not magicians; they serve best to find better and more of the likeliest publishers or producers. And they really do their work after an offer by way of negotiating contracts, selling subsidiary rights, administrating the account(s), advising the writer with objectivity, and acting as the buffer between writer and editor."

JAMES ALLEN, LITERARY AGENCY (III), P.O. Box 278, Milford PA 18337-0278. Estab. 1974. Signatory of WGA. Represents 40 clients. 10% of clients are new/previously unpublished writers. "I handle all kinds of genre fiction (except westerns) and specialize in science fiction and fantasy." Currently handles: 2% nonfiction books; 8% juvenile books; 90% novels.

Handles: Novels. Considers these nonfiction areas: history; true crime/investigative. Considers these fiction areas: action/adventure; detective/police/crime; family saga; fantasy; glitz; historical; horror; mainstream; mystery/suspense; romance (contemporary historical); science fiction; young adult. Query. Responds in 1 week on queries; 2 months on mss. "I prefer first contact to be a query letter with two-three page plot synopsis and SASE with a response time of 1 week. If my interest is piqued, I then ask for the first four chapters, response time two weeks. If I'm impressed by the writing, I then ask for the balance of the manuscript, response time about two months."

Recent Sales: *The Passage*, by David Poyer (St. Martin's Press); *With Pen and Saber*, by Robert Trout (Stackpole).

Terms: Agent receives 10% commission on domestic print sales; 20% on film sales; 20% on foreign sales. Offers written contract, binding for 3 years "automatically renewed. No reading fees or other up-front charges. I reserve the right to charge for extraordinary expenses. I do not bill the author, but deduct the charges from incoming earnings."

Writer's Conferences: First Coast Writers Festival (Jacksonville, Florida); California Writers Club Conference (Pacific Grove, California).

Tips: *"First time at book length need not apply—only* taking on authors who have the foundations of their writing careers in place and can use help in building the rest. A cogent, to-the-point query letter is necessary, laying out the author's track record and giving a brief blurb for the book. The response to a mere 'I have written a novel, will you look at it?' is universally 'NO!' "

‡LINDA ALLEN LITERARY AGENCY (II), 1949 Green St., Suite 5, San Francisco CA 94123. (415)921-6437. Contact: Linda Allen or Amy Kossow. Estab. 1982. Represents 35-40 clients. Specializes in "good books and nice people."

Handles: Nonfiction, novels (adult and juvenile). Considers these nonfiction areas: anthropology/archaeology; art/architecture/design; biography/autobiography; business; child guidance/parenting; computers/electronics; ethnic/cultural interests; gay/lesbian issues; government/politics/law; history; juvenile nonfiction; music/dance/theater/film; nature/environment; New Age/metaphysics; popular culture; psychology; sociology; true crime/investigative; women's issues/women's studies. Considers these fiction areas: action/adventure; contemporary issues; detective/police/crime; ethnic; fantasy; feminist; gay; glitz; horror; juvenile; lesbian; literary; mainstream; mystery/suspense; psychic/supernatural; regional; romance (regency); science fiction; thriller/espionage; young adult. Query with SASE. Reports in 2-3 weeks on queries.

Terms: Agent receives 15% commission. Charges for photocopying.

Tips: Obtains new clients "by referral mostly."

‡MIRIAM ALTSHULER LITERARY AGENCY, (II), 5 Old Post Rd., RR#1 Box 5, Red Hook NY 12571. (914)758-9408. Fax: (914)758-3118. Contact: Miriam Altshuler. Estab. 1994. Member of

AAR. Represents 35 clients. 50% of clients are new/previously unpublished writers. Specializes in literary and commercial fiction and nonfiction. Mostly adult, a little young adult and children's books. Currently handles: 40% nonfiction; 8% juvenile books; 40% novels; 2% short story collections.
Handles: Nonfiction books, novels. Considers these nonfiction areas: biography/autobiography; current affairs; ethnic/cultural interests; gay/lesbian issues; history; nature/environment; psychology; women's issues/women's studies. Considers these fiction areas: ethnic; feminist; gay; literary; mainstream. Query. Must send SASE. Reports in 1 week on queries; 3 weeks on mss.
Terms: Agent receives 10% commission on domestic sales; 20% on foreign sales; 15% on motion picture sales.
Tips: Obtains new clients through recommendations from others.

MARCIA AMSTERDAM AGENCY (II), 41 W. 82nd St., New York NY 10024-5613. (212)873-4945. Contact: Marcia Amsterdam. Estab. 1970. Signatory of WGA. Currently handles: 5% nonfiction books; 80% novels; 10% movie scripts; 5% TV scripts.
Handles: Novels, movie scripts, TV scripts. Considers these fiction areas: action/adventure; detective; glitz; historical; horror; humor; mainstream; mystery/suspense; romance (contemporary, historical); science fiction; thriller/espionage; westerns/frontier; young adult. Send outline plus first 3 sample chapters and SASE. Reports in 1 month on queries.
Recent Sales: *Shadow*, by Joyce Sweeney (Dell); *Relentless*, by Kris Franklin (Zebra); *Keepers of the Misty Time*, by Patricia Rowe (Warner); *White Night*, by William Lovejoy (Zebra).
Terms: Agent receives 15% commission on domestic sales; 20% on foreign sales. Offers written contract, binding for 1 year, "renewable." Charges for extra office expenses, foreign postage, copying, legal fees (when agreed upon).
Tips: "We are always looking for interesting literary voices."

BART ANDREWS & ASSOCIATES INC. (III), 7510 Sunset Blvd., Suite 100, Los Angeles CA 90046. (213)851-8158. Contact: Bart Andrews. Estab. 1982. Member of AAR. Represents 25 clients. 25% of clients are new/previously unpublished authors. Specializes in nonfiction only, and in the general category of entertainment (movies, TV, biographies, autobiographies). Currently handles: 100% nonfiction books.
Handles: Nonfiction books. Considers these nonfiction areas: biography/autobiography; music/dance/theater/film; TV. Query. Reports in 1 week on queries; 1 month on mss.
Recent Sales: *Roseanne*, by J. Randy Taraborrelli (G.P. Putnam's Sons); *Out of the Madness*, by Rose Books (packaging firm) (HarperCollins).
Terms: Agent receives 15% commission on domestic sales; 15% on foreign sales (after subagent takes his 10%). Offers written contract, "binding on a project-by-project basis." Author/client is charged for all photocopying, mailing, phone calls, postage, etc.
Writer's Conferences: Frequently lectures at UCLA in Los Angeles.
Tips: "Recommendations from existing clients or professionals are best, although I find a lot of new clients by seeking them out myself. I rarely find a new client through the mail. Spend time writing a query letter. Sell yourself like a product. The bottom line is writing ability, and then the idea itself. It takes a lot to convince me. I've seen it all! I hear from too many first-time authors who don't do their homework. They're trying to get a book published and they haven't the faintest idea what is required of them. There are plenty of good books on the subject and, in my opinion, it's their responsibility—not mine—to educate themselves before they try to find an agent to represent their work. When I ask an author to see a manuscript or even a partial manuscript, I really must be convinced I want to read it—based on a strong query letter—because I have no intention of wasting my time reading just for the fun of it."

‡APOLLO ENTERTAINMENT (I), 3838 N. Bernard St., 2nd Floor, Chicago IL 60618. (312)267-8126. Contact: Bruce Harrington. Estab. 1993. Signatory of WGA. Represents 5 clients. 20% of clients are new/previously unpublished writers. Specializes in feature screenplays of unordinary topics. Currently handles: 20% nonfiction books; 80% movie scripts; 10% TV scripts.
• See the expanded listing for this agency in Script Agents.

APPLESEEDS MANAGEMENT (II), 200 E. 30th St., Suite 302, San Bernardino CA 92404. (909)882-1667. For screenplays and teleplays only, send to 1870 N. Vermont, Suite 560, Hollywood CA 90027. Executive Manager: S. James Foiles. Estab. 1988. Signatory of WGA, licensed by state of California. Represents 25 clients. 40% of clients are new/previously unpublished writers. Currently handles: 25% nonfiction books; 40% novels; 20% movie scripts; 15% teleplays (mow).
• This agency reports that it is not accepting unsolicited screenplays and teleplays at this time.

Handles: Nonfiction books, novels. Considers these nonfiction areas: biography/autobiography; business; health/medicine; money/finance/economics; music/dance/theater/film; psychology; self-help/personal improvement; true crime/investigative; general nonfiction. Considers these fiction areas: action/adventure; detective/police/crime; fantasy; historical; horror; humor/satire; mainstream; mystery/suspense; occult/horror novels; psychic/supernatural; science fiction; thriller/espionage; true crime/investigative. Query. Reports in 2 weeks on queries; 2 months on mss. **Also Handles:** Movie scripts. Specializes in materials that could be adapted from book to screen; and in screenplays and teleplays. TV scripts (TV mow, no episodic).
Terms: Agent receives 10-15% commission on domestic sales; 20% on foreign sales. Offers written contract, binding for 1-7 years.
Tips: "In your query, please describe your intended target audience and distinguish your book/script from similar works."

AUTHORS' LITERARY AGENCY (III), P.O.Box 610582, DFW Airport TX 75261-0582. Phone: (817)267-1078. Fax: (817)571-4656. Contact: Dick Smith. Estab. 1992. Represents 19 clients. 70% of clients are new/previously unpublished writers. Currently handles: 25% nonfiction books; 75% novels. Member agents: Dick Smith; Jim Campise; Chris Mauno.
Handles: Nonfiction. Considers most nonfiction areas, especially how-to; self-help/personal improvement; true crime/investigative; women's issues/women's studies. Considers these fiction areas: detective/police/crime; literary; mainstream; mystery/suspense; thriller/espionage. Query first always. Unsolicited mss will be returned unread. Reports in 1 month on queries; 2 months on mss.
Recent Sales: *Fourth and Long; The Kent Waldrep Story*, by Kent Waldrep and Susan Malone (Crossroads).
Terms: Agent receives 15% commission on domestic sales; 25% on foreign sales. Offers written contract, binding until cancelled by either party.
Tips: Obtains new clients through recommendations, networking at conferences. "For fiction, always send query letter first with: 1) a synopsis or outline of your work, 2) an author's bio, 3) the first three chapters of your work, and 4) SASE. *Do not send entire manuscript* until the agency requests it. For nonfiction, submit a query letter first with 1) a bio stating your experience and credentials to write the work, 2) a book proposal (we suggest using Michael Larsen's *How To Write A Book Proposal* as a guideline), and 3) SASE. Always send SASE with all queries. We cannot respond to work submitted without SASE and adequate postage for return to you."

THE AXELROD AGENCY (III), 54 Church St., Lenox MA 01240. (413)637-2000. Fax: (413)637-4725. Contact: Steven Axelrod. Estab. 1983. Member of AAR. Represents 30 clients. Specializes in commercial fiction, nonfiction. Currently handles: 40% nonfiction books; 60% fiction.
Handles: Considers these nonfiction areas: art; business; computers; government/politics/law; health/medicine; history; money/finance/economics; music/dance/theater/film; nature/environment; science/technology. Considers these fiction areas: cartoon/comic; detective/police/crime; family saga; glitz; historical; literary; mainstream; mystery/suspense; picture book; romance (contemporary, historical, regency); thriller/espionage. Query. Reports in 10 days on queries; 2-3 weeks on mss.
Terms: Agent receives 10% commission on domestic sales; 20% on foreign sales. Charges for photocopying.
Writer's Conferences: Attends Romance Writers of America and Novelists, Inc. conferences.
Tips: Obtains new clients through referrals.

MALAGA BALDI LITERARY AGENCY (II), P.O. Box 591, Radio City Station, New York NY 10101. (212)222-1221. Contact: Malaga Baldi. Estab. 1985. Represents 40-50 clients. 80% of clients are new/previously unpublished writers. Specializes in quality literary fiction and nonfiction. Currently handles: 60% nonfiction books; 30% novels; 5% novellas; 5% short story collections.
   • See Malaga Baldi's article, *Negotiating a Sale*, in the 1993 edition of the *Guide*.
Handles: Nonfiction books, novels, novellas, short story collections. Considers any well-written nonfiction, but do *not* send child guidance, crafts, juvenile nonfiction, New Age/metaphysics, religious/inspirational or sports material. Considers any well-written fiction, but do *not* send confessional, family saga, fantasy, glitz, juvenile, picture book, psychic/supernatural, religious/inspirational, romance, science fiction, western or young adult. Query first, but prefers entire ms for fiction. Reports within 10 weeks. "Please enclose self-addressed stamped jiffy bag with submission and self-addressed stamped postcard for acknowledgement of consideration of manuscript."
Recent Sales: *What Jane Austen Ate and Charles Dickens Knew: From Fox Hunting to Whist—the Facts of Daily Life in 19th Century England*, by Daniel Pool (Simon & Schuster); *House Rules,*

by Heather Lewis (Nan Talese/Doubleday); *The Monster Show: A Cultural History of Horror*, by David T. Skal (Norton).
Terms: Agent receives 15% commission on domestic sales; 20% on foreign sales. Offers written contract. Charges "initial $50 fee to cover photocopying expenses. If the manuscript is lengthy, I prefer the author to cover expense of photocopying."
Tips: "From the day I agree to represent the author, my role is to serve as his or her advocate in contract negotiations and publicity efforts. Along the way, I wear many different hats. To one author I may serve as a nudge, to another a confidante, and to many simply as a supportive friend. I am also a critic, researcher, legal expert, messenger, diplomat, listener, counselor and source of publishing information and gossip. I work with writers on developing a presentable submission and make myself available during all aspects of a book's publication."

BALKIN AGENCY, INC. (III), P.O. Box 222, Amherst MA 01004. (413)548-9835. Fax: (413)548-9836. President: R. Balkin. Estab. 1972. Member of AAR. Represents 50 clients. 10% of clients are new/previously unpublished writers. Specializes in adult nonfiction. Currently handles: 85% nonfiction books; 5% scholarly books; 5% reference books; 5% textbooks.
Handles: Nonfiction books, textbooks, reference, scholarly books. Considers these nonfiction areas: animals; anthropology/archaeology; biography; current affairs; health/medicine; history; how-to; language/literature/criticism; music/dance/theater/film; nature/environment; pop culture; science/technology; social science; translations; travel; true crime/investigative. Query with outline/proposal. Reports in 2 weeks on queries; 3 weeks on mss.
Recent Sales: *A Natural History of the Grand Canyon*, by Schmidt (H-M); *A Different Mirror*, by Takaki (Little Brown).
Terms: Agent receives 15% commission on domestic sales; 20% on foreign sales. Offers written contract, binding for 1 year. Charges for photocopying, trans-Atlantic long-distance calls or faxes and express mail.
Tips: Obtains new clients through referrals. "I do not take on books described as bestsellers or potential bestsellers. Any nonfiction work that is either unique, paradigmatic, a contribution, truly witty or a labor of love is grist for my mill."

VIRGINIA BARBER LITERARY AGENCY, INC., 101 Fifth Ave., New York NY 10003. Prefers not to share information.

LORETTA BARRETT BOOKS INC. (II), 101 Fifth Ave., New York NY 10003. (212)242-3420. Fax: (212)691-9418. President: Loretta A. Barrett. Associate: Gary Morris. Estab. 1990. Represents 70 clients. Specializes in general interest books. Currently handles: 20% fiction; 80% nonfiction.
Handles: Considers all areas of nonfiction and fiction. Query first, then send partial ms and synopsis. Reports in 4-6 weeks on queries and mss.
Terms: Agent receives 15% commission on domestic sales; 20% on foreign sales. Offers written contract. Charges for "all professional expenses."

GENE BARTCZAK ASSOCIATES INC. (II), Box 715, North Bellmore NY 11710-0766. (516)781-6230. President: Sue Bartczak. Estab. 1980. Represents 18 clients. 100% of clients are new/previously unpublished writers. Currently handles: 33% nonfiction books; 50% juvenile books; 17% novels.
Handles: Nonfiction books, juvenile books, middle readers and up. "No picture books." Considers these nonfiction areas: animals; biography/autobiography; how-to; juvenile nonfiction (middle readers and up); self-help/personal improvement; women's issues/women's studies. Considers these fiction areas: contemporary issues; feminist; humor/satire; juvenile (no picture books); mainstream; young adult. Query. Must have SASE. Reports in 2 weeks on queries; 4-6 weeks on mss.
Recent Sales: *Squank*, by Kathleen Duey (May Haven Publishing).
Terms: Agent receives 15% commission on domestic sales; 20% on foreign sales. Offers written contract, binding for 1 year; automatic renewal for 1-year terms unless given 90 days prior written notice to terminate by either party.
Tips: Obtains new clients through recommendations and agency listings. "Be sure to include SASE with any material sent to an agent if you expect to get an answer. If you want the material you sent returned to you, be sure that your SASE has enough postage to take care of that."

‡THE BEEKMAN LITERARY AGENCY, INC. (I, II), 425 W. 21st St., Apt. 3, New York NY 10011-2947. Phone/fax: (212)759-0408. E-mail: marieke@aol.com. Contact: Michelle Maerov. Estab. 1994. Specializes in fiction and also general nonfiction health and psychology-related books.
Handles: Nonfiction books, novels. Considers these nonfiction areas: animals; anthropology/archaeology; art/architecture/design; biography/autobiography; business; child guidance/parenting; computers/electronics; cooking/food/nutrition; crafts/hobbies; current affairs; education;

ethnic/cultural interests; government/politics/law; health/medicine; history; how-to; humor; language/literature/criticism; money/finance/economics; music/dance/theater/film; nature/environment; New Age/metaphysics; popular culture; psychology; religious/inspirational; science/technology; self-help/personal improvement; sociology; sports; true crime/investigative; women's issues/women's studies. Considers these fiction areas: action/adventure; cartoon/comic; contemporary issues; detective/police/crime; erotica; ethnic; family saga; feminist; glitz; historical; horror; humor/satire; literary; mainstream; psychic/supernatural; regional; romance; westerns/frontier. Query. Reports in 1 week on queries; 6 weeks on mss.
Terms: Agent receives 15% commission on domestic sales; 15% on foreign sales. Offers written contract. Charges for postage, long-distance phone, photocopying if sale is made.
Tips: Obtains new clients through solicitation. "I am a new and eager agent who is looking for clients with whom I can grow. I welcome all genres."

JOSH BEHAR LITERARY AGENCY (I), Empire State Bldg., 350 Fifth Ave., Suite 3304, New York NY 10118. (212)826-4386. Contact: Josh Behar. Estab. 1993. Represents 12 clients. 90% of clients are new/previously unpublished writers. "I specialize in new and unpublished authors." Currently handles: 10% nonfiction books; 90% novels.
Handles: Nonfiction books, novels. Considers these nonfiction areas: biography/autobiography; business; money/finance/economics; New Age/metaphysics; self-help/personal improvement; women's issues/women's studies. Considers these fiction areas: action/adventure; detective/police/crime; fantasy; literary; psychic/supernatural; romance (contemporary, gothic, historical, regency); science fiction; thriller/espionage. Query. Reports in 1 week on queries; 1 month on mss.
Terms: Agent receives 15% commission on domestic sales; 20% on foreign sales. Offers written contract "only after sale has been made."
Writer's Conferences: RWA (NYC), MWA (NY), SciFi (TBA).
Tips: Obtains new clients through "conferences, editors and former agent I worked for. Tell me a good story."

DAVID BLACK LITERARY AGENCY, INC. (II), 156 Fifth Ave., New York NY 10001. (212)242-5080. Fax: (212)924-6609. Associates: Marah B. Rhoades, Susan Raihofer. Estab. 1990. Member of AAR. Represents 150 clients. Specializes in sports, politics, novels. Currently handles: 80% nonfiction; 20% novels.
Handles: Nonfiction books, novels. Considers these nonfiction areas: politics; sports. Query with outline and SASE. Reports in 2 months on queries.
Recent Sales: *Dogs of God*, by Pickney Benedict; *If I Had a Hammer*, by Henry Aaron, Lonnie Wheeler (HarperCollins); *There Are No Children Here*, by Alex Kotlowitz.
Terms: Agent receives 15% commission. Charges for photocopying and books purchased for sale of foreign rights.

BLASSINGAME SPECTRUM CORP. (II), 111 Eighth Ave., Suite 1501, New York NY 10011. (212)691-7556. Contact: Eleanor Wood. Represents 50 clients. Currently handles: 95% fiction, 5% nonfiction books.
Handles: Considers these fiction areas: contemporary issues; fantasy; historical; literary; mainstream; mystery/suspense; science fiction. Query with SASE. Reports in 2 months on queries.
Terms: Agent receives 10% commission on domestic sales.
Tips: Obtains new clients through recommendations from authors and others.

REID BOATES LITERARY AGENCY (II), P.O. Box 328, 274 Cooks Crossroad, Pittstown NJ 08867. (908)730-8523. Fax: (908)730-8931. Contact: Reid Boates. Estab. 1985. Represents 45 clients. 15% of clients are new/previously unpublished writers. Specializes in general fiction and nonfiction, investigative journalism/current affairs; bios and autobiographies; serious self-help; literary humor; issue-oriented business; popular science; "no category fiction." Currently handles: 85% nonfiction books; 15% novels; "very rarely accept short story collections."
Handles: Nonfiction books, novels. Considers these nonfiction areas: animals; anthropology/archaeology; art/architecture/design; biography/autobiography; business; child guidance/parenting; current affairs; ethnic/cultural interests; government/politics/law; health/medicine; history; language/literature/criticism; nature/environment; psychology; science/technology; self-help/personal improvement; sports; true crime/investigative; women's issues/women's studies. Con-

Agents ranked I and II are most open to both established and new writers. Agents ranked III are open to established writers with publishing-industry references.

siders these fiction areas: contemporary issues; crime; family saga; mainstream; mystery/suspense; thriller/espionage. Query. Reports in 2 weeks on queries; 6 weeks on mss.
Terms: Agent receives 15% commission on domestic sales; 20% on foreign sales. Offers written contract, binding "until terminated by either party." Charges for photocopying costs above $50.
Tips: Obtain new clients through recommendations from others.

GEORGES BORCHARDT INC. (III), 136 E. 57th St., New York NY 10022. (212)753-5785. Fax: (212)838-6518. Estab. 1967. Member of AAR. Represents 200+ clients. 10% of clients are new/previously unpublished writers. Specializes in literary fiction and outstanding nonfiction. Currently handles: 60% nonfiction books; 1% juvenile books; 37% novels; 1% novellas; 1% poetry books. Member agents: Denise Shannon, Cindy Klein, Anne Borchardt, George Borchardt.
Handles: Nonfiction books, novels. Considers these nonfiction areas: anthropology/archaeology; biography/autobiography; current affairs; history; women's issues/women's studies. Considers literary fiction. "Must be recommended by someone we know." Reports in 1 week on queries; 3-4 weeks on mss.
Recent Sales: *Wartime Lies*, by Louis Begley (Knopf, rights sold in Germany, England, France, Brazil, Italy, Sweden, Holland, Poland, Japan, Spain, Czech Republic). Has sold fiction book by T. Coraghessan Boyle (Viking); nonfiction book by Tracy Kidder (Houghton Mifflin); and *Memoirs*, by Elie Wiesel (Knopf).
Terms: Agent receives 10% commission on domestic sales; 15% British sales; 20% on foreign sales (translation). Offers written contract. "We charge cost of (outside) photocopying and shipping mss or books overseas."
Tips: Obtains new clients through recommendations from others.

THE BARBARA BOVA LITERARY AGENCY (II), 3951 Gulfshore Blvd., PH1-B, Still Maples FL 33940. (813)649-7237. Estab. 1974. Represents 35 clients. Specializes in fiction and nonfiction hard and soft science. Currently handles: 50% nonfiction books; 50% novels.
Handles: Considers these nonfiction areas: biography; business; cooking/food/nutrition; how-to; money/finance/economics; self-help/personal improvement; social sciences; true crimes/investigative; women's issues/women's studies. Considers these fiction areas: action/adventure; contemporary issues; detective/police/crime; family saga; glitz; mainstream; mystery/suspense; regional; romance (contemporary); science fiction; thrillers/espionage. Query with SASE. Reports in 1 month on queries.
Recent Sales: *In the Drift*, by Borto Milan (Bantam); *Local Knowledge*, by Conor Daly (Kensington).
Terms: Agent receives 15% commission on domestic sales; handles foreign rights.
Tips: Obtains new clients through recommendations from others.

BRANDENBURGH & ASSOCIATES LITERARY AGENCY (III), 24555 Corte Jaramillo, Murrieta CA 92562. (909)698-5200. Contact: Don Brandenburgh. Estab. 1986. Represents 20 clients. "We prefer previously published authors, but will evaluate submissions on their own merits." Works with a small number of new/unpublished authors. Specializes in adult nonfiction for the religious market; limited fiction for religious market and limited nonfiction for the general market. Currently handles: 70% nonfiction books; 20% novels; 10% textbooks.
Handles: Nonfiction books, novels, textbooks. Considers these nonfiction areas: education; psychology; religious/inspirational. Considers these fiction areas: religious/inspirational. Query with outline. Reports in 2 weeks on queries. No response without SASE.
Recent Sales: *The Search for Meaning*, by Naylor/Naylor/Willimon (Abingdon); *Guardians of the Promise*, by Scott/Younce (Thomas Nelson).
Terms: Agent receives 10% commission on domestic sales; 20% on dramatic sales; 20% on foreign sales. Charges $35 mailing/materials fee with signed agency agreement.

THE JOAN BRANDT AGENCY (II), 788 Wesley Dr. NW, Atlanta GA 30305. (404)351-8877. Contact: Joan Brandt. Estab. 1990. Represents 100 clients. Also handles movie rights for other agents.
Handles: Novels, nonfiction books. Considers these fiction areas: contemporary issues; detective/police/crime; literary; mainstream; mystery/suspense; thriller/espionage; "also will consider popular, topical nonfiction." Query with SAE. Reports in 2 weeks on queries.
Terms: Agent receives 15% commission on domestic sales; 20% on foreign sales (co-agents in all major marketplaces). Charges for photocopying and long-distance postage.
Tips: Obtains new clients through recommendations from others and over-the-transom submissions.

BRANDT & BRANDT LITERARY AGENTS INC. (III), 1501 Broadway, New York NY 10036. (212)840-5760. Fax: (212)840-5776. Contact: Carl Brandt, Gail Hochman, Charles Schlessiger. Estab. 1913. Member of AAR. Represents 200 clients.

Handles: Nonfiction books, scholarly books, juvenile books, novels, novellas, short story collections. Considers these nonfiction areas: agriculture/horticulture; animals; anthropology/archaeology; art/architecture/design; biography/autobiography; business; child guidance/parenting; cooking/food/nutrition; crafts/hobbies; current affairs; ethnic/cultural interests; gay/lesbian issues; government/politics/law; health/medicine; history; interior design/decorating; juvenile nonfiction; language/literature/criticism; military/war; money/finance/economics; music/dance/theater/film; nature/environment; psychology; science/technology; self-help/personal improvement; sociology; sports; true crime/investigative; women's issues/women's studies. Considers these fiction areas: action/adventure; contemporary issues; detective/police/crime; erotica; ethnic; experimental; family saga; feminist; gay; historical; humor/satire; lesbian; literary; mainstream; mystery/suspense; psychic/supernatural; regional; romance; science fiction; sports; thriller/espionage; westerns/frontier; young adult. Query. Reports in 2-4 weeks on queries.

Terms: Agent receives 10% commission on domestic sales; 20% on foreign sales. Charges for "manuscript duplication or other special expenses agreed to in advance."

Tips: Obtains new clients through recommendations from others or "upon occasion, a really good letter. Write a letter which will give the agent a sense of you as a professional writer, your long-term interests as well as a short description of the work at hand."

‡PATTI BREITMAN (IV), 12 Rally Ct., Fairfax CA 94930. (414)459-1666. Contact: Patti Breitman. Estab. 1988. Member of AAR. Represents 40 clients. 30% of clients are new/previously unpublished writers. Specializes in self-help, especially vegetarian issues (animal rights, diet/health, environment, compassion). Currently handles: 100% nonfiction books.

Handles: Only nonfiction self-help books. Considers these nonfiction areas: animals; business; child guidance/parenting; cooking/food/nutrition (vegetarian only); health/medicine; how-to; self-help/personal improvement. Query. Reports in 2 weeks on queries. Do not send complete mss.

Recent Sales: *What Your Mother Couldn't Tell You and Your Father Didn't Know,* by John Gray, Ph.D. (HarperCollins); *Short Cut Through Therapy,* by Richard Carlson, Ph.D. (Plume); *Zen in the Markets,* by Edward Toppel (Warner Books).

MARIE BROWN ASSOCIATES INC. (II,III), 625 Broadway, Room 902, New York NY 10012. (212)533-5534. Fax: (212)533-0849. Contact: Marie Brown. Estab. 1984. Represents 100 clients. Specializes in multicultural African-American writers. Currently handles: 50% nonfiction books; 25% juvenile books; 25% other. Member agents: Joanna Blankson, Laini Brown.

Handles: Considers these nonfiction areas: art; biography; business; child guidance/parenting; cooking/food/nutrition; ethnic/cultural interests; gay/lesbian issues; history; juvenile nonfiction; money/finance/economics; music/dance/theater/film; New Age; photography; psychology; religious/inspirational; self-help/personal improvement; sociology; women's issues/women's studies. Considers these fiction areas: contemporary issues; ethnic; family saga; feminist; gay; historical; humor/satire; juvenile; literary; mainstream; mystery/suspense; picture book; regional; science fiction. Query with SASE. Reports in 8-10 weeks on queries.

Recent Sales: *Tar Beach; Aunt Harriet's Underground Railroad,* by Faith Ringgold (Crown Books); *Conversations with My Sisters,* by Dr. J.B. Cole (Doubleday).

Terms: Agent receives 15% commission on domestic sales; 25% on foreign sales. Offers written contract.

Tips: Obtains new clients through recommendations from others.

CURTIS BROWN LTD. (II), 10 Astor Place, New York NY 10003-6935. (212)473-5400. Member of AAR; signatory of WGA. Chairman & CEO: Perry Knowlton. President: Peter L. Ginsberg. Member agents: Laura J. Blake; Ellen Geiger; Emilie Jacobson, vice president; Virginia Knowlton; Timothy Knowlton, COO (films, screenplays, plays); Chris McKerrow (audio rights); Marilyn Marlow, executive vice president; Jess Taylor (film, screenplays, plays); Maureen Walters. Queries to Laura J. Blake.

● Perry Knowlton is the current president of AAR. Ellen Geiger joined Curtis Brown last year.

Handles: Nonfiction books, juvenile books, novels, novellas, short story collections, poetry books. All categories of nonfiction and fiction considered. Query. Reports in 3 weeks on queries; 3-5 weeks on mss (only if requested).

Also Handles: Movie scripts (feature film), TV scripts (TV mow), stage plays. Considers these script subject areas: action/adventure; comedy; detective/police/crime; ethnic; feminist; gay; his-

torical; horror; lesbian; mainstream; mystery/suspense; psychic/supernatural; romantic comedy and drama; thriller; westerns/frontier.
Terms: Agent receives 15% on domestic sales; 20% on foreign sales. Offers written contract. Charges for photocopying, some postage.
Tips: Obtains new clients through recommendations from others, solicitation, at conferences and query letters.

ANDREA BROWN LITERARY AGENCY, INC. (III,IV), P.O. Box 429, El Granada CA 94018-0429. (415)728-1783. Fax: (415)728-1732. Contact: Donna Latte. Estab. 1981. Member of AAR, WNBA. 10% of clients are new/previously unpublished writers. Specializes in "all kinds of children's books—illustrators and authors including multimedia writers and designers." Currently handles: 98% juvenile books; 2% novels. Member agents: Andrea Brown (president; young adult and middle years); Donna Blackett (creative executive; picture books, early readers); Donna Latte (picture books, early readers).
Handles: Juvenile books and multimedia projects. Considers these nonfiction areas: animals; anthropology/archaeology; art/architecture/design; biography/autobiography; current affairs; ethnic/cultural interests; health/medicine; history; how-to; juvenile nonfiction; nature/environment; photography; popular culture; science/technology; sociology; sports. Considers these fiction areas: historical; juvenile; picture book; romance (historical); science fiction; young adult. Query. Reports in 1-3 weeks on queries; 1-3 months on mss.
Recent Sales: *Bully Brothers* series, by Mike Thaler (Scholastic); *Gift of a Traveler*, by Wendy Matthews (TNU).
Terms: Agent receives 15% commission on domestic sales; 20% on foreign sales. No written contract.
Writer's Conferences: SCBWI, Orange County Conferences, Mills College Childrens Literature Conference (Oakland, CA); Asilomar (Pacific Grove, CA).
Tips: Usually obtains new clients through recommendations, editors, clients, agents and slush pile. "Taking on very few picture books. Must be unique—no rhyme, no anthropomorphism. Do not fax queries or manuscripts."

HOWARD BUCK AGENCY, 80 Eighth Ave., Suite 1107, New York NY 10011. (212)807-7855. Contact: Howard Buck or Mark Frisk. Estab. 1981. Represents 75 clients. "All-around agency." Currently handles: 75% nonfiction books; 25% novels.
Handles: Nonfiction, novels. Considers all nonfiction and fiction areas. Query with SASE. Reports in 6 weeks on queries.
Terms: Agent receives 15% commission on domestic sales. Offers written contract. Charges for office expenses, postage and photocopying.
Tips: Obtains new clients through recommendations from others.

JANE BUTLER, ART AND LITERARY AGENT (II, III), P.O. Box 33, Matamoras PA 18336-1530. Estab. 1981. "Prefers published credits, but all queries are welcome; no SASE, no reply." Specializes in fiction. Currently handles: 15% nonfiction books; 80% novels; 5% juvenile books.
Handles: Nonfiction books, novels. Considers nonfiction on Buddhism, Taoism, Shamanism. Considers these fiction areas: science fiction; fantasy; romantic fantasy; romantic suspense; historical fantasy; dark fantasy; children's fiction; some young adult; horror. Query with first chapter and SASE.
Recent Sales: *The Eagle's Daughter*, by Judith Tarr (Tor/Forge, mid-1995); *Untitled*, by S. Andrew Swann (DAW Books, 1996).
Terms: Agent receives 10% commission on domestic sales; 15% on dramatic sales; 20% on foreign sales.

SHEREE BYKOFSKY ASSOCIATES (IV), 211 E. 51st St., Suite 11-D, Box WD, New York NY 10022. Estab. 1984. Member of AAR, ASJA, WNBA. Represents "a limited number of" clients. Specializes in popular reference nonfiction. Currently handles: 80% nonfiction; 20% fiction.
Handles: Nonfiction books. Considers all nonfiction areas, especially biography/autobiography; business; child guidance/parenting; cooking/foods/nutrition; current affairs; ethnic/cultural interests; gay/lesbian issues; health/medicine; history; how-to; humor; music/dance/theater/film; popular culture; psychology; religious/inspirational; self-help/personal improvement; true crime/investigative; women's issues/women's studies. "I have wide-ranging interests, but it really depends on quality of writing, originality, and how a particular project appeals to me (or not). I take on very little fiction unless I completely love it—it doesn't matter what area or genre." Query with SASE. No unsolicited mss or phone calls. Reports in 1 month on queries.
Recent Sales: *Multicultural Manners*, by Norine Dresser (Norton); *Lavender Light: Meditations for Gay Men in Recovery*, by Adrian Milton (Perigee/Putnam's); *Movietime*, by Gene Brown (Macmillan/Prentice Hall).

Terms: Agent receives 15% commission on domestic sales; 15% on foreign sales. Offers written contract, binding for 1 year "usually." Charges for postage, photocopying and fax.
Writer's Conferences: ASJA (New York).
Tips: Obtains new clients through recommendations from others. "Read the agent listing carefully and comply with guidelines."

CANTRELL-COLAS INC., LITERARY AGENCY (II), 229 E. 79th St., New York NY 10021. (212)737-8503. Contact: Maryanne C. Colas. Estab. 1980. Represents 80 clients. Currently handles: 50% nonfiction books; 25% juvenile books; 25% mainstream.
Handles: Considers these nonfiction areas: anthropology; art; biography; child guidance/parenting; cooking/food/nutrition; current affairs; ethnic/cultural interests; government/politics/law; health/medicine; history; juvenile nonfiction; language/literature/criticism; military/war; money/finance/economics; nature/environment; New Age/metaphysics; psychology; science/technology; self-help/personal improvement; sociology; true crime/investigative; women's issues/women's studies. Considers these fiction areas: contemporary issues; detective/police/crime; ethnic; experimental; family saga; feminist; historical; humor/satire; juvenile; literary; mainstream; mystery/suspense; psychic/supernatural; science fiction; thriller/espionage; young adult. Query with SASE and outline plus 2 sample chapters, and "something about author also." Reports in 2 months on queries.
Recent Sales: *Roosevelt and De Gaulle*, by Raoul Aglion; *Miami: A Saga*, by Evelyn Wilde-Mayerson (Viking); *Bride of the Unicorn*, by Kasey Michaels (Pocket Books).
Terms: Agent receives 15% commission on domestic sales; commission varies on foreign sales. Offers written contract. Charges for foreign postage and photocopying.
Tips: Obtains new clients through recommendations from others. "Make sure your manuscript is in excellent condition both grammatically and cosmetically. In other words, check for spelling, typing errors and legibility."

MARIA CARVAINIS AGENCY, INC. (II), 235 West End Ave., New York NY 10023. (212)580-1559. Fax: (212)877-3486. Contact: Maria Carvainis. Estab. 1977. Member of AAR, Authors Guild, signatory of WGA. Represents 35 clients. 10% of clients are new/previously unpublished writers. Currently handles: 25% nonfiction books; 15% juvenile books; 55% novels; 5% poetry books.
 • Maria Carvainis is the chair of the AAR Contracts Committee.
Handles: Nonfiction books, scholarly books, novels, poetry books. Considers these nonfiction areas: biography/autobiography; business; current affairs; government/politics/law; health/medicine; history; military/war; money/finance/economics; psychology; true crime/investigative; women's issues/women's studies; popular science. Considers these fiction areas: action/adventure; detective/police/crime; family saga; fantasy; glitz; historical; humor/satire; juvenile; literary; mainstream; mystery/suspense; romance; thriller/espionage; westerns/frontier; children's; young adult. Query first with SASE. Reports in 2-3 weeks on queries; 3 months on solicited mss.
Recent Sales: New 3 book deal for Sandra Brown (Warner Books); *George Cukor: Master of Elegance*, by Emanuel Levy (William Morrow & Co., Inc.); *Mischief*, by Catherine Hart (Avon Books).
Terms: Agent receives 15% commission on domestic sales; 20% on foreign sales. Offers written contract, binding for 2 years "on a book-by-book basis." Charges for foreign postage and bulk copying.
Tips: "75% of new clients derived from recommendations or conferences. 25% of new clients derived from letters of query."

MARTHA CASSELMAN LITERARY AGENT (III), P.O. Box 342, Calistoga CA 94515-0342. (707)942-4341. Estab. 1978. Member of AAR, IACP, NWBA. Represents 30 clients. Specializes in "nonfiction, especially food books; limited YA, children's. Do not send any submission without query." Member agent: Judith Armenta (New Age and alternative medicine nonfiction).
Handles: Nonfiction proposals only, food-related proposals and cookbooks. Considers these nonfiction areas: agriculture/horticulture; anthropology/archaeology; biography/autobiography; cooking/food/nutrition; film; health/medicine; women's issues/women's studies. Considers only young adult fiction. Send proposal with outline, plus 3 sample chapters. Reports in 2-4 weeks on queries.
Terms: Agent receives 15% commission on domestic sales; 20% on foreign sales (if using subagent). Offers criticism service under special circumstances, on consultation with author. Charges for photocopying, overnight and overseas mailings.
Writer's Conferences: ABA (Chicago); IACP (San Antonio, TX); Fancy Food Show (San Francisco).
Tips: Obtains new clients through referrals. "No tricky letters; no gimmicks; always include SASE or mailer."

JULIE CASTIGLIA LITERARY AGENCY (II), 1155 Camino Del Mar, Suite 510, Del Mar CA 92014. (619)753-4361. Fax: (619)753-5094. Contact: Julie Castiglia. Estab. 1993. Member of AAR, PEN. Represents 50 clients. 25% of clients are new/previously unpublished writers. Currently handles: 70% nonfiction books; 25% novels; 5% short story collections.
Handles: Nonfiction books, novels, short story collections. Considers these nonfiction areas: animals; anthropology/archaeology; art/architecture/design; biography/autobiography; business; child guidance/parenting; cooking/food/nutrition; current affairs; ethnic/cultural interests; health/medicine; history; interior design/decorating; juvenile nonfiction; language/literature/criticism; music/dance/theater/film; nature/environment; New Age/metaphysics; psychology; religious/inspirational; science/technology; self-help/personal improvement; sociology; sports; women's issues/women's studies. Considers these fiction areas: action/adventure; contemporary issues; detective/police/crime; ethnic; family saga; feminist; gay; glitz; literary mainstream; mystery/suspense; picture book; regional; romance (contemporary, gothic, historical, regency); women's fiction especially. Send outline/proposal plus 2 sample chapters; send synopsis with chapters for fiction. Reports in 6-8 weeks on mss.
Recent Sales: *Skywriting*, by Margarita Engle (Bantam); *Science of Desire*, by Dean Hamer and Peter Copeland (Simon & Schuster); *Bridge of No Return*, by Mike Dunn (Avon).
Terms: Agent receives 15% commission on domestic sales; 20% on foreign sales. Offers written contract, 6 week termination. Charges for excessive postage and copying for first-time authors.
Writers' Conferences: Southwestern Writers Conference (Albuquerque). Attends National Writers Club, SDSU Conference, Wilamette Writers Conference, Oregon.
Tips: Obtains new clients through solicitations, conferences, referrals. "Be professional with submissions. Attend workshops and conferences before you approach an agent."

CHADD-STEVENS LITERARY AGENCY (I), P.O. Box 2218, Granbury TX 76048. (817)326-4892. Contact: Lee F. Jordan. Estab. 1991. Represents 25 clients. Specializes in working with previously unpublished authors.
Handles: Novels, novellas, short story collections. Considers all fiction areas except feminist. Send entire ms or 3 sample chapters and SASE. Reports within 6 weeks on mss.
Terms: Agent receives 15% commission on domestic sales; 15% on foreign sales. Offers written contract, binding for 3 months. Charges $35 handling fee for entire ms only. Charges for expenses. Payment of handling fee does not ensure agency representation.
● At press time it was learned that this agency charges a monthly $50 marketing fee.
Tips: "I prefer a query letter and I answer all of them with a personal note. My goal is to look at 80% of everything offered to me. I'm interested in working with people who have been turned down by other agents and publishers. I'm interested in first-time novelists—there's a market for your work if it's good. Don't give up. I think there is a world of good unpublished fiction out there and I'd like to see it."

CIRCLE OF CONFUSION LTD. (II), 666 Fifth Ave., Suite 303, New York NY 10103. (212)969-0653. Fax: (718)997-0512. Contact: Rajeev K. Agarwal, Lawrence Mattis. Estab. 1990. Signatory of WGA. Represents 70 clients. 70% of clients are new/previously unpublished writers. Specializes in screenplays for film and TV. Currently handles: 15% novels; 5% novellas; 80% movie scripts. Member agents: Rageev Agarwal, Lawrence Mattis, Annmarie Negretti, Jasmine Lam.
● See the expanded listing for this agency in Script Agents.

FRANCINE CISKE LITERARY AGENCY (II), P.O. Box 555, Neenah WI 54957. (414)722-5944. Contact: Fran Ciske. Represents 20 clients. Estab. 1993. Member of RWA. Specializes in romance, women's fiction. Currently handles: 80% fiction; 20% nonfiction. Member agent: Patricia Dietz (action/adventure, thrillers, young adult) at NE Office, P.O. Box 193, Greenleaf WI 54126 (414)864-7702.
Handles: Considers these nonfiction areas: cooking/food/nutrition; religious/inspirational; self-help/personal improvement; true crime; women's issues/women's studies. Considers these fiction areas: mystery/suspense; religious/inspiration; romance (contemporary, historical, regency, time travel); thriller; westerns/frontier. Query with outline plus 3 sample chapters and SASE. Reports in 1 month on queries; 2 months on mss.
Terms: Agent receives 15% commission on domestic sales; 20% on foreign sales. Offers nonbinding terms agreement. Expenses for photocopying will be agreed upon in advance.
Writer's Conferences: RWA National Conference, Wisconsin RWA conferences and workshops.
Tips: Obtains new clients through recommendation, solicitation and conferences. No phone queries, please. Agency handles religious/inspirationals for the Evangelical Christian market. No New Age or occult. Prefers sample chapters and synopsis over query letter. No reply without SASE. "Target a market. For a faster response, submit to the agent who specializes in the market you targetted."

CONNIE CLAUSEN ASSOCIATES (II), 250 E. 87th St., #16H, New York NY 10128. (212)427-6135. Fax: (212)996-7111. Contact: Connie Clausen. Estab. 1976. 10% of clients are new/previously unpublished writers. Specializes in true crime, autobiography, biography, health, women's issues, psychology, celebrity, beauty-fashion, how-to, financial. Currently handles: 100% nonfiction books (in New York). Member agents: Genevieve Field, Elyse Cheney.
Handles: Nonfiction books. Considers these nonfiction areas: biography/autobiography; business; cooking/food/nutrition; current affairs; ethnic/cultural interests; gay/lesbian issues; health/medicine; money/finance/economics; music/dance/theater/film; nature/environment; psychology; self-help/personal improvement; true crime/investigative; women's issues/women's studies. Send outline/proposal. Reports in 3 weeks on queries; 4-6 weeks on mss.
Recent Sales: *Eat Smart, Think Smart,* by Robert Haas (HarperCollins); *What to Do if You Get Breast Cancer,* by Lydia Komarnicky, MD, Anne Rosenberg, MD and Marian Betancourt (Little, Brown); *The Rules,* by Ellen Fein and Sherry Shamoon (Warner); *Born To Be Wild,* by Barry Bowe (Warner).
Terms: Agent receives 15% commission on domestic sales; 20% on foreign sales. Offers written contract, terms vary. Charges for office expenses.
Tips: Obtains new clients through referrals by other clients, publishers, magazine editors and *Writer's Digest.* "Always include SASE. Go to the library and read a book or two on publishing and proposal writing."

DIANE CLEAVER INC. (III), 55 Fifth Ave., New York NY 10003. (212)206-5606. Fax: (212)463-8718. Estab. 1979. Member of AAR. Currently handles: 70% nonfiction books; 30% novels.
Handles: Nonfiction books, novels. Generally open to most nonfiction areas. Considers these fiction areas: mainstream; mystery/suspense; thriller/espionage. Query. Reports in 1-2 weeks on queries.
Terms: Agent receives 15% commission on domestic sales; 19% on foreign sales. Charges for photocopying books for foreign submissions.
Tips: Obtains new clients through recommendations from others.

RUTH COHEN, INC. LITERARY AGENCY (II), P.O. Box 7626, Menlo Park CA 94025. (415)854-2054. Contact: Ruth Cohen or associates. Estab. 1982. Member of AAR, Authors Guild, SCBWI. Represents 75 clients. 20% of clients are new/previously unpublished writers. Specializes in "quality writing in juvenile fiction; mysteries; regency and historical romances, adult women's fiction." Currently handles: 15% nonfiction books; 40% juvenile books; 45% novels.
Handles: Juvenile books, adult novels. Considers these nonfiction areas: ethnic/cultural interests; juvenile nonfiction; true crime/investigative; women's issues/women's studies. Considers these fiction areas: detective/police; ethnic; regencies; family saga; historical; juvenile; literary; mainstream; mystery/suspense; picture books; romance (historical, regency); young adult. Send outline plus 2 sample chapters and SASE. Reports in 1 month on queries. No unsolicited mss.
Terms: Agent receives 15% commission on domestic sales; 20% on foreign sales, "if a foreign agent is involved." Offers written contract, binding for 1 year "continuing to next." Charges for foreign postage and photocopying for submissions.
Tips: Obtains new clients through recommendations from others. "A good writer cares about the words he/she uses—so do I. Also, if no SASE is included, material will not be read."

HY COHEN LITERARY AGENCY LTD. (II), 111 W. 57th St., #1400, New York NY 10019. (212)757-5237. Contact: Hy Cohen. Mail ms to P.O. Box 743, Upper Montclair NJ 07043. Estab. 1975. Represents 25 clients. 50% of clients are new/previously unpublished writers. Currently handles: 20% nonfiction books; 5% juvenile books; 75% novels.
Handles: Nonfiction books, novels. All categories of nonfiction and fiction considered. Send 100 pages with SASE. Reports in about 2 weeks (on 100-page submission).
Recent Sales: *The Log of the Jessie Bill,* by Dean Gabbert (M. Evans); *No Effect,* by Daniel Hayes (David Godine).
Terms: Agent receives 10% commission.
Tips: Obtains new clients through recommendations from others and unsolicited submissions. "Send double-spaced, legible scripts and SASE. Good writing helps."

FRANCES COLLIN LITERARY AGENT, (III), P.O. Box 33, Wayne PA 19087-0033. (610)254-0555. Estab. 1948. Member of AAR. Represents 90 clients. 5% of clients are new/previously unpublished writers. Currently handles: 48% nonfiction books; 1% textbooks; 50% novels; 1% poetry books.
Handles: Nonfiction books, novels. Considers these nonfiction areas: anthropology/archaeology; biography/autobiography; business; health/medicine; history; nature/environment; true crime/investigative. Considers these fiction areas: detective/police/crime; ethnic; family saga; fantasy;

torical); science fiction. Query with SASE. Reports in 1 week on queries; 6-8 weeks on mss.
Terms: Agent receives 15% commission on domestic sales; 20% on foreign sales. Offers written contract. Charges for overseas postage for books mailed to foreign agents; photocopying of mss, books, proposals; copyright registration fees; registered mail fees; pass along cost of any books purchased.
Tips: Obtains new clients through recommendations from others.

COLUMBIA LITERARY ASSOCIATES, INC. (II,IV), 7902 Nottingham Way, Ellicott City MD 21043-6721. (410)465-1595. Fax: Call for number. Contact: Linda Hayes, Kathryn Jensen. Estab. 1980. Member of AAR, IACP, RWA, WRW. Represents 40 clients. 10% of clients are new/previously unpublished writers. Specializes in women's fiction (mainstream/genre), commercial nonfiction, especially cookbooks. Currently handles: 40% nonfiction books; 60% novels.
Handles: Nonfiction books, novels. Considers these nonfiction areas: cooking/food/nutrition; health/medicine; self-help. Considers these fiction areas: mainstream; commercial women's fiction; suspense; contemporary romance; psychological/medical thrillers. Reports in 2-4 weeks on queries; 6-8 weeks on mss; "rejections faster."
Recent Sales: *Final Appeal*, by Lisa Scottoline (HarperCollins).
Terms: Agent receives 15% commission on domestic sales. Offers single- or multiple-book written contract, binding for 6-month terms. "Standard expenses are billed against book income (e.g., books for subrights exploitation, tolls, UPS)."
Writer's Conferences: Attends Romance Writers of America and International Association of Culinary Professionals and Novelists, Inc. conferences.
Tips: Obtains new clients through referrals and mail. Submission requirements: "For fiction, send a query letter with author credits, narrative synopsis, first chapter or two, manuscript word count and submission history (publishers/agents); self-addressed, stamped mailer mandatory for response/ms return. (When submitting romances, note whether manuscript is mainstream or category—if category, say which line(s) manuscript is targeted to.) Same for nonfiction, plus include table of contents and note audience, how project is different and better than competition (specify competing books with publisher and publishing date.) Please note that we do *not* handle: historical fiction, regencies, futuristics, westerns, science fiction/fantasy, military books, poetry, short stories or screenplays."

DON CONGDON ASSOCIATES INC. (III), 156 Fifth Ave., Suite 625, New York NY 10010-7002. (212)645-1229. Fax: (212)727-2688. Contact: Don Congdon, Michael Congdon, Susan Ramer. Estab. 1983. Member of AAR. Represents 100+ clients. Currently handles: 50% fiction; 50% nonfiction books.
Handles: Nonfiction books, novels. Considers all nonfiction and fiction areas, especially literary fiction. Query. "If interested, we ask for sample chapters and outline." Reports in 3-4 weeks on manuscript.
Recent Sales: *A Tidewater Morning*, by William Styron (Random House); *Cruel and Unusual*, by Patricia D. Cornwell (Scribner).
Terms: Agent receives 10% commission on domestic sales.
Tips: Obtains new clients through referrals from other authors. "Writing a query letter is a must."

THE DOE COOVER AGENCY (II), 58 Sagamore Ave., Medford MA 02155. (617)488-3937. Fax: (617)488-3153. President: Doe Coover. Agent: Colleen Mohyde. Estab. 1985. Represents 45 clients. Specializes in serious nonfiction and fiction. Currently handles: 80% nonfiction; 20% fiction. Member agents: Doe Coover (cooking, general nonfiction); Colleen Mohyde (fiction, general nonfiction).
Handles: Nonfiction books, fiction. Considers these nonfiction areas: anthropology; biography/autobiography; business; child guidance/parenting; cooking/food; ethnic/cultural interests; finance/economics; health/medicine; history; language/literature/criticism; nature/environment; psychology; religious/inspirational; science/technology; sociology; true crime; women's issues/women's studies. Query with outline. Fiction queries must include SASE and should be addressed to Ms. Mohyde. Reporting time varies on queries.
Recent Sales: *Unplanned Parenthood*, by Liz Carpenter (Random House); *A Season in Hiding*, by Jonathan Wilson (Viking); *Big Flavors of the Hot Sun*, by Chris Schlesinger and John Willoughby (William Morrow).

ALWAYS include a self-addressed, stamped envelope (SASE) for reply or return of your manuscript.

Terms: Agent receives 15% commission on domestic sales; 15% on foreign sales.
Writer's Conferences: ABA (Chicago); Writers at Work (Park City, Utah).
Tips: Obtains new clients through recommendations from others and solicitation.

‡**ROBERT CORNFIELD LITERARY AGENCY (II)**, 145 W. 79th St., New York NY 10024. (212)874-2465. Contact: Robert Cornfield. Estab. 1979. Member of AAR. Represents 60 clients. 20% of clients are new/previously unpublished writers. Specializes in film, art, literary, music criticism, food, fiction. Currently handles: 60% nonfiction books, 20% scholarly books, 20% novels.
Handles: Nonfiction books, novels. Considers these nonfiction areas: animals; anthropology/archaeology; art/architecture/ design; biography/autobiography; cooking/food/nutrition; history; language/literature/criticism/ music/dance/theater/film. Considers literary fiction. Query. Reports in 2-3 weeks on queries.
Recent Sales: *Parenting Cookbook*, by Kathy Gunst & *Parenting* magazine (Holt); *Bean Cookbook*, by Melanie Barnard (Harper); *Adam's Task*, by Vicki Hearne (Harper).
Terms: Agent receives 10% commission on domestic sales; 20% on foreign sales. No written contract. Charges for postage, excessive photocopying.
Tips: Obtains new clients through recommendations.

‡**CRAWFORD LITERARY AGENCY (III)**, 198 Evans Rd., Barnstead NH 03218. (603)269-5851. Fax: (603)269-2533. Contact: Susan Crawford. Estab. 1988. Represents 40 clients. 50% of clients are new/previously unpublished writers. Currently handles: 50% nonfiction books, 49% novels, 1% juvenile books.
Handles: Nonfiction books. Considers these nonfiction areas: biography/autobiography; business; child guidance/parenting; cooking/food/nutrition; how-to; true crime/investigative; women's issues/women's studies. Query with SASE. Reports in 3 weeks on queries.
Recent Sales: *Untitled Bogart bio*, by Stephen Bogart with Gary Provost (Dutton); *Tropical Depression*, by Jeffry Lindsay (Donald I. Fine); *Blind Rage*, by Gary King (Signet); *Prisoners of Fear*, by Gera-Line Kolarik (Avon).
Terms: Agent receives 1% commission on domestic sales; 20% on foreign sales. Offers written contract, binding for 90 days. 100% of business is derived from commissions on sales.
Writers' Conferences: Hemingway Festival/Writers' Conference (Key West FL, July 1995); Writing Today (Birmingham South College, Birmingham AL, March 1995); Write To Sell V (Southeast Nuts & Bolts Workshop, Rock Hill SC, February 11-12, 1995).
Tips: Obtains new clients through recommendations, at conferences.

BONNIE R. CROWN INTERNATIONAL LITERATURE AND ARTS AGENCY (II, IV), 50 E. Tenth St., New York NY 10003-6221. (212)475-1999. Contact: Bonnie Crown. Estab. 1976. Member of Association of Asian Studies. Represents 14 clients. 10% of clients are previously published writers. Specializes in Asian cross-cultural and translations of Asian literary works, American writers influenced by one or more Asian culture. Currently handles: 5% scholarly books; 80% novels; 10% short story collectors; 5% poetry.
Handles: Nonfiction books, novels, short story collections (if first published in literary magazines). Considers these nonfiction areas: ethnic/cultural interests; nature/environment; translations from Asian languages; women's issues/women's studies. Considers these fiction areas: ethnic; experimental; family saga; historical; humor/satire; literary. Query with SASE. Reports in 2 weeks on queries; 2-4 weeks on mss.
Terms: Agent receives 15% commission on domestic sales; 20% on foreign sales. Charges for processing, usually $25, on submission of ms.
Tips: Obtains new clients through "referrals through other authors and listings in reference works. If interested in agency representation, send brief query with SASE."

RICHARD CURTIS ASSOCIATES, INC. (III), 171 E. 74th St., New York NY 10021. (212)772-7363. Fax: (212)772-7393. Contact: Richard Curtis. Estab. 1969. Member of AAR, signatory of WGA. Represents 150 clients. 5% of clients are new/previously unpublished writers. Specializes in genre paperback fiction such as science fiction, women's romance, horror, fantasy, action-adventure. Currently handles: 9% nonfiction books; 1% juvenile books; 90% novels. Member agents: Roberta Cohen, Richard Henshaw.
   • A subsidiary firm, The Content Company®, handles multimedia authors and projects.
   See Richard Curtis's article, *Know What Your Agent Knows About Deal Points*, in the 1994 edition of the *Guide*.
Handles: Nonfiction books, novels. Considers these nonfiction areas: biography/autobiography; business; child guidance/parenting; history; military/war; money/finance/economics; music/dance/theater/film; science/technology; self-help/personal improvement; sports; true crime/investigative. Considers these fiction areas: action/adventure; detective/police/crime; family saga; fantasy; feminist; historical; horror; mainstream; mystery/suspense; romance; science fiction;

thriller/espionage; westerns/frontier. Query, must be accompanied by SASE. Reports in 2 weeks on queries.

Recent Sales: *Deadly Passage*, by Mark Irving (Severn House [UK]; Diva Productions [Denmark]).

Terms: Agent receives 15% commission on domestic sales; 20% on foreign sales. Charges for photocopying, express, fax, international postage, book orders.

Tips: Obtains new clients through recommendations from others.

DARHANSOFF & VERRILL LITERARY AGENTS (II), 1220 Park Ave., New York NY 10128. (212)534-2479. Fax: (212)996-1601. Estab. 1975. Member of AAR. Represents 100 clients. 10% of clients are new/previously unpublished writers. Specializes in literary fiction. Currently handles: 25% nonfiction books; 60% novels; 15% short story collections. Member agents: Liz Darhansoff, Charles Verrill, Leigh Feldman.

Handles: Nonfiction books, novels, short story collections. Considers these nonfiction areas: anthropology/archaeology; biography/autobiography; current affairs; health/medicine; history; language/literature/criticism; nature/environment; science/technology. Considers literary and thriller fiction. Query letter only. Reports in 2 weeks on queries.

Tips: Obtains new clients through recommendations from others.

ELAINE DAVIE LITERARY AGENCY (II), 620 Park Ave., Rochester NY 14607. (716)442-0830. President: Elaine Davie. Estab. 1986. Represents 150+ clients. 30% of clients are new/unpublished writers. Welcomes queries/submissions from new/unpublished authors. Specializes in adult fiction and nonfiction, particularly books by and for women and genre/fiction. Currently handles: 10% nonfiction; 80% novels; 10% juvenile books.

Handles: Nonfiction books, novels (no short stories, children's books or poetry). Considers these nonfiction areas: self-help, true crime, women's issues. Considers these fiction areas: genre fiction, history, horror, mystery, romance, western. Query with outline or synopsis and brief description. Reports in 2 weeks on queries.

Recent Sales: *Come the Night* (Dell) and *Hour of the Rose* (Avon), by Christina Skye; *In Daddy's Arms* and *Sizzle*, by Marcia Evanick (Bantam); *Twice in a Lifetime*, by Christy Cohen (Bantam); *Reckless Angel* and *Twilight Phantasies*, by Maggie Shayne (Silhouette).

Terms: Agent receives 15% commission on domestic sales; 20% on dramatic sales; 20% on foreign sales.

Tips: "Our agency specializes in books by and for women. We pride ourselves on our prompt responses to queries, our accessibility, our personable staff, and that we never charge a fee of any kind."

THE LOIS DE LA HABA AGENCY INC. (III), 1123 Broadway, Suite 810, New York NY 10010. (212)929-4838. Fax: (212)924-3885. Contact: Lois de la Haba. Estab. 1978. Represents 100+ clients. Currently handles: 55% nonfiction books; 3% scholarly books; ½% textbooks; 10% juvenile books; 23% novels; ½% poetry; ½% short story collections; 3% movie scripts; 2% stage plays; 2% TV scripts; ½% syndicated material. Member agent: Luna Carne Ross.

Handles: Nonfiction books, scholarly books, juvenile books, novels, movie scripts, TV scripts, stage plays. Considers these nonfiction areas: animals; anthropology/archaeology; art/architecture/design; biography/autobiography; business; cooking/food/nutrition; current affairs; ethnic/cultural interests; gay/lesbian issues; government/politics/law; health/medicine; history; juvenile nonfiction; money/finance/economics; music/theater/dance/film; nature/environment; New Age/metaphysics; psychology/healing; religious/inspirational; self-help/personal improvement; women's issues/women's studies. Considers these fiction areas: contemporary issues; detective/police/crime; erotica; ethnic; experimental; fantasy; feminist; gay; glitz; historical; humor/satire; juvenile; literary; mainstream; mystery/suspense; religious/inspirational; young adult. Send query with outline/proposal and SASE. Reports in 3-5 weeks on queries; 4-8 weeks on mss.

Recent Sales: *Superself*, by Charles J. Givens (Simon & Schuster); *Power Thoughts*, by Dr. Robert Schuller (HarperCollins).

Terms: Agent receives 15% commission on domestic sales; 25% on foreign sales. Offers written contract, binding for 3 years. Charges for "photocopying, long-distance calls, etc."

Writer's Conferences: Attends Mystery Writers of America.

Tips: Obtains new clients through recommendations from others.

ANITA DIAMANT, THE WRITER'S WORKSHOP, INC. (II), 310 Madison Ave., New York NY 10017. (212)687-1122. Contact: Anita Diamant. Estab. 1917. Member of AAR. Represents 125 clients. 25% of clients are new/previously unpublished writers. Currently handles: 20% nonfiction books; 80% novels. Member agents: Robin Rue (fiction and nonfiction); Garrett Weyr (fiction).

Outsmarting the Typical Diet Book Sale

When agent Sandra Dijkstra gets a manuscript she believes in, she doesn't take no for an answer. "I'm a 'contrarian' agent," she says. "When ten publishers tell me 'you're crazy,' I say no, you're crazy." That drive has helped her market authors like Amy Tan, and books like *Stellaluna*, a children's book that makes bats seem lovable. When Dijkstra first saw Debra Waterhouse's *Outsmarting the Female Fat Cell* (1992 Hyperion Books), she knew she had a winner.

"I don't do a lot of diet books," Dijkstra says, "but this was just in time and so in tune with the zeitgeist. Until this book, everything was '*Thin Thighs in Thirty Days*,' but this was an intelligent woman's diet book."

Dijkstra says she knew the time was right for a new kind of diet book, and that highlighting the differences between men and women's approaches gave the book a unique hook. "One of the hardest things about being an agent," she says, "is you have to know and participate in the entire world of publishing, you have to anticipate the trends."

Although Dijkstra felt the book was brilliant, publishers were hesitant. "When I went to the head of Doubleday he said, 'It's the best *expletive* diet proposal I've ever seen.' So I asked him, 'Then why don't you make me an offer on it?' And he said, 'Because I'm nervous.' "

Dijkstra says there were a few strikes against the book. Waterhouse, a registered nurse, was a first-time author, an unknown. The message of the book was untraditional. But Dijkstra insists she had good material to work with. "The book had a brilliant concept, and inspirational writing," she says. "And we had Deb's brilliant title. Authors tell me titles don't matter, that they can be worked out later, but they do matter. They're the gateway to the author's imagination."

Emphasizing those strengths, Dijkstra prepared a video of Waterhouse to show publishers. She says, "These days, authors need to be mediagenic, and have a distinctive niche." After receiving several possible offers, she decided to go with Hyperion Books, a young publishing house owned by Disney. She thought a young company would be willing to give Waterhouse's book the attention it deserved, and they certainly did. The book has sold over 125,000 copies and Hyperion is about to release the next — *Why Women Need Chocolate*, a food-mood-diet book.

Dijkstra says she has a simple approach to selecting manuscripts: "I have to love it." She has represented a wide range of material, both fiction and nonfiction, and says she always asks herself, "Why does the world need this book?" She believes there is no substitute for good writing and imagination, but there are a few things writers can do to make themselves more marketable, beginning with researching the competition. "Write a few lines about the five or six most similar books and why yours is different," she suggests. Don't send the complete manuscript, but be sure to include a chapter synopsis. And Dijkstra recommends writing to agents, rather than calling. "It's a book business, a print business still; we prefer to see things in writing," she says.

Dijkstra says she still gets excited when she finds a good manuscript. "We're interested in developing a relationship with an author," she says, and getting books into print "is like fulfilling dreams."

—*Alison Holm*

Handles: Nonfiction books, young adults, novels. Considers these nonfiction areas: animals; art/architecture/design; biography/autobiography; business; child guidance/parenting; cooking/food/nutrition; crafts/hobbies; current affairs; government/politics/law; health/medicine; history; juvenile nonfiction; money/finance/economics; nature/environment; New Age/metaphysics; psychology; religious/inspirational; science/technology; self-help/personal improvement; sports; true crime/investigative; women's issues/women's studies. Considers these fiction areas: action/adventure; contemporary issues; detective/police/crime; experimental; family saga; feminist; gay; historical; juvenile; literary; mainstream; mystery/suspense; psychic/supernatural; religious/inspiration; romance; thriller/espionage; westerns/frontier; young adult. Query. Reports "at once" on queries; 3 weeks on mss.
Recent Sales: *Jacqueline Kennedy Onassis*, by Lester David (Carol); *Solomon Organization*, by Andrew Neiderman (Putnam).
Terms: Agent receives 15% commission on domestic sales; 20% on foreign sales. Offers written contract.
Writer's Conferences: Attends the Romance Writers of America Annual Conference and the ABA.
Tips: Obtains new clients through "recommendations from publishers and clients, appearances at writers' conferences, and through readers of my written articles."

DIAMOND LITERARY AGENCY, INC. (III), Non-clients (and specified clients) submit to: Jennifer Niles, 1932 Irving Ave., No. 590, San Francisco CA 94122. Headquarters mailing only to: P.O. Box 117, Arvada CO 80001. (303)759-0291. President: Pat Dalton. Estab. 1982. Represents 20 clients. 10% of clients are new/previously unpublished writers. Specializes in romance, romantic suspense, women's fiction, thrillers, mysteries. Currently handles: 25% nonfiction books; 70% novels; 3% movie scripts; 2% TV scripts.
Handles: Nonfiction books, novels, scripts. Considers these nonfiction areas with mass market appeal: business; health/medicine; money/finance/economics; psychology; self-help/personal improvement. Considers these fiction areas: action/adventure; contemporary issues; detective/police/crime; family saga; feminist; glitz; historical; mainstream; mystery/suspense; romance; thriller/espionage. Reports in 1 month on mss (partials).
Recent Sales: Specializes in romance, including sales to Harlequin and Silhouette. Specifics on request if representation offered.
Terms: Agent receives 10-15% commission on domestic sales; 20% on foreign sales. Offers written contract, binding for 2 years "unless author is well established." Charges a "$15 submission fee for writers who have not previously published/sold the same type of project." Charges for express and foreign postage. "Writers provide the necessary photostat copies."
Tips: Obtains new clients through "referrals from writers, or someone's submitting saleable material. We represent only clients who are professionals in writing quality, presentation, conduct and attitudes—whether published or unpublished. Send a SASE for agency information and submission procedures. People who are not yet clients should not telephone. We consider query letters a waste of time—most of all the writer's, secondly the agent's. Submit approximately first 50 pages and complete synopsis for books, or full scripts, along with SASE and standard-sized audiocassette tape for possible agent comments. Nonclients who haven't sold the SAME TYPE of book or script within five years must include a $15 submission fee by money order or cashier's check. Material not accompanied by SASE is not returned. We are not encouraging submissions from not-yet-published writers at this time."

SANDRA DIJKSTRA LITERARY AGENCY (II), 1155 Camino del Mar, #515, Del Mar CA 92014. (619)755-3115. Contact: Kathryn Miller. Estab. 1981. Member of AAR, Authors Guild, PEN West, Poets and Editors, MWA. Represents 100 clients. 30% of clients are new/previously unpublished writers. "We specialize in a number of fields." Currently handles: 60% nonfiction books; 5% juvenile books; 35% novels. Member agent: Sandra Dijkstra.

Handles: Nonfiction books, novels. Considers these nonfiction areas: anthropology; biography/autobiography; business; child guidance/parenting; nutrition; current affairs; ethnic/cultural interests; government/politics; health/medicine; history; literary studies (trade only); military/war (trade only); money/finance/economics; nature/environment; psychology; science/technology; self-help/personal improvement; sociology; sports; true crime/investigative; women's issues/women's studies. Considers these fiction areas: contemporary issues; detective/police/crime; ethnic; family saga; feminist; literary; mainstream; mystery/suspense; thriller/espionage. Send "outline/proposal with sample chapters for nonfiction, synopsis and first 50 pages for fiction and SASE." Reports in 2-4 weeks on queries; 1-6 weeks on mss.

Recent Sales: *Outsmarting the Female Fat Cell* and *Why Women Need Chocolate*, by Debra Waterhouse (Hyperion); *Trupp*, by Janell Cannon (children's, Harcourt Brace); *Killer Pancake*, by Diane Mott Davidson.

Terms: Agent receives 15% commission on domestic sales; 20% on foreign sales. Offers written contract, binding for 1 year. Charges "an expense fee of $250 (in years we are *active* on author's behalf) to cover domestic costs so that we can spend time selling books instead of accounting expenses. We also charge for the photocopying of the full manuscript or nonfiction proposal and for foreign postage."

Writer's Conferences: Has attended Squaw Valley, Santa Barbara, Asilomar, Southern California Writers Conference, Rocky Mountain Fiction Writers, "to name a few. We also speak regularly for writers groups such as PEN West and the Independent Writers Association."

Tips: Obtains new clients "primarily through referrals/recommendations, but also through queries and conferences and often by solicitation. Be professional and learn the standard procedures for submitting your work. Give full biographical information on yourself, especially for a nonfiction project. Always include SASE with correct return postage for your own protection of your work. Query with a 1 or 2 page letter first and always include postage. Nine page letters telling us your life story, or your book's, are unprofessional and usually not read. Tell us about your book and write your query well. It's our first introduction to who you are and what you can do! Call if you don't hear within a reasonable period of time. Be a regular patron of bookstores and study what kind of books are being published. READ. Check out your local library and bookstores—you'll find lots of books on writing and the publishing industry that will help you! At conferences, ask published writers about their agents. Don't believe the myth that an agent has to be in New York to be successful—we've already disproved it!"

THE JONATHAN DOLGER AGENCY (II), 49 E. 96th St., Suite 9B, New York NY 10128. (212)427-1853. President: Jonathan Dolger. Contact: Tom Wilson. Estab. 1980. Member of AAR. Represents 70 clients. 25% of clients are new/unpublished writers. Writer must have been previously published if submitting fiction. Prefers to work with published/established authors; works with a small number of new/unpublished writers. Specializes in adult trade fiction and nonfiction, and illustrated books.

Handles: Nonfiction books, novels, illustrated books. Query with outline and SASE.

Terms: Agent receives 15% commission on domestic and dramatic sales; 25-30% on foreign sales. Charges for "standard expenses."

‡DONADIO AND ASHWORTH, INC. (II), 231 W. 22nd St., New York NY 10011. (212)691-8077. Fax: (212)633-2837. Contact: Candida Donadio, Neil Olson. Estab. 1970. Member of AAR. Represents 100 clients. Specializes in literary fiction and nonfiction. Currently handles: 40% nonfiction; 50% novels; 10% short story collections.

Handles: Nonfiction books, novels, short story collections. Query with 50 pages and SASE. Reports in 3-4 weeks on mss.

Terms: Agent receives 15% commission on domestic sales; 20% on foreign sales.

THOMAS C. DONLAN (II, IV), 143 E. 43rd St., New York NY 10017. (212)697-1629. Agent: Thomas C. Donlan. Estab. 1983. Represents 12 clients. "Our agency limits itself to philosophy and theology, mainly, but not exclusively Roman Catholic. No special requirements of earlier publication." Prefers to work with published/established authors. Specializes in philosophical and theological writings, including translations. Currently handles: 2% magazine articles; 90% nonfiction books; 8% textbooks.

Handles: Nonfiction books, textbooks. Considers these nonfiction areas: philosophy, theology, translations. Query with outline. Reports in 2 weeks on queries. *Absolutely no unsolicited mss.*

Terms: Agent receives 10% commission on domestic sales; 6% on foreign sales.

DOYEN LITERARY SERVICES, INC. (II), 19005 660th St., Newell IA 50568-7613. (712)272-3300. President: (Ms.) B.J. Doyen. Estab. 1988. Member of RWA, SCBA. Represents 50 clients. 20% of clients are new/previously unpublished writers. Specializes in nonfiction and handles all genre and mainstream fiction mainly for adults (some children's). Currently handles: 60% nonfiction books; 5% juvenile books; 35% novels. No poetry books.

• See B.J. Doyen's article, *Know Your Rights*, in the 1994 edition of the *Guide*.

Handles: Nonfiction books, juvenile books, novels. Considers most nonfiction areas. No gay/lesbian issues, religious/inspirational, or translations. Considers these fiction areas: action/adventure; contemporary issues; detective/police/crime; ethnic; experimental; family saga; fantasy; glitz; historical; horror; humor/satire; juvenile; literary; mainstream; mystery/suspense; psychic/supernatural; romance (contemporary, historical, regency); science fiction; thriller/espionage; westerns/frontier; young adult. Query first with SASE. Reports immediately on queries; 6-8 weeks on mss.

Recent Sales: *Homemade Money*, by Barbara Brabec (Betterway); *Megahealth*, by Sorenson (Evans); *The Family Guide to Financial Aid for Higher Education*, by Black (Putnam/Perigee).

Terms: Agent receives 15% commission on domestic sales; 20% commission on foreign sales. Offers written contract, binding for 1 year.

Tips: "We are very interested in nonfiction book ideas at this time; will consider most topics. Many writers come to us from referrals, but we also get quite a few who initially approach us with query letters. Do *not* use phone queries unless you are successfully published, a celebrity or have an extremely hot, timely idea that can't wait. Send us a sparkling query letter with SASE. It is best if you do not collect editorial rejections prior to seeking an agent, but if you do, be upfront and honest about it. Do not submit your manuscript to more than one agent at a time—querying first can save you (and us) much time. We're open to established or beginning writers—just send us a terrific manuscript!"

ROBERT DUCAS (II), 350 Hudson St., New York NY 10014. (212)924-8120. Fax: (212)924-8079. Contact: R. Ducas. Estab. 1981. Represents 55 clients. 15% of clients are new/previously unpublished writers. Specializes in nonfiction, journalistic exposé, biography, history. Currently handles: 70% nonfiction books; 2% scholarly books; 28% novels.

Handles: Nonfiction books, novels, novellas. Considers these nonfiction areas: animals; biography/autobiography; business; current affairs; gay/lesbian issues; government/politics/law; health/medicine; history; military/war; money/finance/economics; nature/environment; science/technology; sports; true crime/investigative. Considers these fiction areas: action/adventure; contemporary issues; detective/police/crime; family saga; literary; mainstream; mystery/suspense; sports; thriller/espionage. Send outline/proposal. Reports in 2 weeks on queries; 2 months on mss.

Recent Sales: *Tales of the Earth*, by C. Officer (O.U.P.); *Regret Not a Moment*, by N. McGehee (Little Brown).

Terms: Agent receives 15% commission on domestic sales; 20% on foreign sales. Charges for photocopying and postage. "I also charge for messengers and overseas couriers to subagents."

Tips: Obtains new clients through recommendations.

DUPREE/MILLER AND ASSOCIATES INC. LITERARY (II), 100 Highland Park Village, Suite 350, Dallas TX 75205. (214)559-BOOK. Fax: (214)559-PAGE. President: Jan Miller. Estab. 1984. Signatory of WGA west; member of ABA. Represents 120 clients. 20% of clients are new/previously unpublished writers. Specializes in commercial fiction, nonfiction. Currently handles: 75% nonfiction books; 25% novels. Member agents: Jan Miller, Dean Williamson (Vice President); Kay Olsen (Submission Director); Ashley Carroll (Assistant to Vice President).

Handles: Nonfiction books, scholarly books, novels, syndicated material. Considers all nonfiction areas. Considers these fiction areas: action/adventure; cartoon/comic; contemporary issues; detective/police/crime; ethnic; experimental; family saga; fantasy; feminist; gay; glitz; historical; horror; humor/satire; lesbian; literary; mainstream; mystery/suspense; picture book; psychic/supernatural; religious/inspirational; romance (contemporary, historical); science fiction; sports; thriller/espionage; westerns/frontier. Send outline plus 3 sample chapters. Reports in 1 week on queries; 8-12 weeks on mss.

Recent Sales: *Stop the Insanity!*, by Susan Powter (Simon & Schuster); *Untitled*, by Ken Hamblin (Simon & Schuster).

Terms: Agent receives 15% commission on domestic sales. Offers written contract, binding for "no set amount of time. The contract can be cancelled by either agent or client, effective 30 days after cancellation." Charges $20 processing fee and express mail charges.

Writer's Conferences: Southwest Writers (Albuqurque, NM); Brazos Writers (College Station, TX).

Tips: Obtains new client through conferences, lectures, clients and "very frequently through publisher's referrals." If interested in agency representation "it is vital to have the material in the proper working format. As agents' policies differ, it is important to follow their guidelines. The best advice I can give is to work on establishing a strong proposal that provides sample chapters, an overall synopsis (fairly detailed) and some bio information on yourself. Do not send your proposal in pieces; it should be complete upon submission. Remember you are trying to sell your work and it should be in its best condition."

‡JANE DYSTEL LITERARY MANAGEMENT (I, II), One Union Square West, New York NY 10003. (212)627-9100. Fax: (212)627-9313. Contact: Miriam Goderich. Estab. 1994. Member of AAR. Presently represents 150 clients. 50% of clients are new/previously unpublished writers. Specializes in commercial and literary fiction and nonfiction plus cookbooks. Currently handles: 80% nonfiction books; 15% novels; 1% short story collections; 4% cookbooks, photo books, collections.

• Ms. Dystel was a principal agent in Acton, Dystel, Leone and Jaffe before starting her own agency. See her article, *Building a Client List*, in this edition.

Handles: Nonfiction books, novels, cookbooks. Considers these nonfiction areas: animals; anthropology/archaeology; biography/autobiography; business; child guidance/parenting; cooking/food/nutrition; current affairs; education; ethnic/cultural interests; gay/lesbian issues; government/politics/law; health/medicine; history; humor; military/war; money/finance/economics; New Age/metaphysics; popular cultures; psychology; religious/inspirational; science/technology; true crime/investigative; women's issues/women's studies. Considers these fiction areas: Action/adventure; contemporary issues; detective/police/crime; ethnic; family saga; gay; lesbian; literary; mainstream; thriller/espionage. Query. Reports in 2 weeks on queries; 1 month on mss.
Recent Sales: *Tiger's Tale*, by Gus Lee (Knopf); *I Never Forget A Meal*, by Michael Tucker (Little Brown); *Entries From a Hot Pink Diary*, by Todd Brown (Pocket Books).
Terms: Agent receives 15% commission on domestic sales; 19% of foreign sales. Offers written contract on a book to book basis. Charges for photocopying. Galley charges and book charges from the publisher are passed on to the author.
Writer's Conferences: West Coast Writers Conference (Whidbey Island WA, Columbus Day weekend); University of Iowa Writers' Conference.
Tips: Obtains new clients through recommendations from others, solicitation, at conferences.

EDUCATIONAL DESIGN SERVICES, INC. (II, IV), P.O. Box 253, Wantagh NY 11793. (718)539-4107 or (516)221-0995. President: Bertram L. Linder. Vice President: Edwin Selzer. Estab. 1979. Represents 17 clients. 70% of clients are new/previously unpublished writers. Specializes in textual material for educational market. Currently handles: 100% textbooks.
Handles: Textbooks, scholarly books. Considers these nonfiction areas: anthropology/archaeology; business; child guidance/parenting; current affairs; ethnic/cultural interests; government/politics/law; history; juvenile nonfiction; language/literature/criticism; military/war; money/finance/economics; science/technology; sociology; women's issues/women's studies. Query with outline/proposal or outline plus 1-2 sample chapters. Reports in 1 month on queries; 4-6 weeks on mss.
Recent Sales: *New York in U.S. History* (Amsco); *Nueva Historia de Los Estados Unidos* (Minerva Books).
Terms: Agent receives 15% commission on domestic sales; 25% on foreign sales. Offers written contract. Charges for photocopying.
Tips: Obtains new clients through recommendations; at conferences; queries.

PETER ELEK ASSOCIATES (II, IV), Box 223, Canal Street Station, New York NY 10013-2610. (212)431-9368. Fax: (212)966-5768. E-mail: CompuServe, 713714,2515. Contact: Debbie Marketta. Estab. 1979. Represents 20 clients. Specializes in children's picture books, adult nonfiction. Currently handles: 30% juvenile books. Staff includes Gerardo Greco (Director of Project Development/Multimedia).
Handles: Juvenile books (nonfiction, picture books). Considers anthropology; parenting; juvenile nonfiction; nature/environment; popular culture; science; true crime/investigative. Considers juvenile picture books. Query with outline/proposal and SASE. Reports in 2 weeks on queries; 3 weeks on mss.
Recent Sales: *Tsar: The Lost World of Nicholas & Alexandra*, by Peter Kurth (Little, Brown).
Terms: Agent receives 15% commission on domestic sales; 20% on foreign sales. If required, charges for photocopying, typing, courier charges.
Writer's Conferences: Internet (Atlanta,GA); Frankfurt Book Fair (Frankfurt, Germany); Milia (Cannes, France); Bologna Children's Book Fair (Italy).
Tips: Obtains new clients through recommendations and studying consumer and trade magazines. "No work returned unless appropriate packing and postage is remitted. Actively seeking intellectual property/content, text and images for strategic partnering for multimedia. We are currently licensing series and single projects (juvenile, YA and adult) for electronic platforms such as CD-ROM, and CD-I. Our subsidiary company for this is The Content Company Inc.—contact: Gerardo Greco, at the same address."

ETHAN ELLENBERG LITERARY AGENCY (II), 548 Broadway, #5-E, New York NY 10012. (212)431-4554. Fax: (212)941-4652. Contact: Ethan Ellenberg. Estab. 1983. Represents 70 clients. 25% of clients are new/previously unpublished writers. Specializes in commercial and literary fiction, including first novels, thrillers, mysteries, science fiction, fantasy, all categories of romance fiction, quality nonfiction, including biography, history, health, spirituality, business and popular science. Currently handles: 25% nonfiction books; 75% novels. Member agent: Steve Seitz (commercial fiction/nonfiction, health, psychology).

• See Ethan Ellenberg's articles, *On the Merits: The Case Against Reading Fees*, in this edition, and *Building a Career* in the 1993 edition of the *Guide*.

Handles: Nonfiction books, novels. Considers these nonfiction areas: biography/autobiography; business; child guidance/parenting; cooking/food/nutrition; current affairs; health/medicine; history; juvenile nonfiction; New Age/metaphysics; psychology; religious/inspirational; science/technology; self-help/personal improvement; true crime/investigative. Considers these fiction areas: detective/police/crime; family saga; fantasy; historical; humor; juvenile; literary; mainstream; mystery/suspense; picture book; romance; science fiction; thriller/espionage; westerns/frontier; young adult. Send outline plus 3 sample chapters. Reports in 10 days on queries; 3-4 weeks on mss.

Recent Sales: *Radiant Health*, by Ron Teeguarden (Warner); *Patient's Guide to Prostate Cancer*, by Dr. Marc Garnick (Dutton); *two untitled Civil War novels*, by Leonard Scott (Ballantine); *The Rock*, and *untitled science thriller*, by Bob Mayer (Dell); *American Regional Cooking*, by Anthony Dias Blue; *The Movie Studio*, CD-ROM by Kim and Sunny Baker (Putnam New Media); *Battletech*, electronic game script by Bill Keith (Absolute/Sega).

Terms: Agent receives 15% on domestic sales; 10% on foreign sales. Offers written contract, "flexible." Charges for "direct expenses only: photocopying, postage."

Writer's Conferences: Speaks at Vassar Conference on Children's Publishing, attends a number of other RWA conferences (including Hawaii) and Novelists, Inc.

Tips: "We do consider new material from unsolicited authors. Write a good clear letter with a succinct description of your book. We prefer the first three chapters when we consider fiction. For all submissions you must include SASE for return or the material is discarded. It's always hard to break in, but talent will find a home. We continue to see natural storytellers and nonfiction writers with important books."

NICHOLAS ELLISON, INC. (II), 55 Fifth Ave., 15th Floor, New York NY 10003. (212)206-6050. Affiliated with Sanford J. Greenburger Associates. Contact: Elizabeth Ziemska. Estab. 1983. Represents 70 clients. Currently handles: 25% nonfiction books; 75% novels.

Handles: Nonfiction, novels. Considers most nonfiction areas. No biography, gay/lesbian issues or self-help. Considers literary and mainstream fiction. Query with SASE. Reporting time varies on queries.

Recent Sales: *Spencerville* and *The General's Daughter*, by Nelson DeMille (Warner Books); *Tygers of Wrath*, by Philip Rosenberg (St. Martin's Press); *Bijou*, by Mark Joseph (HarperCollins).

Terms: Agent receives 15% commission on domestic sales; 20% commission on foreign sales.

Tips: Usually obtains new clients from word-of-mouth referrals.

ANN ELMO AGENCY INC. (III), 60 E. 42nd St., New York NY 10165. (212)661-2880, 2881. Fax: (212)661-2883. Contact: Ann Elmo or Lettie Lee. Estab. 1961. Member of AAR, MWA, Authors Guild. Member agents: Ann Elmo, Lettie Lee, Mari Cronin (plays).

Handles: Nonfiction, novels. Considers these nonfiction areas: anthropology/archaeology; art/architecture/design; biography/autobiography; business; child guidance/parenting; computers/electronics; cooking/food/nutrition; crafts/hobbies; current affairs; education; health/medicine; history; how-to; juvenile nonfiction; money/finance/economics; music/dance/theater/film; photography; popular culture; psychology; self-help/personal improvement; true crime/investigative; women's issues. Considers these fiction areas: action/adventure; contemporary issues; detective/police/crime; ethnic; family saga; feminist; glitz; historical; juvenile; literary; mainstream; mystery/suspense; psychic/supernatural; regional; romance (contemporary, gothic, historical, regency); thriller/espionage; young adult. Query with outline/proposal. Reports in 4-6 weeks "average" on queries.

Terms: Agent receives 15% commission on domestic sales; 20% on foreign sales. Offers written contract (standard AAR contract).

Tips: Obtains new clients through referrals. "Send properly prepared manuscript. A readable manuscript is the best recommendation. Double space."

‡EMERALD LITERARY AGENCY (I, II), 1212 N. Angelo Dr., Beverly Hills CA 90210. (310)247-0488. (310)247-0885. Contact: Debra Rodman. Estab. 1994. Represents 16 clients. 75% of clients are new/previously published writers. Currently handles: 10% nonfiction books; 5% juvenile books; 65% novels; 10% movie scripts; 10% TV scripts. Member agent: Cheryl Pereira (film scripts).

Handles: Nonfiction books, scholarly books, novels, novellas. Considers these nonfiction areas: art/architecture/design; biography/autobiography; business; child guidance/parenting; computers/electronics; current affairs; ethnic/cultural interests; government/politics/law; how-to; juvenile nonfiction; language/literature/criticism; money/finance/economics; music/dance/theater/film; nature/environment; New Age/metaphysics; photography; popular culture; psychology; religious/inspirational; self-help/personal improvement; sociology; sports; true crime/investigative; women's issues/women's studies. Considers these fiction areas: action/adventure; contemporary issues; detective/police/crime; fantasy; literary; mainstream; mystery/suspense; psychic/supernatural; religious/inspirational; romance (contemporary); science fiction. Query with outline and 3 sample chapters with SASE. Reports in 2 weeks on queries; 1 month on mss.

Recent Sales: *The Rolling Stones, Black & White Blues 1963—*, by David Muckley and Debra Rodman, ed. by Kevin Mulroy (Turner Publications).

Also Handles: Movie scripts (feature film, animation), TV scripts (TV mow, miniseries, episodic drama). Considers these script subjects: action/adventure; contemporary issues; feminist; mainstream; mystery/suspense; psychic/supernatural; religious/inspirational; sports; teen; thriller. Query. Reports in 10 days on queries; 3 weeks on mss.

Terms: Agent receives 15% commission on domestic sales; 20% on foreign sales. Offers written contract, binding for 9 months. Charges $10 reading fee for scripts. Charges for postage, photocopying.

Writers' Conferences: Maui Writers conference.

Tips: Obtains new clients through referrals, luck, conferences and listings in LMP and Hollywood Directory.

ESQUIRE LITERARY PRODUCTIONS (II), 1492 Cottontail Lane, La Jolla CA 92037. (619)551-9383. Contact: Sherrie Dixon, Esq. Estab. 1993. Represents 12 clients. 75% of clients are new/previously unpublished writers. Currently handles: 10% nonfiction books; 90% novels. Agency specializes in adult mainstream fiction. Member agent: D.S. Lada (mainstream fiction.)

Handles: Fiction. Considers these fiction areas: action/adventure; contemporary issues; detective/police/crime; family saga; mainstream; mystery/suspense; thriller/espionage. Send outline, SASE and 3 sample chapters. Reports in 1-2 weeks on queries; 3-4 weeks on mss.

Terms: Agent receives 15% commission on domestic sales; 20% on foreign sales. Offers written contract.

FELICIA ETH LITERARY REPRESENTATION (II), 555 Bryant St., Suite 350, Palo Alto CA 94301-1700. (415)375-1276. Fax: (415)375-1277. Contact: Felicia Eth. Estab. 1988. Member of AAR. Represents 25-30 clients. Works with established and new writers; "for nonfiction, established expertise is certainly a plus, as is magazine publication—though not a prerequisite. I specialize in provocative, intelligent, thoughtful nonfiction on a wide array of subjects which are commercial and high-quality fiction; preferably mainstream and contemporary. I am highly selective, but also highly dedicated to those projects I represent." Currently handles: 85% nonfiction; 15% novels.

Handles: Nonfiction books, novels. Considers these nonfiction areas: animals; anthropology; biography/autobiography; business; child guidance/parenting; current affairs; ethnic/cultural interests; gay/lesbian issues; government/politics/law; health/medicine; history; nature/environment; popular culture; psychology; science/technology; sociology; true crime/investigative; women's issues/women's studies. Considers these fiction areas: ethnic; feminist; gay; lesbian; literary; mainstream; thriller/espionage. Query with outline. Reports in 3 weeks on queries; 1 month on proposals and sample pages.

Recent Sales: *Womanhood: Real Life After Feminism*, by Meredith Maran (Bantam Books); *A Time for Every Purpose*, by Dr. Lonnie Shavelson (Simon & Schuster); *Riding the Windhorse: Psychological Health & The Experience of Transcendence*, by Dr. Kate Noble (Ballantine Books).

Terms: Agent receives 15% commission on domestic sales; 20% on dramatic sales; 20% on foreign sales. Charges for photocopying, express mail service—extraordinary expenses.

Writer's Conferences: Independent Writers of South Carolina (LA); Conference of National Coalition of Independent Scholars (Berkeley, CA).

‡MARY EVANS INC. (II), 242 E. Fifth St., New York NY 10003. (212)979-0880. Fax: (212)979-5344. Contact: Mary Evans. Estab. 1994. Member of AAR. Represents 25 clients. 8% of clients are new/previously unpublished writers. Specializes in upmarket, literary, commercial fiction and nonfiction. Currently handles: 30% nonfiction books; 60% novels; 5% movie scripts; 5% short story collections.

Handles: Nonfiction books, novels. Considers all nonfiction and fiction areas. "Anything if it's good!" Query. Reports in 1 week on queries.

The Agent Who Hasn't Come In From the Cold

In *Spencerville*, the Cold War is over and intelligence agent Keith Landry has returned home. But literary agent Nick Ellison is still out there, working to make Nelson Demille one of the most popular mainstream authors, not only in the U.S., but internationally as well. And he is succeeding, with seven out of eight novels main selections of the Book of the Month Club or Literary Guild, and three feature films due out within 20 months of each other.

Nick Ellison and Nelson Demille began working together in 1980. "I was Nelson's editor on *Cathedral* when I was editor-in-chief at Delacorte Press. When I switched roles eleven years ago and became a literary agent, soon thereafter he became my client." Ellison and Demille continue to work together on the content of the books. "When he's starting a new book, I block out an afternoon and we get a cup of coffee and go to the park. We talk about general themes in the book, not so much about the plot. I offer suggestions."

Spencerville is DeMille's eighth novel, the second in a four-book deal with Warner Books. While three of his books were published by other houses, in 1985 Warner published *Word of Honor* and through Ellison gradually acquired the backlist, which it redesigned for continuity and reissued in paperback. Two more books followed, rounding out the contracts. In 1991, when it came time to negotiate a new contract, Ellison and Demille were faced with the option of leaving Warner and going to another major publisher, or staying and redesigning their relationship with Warner. They chose the latter, but based their discussion "in the spirit of the marketplace" in determining price, as Ellison puts it.

"Since the last negotiation, Warner had made a break with Random House, who used to distribute them, and we saw it as a healthy phenomenon when they united with Little, Brown," explains Ellison. "We found it encouraging, that they took on more critical mass as a legitimate hardcover publisher, not just a mass market house doing hardcover as an afterthought."

Another consideration for both author and agent was the fact Warner had the backlist, which still generates a great deal of money. Ellison considered the existing backlist connection carefully, noting "Warner was enjoying some success themselves, and had the backing of the Little, Brown sales force as well as their own. Their mass market success was self-evident." In continuing with Warner, Ellison reasoned, that backlist would continue to be pushed by the combined sales forces. Demille agrees. "Sometimes an agent doesn't think the backlist is important, they are more interested in the money upfront, but to an author it's a primary concern," he says.

"I would say money was key, but also important was the notion that Nelson could be a very big fish in a less-populated pond, rather than at a big house where there was the danger of him not having quite the preeminence he would otherwise have," states Ellison. "Time Warner showed a lot of zeal, and conversations took place on that level, too."

Demille attended one day of the negotiations, to get the feel for what was happening, and to ensure that several "author-friendly" clauses were included. "Sometimes," he adds, "an agent doesn't want the author to be anywhere near. It's like Kissinger not wanting Nixon to be in Moscow at the same time. It's easier for an agent to say 'I don't know if my client would like that' if the client isn't sitting right next to him." Ellison made sure he and his client had input into various levels of producing and marketing the books. "We have terms with Warner with a high degree of participation."

One area of mutual benefit was the sale of subsidiary rights. "Book of the Month Club took *Spencerville* as part of a multi-book deal, too. This was negotiated by the subrights department at Warner, but because of the nature of our agreement, although it was their deal, we were party to the conversation, in a very supportive way. There is a mutuality," adds Ellison. Also included in the deal with BOMC were performance bonuses. "Performance clauses are more complicated than weeks on the bestseller list, it's a formula. Sometimes these are called bestseller, performance or sell-through clauses."

Film rights were offered by Ellison to Alan Ladd, then chairman and president of MGM, and Paramount. The studios were given 70 pages, which were promptly collected as soon as the executives finished reading. Ellison started accepting bids 72 hours later. "Interestingly enough, when I was selling it, I received bids from both MGM and Paramount. Alan Ladd was asked to resign on Friday, when I was going to close the deal the following Monday. So I wound up selling the option to Paramount. A few weeks later he turned up as an independent producer in the Alan Ladd Company at Paramount, so though Paramount bought it, they obviously held him in such high regard that he is now the producer."

Ellison sold a one year option for *Spencerville* to Paramount for $525,000 against a buyout of one million dollars. "They already have a screenwriter and are very high on the project, Sherry Lansing, Alan Ladd and Paramount. The option only lasts for a year, so if it's made, that's great, if not, there's a list a mile long, so we'll sell it." He adds, "That's good money for an option; a buyout now with his stature, you see deals with a half million, two or three million for major authors, and as astounding as it is, it's not uncommon. But an option at that price, for a year, it doesn't matter who it is, that's still extraordinary.

"Also at Paramount is *The General's Daughter*, a buyout by Bob Rahme (President of the Motion Picture Association) and Mace Neufeld. *Gold Coast* is under option to Michael and Martin Bregman at Universal, and they have Bob Garland doing the screenplay. All the producers have first-rate screenwriters attached, so we have three feature films coming out within 20 months. With two major ones with Paramount and another at Universal, we are persuaded we can take Nelson to a whole new level."

With *Spencerville*, Warner's marketing department arranged a one-day lay-down, which Ellison explains. "When the sales force goes out and solicits orders for the book, and the book comes in from the printer, it takes a couple of weeks to end up distributed around the country. With this book it was all done in one day for high impact. October 12 about 500,000 copies hit the shelves. We've been hearing phenomenal sales from Warner, which has cooperated by immediately forwarding the sales data they've received."

Ellison also conducts his own informal sales research to track how the book is doing. "I checked the Barnes & Noble in Grand Central, where you get more of a cross-section of people coming in, perhaps, than another bookstore. Between 8 and 11 a.m. they sold 70 copies, 30 more than any other book. In Denver, at The Tattered Cover bookstore," he added, "the management is expecting a crowd at Nelson's book signing and is giving out numbers like a bakery to accomodate all the fans."

While we spoke he was handed a memo notifying him that with only three days' sales reported, *Spencerville* had hit number ten on the *Wall Street Journal* bestseller list. Perusing numbers one through nine, Ellison predicted confidently, "Stephen King is his own world. But all these guys are touchable, definitely. This book is going to knock 'em all down."

Recent Sales: *Green*, by Frances Sherwood (Farrar, Straus and Giroux); *Dead Man's Dance*, by Robert Ferrigno (Peterson's).
Also Handles: Movie scripts (feature film).
Recent Sales: *Gentlemen Host*, by Michael Chabon (Paramount Pictures).
Terms: Agent receives 15% commission on domestic sales; 20% on foreign sales. Offers written contract if requested.
Writer's Conferences: Columbia County Writers Conference (Chatham NY, July 1995); Squaw Valley (Squaw Valley CA, August 1995).
Tips: Obtains new clients through writers' conferences. "Remember that good writing isn't enough — there must be a *market* for the writing."

FARBER LITERARY AGENCY INC. (II), 14 E. 75th St., #2E, New York NY 10021. (212)861-7075. Fax: (212)861-7076. Contact: Ann Farber. Estab. 1989. Signatory of WGA. Represents 30 clients. 84% of clients are new/previously unpublished writers. Currently handles: 65% nonfiction books; 5% scholarly books; 20% stage plays.
Handles: Nonfiction books, textbooks, juvenile books, novels, stage plays. Considers these nonfiction areas: child guidance/parenting; cooking/food/nutrition; music/dance/theater/film; psychology. Considers these fiction areas: action/adventure; contemporary issues; humor/satire; juvenile; literary; mainstream; mystery/suspense; thriller/espionage; young adult. Send outline/proposal plus 3 sample chapters. Reports in 1 week on queries; 1 month on mss.
Terms: Agent receives 15% commission on domestic sales; 20% on foreign sales. Offers written contract, binding for 2 years.
Tips: Obtains new clients through recommendations from others. Client must furnish copies of ms. "Our attorney, Donald C. Farber, is the author of many books. His services are available to the clients of the agency as part of the agency service."

FLORENCE FEILER LITERARY AGENCY (III), 1524 Sunset Plaza Dr., Los Angeles CA 90069. (213)652-6920. Fax: (213)652-0945. Associate: Joyce Boorn. Estab. 1976. Member of PEN American Center, Women in Film, California Writers Club, MWA. Represents 40 clients. No unpublished writers. "Quality is the criterion." Specializes in fiction, nonfiction, screenplays, TV. No short stories.
  ● See the expanded listing for this agency in Script Agents.

*JOYCE A. FLAHERTY, LITERARY AGENT (II, III), 816 Lynda Court, St. Louis MO 63122-5531. (314)966-3057. Contact: Joyce or John Flaherty. Estab. 1980. Member of AAR, RWA, MWA, Author's Guild. Represents 60 clients. 10% of clients are new/previously unpublished writers. Currently handles: 25% nonfiction books; 75% novels. Member agents: Joyce A. Flaherty (women's fiction, romance, mystery and suspense, general fiction and nonfiction); John Flaherty (thrillers, male-oriented mysteries and espionage novels; also military fiction and nonfiction).
Handles: Nonfiction books, novels. Considers these nonfiction areas: collectibles; Americana; animals; biography/autobiography (celebrity); child guidance/parenting; crafts/hobbies; health/medicine; history (Americana); how-to; military/war; nature/environment; popular culture; psychology; self-help/personal improvement; sociology; true crime/investigative; women's issues/

women's studies. Considers these fiction areas: contemporary issues; crime; family saga; feminist; frontier; historical; literary; mainstream; military/aviation/war; mystery/suspense; psychic/supernatural; romance (contemporary, regency); thriller/espionage; women's fiction. Send outline plus 1 sample chapter and SASE. No unsolicited mss. Reports in 6 weeks on queries; 2 months on mss unless otherwise agreed on.

Recent Sales: *Splendor*, by Charlene Cross (Pocket Books); *Riverbend*, by Marcia Martin (Penguin-Onyx).

Terms: Agent receives 15% commission on domestic sales; 25-30% on foreign sales. Charges $50 marketing fee for new clients unless currently published book authors.

Writer's Conferences: Attends Romance Writers of America; Virginia Romance Writers (Williamsburg, VA); Moonlight & Magnolias (Atlanta, GA); California Writers Club (Asilomar Conference Center, Pacific Grove, CA).

Tips: Obtains new clients through recommendations from editors and clients, writers' conferences and from queries. "Be concise in a letter or by phone and well focused. Always include a SASE as well as your phone number. If you want an agent to return your call, leave word to call you collect if you're not currently the agent's client. If a query is a multiple submission, be sure to say so and mail them all at the same time so that everyone has the same chance. Know something about the agent beforehand so that you're not wasting each other's time. Be specific about word length of project and when it will be completed if not completed at the time of contact. Be brief!"

FLAMING STAR LITERARY ENTERPRISES (II), 320 Riverside Dr., New York NY 10025. Contact: Joseph B. Vallely or Janis C. Vallely. Estab. 1985. Represents 50 clients. 25% of clients are new/previously unpublished writers. Specializes in upscale commercial fiction and nonfiction. Currently handles: 75% nonfiction books; 25% novels.

Handles: Nonfiction books, novels. Considers these nonfiction areas: current affairs; government/politics/law; health/medicine; nature/environment; New Age/metaphysics; science/technology; self-help/personal improvement; sports. Considers only upscale literary fiction. Query with SASE. Reports in 1 week on queries.

Terms: Agent receives 15% commission on domestic sales; 20% on foreign sales. Offers written contract. Charges for photocopying, postage, long distance phone calls only.

Tips: Obtains new clients through over the transom and referrals.

‡FLANNERY LITERARY (II), 34-36 28th St., #5, Long Island City NY 11106-3516. (718)472-0523. Fax: (718)482-0718. Contact: Jennifer Flannery. Estab. 1992. Represents 18 clients. 25% of clients are new/previously unpublished writers. Specializes in children's and young adult, juvenile fiction and nonfiction. Currently handles: 5% nonfiction books; 90% juvenile books; 5% novels.

Handles: Nonfiction books, juvenile books, novels. Considers these nonfiction areas: child guidance/parenting; juvenile nonfiction. Considers these fiction areas: action/adventure; contemporary issues; ethnic; experimental; family saga; historical; humor/satire; juvenile; literary; mainstream; mystery/suspense; picture book; sports; western/frontier; young adult. Query. Reports in 2 weeks on queries; 4-6 weeks on mss.

Also Handles: Movie scripts (feature film, animation), TV scripts (TV mow, miniseries, animation). Considers these script subject areas: action/adventure; comedy; ethnic; family saga; historical; humor; juvenile; mainstream; mystery/suspense; teen. Query. Reports in 2 weeks on queries; 4-6 weeks on scripts.

Terms: Agent receives 15% commission on domestic sales; 20% on foreign sales. Offers written contract, binding for life of book in print, with 30 day cancellation clause. 100% of business is derived from commissions on sales.

Writers' Conferences: Rice University Writers' Conference (Houston, June 10-11, 1995); SCBWI/Bank Street College (New York City, November 1994).

Tips: Obtains new clients through referrals. "Write an engrossing succinct query describing your work."

PETER FLEMING AGENCY (IV), P.O. Box 458, Pacific Palisades CA 90272. (310)454-1373. Contact: Peter Fleming. Estab. 1962. Specializes in "nonfiction books: innovative, helpful, contrarian, individualistic, pro-free market . . . with bestseller big market potential." Currently handles: 100% nonfiction books.

Handles: Nonfiction books. Considers "any nonfiction area with a positive, innovative, helpful, professional, successful approach to improving the world (and abandoning special interests, corruption and patronage)." Query with SASE.

Recent Sales: "2 revisions of bestselling *The Living Trust*, by Henry Abts (Contemporary Books—Chicago, Harvey Plotnick-Publisher), over 400,000 sold.

Terms: Agent receives 15% commission on domestic sales; 25% on foreign sales. Offers written contract, binding for 1 year. Charges "only those fees agreed to in *writing*, i.e., NY-ABA expenses shared. We may ask for a TV contract, too."
Tips: Obtains new clients "through a *sensational*, different, one of a kind idea for a book usually backed by the writer's experience in that area of expertise. If you give seminars, you can begin by self-publishing, test marketing with direct sales. One of my clients sold 70,000 copies through his speeches and travels."

‡B.R. FLEURY AGENCY, 1228 E. Colonial Dr., Orlando FL 32803. (407)896-4976. Contact: Blanche or Margaret. Estab. 1994. Signatory of WGA. Currently handles: 50% books; 50% scripts.
   ● See the expanded listing for this agency in Script Agents.

FOGELMAN LITERARY AGENCY (I), 7515 Greenville Ave., Suite 712, Dallas TX 75231. (214)361-9956. Fax: (214)361-9553. Contact: Evan Fogelman or Linda Diehl Kruger. Estab. 1990. Member of AAR. Represents 85-100 clients. Specializes in romance fiction and nonfiction. Currently handles: 40% nonfiction books; 60% novels.
Handles: Considers these nonfiction areas: biography; business; current affairs; government/politics/law; money; nutrition; parenting; popular culture; self-help; true crime; contemporary women's issues/women's studies. Query with SASE. Reports in 1-2 working days on 1-page query. Unsolicited mss not accepted.
Terms: Agent receives 15% commission on domestic sales; varying on foreign sales.
Writer's Conferences: Many RWA and multi-genre conferences throughout the world.
Tips: Obtains new clients through referrals, through writers conferences and solicited submissions. Published authors may call; unpublished authors please query.

JAY GARON-BROOKE ASSOC. INC. (II), 101 W. 55th St., Suite 5K, New York NY 10019. (212)581-8300. President: Jay Garon. Vice President: Jean Free. Agent: Nancy Coffey. Estab. 1952. Member of AAR, signatory of WGA. Represents 80 clients. 10% of clients are new/previously unpublished writers. Specializes in mainstream fiction and nonfiction. Currently handles: 15% nonfiction books; 75% novels; 5% movie scripts; 3% TV scripts.
Handles: Nonfiction books, novels, movie scripts, TV scripts, stage plays. Considers these nonfiction areas: biography/autobiography; child guidance/parenting; gay/lesbian issues; health/medicine; history; military/war; music/dance/theater/film; psychology; self-help/personal improvement; true crime/investigative. Considers these fiction areas: action/adventure; contemporary issues; detective/police/crime; family saga; fantasy; gay; glitz; historical; literary; mainstream; mystery/suspense; romance; science fiction. Query. Reports in 3 weeks on queries; 5-8 weeks on mss.
Recent Sales: *The Chamber*, by John Grisham (Doubleday-Dell); *Arc Light*, by Eric Harry (Simon & Schuster); *Judgement Day*, by Patrick Reinken (Simon & Schuster); *Intimate*, by Elizabeth Gage (Pocket Book—hardcover & paperback).
Terms: Agent receives 15% on domestic sales; 30% on foreign sales. Offers written contract, binding for 3-5 years. Charges for "photocopying if author does not provide copies."
Tips: Obtains new clients through referrals and from queries. "Send query letter first giving the essence of the manuscript and a personal or career bio with SASE."

MAX GARTENBERG, LITERARY AGENT (II,III), 521 Fifth Ave., Suite 1700, New York NY 10175-0105. (212)860-8451. Contact: Max Gartenberg. Estab. 1954. Represents 30 clients. 5% of clients are new writers. Currently handles: 90% nonfiction books; 10% novels.
Handles: Nonfiction books. Considers these nonfiction areas: agriculture/horticulture; animals; art/architecture/design; biography/autobiography; child guidance/parenting; current affairs; health/medicine; history; military/war; money/finance/economics; music/dance/theater/film; nature/environment; psychology; science/technology; self-help/personal improvement; sports; true crime/investigative; women's issues/women's studies. Query. Reports in 2 weeks on queries; 6 weeks on mss.
Recent Sales: *Ling Ch'I Ching*, edited and translated by Ralph D. Sawyer (Shambhala Publications); *Joan Crawford: The Last Word*, by Fred Lawrence Guiles (Carol Publishing); *Wilhelm Reich vs. the USA*, by Jerome Greenfield (Verlag Zweitausendeins [Germany]).

Agents who specialize in a specific subject area such as computer books or in handling the work of certain writers such as gay or lesbian writers are ranked IV.

Terms: Agent receives 10% commission on domestic sales; 15% on foreign sales. Offers written contract.
Tips: Obtains new clients "primarily, by recommendations from others, but often enough by following up on good query letters. However, this is a small agency serving established writers, and new writers whose work it is able to handle are few and far between. Nonfiction is more likely to be of interest here than fiction, and category fiction not at all."

‡RICHARD GAUTREAUX—A LITERARY AGENCY (II), 729 Frisella St., Gretna LA 70056. (504)362-6019. Contact: Jay Richards. Estab. 1985. Signatory of WGA. Represents 6 clients. 75% of clients are new/previously unpublished writers. Currently handles: 45% novels; 25% movie scripts; 20% TV scripts; 5% short story collections.
• See the expanded listing for this agency in Script Agents.

CONNIE GODDARD: BOOK DEVELOPMENT (II), 203 N. Wabash Ave., Chicago IL 60601-2415. (312)759-5822. Fax: (312)759-5823. Contact: Connie Goddard. Estab. 1992. Represents 25 clients. 30% of clients are new/previously unpublished writers. Specializes in Chicago-area writers and projects with Midwest origins. Currently handles: 70% nonfiction books; 30% novels.
Handles: Nonfiction books, novels. Considers these nonfiction areas: agriculture/horticulture; animals; anthropology/archaeology; art/architecture/design; biography/autobiography; business; child guidance/parenting; computers/electronics; cooking/food/nutrition; crafts/hobbies; current affairs; ethnic/cultural interests; government/politics/law; health/medicine; history; interior design/decorating; language/literature/criticism; military/war; money/finance/economics; music/dance/theater/film; nature/environment; photography; psychology; religious/inspirational; science/technology; self-help/personal improvement; sociology; sports; translations; true crime/investigative; women's issues/women's studies. Considers these fiction areas: detective/police/crime; historical; mainstream; mystery/suspense; thriller/espionage. Query with letter before sending ms or proposal. Always include SASE. Reports in 1 month.
Recent Sales: *Wisconsin Trivia*, by Kristin Visser (Rutledge Hill); *Encyclopedia of Television*, by Museum of Broadcast Communications (Fitzroy-Dearborn).
Terms: Agent receives 10-20% commission on domestic sales. Offers written contract; binding for 6-12 months to begin. Charges for express postage, long distance phone calls, and photocopying; deducted from advance. "All unsolicited inquiries will be briefly reviewed by myself or a reader. Chicago-area writers needing guidance in developing/marketing a proposal are welcome to attend one of my frequent workshops. If specific arrangements are made, I will do a written or oral evaluation for a fee of $100-500 depending upon material submitted. This usually would preclude representation."
Writers Conferernces: ABA (Chicago); Printer's Row Book Fair (Chicago); Blooming Grove Writers (Bloomington, IL).
Tips: Obtains new clients "mainly by referral. I make frequent appearances, giving 'Getting Published; Why Writers Don't Need New York Any More' workshops and speaking frequently about publishing and bookselling in Chicago, Illinois, and Midwest. I want to work with people who want to work; writing books is a business as well as all the other fine things it might be."

GOLDFARB & GRAYBILL, ATTORNEY AT LAW (II), (formerly Ronald Goldfarb & Associates), 918 16th St. NW, Washington DC 20006. (202)466-3030. Contact: Nina Graybill. Estab. 1966. Signatory of WGA. Represents "hundreds" of clients. "Minority" of clients are new/previously unpublished writers. Specializes in nonfiction, "books with TV tie-ins." Currently handles: 80% nonfiction books; 15% fiction; 5% other. Member agents: Ronald Goldfarb, Nina Graybill.
Handles: Nonfiction books, fiction. Considers all nonfiction areas except children's books. No poetry. Considers these fiction areas: action/adventure; contemporary issues; detective/police/crime; ethnic; feminist; gay; glitz; historical; literary; mainstream; mystery/suspense; thriller/espionage. Send outline or synopsis plus 1-2 sample chapters. Reports in 1 month on queries; 2 months on mss.
Recent Sales: *The Sheltering Circle*, by Susan Eisenhower (Farrar, Straus & Giroux, Inc.); *Firewall: Iran-Contra*, by Lawrence Walsh with Alfred Friendly, Jr. (W.W. Norton).
Writer's Conferences: Attends Washington Independent Writers Conference; Medical Writers Conference, ABA, VCCA.
Tips: Obtains new clients mostly through recommendations from others. "We are a law firm which can help writers with related problems, Freedom of Information Act requests, libel, copyright, contracts, etc. We are published writers."

GOODMAN ASSOCIATES (III), 500 West End Ave., New York NY 10024. (212)873-4806. Contact: Elise Simon Goodman. Estab. 1976. Member of AAR. Represents 100 clients. "Presently accepting new clients on a very selective basis."

• Arnold Goodman is current chair of the AAR Ethics Committee. See his article, *Write and Wrong: Literary Agents and Ethics*, in this edition.
Handles: Nonfiction, novels. Considers most adult nonfiction and fiction areas. No "poetry, articles, individual stories, children's or YA material." Query with SASE. Reports in 10 days on queries; 1 month on mss.
Terms: Agent receives 15% commission on domestic sales; 20% on foreign sales. Charges for certain expenses: faxes, toll calls, overseas postage, photocopying, book purchases.

CHARLOTTE GORDON AGENCY (II), 235 E. 22nd St., New York NY 10010-4633. (212)679-5363. Contact: Charlotte Gordon. Estab. 1986. Represents 30 clients. 10% of clients are new/unpublished writers. "I'll work with writers whose work is interesting to me. Specializes in books (not magazine material, except for my writers, and then only in special situations). My taste is eclectic." Currently handles: 40% nonfiction; 40% novels; 20% juvenile.
Handles: Nonfiction books, novels; juvenile fiction and nonfiction. Considers these nonfiction areas: anthropology/archaeology; business; health/medicine; history; juvenile nonfiction; money/finance/economics; nature/environment; New Age/metaphysics; psychology; sociology; women's issues/women's studies. Considers these fiction areas: contemporary issues; family saga; feminist; gay; juvenile; lesbian; literary; mystery/suspense; romance (regency); young adult. Must query first with first chapter. No unsolicited mss. Reports in 2 weeks on queries.
Recent Sales: *Untitled mystery*, by Grif Stockley (Simon & Schuster).
Terms: Agent receives 15% commission on domestic sales; 10% on dramatic sales; 10% on foreign sales, if another agent involved.

GOTHAM ART & LITERARY AGENCY INC. (V), 25 Tudor City Place, Suite 1504, New York NY 10017-6843. (212)599-0059. Fax: (212)599-2070. Contact: Anne Elisabeth Suter. Estab. 1983. Currently handles: 10% nonfiction books; 45% juvenile books; 45% novels.
• This agency is currently restructuring and will not accept any unsolicited manuscripts at this time.

SANFORD J. GREENBURGER ASSOCIATES (II), 55 Fifth Ave., New York NY 10003. (212)206-5600. Fax: (212)463-8718. Contact: Heide Lange. Estab. 1945. Member of AAR. Represents 500 clients. Member agents: Heide Lange, Faith Hamlin, Beth Vesel, Diane Cleaver.
Handles: Nonfiction books, novels. Considers all nonfiction areas. Considers these fiction areas: action/adventure; contemporary issues, detective/police/crime; ethnic; family saga; feminist; gay; glitz; historical; humor/satire; juvenile; lesbian; literary; mainstream; mystery/suspense; picture books; psychic/supernatural; regional; sports; thriller/espionage. Query first. Reports in 1-2 weeks on queries; 1-2 months on mss.
Recent Sales: *Let Me Hear Your Voice*, by Catherine Maurice (Knopf); *Your Money or Your Life*, by Joe Domiguez and Vicki Robin (Viking).
Terms: Agent receives 15% commission on domestic sales; 19% on foreign sales. Charges for photocopying, books for foreign and subsidiary rights submissions.

‡RANDALL ELISHA GREENE, LITERARY AGENT (II), 620 S. Broadway, Suite 210, Lexington KY 40508. (606)225-1388. Contact: Randall Elisha Greene. Estab. 1987. Represents 20 clients. 30% of clients are new/previously unpublished writers. Specializes in adult fiction and nonfiction only. No juvenile or children's books. Currently handles: 50% nonfiction books; 50% novels.
Handles: Nonfiction books, novels. Considers these nonfiction areas: agriculture/horticulture; biography/autobiography; business; current affairs; government/politics/law; history; how-to; language/literature/criticism; psychology; religious/inspirational; true crime/investigative. Considers these fiction areas: action/adventure; contemporary issues; detective/police/crime; family saga; humor/satire; literary; mainstream; regional; romance (contemporary); thriller/espionage. Query. Reports in 1 month on queries; 2 months on mss.
Terms: Agent receives 15% commission on domestic sales; 20% on foreign sales. Charges for extraordinary expenses such as photocopying and foreign postage.

MAIA GREGORY ASSOCIATES (II), 311 E. 72nd St., New York NY 10021. (212)288-0310. Contact: Maia Gregory. Estab. 1978. Represents 10-12 clients. Currently handles: 98% nonfiction books.
Handles: Considers these nonfiction areas: art; history; language; music/dance/theater/film. Query with outline plus 1 sample chapter and SASE. Reports in 2 weeks on queries.
Terms: Agent receives 15% commission on domestic sales; varies on foreign sales.
Writer's Conferences: PEN (Prague).
Tips: Obtains new clients "through recommendations and queries."

on line

LEW GRIMES LITERARY AGENCY (II), 250 W. 54th St., Suite 800, New York NY 10019-5586. (212)974-9505. Fax: (212)974-9525. Contact: Lew Grimes. Estab. 1991. 50% of clients are new/previously unpublished writers. Currently handles: 40% nonfiction books; 5% scholarly books; 1% textbooks; 50% novels; 2% poetry books; 2% movie scripts.
Handles: Nonfiction books, novels. Query. Reports in 3-4 weeks on queries; 3 months on mss.
Recent Sales: *Don't Speak to Strangers*, by Marion Rosen (St. Martin's); *The Boy, the Devil & Divorce*, by Richard Frede (Pocket).
Terms: Agent receives 15% commission on domestic sales; 20% on foreign sales. Offers written contract. Charges $15 postage and handling for return of ms. "Expenses are reimbursed for unpublished authors and for non-commercial projects."
Tips: Obtains new clients through referral and by query. "Provide brief query and resume showing publishing history clearly. Always put phone number and address on correspondence and enclose SASE. No faxed queries."

THE CHARLOTTE GUSAY LITERARY AGENCY (II, IV), 10532 Blythe, Suite 211, Los Angeles CA 90064. (310)559-0831. Fax: (310)559-2639. Contact: Charlotte Gusay. Estab. 1988. Member of SPAR, signatory of WGA. Represents 30 clients. 50% of clients are new/previously unpublished writers. Specializes in fiction, nonfiction, children's (multicultural, nonsexist), children's illustrators, screenplays, books to film. "Percentage breakdown of the manuscripts different at different times."
Handles: Nonfiction books, scholarly books, juvenile books, travel books, novels, movie scripts. Considers all nonfiction and fiction areas. No romance, short stories, science fiction or horror. Query. Reports in 4-6 weeks on queries; 6-10 weeks on mss.
Recent Sales: *Groucho Marx and Other Short Stories and Tall Tales: Selected Writings of Groucho Marx*, edited by Robert Bader (Faber & Faber Pubs).
Terms: Agent receives 15% commission on domestic sales; 10% on dramatic sales; 25% on foreign sales. Offers written contract, binding for "usually 1 year." Charges for out-of-pocket expenses for long distance phone, fax, express mail, postage, etc.
Writer's Conferences: Attends Writers Connection, in San Jose, California; Scriptwriters Connection, in Studio City, California; National Women's Book Association, in Los Angeles.
Tips: Usually obtains new clients through referrals, queries. "Please be professional."

‡REECE HALSEY AGENCY (II, III), 8733 Sunset Blvd., Suites 101, 102, Los Angeles CA 90069. (310)652-2409. Fax: (310)652-7595. Contact: Dorris Halsey (#101), Kimberley Cameron (#102); (310)652-0271. Estab. 1957. Signatory of WGA. Represents 30 clients. 20% of clients are new/previously unpublished writers. Specializes mostly in books/excellent writing. Currently handles: 10% nonfiction books; 60% novels; 30% movie scripts. Member agents: Dorris Halsey; Kimberley Cameron.
Handles: Nonfiction books, novels. Considers these nonfiction areas: biography/autobiography; current affairs; history; language/literature/criticism; popular culture; true crime/investigative; women's issues/women's studies. Considers these fiction areas: action/adventure; contemporary issues; detective/police/crime; ethnic; family saga; historical; literary; mainstream; mystery/suspense; romance (contemporary); science fiction; thriller/espionage. Query with SASE. Reports in 2 days on queries; 1-3 months on mss.
Also Handles: Movie scripts.
Terms: Agent receives 15% commission on domestic sales. Offers written contract, binding for 1 year. Requests four copies of ms if representing an author.
Writer's Conferences: Attends ABA every year.
Tips: Obtains new clients through recommendations from others and solicitation. "Always send a well-written query and include an SASE with it!"

THE MITCHELL J. HAMILBURG AGENCY (II), 292 S. La Cienega Blvd., Suite 312, Beverly Hills CA 90211. (310)657-1501. Contact: Michael Hamilburg. Estab. 1960. Signatory of WGA. Represents 40 clients. Currently handles: 75% nonfiction books; 25% novels.
Handles: Nonfiction, novels. Considers all nonfiction areas and most fiction areas. No romance. Send outline plus 2 sample chapters. Reports in 3-4 weeks on mss.

The publishing field is constantly changing! If you're still using this book and it is 1996 or later, buy the newest edition of Guide to Literary Agents *at your favorite bookstore or order directly from Writer's Digest Books.*

Recent Sales: *A Biography of the Leakey Family,* by Virginia Morrell (Simon & Schuster); *A Biography of Agnes De Mille,* by Carol Easton (Little, Brown).
Terms: Agent receives 10-15% commission on domestic sales.
Tips: Usually obtains new clients through recommendations from others, at conferences or personal search. "Good luck! Keep writing!"

‡**THE HANSON AGENCY (II, IV),** P.O. Box 1335, Southampton NY 11969. (516)287-2525. Fax: (516)287-2582. Contact Ralph Schiano or Leslie Jennemann. Estab. 1992. Signatory of WGA. Represents 46 clients. 80% of clients are new/previously unpublished writers. Specializes in science fiction, horror, fantasy. Currently handles: 5% nonfiction books; 10% juvenile books; 60% novels; 20% movie scripts; 5% short story collections.
Handles: Considers these fiction areas: action/adventure; contemporary issues; ethnic (juvenile multicultural); experimental; fantasy; feminist; gay; glitz; historical; horror; humor/satire; juvenile; literary; picture book; psychic/supernatural; romance (with science fiction twist); science fiction; young adult. Query with outline/proposal and/or 1 sample chapter and SASE.
Terms: Agent receives 10-15% commission on domestic sales. Offers written contract, binding for 1 year with cancellation clause. Charges for photocopying and postage.
Tips: Obtains new clients through referrals. "Keep it in the mail and don't give up!"

JOHN HAWKINS & ASSOCIATES, INC. (II), 71 W. 23rd St., New York NY 10010. (212)807-7040. Fax: (212)807-9555. Contact: John Hawkins, William Reiss, Sharon Friedman. Estab. 1893. Member of AAR. Represents 100+ clients. 5-10% of clients are new/previously unpublished writers. Currently handles: 40% nonfiction books; 20% juvenile books; 40% novels.
Handles: Nonfiction books, juvenile books, novels. Considers all nonfiction areas except computers/electronics; religion/inspirational; translations. Considers all fiction areas except confessional; erotica; fantasy; romance. Query with outline/proposal. Reports in 1 month on queries.
Terms: Agent receives 15% commission on domestic sales; 20% on foreign sales. Charges for photocopying.
Tips: Obtains new clients through recommendations from others.

GARY L. HEGLER LITERARY AGENCY (III), P.O. Box 890101, Houston TX 77289-0101. (713)333-0173. Contact: Gary L. Hegler or Nikki Cane. Estab. 1985. Signatory of WGA. 10% of clients are new/previously unpublished writers. Specializes in young adult, nonfiction and adult westerns. Currently handles: 50% nonfiction books; 30% juvenile books; 5% novels; 5% movie scripts; 10% TV scripts.
Handles: Nonfiction books, textbooks, juvenile books, poetry books, movie and TV scripts. Considers these nonfiction areas: animals; biography/autobiography; health/medicine; juvenile nonfiction; military/war; money/finance/economics; nature/environment; psychology; religious/inspirational; true crime/investigative; science/technology; self-help/personal improvement. Considers these fiction areas: action/adventure; detective/police/crime; juvenile; mainstream; mystery/suspense; regional (Texas only); romance (contemporary); westerns; young adult. Query with outline plus 3 sample chapters. "First query; then we'll ask for the outline." Reports in 1 week on queries; 2 months on mss.
Recent Sales: *The Whiskey City* series, by Robin Gibson (Avalon Books); *Blue Hills Robbery,* by Leola Kahrimanis (Eakin Press).
Terms: Agent receives 10% commission on domestic sales; 10% on foreign sales. Offers written contract, binding for 1 year.
Writer's Conferences: Attends Bay Area Writers Conference; Golden Triangle Writers Guild Conference.
Tips: Obtains new clients through recommendations from authors, from WGA referral listing and conferences. "Be sure the submission is the best you can do, this includes its neatness, accuracy and suspense (if fictional). We will not represent writers who won't actively promote their books."

‡**HENDERSON LITERARY REPRESENTATION (I, II),** P.O. Box 476, 415 Sicklerville Ave., Sicklerville NJ 08081. Contact: Rita Elizabeth Henderson. Estab. 1994. Represents 5 clients. Specializes in autobiography and biography, especially celebrity bios. Currently handles: 100% nonfiction books.
Handles: Nonfiction books. Considers these nonfiction areas: art/architecture/design; biography/autobiography; biography (celebrity); business; child guidance/parenting; computers/electronics; cooking/food/nutrition; current affairs; education; ethnic/cultural interests; gay/lesbian issues; government/politics/law; health/medicine; history; how-to; humor; interior design/decorating; juvenile nonfiction; money/finance/economics; music/dance/theater/film; photography; popular culture; psychology; religious/inspirational; science/technology; self-help/personal improvement; sociology; sports; true crime/investigative; women's issues/women's studies. Query

by mail with outline/proposal and 3 sample chapters. Reports in 2 weeks on queries; 1 month on mss.

Recent Sales: *The Boyz II Men Success Story: Defying the Odds*, by Rita Elizabeth Henderson (Aynderson Press Publishing).

Terms: Agent receives 10% commission on domestic sales; 20% on foreign sales. Offers written contract, binding for life of book or until mutually terminated. 100% of business derived from commissions on book sales.

Writers' Conferences: Meet the Agents (New York City, October).

Tips: Obtains new clients through conferences, solicitation and referrals from others. "Please be organized in your proposal. If you think you have a good manuscript, and know that there is a marketplace for it, continue to work diligently to get it sold and don't give up. Have patience because some books sell quickly and others can take more time. In preparing your manuscript, please follow the Chicago Manual of Style."

‡DAVID HENDIN LITERARY (I, II), P.O. Box 990, Nyack NY 10960. (212)753-7942. Fax: (212)758-3437. E-mail: CompuServe: 74242,2240. Contact: David Hendin. Estab. 1993. Represents 25 clients. 75% of clients are new/previously unpublished writers. Specializes in trade fiction, nonfiction and newspaper syndication of columns or comic strips. Currently handles: 60% nonfiction books; 10% scholarly books; 20% novels; 10% syndicated material.

Handles: Nonfiction books, scholarly books, novels, syndicated material. Considers these nonfiction areas: agriculture/horticulture; animals; anthropology/archaeology; art/architecture/design; biography/autobiography; business; child guidance/parenting; cooking/food/nutrition; current affairs; education; ethnic/cultural interests; gay/lesbian issues; government/politics/law; health/medicine; history; how-to; humor; language/literature/criticism; military/war; money/finance/economics; music/dance/theater/film; nature/environment; New Age/metaphysics; photography; popular culture; psychology; religious/inspirational; science/technology; self-help/personal improvement; sociology; sports; true crime/investigative; women's issues/women's studies. Considers these fiction areas: action/adventure; cartoon/comic; contemporary issues; detective/police/crime; ethnic; feminist; gay; glitz; historical; horror; humor/satire; lesbian; literary; mainstream; psychic/supernatural; thriller/espionage; westerns/frontier. Reports in 2 weeks on queries; 1 month on mss.

Recent Sales: *Miss Manners* (multiple books contract), by Judith Martin (Crown); *You're Too Good For This*, by Abraham Twerski, M.D. (St. Martin's); *Power Language*, by Jeffrey McQuain (Houghton-Mifflin).

Terms: Agent receives 15% commission on domestic sales; 20% on foreign sales. Offers written contract, binding for 1 year. Charges for out of pocket expenses for postage, photocopying manuscript, and overseas phone calls specifically related to a book.

Tips: Obtains new clients through referrals from others (clients, writers, publishers). "Have your project in mind and on paper before you submit. Too many writers/cartoonists say 'I'm good . . . get me a project.' Publishers want writers with their own great ideas and their own unique voice."

THE JEFF HERMAN AGENCY INC. (II), 500 Greenwich St., #501C, New York NY 10013. (212)941-0540. Contact: Jeffrey H. Herman. Estab. 1985. Member of AAR. Represents 100 clients. 10% of clients are new/previously unpublished writers. Specializes in adult nonfiction. Currently handles: 85% nonfiction books; 5% scholarly books; 5% textbooks; 5% novels. Member agent: Deborah Adams (vice president, nonfiction book doctor).

• See Jeff Herman's article, *The Literary Agent: A User's Guide*, in the 1992 edition of the *Guide*.

Handles: Business, computers; health; history; how-to; politics; popular psychology; popular reference; recovery; self-help; spirituality. Query. Reports in 2 weeks on queries; 1 month on mss.

Recent Sales: *How to Drive Your Woman Wild In Bed* (Warner); *The Coopers & Lybrand Investment Guide* (Penguin).

Terms: Agent receives 15% commission on domestic sales. Offers written contract.

SUSAN HERNER RIGHTS AGENCY (II), P.O. Box 303, Scarsdale NY 10583. (914)725-8967. Fax: (914)725-8969. Contact: Susan Herner or Sue Yuen. Estab. 1987. Represents 75 clients. 30% of clients are new/unpublished writers. Eager to work with new/unpublished writers. Currently handles: 60% nonfiction books; 40% novels. Member agent: Sue Yuen (commercial genre fiction).

Handles: Adult nonfiction books, novels. Consider these nonfiction areas: anthropology/archaeology; biography/autobiography; business; child guidance/parenting; cooking/food/nutrition; current affairs; ethnic/cultural interests; gay/lesbian issues; government/politics/law; health/medicine; history; how-to; language/literature/criticism; nature/environment; New Age/metaphysics;

popular culture; psychology; religious/inspirational; science/technology; self-help/personal improvement; sociology; true crime/investigative; women's issues/women's studies. "I'm particularly interested in women's issues, popular science, and feminist spirituality." Considers these fiction areas: action/adventure; contemporary issues; detective/police/crime; ethnic; family/saga; fantasy; feminist; glitz; historical; horror; literary; mainstream; mystery; romance (contemporary, gothic, historical, regency); science fiction; thriller; "I'm particularly looking for strong women's fiction." Query with outline and sample chapters. Reports in 1 month on queries.
Recent Sales: *Everything You Need to Know About Latino History*, by Himilce Novas (Dutton); *Something's Cooking*, by Joanna Pence (Harper); *Until Spring*, by Libby Sydes (Dell).
Terms: Agent receives 15% commission on domestic sales; 20% on dramatic sales; 20% on foreign sales. Charges for extraordinary postage, handling and photocopying. "Agency has two divisions: one represents writers on a commission-only basis; the other represents the rights for small publishers and packagers who do not have inhouse subsidiary rights representation. Percentage of income derived from each division is currently 70-30."
Writer's Conferences: Vermont League of Writers (Burlington, Vt); Gulf States Authors League (Mobile, AL).

FREDERICK HILL ASSOCIATES, 8446½ Melrose Place, Los Angeles CA 90069-5308. (213)852-0830. Fax: (213)852-0426. Contact: Bonnie Nadell. Estab. 1979. Represents 100 clients. 50% of clients are new/unpublished writers. Specializes in general nonfiction, fiction.
Handles: Nonfiction books, novels. Considers these nonfiction areas: biography/autobiography; current affairs; government/politics/law; language/literature/criticism; women's issues/women's studies. Considers literary and mainstream fiction.
Recent Sales: *Making Monsters*, by Richard Ofshe and Ethan Walters (Scribner); *Grand Avenue*, by Greg Sams (Hyperion).
Terms: Agent receives 15% commission on domestic sales; 15% on dramatic sales; 20% on foreign sales. Charges for overseas airmail (books, proofs only).

JOHN L. HOCHMANN BOOKS (III, IV), 320 E. 58th St., New York NY 10022-2220. (212)319-0505. President: John L. Hochmann. Estab. 1976. Represents 23 clients. Member of AAR, PEN. Specializes in nonfiction books. Writers must have demonstrable eminence in field or previous publications. Prefers to work with published/established authors. Currently handles: 80% nonfiction; 20% textbooks. Member agent: Theodora Eagle (popular medical and nutrition books).
Handles: Nonfiction trade books, textbooks. Considers these nonfiction areas: anthropology/archaeology; art/architecture/design; biography/autobiography; cooking/food/nutrition; current affairs; gay/lesbian issues; government/politics/law; health/medicine; history; military/war; music/dance/theater/film; sociology. Query with outline, titles of previous books and SASE first. Reports in 1 week on queries; 1 month on mss (solicited).
Recent Sales: *Granite and Rainbow: A Life of Virginia Woolf*, by Mitchell A. Leaska (Farrar, Straus); *Philip Johnson: A Man of Affairs*, by Lee Hall (Little, Brown); *What Makes a Picasso a Picasso*, by Richard Mühlberger (Metropolitan Museum of Art).
Terms: Agent receives 15% commission on domestic sales; 25% on foreign sales.
Tips: Obtains new clients through recommendations from authors and editors. "Detailed outlines are read carefully; letters and proposals written like flap copy get chucked. We make multiple submissions to editors, but we do not accept multiple submissions from authors. Why? Editors are on salary, but we work for commission, and do not have time to read manuscripts on spec."

BERENICE HOFFMAN LITERARY AGENCY (III), 215 W. 75th St., New York NY 10023. (212)580-0951. Fax: (212)721-8916. Contact: Berenice Hoffman. Estab. 1978. Member of AAR. Represents 55 clients.
Handles: Nonfiction, novels. Considers all nonfiction areas and most fiction areas. No romance. Query with SASE. Reports in 3-4 weeks on queries.
Terms: Agent receives 15% on domestic sales. Sometimes offers written contract. Charges of out of the ordinary postage, photocopying.
Tips: Usually obtains new clients through referrals from people she knows.

‡**BARBARA HOGENSON AGENCY (III)**, 2472 Broadway, Suite 255, New York NY 10025. (212)580-3293. Estab. 1994. Signatory of WGA. Represents 25 clients. 10% of clients are new/previously unpublished writers. Currently handles: 30% nonfiction books; 10% novels; 30% movie scripts; 30% stage plays.
• See the expanded listing for this agency in Script Agents.

HOLUB & ASSOCIATES (II), 24 Old Colony Rd., North Stonington CT 06359. (203)535-0689. Contact: William Holub. Estab. 1967. Specializes in Roman Catholic publications. Currently handles: 100% nonfiction books.
Handles: Nonfiction books. Considers these nonfiction areas: biography; religious/inspirational; self-help; spirituality; theology. Query with outline plus 2 sample chapters and SASE.
Terms: Agent receives 15% commission on domestic sales. Charges for postage and photocopying.
Tips: Obtains new clients through recommendations from others.

HULL HOUSE LITERARY AGENCY (II), 240 E. 82nd St., New York NY 10028-2714. (212)988-0725. Fax: (212)794-8758. President: David Stewart Hull. Associate: Lydia Mortimer. Estab. 1987. Represents 38 clients. 15% of clients are new/previously unpublished writers. Specializes in military and general history, true crime, mystery fiction, general commercial fiction. Currently handles: 60% nonfiction books; 40% novels. Member agents: David Stewart Hull (history, biography, military books, true crime, mystery fiction, commercial fiction by published authors); Lydia Mortimer (new fiction by unpublished writers, nonfiction of general nature including women's studies).
Handles: Nonfiction books, novels. Considers these nonfiction areas: anthropology/archaeology; art/architecture/design; biography/autobiography; business; current affairs; ethnic/cultural interests; government/politics/law; history; military/war; money/finance/economics; music/dance/theater/film; sociology; true crime/investigative. Considers these fiction areas: detective/police/crime; literary; mainstream; mystery/suspense. Query with SASE. Reports in 1 week on queries; 1 month on mss.
Recent Sales: *Biography of Ambrose Bierce*, by Peter Cozzens (W.W. Norton).
Terms: Agent receives 15% commission on domestic sales; 20% on foreign sales, "split with foreign agent." Written contract is optional, "at mutual agreement between author and agency." Charges for photocopying, express mail, extensive overseas telephone expenses.
Tips: Obtains new clients through "referrals from clients, listings in various standard publications such as *LMP, Guide to Literary Agents*, etc. If interested in agency representation, send a single-page letter outlining your project, always accompanied by an SASE. If nonfiction, sample chapter(s) are often valuable. A record of past publications is a big plus."

IMG-JULIAN BACH LITERARY AGENCY (II), 22 E. 71st St., New York NY 10021. (212)772-8900. Fax: (212)772-2617. Contact: Julian Bach. Estab. 1956. Member of AAR. Represents 300 clients. Currently handles: 60% nonfiction books; 40% novels. Member agents: Julian Bach, Trish Lande, Carolyn Krupp, Mark Reiter. Contacts: Geraldine Seidell, Ann Torrago.
Handles: Nonfiction books, novels. Considers these nonfiction areas: anthropology/archaeology; biography; business; cooking/food/nutrition; current affairs; government/politics; history; language/literature/criticism; military/war; music/dance/theater/film; nature/environment; psychology; self-help/personal improvement; sports; true crime/investigative; women's issues/women's studies. Considers these fiction areas: detective/police/crime; literary; mainstream. Query.
Terms: No information provided. Offers written contract.

INTERNATIONAL CREATIVE MANAGEMENT (III), 40 W. 57th St., New York NY 10019. (212)556-5600. Fax: (212)556-5665. West Coast office: 8942 Wilshire Blvd., Beverly Hills CA 90211. (310)550-4000. Member of AAR, signatory of WGA. Member agents: Esther Newberg and Amanda Urban, department heads; Lisa Bankoff; Kristine Dahl; Mitch Douglas; Suzanne Gluck; Sloan Harris; Gordon Kato; Heather Schroder.
Terms: Agent receives 10% commission on domestic sales; 15% on UK sales; 20% on translations.

INTERNATIONAL PUBLISHER ASSOCIATES INC. (II), 304 Guido Ave., Lady Lake FL 32159. Contact: Joseph De Rogatis. Estab. 1983. Represents 15 clients. Currently handles: 100% nonfiction books.
Handles: Nonfiction books. Considers all nonfiction areas. Considers "mostly" mainstream fiction. Query with SASE. Reports in 3 weeks on queries.
Recent Sales: *The Pocket Pediatrician*, by Dr. David Ziggelman (Doubleday).
Terms: Agent receives 15% commission on domestic sales; 20% on foreign sales. Offers written contract, binding for life of book. Charges for postage and photocopying.

If you're looking for a particular agent, check the Agents Index to find at which agency the agent works. Then check the listing for that agency in the appropriate section.

Tips: Obtains new clients through word of mouth and *Guide to Literary Agents*.

J DE S ASSOCIATES INC. (II), 9 Shagbark Rd., Wilson Point, South Norwalk CT 06854. (203)838-7571. Contact: Jacques de Spoelberch. Estab. 1975. Represents 50 clients. Currently handles: 50% nonfiction books; 50% novels.
Handles: Nonfiction books, novels. Considers these nonfiction areas: biography/autobiography; business; current affairs; ethnic/cultural interests; government/politics/law; health/medicine; history; military/war; New Age; self-help/personal improvement; sociology; sports; translations. Considers these fiction areas: detective/police/crime; historical; juvenile; literary; mainstream; mystery/suspense; New Age; westerns/frontier; young adult. Query with SASE. Reports in 2 months on queries.
Terms: Agent receives 15% commission on domestic sales; 20% on foreign sales. Charges for foreign postage and photocopying.
Tips: Obtains new clients through recommendations from others, authors and other clients.

JAMES PETER ASSOCIATES, INC. (II), P.O. Box 772, Tenafly NJ 07670-0772. (201)568-0760. Fax: (201)568-2959. ATT Easylink: BHOLTJE. Contact: Bert Holtje. Estab. 1971. Member of AAR. Represents 84 clients. 15% of clients are new/previously unpublished writers. Specializes in nonfiction, all categories. "We are especially interested in trade and general reference projects." Currently handles: 100% nonfiction books.
Handles: Nonfiction books. Considers these nonfiction areas: anthropology/archaeology; art/architecture/design; biography/autobiography; business; child guidance/parenting; current affairs; ethnic/cultural interests; gay/lesbian issues; government/politics/law; health/medicine; history; language/literature/criticism; military/war; money/finance/economics; music/dance/theater/film; popular culture; psychology; self-help/personal improvement; women's issues/women's studies. Send outline/proposal and SASE. Reports in 3-4 weeks on queries.
Recent Sales: *Out West: A Narrative History*, by Alan Axelrod, Charles Phillips (Bob Adams Inc.); *Men's Health Encyclopedia*, by Michael Oppenheim, M.D. (Prentice-Hall).
Terms: Agent receives 15% commission on domestic sales; 20% on foreign sales. Offers written contract "on a per book basis." Charges for foreign postage.
Tips: Obtains new clients through recommendations from other clients and editors, contact people who are doing interesting things, and over-the-transom queries. "Phone me! I'm happy to discuss book ideas any time."

JET LITERARY ASSOCIATES, INC. (III), 124 E. 84th St., New York NY 10028. (212)879-2578. President: James Trupin. Estab. 1976. Represents 85 clients. 5% of clients are new/unpublished writers. Writers must have published articles or books. Prefers to work with published/established authors. Specializes in nonfiction. Currently handles: 50% nonfiction books; 50% novels.
Handles: Nonfiction books, novels. No unsolicited mss. Reports in 2 weeks on queries; 1 month on mss.
Recent Sales: *Deeper Thoughts*, by Jack Handey (Hyperion); *How Does Aspirin Find a Headache?*, by David Feldman (The Imponderable Series).
Terms: Agent receives 15% commission on domestic sales; 15% on dramatic sales; 25% on foreign sales. Charges for international phone and postage expenses.

LAWRENCE JORDAN LITERARY AGENCY (II), A Division of Morning Star Rising, Inc., 250 W. 57th St., Suite 1527, New York NY 10107. (212)662-7871. Fax:(212)662-8138. President: Lawrence Jordan. Estab. 1978. Represents 50 clients. 25% of clients are new/unpublished writers. Works with a small number of new/unpublished authors. Specializes in general adult fiction and nonfiction. Currently handles: 60% nonfiction; 25% novels; 3% textbooks; 2% juvenile books; 3% movie scripts; 7% stage plays.
Handles: Nonfiction books, novels, textbooks, juvenile books, movie scripts, stage plays. Handles these nonfiction areas: autobiography; business; computer manuals; health; religion; science; self-help; sports. Query with outline. Reports in 3 weeks on queries; 6 weeks on mss.
Recent Sales: *A Way Out of No Way; A Spiritual Memoir*, by Andrew Young (Thomas Nelson); *Southern Journey: A Personal Voyage Through the New South*, by Tom Dent (Harcourt Brace); *Club Grandma: Handbook for Happiness*, by Leslie Lehr Spirson and Claire Lehr (Longmeadow Press).
Terms: Agent receives 15% commission on domestic sales; 20% on dramatic sales; 20% on foreign sales. Charges long-distance calls, photocopying, foreign submission costs, postage, cables and messengers. Makes 99% of income from commissions.

THE KARPFINGER AGENCY (II), 500 5th Ave., Suite 2800, New York NY 10110. Prefers not to share information.

THE KELLOCK COMPANY INC. (III) 222 Park Ave. S., New York NY 10003-1504. (212)529-7122. Contact: Alan C. Kellock. Estab. 1990. Represents 50 clients. 10% of clients are new/previously unpublished writers. Specializes in nonfiction only, especially general reference and illustrated books. Currently handles: 100% nonfiction books.
Handles: Nonfiction books. Considers these nonfiction areas: anthropology/archaeology; art/architecture/design; biography/autobiography; business; child guidance/parenting; cooking/food/nutrition; crafts/hobbies; current affairs; education; government/politics/law; health/medicine; history; how-to; interior design/decorating; juvenile nonfiction; military/war; money/finance/economics; music/dance/theater/film; nature/environment; photography; popular culture; religious/inspirational; psychology; self-help/personal improvement; sociology; sports; women's issues/women's studies. Query. Reports in 2 weeks on queries, 1 month on mss.
Recent Sales: *The Parents' Desk Reference*, by Brownstone & Franck (HarperCollins); *Free Money for Small Business*, fourth edition, by Blum (Wiley).
Terms: Agent receives 15% commission on domestic sales; 25% on foreign and multimedia sales. Offers written contract. Charges for postage, photocopying.
Tips: Obtains most new clients through referrals.

LOUISE B. KETZ AGENCY (II), 1485 First Ave., Suite 4B, New York NY 10021. (212)535-9259. Contact: Louise B. Ketz. Estab. 1983. Represents 25 clients. 15% of clients are new/previously unpublished writers. Specializes in science, business, sports, history and reference. Currently handles: 100% nonfiction books.
Handles: Nonfiction books. Considers these nonfiction areas: anthropology/archaeology; biography/autobiography; business; current affairs; history; military/war; money/finance/economics; science/technology; sports; true crime/investigative. Send outline plus 2 sample chapters. Reports in 4-6 weeks on queries and mss.
Recent Sales: *1001 Things Everyone Should Know About Science*, by James Trefil (Doubleday).
Terms: Agent receives 10-15% commission on domestic sales; 10% on foreign sales. Offers written contract.
Tips: Obtains new clients through recommendations, idea development.

‡VIRGINIA KIDD, LITERARY AGENT (V), 538 E. Harford St., P.O. Box 278, Milford PA 18337. (717)296-6205. Fax: (717)296-7266. E-mail: 73107,3311. Contact: Virginia Kidd. Estab. 1965. Member of Author Guild, SFWA, NWU, SFRA. Represents 80 clients. Very small percentage of clients are new previously unpublished writers. Specializes in speculative fiction. Currently handles: 15% juvenile books; 75% novels; 5% short story collections; 4% novellas; 1% poetry. Member agents: Linn Prentis (mainstream novels).
Handles: Fiction. Considers science fiction, but only from previously published writers. Query. Reports immediately on queries; a month or more on mss.
Terms: Agent receives 10% commission on domestic sales; 20% on foreign sales; 20% on dramatic sales. Offers written contract, binding until canceled by either party.
Tips: Seldom takes on new clients. "Never forget the SASE."

KIDDE, HOYT & PICARD (III), 335 E. 51st St., New York NY 10022. (212)755-9461. Contact: Katharine Kidde, Wendy Wylegala. Estab. 1980. Member of AAR. Represents 50 clients. Specializes in mainstream fiction and nonfiction. Currently handles: 15% nonfiction books; 5% juvenile books; 80% novels. Member agents: Kay Kidde (mainstream fiction, romances, mysteries, suspense, literary fiction); W. Wylegula (mainstream fiction, trade nonfiction).
Handles: Nonfiction books, novels. Considers these nonfiction areas: African studies; the arts; biography; current events; dance; ethnic/cultural interests; gay/lesbian issues; government/politics/law; history; language/literature/criticism; popular culture; psychology; self-help/personal improvement; sociology; women's issues. Considers these fiction areas: action/adventure; contemporary issues; detective/police/crime; ethnic; feminist; gay; glitz; historical; humor; lesbian; literary; mainstream; mystery/suspense; regional; romance (contemporary, historical, regency); thriller/espionage. Query. Reports in a few weeks on queries; 3-4 weeks on mss.
Recent Sales: *Skyscape*, by Michael Cadnum (Carroll & Graf); *Julia*, by Barrie King (Ballantine); *Pacific Passions*, by Frank Sherry (Morrow).
Terms: Agent receives 10% commission on domestic sales; 10% on foreign sales. Charges for photocopying.
Tips: Obtains new clients through query letters, recommendations from others, "former authors from when I was an editor at NAL, Harcourt, etc.; listings in *LMP*, writers' guides."

KIRCHOFF/WOHLBERG, INC., AUTHORS' REPRESENTATION DIVISION (II), 866 United Nations Plaza, #525, New York NY 10017. (212)644-2020. Fax: (212)223-4387. Director of Operations: John R. Whitman. Estab. 1930s. Member of AAR, AAP, Society of Illustrators, SPAR, Bookbuilders of Boston, New York Bookbinders' Guild, AIGA. Represents 50 authors. 10% of clients are new/previously unpublished writers. Specializes in juvenile through young adult trade books and textbooks. Currently handles: 5% nonfiction books; 80% juvenile books; 5% novels; 5% novellas; 5% young adult. Member agent: Elizabeth Pulitzer-Voges (juvenile and young adult authors); Julie Alperen (juvenile and young adult authors).

Handles: "We are interested in any original projects of quality that are appropriate to the juvenile and young adult trade book markets. Send a query that includes an outline and a sample; SASE required." Reports in 1 month on queries; 6 weeks on mss. Please send queries to the attention of: Liza Pulitzer-Voges

Recent Sales: *Alvin Ailey*, by Andrea Davis Pinkney (Hyperion); *Nuts to You!*, by Lois Ehlert (Harcourt Brace); *Black Dog, Red House*, by Lizi Boyd (Little, Brown); *Bennie's Pennies*, by Pat Brisson (Doubleday).

Terms: Agent receives standard commission "depending upon whether it is an author only, illustrator only, or an author/illustrator book." Offers written contract, binding for not less than 1 year.

Tips: "Usually obtains new clients through recommendations from authors, illustrators and editors. Kirchoff/Wohlberg has been in business for over 50 years."

HARVEY KLINGER, INC. (III), 301 W. 53rd St., New York NY 10019. (212)581-7068. Fax: (212)315-3823. Contact: Harvey Klinger. Estab. 1977. Member of AAR. Represents 100 clients. 25% of clients are new/previously unpublished writers. Specializes in "big, mainstream contemporary fiction and nonfiction." Currently handles: 50% nonfiction books; 50% novels. Member agents: Carol McCleary (mysteries, science fiction, fantasy, category fiction), Laurie Liss (politics, women's issues).

Handles: Nonfiction books, novels. Considers these nonfiction areas: biography/autobiography; cooking/food/nutrition; health/medicine; psychology; science/technology; self-help/personal improvement; sports; true crime/investigative; women's issues/women's studies. Considers these fiction areas: action/adventure; detective/police/crime; family saga; glitz; horror (dark); literary; mainstream; mystery/suspense; romance (contemporary); thriller/espionage. Query. Reports in 2 weeks on queries; 6-8 weeks on mss.

Recent Sales: *Untitled*, by Stephen Collins (Bantam); *Blue Crystal*, by Philip Lee Williams (Grove); *Run with the Hunted*, by Charles Bukowski (HarperCollins).

Terms: Agent receives 15% commission on domestic sales; 25% on foreign sales. Offers written contract. Charges for photocopying manuscripts, overseas postage for mss.

Tips: Obtains new clients through recommendations from others.

BARBARA S. KOUTS, LITERARY AGENT (II), P.O. Box 558, Bellport NY 11713. (516)286-1278. Contact: Barbara Kouts. Estab. 1980. Member of AAR. Represent 50 clients. 10% of clients are new/previously unpublished writers. Specializes in adult fiction and nonfiction and children's books. Currently handles: 20% nonfiction books; 40% juvenile books; 40% novels.

Handles: Nonfiction books, juvenile books, novels. Considers these nonfiction areas: biography/autobiography; business; child guidance/parenting; current affairs; ethnic/cultural interests; health/medicine; history; juvenile nonfiction; music/dance/theater/film; nature/environment; psychology; self-help/personal improvement; women's issues/women's studies. Considers these fiction areas: contemporary issues; family saga; feminist; historical; juvenile; literary; mainstream; mystery/suspense; picture book; romance (gothic, historical); young adult. Query. Reports in 2-3 days on queries; 4-6 weeks on mss.

Recent Sales: *Ordinary Time*, by Nancy Mairs (Beacon); *Sukey and the Mermaid*, by Robert San Souci (4 Winds Press).

Terms: Agent receives 10% commission on domestic sales; 20% on foreign sales. Charges for photocopying.

Tips: Obtains new clients through recommendations from others, solicitation, at conferences, etc. "Write, do not call. Be professional in your writing."

LUCY KROLL AGENCY (II,III), 390 W. End Ave., New York NY 10024. (212)877-0627. Fax: (212)769-2832. Member of AAR, signatory of WGA. Represents 60 clients. 5% of clients are new/unpublished writers. Specializes in nonfiction, screenplays, plays. Currently handles: 45% nonfiction books; 15% novels; 15% movie scripts; 25% stage plays.

Handles: Nonfiction, movie scripts, TV scripts, stage plays. Query with outline and SASE. No unsolicited mss. Reports in 1 month.

Recent Sales: *Great American Anecdotes*, by John and Claire Whitcomb (Morrow); *Mittel Europa*, by Cliff Slesin, et al. (Clarkson N. Potter).

Terms: Agent receives 10% commission on domestic sales; 10% on dramatic sales; 20% on foreign sales.

EDITE KROLL LITERARY AGENCY (II), 12 Grayhurst Park, Portland ME 04102. (207)773-4922. Fax: (207)773-3936. Contact: Edite Kroll. Estab. 1981. Represents 40 clients. Currently handles: 60% adult books; 40% juvenile books.
Handles: Nonfiction, juvenile books, humor, novels. Considers these nonfiction areas: current affairs; social and political issues (especially feminist). Considers these fiction areas: contemporary issues; feminist; literary; mainstream; mystery/suspense; juvenile; picture books by author/artists. Query in writing only with SASE. For nonfiction, send outline/proposal. For fiction, send outline plus 1 sample chapter or dummy. Reports in 2 weeks on queries; 6 weeks on mss.

PETER LAMPACK AGENCY, INC. (II), 551 Fifth Ave., Suite 1613, New York NY 10176-0187. (212)687-9106. Fax: (212)687-9109. Contact: Deborah T. Brown. Estab. 1977. Represents 50 clients. 10% of clients are new/previously unpublished writers. Specializes in commercial fiction, male-oriented action/adventure, contemporary relationships, distinguished literary fiction, nonfiction by a recognized expert in a given field. Currently handles: 15% nonfiction books; 85% novels. Member agents: Peter Lampack (psychological suspense, action/adventure, literary fiction, nonfiction, contemporary relationships); Sandra Blanton (contemporary relationships, psychological thrillers, mysteries, literary fiction, nonfiction including literary and theatrical biography); Deborah Brown (literary fiction, historical fiction, nonfiction, especially interested in history and art, and women's issues).
Handles: Nonfiction books, novels. Considers these nonfiction areas: anthropology/archaeology; art/architecture/design; biography/autobiography; business; current affairs; government/politics/law; health/medicine; history; humor; money/finance/economics; music/dance/theater/film; popular culture; high profile true crime/investigative; women's issues. Considers these fiction areas: action/adventure; contemporary relationships; detective/police/crime; family saga; glitz; historical; horror; humor/satire; literary; mainstream; mystery/suspense; thriller/espionage. Query. No unsolicited mss. Reports in 3 weeks on queries; 2 months on mss.
Recent Sales: *Inca Gold,* by Clive Cussler (Simon & Schuster); *One Last Kiss,* by Judith Kelman (Bantam Books); *True Colors,* by Doris Mortman (Crown/Ballantine); *Argue to Win,* by Gerry Spence, Esq. (St. Martin's Press); *The Master of Petersburg,* by J.M. Coeztee (Viking/Penguin); *The Living Trust Workbook,* by Robert A. Esperti, Esq. and Renno L. Peterson, Esq. (Viking/Penguin); *Second Vision,* by Ralph Vallone, Jr. (NAL/Dutton).
Terms: Agent receives 15% commission on domestic sales; 20% on foreign sales. Offers written contract, binding for 1-3 years. "Writer is required to furnish copies of his/her work for submission purposes."
Writer's Conferences: ABA in Chicago.
Tips: Obtains new clients from referrals made by clients. "Submit only your best work for consideration. Have a very specific agenda of goals you wish your prospective agent to accomplish for you. Provide the agent with a comprehensive statement of your credentials—educational and professional."

THE ROBERT LANTZ-JOY HARRIS LITERARY AGENCY INC. (II), 156 Fifth Ave., Suite 617, New York NY 10010. (212)924-6269. Fax: (212)924-6609. Contact: Joy Harris. Member of AAR. Represents 150 clients. Currently handles: 50% nonfiction books; 50% novels.
Handles: Considers "adult-type books, not juvenile." Considers all fiction areas except fantasy; juvenile; science fiction; westerns/frontier. Query with outline/proposal and SASE. Reports in 1-2 months on queries.
Terms: Agent receives 15% commission on domestic sales; 20% on foreign sales. Offers written contract. Charges for extra expenses.
Tips: Obtains new clients through recommendations from clients and editors. "No unsolicited manuscripts, just query letters."

MICHAEL LARSEN/ELIZABETH POMADA LITERARY AGENTS (II), 1029 Jones St., San Francisco CA 94109-5023. (415)673-0939. Contact: Mike Larsen or Elizabeth Pomada. Estab. 1972. Member of AAR, Authors Guild, NWA, PEN, WNBA, California Writers Club. Represents 100 clients. 50-55% of clients are new/unpublished writers. Eager to work with new/unpublished writers. "We have very diverse tastes and do not specialize. We look for fresh voices with new ideas. We handle literary, commercial and genre fiction, and the full range of nonfiction books." Currently handles: 60% nonfiction books; 40% novels. Member agents: Michael Larsen (nonfiction), Elizabeth Pomada (fiction, women's issues).
• See Michael Larsen's article, *When the Honeymoon's Over,* in the 1994 edition.
Handles: Adult nonfiction books, novels. Considers these nonfiction areas: anthropology/archaeology; art/architecture/design; biography/autobiography; business; child guidance/parenting; cooking/food/nutrition; crafts/hobbies; current affairs; ethnic/cultural interests; gay/lesbian issues; government/politics/law; health/medicine; history; how-to; humor; interior design/decorating; language/literature/criticism; money/finance/economics; music/dance/theater/film; na-

ture/environment; New Age/metaphysics; photography; popular culture; psychology; religious/inspirational; science/technology; self-help/personal improvement; sociology; sports; true crime/investigative; women's issues/women's studies. Considers these fiction areas: action/adventure; contemporary issues; detective/police/crime; ethnic; experimental; family saga; fantasy; feminist; gay; glitz; historical; horror; humor/satire; lesbian; literary; mainstream; mystery/suspense; psychic/supernatural; religious/inspirational; romance (contemporary, gothic, historical, regency). Query with synopsis and first 30 pages of completed novel. Reports in 2 months on queries. For nonfiction, call first. "Always include SASE. Send SASE for brochure."

Recent Sales: *A Crack In Forever*, by Jeannie Brewer (Simon & Schuster); *The Water Book*, by Scott Lewis (Sierra Club).

Terms: Agent receives 15% commission on domestic sales; 15% on dramatic sales; 20% on foreign sales. May charge writer for printing, postage for multiple submissions, foreign mail, foreign phone calls, galleys, books, and legal fees.

Writer's Conferences: ABA (Chicago); Santa Barbara Writers Conference (Santa Barbara); Maui Writers Conference (Maui, Hawaii); Writers Connection (Cupertino, CA); WORLDCON (Glasgow, Scotland).

‡THE MAUREEN LASHER AGENCY (II, III), P.O. Box 888, Pacific Palisades CA 90272. (310)459-8415. Contact: Ann Cashman. Estab. 1980.

Handles: Nonfiction books, novels. Considers these nonfiction areas: animals; anthropology/archaeology; art/architecture/design; biography/autobiography; business; child guidance/parenting; cooking/food/nutrition; current affairs; ethnic/cultural interests; govenment/politics/law; health/medicine; history; how-to; nature/environment; popular culture; psychology; science/technology; self-help/personal improvement; sociology; sports; true crime/investigative; women's issues/women's studies. Considers these fiction areas: action/adventure; contemporary issues; detective/police/crime; family saga; feminist; historical; literary; mainstream; sports; thriller/espionage. Send outline/proposal and 1 sample chapter.

Terms: No information provided. Does not charge a reading fee or offer criticism service.

LAZEAR AGENCY INCORPORATED (II), 430 First Ave., Suite 416, Minneapolis MN 55401. (612)332-8640. Fax: (612)332-4648. Contact: Editorial Board. Estab. 1984. Represents 250 clients. Currently handles: 40% nonfiction books; 20% juvenile books; 29% novels; 1% short story collections; 5% movie scripts; 2.5% TV scripts; 2.5% syndicated material. Member agents: Jonathon Lazear (president); Eric Vrooman (agent); Dennis Cass (director of subsidiary rights).

Handles: Nonfiction books, juvenile books, novels, movie scripts, TV scripts, syndicated material. Considers all nonfiction areas. Considers all fiction areas. Query with outline/proposal. Reports in 3 weeks on queries; 6-8 weeks on ms. Highly selective. No phone calls.

Terms: Agent receives 15% commission on domestic sales; 20% on foreign sales. Offers written contract, binding "for term of copyright." Charges for "photocopying, international express mail."

Tips: Obtains new clients through recommendations from others, "through the bestseller lists, word-of-mouth. The writer should first view himself as a salesperson in order to obtain an agent. Sell yourself, your idea, your concept. Do your homework. Notice what is in the marketplace. Be sophisticated about the arena in which you are writing."

LESCHER & LESCHER LTD. (II), 67 Irving Place, New York NY 10003. (212)529-1790. Fax: (212)529-2716. Contact: Robert or Susan Lescher. Estab. 1966. Member of AAR. Represents 150 clients. Currently handles: 75% nonfiction books; 13% juvenile books; 12% novels.

Handles: Nonfiction books, novels. Query with SASE.

Terms: Agent receives 15% commission on domestic sales; 20-25% on foreign sales. Charges for photocopying mss and copyrighting fees.

Tips: Usually obtains new clients through recommendations from others.

LEVANT & WALES, LITERARY AGENCY, INC. (II, IV), 108 Hayes St., Seattle WA 98109-2808. (206)284-7114. Fax: (206)284-0190. Contact: Elizabeth Wales and Valerie Griffith. Estab. 1988. Member of AAR, Pacific Northwest Writers' Conference, Book Publishers' Northwest. Represents 50 clients. We are interested in published and not-yet-published writers. Prefers writers from the Pacific Northwest, West Coast, Alaska and Pacific Rim countries. Specializes in nonfiction and mainstream fiction. Currently handles: 75% nonfiction books; 25% novels.

Handles: Nonfiction books, novels. Considers these nonfiction areas: animals; anthropology/archaeology; art/architecture/design; biography/autobiography; business; child guidance/parenting; current affairs; education; ethnic/cultural interests; gardening; gay/lesbian issues; health; language/literature/criticism; lifestyle; memoir; music/dance/theater/film; nature; New Age/metaphysics; popular culture; psychology; science; self-help/personal improvement; sports; women's issues/women's studies—open to creative or serious treatments of almost any nonfiction subject. Considers these fiction areas: cartoon/comic/women's; ethnic; experimental; feminist; gay; lesbian; literary; mainstream (no genre fiction). Query first. Reports in 3 weeks on queries; 6 weeks on mss.

Recent Sales: *Girlfriend To Girlfriend: Affirmations From The Sister Circle*, by Julia Boyd (Dutton, 1995); *The Family Guide To Media Literacy*, by Gloria DeGaetano and Kathleen Bander (Houghton Mifflin, 1995).

Terms: Agent receives 15% commission on domestic sales. "We make all our income from commissions. We offer editorial help for some of our clients and help some clients with the development of a proposal, but we do not charge for these services. We do charge, after a sale, for express mail, manuscript photocopying costs, foreign postage and outside USA telephone costs."

Writer's Conferences: Pacific NW Writers Conference (Vancouver, British Columbia, Canada); Yachats, Oregon Literary Festival.

ELLEN LEVINE LITERARY AGENCY, INC. (II, III), 15 E. 26th St., Suite 1801, New York NY 10010. (212)889-0620. Fax: (212)725-4501. Contact: Ellen Levine, Diana Finch, Elizabeth Kaplan. Estab. 1980. Member of AAR. Represents over 100 clients. 20% of clients are new/previously unpublished writers. "My three younger colleagues at the agency (Anne Dubuisson, Diana Finch and Elizabeth Kaplan) are seeking both new and established writers. I prefer to work with established writers, mostly through referrals." Currently handles: 45% nonfiction books; 8% juvenile books; 45% novels; 2% short story collections.
• Ellen Levine is the current Secretary of AAR.
Handles: Nonfiction books, juvenile books, novels, short story collections. Considers these nonfiction areas: anthropology; biography; current affairs; health; popular culture; psychology; science; women's issues/women's studies; books by journalists. Considers these fiction areas: literary; mystery; women's thrillers. Query. Reports in 2-3 weeks on queries, if SASE provided; 4-6 weeks on mss, if submission requested.
Recent Sales: *Past the Bleachers*, by Christopher Bohjalian (Carroll & Graf; dramatic rights to Hallmark).
Terms: Agent receives 15% commission on domestic sales; 20% on foreign sales. Charges for overseas postage, photocopying, messenger fees, overseas telephone and fax, books ordered for use in rights submissions.
Tips: Obtains new clients through recommendations from others.

ROBERT LEWIS (V), 65 E. 96th St., New York NY 10128. Agency not currently seeking new clients. Published writers may query.

‡LICHTMAN, TRISTER, SINGER, & ROSS (III), 1666 Connecticut Ave. NW, #501, Washington DC 20009. (202)328-1666. Fax: (202)328-9162. Contact: Gail Ross, Leslie Breed, Howard Yoon. Estab. 1988. Member of AAR. Represents 200 clients. 20% of clients are new/previously unpublished writers. Specializes in adult trade nonfiction. Currently handles: 90% nonfiction books; 10% novels. Member agents: Gail Ross (nonfiction); Leslie Breed; Howard Yoon.
Handles: Nonfiction books, novels. Considers these nonfiction areas: anthropology/archaeology; biography/autobiography; business; cooking/food/nutrition; education; ethnic/cultural interests; gay/lesbian issues; government/politics/law; humor; money/finance/economics; nature/environment; psychology; religious/inspirational; science/technology; self-help/personal improvement; sociology; sports; true crime/investigative. Considers these fiction areas: ethnic; feminist; gay; literary. Query. Reports in 1 month.
Terms: Agent receives 15% commission on domestic sales; 25% on foreign sales. Charges for office expenses (i.e., postage, copying).
Tips: Obtains new clients through referrals.

RAY LINCOLN LITERARY AGENCY (II), Elkins Park House, Suite 107-B, 7900 Old York Rd., Elkins Park PA 19117. (215)635-0827. Contact: Mrs. Ray Lincoln. Estab. 1974. Represents 34 clients. 35% of clients are new/previously unpublished writers. Specializes in biography, nature, the sciences, fiction in both adult and children's categories. Currently handles: 30% nonfiction books; 20% juvenile books; 50% novels. Member agent: Jerome A. Lincoln.
Handles: Nonfiction books, scholarly books, juvenile books, novels. Considers these nonfiction areas: horticulture; animals; anthropology/archaeology; art/architecture/design; biography/autobiography; business; child guidance/parenting; cooking/food/nutrition; crafts/hobbies; current affairs; ethnic/cultural interests; gay/lesbian issues; government/politics/law; health/medicine; history; interior design/decorating; juvenile nonfiction; language/literature/criticism; money/finance/economics; music/dance/theater/film; nature/environment; psychology; science/technology; self-help/personal improvement; sociology; sports; women's issues/women's studies. Considers these fiction areas: action/adventure; contemporary issues; detective/police/crime; ethnic;

family saga; fantasy; feminist; gay; historical; humor/satire; juvenile; lesbian; literary; mainstream; mystery/suspense; psychic/supernatural; regional; romance (contemporary, gothic, historical); science fiction; sports; thriller/espionage; young adult. Query "first, then send outline plus 2 sample chapters with SASE. I send for balance of manuscript if it is a likely project." Reports in 2 weeks on queries; 1 month on mss.

Recent Sales: *Sophie's Masterpiece*, by Eileen Spinelli (Simon & Schuster); *Hostile Witness*, by William Lashner (HarperCollins); *Soulfire*, by Lorri Hewett (Dutton).

Terms: Agent receives 15% commission on domestic sales; 20% on foreign sales. Offers written contract, binding "but with notice, may be cancelled. Charges only for overseas telephone calls. I request authors to do manuscript photocopying themselves. Postage, or shipping charge, on manuscripts accepted for representation by agency."

Tips: Obtains new clients usually from recommendations. "I always look for polished writing style, fresh points of view and professional attitudes."

‡LINDSTROM LITERARY GROUP (I), 871 N. Greenbrier St., Arlington VA 22205. (703)522-4730. Fax: (703)527-7624. Contact: Kristin Lindstrom. Estab. 1994. Represents 22 clients. 75% of clients are new/previously unpublished writers. Currently handles: 50% nonfiction books; 30% novels; 10% movie scripts; 10% TV scripts.

Handles: Nonfiction books; novels. Considers these nonfiction areas: animals; biography/autobiography; business; computers/electronics; cooking/food/nutrition; current affairs; education; ethnic/cultural interests; government/politics/law; health/medicine; history; how-to; humor; money/finance/economics; nature/environment; popular culture; psychology; science/technology; self-help/personal improvement; sociology; true crime/investigative; women's issues/women's studies. Considers these fiction areas: action/adventure; contemporary issues; detective/police/crime; ethnic; family saga; fantasy; glitz; historical; horror; literary; mainstream; science fiction; thriller/espionage; westerns/frontier. Send entire ms if fiction with SASE. Send outline/proposal if nonfiction with SASE. Reports in 3-4 weeks on queries; 6 weeks on mss.

Also Handles: Movie scripts (feature film), TV scripts (TV mow, miniseries). Considers these script subject areas: action/adventure; comedy; detective/police/crime; ethnic; family saga; historical; horror; mainstream; mystery/suspense; romantic comedy and drama; thriller.

Terms: Agent receives 15% commission on domestic sales; 15% on foreign sales. Offers written contract. Charges for mailing expense, express mail, UPS, etc.

Tips: Obtains new clients through references, advertising. "Include biography of writer. Send enough material for an overall review of project scope."

WENDY LIPKIND AGENCY (II), 165 E. 66th St., New York NY 10021. (212)628-9653. Fax: (212)628-2693. Contact: Wendy Lipkind. Estab. 1977. Member of AAR. Represents 60 clients. Specializes in adult nonfiction. Currently handles: 80% nonfiction books; 20% novels.

Handles: Nonfiction, novels. Considers these nonfiction areas: biography; current affairs; health/medicine; history; science; social history. Considers mainstream and mystery/suspense fiction. No mass market originals. For nonfiction, query with outline/proposal. For fiction, query with SASE only. Reports in 1 month on queries.

Recent Sales: *Where's The Baby* and *Animal's Lullaby*, both by Tom Paxton (Morrow Junior Books).

Terms: Agent receives 15% commission on domestic sales; 20% on foreign sales. Sometimes offers written contract. Charges for foreign postage and messenger service.

Tips: Usually obtains new clients through recommendations from others. "Send intelligent query letter first. Let me know if you sent to other agents."

LITERARY AND CREATIVE ARTISTS AGENCY INC. (III), 3543 Albemarle St. NW, Washington DC 20008. (202)362-4688. Fax: (202)362-8875. Contact: Muriel Nellis, Jane Roberts, Deborah Estes, Karen Gerwin. Estab. 1982. Member of Authors Guild, associate member of American Bar Association. Represents over 75 clients. "While we prefer published writers, it is not required if the proposed work has great merit." Requires exclusive review of material; no simultaneous submissions. Currently handles: 70% nonfiction books; 15% novels; 10% audio/video; 5% film/TV.

Handles: Nonfiction, novels, audio, film/TV rights. Considers these nonfiction areas: business; cooking; health; how-to; human drama; lifestyle; memoir; philosophy; politics. Query with outline, bio and SASE. No unsolicited mss. Reports in 2-3 weeks on queries.

 The double dagger before a listing indicates the listing is new in this edition.

Recent Sales: *Ageless Body, Timeless Mind*, by Dr. D. Chopra (Harmony); *A Temple in the House*, by A. Lawlor (Tarcher/Putnam); *Lessons from the Art of Juggling*, by M. Gelb and T. Bozan (Harmony); *Putting America on the Couch*, by P. Peay (Riverhead); *Growing Younger*, by Dr. D. Chopra (Time-Life Video).
Terms: Agent receives 15% commission on domestic sales; 20% on dramatic sales; 25% on foreign sales. Charges for long-distance phone and fax, photocopying and shipping.

THE LITERARY GROUP (II), 270 Lafayette St., #1505, New York NY 10012. (212)274-1616. Fax: (212)274-9876. Contact: Frank Weimann. Estab. 1985. Represents 90 clients. 75% of clients are new/previously unpublished writers. Specializes in nonfiction (true crime; biography; sports; how-to). Currently handles: 80% nonfiction books; 20% novels. Member agents: Frank Weimann (nonfiction in all areas); Jessica Wainwright (women's issues, romance); Jimmy Vines (all areas of fiction).
• See Frank Weimann's article, *How to Find an Agent: One Agent's View*, in the 1992 edition of the *Guide*.
Handles: Nonfiction books, novels. Considers these nonfiction areas: animals; anthropology/archaeology; biography/autobiography; business; child guidance/parenting; crafts/hobbies; current affairs; education; ethnic/cultural interests; gay/lesbian issues; government/politics/law; health/medicine; history; how-to; humor; juvenile nonfiction; language/literature/criticism; military/war; money/finance/economics; music/dance/theater/film; nature/environment; New Age/metaphysics; popular culture; psychology; religious/inspirational; science/technology; self-help/personal improvement; sociology; sports; true crime/investigative; women's issues/women's studies. Considers these fiction areas: action/adventure; cartoon/comic; contemporary issues; detective/police/crime; ethnic; family saga; fantasy; feminist; gay; historical; horror; humor/satire; lesbian; mystery/suspense; psychic/supernatural; romance (contemporary, gothic, historical, regency); science fiction; sports; thriller/espionage; westerns/frontier; young adult. Query with outline plus 3 sample chapters. Reports in 1 week on queries; 1 month on mss.
Recent Sales: *The Emmitt Zone*, by Emmitt Smith (Crown); *I Get No Respect*, by Rodney Dangerfield (HarperCollins).
Terms: Agent receives 15% commission on domestic sales; 20% on foreign sales. Offers written contract, which can be cancelled after 30 days.
Writer's Conferences: Detroit Women's Writers (MI); Kent State University (OH); San Diego Writers Conference (CA).
Tips: Obtains new clients through referrals, writers conferences, query letters.

STERLING LORD LITERISTIC, INC. (III), One Madison Ave., New York NY 10010. (212)696-2800. Fax: (212)686-6976. Contact: Peter Matson. Estab. 1952. Member of AAR, signatory of WGA. Represents 500+ clients. Specializes in "nonfiction and fiction." Currently handles: 50% nonfiction books, 50% novels. Member agents: Peter Matson, Sterling Lord; Jody Hotchkiss (film scripts); Philippa Brophy; Stuart Krichevsky; Elizabeth Grossman, Chris Calhoun; Jennifer Hengen.
Handles: Nonfiction books, novels. Considers "mainstream nonfiction and fiction." Query. Reports in 1 month on mss.
Terms: Agent receives 15% commission on domestic sales; 20% on foreign sales. Offers written contract. Charges for photocopying.
Tips: Obtains new clients through recommendations from others.

NANCY LOVE LITERARY AGENCY (III), 250 E. 65th St., New York NY 10021. (212)980-3499. Fax: (212)308-6405. Contact: Nancy Love. Estab. 1984. Member of AAR. Represents 60 clients. Specializes in adult nonfiction. Currently handles: 90% nonfiction books; 10% novels.
Handles: Nonfiction books, novels. Considers these nonfiction areas: animals, biography/autobiography; child guidance/parenting; cooking/food/nutrition; current affairs; ethnic/cultural interests; gay/lesbian issues; government/politics/law; health/medicine; history; how-to; nature/environment; New Age/metaphysics; popular culture; psychology; science/technology; self-help/personal improvement; sociology; true crime/investigative; women's issues/women's studies. Considers these fiction areas: action/adventure; contemporary issues; detective/police/crime; erotica; ethnic; gay; glitz; literary; mainstream; mystery/suspense; thriller/espionage. "For nonfiction, send a proposal, chapter summary and sample chapter. For fiction, send the first 40-50 pages plus summary of the rest (will consider only *completed* novels)." Reports in 2 weeks on queries; 3 weeks on mss.
Recent Sales: *Children's Hospital of Philadelphia Handbook of Infectious Diseases* (Macmillan Reference); *Anasazi*, by Micah S. Hachler (Dell 2-book contract for mystery series).
Terms: Agent receives 15% commission on domestic sales; 20% on foreign sales. Offers written contract. Charges for photocopying, "if it runs over $20."

Tips: Obtains new clients through recommendations and solicitation. "Many also come through the National Writer's Union, where I have a number of clients and a very high rating. I prefer a call to a query letter. That cuts out a step and allows me to express my preference for an exclusive and to discuss the author's credentials. I can also tell a writer that I won't return material without a SASE."

LOWENSTEIN ASSOCIATES, INC. (II), 121 W. 27th St., Suite 601, New York NY 10001. (212)206-1630. President: Barbara Lowenstein. Estab. 1976. Member of AAR. Represents 120 clients. 15% of clients are new/unpublished writers. Specializes in nonfiction—especially science and medical-topic books for the general public—general fiction. Currently handles: 2% magazine articles; 55% nonfiction books; 43% novels. Member agents: Norman Kurz, Nancy Yost.
Handles: Nonfiction books, novels. Considers these nonfiction areas: medicine, science. Considers these fiction areas: romance (historical, contemporary), mainstream, and "bigger women's fiction." Query. Does not accept unsolicited mss.
Recent Sales: *The Best Kind of Loving: A Black Woman's Guide to Finding Intimacy*, by Dr. Gwendolyn Goldsby Grant (HarperCollins).
Terms: Agent receives 15% commission on domestic and dramatic sales; 20% on foreign sales. Charges for photocopying, foreign postage, messenger expenses.

LYCEUM CREATIVE PROPERTIES, INC. (I, II), P.O. Box 12370, San Antonio TX 78212. (210)732-0200. President: Guy Robin Custer. Estab. 1992. Signatory of WGA. Represents 25 clients. 50% of clients are new/previously unpublished writers. Currently handles: 20% nonfiction books; 5% scholarly books; 40% novels; 25% movie scripts; 5% stage plays; 5% TV scripts. Member agents: Guy Robin Custer (novels, nonfiction, some screenplays); Dave Roy (novels, screenplays, stage plays); Geoff Osborne (nonfiction, screenplays, stage plays).
Handles: Nonfiction books, textbooks, scholarly books, juvenile books, novels, novellas, movie scripts, stage plays, features for TV (no episodics). Considers these nonfiction areas: anthropology/archaeology; art/architecture/design; biography/autobiography; business; child guidance/parenting; computers/electronics; cooking/food/nutrition; current affairs; ethnic/cultural interests; gay/lesbian issues; government/politics/law; history; juvenile nonfiction; language/literature/criticism; music/dance/theater/film; nature/environment; New Age/metaphysics; psychology; sociology; translations; travel; true crime/investigative; exposé. Considers these fiction areas: action/adventure; cartoon/comic; contemporary issues; detective/police/crime; erotica; ethnic; experimental; fantasy; feminist; gay; historical; humor/satire; juvenile; lesbian; literary; mainstream; mystery/suspense; picture book; psychic/supernatural; science fiction; thriller/espionage; westerns/frontier; political satire. Query. Reports in 2 weeks on queries; 6-8 weeks on solicited mss.
Terms: Agent receives 10% commission on domestic sales; 20% on foreign sales. Offers written contract, binding for 6 months-2 years. "Some editorial support is available to our signed clients." Writer offsets expenses for long distance tolls, postage, photocopying and any unusual expenses, all agreed upon in advance.
Tips: Obtains new clients through well-written queries and referrals. "Always include SASE with your letter of query. All our agents will consider a new writer. We'd rather not read first drafts or unfinished work. Please, no phone queries."

DONALD MAASS LITERARY AGENCY (III), 157 West 57th St., Suite 1003, New York NY 10019. (212)757-7755. Contact: Donald Maass. Estab. 1980. Member of AAR, SFWA, MWA. Represents 75 clients. 5% of clients are new/previously unpublished writers. Specializes in commercial fiction, especially science fiction, fantasy, mystery, suspense. Currently handles: 100% novels. Member agent: Jennifer Jackson.
Handles: Novels. Considers these fiction areas: detective/police/crime; family saga; fantasy; historical; horror; literary; mainstream; mystery/suspense; psychic/supernatural; science fiction; thriller/espionage. Query with SASE. Reports in 2 weeks on queries, 2-3 months on mss (if requested following query).
Recent Sales: *Sins of the Wolf*, by Anne Perry (Fawcett Columbine); *Death Masque*, by P.N. Elrod (ACE Books); *Pasquale's Angel*, by Paul J. McAuley (Morrow); *The Venom Factor*, by Dianne Duane (Putnam's); *Cradle of Splendor*, Patricia Anthony (ACE Books).
Terms: Agent receives 15% commission on domestic sales; 20% on foreign sales. "Manuscript copying for auction charged separately."
Writer's Conferences: Attends World Science Fiction Convention (Glasgow, Scotland).
Tips: "Most new clients are established authors referred by clients, publishers and other writers. We are fiction specialists. Few new clients are accepted, but interested authors should query with SASE. Subagents in all principle foreign countries and Hollywood. No nonfiction or juvenile works considered."

✓

MARGRET MCBRIDE LITERARY AGENCY (II), 7744 Fay Ave., Suite 201, La Jolla CA 92037. (619)454-1550. Fax: (619)454-2156. Contact: Winifred Golden or Susan Travis. Estab. 1980. Member of AAR, Authors Guild. Represents 50 clients. 15% of clients are new/unpublished writers. Specializes in mainstream fiction and nonfiction.
Handles: Nonfiction books, novels, audio, video film rights. Considers these nonfiction areas: biography/autobiography; business; child guidance/parenting; cooking/food/nutrition; current affairs; ethnic/cultural interests; gay/lesbian issues; government/politics/law; health/medicine; history; how-to; money/finance/economics; music/dance/theater/film; popular culture; psychology; religious/inspirational; science/technology; self-help/personal improvement; sociology; sports; true crime/investigative; women's issues/women's studies. Considers these fiction areas: action/adventure; detective/police/crime; ethnic; historical; literary; mainstream; mystery/suspense; thriller/epionage; westerns/frontier. Query with synopsis or outline. No unsolicited mss. Reports in 6 weeks on queries.
Recent Sales: *Advantage Selling*, by Brian Tracy (Simon & Schuster); *Youth in Revolt*, by C.D. Payne (Doubleday); *Sherman's March*, by Cynthia Bass (Villard); *Portable Therapist*, by Susanna McMahon (Dell).
Terms: Agent receives 15% commission on domestic sales; 10% on dramatic sales; 25% on foreign sales.

DONALD MACCAMPBELL INC. (III), 12 E. 41st St., New York NY 10017. (212)683-5580. Editor: Maureen Moran. Estab. 1940. Represents 50 clients. "The agency does not handle unpublished writers." Specializes in women's book-length fiction in all categories. Currently handles: 100% novels.
Handles: Novels. Query; does not read unsolicited mss. Reports in 1 week on queries.
Recent Sales: *One of Our Own*, by Cheryl Ravis (Silhouette); *Toast of the Town*, by Margaret Porter (NAL); *Alpine* mystery series, by Mary Daheim (Ballentine).
Terms: Agent receives 10% commission on domestic sales; 20% on foreign sales.

GERARD MCCAULEY (III), P.O. Box 844, Katonah NY 10536. (914)232-5700. Fax: (914)232-1506. Estab. 1970. Member of AAR. Represents 60 clients. 5% of clients are new/previously unpublished writers. Specializes in history, biography and general nonfiction. Currently handles: 65% nonfiction books; 15% scholarly books; 20% textbooks. "Developing commercial fiction list through Henry O. Houghton (53 Garland Rd., Concord MA 01742) and Anne McAttee (P.O. Box 844, Katonah NY 10536).
Handles: Nonfiction books, textbooks, novels ("novels go to Henry Houghton"). Considers these nonfiction areas: biography/autobiography; current affairs; history; military/war; sports. Query. Reports in 1 month on queries; 2 months on mss.
Recent Sales: *Baseball*, by Geoffrey Ward and Ken Burns; *The Unredeemed Capture*, by John Demos.
Terms: Agent receives 15% commission on domestic sales; 20% on foreign sales. Charges for "postage for all submissions and photocopying."
Tips: Obtains new clients through recommendations. "Always send a personal letter—not a form letter with recommendations from published writers."

ANITA D. MCCLELLAN ASSOCIATES (III), 50 Stearns St., Cambridge MA 02138. Estab. 1988. Member of AAR, Boston Literary Agents' Society. 25% of clients are new/previously unpublished writers. Specializes in general book-length trade fiction and nonfiction.
Handles: Query with SASE only. No computer or technical books, cookbooks, science fiction or horror fiction, or young adult fiction. "No certified mail, no telephone queries, no unsolicited manuscripts." 50-page maximum on sample material. Reports in 3 weeks on queries.
Terms: Agent receives 15% commission on domestic sales; 20% on foreign sales. Charges for photocopying, postage, copies of galleys and books, fax and telephone.

GINA MACCOBY LITERARY AGENCY (II), 1123 Broadway, Suite 1009, New York NY 10010. (212)627-9210. Contact: Gina Maccoby. Estab. 1986. Represents 30 clients. Currently handles: 33% nonfiction books; 33% juvenile books; 33% novels. Represents illustrators of children's books.
Handles: Nonfiction, juvenile books, novels. Considers these nonfiction areas: biography; current affairs; ethnic/cultural interests; juvenile nonfiction; women's issues/women's studies. Considers these fiction areas: juvenile; literary; mainstream; mystery/suspense; thriller/espionage; young adult. Query with SASE. Reports in 4-6 weeks.
Recent Sales: *Snapshot*, by Linda Barnes (Delacorte); *The Old Woman & Her Pig*, by Rosanne Litzinger (Harcourt Brace Jovanovich).
Terms: Agent receives 15% commission on domestic sales; 25% on foreign sales. May recover certain costs such as airmail postage to Europe or Japan or legal fees.

Tips: Usually obtains new clients through recommendations from own clients.

RICHARD P. MCDONOUGH, LITERARY AGENT (II), P.O. Box 1950, Boston MA 02130. (617)522-6388. Contact: Richard P. McDonough. Estab. 1986. Represents 30 clients. 50% of clients are new/unpublished writers. Works with unpublished and published writers "whose work I think has merit and requires a committed advocate." Specializes in nonfiction for general contract and fiction. Currently handles: 80% nonfiction books; 10% novels.
Handles: Nonfiction books, novels. Query with outline and SASE or send 3 chapters and SASE. Reports in 2 weeks on queries; 5 weeks on mss.
Recent Sales: *Parents Who Love Reading, Kids Who Don't*, by M. Leonhardt (Crown); *We Will Gather at the River*, by M.R. Montgomery (Simon & Schuster).
Terms: Agent receives 15% commission on domestic sales; 15% on dramatic sales; 15% on foreign sales. Charges for photocopying, phone beyond 300 miles; postage for sold work only.

HELEN MCGRATH (III), 1406 Idaho Ct., Concord CA 94521. (510)672-6211. Contact: Helen McGrath. Estab. 1977. Currently handles: 50% nonfiction books; 50% novels. Member agent: Doris Johnson.
Handles: Nonfiction books, novels. Considers these nonfiction areas: biography; business; current affairs; health/medicine; history; how-to; military/war; psychology; self-help/personal improvement; sports; women's issues/women's studies. Considers these fiction areas: contemporary issues; detective/police/crime; family saga; literary; mainstream; mystery/suspense; psychic/supernatural; romance; science fiction; sports; thriller/espionage; westerns/frontier. Query with proposal and SASE. No unsolicited mss. Reports in 6-8 weeks on queries.
Terms: Agent receives 15% commission on domestic sales. Sometimes offers written contract. Charges for photocopying.
Tips: Usually obtains new clients through recommendations from others.

ROBERT MADSEN AGENCY (I), 1331 E. 34th St., Suite #1, Oakland CA 94602. (510)223-2090. Agent: Robert Madsen. Senior Editor: Kim Van Nguyen. Estab. 1992. Represents 5 clients. 100% of clients are new/previously unpublished writers. Currently handles 25% nonfiction books; 25% fiction books; 25% movie scripts; 25% TV scripts.
Handles: Nonfiction books, fiction, TV scripts, radio script, video, stage plays. Considers all nonfiction and fiction areas. Considers all script subject areas. "Willing to look at subject matter that is specialized, controversial, even unpopular, esoteric and outright bizarre. However, it is strongly suggested that authors query first, to save themselves and this agency time, trouble and expense." Query. Reports in 1 month on queries; 2-3 months on mss.
Terms: Agent receives 10% commission on domestic sales; 20% on foreign sales. Offers written contract, binding for 3 years.
Tips: Obtains new clients through recommendations, or by query. "Be certain to take care of business basics in appearance, ease of reading and understanding proper presentation and focus. Be sure to include sufficient postage and SASE with all submissions."

‡RICIA MAINHARDT AGENCY (II), 612 Argyle Rd., #L5, Brooklyn NY 11230. (718)434-1893. Fax: (718)434-2157. Contact: Ricia. Estab. 1987. Member of AAR. 40% of clients are new/previously unpublished writers. Currently handles: 20% nonfiction books; 30% juvenile books; 50% novels.
Handles: Nonfiction books, juvenile books, novels. Considers these nonfiction areas: agriculture/horticulture; animals; anthropology/archaeology; biography/autobiography; business; child guidance/parenting; cooking/food/nutrition; crafts/hobbies; current affairs; ethnic/cultural interests; government/politics/law; health/medicine; history; how-to; humor; interior design/decorating; juvenile nonfiction; money/finance/economics; nature/environment; New Age/metaphysics; popular culture; psychology; science/technology; self-help/personal improvement; sociology; sports; true crime/investigative; women's issues/women's studies. Considers these fiction areas: action/adventure; contemporary issues; detective/police/crime; erotica; ethnic; family saga; fantasy; feminist; glitz; historical; horror; humor/satire; juvenile; literary; mainstream; picture book; psychic/supernatural; romance (contemporary, gothic, historical, regency); science fiction; sports; thriller/espionage; westerns/frontier; young adult. Send outline and 3 sample chapters. Reports in 1 month on queries; 2-3 months on mss.
Terms: Agent receives 15% commission on domestic sales; 20% on foreign sales. No written contract. Charges new writers $10 to cover postage and handling. Charges for photocopying.
Writer's Conferences: "I attend the major genre conferences—World Fantasy, Bouchercon, Malice Domestic, Romance Writers."
Tips: Obtains most new clients through recommendations of established writers and editors.

CAROL MANN AGENCY (II,III), 55 Fifth Ave., New York NY 10003. (212)206-5635. Fax: (212)463-8718. Contact: Carol Mann. Estab. 1977. Member of AAR. Represents 100+ clients. 25% of clients are new/previously unpublished writers. Specializes in current affairs; self-help; psychology; parenting; history. Currently handles: 80% nonfiction books; 15% scholarly books; 5% novels. Member agent: Gareth Esersky (contemporary nonfiction).
Handles: Nonfiction books. Considers these nonfiction areas: anthropology/archaeology; art/ architecture/design; biography/autobiography; business; child guidance/parenting; current affairs; ethnic/cultural interests; government/politics/law; health/medicine; history; interior design/ decorating; money/finance/economics; psychology; self-help/personal improvement; sociology; true crime/investigative; women's issues/women's studies. Considers literary fiction. Query with outline/proposal and SASE. Reports in 3 weeks on queries.
Recent Sales: *Holistic Health for Children*, by Dr. Kathi Kemper (Villard); *Smart Exercise*, by Covert Bailey (Houghton); *Untitled*, by Shelby Sleek (HarperCollins); *Entitled to Good Loving*, by Audrey Chapman (Henry Holt).
Terms: Agent receives 15% commission on domestic sales; 20% on foreign sales. Offers written contract.

‡MANUS & ASSOCIATES LITERARY AGENCY, INC. (II), 417 E. 57th St., Suite 5D, New York NY 10022. (212)644-8020. Fax: (212)644-3374. Contact: Janet Wilkens Manus. Also 430 Cowper St., Palo Alto CA 94301. (415)617-4556. Fax: (415)617-4546. Contact: Jillian Manus. Estab. 1985. Member of AAR. Represents 60 clients. 15% of clients are new/previously unpublished writers. Specializes in quality fiction, mysteries, thrillers, true crime, health, pop psychology. Currently handles: 60% nonfiction books; 10% juvenile books; 20% novels; 10% film rights, TV and feature films.
Handles: Nonfiction books, novels. Considers these nonfiction areas: anthropology/archaeology; biography/autobiography; business; child guidance/parenting; current affairs; ethnic/cultural interests; health/medicine; how-to; nature/environment; popular culture; psychology; self-help/ personal improvement; true crime/investigative; women's issues/women's studies. Considers these fiction areas: action/adventure; confessional; contemporary issues; detective/police/crime; ethnic; family saga; feminist; mainstream; mystery/suspense; thriller/espionage. Send outline and 2-3 sample chapters with SASE. Reports in 3 weeks on queries; 6 weeks on mss.
Terms: Agent receives 15% commission on domestic sales; 20% on foreign sales. Offers written contract, binding for 1.3 years, with 45 days cancellation clause. 100% of business is derived from commissions on sales.
Writers' Conferences Squaw Valley Community of Writers; San Diego State University Writers Conference; Writer's Connection/Agent's Day Conference; Maui Writers Conference; ABA (Chicago).
Tips: Obtains new clients through recommendations from others, at conferences.

MARCH TENTH, INC. (III), 4 Myrtle St., Haworth NJ 07641. (201)387-6551. Fax: (201)387-6552. President: Sandra Choron. Estab. 1982. Represents 40 clients. 30% of clients are new/ unpublished writers. "Writers must have professional expertise in the field in which they are writing." Prefers to work with published/established writers. Currently handles: 75% nonfiction books; 25% fiction.
Handles: Nonfiction books, fiction. Considers these nonfiction areas: biography/autobiography; current affairs; ethnic/cultural interests; health/medicine; history; humor; language/literature/ criticism; music/dance/theater/film; popular culture; true crime/investigative. Considers these fiction areas: confessional; ethnic; family saga; glitz; historical; horror; humor/satire; literary; mainstream; mystery/suspense; regional; thriller/espionage. Query. Does not read unsolicited mss. Reports in 1 month.
Recent Sales: *Schindler's Legacy*, by Elinor Brecher (Dutton); *Louie Louie: A Social History Of The Song*, by Dave Marsh (Hyperion); *The Big Book of Blues*, by Robert Santelli (Penguin).
Terms: Agent receives 15% commission on domestic sales; 20% on dramatic sales; 20% on foreign sales. Charges writers for postage, photocopying, overseas phone expenses.

BARBARA MARKOWITZ LITERARY AGENCY (II), 117 N. Mansfield Ave., Los Angeles CA 90036. (213)939-5927. Literary Agent/President: Barbara Markowitz. Estab. 1980. Represents 14 clients. Works with a small number of new/unpublished authors. Specializes in mid-level and YA; contemporary fiction; adult trade fiction and nonfiction. Currently handles: 25% nonfiction books; 25% novels; 50% juvenile books. Member agent: Judith Rosenthal (psychology, current affairs, women's issues, biography).
Handles: Nonfiction books, novels, juvenile books. Considers these nonfiction areas: biography/ autobiography; current affairs; juvenile nonfiction; music/dance/theater/film; nature/environ-ment; popular culture; sports; women's issues/women's studies. Considers these fiction areas: contemporary issues; detective/police/crime; ethnic; humor/satire; juvenile; mainstream; mys-

tery/suspense; sports; thriller/espionage; young adult. No illustrated books. Query with outline. SASE required for return of any material. Reports in 3 weeks.

Recent Sales: *Moondog*, by Henry Garfield (St. Martin's Press); *Embracing the Other*, by Ellen McClain (Basic Books); *Jimmy Spoon & the Pony Express*, by Kristiana Gregory (Scholastic Books).

Terms: Agent receives 15% commission on domestic sales; 15% on dramatic sales; 15% on foreign sales. Charges writers for mailing, postage.

Tips: "We do *not* agent pre-school or early reader books. Only mid-level and YA contemporary fiction and historical fiction. We receive an abundance of pre-school and early reader mss, which our agency returns if accompanied by SASE."

ELAINE MARKSON LITERARY AGENCY (II), 44 Greenwich Ave., New York NY 10011. (212)243-8480. Estab. 1972. Member of AAR. Represents 200 clients. 10% of clients are new/unpublished writers. Specializes in literary fiction, commercial fiction, trade nonfiction. Currently handles: 35% nonfiction books; 55% novels; 10% juvenile books; 5% movie scripts. Member agents: Geri Thomas, Sally Wofford-Girand, Elaine Markson.

Handles: Novels, nonfiction books. Query with outline (must include SASE). SASE is required for the return of any material.

Recent Sales: *Rhinegold*, by Stephen Grundy (Kruger [Germany], Bantam [US], Michael Joseph [UK]).

Terms: Agent receives 15% commission on domestic sales; 10% on dramatic sales; 20% on foreign sales. Charges for postage, photocopying, foreign mailing, faxing, long-distance telephone and other special expenses.

MILDRED MARMUR ASSOCIATES LTD. (II), 2005 Palmer Ave., Suite 127, Larchmont NY 10538. (914)834-1170. Fax: (914)834-2840. Contact: Mildred Marmur. Estab. 1987. Member of AAR. Specializes in serious nonfiction. Member agent: Mildred Marmur.

Handles: Nonfiction books, novels. Considers these nonfiction areas: biography/autobiography; business; cooking/food/nutrition; current affairs; ethnic/cultural interests; government/politics/law; health/medicine; history; juvenile nonfiction; money/finance/economics; music/dance/theater/film; nature/environment; religious/inspirational; science/technology; sports; true crime/investigative; women's issues/women's studies. Considers these fiction areas: contemporary issues; detective/police/crime; family saga; feminist; juvenile; literary; mainstream; mystery/suspense; thriller/espionage; young adult. Query with SASE. Reports in 4 weeks on queries.

Terms: Agent receives 15% commission on domestic sales; 20% on foreign sales. Sometimes offers written contract (book-by-book).

Tips: Obtains new clients through recommendations from other clients. "Browse in a bookstore or library and look at the acknowledgments in books similar to yours. If an author of a nonfiction book in your general area thanks his or her agent, send your manuscript to that person and point out the link. If you can't figure out who the agent is, try phoning the publisher. At least you'll have a more targeted person. Also, agents are more receptive to written submissions than to pitches over the phone."

THE MARTELL AGENCY (III), 555 Fifth Ave., Suite 1900, New York NY 10017. (212)692-9770. Contact: John Sanful or Alice Fried Martell. Estab. 1984. Represents 75 clients. Currently handles: 65% nonfiction books; 35% novels.

Handles: Nonfiction books, novels. Considers all nonfiction areas. Considers most fiction areas. No science fiction or poetry. Query with outline plus 2 sample chapters and SASE. Will report in 3 weeks on queries, only if interested.

Terms: Agent receives 15% commission on domestic sales; 20% on foreign sales. Offers written contract, binding for 1 year. Charges for foreign postage, photocopying.

Tips: Usually obtains new clients by recommendations from agents and editors.

ROBERTA D. MILLER ASSOCIATES (I), 42 E. 12th St., New York NY 10003-4640. Contact: Roberta D. Miller. Estab. 1991. Represents 8 clients. 75% of clients are new/previously unpublished writers. Specializes in literary fiction, young adult. Currently handles: 75% adult fiction and nonfiction; 25% young adult. Member agents: Roberta Miller; Elisabeth Whelan (young adult).

Handles: Nonfiction books, juvenile books, novels. Considers these nonfiction areas: art/architecture/design; biography/autobiography; current affairs; ethnic/cultural interests; language/literature/criticism. Considers these fiction areas: contemporary issues; detective/police/crime; humor/satire; literary; mainstream; young adult. Query with outline plus 1 sample chapter. Reports in 1 month on mss.

Recent Sales: *Kingsland*, by Rosemary Cassata (Viking).
Terms: Agent receives 15% commission on domestic sales; 25% on foreign sales. Offers written contract. Charges for photocopying, postage, fax charges.
Tips: Obtains new clients from recommendations, agent listings, editors. "U.S. authors only, please."

MOORE LITERARY AGENCY (IV), 4 Dove St., Newburyport MA 01950. (508)465-9015. Contact: Claudette Moore. Estab. 1989. 20% of clients are new/previously unpublished writers. Specializes in trade computer books. Currently handles: 100% computer-related books.
Handles: Computer books only. Send outline/proposal. Reports in 3 weeks on queries.
Recent Sales: *How to Use Windows*, by Douglas Hergert (Ziff-Davis Press); *The Windows Scanning Book*, by Luisa Simone (John Wiley & Sons).
Terms: Agent receives 15% commission on all sales. Offers written contract.
Writer's Conferences: ABA (Chicago); Comdex (Las Vegas).
Tips: Obtains new clients through recommendations/referrals and conferences.

HOWARD MORHAIM LITERARY AGENCY (II), 175 Fifth Ave., Suite 709, New York NY 10010-7703. (212)529-4433. Fax: (212)995-1112. Contact: Howard Morhaim or Allison Mullen. Estab. 1978. Member of AAR. Represents 80 clients. 15% of clients are new/previously unpublished writers. Currently handles: 15% nonfiction books; 5% juvenile books; 75% novels; 2% novellas; 3% short story collections. Member agent: Allison Mullen (women's fiction, romance, mysteries/thrillers).
Handles: Nonfiction books, novels. Considers these nonfiction areas: art/architecture/design; biography/autobiography; child guidance/parenting; current affairs; ethnic/cultural interests; popular culture; psychology; self-help/personal improvement; true crime/investigative; women's issues/women's studies. Considers these fiction areas: detective/police/crime; family saga; glitz; historical; mainstream; mystery/suspense; romance (contemporary, historical); thriller/espionage. Send outline plus 3 sample chapters. Reports in 2 weeks on queries; 6-8 weeks on ms.
Terms: Agent receives 15% commission on domestic sales; 20% on foreign sales. Charges for photocopying only.
Writer's Conferences: Bouchercon (Seattle, WA); Moonlight & Magnolias (Atlanta, GA); World Fantasy (New Orleans, LA).
Tips: Obtains new clients through recommendations from others; conferences.

WILLIAM MORRIS AGENCY (III), 1350 Avenue of the Americas, New York NY 10019. (212)586-5100. Estab. 1898. West Coast office: 151 El Camino Dr., Beverly Hills CA 90212. (310)274-7451. Member of AAR. Works with a small number of new/unpublished authors. Specializes in novels, nonfiction.
Handles: Nonfiction books, novels. Query only. Reports in 6 weeks.
Recent Sales: *The Quiet Room*, by Lori Schiller and Amanda Bennett (Warner Books; optioned by Touchstone Pictures).
Terms: Agent receives 10% commission on domestic sales; 10% on dramatic sales; 20% on foreign sales.

HENRY MORRISON, INC. (II, III), 320 McLain St., Bedford Hills NY 10507. (914)666-3500. Fax: (914)241-7846. Contact: Henry Morrison. Estab. 1929. Signatory of WGA. Represents 48 clients. 5% of clients are new/previously unpublished writers. Currently handles: 5% nonfiction books; 5% juvenile books; 85% novels; 5% movie scripts.
Handles: Nonfiction books, novels. Considers these nonfiction areas: anthropology/archaeology; biography; government/politics/law; history; juvenile nonfiction. Considers these fiction areas: action/adventure; detective/police/crime; family saga. Query. Reports in 2 weeks on queries; 2-3 months on mss.
Recent Sales: *Desperate Measures*, by David Morrel (Warner); *Prisoners of Hope: The MIA Scandal*, by Susan Keating (Random); *The Omega Countdown*, by Robert Ludlum (Bantam); *Thinning the Predators*, by Daina Graziunas and Jim Starlin (Warner Books).
Terms: Agent receives 15% commission on domestic sales; 20% on foreign sales. Charges for ms copies, bound galleys and finished books for submission to publishers, movie producers, foreign publishers.
Tips: Obtains new clients through recommendations from others.

Agents who specialize in a specific subject area such as computer books or in handling the work of certain writers such as gay or lesbian writers are ranked IV.

MULTIMEDIA PRODUCT DEVELOPMENT, INC. (III), 410 S. Michigan Ave., Suite 724, Chicago IL 60605. (312)922-3063. Fax: (312)922-1905. President: Jane Jordan Browne. Estab. 1971. Member of AAR, RWA, MWA, SCBWI. Represents 150 clients. 5% of clients are new/previously unpublished writers. "We are generalists." Currently handles: 60% nonfiction books; 8% juvenile books; 30% novels; 1% scholarly books; 1% textbooks. Member agent: Danielle Egan-Miller (popular culture).

Handles: Nonfiction books, novels. Considers these nonfiction areas: agriculture/horticulture; animals; anthropology/archaeology; biography/autobiography; business; child guidance/parenting; cooking/food/nutrition; crafts/hobbies; current affairs; ethnic/cultural issues; health/medicine; how-to; humor; juvenile nonfiction; money/finance; nature; popular culture; psychology; religious/inspirational; science/technology; self-help/personal improvement; sociology; sports; true crime/investigative; women's issues/women's studies. Considers these fiction areas: contemporary issues; detective/police/crime; ethnic; family saga; glitz; historical; horror; juvenile; literary; mainstream; mystery/suspense; picture book; religious/inspirational; romance (contemporary, gothic, historical, regency, western); sports; thriller/espionage; westerns/frontier. Query "by mail with SASE required." Reports in 2 days on queries; 4-6 weeks on mss.

Recent Sales: *The Chile Pepper Kitchen*, by Dave Dewitt and Gloria Moore (Little, Brown); *Unforgettable*, by Danice Allen (Avon); *The Sewing Circle*, by Axel Madsen (Birch Lane).

Terms: Agent receives 15% commission on domestic sales; 20% on foreign sales. Offers written contract, binding for 2 years. Charges for photocopying, overseas postage, faxes, phone calls.

Writer's Conferences: ABA (Chicago, IL); Frankfurt Book Fair (Frankfurt, Germany); RWA.

Tips: Obtains new clients through "referrals, queries by professional, marketable authors. If interested in agency representation, be well informed."

‡DEE MURA ENTERPRISES, INC. (II), 269 West Shore Dr., Massapequa NY 11758-8225. (516)795-1616. Fax: (516)795-8797. E-mail: samurai5@netcom.com. Contact: Dee Mura. Estab. 1987. Signatory of WGA. 50% of clients are new/previously published writers. "We work on everything, but are especially interested in true life stories, true crime and women's stories and issues." Currently handles: 20% nonfiction books; 15% scholarly books; 15% juvenile books; 20% novels; 15% movie scripts; 15% TV scripts.

Handles: Nonfiction books, scholarly books, juvenile books, novels. Considers these nonfiction areas: agriculture/horticulture; animals; anthropology/archaeology; biography/autobiography; business; child guidance/parenting; computers/electronics; current affairs; education; ethnic/cultural interests; gay/lesbian issues; government/politics/law; health/medicine; history; how-to; humor; juvenile nonfiction; military/war; money/finance/economics; nature/environment; science/technology; self-help/personal improvement; sociology; sports; true crime/investigative; women's issues/women's studies. Considers these fiction areas: action/adventure; contemporary issues; detective/police/crime; ethnic; experimental; family saga; fantasy; feminist; gay; glitz; historical; humor/satire; juvenile; lesbian; literary; mainstream; mystery/suspense; psychic/supernatural; regional; romance (contemporary, gothic, historical, regency); science fiction; sports; thriller/espionage; westerns/frontier; young adult. Query. Reports in approximately 2 weeks on queries.

Also Handles: Movie scripts (feature film, documentary, animation), TV scripts (TV mow, miniseries, episodic drama, sitcom, variety show, animation). Considers these script subject areas: action/adventure; cartoon/animation; comedy; contemporary issues; detective/police/crime; family saga; fantasy; feminist; gay; glitz; historical; horror; humor; juvenile; mainstream; mystery/suspense; psychic/supernatural; religious/inspirational; romantic comedy and drama; science fiction; sports; teen; thriller; western/frontier.

Terms: Agent receives 15% commission on domestic sales; 20-25% on foreign sales. Offers written contract. Charges for photocopying and mailing expenses directly pertaining to writer.

Tips: Obtains new clients through recommendations from others. Query solicitation. "Please include a paragraph on writer's background and a brief synopsis of the project. We enjoy well-written query letters that tell us about the project and the author."

JEAN V. NAGGAR LITERARY AGENCY (III), 216 E. 75th St., Suite 1E, New York NY 10021. (212)794-1082. Contact: Jean Naggar. Estab. 1978. Member of AAR. Represents 100 clients. 20% of clients are new/previously unpublished writers. Currently handles: 30% nonfiction books;

Agents ranked I-IV are actively seeking new clients. Those ranked V or those who prefer not to be listed have been included to inform you they are not currently looking for new clients.

5% scholarly books; 15% juvenile books; 40% novels; 5% short story collections. Member agents: Teresa Cavanaugh, Frances Kuffel. Agent-at-large: Anne Engel (nonfiction).

Handles: Nonfiction books, some juvenile books, novels. Considers these nonfiction areas: biography/autobiography; business; child guidance/parenting; cooking/food/nutrition; current affairs; gay/lesbian issues; government/politics/law; health/medicine; history; interior design/decorating; juvenile nonfiction; money/finance/economics; music/dance/theater/film; New Age/metaphysics; psychology; religious/inspirational; self-help/personal improvement; sociology; true crime/investigative; women's issues/women's studies. "We would, of course, consider a query regarding an exceptional mainstream manuscript touching on any area." Considers these fiction areas: action/adventure; contemporary issues; detective/police/crime; ethnic; family saga; fantasy; feminist; gay; glitz; historical; juvenile; lesbian; literary; mainstream; mystery/suspense; picture book; psychic/supernatural; regional; science fiction; thriller/espionage. Query. Reports in 24 hours on queries; 2 months on mss.

Recent Sales: *Clouds of Heaven*, by Joe De Mers (Dutton/Signet); *Down Came the Rain*, by Jessica Auerbach (Putnam); *Final Design*, by Noreen Gilpatrick (Mysterious Press).

Terms: Agent receives 15% commission on domestic sales; 20% on foreign sales. Offers written contract. Charges for overseas mailing; messenger services; book purchases; long-distance telephone; photocopying. "These are deductible from royalties received."

Writer's Conferences: Virginia Women's Press Conference (Richmond VA).

Tips: Obtains new clients through "recommendations from publishers, editors, clients and others, and from writers' conferences. Use a professional presentation. Because of the avalanche of unsolicited queries that flood the agency every week, we have had to modify our policy. We will now only guarantee to read responds to queries from writers who come recommended by someone we knoww. Our areas are general fiction and nonfiction, no children's books by unpublished writers, no multimedia, no screenplays, no formula fiction, no mysteries by unpublished writers."

RUTH NATHAN (II), 80 Fifth Ave., Room 706, New York NY 10011. Phone/fax: (212)675-6063. Estab. 1980. Member of AAR. Represents 12 clients. 10% of clients are new/previously unpublished writers. Specializes in art, decorative arts, fine art; theater; film; show business. Currently handles: 90% nonfiction books; 10% novels.

Handles: Nonfiction books, novels. Considers these nonfiction areas: art/architecture/design; biography/autobiography; theater/film; true crime/investigative. Query. Reports in 2 weeks on queries; 1 month on mss.

Recent Sales: *A Dangerous Gift*, by Claudia Crawford (Dutton); *Faking It*, by K.J. Lane (Harry Abrams).

Terms: Agent receives 15% commission on domestic sales; 20% on foreign sales. Charges for office expenses, postage, photocopying, etc.

Tips: "Read carefully what my requirements are before wasting your time and mine."

‡KAREN NAZOR LITERARY AGENCY (II, III), Opera Plaza, 601 Van Ness Ave., Suite E3124, San Francisco CA 94102. (415)648-2281. Fax: (415)648-2348. E-mail: AgentNazor@aol.com or agentKN@well.com. Contact: Karen Nazor. Estab. 1991. Represents 25 clients. 15% of clients are new/previously unpublished writers. Specializes in "good writers! Mostly nonfiction—arts, culture, politics, technology, civil rights, etc." Currently handles: 80% nonfiction books; 15% novels; 5% novellas.

Handles: Nonfiction books, novels, novellas. Considers these nonfiction areas: biography/autobiography; business; computers/electronics; cooking/food; current affairs; ethnic/cultural interests; gay/lesbian issues; government/politics/law; history; how-to; music/dance/theater/film; nature/environment; photography; popular culture; science/technology; sociology; sports; women's issues/women's studies. Considers these fiction areas: action/adventure; cartoon/comic; contemporary issues; erotica; ethnic; feminist; literary; regional. Query (preferred) or send outline/proposal (accepted). Reports in 2 weeks on queries; up to 2 months on mss.

Recent Sales: *Ebbetts Field*, by Bob McGee (W.W. Norton); *Happy Mutant Handbook*, by Carla Sinclair, Mark Fraunfelder, Gareth Branwyn, Will Kreth (Riverhead Press—new division of Putnam); *Garage Virtual Reality*, by Linda Jacobson (SAMS).

Terms: Agent receives 15% commission on domestic sales; 20% on foreign sales. Offers written contract. Charges for express mail services and photocopying costs.

Tips: Referrals from editors and writers; online; teaching classes on publishing; newspaper article on agency. "I'm interested in writers that want a long term, long haul relationship. Not a one-book writer, but a writer who has many ideas, is productive, professional, passionate and meets deadlines!"

NEW ENGLAND PUBLISHING ASSOCIATES, INC. (II), P.O. Box 5, Chester CT 06412. (203)345-READ and (203)345-4976. Fax: (203)345-3660. Contact: Elizabeth Frost Knappman, Edward

W. Knappman. Estab. 1983. Member of AAR. Represents over 100 clients. 15% of clients are new/previously unpublished writers. Specializes in adult nonfiction books of serious purpose.
Handles: Nonfiction books. Considers these nonfiction areas: biography/autobiography; business; child guidance/parenting; government/politics/law; health/medicine; history; language/literature/criticism; military/war; money/finance/economics; nature/environment; psychology; science/technology; self-help/personal improvement; sociology; true crime/investigative; women's issues/women's studies. Send outline/proposal. Reports in 2-3 weeks on queries; 4-5 weeks on mss.
Recent Sales: *Eudora Welty*, by Ann Waldron; *The Importance of Being Different*, by Robert Sherril.
Terms: Agent receives 15% commission on domestic sales; 20% foreign sales (split with overseas agent). Offers written contract, binding for 6 months.
Tips: "Send us a well-written proposal that clearly identifies your audience—who will buy this book and why."

NINE MUSES AND APOLLO (II), 2 Charlton St., New York NY 10014. (212)243-0065. Contact: Ling Lucas. Estab. 1991. Represents 50 clients. 50% of clients are new/previously unpublished writers. Specializes in nonfiction. Currently handles: 90% nonfiction books; 10% novels. Member agents: Ling Lucas, Ed Vesneske, Jr.
Handles: Nonfiction books. Considers these nonfiction areas: animals; biography/autobiography; business; current affairs; ethnic/cultural interests; gay/lesbian issues; government/politics/law; health/medicine; history; language/literature/criticism; money/finance/economics; psychology; science/technology; true crime/investigative; women's issues/women's studies. Considers these fiction areas: commercial; ethnic; humor/satire; mainstream. Send outline plus 2 sample chapters. Reports in 1 month on mss.
Recent Sales: *Use Your Anger, A Woman's Guide*, by Dr. Sandra Thomas (Pocket Books); *Ida B. Wells Reader*, by Lisa Kennedy (William Morrow).
Terms: Agent receives 15% commission on domestic sales; 25% on foreign sales. Offers written contract. Charges for photocopying proposals and mss.
Tips: "Your outline should already be well developed, cogent and reveal clarity of thought about the general structure and direction of your project."

THE BETSY NOLAN LITERARY AGENCY (II), 224 W. 29th St., 15th Floor, New York NY 10001. (212)967-8200. Fax: (212)967-7292. President: Betsy Nolan. Estab. 1980. Represents 200 clients. 10% of clients are new/unpublished writers. Works with a small number of new/unpublished authors. Currently handles: 80% nonfiction books; 20% novels. Member agents: Donald Lehr, Corrina Wright and Carla Glasser.
Handles: Nonfiction books. Query with outline. Reports in 3 weeks on queries; 2 months on mss.
Terms: Agent receives 15% commission on domestic sales; 20% on foreign sales.

‡THE NORMA-LEWIS AGENCY (II), 360 W. 53rd St., Suite B-A, New York NY 10019-5720. (212)664-0807. Fax: (212)664-0462. Contact: Norma Liebert. Estab. 1980. 50% of clients are new/previously unpublished writers. Specializes in juvenile books (pre-school-high school). Currently handles: 60% juvenile books; 40% adult books.
Handles: Juvenile and adult nonfiction and fiction, movie scripts, TV scripts, radio scripts, stage plays. Considers these nonfiction areas: art/architecture/design; biography/autobiography; child guidance/parenting; cooking/food/nutrition; crafts/hobbies; current affairs; ethnic/cultural interests; government/politics/law; health/medicine; history; juvenile nonfiction; music/dance/theater/film; nature/environment; photography; popular culture; self-help/personal improvement; true crime/investigative; women's issues/women's studies. Considers these fiction areas: action/adventure; contemporary issues; detective/police/crime; family saga; historical; horror; humor/satire; juvenile; mainstream; mystery/suspense; picture book; romance (contemporary, gothic, historical, regency); thriller/espionage; westerns/frontier; young adult.
Recent Sales: *Viper Quarry* and *Pitchfork Hollow*, both by Dean Feldmayer (Pocket Books).
Terms: Agent receives 15% commission on domestic sales; 20% on foreign sales.

EDWARD A. NOVAK III LITERARY REPRESENTATION (II), 711 N. Second St., Suite 1, Harrisburg PA 17102. (717)232-8081. Fax: (717)232-7020. Contact: Ed Novak. Estab. 1991. Represents 30 clients. 65% of clients are new/previously unpublished writers. Currently handles: 70% nonfiction books; 30% novels.
• See Edward Novak's article, *The Literary Agent: Savant, Savior or Svengali?*, in this edition.
Handles: Nonfiction books, novels. Considers these nonfiction areas: art/architecture/design; biography/autobiography; business; child guidance/parenting; current affairs; ethnic/cultural in-

terests; gay/lesbian issues; government/politics/law; health/medicine; history; military/war; money/finance/economics; music/dance/theater/film; nature/environment; science/technology; self-help/personal improvement; sports; true crime/investigative; women's issues/women's studies. Considers these fiction areas: contemporary issues; detective/police/crime; historical; literary; mainstream; mystery/suspense; romance (contemporary, historical); sports; thriller/espionage. Query. Reports in 1 month on queries; 2 months on mss.
Recent Sales: *Rogue's Isles: A Michael Carolina Murder Mystery*, by Thomas G. Briody (Dunne/St. Martin's Press); *Elvis in the Army*, by Col. Bill Taylor (Presidio Press); *Bear Bryant: The Legend and the Man*, by Keith Dunnavant (Simon & Schuster).
Terms: Agent receives 15% commission on domestic sales; 19% on foreign sales. Offers written contract. Charges for photocopying only.
Tips: Obtains new clients "mostly through referrals, some through my own solicitation, a few through unsolicited queries."

‡NUGENT LITERARY (III), 170 Tenth St. N, Naples FL 33940. Phone/fax: (813)262-3683. Contact: Ray Nugent. Estab. 1976. Represents 10 clients. No new previously unpublished writers. Specializes in nonfiction. Currently handles: 100% nonfiction books.
Handles: Nonfiction books. Considers these nonfiction areas: biography/autobiography; health/medicine; true crime/investigative. Query. Reports in 1 month on queries; 2 months on mss.
Recent Sales: *Moonshot*, by Shepard (Turner); *Suffer the Children*, by Jose (New Horizon).
Terms: Agent receives 20% commission on domestic sales; 25% on foreign sales. Offers written contract, binding for 1 year. 100% of business derived from commission on sales.
Tips: Obtains new clients through referrals.

HAROLD OBER ASSOCIATES (III), 425 Madison Ave., New York NY 10017. (212)759-8600. Fax: (212)759-9428. Estab. 1929. Member of AAR. Represents 250 clients. 15% of clients are new/previously unpublished writers. Currently handles: 35% nonfiction books; 15% juvenile books; 50% novels. Member agents: Claire Smith, Phyllis Westberg, Peter Shepherd, Henry Dunow, Wendy Schmalz.
Handles: Nonfiction books, juvenile books, novels. Considers all nonfiction and fiction subjects. Query letter *only*. Reports in 1 week on queries; 2-3 weeks on mss.
Terms: Agent receives 10-15% commission on domestic sales; 15-20% on foreign sales. Charges for photocopying for multiple submissions.
Tips: Obtains new clients through recommendations from others.

FIFI OSCARD AGENCY INC. (II), 24 W. 40th St., New York NY 10018. (212)764-1100. Contact: Ivy Fischer Stone, Literary Department. Estab. 1956. Member of AAR, signatory of WGA. Represents 108 clients. 5% of clients are new/unpublished writers. "Writer must have published articles or books in major markets or have screen credits if movie scripts, etc." Specializes in literary novels, commercial novels, mysteries and nonfiction, especially celebrity biographies and autobiographies. Currently handles: 40% nonfiction books; 40% novels; 5% movie scripts; 5% stage plays; 10% TV scripts.
Handles: Nonfiction books, novels, movie scripts, stage plays. Query with outline. Reports in 1 week on queries if SASE enclosed.
Recent Sales: *Bruised Hibiscus*, by Elizabeth Nunez (Amistad); *The Gainesville Ripper* (Donald I. Fine).
Terms: Agent receives 15% commission on domestic sales; 10% on dramatic sales; 20% on foreign sales. Charges for photocopying expenses.

OTITIS MEDIA (II), 1926 DuPont Ave. S., Minneapolis MN 55403. (612)377-4918. Fax: (612)377-3096. Contact: Richard Boylan or Hannibal Harris. Signatory of WGA. Currently handles: novels; movie scripts; stage plays; TV scripts. Member agents: B.R. Boylan (novels, nonfiction, screenplays, stage plays); Hannibal Harris (queries, evaluation of proposals, books); Greg Boylan (screenplays, TV scripts); Ingrid DiLeonardo (script and ms evaluation, story development).
• See the expanded listing for this agency in Script Agents.

THE OTTE COMPANY (II), 9 Goden St., Belmont MA 02178-3002. (617)484-8505. Contact: Jane H. Otte or L. David Otte. Estab. 1973. Represents 35 clients. 33% of clients are new/unpublished writers. Works with a small number of new/unpublished authors. Specializes in quality adult trade books. Currently handles: 40% nonfiction books; 60% novels.
Handles: Nonfiction books, novels. Considers these nonfiction areas: anthropology/archaeology; biography/autobiography; business; government/politics/law; health/medicine; history; language/literature/criticism; military/war; money/finance/economics; sociology; true crime/investigative. Considers these fiction areas: action/adventure; contemporary issues; detective/police/crime; historical; horror; literary; mainstream; mystery/suspense. Does not handle poetry, juvenile or

"by-the-number" romance. Query should include SASE. Reports in 1 week on queries; 1 month on requested mss.
Recent Sales: *The Knowledge of Water*, by Sarah Smith (Ballantine); *Where the Wicked Dwell* (tentative title #7 of mystery series), by Philip Craig (Scribner).
Terms: Agent receives 15% commission on domestic sales; 7½% on dramatic sales; 10% on foreign sales plus 10% to foreign agent. Charges for photocopying, overseas phone and postage expenses.

THE RICHARD PARKS AGENCY (III), 138 E. 16th St., 5th Floor, New York NY 10003. (212)254-9067. Contact: Richard Parks. Estab. 1988. Member of AAR. Currently handles: 50% nonfiction books; 5% young adult books; 40% novels; 5% short story collections.
Handles: Nonfiction books, novels. Considers these nonfiction areas: horticulture; animals; anthopology/archaeology; art/architecture/design; biography/autobiography; business; child guidance/parenting; cooking/food/nutrition; crafts/hobbies; current affairs; ethnic/cultural interests; gay/lesbian issues; government/politics; health/medicine; history; how-to; humor; language/literature/criticism; military/war; money/finance/economics; music/dance/theater/film; nature/environment; popular culture; psychology; science/technology; self-help/personal improvement; sociology; women's issues/women's studies. Considers these fiction areas: action/adventure; contemporary issues; detective/police/crime; ethnic; family saga; feminist; gay; glitz; historical; horror; lesbian; literary; mainstream; mystery/suspense; psychic/supernatural; romance (contemporary, gothic, historical); thriller/espionage; westerns/frontier; young adult. Query with SASE. "We will not accept any unsolicited material." Reports in 2 weeks on queries.
Recent Sales: *The Gettin' Place*, by Susan Straight (Hyperion); *The Working Parents Handbook*, by Ellen Melinkoff, June Sale and Kit Kollenberg (Simon & Schuster).
Terms: Agent receives 15% commission on domestic sales; 20% on foreign sales. Charges for photocopying or any unusual expense incurred at the writer's request.
Tips: Obtains new clients through recommendations and referrals.

KATHI J. PATON LITERARY AGENCY (II), 19 W. 55th St., New York NY 10019-4907. (212)265-6586. Fax: call first. Contact: Kathi Paton. Estab. 1987. Specializes in adult nonfiction. Currently handles: 65% nonfiction books; 35% fiction.
Handles: Nonfiction, novels, short story collections. Considers these nonfiction areas: business; sociology; psychology; women's issues/women's studies; how-to. Considers literary and mainstream fiction; short stories. For nonfiction, send proposal, sample chapter and SASE. For fiction, send first 40 pages and plot summary or 3 short stories.
Recent Sales: *Total Customer Service*, by Bro Uttal (HarperCollins); *The Myth of the Bad Mother*, by Jane Swigart (Doubleday); *White Trash, Red Velvet*, by Donald Secreast (HarperCollins).
Terms: Agent receives 15% commission on domestic sales; 20% on foreign sales. Offers written contract. Charges for photocopying.
Writer's Conferences: Attends International Womens Writing Guild panels and the Pacific Northwest Writers Conference.
Tips: Usually obtains new clients through recommendations from other clients. "Write well."

RODNEY PELTER (II), 129 E. 61st St., New York NY 10021. (212)838-3432. Contact: Rodney Pelter. Estab. 1978. Represents 10-12 clients. Currently handles: 25% nonfiction books; 75% novels.
Handles: Nonfiction books, novels. Considers all nonfiction areas. Considers most fiction areas. No juvenile, romance, science fiction. For nonfiction, query with SASE. For fiction, send outline, first 50-75 pages and SASE. Reports in 1-3 months.
Terms: Agent receives 15% commission on domestic sales; 20% on foreign sales. Offers written contract. Charges for foreign postage, photocopying.
Tips: Usually obtains new clients through recommendations from others.

L. PERKINS ASSOCIATES (IV), 5800 Arlington Ave., Riverdale NY 10471. (718)543-5354. Fax: (718)543-5354. Contact: Lori Perkins, Peter Rubie. Estab. 1990. Member of AAR, HWA. Represents 100 clients. 15% of clients are new/previously unpublished writers. Perkins specializes in horror, dark thrillers, literary fiction, pop culture, Latino and gay issues (fiction and nonfiction). Rubie specializes in science fiction, fantasy, mysteries, history, fiction thrillers, journalistic nonfiction. Currently handles: 60% nonfiction books; 40% novels.
   • See Lori Perkins' article, *How to Find (and Keep) the Right Agent*, in the 1994 edition of the *Guide*.
Handles: Nonfiction books, novels. Considers these nonfiction areas: art/architecture/design; current affairs; ethnic/cultural interests; music/dance/theater/film; "subjects that fall under pop culture—TV, music, art, books and authors, film, current affairs etc." Considers these fiction areas: adventure; detective/police/crime; ethnic; horror; literary; mainstream; mystery/suspense;

psychic/supernatural; thriller. Query with SASE. Reports immediately on queries "with SASE"; 6-10 weeks on mss.

Recent Sales: *A Darker Shade of Crimson: Memoirs of a Harvard-Chicano* (Bantam); *Burning Down the House*, by Merry McInerny (Tor).

Terms: Agent receives 15% commission on domestic sales; 20% on foreign sales. Offers written contract, only "if requested." Charges for photocopying.

Writer's Conferences: Attends Horror Writers of America Conference; World Fantasy Conference; Necon and Lunacon; Southwest Writers Conference; MidAtlantic Writers Conference; ABA; Cape Cod Writers Conference.

Tips: Obtains new clients through recommendations from others, solicitation, at conferences, etc. "Sometimes I come up with book ideas and find authors (*Coupon Queen*, for example). Be professional. Read *Publishers Weekly* and genre-related magazines. Join writers' organizations. Go to conferences. Know your market."

ALISON J. PICARD LITERARY AGENT (II), P.O. Box 2000, Cotuit MA 02635-2000. Contact: Alison Picard. Assistant: Janet Burke. Estab. 1985. Represents 60 clients. 25% of clients are new/previously unpublished writers. "Most interested in nonfiction at this time, especially self-help/recovery, pop psychology, how-to, business and current affairs." Currently handles: 40% nonfiction books; 30% juvenile books; 30% novels.

Handles: General trade nonfiction. Considers these nonfiction areas: animals; anthropology/ archaeology; art/architecture/design; biography/autobiography; business; child guidance/parenting; computers/electronics; cooking/food/nutrition; crafts/hobbies; current affairs; education; ethnic/cultural interests; gay/lesbian issues; government/politics/law; health/medicine; history; how-to; humor; interior design/decorating; juvenile nonfiction; language/literature/criticism; military/war; money/finance/economics; music/dance/theater/film; nature/environment; New Age/metaphysics; photography; popular culture; psychology; religious/inspirational; science/ technology; self-help/personal improvement; sociology; sports; translations; true crime/investigative; women's issues/women's studies. Considers these fiction areas: action/adventure; cartoon/ comic; contemporary issues; detective/police/crime; erotica; ethnic; family saga; feminist; gay; glitz; historical; horror; humor/satire; juvenile; lesbian; mainstream; mystery/suspense; picture book; psychic/supernatural; religious/inspirational; romance (contemporary, gothic, historical, regency); sports; thriller/espionage; westerns/frontier; young adult. Query with SASE. Send written query first. No phone/fax queries. Reports in 1 week on queries; 1 month on mss.

Recent Sales: *Unsafe Keeping*, by Carol Cail (St. Martin's Press); *The Best of Enemies*, by Osha Davidson (Scribner).

Terms: Agent receives 15% commission on domestic sales; 15% on foreign sales.

Writer's Conferences: Attends Cape Cod Writer's Conference.

Tips: Obtains new clients through recommendations.

‡POCONO LITERARY AGENCY (II), RR5, Box 5543, Saylorsburg PA 18353. (610)381-2643. Contact: Carolyn Hopwood Blick. Estab. 1993. Represents 5 clients. 80% of clients are new/previously unpublished writers. Specializes in young adult/juvenile novels and romance (all categories). Currently handles: 50% juvenile books; 50% novels.

Handles: Nonfiction books, juvenile books, novels, poetry books (for children). Considers these nonfiction areas: education, history, how-to, interior design/decorating, juvenile nonfiction, sports. Considers these fiction areas: action/adventure; family saga; historical; horror; juvenile; picture book; romance (contemporary, gothic, historical, regency); science fiction; sports; thriller/espionage; westerns/frontier; young adult. Query with 1 page synopsis. Reports in 2 weeks on queries; 1 month on mss.

Terms: Agent receives 15% commission on domestic sales; 20% on foreign sales. Offers written contract, binding for 6 months. Charges for photocopying, postage, long-distance telephone, UPS, and all other reasonable expenses.

Tips: Obtains clients through recommendations from others and direct submissions from authors. "I spent ten years teaching elementary school students prior to beginning my agency, so I know what types of books children like best."

‡THE POTOMAC LITERARY AGENCY, (II), 19062 Mills Choice Rd., Suite 5, Gaithersburg MD 20879. (301)208-0674. Fax: (301)869-7513. Contact: Thomas F. Epley. Estab. 1993. Represents 11 clients. 60% of clients are new/previously unpublished writers. Currently handles: 80% novels;

To find an agent located near you, check the Geographic Index.

20% nonfiction. Currently handling novels—mostly literary fiction, but will consider commercial fiction, novellas, and general nonfiction.

Handles: Nonfiction books, novels, novellas. Considers these nonfiction areas: biography/autobiography; business; current affairs; education; ethnic/cultural interests; gay/lesbian issues; history; language/literature/criticism; military/war; money/finance/economics; nature/environment; psychology; science/technology; self-help/personal improvement; sports; true crime/investigative. Considers these fiction areas: action/adventure; contemporary issues; detective/police/crime; ethnic; experimental; family saga; feminist; gay; historical; humor/satire; lesbian; literary; mainstream; sports; thriller/espionage; westerns/frontier. Query with outline and brief synopsis (no more than 1 page) and SASE. Reports in 2 weeks on queries; 6 weeks on mss.

Recent Sales: *Walking West*, by Noelle Sickels (St. Martin's Press); *The Rickover Effect*, by T. Rockwell (John Wiley & Sons).

Terms: Agents receive 15% commission on domestic sales; 20% on foreign sales (if co-agent used). Offers written contract.

Tips: Obtains new clients through referrals.

AARON M. PRIEST LITERARY AGENCY (II), 708 Third Ave., 23rd Floor, New York NY 10017. (212)818-0344. Contact: Aaron Priest or Molly Friedrich. Member of AAR. Currently handles: 25% nonfiction books; 75% fiction. Member agents: Lisa Erbach Vance, Sheri Holman.

Handles: Nonfiction books, fiction. Query only (must be accompanied by SASE). Unsolicited mss will be returned unread.

Recent Sales: *The Juror*, by George Green, Robert James Waller; *Waiting to Exhale*, by Terry McMillan; *A Thousand Acres*, by Jane Smiley; *Day After Tomorrow*, by Allan Folsom.

Terms: Agent receives 15% commission on domestic sales. Charges for photocopying, foreign postage expenses.

‡PRINTED TREE INC., (II), 2357 Trail Dr., Evansville IN 47711. (812)476-9015. Fax: (812)476-9015 (*51). Contact: Jo Frohbieter-Mueller. Estab. 1990. Represents 45 clients. 60% of clients are new/previously unpublished writers. Currently handles: 30% nonfiction books; 20% scholarly books; 30% novels; 20% textbooks. Member agents: Janet McCormick (novels, juvenile books).

Handles: Nonfiction books, scholarly books, textbooks, juvenile books, novels. Considers these nonfiction areas: business; child guidance/parenting; cooking/food/nutrition; crafts/hobbies; education; how-to; juvenile nonfiction; military/war; religious/inspirational; self-help/personal improvement; women's issues/women's studies. Considers these fiction areas: action/adventure; contemporary issues; family saga; horror; juvenile; mainstream; religious/inspirational; science fiction; thriller/espionage; young adult. Query. Reports in 2 weeks on queries; 2 months on mss.

Terms: Agent receives 15% commission on domestic sales; 20% on foreign sales. Offers written contract. Charges $50 upon acceptance for marketing expenses; taken from commission when book sold.

Writers' Conferences: "I speak at libraries throughout the country on the subject of 'getting into print.' This is an ongoing commitment—I lecture at approximately 50-75 libraries each year. I'm always amazed at the crowds that gather to learn about this subject."

Tips: Obtains new clients from lectures, listing in references. "Write a good query letter that includes 1) target readers of proposed book, 2) brief synopsis of proposed book, 3) explain how it differs from others on market, 4) your qualification for writing book."

SUSAN ANN PROTTER LITERARY AGENT (II), 110 W. 40th St., Suite 1408, New York NY 10018. (212)840-0480. Contact: Susan Protter. Estab. 1971. Member of AAR. Represents 50 clients. 10% of clients are new/unpublished writers. Writer must have book-length project or ms that is ready to be sold. Works with a very small number of new/unpublished authors. Currently handles: 40% nonfiction books; 60% novels; occasional magazine or short story (for established clients only).

Handles: Nonfiction books, novels. Considers these nonfiction areas: general nonfiction; biography; child guidance/parenting; health; medicine; psychology; science. Considers these fiction areas: detective/police/crime; historical; mystery; science fiction, thrillers. Send short query with brief description of project/novel. Please include publishing history. "Must include SASE." Reports in 2-3 weeks on queries; 2 months on solicited mss. "Please do not call; mail queries only."

Recent Sales: *Freeware*, by Rudy Rucker (Morrow/Avonova); *Dr. Nightingale* and *Alice Nestleton* (mystery series), by Lydia Adamson (Signet); *Northern Stars*, by David G. Hartwell and Glenn Grent (TOR); *20 Teachable Virtues*, by Barbara C. Unell and Jerry L. Wyckoff, PhD (Perigee Berkley); *Am I Crazy for Feeling So Bad?*, by Kathleen McCoy, PhD, and Charles Wibbelsmen, MD.

Terms: Agent receives 15% commission on domestic sales; 15% on TV, film and dramatic sales; 25% on foreign sales. Charges for long distance, photocopying, messenger, express mail, airmail expenses.

Tips: "Please send neat and professionally organized queries. Make sure to include an SASE or we cannot reply. We receive up to 100 queries a week and read them in the order they arrive. We usually reply within two weeks to any query. Do not call. If you are sending a multiple query, make sure to note that in your letter."

ROBERTA PRYOR, INC. (II), 24 W. 55th St., New York NY 10019. (212)245-0420. President: Roberta Pryor. Estab. 1985. Member of AAR. Represents 50 clients. Prefers to work with published/established authors; works with a small number of new/unpublished writers. Specializes in serious nonfiction and (tends toward) literary fiction. Special interest in natural history, good cookbooks. Currently handles: 50% nonfiction books; 30% novels; 10% textbooks; 10% juvenile books.
Handles: Nonfiction books, novels, textbooks, juvenile books. Considers these nonfiction areas: animals; anthropology/archaeology; art/architecture/design; biography/autobiography; cooking/food; current affairs; ethnic/cultural interests; gay/lesbian issues; government/politics/law; history; interior design/decorating; juvenile nonfiction; literature/criticism; military/war; nature/environment; photography; popular culture; sociology; theater/film; true crime/investigative; women's issues/women's studies. Considers these fiction areas: contemporary issues; detective/police/crime; historical; juvenile; literary; mainstream; mystery/suspense; picture book; young adult. Query. SASE required for any correspondence. Reports in 10 weeks on queries.
Recent Sales: *A Nation of Salesmen*, by Earl Sherris (W.W. Norton, also *Harper's* Magazine); *The Phalanx Dragon*, by Timothy Rizzi (Donald I. Fine, techno-thriller); *The Dangerous Lives of Altar Boys*, by Chris Fuhrman (University of Georgia Press); *Literary Biography of Paul Bowles*, by Virginia Spencer Carr (Scribner); *Decision of Dissent: With Halsey at Leyte Gulf*, by Carl Solberg (Naval Institute Press).
Terms: Charges 15% commission on domestic sales; 10% on film sales; 20% on foreign sales. Charges for photocopying, express mail service sometimes.
Writer's Conferences: Attends Antioch Writers Conference.

‡PUBLISHING SERVICES (I), 525 E. 86th St., New York NY 10028. (212)535-6248. Fax: (212)988-1073. Contact: Amy Goldberger. Estab. 1993. Represents 20 clients. 50% of clients are new/previously unpublished writers. Currently handles: 75% nonfiction books; 25% novels.
Handles: Nonfiction books, novels. Considers these nonfiction areas: biography/autobiography; child guidance/parenting; cooking/food/nutrition; education; ethnic/cultural interests; health/medicine; New Age/metaphysics; popular culture; self-help/personal improvement; women's issues/women's studies. Considers these fiction areas: contemporary issues; ethnic; feminist; historical; literary; mainstream. Query with SASE. Reports in 2 weeks on queries.
Terms: Agent receives 15% commission on domestic sales; 20% on foreign sales. Offers written contract. Charges for photocopying, postage, long distance calls.
Tips: Obtains new clients from queries and referrals. Query first and always include a SASE.

QUICKSILVER BOOKS-LITERARY AGENTS (II), 50 Wilson St., Hartsdale NY 10530. (914)946-8748. Contact: Bob Silverstein. Estab. 1973 as packager; 1987 as literary agency. Represents 50+ clients. 50% of clients are new/previously unpublished writers. Specializes in literary and commercial mainstream fiction and nonfiction (especially psychology, New Age, holistic healing, consciousness, ecology, environment, spirituality). Currently handles: 75% nonfiction books; 25% novels.
Handles: Nonfiction books, novels. Considers these nonfiction areas: anthropology/archaeology; biography; business; child guidance/parenting; cooking/food/nutrition; current affairs; ethnic/cultural interests; health/medicine; history; how-to; literature; nature/environment; New Age/metaphysics; popular culture; psychology; inspirational; science/technology; self-help/personal improvement; sociology; sports; true crime/investigative; women's issues/women's studies. Considers these fiction areas: action/adventure; glitz; mystery/suspense. Query, "always include SASE." Reports in up to 2 weeks on queries; up to 1 month on mss.
Recent Sales: *Sound Mind/Sound Body*, by James Brooks, M.D. and Jack Forem (Simon & Schuster); *Bears at Work*, by Gage Taylor (Chronicle Books); *Headaches and How to Relieve Them*, by Susan Lang and Lawrence Robbins, M.D. (Houghton Mifflin).
Terms: Agent receives 15% commission on domestic sales; 20% on foreign sales. Offers written contract, "only if requested. It is open ended, unless author requests time frame." Charges for postage. Authors are expected to supply SASE for return of mss and for query letter responses.
Writer's Conferences: Attends National Writers Union Conference.
Tips: Obtains new clients through recommendations, listings in sourcebooks, solicitations, workshop participation.

CHARLOTTE CECIL RAYMOND, LITERARY AGENT (III), 32 Bradlee Rd., Marblehead MA 01945. Contact: Charlotte Cecil Raymond. Estab. 1983. Represents 30 clients. 20% of clients

are new/previously unpublished writers. Currently handles: 70% nonfiction books; 10% juvenile books; 20% novels.
Handles: Nonfiction books, juvenile books, novels. Considers these nonfiction areas: biography; current affairs; ethnic/cultural interests; gay/lesbian issues; history; juvenile nonfiction; nature/environment; politics; psychology; sociology; translations; women's issues/women's studies. No self-help/personal improvement. Considers these fiction areas: contemporary issues; ethnic; feminist; gay; lesbian; literary; mainstream; regional; young adult. Query with outline/proposal. Reports in 2 weeks on queries; 6 weeks on mss.
Terms: Agent receives 15% commission on domestic sales. 100% of business derived from commissions on ms sales.

HELEN REES LITERARY AGENCY (II, III), 308 Commonwealth Ave., Boston MA 02116. (617)262-2401. Fax: (617)262-2401. Contact: Joan Mazmanian. Estab. 1981. Member of AAR. Represents 50 clients. 50% of clients are new/previously unpublished writers. Specializes in general nonfiction, health, business, world politics, autobiographies, psychology, women's issues. Currently handles: 60% nonfiction books; 30% novels; 10% syndicated material.
Handles: Nonfiction books, novels. Considers these nonfiction areas: biography/autobiography; business; current affairs; ethnic/cultural interests; government/politics/law; health/medicine; history; money/finance/economics; New Age/metaphysics; self-help/personal improvement; sociology; true crime/investigative; women's issues/women's studies. Considers these fiction areas: action/adventure; contemporary issues; detective/police/crime; family saga; feminist; glitz; historical; humor/satire; literary; mainstream; mystery/suspense; thriller/espionage. Query with outline plus 2 sample chapters. Reports in 1 week on queries; 3 weeks on mss.
Recent Sales: *Reengineering the Corporation*, by Hammer and Champy (Harper Business).
Terms: Agent receives 15% commission on domestic sales; 20% on foreign sales.
Tips: Obtains new clients through recommendations from others, solicitation, at conferences, etc.

RENAISSANCE: A LITERARY/TALENT AGENCY (III), 152 N. La Peer Dr., Los Angeles CA 90048-3011. (310)246-6000. Fax: (310)246-1633. Contact: Joel Gotler. Member of SAG, AFTRA, DGA; signatory of WGA. Represents 50 clients. Specializes in selling movies and TV rights from books. Member agents: Irv Schwartz, partner (TV writers); Allan Nevins, partner (book publishing); Brian Lipson, associate (motion picture writers).
  ● This agency recently acquired H.N. Swanson, recognized as the first Hollywood literary agency. Mr. Gotler started his agenting career under H.N. Swanson. The new company will be called Renaissance—H.N. Swanson.
Handles: Nonfiction books, novels. Considers these nonfiction areas: biography/autobiography; history; film; true crime/investigative. Considers these fiction areas: action/adventure; contemporary issue; detective/police/crime; ethnic; family saga; fantasy; historical; humor/satire; literary; mainstream; mystery/suspense; science fiction; thriller/espionage. Query with outline and SASE. Reports in 1 month on queries.
Recent Sales: *Black Eagle*, by Larry Collins (Dutton); *Last Tango in Brooklyn*, by Kirk Douglas (Warner Books); *The Deaths of Sybil Bolton*, by Dennis McAuliffe Jr. (Patchett Kaufman Entertainment).
Terms: Agent receives 15% commission on domestic books; 10% on film sales.
Tips: Obtains news clients through recommendations from others.

RIVERSIDE LITERARY AGENCY (III), Keets Brook Rd., Leyden MA 01337. (413)772-0840. Fax: (413)772-0969. Contact: Susan Lee Cohen. Estab. 1991. Represents 55 clients. 20% of clients are new/previously unpublished writers. Currently handles: 65% nonfiction books; 30% novels; 5% short story collections.
Handles: Nonfiction books, novels.
Tips: Only accepts new clients through referrals.

THE ROBBINS OFFICE, INC. (II), 405 Park Ave., New York NY 10022. (212)223-0720. Fax: (212)223-2535. Contact: Kathy P. Robbins, Elizabeth Mackey. Specializes in selling mainstream nonfiction, commercial and literary fiction.
Handles: Nonfiction books, novels, magazine articles for book writers under contract. Does not read unsolicited mss.
Terms: Agent receives 15% commission on all domestic, dramatic and foreign sales. Bills back specific expenses incurred in doing business for a client.

ROCK LITERARY AGENCY (II), P.O. Box 625, Newport RI 02840. (401)849-4442. Fax: (401)849-4442. Contact: Andrew T. Rock. Estab. 1988. Represents 46 clients. Currently handles: 75% nonfiction books; 25% fiction; packages some projects.

Handles: Fiction (literary and mainstream); nonfiction (literary); body/mind/spirit (consciousness); Middle East; business (general and professional); reference (general and professional). Query with SASE. Reports in 10 days on queries.
Terms: Agent receives 15% commission on domestic sales; 20% on foreign sales. Offers written contract. Charges for photocopying, postage, fax, phone and packages.
Tips: Usually obtains new clients through recommendations from editors and other clients or "I go out and get people to write books I want to represent."

ROSE LITERARY AGENCY (II), 215 Park Ave. S., Suite 1403, New York NY 10003. (212)353-9600. Fax: (212)353-9757. Contact: Mitchell Rose. Estab. 1986. Represents 60 clients. 25% of clients are new/previously unpublished writers. "We have a broad list, but do have a few areas in which we specialize: film, exposé, history, politics, psychology, nutrition and innovative literary fiction." Currently handles: 80% nonfiction books; 15% novels; 5% short story collections.
Handles: Nonfiction books, novels, short story collections. Considers these nonfiction areas: anthropology/archaeology; art/architecture/design; biography/autobiography; business; child guidance/parenting; cooking/food/nutrition; current affairs; ethnic/cultural interests; gay/lesbian issues; government/politics/law; health/medicine; history; language/literature/criticism; military/war; money/finance/economics; music/dance/theater/film; nature/environment; psychology; science/technology; self-help/personal improvement; sociology; sports; women's issues/women's studies. Considers these fiction areas: contemporary issues; ethnic; feminist; gay; humor/satire; literary; thriller/espionage. Query. Reports in 2 weeks on queries; 1 month on mss.
Recent Sales: *Lawrence of Arabia*, by Morris and Raskin (Doubleday); *Kennedy as President*, by Gerald Strober (HarperCollins); *Healing Through Nutrition*, by Melvyn Werbach (HarperCollins); *Consumer's Guide to Today's Health Care*, by Stephen Isaacs and Ava Swartz (Houghton Mifflin); *Love Awaits*, by Courtney Lang (Bantam).
Terms: Agent receives 15% commission on domestic sales; 20% on foreign sales. Offers written contract. "For projects and authors that show promise, we offer extensive editorial feedback at no charge. Critiques are written by myself and staff project developers." Charges fees "but only for very high volume photocopying. Any expense would be approved by the client before it is incurred."
Tips: Obtains new clients mostly through recommendations of existing clients and from editors. "We have taken on several clients whose initial contacts were through query letters."

JEAN ROSENTHAL LITERARY AGENCY (V), 28 E. 11th St., New York NY 10003. Agency not currently seeking new clients.

JANE ROTROSEN AGENCY (II), 318 E. 51st St., New York NY 10022. (212)593-4330. Estab. 1974. Member of AAR. Represents 100 clients. Works with published and unpublished writers. Specializes in trade fiction and nonfiction. Currently handles: 40% nonfiction books, 60% novels.
Handles: Adult fiction, nonfiction. Query with short outline. Reports in 2 weeks.
Recent Sales: *River of Sky* and *O Christmas Tree*, by Karen Harper (Dutton); *Night Sins*, by Tami Hoag (Bantam).
Terms: Receives 15% commission on domestic sales; 15% on dramatic sales; 20% on foreign sales. Charges writers for photocopying, long-distance/transoceanic telephone, telegraph, Telex, messenger service and foreign postage.

PESHA RUBINSTEIN LITERARY AGENCY, INC. (II), 37 Overlook Terrace, #1D, New York NY 10033-2216. (212)781-7845. Contact: Pesha Rubinstein. Estab. 1990. Member of AAR, RWA, MWA, SCBWI. Represents 35 clients. 25% of clients are new/previously unpublished writers. Specializes in women's fiction and romance, and children's books. Currently handles: 20% juvenile books; 80% novels.
Handles: Genre fiction, juvenile books, picture book illustration. Considers these nonfiction areas: child guidance/parenting; juvenile nonfiction; nature/environment. Considers these fiction areas: detective/police/crime; ethnic; glitz; historical; horror; juvenile; mainstream; mystery/suspense; picture book; psychic/supernatural; romance (contemporary, historical). "No science fiction or poetry." Send query plus first 10 pages and SASE. Reports in 2 weeks on queries; 6 weeks on requested mss.
Recent Sales: *Surrender to a Stranger*, by Karyn Monk (Bantam); *With One Look*, by Jennifer Horsman (Avon).
Terms: Agent receives 15% commission on domestic sales; 20% on foreign sales. Offers written contract. Charges for photocopying. No collect calls accepted.
Writer's Conferences: Romantic Times (Fort Worth, TX).
Tips: "Keep the query letter and synopsis short. Please send first ten pages of manuscript rather than selected chapters from the manuscript. The work speaks for itself better than any descrip-

tion can. Never send originals. A phone call after one month is acceptable. Always include a SASE covering return of the entire package with the material."

RUSSELL-SIMENAUER LITERARY AGENCY INC. (II), P.O. Box 43267, Upper Montclair NJ 07043-2501. (201)746-0539, (201)992-4198. Fax: (201)746-0754. Contact: Jacqueline Simenauer or Margaret Russell. Estab. 1990. Member of Authors Guild, Authors League, NASW. Represents 45-50 clients. 60% of clients are new/previously unpublished writers. Subject matter most interested in agenting: self-help books, especially those by psychiatrists and psychologists. Currently handles: 90% nonfiction books; 8% novels; 1% movie scripts; 2% TV scripts. Member agents: Jacqueline Simenauer, Margaret Russell.

Handles: Nonfiction books, novels. Considers these nonfiction areas: animals; biography/autobiography; business; child guidance/parenting; cooking/food/nutrition; current affairs; education; gay/lesbian issues; health/medicine; history; how-to; humor; language/literature/criticism; money/finance; music/dance/theater/film; nature/environment; New Age/metaphysics; popular culture; psychology; religious/inspirational; self-help/personal improvement; sociology; sports; true crime/investigative; women's issues/women's studies. Considers these fiction areas: contemporary issues; detective/police/crime; family saga; feminist; gay; glitz; historical; humor/satire; lesbian; literary; mainstream; mystery/suspense; psychic/supernatural; romance (contemporary); science fiction; thriller/espionage. Query with outline/proposal. Reports in 3-4 weeks on queries; 4-6 weeks on mss.

Recent Sales: *The Secret Language of Your Body*, by Martin Rush, M.D. (Simon & Schuster); *Why Did It Happen*, by Janice Cohn, Ph.D. (William Morrow); *Dream Girls*, by Anthony Pietropinto, M.D. (Bob Adams); *365 Wealth-Building Tips*, by Stephanie Gallagher (AMACOM); *Power Thoughts*, by Daniel Araoz, Ph.D. (Bob Adams).

Also Handles: Movie scripts (feature films), TV scripts (MOW, episodic drama, documentary). Considers these script subjects: Considers these script subject areas: action/adventure; contemporary issues; detective/police/crime; family saga; feminist; gay; glitz; lesbian; mainstream; mystery/suspense; psychic/supernatura; romance; thriller.

Recent Sales: *Eight Years of Silence*, by Harvey Rosenstock M.D. (David Simons Productions).

Terms: Agent receives 15% commission on domestic sales; 25% on foreign sales. "There are no reading fees." Charges for postage, photocopying, phone, fax. 100% of business is derived from commissions on ms sales.

Tips: Obtains new clients through recommendations from others; advertising in various journals, newsletters, publications, etc. and professional conferences.

‡VICTORIA SANDERS LITERARY AGENCY (II), 241 Avenue of the Americas, New York NY 10014. (212)633-8811. Fax: (212)633-0525. Contact: Victoria Sanders and/or Diane Dickensheid. Estab. 1993. Member of AAR, signatory of WGA. Represents 25 clients. 50% of clients are new/previously unpublished writers. Currently handles: 50% nonfiction books; 30% novels; 10% movie scripts; 10% short story.

Handles: Nonfiction, novels. Considers these nonfiction areas: biography/autobiography; current affairs; ethnic/cultural interests; gay/lesbian issues; govenment/politics/law; history; humor; language/literature/criticism; music/dance/theater/film; popular culture; psychology; translations; women's issues/women's studies. Considers these fiction areas: action/adventure; contemporary issues; family saga; feminist; gay; lesbian; literary; thriller/espionage. Query and SASE. Reports in 1 week on queries; 1 month on mss.

Recent Sales: *Sisters and Lovers*, by Connie Briscoe (HarperCollins—book; CBS/Citadel Entertainment—TV mini series); *The Intersection of Law and Desire*, by J.M. Redmann (Norton); *Skinflicks*, by Dave Blander (Zebra).

Terms: Agent receives 15% commission on domestic sales; 20% on foreign sales. Offers written contract binding at will. Charges for photocopy, messenger, express mail and extraordinary fees. If in excess of $100, client approval is required.

Tips: Obtains new clients through recommendations, "or I find them through my reading and pursue. Limit query to letter, no calls and give it your best shot. A good query is going to get good responses."

For explanation of symbols, see the Key to Symbols and Abbreviations. For translation of an organization's acronym, see the Table of Acronyms. For unfamiliar words, check the Glossary.

SANDUM & ASSOCIATES (II), 144 E. 84th St., New York NY 10028-2035. (212)737-2011. Fax number on request. Managing Director: Howard E. Sandum. Estab. 1987. Represents 35 clients. 20% of clients are new/unpublished writers. Specializes in general nonfiction—all categories of adult books; commercial and literary fiction. Currently handles: 60% nonfiction books; 40% novels.
Handles: Nonfiction books, novels. Query with proposal, sample pages. Do not send full ms unless requested. Include SASE. Reports in 2 weeks on queries.
Terms: Agent receives 15% commission. Agent fee adjustable on dramatic and foreign sales. Charges writers for photocopying, air express, long-distance telephone/fax.

‡BLANCHE SCHLESSINGER AGENCY (III, V), 433 Old Gulph Rd., Penn Valley PA 19072. (610)664-5513. Fax: (610)664-5959. Contact: Blanche Schlessinger. Estab. 1984. Particular interests: mysteries, true crime, cookbooks.
Handles: Nonfiction books, novels. Considers these nonfiction areas: biography/autobiography; cooking/food/nutrition; health/medicine; how-to; self-help/personal improvement; true crime/investigative. Considers these fiction areas: detective/police/crime; glitz; mainstream; mystery; thriller/espionage. No children's, horror or science fiction. Send outline and 2 sample chapters. Reports in 10 days on queries; 4-6 weeks on mss. SASE essential.
Recent Sales: *Pennsylvania Dutch Country Cooking*, by William Woys Weaver (Abbeville); *Cruel April*, by Neil Albert (Dutton); *The Seventh Sacrament*, by James Bradberry (St. Martin's).
Terms: Agent receives 15% commission on domestic sales; 20% on foreign sales. Offers written contract. Charges for office expenses (long distance telephone, UPS charges, copying and bound galleys).
Tips: Obtains new clients primarily through recommendations from others.

HAROLD SCHMIDT LITERARY AGENCY (II), 343 W. 12th St., #1B, New York NY 10014. (212)727-7473. Fax: (212)807-6025. Contact: Harold Schmidt. Estab. 1983. Member of AAR. Represents 30 clients. 20% of clients are new/previously unpublished writers. Currently handles: 45% nonfiction books; 5% scholarly books; 50% novels.
Handles: Nonfiction books, scholarly books, novels, short story collections. Considers these nonfiction areas: anthropology/archaeology; art/architecture/design; biography/autobiography; business; current affairs; ethnic/cultural interests; gay/lesbian issues; government/politics/law; health/medicine; history; language/literature/criticism; military/war; money/finance/economics; music/dance/theater/film; nature/environment; New Age/metaphysics; psychology; science/technology; self-help/personal improvement; sociology; translations; true crime/investigative; women's issues/women's studies. Considers these fiction areas: action/adventure; contemporary issues; detective/police/crime; ethnic; family saga; feminist; gay; glitz; historical; horror; lesbian; literary; mainstream; mystery/suspense; psychic/supernatural; science fiction; thriller/espionage; westerns/frontier. Query before sending any material. Endeavors to report 2 weeks on queries; 4-6 weeks on mss.
Recent Sales: *The Gifts of the Body*, by Rebecca Brown (HarperCollins); *The Other World*, by John Wynne (City Lights Books); *Growing Your Own Business*, by Gregory and Patricia Kishel (Putnam's).
Terms: Agent receives 15% commission on domestic sales; 20% commission on foreign sales. Offers written contract "on occasion—time frame always subject to consultation with author." Charges for "photocopying, long distance telephone calls and faxes, ms submission postage costs."
Tips: Obtains new clients through recommendations from others and solicitation. "I cannot stress enough how important it is for the new writer to present a clear, concise and professionally presented query letter. And, please, NEVER send material until requested."

SUSAN SCHULMAN, A LITERARY AGENCY (III), 454 W. 44th St., New York NY 10036-5205. (212)713-1633/4/5. Fax: (212)586-8830. President: Susan Schulman. Estab. 1979. Member of AAR, Dramatists Guild, Women's Media Group, signatory of WGA. 10-15% of clients are new/unpublished writers. Prefers to work with published/established authors; works with a small number of new/unpublished authors. Currently handles: 70% nonfiction books; 20% novels; 10% stage plays. Member agents: Jake Holder (submissions); Holly Frederick (foreign rights).
Handles: Nonfiction, fiction, plays, emphasizing contemporary women's fiction and nonfiction books of interest to women. Considers these nonfiction areas: anthropology/archaeology; biography/autobiography; business; child guidance/parenting; current affairs; education; ethnic/cultural interests; gay/lesbian issues; government/politics/law; health/medicine; history; how-to; juvenile nonfiction; military/war; money/finance/economics; music/dance/theater/film; nature/environment; New Age/metaphysics; popular culture; psychology; religious/inspirational; self-help/personal improvement; sociology; translations; true crime/investigative; women's issues/women's studies. Considers these fiction areas: contemporary issues; detective/police/crime; his-

torical; lesbian; literary; mainstream; mystery/suspense; young adult. Query with outline. Reports in 2 weeks on queries; 6 weeks on mss. SASE required.

Recent Sales: *The Psychic Pathway*, by Sonia Choquette (Crown Publishing); *The Vein of Gold*, by Julia Cameron.

Also Handles: Movie rights, stage plays.

Recent Sales: *The English Patient*, by Michael Ondaate (Saul Zaentz); *Voodoo Dreams*, by Jewell Parker Rhodes (Steve Tisch Co.); *Evelyn & the Polka King*, by John Olive (Amblin Entertainment).

Terms: Agent receives 15% commission on domestic sales; 10-20% on dramatic sales; 7½-10% on foreign sales (plus 7½-10% to co-agent). Charges for special messenger or copying services, foreign mail and any other service requested by client.

LAURENS R. SCHWARTZ AGENCY (II), 5 E. 22nd St., Suite 15D, New York NY 10010-5315. (212)228-2614. Contact: Laurens R. Schwartz. Estab. 1984. Represents 100 clients. "General mix of nonfiction and fiction. Also handles movie and TV tie-ins, all licensing and merchandising. Works world-wide. *Very* selective about taking on new clients. Only takes on 2-3 new clients per year."

Handles: Does not read unsolicited mss. Reports in 1 month.

Terms: Agent receives 15% commission on domestic sales; up to 25% on foreign sales. "No fees except for photocopying, and that fee is avoided by an author providing necessary copies or, in certain instances, transferring files on diskette—must be IBM compatible." Where necessary to bring a project into publishable form, editorial work and some rewriting provided as part of service. Works with authors on long-term career goals and promotion.

Tips: "Do not like receiving mass mailings sent to all agents. Be selective—do your homework. Do not send *everything* you have ever written. Choose *one* work and promote that. *Always* include an SASE. *Never* send your only copy. *Always* include a background sheet on yourself and a *one*-page synopsis of the work (too many summaries end up being as long as the work)."

LYNN SELIGMAN, LITERARY AGENT (II), 400 Highland Ave., Upper Montclair NJ 07043. (201)783-3631. Contact: Lynn Seligman. Estab. 1985. Member of Women's Media Group. Represents 32 clients. 15% of clients are new/previously unpublished writers. Currently handles: 75% nonfiction books; 15% novels; 10% photography books.

Handles: Nonfiction books, novels, photography books. Considers these nonfiction areas: anthropology/archaeology; art/architecture/design; biography/autobiography; business; child guidance/parenting; cooking/food/nutrition; current affairs; education, ethnic/cultural interests; government/politics/law; health/medicine; history; how-to; humor; interior design/decorating; language/literature/criticism; money/finance/economics; music/dance/theater/film; nature/environment; photography; popular culture; psychology; science/technology; self-help/personal improvement; sociology; translations; true crime/investigative; women's issues/women's studies. Considers these fiction areas: contemporary issues; detective/police/crime; ethnic; fantasy; feminist; gay; historical; horror; humor/satire; lesbian; literary; mainstream; mystery/suspense; romance (contemporary, gothic, historical, regency); science fiction. Query with letter or outline/proposal plus 1 sample chapter and SASE. Reports in 2 weeks on queries; 1-2 months on mss.

Recent Sales: *Big Fat Legs*, by Dr. Glenn Gaesser (Ballentine); *Lost and Found: A Girl's Journey Through Eighth Grade*, by Roberta Israeloff (Simon & Schuster).

Terms: Agent receives 15% commission on domestic sales; 25% on foreign sales. Charges for photocopying, unusual postage or telephone expenses (checking first with the author), express mail.

Writer's Conferences: Attends Dorothy Canfield Fisher Conference.

Tips: Obtains new clients usually from other writers or from editors.

THE SEYMOUR AGENCY (II, IV), 7 Rensselaer Ave., Heuvelton NY 13654. Phone/fax: (315)344-7223. Contact: Mike Seymour/Mary Sue Seymour. Estab. 1992. Member of RWA, New York State Outdoor Writers, OWAA. 50% of clients are new/previously unpublished writers. Specializes in women's fiction and romance. Member agents: Mary Sue Seymour (fiction); Mike Seymour (nonfiction).

Handles: Considers these nonfiction areas: art/architecture/design; juvenile nonfiction; religious/inspirational. Considers these fiction areas: action/adventure; detective/police/crime; ethnic; glitz; historical; horror; humor/satire; mainstream; mystery/suspense; religious/inspirational; romance (contemporary, gothic, historical, medieval, regency); westerns/frontier. Accepts a few young adult horror or humor or upbeat romance or adventure. Will read well thought out nonfiction proposals, and any good fiction in any genre. Query with first chapter and synopsis. No certified mail, please. Reports in 2 weeks on queries; 1 month on mss.

Recent Sales: *Warrior Bride, Virgin Bride* and 2 untitled, all by Tamara Leigh (Bantam); *Under the Greenwood Tree* (Harlequin); *The Bought Bride* (Chartin Pub.); *Beyond Forever*, by Lee Ann Dansby (Lion Hearted Pub.).
Terms: Agent receives 15% commission on domestic sales; 15% on foreign sales. Offers written contract, binding for 1 year. Offers criticism service for prospective clients only. Postage fee refundable when/if ms sells. 99% of business derived from commissions on ms sales.
Tips: "Send query, synopsis and first chapter. If you don't hear from us, you didn't send SASE. Our critique service is only for works we plan on representing. We are looking for romance— women in jeopardy, suspense, contemporary, historical, some regency and any well written women's fiction. Both agents are New York state certified teachers who have taught writing and are published authors."

CHARLOTTE SHEEDY LITERARY AGENCY, INC. (II), 611 Broadway, Suite 428, New York NY 10012. Prefers not to share information.

THE SHEPARD AGENCY (II), Pawling Savings Bank Bldg., Suite 3, Southeast Plaza, Brewster NY 10509. (914)279-2900 or (914)279-3236. Fax: (914)279-3239. Contact: Jean or Lance Shepard. Specializes in "some fiction; nonfiction: business, biography, homemaking; inspirational; self-help." Currently handles: 75% nonfiction books; 5% juvenile books; 20% novels.
Handles: Nonfiction books, scholarly books, novels. Considers these nonfiction areas: agriculture; horticulture; animals; biography/autobiography; business; child guidance/parenting; computers/electronics; cooking/food/nutrition; crafts/hobbies; current affairs; government/politics/law; health/medicine; history; interior design/decorating; juvenile nonfiction; language/literature/criticism; money/finance/economics; music/dance/theater/film; nature/environment; psychology; religious/inspirational; self-help/personal improvement; sociology; sports; women's issues/women's studies. Considers these fiction areas: contemporary issues; family saga; historical; humor/satire; literary; regional; sports; thriller/espionage. Query with outline, sample chapters and SASE. Reports in 1 month on queries; 2 months on mss.
Recent Sales: *Crane's Wedding Blue Book*, by Steven Feinberg (Simon & Schuster).
Terms: Agent receives 15% on domestic sales. Offers written contract. Charges for extraordinary postage, photocopying and long-distance phone calls.
Tips: Obtains new clients through referrals and listings in various directories for writers and publishers. "Provide info on those publishers who have already been contacted, seen work, accepted or rejected same. Provide complete bio and marketing info."

BOBBE SIEGEL LITERARY AGENCY (II), 41 W. 83rd St., New York NY 10024-5246. (212)877-4985. Fax: (212)877-4985. Contact: Bobbe Siegel. Estab. 1975. Member of West Side Agents Group. Represents 60 clients. 30% of clients are new/previously unpublished writers. Currently handles: 65% nonfiction books; 35% novels.
Handles: Nonfiction books, novels. Considers these nonfiction areas: archaeology; biography/autobiography; child guidance/parenting; current affairs; nutrition; ethnic; health/medicine; history; juvenile nonfiction; literature; music/dance/theater/film; nature/environment; psychology; self-help/personal improvement; sports; true crime/investigative; women's issues. Considers these fiction areas: action/adventure; contemporary issues; detective/police/crime; ethnic; family saga; fantasy; feminist; glitz; historical; horror; literary; mainstream; mystery/suspense; psychic/supernatural; romance (historical); thriller/espionage. Query. Reports in 2 weeks on queries; 2 months on mss.
Recent Sales: *The Music Club Mystery*, by Graham Landrum (St. Martin's); *The Storytellers*, by Curt Smith (Macmillan); *Beginning the Divorce Wars*, by Ronald Sharp (Kensington).
Terms: Agent receives 15% on domestic sales; 20% on foreign sales. Offers written contract. Charges for photocopying; long-distance or overseas telephone calls or fax messages; airmail postage, both foreign and domestic.
Writer's Conferences: Vermont Writer's Conference (Burlington).
Tips: Obtains new clients through "word of mouth; editors' and authors' recommendations; through conferences and from people who see my name in publications. Write clear and neat letters of inquiry; always remember to include SASE. Never use dot matrix. In your letter never tell the agent why your book is great. Letters should be spaced and paragraphed so they are easy to read and should not be more than two pages."

SIERRA LITERARY AGENCY (II), P.O. Box 1090, Janesville CA 96114-1090. (916)253-3250. Contact: Mary Barr. Estab. 1988. Specializes in contemporary women's novels, mainstream fiction and nonfiction, self-help, self-esteem books.
Handles: Fiction, nonfiction books, novels. Considers these nonfiction areas: gay/lesbian issues; government/politics/law; how-to; nature/environment; self-help/personal improvement; wom-

en's issues/women's studies. Considers these fiction areas: action/adventure; detective/police/crime; feminist; mainstream. Query with outline or entire ms. Reports in 2 weeks on queries; 6 weeks on mss.
Recent Sales: *Open and Shut Case*, by Gary Roberts (Ocelot Press).
Terms: Agent receives 10% commission on domestic sales; 15% on dramatic sales; 20% on foreign sales. Charges writers for photocopying, phone and overseas postage.
Writer's Conferences: Surrey Writers' Conference (Surrey, British Columbia, Canada).

EVELYN SINGER LITERARY AGENCY INC. (III), P.O. Box 594, White Plains NY 10602-0594. Contact: Evelyn Singer. Estab. 1951. Represents 30 clients. 25% of clients are new/previously unpublished writers. Specializes in nonfiction (adult/juvenile, adult suspense).
Handles: Nonfiction books, juvenile books, novels. Considers these nonfiction areas: anthropology/archaeology; biography; business; child guidance; computers/electronics; current affairs; ethnic/cultural interests; government/politics/law; health/medicine; how-to; juvenile nonfiction; money/finance/economics; nature/environment; psychology; religious/inspirational; science; self-help/personal improvement; women's issues/women's studies. Considers these fiction areas: contemporary issues; detective/police/crime; ethnic; feminist; historical; literary; mainstream; mystery/suspense; regional; thriller/espionage. Query. Reports in 2 weeks on queries; 6-8 weeks on mss. "SASE must be enclosed for reply or return of manuscript."
Recent Sales: *Delanna*, series by Nancy Smith (Avon); *Legacy of Vengeance*, by John Armistead (Carroll & Graf).
Terms: Agent receives 15% commission on domestic sales; 20% on foreign sales. Offers written contract, binding for 3 years. Charges for long-distance phone calls, overseas postage ("authorized expenses only").
Tips: Obtains new clients through recommendations. "I am accepting writers who have earned at least $20,000 from freelance writing. SASE must accompany all queries and material for reply and or return of ms." Enclose biographical material and double-spaced book outline or chapter outline.

VALERIE SMITH, LITERARY AGENT (III), 1746 Rt. 44/55, Modena NY 12548-5205. (914)883-5848. Contact: Valerie Smith. Estab. 1978. Represents 30 clients. 1% of clients are new/previously unpublished writers. Specializes in science fiction and fantasy. Currently handles: 2% nonfiction books; 96% novels; 1% novellas; 1% short story collections.
Handles: Novels. Considers these fiction areas: fantasy; literary; mainstream; science fiction; young adult. Query. Reports in 2 weeks on queries; 2 months on mss.
Recent Sales: *Syrtis*, by Alexander Jablokov (Morrow); *Two Hundred Years Later*, by Steven Brust (Tor Books).
Terms: Agent receives 15% commission on domestic sales; 20% on foreign sales. Offers written contract. Charges for "extraordinary expenses by mutual consent."
Tips: Obtains new clients through recommendations from other clients, various respected contacts.

MICHAEL SNELL LITERARY AGENCY (II), P.O. Box 1206, Truro MA 02666-1206. (508)349-3718. Contact: Michael Snell. Estab. 1980. Represents 200 clients. 25% of clients are new/previously unpublished authors. Specializes in how-to, self-help and all types of business and computer books, from low-level how-to to professional and reference. Currently handles: 90% nonfiction books, 10% novels. Member agents: Michael Snell (nonfiction); Patricia Smith (fiction and children's books).
Handles: Nonfiction books. Open to all nonfiction categories, especially health, law, medicine, psychology, science, women's issues. Query with SASE. Reports in 1 week on queries; 2 weeks on mss.
Recent Sales: *Women Inventors*, by Autumn Stanley (Doubleday/Currency); *Multipreneuring*, by Tom Gorman (Simon & Schuster); *The 20% Solution*, by John Cotler (Oliver Wight); *The MBA Advantage*, by Ron Yeaple (Bob Adams).
Terms: Agent receives 15% on domestic sales; 15% on foreign sales.
Tips: Obtains new clients through unsolicited mss, word-of-mouth, *LMP* and *Guide to Literary Agents*. "Send a half- to a full-page query, with SASE. Brochure 'How to Write a Book Proposal' available on request and SASE."

ELYSE SOMMER, INC. (II), P.O. Box 1133, Forest Hills NY 11375. (718)263-2668. President: Elyse Sommer. Estab. 1952. Member of AAR. Represents 20 clients. Works with a small number of new/unpublished authors. Specializes in nonfiction: reference books, dictionaries, popular culture. Currently handles: 90% nonfiction books; 5% novels; 5% juvenile.
Handles: Nonfiction books, novels (some mystery but no science fiction), juvenile (no preschool). Query with outline. Reports in 2 weeks on queries.

Terms: Agent receives 15% commission on domestic sales (when advance is under 5,000, 10% over); 5% on dramatic sales; 20% on foreign sales. Charges for photocopying, long distance, express mail, extraordinary expenses.

F. JOSEPH SPIELER (V), 154 W. 57th St., 13th Floor, Room 135, New York NY 10019. (212)757-4439. Fax: (212)333-2019. Contact: Joe Spieler, Lisa Ross or John Thornton. Estab. 1981. Represents 47 clients. 2% of clients are new/previously unpublished writers. Member agents: John Thornton (nonfiction; Lisa M. Ross (fiction/nonfiction); Ginger Wade (fiction).
Handles: Nonfiction books, novels. Considers these nonfiction areas: biography/autobiography; business; child guidance/parenting; cooking/food/nutrition; current affairs; ethnic/cultural interests; gay/lesbian issues; government/politics/law; history; money/finance/economics; sociology; women's issues/women's studies. Considers these fiction areas: ethnic; family saga; feminist; gay; humor/satire; lesbian; literary; mainstream. Query. Reports in 1-2 weeks on queries; 3-5 weeks on mss.
Recent Sales: *The Fifth Discipline Fieldbook*, by Bryan Smith/Peter Senye (Doubleday); *Blindside*, by Eamonn Fingeleton (Houghton Mifflin).
Terms: Agent receives 15% commission on domestic sales. Charges for long distance phone/fax, photocopying, postage.
Tips: Obtains new clients through recommendations and *Literary Marketplace* listing.

GRETCHEN SPIELER LITERARY AGENCY (V), 4732 California St., San Francisco CA 94118-1129. (415)668-8162. Contact: Gretchen Spieler. Estab. 1993. Represents 5 clients. 50% of clients are new/previously unpublished writers. Specializes in cookbooks, crafts and hobbies, literature, child-guidance/parenting, self-help/psychology. Currently handles: 50% nonfiction books; 50% novels.
• This agency is not accepting new clients at this time.
Handles: Nonfiction books, novels. Considers these nonfiction areas: specialities in: art/architecture/design; child guidance/parenting; cooking/food/nutrition; crafts/hobbies; history; interior design/decorating; literature; psychology; self-help/personal improvement; women's issues/women's studies. Considers literary fiction. Query with outline/proposal or outline plus 2-3 sample chapters. Reports in 6-8 weeks on queries; 2-3 months on mss. Please send query before sending ms.
Terms: Agent receives 15% commission on domestic sales; 20% on foreign sales. Offers written contract, cancellable with notice. Charges for postage, photocopying, fax services, "any other fees that are necessary, always with author's consent."
Writer's Conferences: ABA.
Tips: Obtains new clients through recommendations from others, word of mouth, writing groups. "Please send queries first. Make sure manuscript or proposal is typed and cleanly photocopied. Always send a SASE."

PHILIP G. SPITZER LITERARY AGENCY (III), 50 Talmage Farm Lane, East Hampton NY 11937. (516)329-3650. Fax: (516)329-3651. Contact: Philip Spitzer. Estab. 1969. Member of AAR. Represents 60 clients. 10% of clients are new/previously unpublished writers. Specializes in mystery/suspense, literary fiction, sports, general nonfiction (no how-to). Currently handles: 50% nonfiction books; 50% novels.
Handles: Nonfiction books, novels. Considers these nonfiction areas: biography/autobiography; business; current affairs; ethnic/cultural interests; government/politics/law; health/medicine; history; language/literature/criticism; military/war; music/dance/theater/film; nature/environment; psychology; popular culture; sociology; sports; true crime/investigative. Considers these fiction areas: contemporary issues; detective/police/crime; literary; mainstream; mystery/suspense; sports; thriller/espionage. Send outline plus 1 sample chapter and SASE. Reports in 1 week on queries; 6 weeks on mss.
Recent Sales: *Dixie City Jam*, by James Lee Burke (Hyperion); *The Concrete Blonde*, by Michael Connelly (Little, Brown).
Terms: Agent receives 15% commission on domestic sales; 20% on foreign sales. Charges for photocopying.
Writer's Conferences: ABA (Chicago).
Tips: Usually obtains new clients on referral.

NANCY STAUFFER ASSOCIATES (II, III), 171 Newbury St., Boston MA 02116-2839. (617)247-0356. Contact: Nancy Stauffer Cahoon. Estab. 1989. Member of PEN Center USA West. 10% of clients are new/previously unpublished writers. Currently handles: 50% nonfiction books; 50% fiction.
Handles: Nonfiction books, novels, novellas, short story collections. Considers these nonfiction areas: animals; biography/autobiography; business; current affairs; ethnic/cultural interests; na-

ture/environment; popular culture; self-help/personal improvement; sociology; translations. Considers these fiction areas: contemporary issues; literary; mainstream; regional. No unsolicited queries.

Recent Sales: *Nemesis*, by Arthur Hailey (Crown Publishers); *Skins*, by Adrian C. Louis (Orion Books).

Terms: Agent receives 15% commission on domestic sales; 20% on foreign sales. Charges for messenger and express delivery; photocopying."

Writer's Conferences: "I teach a seminar at the UCLA Extension Writers' Program titled 'Getting Published: A One Day Tour Through the World of New York Publishing,' and participate in writers conferences around the country." Writers At Work (Park City, Utah).

Tips: Obtains new clients primarily through referrals from existing clients.

LYLE STEELE & CO., LTD. (II), 511 E. 73rd St., Suite 6, New York NY 10021. (212)288-2981. Contact: Lyle Steele. Estab. 1985. Signatory of WGA. Represents 125 clients. 20% of clients are new/previously unpublished writers. "In nonfiction we are particularly interested in current events, unique personal stories, biography and autobiography, popular business, true crime, health, parenting, personal growth and psychological self-help. In fiction we are interested in good mysteries not of the hard-boiled type, horror and occult of all types, thrillers and historical novels. We are also open to quality fiction." Currently handles: 70% nonfiction books; 30% novels. Member agents: Jim Kepler (Chicago, nonfiction).

Handles: Nonfiction books, novels. Considers these nonfiction areas: anthropology/archaeology; biography/autobiography; business; child guidance/parenting; cooking/food/nutrition; current affairs; ethnic/cultural interests; gay/lesbian issues; government/politics/law; health/medicine; history; money/finance/economics; nature/environment; New Age/metaphysics; psychology; science/technology; self-help/personal improvement; sociology; sports; true crime/investigative. Considers these fiction areas: detective/police/crime; family saga; gay; historical; horror; lesbian; literary; mystery/suspense; psychic/supernatural; thriller/espionage; horror. Send outline plus 2 sample chapters. Reports in 10 days on queries; 2 weeks on mss.

Recent Sales: *How to License Your Million Dollar Idea*, by Harvey Reese (Wiley); *The House of Real Love*, by Carla Tomaso (NAL/Dutton).

Terms: Agent receives 15% commission on domestic sales. Offers written contract, binding for 1 year.

Tips: Obtains new clients through recommendations and solicitations. "Our goal is to represent books that provide readers with solid information they can use to improve and change their personal and professional lives. In addition, we take the long view of an author's career. A successful writing career is built step by step, and our goal is to provide the long-term professional management required to achieve it. Be prepared to send your material quickly once an agent has responded. Frequently, we'll have room to take on only a few new clients and a slow response may mean the openings will be filled by the time your material arrives."

STEPPING STONE (IV), 59 W. 71st St., New York NY 10023. (212)362-9277. Fax: (212)362-1998. Contact: Sarah Jane Freymann. Member of AAR. Represents 75 clients. 20% of clients are new/previously unpublished writers. Currently handles: 75% nonfiction books; 2% juvenile books; 23% novels.

Handles: Nonfiction books, novels, lifestyle-illustrated. Considers these nonfiction areas: animals; anthropology/archaeology; art/architecture/design; biography/autobiography; business; child guidance/parenting; cooking/food/nutrition; current affairs; ethnic/cultural interests; gay/lesbian issues; government/politics/law; health/medicine; history; interior design/decorating; nature/environment; New Age/metaphysics; psychology; religious/inspirational; self-help/personal improvement; true crime/investigative; women's issues/women's studies. Considers these fiction areas: contemporary issues; ethnic; literary; mainstream; mystery/suspense; thriller/espionage. Query. Reports in 2 weeks on queries; 6 weeks on mss.

Recent Sales: *From Aging to Saging*, by Zalman Schchter Shalomi and Ron Miller (Warner); *Spell of the Tiger*, by Sy Montgomery (Houghton Mifflin).

Terms: Agent receives 15% commission on domestic sales; 20% on foreign sales. Offers written contract. Offers criticism service. Charges for long distance, overseas postage, photocopying. 99% of business is derived from commissions on ms sales; 1% is derived from criticism services. Payment of a criticism fee does not ensure representation.

Tips: Obtains new clients through recommendations from others. "I love fresh new passionate works by authors who love what they are doing and have both natural talent and carefully honed skill."

GLORIA STERN LITERARY AGENCY (II,III,IV), 2929 Buffalo Speedway, Houston TX 77098-1707. (713)963-8360. Fax: (713)963-8460. Contact: Gloria Stern. Estab. 1976. Member of AAR. Represents 35 clients. 20% of clients are new/previously unpublished writers. Specializes in history, biography, women's studies, child guidance, parenting, business, cookbooks, health, cooking, finance, sociology, true crime. Currently handles: 80% nonfiction books; 5% scholarly books; 15% novels.

• This agency is not affiliated with the Gloria Stern Agency located in California.

Handles: Nonfiction books, scholarly books, novels. Considers these nonfiction areas: anthropology/archaeology; art/architecture/design; biography; business; child guidance/parenting; cooking/food/nutrition; current affairs; ethnic/cultural interests; government/politics/law; health/medicine; history; how-to; language/literature/criticism; money/finance/economics; psychology; science/technology; self-help/personal improvement; sociology; sports; true crime/investigative; women's issues/women's studies. Considers these fiction areas: contemporary issues; detective/police/crime; ethnic; experimental; family saga; feminist; literary; mainstream; mystery/suspense; thriller/espionage. Query with outline plus 2 sample chapters and SASE. Reports in 1 week on queries; 1 month on mss.

Recent Sales: *Stefan in Love*, by Joseph Machlis (WW Norton); *Breaking the Science Barrier*, by Sheila Tobias and Carl Tomizoka (College Board); *Big Noise from Winnetka*, by Jeanne N. Clark (biography of Harold Ikes).

Terms: Agent receives 15% commission on domestic sales; 20% on foreign sales (shared). Offers written contract, binding for 60 days.

Tips: Obtain new clients through editors, previous clients, listings. "I prefer fiction authors that have some published work such as short stories in either commercial or literary magazines or come recommended by an editor or writer. I need a short outline of less than a page, one-two chapters and SASE. For nonfiction, I need credentials, an outline, competitive books, one-two chapters and SASE. No unsolicited mss."

H.N. SWANSON INC. (III), 8523 Sunset Blvd., Los Angeles CA 90069. President: Thomas J. Shanks. Estab. 1934. Contact: Anna Courtney. Signatory of WGA. Represents over 100 clients. 10% of clients are new/previously unpublished writers. Currently handles: 60% novels; 40% movie and TV scripts. Member agents: Steven Fisher, Gail Barrick, Jim Anderson, Larry Kennar.

• See the expanded listing for this agency in Script Agents.

‡TCA (III), (formerly The Chalfant Agency), 111 W. 57th St., New York NY 10019. Contact: David Chalfant. Estab. 1991. Represents 40 clients. No new/previously unpublished writers. Specializes in general nonfiction. Currently handles: 95% nonfiction books; 5% novels.

Handles: Nonfiction books. Considers these nonfiction areas: biography/autobiography; business; cooking/food/nutrition; current affairs; history; money/finance/economics; true crime/investigative; women's issues/women's studies.

Terms: Agent receives 15% commission on domestic sales; 20% on foreign sales. No written contract.

Tips: Obtains new clients through solicitation by the agent, referrals from existing clients.

PATRICIA TEAL LITERARY AGENCY (III), 2036 Vista Del Rosa, Fullerton CA 92631. (714)738-8333. Contact: Patricia Teal. Estab. 1978. Member of AAR, RWA, Authors Guild. Represents 60 clients. Published authors only. Specializes in category fiction and commercial, how-to and self-help nonfiction. Currently handles: 10% nonfiction books, 90% novels.

Handles: Nonfiction books, novels. Considers these nonfiction areas: animals; biography/autobiography; child guidance/parenting; health/medicine; how-to; psychology; self-help/personal improvement; true crime/investigative; women's issues. Considers these fiction areas: glitz, mainstream, mystery/suspense, romance (contemporary, historical, regency). Query. Reports in 10 days on queries; 6 weeks on requested mss.

Recent Sales: *After All*, by Jill Marie Landis (Berkeley/Jove); *Guilty By Choice, Justice*, by Patricia D. Benke (Avon).

Terms: Agent receives 10-15% commission on domestic sales; 20% on foreign sales. Offers written contract, binding for 1 year. Charges for postage, photocopying.

Writer's Conferences: Attends several Romance Writers of America conferences, Asilomar (California Writers Club); Bouchercon; Emerald City (Seattle).

Tips: Usually obtains new clients through recommendations from authors and editors or at conferences. "Include SASE with all correspondence."

2M COMMUNICATIONS LTD. (II), 121 W. 27 St., #601, New York NY 10001. (212)741-1509. Fax: (212)691-4460. Contact: Madeleine Morel. Estab. 1982. Represents 40 clients. 20% of clients are new/previously unpublished writers. Specializes in adult nonfiction. Currently handles: 100% nonfiction books.

Handles: Nonfiction books. Considers these nonfiction areas: biography/autobiography; child guidance/parenting; ethnic/cultural interests; gay/lesbian issues; health/medicine; music/dance/

theater/film; self-help/personal improvement; women's issues/women's studies. Query. Reports in 1 week on queries, weeks on outlines.

Recent Sales: *Michael Jordan*, by M. Krupel (St. Martin's Press); *Breast Cancer Prevention*, by Epstein and Steinman (Macmillan); *Emergency Baby Care Book*, by Salmans/Phillips (Avon).

Terms: Agent receives 15% commission on domestic sales; 20% on foreign sales. Offers written contract, binding for 2 years. Charges for postage, photocopying, long distance calls and faxes.

Tips: Obtains new clients through recommendations from others, solicitation.

*SUSAN P. URSTADT INC. WRITERS AND ARTISTS AGENCY (II), P.O. Box 1676, New Canaan CT 06840-4208. (203)966-6111. Contact: Susan P. Urstadt. Estab. 1975. Member of AAR. Represents 45 clients. 10% of clients are new/previously unpublished authors. Specializes in history, biography, current affairs and journalism, natural history and environment, illustrated books, popular reference, art, antiques, decorative arts, gardening, travel, horses, armchair cookbooks, business, self-help, crafts, hobbies, collectibles. Currently handles: 95% nonfiction books.

Handles: Nonfiction books and select quality commercial literary fiction. Considers these non-fiction areas: agriculture/horticulture; animals; anthropology/archaeology; art/architecture/design; biography/autobiography; business; child guidance/parenting; cooking/food/nutrition; crafts/hobbies; current affairs; education; ethnic/cultural interests; health/medicine; history; how-to; interior design/decorating; juvenile nonfiction; military/war; money/finance/economics; music/dance/theater/film; nature/environment; photography; popular culture; self-help/personal improvement; sports; women's issues/women's studies. "No unsolicited fiction please." Send outline plus 2 sample chapters, short author bio and SASE. Reports in 3 weeks on queries.

Recent Sales: *Biography of Eric Sevareid*, by Ray Schroth (Steerforth Press); *Gardening on a Budget*, by Maureen Gilmer (Viking/Penguin).

Terms: Agent receives 15% commission on domestic sales; 20% on foreign sales. Offers written contract.

Writer's Conferences: ABA (Chicago).

Tips: Obtains new clients through recommendations from others. "We are interested in building a writer's career through the long term and only want dedicated writers with special knowledge, which they share in a professional way."

VAN DER LEUN & ASSOCIATES (II), 22 Division St., Easton CT 06612. (203)259-4897. Contact: Patricia Van der Leun. Estab. 1984. Represents 30 clients. Specializes in fiction, science, biography. Currently handles: 60% nonfiction books; 40% novels.

Handles: Nonfiction books, novels. Considers all nonfiction areas. Considers these fiction areas: art/architecture/design; contemporary issues; ethnic; history; literary; mainstream. Query. Reports in 2 weeks on queries; 1 month on mss.

Recent Sales: *Wherever You Go, There You Are*, by John Kabat-Zinn (Hyperion); *The Object Stares Back*, by James Elkins (Simon & Schuster).

Terms: Agent receives 15% on domestic sales; 25% on foreign sales. Offers written contract.

Tips: "We are interested in high-quality, serious writers only."

MARY JACK WALD ASSOCIATES, INC. (III), 111 E. 14th St., New York NY 10003. (212)254-7842. Contact: Danis Sher. Estab. 1985. Member of Authors Guild, SCBWI. Represents 55 clients. 10% of clients are new/previously unpublished writers. Specializes in literary works, juvenile. Currently handles: adult and juvenile fiction and nonfiction, including some original film/TV scripts. Member agents: Danis Sher, Lem Lloyd. Foreign rights representative: Lynne Rabinoff, Lynne Rabinoff Associates.

Handles: Nonfiction books, juvenile books, novels, novellas, short story collections, movie scripts, TV scripts. Considers these nonfiction areas: biography/autobiography; current affairs; ethnic/cultural interests; history; juvenile nonfiction; language/literature/criticism; military/war; music/dance/theater/film; nature/environment; photography; sociology; sports; translations; true crime/investigative. Considers these fiction areas: action/adventure; contemporary issues; detective/police/crime; ethnic; experimental; family saga; fantasy; feminist; gay; glitz; historical; humor/satire; juvenile; literary; mainstream; mystery/suspense; picture book; thriller; young adult. Query. Reports in 1 month on queries; 2 months on mss.

Recent Sales: *The Dictionary of Rap, Hip Hop and Slang*, by I.E. Mozeson and Lois Stavsky (The Berkley Publishing Group); two (2-book) John Peel (Pocket Books).

Terms: Agent receives 15% commission on domestic sales; 15-30% on foreign sales. Offers written contract, binding for 1 year.

ALWAYS include a self-addressed, stamped envelope (SASE) for reply or return of your manuscript.

Tips: Obtains new clients through recommendations from others. "Send a query letter with brief description and credits, if any. If we are interested, we'll request 50 pages. If that interests us, we'll request entire manuscript, which should be double-spaced. SASE should be enclosed."

WALLACE LITERARY AGENCY, INC. (III), 177 E. 70 St., New York NY 10021. (212)570-9090. Contact: Lois Wallace, Thomas C. Wallace. Estab. 1988. Member of AAR. Represents 125 clients. 5% of clients are new/previously unpublished writers. Specializes in fiction and nonfiction by good writers. Currently handles: 60% nonfiction books, 35% novels, 5% magazine articles and short stories. "We handle poetry, movie scripts, juveniles and stage plays ONLY if written by clients who write trade books."
Handles: Nonfiction books, novels. Considers these nonfiction areas: anthropology/archaeology, biography/autobiography, current affairs, history, literature, military/war, science; true crime/investigative. Considers these fiction areas: literary, mainstream, mystery/suspense. Send outline plus 1-2 sample chapters, reviews of previously published books, curriculum vitae, return postage. Reports in 2 weeks on queries; 3 weeks on mss.
Terms: Agent receives 10-15% commission on domestic sales; 20% on foreign sales. Offers written contract; binding until terminated with notice. Charges for photocopying, book shipping (or ms shipping) overseas, legal fees (if needed, with writer's approval), galleys and books needed for representation and foreign sales.
Tips: Obtains new clients through "recommendations from editors and writers we respect."

JOHN A. WARE LITERARY AGENCY (II), 392 Central Park West, New York NY 10025-5801. (212)866-4733. Fax: (212)866-4734. Contact: John Ware. Estab. 1978. Represents 60 clients. 40% of clients are new/previously unpublished writers. Currently handles: 75% nonfiction books; 25% novels.
Handles: Nonfiction books, novels. Considers these nonfiction areas: agriculture/horticulture; animals; anthropology; biography/autobiography (memoirs); business; child guidance/parenting; current affairs; ethnic/cultural interests; gay/lesbian issues; government/politics/law; health/medicine; history (including oral history, Americana and folklore); investigative journalism; language/literature/criticism; military/war; music/dance/theater/film; nature/environment; popular culture; psychology and health (academic credentials required); science; sports; true crime/investigative; women's issues/women's studies; 'bird's eye' views of phenomena. Considers these fiction areas: accessible literate noncategory fiction; contemporary issues; detective/police/crime; ethnic; literary; mystery/suspense; sports; thriller/espionage. Query by mail first, include SASE. Reports in 2 weeks on queries.
Recent Sales: *Redneck Heaven*, by Bethany Bultman (Bantam); *Denmark Vesey: A Biography*, by David Robertson (Alfred A. Knopf); *Let's Put the Future Behind Us: A Novel*, by Jack Womack (Grove/Atlantic).
Terms: Agent receives 15% commission on domestic sales; 15% on dramatic sales; 20% on foreign sales. Charges for messenger service, photocopying, extraordinary expenses.
Writer's Conferences: Austin Writers' Conference (Austin, TX); Southern Connecticut Writer's Conference (Greenwich, CT).
Tips: "Writers must have appropriate credentials for authorship of proposal (nonfiction) or manuscript (fiction); no publishing track record required. Open to good writing and interesting ideas by new or veteran writers."

HARRIET WASSERMAN LITERARY AGENCY (III), 137 E. 36th St., New York NY 10016. (212)689-3257. Contact: Harriet Wasserman. Member of AAR. Specializes in fiction and nonfiction, some young adult and children's.
Handles: Nonfiction books, novels. Considers "mostly quality fiction (novels)." Referrals only. No unsolicited material.
Terms: Information not provided.

WATERSIDE PRODUCTIONS, INC. (II), 2191 San Elijo Ave., Cardiff-by-the-Sea CA 92007. (619)632-9190. Fax: (619)632-9295. E-mail: CompuServe 75720,410. President: Bill Gladstone. Contact: Matt Wagner, Margot Maley. Estab. 1982. Represents 300 clients. 20% of clients are new/previously unpublished writers. Currently handles: 100% nonfiction. Member agents: Bill Gladstone (trade computer titles, business); Margot Maley (women's issues, serious nonfiction, trade computer titles); Matthew Wagner (trade computer titles, nonfiction); Carole McClendon (trade computer titles).
Handles: Nonfiction books. Considers these nonfiction areas: anthropology/archaeology; art/architecture/design; biography/autobiography; business; child guidance/parenting; computers/electronics; ethnic/cultural interests; health/medicine; money/finance/economics; music/dance/theater/film; nature/environment; New Age/metaphysics; psychology; sociology; sports; true

crime/investigative; women's issues/women's studies. Query with outline/proposal. Reports in 2 weeks on queries; 6-8 weeks on mss.
Recent Sales: *The Internet Business Book*, by Jill Ellsworth (Wiley).
Terms: Agent receives 15% commission on domestic sales; 25% on foreign sales. Offers written contract. Charges for photocopying and other unusual expenses.
Writer's Conferences: Waterside Computer Boom Conference (San Diego, CA); MacWorld (San Francisco); Comdex (Las Vegas).
Tips: Usually obtains new clients through recommendations from others. "Be professional. The more professional a submission, the more seriously it's viewed. Beginning writers should go to a writers workshop and learn how a presentation should be made."

WATKINS LOOMIS AGENCY, INC. (II), 133 E. 35th St., Suite 1, New York NY 10016. (212)532-0080. Contact: Andrea Basserman. Estab. 1908. Represents 150 clients. Specializes in literary fiction, London/UK translations. Member agent: Nicole Aragi.
Handles: Nonfiction books, novels. Considers these nonfiction areas: art/architecture/design; biography/autobiography; cooking/food/nutrition; current affairs; ethnic/cultural interests; gay/. lesbian issues; history; nature/environment; popular culture; science/technology; translations; true crime/investigative; women's issues/women's studies; journalism. Considers these fiction areas: contemporary issues; detective/police/crime; ethnic; gay; literary; mainstream; mystery/suspense; young adult. Query with SASE. Reports within 3 weeks on queries.
Recent Sales: *Wilder*, by Nina Bernstein (Pantheon); *If Mama Ain't Happy*, by Helen Prejean (Random House).
Terms: Agent receives 10% commission on domestic sales; 15% on foreign sales.

WECKSLER-INCOMCO (II), 170 West End Ave., New York NY 10023. (212)787-2239. Fax: (212)496-7035. Contact: Sally Wecksler. Estab. 1971. Represents 20 clients. 50% of clients are new/previously unpublished writers. Specializes in nonfiction with illustrations (photos and art). Currently handles: 50% nonfiction books; 15% novels; 35% juvenile books. Member agents: Joann Amparan (general), S. Wecksler (foreign rights/co-editions).
Handles: Nonfiction books, novels, juvenile books. Considers these nonfiction areas: art/architecture design; biography/autobiography; business; current affairs; history; juvenile nonfiction; music/dance/theater/film; nature/environment; photography. Considers these fiction areas: contemporary issues; historical; juvenile; literary; mainstream; picture book. Query with outline plus 3 sample chapters. Reports in 1 month on queries; 2 months on mss.
Recent Sales: *Do's & Taboos — Public Speaking*, by Roger Axtell (Wiley); *Making Good*, by Loren Singer (Holt).
Terms: Agent receives 12-15% commission on domestic sales; 20% on foreign sales. Offers written contract, binding for 3 years.
Tips: Obtains new clients through recommendations from others and solicitations. "Make sure a SASE is enclosed. Send a clearly typed or word processed manuscript, written with punctuation and grammar in approved style."

CHERRY WEINER LITERARY AGENCY (IV,V), 28 Kipling Way, Manalapan NJ 07726. (908)446-2096. Fax: (908)446-20963*. Contact: Cherry Weiner. Estab. 1977. Represents 40 clients. 10% of clients are new/previously unpublished writers. Specializes in science fiction, fantasy, westerns, all the genre romances. Currently handles: 2-3% nonfiction books; 97% novels.
 • This agency is not currently looking for new clients except by referral or by contact at writers' conferences.
Handles: Nonfiction books, novels. Considers self-help/improvement, sociology nonfiction. Considers these fiction areas: action/adventure; contemporary issues; detective/police/crime; family saga; fantasy; glitz; historical; mainstream; mystery/suspense; psychic/supernatural; romance; science fiction; thriller/espionage; westerns/frontier. Query. Reports in 1 week on queries; 6-8 weeks on mss.
Recent Sales: *Maze of Moonlight*, by Gael Baudino (NAL/ROC); *Lady Valient*, by Suzanne Robinson (Bantam/Fanfare).
Terms: Agent receives 15% on domestic sales; 15% on foreign sales. Offers written contract. Charges for extra copies of mss "but would prefer author do it"; 1st class postage for author's copies of books; Express Mail for important document/manuscripts.
Writer's Conferences: Attends Western Writers Convention; Golden Triangle; Fantasy Convention.
Tips: "Meet agents and publishers at conferences. Establish a relationship, then get in touch with them reminding them of meetings and conference."

THE WEINGEL-FIDEL AGENCY (III), 310 E. 46th St., #21E, New York NY 10017. (212)599-2959. Contact: Loretta Fidel. Estab. 1989. Represents 35 clients. 10% of clients are new writers.

Specializes in commercial, literary fiction and nonfiction. Currently handles: 50% nonfiction books; 50% novels.

Handles: Nonfiction books, novels. Considers these nonfiction areas: anthropology/archaeology; art/architecture/design; biography/autobiography; investigative; music/dance/theater/film; psychology; science; sociology; women's issues/women's studies. Considers these fiction areas: contemporary issues; detective/police/crime; literary; mainstream; mystery/suspense. Query with cover letter, résumé and SASE. Previously published or referred writers only. Do not send mss.

Recent Sales: *Too Easy*, by Bruce Deitrick Price (Simon & Schuster).

Terms: Agent receives 15% on domestic sales; 20% on foreign sales. Offers written contract, binding for 1 year automatic renewal. Bills back to clients all reasonable expenses such as UPS, express mail, photocopying, etc.

Tips: Obtains new clients through referrals. "Be forthcoming about prior representation and previous submissions to publishers."

WESTCHESTER LITERARY AGENCY, INC. (II), 4278 D'Este Court, Suite 203, Lake Worth FL 33467. (407)642-2908. Fax: (407)965-4258. Contact: Neil G. McCluskey. Estab. 1991. Represents 55 clients. 30% of clients are new/previously unpublished writers. Specializes in trade mss and proposals from quality writers with an academic or school background. Currently handles: 75% nonfiction books; 3% juvenile books; 22% novels and novellas. Member agents: Medved Jeffers (ML fiction/adventure); Elaine Jacobs (ML fiction/romance); Arthur Rosenfeld (mystery/western).

Handles: Nonfiction books, juvenile books, novels, novellas, short story collections. Considers these nonfiction areas: biography/autobiography; business; child guidance/parenting; current affairs; education; ethnic/cultural interests; gay/lesbian issues; government/politics; health/medicine; history; how-to; humor; juvenile nonfiction; language/literature; nature/environment; popular culture; psychology; religious/inspirational; self-help/personal improvement; sociology; sports; translations; true crime/investigative; women's issues/women's studies. Considers these fiction areas: action/adventure; contemporary/issues; detective/police/crime; family saga; historical; juvenile; lesbian; literary; mainstream; mystery/suspense; regional; religious/inspiration; romance (contemporary, gothic, historical, regency); thriller/espionage; westerns/frontier; young adult. Query with outline/proposal. Reports in 1 month on queries; 6 weeks on mss. "Ordinarily, fiction manuscripts should be submited only after professional editing by a book doctor."

Recent Sales: *Pawnee*, by T. Jensen Lacey (Chelsea House); *Please Don't Let Him Hurt Me Anymore*, by Alexis Asher (Burning Gate).

Terms: Agent receives 15% commission on domestic sales; 20% on foreign sales. Offers written contract, binding for 1 year and renewable. Client pays for all submission costs.

Writer's Conferences: ABA (Chicago).

Tips: Obtains new clients through *LMP*, *Guide to Literary Agents*, stories in WD, recommendations from clients and editors.

RHODA WEYR AGENCY (II, III), 151 Bergen St., Brooklyn NY 11217. (718)522-0480. President: Rhoda A. Weyr. Estab. 1983. Member of AAR. Prefers to work with published/established authors; works with a small number of new/unpublished authors. Specializes in general nonfiction and fiction.

Handles: Nonfiction books, novels. Query with outline, sample chapters and SASE.

Terms: Agent receives 15% commission on domestic sales; 20% on foreign sales.

WIESER & WIESER, INC. (III), 118 E. 25th St., 7th Floor, New York NY 10010-2915. (212)260-0860. Contact: Olga Wieser. Estab. 1975. 30% of clients are new/previously unpublished writers. Specializes in mainstream fiction and nonfiction. Currently handles: 50% nonfiction books; 50% novels. Member agents: Jake Elwell (history, contemporary, sports); George Wieser (contemporary fiction, thrillers, current affairs); Olga Wieser (psychology, fiction, historicals, translations, literary fiction).

Handles: Nonfiction books, novels. Considers these nonfiction areas: business; cooking/food/nutrition; current affairs; health/medicine; history; money/finance/economics; nature/environment; psychology; translations; true crime/investigative. Considers these fiction areas: contemporary issues; detective/police/crime; family saga; historical; literary; mainstream; mystery/suspense; thriller/espionage. Query with outline/proposal. Reports in 1 week on queries.

Recent Sales: *Phoenix Rising*, by John Nance (Crown Publishers, Inc.); *For King and Country*, by Dewey Lambdin (Donald I. Fine, Inc.).

Terms: Agent receives 15% commission on domestic sales; 20% on foreign sales. Offers written contract. Offers criticism service. "No charge to our clients or potential clients." Charges for duplicating of ms and overseas mailing of ms or promotional material.

Writer's Conferences: ABA '95 (Chicago, IL); Frankfurt Book Fair '95 (Frankfurt, Germany).

Tips: Obtains new clients through author's recommendations and industry professionals.

WITHERSPOON & ASSOCIATES, INC. (II), 157 W. 57th St., Suite 700, New York NY 10019. (212)757-0567. Fax: (212)757-2982. Contact: Kimberly Witherspoon. Estab. 1990. Represents 100 clients. 20% of clients are new/previously unpublished writers. Currently handles: 50% nonfiction books; 45% novels; 5% short story collections.
Handles: Nonfiction books, novels. Considers these nonfiction areas: anthropology/archaeology; biography/autobiography; business; current affairs; ethnic/cultural interests; gay/lesbian issues; government/politics/law; health/medicine; history; money/finance/economics; music/dance/theater/film; science/technology; self-help/personal improvement; true crime/investigative; women's issues/women's studies. Considers these fiction areas: contemporary issues; detective/police/crime; ethnic; family saga; feminist; gay; glitz; historical; humor/satire; lesbian; literary; mainstream; mystery/suspense; romance (contemporary); thriller/espionage. Query. Reports in 1-2 weeks on queries; 6-8 weeks on mss.
Terms: Agent receives 15% commission on domestic sales; 20% on foreign sales. Offers written contract.
Writer's Conferences: Attended Recursos de Santa Fe in Santa Fe, NM; Fishtrap in Oregon.
Tips: Obtains new clients through recommendations from others, solicitation and conferences.

GARY S. WOHL LITERARY AGENCY (II,III), One Fifth Ave., New York NY 10003. (212)254-9126. Estab. 1983. 10% of clients are new/previously unpublished writers. Specializes in textbooks, ESL/bilingual books, how-to books and consumer guides.
Handles: Nonfiction books, textbooks. Considers these nonfiction areas: business; cooking/food/nutrition; crafts/hobbies; sports. Query with outline/proposal.
Terms: Agent receives 15% commission on domestic sales; 15% on foreign sales. Offers written contract.

RUTH WRESCHNER, AUTHORS' REPRESENTATIVE (II, III), 10 W. 74th St., New York NY 10023-2403. (212)877-2605. Fax: (212)595-5843. Contact: Ruth Wreschner. Estab. 1981. Represents 80 clients. 70% of clients are new/unpublished writers. "In fiction, if a client is not published yet, I prefer writers who have written for magazines; in nonfiction, a person well qualified in his field is acceptable." Prefers to work with published/established authors; works with new/unpublished authors. "I will always pay attention to a writer referred by another client." Specializes in popular medicine, health, how-to books and fiction (no pornography, screenplays or dramatic plays). Currently handles: 80% nonfiction books; 10% novels; 5% textbooks; 5% juvenile books.
Handles: Nonfiction books, textbooks, adult and young adult fiction, magazine articles (only if appropriate for commercial magazines). Considers these nonfiction areas: biography/autobiography; business; child guidance/parenting; cooking/food/nutrition; crafts/hobbies; current affairs; ethnic/cultural interests; gay/lesbian issues; government/politics/law; health/medicine; history; how-to; juvenile nonfiction; money/finance/economics; popular culture; psychology; religious/inspirational; science/technology; self-help/personal improvement; true crime/investigative; women's issues/women's studies. Considers these fiction areas: action/adventure; contemporary issues; detective/police/crime; ethnic; family saga; gay; glitz; historical; horror; juvenile; lesbian; literary; mainstream; mystery/suspense; romance (contemporary, historical, regency); thriller/espionage; young adult. Particularly interested in literary, mainstream and mystery fiction. Query with outline. Reports in 2 weeks on queries.
Recent Sales: *Making It Big in America: How to Succeed in Business and in Life*, by Andrew Wood (Prima); *Winning with Chronic Pain* and *Winning with Heart Attack*, by Harris McIlwain, M.D. and Debra F. Bruce (Prometheus).
Terms: Agent receives 15% commission on domestic sales; 20% on foreign sales. Charges for photocopying expenses. "Once a book is placed, I will retain some money from the second advance to cover airmail postage of books, long-distance calls, etc. on foreign sales. I may consider charging for reviewing contracts in future. In that case I will charge $50/hour plus long-distance calls, if any."
Writer's Conference: ABA (Chicago, 1995).

ANN WRIGHT REPRESENTATIVES (II), 136 E. 56th St., Suite 9J, New York NY 10022-3619. (212)832-0110. Fax: (212)750-9680. Head of Literary Department: Dan Wright. Estab. 1961. Signatory of WGA. Represents 50 clients. 50% of clients are new/unpublished writers. Prefers to work with published/established authors; works with a small number of new/unpublished authors. "Eager to work with any author with material that we can effectively market in the motion picture business worldwide." Specializes in "book or screenplay with strong motion picture potential." Currently handles: 40% novels; 40% movie scripts; 20% TV scripts.
● See the expanded listing for this agency in Script Agents.

WRITERS HOUSE (III), 21 W. 26th St., New York NY 10010. (212)685-2400. Fax: (212)685-1781. Contact: John Abrahams. Estab. 1974. Member of AAR. Represents 280 clients. 50% of clients

are new/unpublished writers. Specializes in all types of popular fiction, nonfiction as well as the writing for multimedia projects such as "The Seventh Guest." No scholarly, professional, poetry or screenplays. Currently handles: 25% nonfiction books; 35% juvenile books; 40% novels. Member agents: Albert Zuckerman (major novels, thrillers, women's fiction, important nonfiction); Amy Berkower (major juvenile authors, women's fiction, art and decorating, cookbooks, psychology); Merrillee Heifetz (science fiction and fantasy, popular culture, literary fiction); Susan Cohen (juvenile and young adult fiction and nonfiction, Judaism, women's issues); Susan Ginsberg (serious and popular fiction, true crime, narrative nonfiction, personality books, cookbooks); Fran Lebowitz (juvenile and young adult, mysteries, computer-related books, popular culture); Michele Rubin (serious nonfiction); Liza Landsman (multimedia).
- See Liza Landsman's article, *New Media and the Agent*, in this edition of the *Guide*.
Handles: Nonfiction books, juvenile books, novels, proposals for multimedia project. Considers these nonfiction areas: animals; art/architecture/design; biography/autobiography; business; child guidance/parenting; cooking/food/nutrition; health/medicine; history; interior design/decorating; juvenile nonfiction; military/war; money/finance/economics; music/dance/theater/film; nature/environment; psychology; science/technology; self-help/personal improvement; true crime/investigative; women's issues/women's studies. Considers any fiction area. "Quality is everything." Query. Reports in 1 month on queries.
Recent Sales: *Blessing In Disguise*, by Eileen Goudge (Viking).
Terms: Agent receives 15% commission on domestic sales; 20% on foreign sales. Offers written contract, binding for 1 year.
Tips: Obtain new clients through recommendations from others. "Do not send manuscripts. Write a compelling letter. If you do, we'll ask to see your work."

WRITERS' PRODUCTIONS (II), P.O. Box 630, Westport CT 06881-0630. (203)227-8199. Contact: David L. Meth. Estab. 1982. Represents 25 clients. Specializes in literary-quality fiction and nonfiction, with a special interest in Asia. Currently handles: 40% nonfiction books; 60% novels.
Handles: Nonfiction books, novels. "Literary quality fiction." Send outline plus 2-3 sample chapters (30-50 pages). Reports in 1 week on queries; 1 month on mss.
Terms: Agent receives 15% on domestic sales; 25% on foreign sales; 25% on dramatic sales; 25% on new media or multimedia sales. Offers written contract. Charges for electronic transmissions, long-distance calls, express or overnight mail, courier service, etc.
Tips: Obtain new clients through word of mouth. "Send only your best, most professionally prepared work. Do not send it before it is ready. We must have SASE for all correspondence and return of manuscripts. No telephone calls, please."

WRITERS' REPRESENTATIVES, INC. (II), 25 W. 19th St., New York NY 10011-4202. (212)620-9009. Contact: Glen Hartley or Lynn Chu. Estab. 1985. Represents 100 clients. 5% of clients are new/previously unpublished writers. Currently handles: 90% nonfiction books; 10% novels.
- See *How Things Work: Book Auctions*, an interview with Glen Hartley, in this edition of the *Guide*.
Handles: Nonfiction books, novels. Considers literary fiction. "Nonfiction submissions should include book proposal, detailed table of contents and sample chapter(s). For fiction submissions send sample chapters—not synopses. All submissions should include author biography and publication list. SASE required." Does not accept unsolicited mss.
Recent Sales: *How We Die*, by Sherwin Nuland (Alfred A. Knopf); *The Real Anita Hill*, by David Brock (Free Press); *The Divorce Culture*, by Barbara DaFoe Whitehead; *The Western Canon*, by Harold Bloom (Harcourt Brace); *The Moral Sense*, by James Q. Wilson (Free Press).
Terms: Agent receives 15% commission on domestic sales; 20% on foreign sales. "We charge for out-of-house photocopying as well as messengers, courier services (e.g., Federal Express), etc."
Tips: Obtains new clients "mostly on the basis of recommendations from others. Always include a SASE that will ensure a response from the agent and the return of material submitted."

‡KAREN GANTZ ZAHLER LITERARY AGENCY (III), 860 Fifth Ave., New York NY 10021. Contact: Karen Gantz Zahler. Estab. 1990. Represents 40 clients. 40% of clients are new/previously unpublished writers. Specializes in nonfiction, cookbooks. Currently handles: 70% nonfiction books; 20% novels; 10% movie scripts.
Handles: Nonfiction books, novels, movie scripts. Considers all nonfiction and fiction areas; "anything great." Query. Reports in 1-2 months.
Recent Sales: *Medal of Drought*, by Joyce Starr (Henry Holt); *Faxes to God*, by Joyce Starr (HarperCollins); *Food From My Heart*, by Zarela Martinez (Macmillan); *Taste of New York*, by Karen Gantz Zahler (Addison Wesley).
Terms: Agent receives 12-15% commission on domestic sales; 20% commission on foreign sales. Offers written contract, binding for 1 year.

Writer's Conferences: ABA.

Tips: Obtains new clients through recommendations from others. "I'm a literary property lawyer and provide excellent negotiating services and exploitation of subsidiary rights."

SUSAN ZECKENDORF ASSOC. INC. (II), 171 W. 57th St., New York NY 10019. (212)245-2928. Contact: Susan Zeckendorf. Estab. 1979. Member of AAR. Represents 35 clients. 25% of clients are new/previously unpublished writers. Currently handles: 50% nonfiction books; 50% fiction. **Handles:** Nonfiction books, novels, short story collections. Considers these nonfiction areas: art/architecture/design; biography/autobiography; business; child guidance/parenting; health/medicine; history; music/dance/theater/film; psychology; science/technology; sociology; true crime/investigative; women's issues/women's studies. Considers these fiction areas: action/adventure; contemporary issues; detective/police/crime; ethnic; family saga; glitz; historical; literary; mainstream; mystery/suspense; thriller/espionage. Query. Reports in 10 days on queries; 2-3 weeks mss.
Recent Sales: *The True Life Story of Isobel Roundree* and *Maybelleen*, by Kathleen Wallace King; *Cry For Help*, by Karen Hansan Sruyck.
Terms: Agent receives 15% commission on domestic sales; 20% on foreign sales. Charges for photocopying, messenger services.
Writer's Conferences: Central Valley Writers Conference, the Tucson Publishers Association Conference, Writer's Connection, Frontiers in Writing Conference (Amarillo), Golden Triangle Writers Conference (Beaumont, Texas), Oklahoma Festival of Books (Claremont OK).
Tips: Obtains new clients through recommendations, listings in writer's manuals.

‡GEORGE ZIEGLER LITERARY AGENCY (II), 160 E. 97th St., New York NY 10029. (212)348-3637. Contact: George Ziegler. Estab. 1977. Represents 25 clients. 50% of clients are new/previously unpublished writers. Specializes in nonfiction. Currently handles: 80% nonfiction books; 15% novels; 5% stage plays.
Handles: Nonfiction books, novels. Considers these nonfiction areas: animals; anthropology/archaeology; biography/autobiography; cooking/food/nutrition; crafts/hobbies; gay/lesbian issues; health/medicine; history; music/dance/theater/film; nature/environment; religious/inspirational; self-help/personal improvement. Considers these fiction areas: contemporary issues; family saga; gay; historical; horror; lesbian; literary; mainstream; psychic/supernatural. Query. Reports in 2 weeks on queries.
Recent Sales: *Child of Two Worlds*, by Norman Reyes (Three Continents Press); *Portrait of a Woman*, by Joseph Roccasalvo (Ignatius Press); *Democracy & the Dictator*, by Robert Amerson (American University Press).
Terms: Agent receives 15% commission on domestic sales; 20% on foreign sales if subagent is used. No written contract.
Tips: Obtains new clients through mail queries and recommendations. "Be professional."

Additional Nonfee-charging Agents

The following nonfee-charging agencies have indicated that they are *primarily* interested in handling the work of scriptwriters, but also handle less than ten to fifteen percent book manuscripts. After reading the main listing (you can find the page number in the Listings Index), send them a query to obtain more information on their needs and manuscript submission policies.

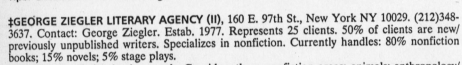

All-Star Talent Agency
Cinema Talent International
Client First—A/K/A Leo P.
   Haffey Agency
The Coppage Company
Dragon Literary, Inc.

Legacies
Lenhoff/Robinson Talent and
   Literary Agency, Inc.
Montgomery-West Literary
   Agency
Jack Scagnetti Talent & Liter-

ary Agency
The Tantleff Office
The Turtle Agency
Erika Wain Agency
Ann Wright Representataives

The publishing field is constantly changing! If you're still using this book and it is 1996 or later, buy the newest edition of Guide to Literary Agents at your favorite bookstore or order directly from Writer's Digest Books.

Nonfee-charging Agents/'94-'95 changes

The following agencies appeared in the last (1994) edition of *Guide to Literary Agents* but are absent from the 1995 edition. These agencies failed to respond to our request for an update of their listing, or were left out for the reasons indicated in parentheses following the agency name.

Bernsen, Jamail & Goodson, L.L.P. (no longer agenting)
The Dark Horse Group
Vicki Eisenberg Literary Agency (out of business)
Embers Literary Agency (out of business)
Frontier Talents (unable to contact)
Candice Fuhrman Literary Agency (deleted by request)
Ellen Geiger Literary Agency (joined Curtis Brown Ltd.)
Irene Goodman Literary Agency

Lloyd Jones Literary Agency
Los Angeles Literary Associates
MGA Agency Inc. (represents Canadian authors only)
Rhodes Literary Agency (out of business)
Jean Rosenthal Literary Agency (not taking on new clients)
The Roth Agency (removed for one year by request)
Schaffner Agency (out of business)
Richard R. Shreves Agency

Larry Sternig Literary Agency (not taking on new clients)
Gunther Stuhlmann, Author's Representative (not taking on new clients)
Maya Swamy, Literary Agency (removed for 1 year by request)
Roslyn Targ Literary Agency, Inc. (removed by request due to inappropriate submissions)
The Wendy Weil Agency Inc.

Literary Agents: Fee-charging

This section contains literary agencies that charge a fee to writers in addition to taking a commission on sales. The sales commissions are the same as those taken by nonfee-charging agents: 10 to 15 percent for domestic sales, 10 to 20 percent for foreign and dramatic sales, with the difference going to the subagent.

Several agencies charge fees only under certain circumstances, generally for previously unpublished writers. These agencies are indicated by an asterisk (*). Most agencies will consider you unpublished if you have subsidy publishing, local or small press publication credits only; check with a prospective agency before sending material to see if you fit their definition of published.

Agents who charge one-time marketing fees in excess of $50 are also included in this section. Those who charge less than $50 and do not charge for other services appear in the Literary Agents: Nonfee-charging section.

Reading fees and critique services

The issue of reading fees is as controversial for literary agents as for those looking for representation. While some agents dismiss the concept as inherently unethical and a scam, others see merit in the system, provided an author goes into it with his eyes open. Some writers spend hundreds of dollars for an "evaluation" that consists of a poorly written critique full of boilerplate language that says little, if anything, about their individual work. Others have received the helpful feedback they needed to get their manuscript in shape and have gone on to publish their work successfully.

Ethan Ellenberg and Denise Marcil, both members of the Association of Authors Representatives (AAR), present different views on reading fees in their articles, *On the Merits: The Case For* and *The Case Against Reading Fees*. Effective January 1, 1996, however, all members of the AAR are prohibited from directly or indirectly charging reading fees. Until that time some members are allowed to continue to do so, provided they adhere to guidelines designed to protect the client. Arnold Goodman discusses these guidelines in his article, Write and Wrong: Literary Agents and Ethics.

In discussing consideration of a fee-charging agent, we must underscore the importance of research. Don't be bowled over by an impressive brochure or an authoritative manner. At the same time, overly aggressive skepticism may kill your chances with a legitimate agent. Business-like, professional behavior will help you gather the material you need to make an informed decision.

● Obtain a fee schedule and ask questions about the fees. Be sure you understand what the fees cover and what to expect for your money.

● Request a sample critique the agent has done for another person's manuscript. Are the suggestions helpful and specific? Do they offer advice you couldn't get elsewhere, such as in writing groups, conferences and seminars or reference books?

● Ask for recent sales an agent has made. Many agents have a pre-printed list of sales they can send you. If there haven't been any sales made in the past two years, what is the agent living on? In the listings we provide information on the percentage of income an agency receives from commissions on sales, and the percentage from reading or critique fees.

● Verify a few of these sales. To verify that the publisher has a book by that title, check *Books in Print*. To verify that the agent made the sale, call the contracts department of the publisher and ask who the agent of record is for a particular title.

Don't hesitate to ask the questions that will help you decide. The more you know about an agent and her abilities, the fewer unpleasant surprises you'll receive.

Fees range from one agency to another in nomenclature, price and purpose. Here are some of the more frequent terms and their generally-accepted definitions.

● *Reading fee*. This is charged for reading a manuscript (most agents do not charge to look at queries alone). Often the fee is paid to outside readers. It is generally a one-time, nonrefundable fee, but some agents will return the fee or credit it to your account if they decide to take you on as a client. Often an agent will offer to refund the fee upon sale of the book, but that isn't necessarily a sign of good faith. If the agency never markets your manuscript no sale would ever be made and the fee never refunded.

● *Evaluation fee*. Sometimes a reading fee includes a written evaluation, but many agents charge for this separately. An evaluation may be a one-paragraph report on the marketability of a manuscript or a several-page evaluation covering marketability along with flaws and strengths.

● *Marketing fees*. Usually a one-time charge to offset the costs of handling work, marketing fees cover a variety of expenses and may include initial reading or evaluation. Beware of agencies charging a monthly marketing fee; there is nothing to compel them to submit your work in a timely way if they are getting paid anyway.

● *Critiquing service*. Although "critique" and "evaluation" are sometimes used interchangeably, a critique is usually more extensive, with suggestions on ways to improve the manuscript. Many agents offer critiques as a separate service and have a standard fee scale, based on a per-page or word-length basis. Some agents charge fees based on the extent of the service required, ranging from overall review to line-by-line commentary.

● *Editing service*. While we do not list businesses whose primary source of income is from editing, we do list agencies who also offer this service. Many do not distinguish between critiques and edits, but we define editing services as critiques that include detailed suggestions on how to improve the work and reduce weaknesses. Editing services can be charged on similar bases as critiquing services.

● *Consultation services*. Some agents charge an hourly rate to act as a marketing consultant, a service usually offered to writers who are not clients and who just want advice on marketing. Some agents are also available on an hourly basis for advice on publishers' contracts.

● *Other services*. Depending on an agent's background and abilities, the agent may offer a variety of other services to writers including ghostwriting, typing, copyediting, proofreading, translating, book publicity, and legal advice.

Be forewarned that payment of a critique or editing fee does not ensure that an agent will take you on as a client. However, if you feel you need more than sales help and would not mind paying for an evaluation or critique from a professional, the agents listed in this section may interest you.

Special indexes and additional help

To help you with your search, we've included a number of special indexes in the back of the book. The Subject Index is divided into sections for nonfee-charging and fee-charging literary agents and script agents. Each of these sections in the index is then divided by nonfiction and fiction subject categories. Some agencies indicated that they were open to all nonfiction or fiction topics. These have been grouped under the subject heading "open" in each section. This year we have added a number of new topics, including education, how-to, humor and popular culture in nonfiction, and horror in fiction. Many agents have indicated additional areas of interest that were not represented in their listings last year.

We've included an Agents Index as well. Often you will read about an agent who is an employee of a larger agency and may not be able to locate her business phone or address. We asked agencies to list the agents on staff, then listed the names in alphabetical order along with the name of the agency they work for. Find the name of the person you would like to contact and then check the agency listing. You will find the page number for the agency's listing in the Listing Index.

A Geographic Index lists agents state by state, for those authors looking for an agent close to home.

Many literary agents are also interested in scripts; many script agents will also consider book manuscripts. Fee-charging agents who primarily sell scripts but also handle at least 10 to 15 percent book manuscripts appear among the listings in this section, with the contact information, breakdown of work currently handled and a note to check the full listing in the script section, if they are a signatory of the WGA or report a sale. Those nonfee-charging script agencies that sell scripts and less than 10 to 15 percent book manuscripts appear in "Additional Fee-charging Agents" at the end of this section. Complete listings for these agents appear in the Script Agent section.

Before contacting any agency, check the listing to make sure it is open to new clients. Those designated (V) are currently not interested in expanding their rosters.

For more information on approaching agents and the specifics of the listings, read *How to Use Your Guide to Literary Agents* and *The Right Agent for You*. Also see the various articles at the beginning of the book for explorations of different aspects of the author/agent relationship.

We've ranked the agencies listed in this section according to their openness to submissions. Below is our ranking system:

  I Newer agency actively seeking clients.
 II Agency seeking both new and established writers.
III Agency prefers to work with established writers, mostly obtains new clients through referrals.
IV Agency handling only certain types of work or work by writers under certain circumstances.
 V Agency not currently seeking new clients. We have included mention of agencies rated **V** to let you know they are currently not open to new clients. In addition to those ranked **V**, we have included a few well-known agencies' names who have declined the opportunity to receive full listings at this time. *Unless you have a strong recommendation from someone well respected in the field, our advice is to approach only those agents ranked I-IV.*

A & R BURKE CORPORATION (II), P.O. Box 11794, Ft. Lauderdale FL 33339-1794. (305)525-0531. Fax: (305)761-1952. Contact: Anna Mae Burke or Robert Burke. Corporation formed

1977, expanded to non-insider writers in 1991. Represents 15 clients. 60% of clients are new/previously unpublished writers. "In addition to adult and young adult fiction, the agency handles technical books, textbooks and computer software among its nonfiction specialties." Currently handles: 5% nonfiction books; 5% scholarly books; 5% textbooks; 10% juvenile books; 60% novels; 15% computer. Member agents: Anna Mae Burke (fiction: adult and young readers; nonfiction: technical); Robert Burke (nonfiction, technical and computer software).

Handles: Nonfiction books, textbooks, scholarly books, juvenile books, novels. Considers these nonfiction areas: art/architecture/design; biography/autobiography; business; computers/electronics; current affairs; psychology; government/politics/law; history; juvenile nonfiction; language/literature/criticism; military/war; money/finance/economics; music/dance/theater/film; science/technology; self-help/personal improvement; sociology; sports; true crime/investigative; women's issues/women's studies. Considers these fiction areas: action/adventure; contemporary issues; detective/police/crime; ethnic; family saga; fantasy; feminist; historical; humor/satire; juvenile; literary; mainstream; mystery/suspense; picture book; romance (contemporary, gothic, historical, regency); science fiction; sports; thriller/espionage; young adult; computer software. Does not accept unsolicited mss from unpublished writers at this time

Terms: Agent receives 15% commission on domestic sales; 20% on foreign sales. Offers written contract, binding for 1 year.

Fees: Charges $35 reading fee. Offers criticism service. 85% of business derived from commissions of ms sales; 15% derived from reading fees or criticism service.

Writer's Conferences: North Carolina Writers Conference, Mystery Writers of America (Florida chapter), Florida Freelance Writers Conference.

Tips: "We are always conscious of seeking new clients and may meet one almost anywhere."

‡THE ABACUS GROUP (II), P.O. Box 35, Ridgecrest CA 93556. (619)375-5243. Fax: (619)375-6284. Director: G. Terry Dawson. Estab. 1982. Represents 56 clients. 90% of clients are new/previously unpublished writers. Currently handles: 15% nonfiction books; 55% novels; 20% movie scripts; 10% TV scripts. Member agents: Terry Dawson (fiction, novels); Rita Dufresne (fiction, nonfiction, novels); William Russell (screenplays/teleplays).

Handles: Nonfiction books, scholarly books, poetry books, novels, short story collections, syndicated material. Considers these nonfiction areas: animals; anthropology/archaeology; art/architecture/design; biography/autobiography; business; cooking/food/nutrition; current affairs; education; ethnic/cultural interests; government/politics/law; health/medicine; history; how-to; humor; language/literature/criticism; military/war; music/dance/theater/film; nature/environment; psychology; religious/inspirational; science/technology; sociology; sports; true crime/investigative. Considers these fiction areas: action/adventure; contemporary issues; detective/police/crime; erotica; family saga; fantasy; historical; horror; humor/satire; literary; mainstream; psychic/supernatural; religious/inspirational; romance (contemporary); science fiction; sports; thriller/espionage; westerns/frontier. Query. Reports immediately on queries; 2 weeks on mss.

Recent Sales: *Whipping Hidden Allergies,* by Dr. A. Hosen (Morgan Press, Austin, TX).

Also Handles: Movie scripts, TV scripts.

Recent Sales: *"Silk Stalkings,"* by G.T. Dawson (USA-Network Films Television: 5 episodes).

Terms: Agent receives 10% commission on domestic sales; 20% on foreign sales. Offers written contract, binding for 2 years.

Fees: Charges a reading fee: novels: 50¢/page; screenplays: 70¢/page; refundable to client upon sale of ms. Criticism service included within initial per page charge, "indicating areas of strength, weakness (e.g., marketability, literary skill, crescendo, etc.) plus a reworked written version of a few pages of how we would do it, written by G.T. Dawson." Charges for client setup, duplicating, phone calls.

Tips: Obtains new clients through word-of-mouth, *LMP*, advertising. "It is not whether an agency charges fees but, rather, the professional services the client receives that determines the value of the agency to the client. The fact is The Abacus Group stands behind what it does, what it says, and produces the highest quality critique in the business. We have clients from Naples, Florida, to Farmingdale, New York, to San Diego, California, who can testify to exactly that."

*ACACIA HOUSE PUBLISHING SERVICES LTD. (II, III), 51 Acacia Rd., Toronto, Ontario M4S 2K6 Canada. Phone/fax: (416)484-8356. Contact: Frances Hanna. Estab. 1985. Represents 30 clients. "I prefer that writers be previously published, with at least a few articles to their credit. Strongest consideration will be given to those with, say, three or more published books. However, I *would* take on an unpublished writer of outstanding talent." Works with a small number of new/unpublished authors. Specializes in contemporary fiction: literary or commercial (no horror, occult or science fiction); nonfiction: all categories but business/economics—in the trade, not textbook area; children's: a few picture books; young adult, mainly fiction. Currently handles: 30% nonfiction books; 60% novels; 10% juvenile books.

Handles: Nonfiction books, novels, juvenile books. Considers these nonfiction areas: animals; biography/autobiography; cooking/food/nutrition; crafts/hobbies; current affairs; health/medicine; language/literature/criticism; military/war; music/dance/theater/film; nature/environment; popular culture; psychology. Considers these fiction areas: action/adventure; detective/police/crime; historical; juvenile; literary; mainstream; mystery/suspense; romance (historical); thriller/espionage. Query with outline. Does not read unsolicited mss. Reports in 3 weeks on queries.
Recent Sales: *Mannequin* and *Dollmaker* (mystery series), by Robert Janes (Constable [UK]); *The Last Castrato*, by John Spencer Hill (Constable [UK]; St. Martin's [US]).
Terms: Agent receives 20% commission on English language sales; 20% on dramatic sales; 30% on foreign language sales.
Fees: Charges reading fee on mss over 200 pages (typed, double-spaced) in length; $200/200 pages. Waives reading fee when representing the writer. 4% of income derived from reading fees. "If a critique is wanted on a manuscript under 200 pages in length, then the charge is the same as the reading fee for a longer manuscript (which incorporates a critique)." 5% of income derived from criticism fees. Critique includes 2-3-page overall evaluation "which will contain any specific points that are thought important enough to detail. Marketing advice is not usually included, since most manuscripts evaluated in this way are not considered to be publishable." Charges writers for photocopying, courier, postage, telephone/fax "if these are excessive."
Writer's Conferences: LIBER (Barcelona); London International Book Fair (London); Bologna Book Fair (Bologna); ABA (Chicago); Frankfurt Book Fair (Frankfurt).

ACKERMAN LITERARY SERVICES (I), 108 E. Derenne Ave, Savannah GA 31405. (912)352-7646. Contact: Sharon Ackerman. Estab. 1992. Member of RWA. Represents 25 clients. 80% of new clients are new/previously unpublished writers. Currently handles: 100% novels. Member agents: Jodi Ceriale, Christine Hoskins.
Handles: Novels. Considers these nonfiction areas: crafts/hobbies; true crime/investigative. Considers these fiction areas: confessional; detective/police/crime; glitz; mystery/suspense; psychic/supernatural; romance (contemporary, gothic). Query with entire ms. Reports in 1 week on queries; 2 months on mss.
Terms: Agent receives 12% commission on domestic sales; 15% on foreign sales.
Fees: Does not charge a reading fee. Criticism service: $75 up to 100,000 words; $100 over 100,000; refundable upon sale of ms. "I prefer to make notations on manuscripts, in addition to a two to three page report on marketability, characterization, plot, style, etc. We work with the author on correcting weak points." Charges for postage, photocopying, telephone, etc. "We also offer a manuscript typing service for $2 per page. Always include SASE with your transcript."
Writer's Conferences: Attended Romance Writers of America Conference, Savannah GA.
Tips: Obtains new clients through advertising and recommendations. "Manuscripts should have a professional look, correct grammar, no typing errors. We want new writers to know we're here to help. We're interested in long-term career goals. Know the market you're writing for. Don't give up. Make a commitment to writing. Always include a SASE with your manuscript."

*THE AHEARN AGENCY, INC. (I), 2021 Pine St., New Orleans LA 70118-5456. (504)861-8395. Fax: (504)866-6434. Contact: Pamela G. Ahearn. Estab. 1992. Member of RWA. Represents 22 clients. 20% of clients are new/previously unpublished writers. Specializes in historical romance; also very interested in mysteries and suspense fiction. Currently handles: 10% nonfiction books; 10% juvenile books; 80% novels.
Handles: Nonfiction books, juvenile books, novels, short story collections (if stories previously published), young adult (no picture books). Considers these nonfiction areas: animals; biography; business; child guidance/parenting; current affairs; ethnic/cultural interests; gay/lesbian issues; health/medicine; history; juvenile nonfiction; music/dance/theater/film; popular culture; self-help/personal improvement; true crime/investigative; women's issues/women's studies. Considers these fiction areas: action/adventure; contemporary issues; detective/police/crime; ethnic; family saga; fantasy; feminist; gay; glitz; historical; horror; humor/satire; juvenile; lesbian; literary; mainstream; mystery/suspense; psychic/supernatural; regional; romance (contemporary, gothic, historical, regency); science fiction; thriller/espionage; westerns/frontier; young adult. Query. Reports in 2-4 weeks on queries; 8-10 weeks on mss.
Recent Sales: *Heart of the Storm*, by Rexanne Becnel (St. Martin's); *Still Waters*, by Margaret Woodward (Putnam).

The double dagger before a listing indicates the listing is new in this edition.

Terms: Agent receives 15% commission on domestic sales; 20% on foreign sales. Offers written contract, binding for 1 year; renewable by mutual consent.

Fees: "I charge a reading fee to previously unpublished authors, based on length of material. Fees range from $125-400 and are non-refundable. When authors pay a reading fee, they receive a three to five single-spaced-page critique of their work, addressing writing quality and marketability." Critiques written by Pamela G. Ahearn. Charges for photocopying. 90% of business derived from commissions; 10% derived from reading fees or criticism services. Payment of reading fee does not ensure representation.

Writers' Conferences: Attends Midwest Writers Workshop, Moonlight & Magnolias, RWA National conference (Hawaii); Virginia Romance Writers (Williamsburg, VA); Florida Romance Writers (Ft. Lauderdale, FL), Golden Triangle Writers Conference.

Tips: Obtains new clients "usually through listings such as this one and client recommendations. Sometimes at conferences. Be professional! Always send in exactly what an agent/editor asks for, no more, no less. Keep query letters brief and to the point, giving your writing credentials and a very brief summary of your book. If one agent rejects you, keep trying—there are a lot of us out there!"

‡ALP ARTS CO. (I, II), 63 Coyote Circle, RR6, Golden CO 80403. Phone/fax: (303)642-0916. E-mail: sffuller@alparts.com. Contact: Ms. Sandy Ferguson Fuller. Estab. 1994. Represents 20 clients. 90% of clients are new/previously unpublished writers. "Specializes in children's books. Works with picture book authors and illustrators, also middle-grade and YA writers, nonfiction and fiction." Currently handles: 100% juvenile books.

Handles: Juvenile books, all types. Considers juvenile nonfiction. Considers juvenile and young adult fiction, picture books. Query. For picture books and easy readers send entire ms. Reports in 2-3 weeks on queries; 4-6 weeks on mss.

Terms: 10% commission on domestic sales. Offers written contract, with 30 day cancellation clause.

Fees: Criticism service: $25/hour for critique and consulting session. Basic consultation is $25/hour or $25/submission. Contract varies upon client's needs. Charges for postage, photocopying costs. Long-distance phone consultation at $25/hour plus phone bill. Receipts supplied to client for all of the above. 50% of business derived from criticism fees.

Writers' Conferences: ABA (Chicago, 5/95); SCBWI (8/95).

Tips: Obtains new clients from referrals, solicitation and at conferences. "Several mailings per year through advertising services, workshops and seminars. Referrals. Networking in publishing industry. Society of Children's Book Writers and Illustrators. Usually establish a working relationship via consulting or workshop prior to agenting. Agency representation is not for everyone. Some aspiring or published authors and/or illustrators have more confidence in their own abilities to target and market work. Others are 'territorial' or prefer to work directly with the publishers. The best agent/client relationships exist when complete trust is established prior to representation. I recommend at least one (or several) consultations via phone or in person with a prospective agent. References are important. Also, the author or illustrator should have a clear idea of the agent's role i.e., editorial/critiquing input, 'post-publication' responsibilities, exclusive or non-exclusive representation, fees, industry reputation, etc. Each author or illustrator should examine his or her objectives, talents, time constraints, and perhaps more important, personal rapport with an individual agent prior to representation."

JOSEPH ANTHONY AGENCY (II), 15 Locust Court, R.D. 20, Mays Landing NJ 08330. (609)625-7608. Contact: Joseph Anthony. Estab. 1964. Signatory of WGA. Represents 30 clients. 80% of clients are new/previously unpublished writers. "Specializes in general fiction and nonfiction. Always interested in screenplays." Currently handles: 5% juvenile books; 80% novellas; 5% short story collections; 2% stage plays; 10% TV scripts. Member agent: Lena Fortunato.

Handles: Nonfiction books, juvenile books, novels, movie scripts, TV scripts. Considers these nonfiction areas: health/medicine; military/war; psychology; science/technology; self-help/personal improvement; true crime/investigative. Considers these fiction areas: action/adventure; confessional; detective/police/crime; erotica; fantasy; mystery/suspense; psychic/supernatural; romance (gothic, historical, regency); science fiction; thriller/espionage; young adult. Query, SASE required. Reports in 2 weeks on queries; 1 month on mss.

Terms: Agent receives 15% commission on domestic sales; 20% on foreign sales.

Fees: Charges $85 reading fee for novels up to 100,000 words. "Fees are returned after a sale of $3,000 or more." Charges for postage and photocopying up to 3 copies. 10% of business is derived from commissions on ms sales; 90% is derived from reading fees ("because I work with new writers").

Tips: Obtains new clients through recommendations from others, solicitation. "If your script is saleable, I will try to sell it to the best possible markets. I will cover sales of additional rights through the world. If your material is unsaleable as it stands but can be rewritten and repaired,

I will tell you why it has been turned down. After you have rewritten your script, you may return it for a second reading without *any additional fee*. But ... if it is completely unsaleable in our evaluation for the markets, I will tell you why it has been turned down again and give you specific advice on how to avoid these errors in your future material. I do not write on, edit or blue pencil your script. I am an *agent* and an agent is out to sell a script."

‡ARGONAUT LITERARY AGENCY (I), P.O. Box 8446, Clearwater FL 34618. (813)442-2511. Contact: R.R. Reed. Estab. 1992. Represents 3 clients. 66% of clients are new/previously unpublished authors. Currently handles: 30% nonfiction books; 20% scholarly books; 50% novels.
Handles: Nonfiction books, novels. Considers these nonfiction areas: biography/autobiography; current affairs; history; military/war; money/finance/economics; sports; true crime/investigative. Considers these fiction areas: action/adventure; confessional; contemporary issues; detective/police/crime; historical; humor/satire; mystery/suspense; sports; thriller/espionage; westerns/frontier. Query. Reports in 1 month on queries; 3 months on mss.
Terms: Agent receives 10% commission on domestic sales; 15% on foreign sales. Offers written contract, binding for 2 years.
Fees: Charges $35 reading fee. Criticism service: $100.

*AUTHOR AID ASSOCIATES (II), 340 E. 52nd St., New York NY 10022. (212)758-4213; 980-9179. Editorial Director: Arthur Orrmont. Estab. 1967. Represents 175 clients. Specializes in aviation, war, biography, novels, autobiography. Currently handles: 5% magazine fiction; 35% nonfiction books; 38% novels; 5% juvenile books; 5% movie scripts; 2% stage plays; 10% other. Member agent: Leonie Rosenstiel, vice president, "a musicologist and authority on New Age subjects and nutrition."
Handles: Magazine fiction, nonfiction books, novels, juvenile books, movie scripts, stage plays, TV scripts. Considers these nonfiction areas: animals; anthropology/archaeology; biography/autobiography; current affairs; ethnic/cultural interests; health/medicine; history; how-to; humor; juvenile nonfiction; language/literature/criticism; military/war; music/dance/theater/film; nature/environment; New Age/metaphysics; popular culture; psychology; religious/inspirational; science/technology; self-help/personal improvement; sociology; sports; translations; true crime/investigative; women's issues/women's studies. Considers these fiction areas: action/adventure; confessional; contemporary issues; detective/police/crime; erotica; ethnic; experimental; family saga; fantasy; glitz; historical; horror; humor/satire; juvenile; lesbian; literary; mainstream; mystery/suspense; picture book; psychic/supernatural; regional; religious/inspirational; romance (contemporary, gothic, historical, regency); science fiction; sports; thriller/espionage; westerns/frontier; young adult. Query with outline. "Short queries answered by return mail." Reports within 6 weeks on mss.
Recent Sales: *World Series*, by John S. Snyder (Chronicle Books); *Guide to The American Southwest*, by Larry Ludmar (Hunter Publishers).
Terms: Agent receives 15% commission on domestic and dramatic sales; 20% on foreign sales.
Fees: Charges a reading fee to new authors, refundable from commission on sale. Charges for cable, photocopying and messenger express. Offers consultation service through which writers not represented can get advice on a contract. 85% of income from sales of writers' work; 15% of income derived from reading fees.
Tips: Publishers of *Literary Agents of North America* (5th edition).

AUTHOR AUTHOR LITERARY AGENCY (I, II), P.O. Box 34051, 1200-37 St. SW, Calgary, Alberta T3C 3W2 Canada. (403)242-0226. Fax: (403)242-0226. President: Joan Rickard. Estab. 1992. Member of Writers' Guild of Alberta and CAA. Represents 40 clients. 50% of clients are new/previously unpublished writers. "Welcomes new writers." Currently handles: 10% nonfiction books; 5% scholarly books; 5% textbooks; 25% juvenile books; 45% novels; 5% novellas; 5% short story collections.
Handles: Fiction and nonfiction, adult and juvenile, textbooks, scholarly books, novels, novellas, short story collections. No poetry or screenplays. Considers these nonfiction areas: anthropology/archaeology; biography/autobiography; business; child guidance/parenting; cooking/food/nutrition; crafts/hobbies; education; ethnic/cultural interests; gay/lesbian issues; government/politics/law; health/medicine; history; how-to; humor; interior design/decorating; juvenile nonfiction; language/literature/criticism; military/war; money/finance/economics; nature/environment; New Age/metaphysics; photography; popular culture; psychology; self-help/personal improvement; sociology; sports; true crime/investigative; women's issues/women's studies. Considers these fiction areas: action/adventure; contemporary issues; detective/police/crime; erotica;experimental; family saga; fantasy; feminist; gay; historical; horror; humor/satire; juvenile; lesbian; literary; mainstream; mystery/suspense; picture book; psychic/supernatural; regional; romance (contemporary, gothic, historical, regency); science fiction; sports; thriller/espionage; westerns/frontier;

young adult. "Responds to all letters of inquiry promptly." Reports in about 2 weeks on queries, ms outlines and/or sample chapters; 2 months on complete mss.

Recent Sales: *Backyard Trampolining*, by Darlene Traviss (Life Line Books); *Taming The Dragon, Module I*, by Helen Webster and Lorraine Parker (Detselig/Temeron).

Terms: Agent receives 15% commission on domestic sales; 20% on foreign sales. Offers written contract.

Fees: "We provide a complete package: manuscript critique, editing, ghostwriting and marketing services. Will read at no charge unsolicited queries and outlines. Reads queries, edits and evaluates outlines and partial manuscripts of up to three sample chapters (about 30 pages) for $75, which is applied toward entire fee if agency agrees to study complete work. Manuscript must be accompanied by handling fee: up to 65,000 words $350; up to 85,000 words $450; 85,000+ words flat rate $475 (certified check or money order, please). Due to publishers constraints, manuscripts should rarely exceed 100,000 words. Payment of partial or complete evaluation fee does not ensure representation. We discuss methods to improve and/or make the manuscripts marketable. Once we place an author's work, there are no further evaluating fees. Charges for additional photocopying of manuscripts submitted to publishers, long-distance telephone/fax to promote sales and express of manuscripts. Consults with and reports promptly to writers on all communications concerning handling and marketing of their manuscripts!"

Tips: "If we agree to representation we work closely with clients when necessary to assist with honing their writing to as fine a polish as is possible; but the key word is ASSIST. It is not the agent's (or publisher's) job to revise the entire mechanics of formatting, punctuation and literary content/context. Many potentially good stories/novels are rejected by publishers and agents due to improperly, hastily prepared/presented manuscripts. Study your chosen genre thoroughly to learn technique and what publishers are buying. Excellent instructional manuals are available at bookstores or libraries. We provide *'A Crash Course' Kit on Business Letters, Basic Punctuation Guide & Manuscript Formatting* free of charge to clients, or this may be obtained upon request from our agency ($7.95 including postage/handling). Obtains new clients primarily through referrals and writers' manuals. Always enclose SASE for queries/manuscripts."

THE AUTHORS AND ARTISTS RESOURCE CENTER/TARC LITERARY AGENCY (II), 4725 E. Sunrise, #219, Tucson AZ 85718. (602)325-4733. Contact: Martha R. Gores. Estab. 1984. Represents 30 clients. Specializes in mainstream adult fiction and nonfiction books. Currently handles: 80% nonfiction books; 20% novels.

Handles: Nonfiction books, novels. Considers all nonfiction areas except essays, autobiography (unless celebrity) and journals. "Especially interested in how-to or self-help books by professionals; parenting books by psychologists or M.D.s." Query with outline. Does not read unsolicited mss. Reports in 2 months if SASE included.

Recent Sales: *Walker of Time* (Harbinger House).

Terms: Agent receives 15% commission on domestic sales; 20% on dramatic sales; 20% on foreign sales.

Fees: Does not charge a reading fee. Criticism service "only if is requested by the author." No set fee. "Each critique is tailored to the individual needs of the writer. We hire working editors who are employed by book publishers to do critiquing, editing, etc." Charges writers for mailing, photocopying, faxing, telephone calls.

Tips: "We do ghosting for professional people. In order to do ghosting, you must be published by a professional, reputable publisher. To be considered, send a business card with your résumé to our Arizona address."

*AUTHORS' MARKETING SERVICES LTD. (II), 200 Simpson Ave., Toronto, Ontario M4K 1A6 Canada. (416)463-7200. Fax: (416)469-4494. Contact: Larry Hoffman. Estab. 1978. Represents 17 clients. 25% of clients are new/previously unpublished writers. Specializes in thrillers, romance, parenting and self-help. Currently handles: 65% nonfiction books; 10% juvenile books; 20% novels; 5% other. Member agents: Paula Newton (romance, women's fiction); Bok Busboom (adventure).

Handles: Nonfiction books, novels. Considers these nonfiction areas: biography/autobiography; business; child guidance/parenting; cooking/food/nutrition; current affairs; education; health/medicine; history; how-to; military/war; money/finance/economics; nature/environment; popular culture; psychology; science/technology; self-help/personal improvement; sports; true crime/investigative. Considers these fiction areas: action/adventure; cartoon/comic; detective/police/crime; family saga; fantasy; historical; horror; humor/satire; literary; mainstream; mystery/suspense; psychic/supernatural; romance (contemporary, gothic, historical, regency); science fiction; thriller/espionage. Query. Reports in 1 week on queries; 1-2 months on mss.

Recent Sales: *Leonard Cohen: A Biography*, by Ira Nadel (Random House); *Duped*, by David Kilgour, M.P. (Prentice-Hall).

Terms: Agent receives 15% commission on domestic sales; 20% on foreign sales. Offers written contract, binding for 6-9 months to complete first sale.
Fees: Charges $325 reading fee. "A reading/evaluation fee of $325 applies only to unpublished authors, and the fee must accompany the completed manuscript. Criticism service is included in the reading fee. The critique averages three to four pages in length, and discusses strengths and weaknesses of the execution, as well as advice aimed at eliminating weaknesses." 95% of business is derived from commissions on ms sales; 5% is derived from reading fees. Payment of criticism fee does not ensure representation.
Tips: Obtains new clients through recommendations from other writers and publishers, occasional solicitation. "Never submit first drafts. Prepare the manuscript as cleanly and as perfectly, in the writer's opinion, as possible."

‡**ELIZABETH H. BACKMAN (II)**, 86 Johnnycake Hollow Rd., Pine Plains NY 12567. (518)398-6408. Fax: (518)398-6449. Contact: Elizabeth H. Backman. Estab. 1981. Represents 50 clients. Specializes in nonfiction, women's interest and positive motivation. Currently handles: 33-66% nonfiction books; 33% scholarly books; 33-50% novels.
Handles: Considers these nonfiction areas: biography/autobiography; business; child guidance/parenting; cooking/food/nutrition; crafts/hobbies; current affairs; ethnic/cultural interests; government/politics/law; health/medicine; history; interior design/decorating; dance; photography; psychology; religious/inspirational; pop science; self-help/personal improvement; sports; women's issues/women's studies. Considers these fiction areas: ethnic; fantasy; historical; mystery/suspense; regional; science fiction; sports; thriller/espionage; men's adventure and suspense; women's contemporary fiction. Query with sample ms. Reports in 3 weeks on queries; 3-6 weeks on mss.
Recent Sales: *And Soon I'll Come to Kill You* and *Out of the Darkness*, by Susan Kelly; *The New Toughness Training for Sports*, Jim Loehr.
Terms: Agent receives 15% commission on domestic sales; commission varies on foreign sales. Offers written contract on request, binding for 1-3 years.
Fees: Charges $25 reading fee for proposal/3 sample chapters, $50 for complete ms. Offers criticism service. Charges for photocopying, postage, telephone, fax, typing, editing, special services.
Writers' Conferences: Attends International Women's Writing Guild Conferences.
Tips: Obtains new clients through referrals from other editors. "I help writers prepare their proposals in best possible shape so they can get best possible deal with publisher. May not be the highest advance, but best overall deal."

*****MEREDITH BERNSTEIN LITERARY AGENCY (II)**, 2112 Broadway, Suite 503 A, New York NY 10023. (212)799-1007. Fax: (212)799-1145. Contact: Meredith Bernstein. Estab. 1981. Member of AAR. Represents approximately 75 clients. 20% of clients are new/previously unpublished writers. Does not specialize, "very eclectic." Currently handles: 50% nonfiction books; 50% fiction. Member agent: Elizabeth Cavanaugh.
Handles: Fiction and nonfiction books. Query first.
Recent Sales: *What Women Want*, by Patricia Ireland (Dutton/NAL); *Best Friends*, Terri Crisp and Samantha Glen (Pocket); *Superior Spirit*, by Ann Linnea (Little/Brown).
Terms: Agent receives 15% commission on domestic sales; 20% on foreign sales.
Fees: Charges reading fee of up to $100 for unpublished writers only. Charges $75 disbursement fee per year. 98% of business is derived from commissions on ms sales; 2% is derived from reading fees. Payment of fees does not ensure representation.
Tips: Obtains new clients through recommendations from others, solicitation, at conferences; own ideas developed and packaged.

*****THE MARIAN BERZON AGENCY (II)**, 1614 Victory Blvd., #110, Glendale CA 91201. (818)552-2699. Fax: (818)548-1560. Also: 336 E. 17th St., Costa Mesa CA 92627. Contact: Mike Ricciardi or Eric Sagucio. Estab. 1979. Signatory of WGA. "We are also a talent agent and signatory of SAG, AFTRA, Equity and AGVA." 80% of clients are new/previously unpublished writers. Specializes in screenplays of all genres, especially comedy (must be honest), family movies and thrillers. Currently handles: 2% juvenile books; 20% novels; 65% movie scripts; 6% stage plays; 12% TV scripts; 5% songs for movies and musical theater (cassettes only).
  • See the expanded listing for this agency in Script Agents.

THE BRINKE LITERARY AGENCY (II), 4498 B Foothill Rd., Carpinteria CA 93013-3075. (805)684-9655. Contact: Jude Barvin. Estab. 1988. Represents 24 clients. Currently handles: 30% nonfiction books; 60% novels; 10% movie scripts.
Handles: Considers these nonfiction areas: animals; anthropology/archaeology; biography/autobiography; child guidance/parenting; history; how-to; New Age/metaphysics; religious/inspira-

tional; self-help/personal improvement. Considers these fiction areas: action/adventure; detective/police/crime; fantasy; mystery/suspense; psychic/supernatural; religious/inspirational; romance (contemporary); science fiction; thriller/espionage; New Age; meditation. Query with SASE.

Also Handles: Movie scripts (feature film). Considers these script subject areas: action/adventure; contemporary issues; detective/police/crime; mystery/suspense; psychic/supernatural; religious/inspirational; science fiction; thriller.

Terms: Agent receives 15% commissions on domestic sales; 20% on foreign sales. Offers written contract, binding for 1 year.

Fees: Charges $125 reading fee for novel ms; $100 for screenplays. No charges for office expenses, postage, photocopying.

Writers' Conferences: Attends Santa Barbara Writers Conference.

Tips: Obtains new clients through recommendations from others, queries, mail. Offers complete critique/evaluation or a contract.

*PEMA BROWNE LTD. (II), HCR Box 104B, Pine Rd., Neversink NY 12765-9603. (914)985-2936. Contact: Perry Browne or Pema Browne. Estab. 1966. Member of SCBWI, RWA. Represents 50 clients. Handles any commercial fiction, nonfiction, romance, juvenile and children's picture books. Currently handles: 25% nonfiction books; 25% juvenile books; 45% novels; 5% movie scripts. Member agents: Pema Browne (juvenile nonfiction); Perry Browne (fiction, nonfiction).

Handles: Nonfiction books, scholarly books, juvenile books, novels. Considers these nonfiction areas: anthropology/archaeology; art/architecture/design; biography/autobiography; business; child guidance/parenting; cooking/food/nutrition; current affairs; education; ethnic/cultural interests; gay/lesbian issues; government/politics/law; health/medicine; how-to; juvenile nonfiction; military/war; money/finance/economics; nature/environment; New Age/metaphysics; popular culture; psychology; religious/inspirational; science/technology; self-help/personal improvement; sports; true crime/investigative; women's issues/women's studies. Considers these fiction areas: action/adventure, contemporary issues; detective/police/crime; ethnic; feminist; gay; glitz; historical; humor/satire; juvenile; lesbian; literary; mainstream; mystery/suspense; picture book; psychic/supernatural; religious/inspiration; romance (contemporary, gothic, historical, regency); science fiction; thriller/espionage; westerns/frontier; young adult. Query with SASE. Reports in 1 week on queries; 2 weeks on mss.

Recent Sales: *Always In My Dreams*, by Jo Goodman (Zebra); *Phantom Surfer*, by Linda Cargill (Coraverlag/Scholastic); *Debt Free Living*, by Bob Hammond (Career Press); *The Baboon, Python, Hare Collection*, by Teresa Rantaoogle (Lothrup Lee & Shepard).

Terms: Agent receives 15% commission on domestic sales; 20% outside USA.

Fees: Charges reading fee *only* on *selective adult* novels by unpublished authors.

Tips: Obtains new clients through "editors, authors, *LMP, Guide to Literary Agents* and as a result of longevity! If writing romance, be sure to receive guidelines from various romance publishers. In nonfiction, one must have credentials to lend credence to a proposal. Make sure of margins, double-space and use clean, dark type."

THE CATALOG™ LITERARY AGENCY (II), P.O. Box 2964, Vancouver WA 98668. (206)694-8531. Contact: Douglas Storey. Estab. 1986. Represents 50 clients. 50% of clients are new/previously unpublished writers. Specializes in business, health, psychology, money, science, how-to, self-help, technology, parenting, women's interest. Currently handles: 50% nonfiction books; 20% juvenile books; 30% novels.

Handles: Nonfiction books, textbooks, juvenile books, novels. Considers these nonfiction areas: agriculture/horticulture; animals; anthropology/archaeology; business; child guidance/parenting; computers/electronics; cooking/food/nutrition; crafts/hobbies; current affairs; education; ethnic/cultural interests; government/politics/law; health/medicine; how-to; juvenile nonfiction; military/war; money/finance/economics; nature/environment; photography; popular culture; psychology; science/technology; self-help/personal improvement; sociology; sports; women's issues/women's studies. Considers these fiction areas: action/adventure; family saga; horror; juvenile; mainstream; romance; science fiction; thriller/espionage; young adult. Query. Reports in 2 weeks on queries; 3 weeks on mss.

Recent Sales: *Home Checklist Almanac*, by Lizabeth Healy (Prentice Hall); *The Video Producers Notebook*, by Aleks Matza (Focal Press).

Terms: Agent receives 15% on domestic sales; 20% on foreign sales. Offers written contract, binding for about 9 months.

Fees: Does not charge a reading fee. Charges an upfront handling fee from $85-250 that covers photocopying, telephone and postage expense.

*THE CHANDELYN LITERARY AGENCY (II), P.O. Box 50162, 7750 Maryland, Clayton MO 63105. Fax: (314)531-2627. President: T. Patrick Miller (Tim). Estab. 1991. Signatory of WGA,

AFTRA. Represents 30 clients. 50% of clients are new/previously unpublished writers. Currently handles: 10% nonfiction books; 10% juvenile books; 10% novels; 50% movie scripts; 10% stage plays; 10% TV scripts. Member agents: T. Patrick Miller (picture books, novels, plays, screenplays, teleplays), N. Rochelle Collins (children's books).
  ● See the expanded listing for this agency in Script Agents.

SJ CLARK LITERARY AGENCY (IV), 56 Glenwood, Hercules CA 94547. Fax: (510)236-1052. Contact: Sue Clark. Estab. 1982. Represents 12 clients. 95% of clients are new/previously unpublished writers. Specializes in mysteries/suspense, children's books. Currently handles: 35% juvenile books; 65% novels.
Handles: Juvenile books, novels. Considers these nonfiction areas: New Age/metaphysics; true crime/investigative. Considers these fiction areas: detective/police/crime; juvenile; mystery/suspense; picture book; psychic/supernatural; thriller/espionage; young adult. Query with entire ms. Reports in 1 month on queries; 2 months on mss.
Recent Sales: *Three Is A Crowd*, by D.B. Borton (Berkley); *Four Elements of Murder*, by D.B. Borton (Berkley).
Terms: Agent receives 20% commission on domestic sales. Offers written contract.
Fees: "I specialize in working with previously unpublished writers. If the writer is unpublished, I charge a reading fee of $50 which includes a detailed two to three page single-spaced critique. Fee is nonrefundable. If the writer is published, the reading fee is refundable from commission on sale if I agree to represent author. I also offer an editing service for unpublished or published authors. Payment of criticism fee does not ensure representation. Clients are asked to keep all agreed upon amounts in their account to cover postage, phone calls, fax, etc. (Note: Since February 1994, 38% of income from commissions, 62% from reading and critiquing fees from unpublished authors.)"
Tips: Obtains new clients by word of mouth, listing in *Guide to Literary Agents* and *Mystery Writer's Marketplace & Sourcebook*.

COAST TO COAST TALENT AND LITERARY (II), 4942 Vineland Ave., Suite 200, North Hollywood CA 91601. (818)762-6278. Fax: (818)762-7049. Estab. 1986. Signatory of WGA. Represents 20 clients. 35% of clients are new/previously unpublished writers. Specializes in "true stories and true crime books that can be packaged into movies/scripts." Currently handles: 25% nonfiction books; 50% movie scripts; 25% TV scripts.
  ● See the expanded listing for this agency in Script Agents.

COLBY: LITERARY AGENCY (I), 2864-20 Jefferson Ave., Yuba City CA 95993. (916)674-3378. Contact: Pat Colby. Estab. 1990. Represents 15 clients. 93% of clients are new/previously unpublished writers. Specializes in fiction—mystery and comedy. Currently handles: 100% novels. Member agent: Richard Colby.
Handles: Novels, novellas, short story collections. Considers these fiction areas: cartoon/comic; detective/police/crime; humor/satire; mystery/suspense; sports; thriller/espionage; westerns/frontier. Query or send entire ms. Reports within 1 week on queries; 2 months on mss.
Terms: Agent receives 12% commission on domestic sales; 15% commission on foreign sales. Offers written contract, binding for 1 year.
Fees: No reading fee. Offers criticism service. Send query or 30 pages of ms for a prompt reply with full explanation of any charges. Critiques are done by Pat or Richard Colby. Charges for editing, photocopying, postage. Payment of criticism fee does not ensure representation.

*COLLIER ASSOCIATES (III), P.O. Box 688, Boca Raton FL 33429-0689. (407)998-8537. Contact: Dianna Collier. Estab. 1976. Represents 75 + clients. 10% of clients are new/previously unpublished writers. Specializes in "adult fiction and nonfiction books only." Currently handles: 50% nonfiction books; 50% novels. Member agents: Dianna Collier (adult fiction, nonfiction); Oscar Collier (biography, autobiography, financial). "This is a small agency that rarely takes on new clients because of the many authors it represents already."
Handles: Nonfiction, novels. Considers these nonfiction areas: biography/autobiography; business; computers/electronics; cooking/food/nutrition; crafts/hobbies; history; how-to; self-help/personal improvement; true crime/investigative; women's issues/women's studies. Considers these fiction areas: action/adventure; detective/police/crime; fantasy; historical; mainstream; mystery/suspense; romance (contemporary, gothic, historical, regency); science fiction; thriller/espionage; westerns/frontier. Query with SASE. Reports in 6-8 weeks on queries; 3-4 months "or longer" on mss.
Recent Sales: *Me and the Boys*, by Ellen Ricknor (Berkley Books); *Lew Fields and the Roots of American Popular Theater*, by Armand Fields and Marc Fields (Oxford University Publishing); *Fools Errant*, by Matt Hughes (Maxwell-Macmillan).

Terms: Agent receives 10-15% commission on domestic sales; 20% on foreign sales. Offers written contract "sometimes."

Fees: Charges $50 reading fee for unpublished trade book authors. "Reserves the right to charge a reading fee on longer fiction of unpublished authors." Charges for photocopying and express mail, "if requested, with author's consent, and for copies of author's published books used for rights sales."

Tips: Obtains new clients through recommendations from others. "Send biographical information with query; must have SASE. Don't telephone. Read Oscar Collier's books *How to Write and Sell Your First Novel* and *How to Write and Sell Your First Nonfiction Book*."

‡CONNOR LITERARY AGENCY (III, IV), 640 W. 153rd St., New York NY 10031. (212)491-5233. Fax: (212)491-5233. Also: 7333 Gallagher Dr., #221D, Edina MN 55435. Phone/fax: (612)835-7251. Contact: Marlene K. Connor. Estab. 1985. Represents 50 clients. 30% of clients are new/previously unpublished writers. Specializes in popular fiction and nonfiction. Currently handles: 50% nonfiction books; 50% novels. Member agents: Deborah Connor Coker (children's books); John Lynch (sports, success/inspiration).

Handles: Nonfiction books, novels, children's books (especially with a minority slant). Considers these nonfiction areas: business; child guidance/parenting; cooking/food/nutrition; crafts/hobbies; current affairs; ethnic/cultural interests; government/politics/law; health/medicine; how-to; humor; interior decorating; language/literature/criticism; money/finance/economics; photography; popular culture; self-help/personal improvement; sports; true crime/investigative; women's issues/women's studies. Considers these fiction areas: contemporary issues; detective/police/crime; ethnic; experimental; family saga; horror; literary; mystery/suspense; thriller/espionage. Query with outline/proposal. Reports in 4 weeks on queries; 4-6 weeks on mss.

Recent Sales: *Essence: 25 Years of Celebrating the Black Woman* (Abrams); *Are You Compatible*, by Susan Adams (Carol Publishing Group).

Terms: Agent receives 15% commission on domestic sales; 25% on foreign sales. Offers a written contract, binding for 1 year.

Fees: Charges a reading fee. "Fee depends on length: $75-125. Deductible from commissions; reader's reports provided for all manuscripts read with fees charged." Charges for general expenses—messenger, photocopying, postage. "Less than $100 in most cases. Deducted from commissions and explained." 99% of business derived from commissions on ms sales; 1% is derived from reading fees or criticism services.

Writers' Conferences: Howard University Publishing Institute; ABA; Oklahoma Writer's Federation.

Tips: Obtains new clients through queries, recommendations, conferences, grapevine, etc. "Seeking previously published writers with good sales records and new writers with real talent."

BRUCE COOK AGENCY (I), P.O. Box 75995, St. Paul MN 55175-0995. (612)487-9355. Estab. 1992. 50% of clients are new/previously unpublished writers. Subject areas include romance, mystery, science fiction, juvenile, history, education and religion. Currently handles: 20% nonfiction books; 10% scholarly books; 30% novels; 10% short story collections; 10% movie scripts; 10% TV scripts. Literary Manager: Elizabeth Young (15 years experience with two other agencies). Member agent: Edward Young.

Handles: Nonfiction books, textbooks, scholarly books, juvenile books, novels, short story collections. Considers these nonfiction areas: biography/autobiography; business; child guidance/parenting; cooking/food/nutrition; health/medicine; history; juvenile nonfiction; language/literature/criticism; music/dance/theater/film; nature/environment; psychology; religious/inspirational; self-help/personal improvement; sociology. Considers these fiction areas: action/adventure; cartoon/comic; family saga; fantasy; historical; humor/satire; juvenile; literary; mystery/suspense; regional; religious/inspiration; science fiction; thriller/espionage; young adult. Query with 1-page outline. Reports in 2 weeks on queries; 1-2 months on mss.

Recent Sales: *Successful Student Teaching*, by F.D. Kreamelmeyer (Sheffield Publishing Company).

Also Handles: Movie scripts, TV scripts, stage plays.

Terms: Agent receives 15% commission on domestic sales; 25% on foreign sales. Offers written contract.

Fees: "Reading fee for a published author is minimal. Evaluation by qualified professionals based on number of pages to be reviewed and primarily for new authors. Critiques are five to ten pages long. Charges for out-of-pocket expenses incurred in marketing the ms are charged to the client. Services for marketing are on a contingency basis." 60% of business is derived from commissions on ms sales; 40% is derived from reading fees or criticism services. "Payment must be made in advance of service rendered, and is nonrefundable. Payment of criticism fee does not ensure representation."

Writers' Conferences: Lectured at Minneapolis Writers Workshop; Association of PEN Women, Minneapolis.
Tips: Obtains new clients through referrals, networking and advertising. "Make a point of meeting your agent in person. Insist on regular communication. Your manuscript should be legible, typed, double-spaced and with pages marked. Be open to suggestions for improving your manuscripts."

ALETA M. DALEY/MAXIMILIAN BECKER, 444 East 82nd St., New York NY 10028. (212)744-1453. Head: Aleta M. Daley. Estab. 1950. Looking for exciting literary and mainstream fiction, suspense, science fiction.
Handles: Provocative nonfiction including women's, black and ethnic studies, biography and selected scholarly works. Children's books. Query with sample chapters or a well-developed proposal (nonfiction) with a brief resume. No unsolicited mss.
Recent Sales: *The First Duelist*, by Rutledge Etheridge (Berkley Publishing Group); *Open Womb: Anthology on Motherhood*, by J.B. Bernstein and Karen J. Donnelly (Greenwood Publishing); *Marketing Success for Interior Designers*, by Jane Martin and Nancy Knoohuizen (John Wiley & Sons).
Terms: Agent receives 15% on domestic sales including dramatic and film rights; 20% on foreign sales.
Fees: Does not charge a reading fee. Criticism service: if requested. This includes editorial suggestions. Normal handling fee.

DORESE AGENCY LTD. (III), 37965 Palo Verde Dr., Cathedral City CA 92234. (619)321-1115. Fax: (619)321-1049. Contact: Alyss Barlow Dorese. Estab. 1977. Represents 30 clients. Currently handles: 65% nonfiction books; 35% novels.
Handles: Considers these nonfiction areas: art; biography/autobiography; business; child guidance/parenting; cooking/food/nutrition; crafts/hobbies; current affairs; gay/lesbian issues; government/politics/law; health/medicine; history; interior design/decorating; language/literature/criticism; military/war; money/finance/economics; music/dance/theater/film; New Age/metaphysics; photography; psychology; self-help/personal improvement; sociology; sports; true crime/investigative; women's issues/women's studies. Considers these fiction areas: action/adventure; contemporary issues; detective/police/crime; ethnic; family saga; feminist; gay; glitz; historical; lesbian; literary; mainstream; mystery/suspense; psychic/supernatural; regional; inspirational; sports; young adult. Send outline/proposal and SASE. Reports in 6 weeks on queries.
Recent Sales: *Rape of Kuwait*, by Jean Sassoon (Knightsbridge); *Get Married Now*, by Hilary Rich (Bob Adams).
Terms: Agent receives 15% commission on domestic sales; 20% on foreign sales. Offers written contract, binding for 2 years.
Fees: Does not charge a reading fee. Offers criticism service, cost depends on length of book.
Tips: Obtains new clients through referrals from past clients. "Don't say, 'I've written The Great American Novel.' It's an immediate turnoff."

EASTWIND WRITERS (II), P.O. Box 348, Los Angeles CA 90053. Phone/fax: (818)951-6609. "For first contact, send direct mail with your queries." President: Paul Lee. Estab. 1991. Represents 30 clients. 50% of clients are new/previously unpublished writers. Specializes in English, Korean, Japanese translations; copyright registration to the US Library of Congress copyright office. Currently handles: 10% novels; 30% poetry books; 20% short story collections; 30% translations; 10% criticism.
Handles: Novels, novellas, short story collections, poetry books, translations. Considers these nonfiction areas: biography/autobiography; ethnic/cultural interests; nature/environment; translations for English, Korean, Japanese. Considers these fiction areas: erotica; ethnic; humor/satire; literary; mystery/suspense; picture book; romance (contemporary, gothic, historical, regency); science fiction; translations; westerns/frontier; young adult. Query with entire ms, proposal or outline. Reports in 2 weeks on queries; 1 month on mss. "Must include SASE. Mail queries only."
Terms: Agent receives 15% commission on domestic sales; 20% on foreign sales. Offers written contract, binding for 1-5 years.
Fees: Charges $200-300 reading fee, nonrefundable; includes evaluation/critique of 2 to 4 pages, written by professional critics. Charges copyright registration fee of $200. Translation, editing, proofreading fees vary. Payment of criticism fee does not ensure representation. Charges for photocopying, postage, fax expenses.
Tips: Obtains new clients through recommendations from others and direct inquiries, as well as solicitation.

EDEN LITERARY AGENCY (I), P.O. Box 11033, Boulder CO 80301. (303)441-7877. Contact: Jodi Jill. Estab. 1992. Member of NWA, CAL, SCBWI. Represents 26 clients. 75% of clients are new/previously unpublished writers. Currently handles: 25% nonfiction books; 25% juvenile books; 25% novels; 25% puzzles/games. Member agents: Jodi Jill (nonfiction, juvenile), Karen Eden (fiction, special projects).
Handles: Nonfiction books, juvenile books, novels, poetry books, syndicated material. Considers these nonfiction areas: agriculture/horticulture; animals; business; computers/electronics; cooking/food/nutrition; crafts/hobbies; current affairs; government/politics/law; history; how-to; humor; juvenile nonfiction; language/literature/criticism; military/war; money/finance/economics; music/dance/theater/film; nature/environment; photography; science/technology; sports; translations; true crime/investigative; women's issues/women's studies; games and puzzles. Considers these fiction areas: action/adventure; cartoon/comic; confessional; detective/police/crime; experimental; fantasy; historical; horror; humor/satire; juvenile; literary; mystery/suspense; picture book; romance (contemporary, gothic, historical, regency); science fiction; westerns/frontier; young adult. Query or send entire ms. Reports in 1 month on queries and mss.
Recent Sales: *Puzzles, Plus*, by Caton Anderson (Jelm Publishing); *On An Aircraft Carrier*, by J. McGuire (JJF Publishing).
Terms: Agent receives 10-25% commission on domestic sales; 14% on foreign sales. Offers written contract, binding for 1-2 years, depending on project.
Fees: Does not charge a reading fee. Criticism service: $50. "Our critique includes a written report plus suggestions for improvements and markets. It is done by our three literary agents who together have published five books in the last three years and over 150 articles." Charges for photocopying, postage and telephone fees. Fees waived if on retainer. 80% of business is derived from commissions on ms sales; 20% is derived from reading fees or criticism services. Payment of criticism fee does not ensure representation.
Writer's Conferences: Locations in: Wisconsin, Colorado, California, Wyoming, Florida.
Tips: "We thrive on recommendations from others. We are new, ambitious and would like the opportunity to help you. Send us your manuscripts and SASE with a description on where you want your work at in two years. Then we'll see if we can help. Listen to other writers and you'll know where to send your material for a literary agent."

‡EVANS & ASSOCIATES, 14330 Caves Rd., Novelty OH 44072-9503. Phone/fax: (216)338-3264. Contact: Bryan Evans. Estab. 1987. Represents 6 clients. 50% of clients are new/previously published writers. Currently handles: 20% nonfiction books; 20% scholarly books; 10% juvenile books; 30% novels; 20% short story collections. Member agents: Bryan Evans (scholarly books, nonfiction, short story collections, juvenile); Clyde Evans (mysteries, self-help).
Handles: Nonfiction books, scholarly books, juvenile books, novels, short story collections. Considers all nonfiction and fiction areas. Query. Send outline and 3 sample chapters. Reports in 2 months on queries; 4 months on mss.
Recent Sales: Recently returned from sabbatical.
Terms: Agent receives 15% commission on domestic sales; 20% on foreign sales (with 10% to foreign agent). Offers written contract, binding for 1 year, but negotiable.
Fees: Criticism service: Negotiated individually with each ms, generally $50-100 which includes "at least one typewritten report which reviews the work with practical suggestions for improvement." Charges for "expenses that should be borne by writer. Only a reimbursement and with author's permission."
Tips: Listings such as the *Guide to Literary Agents* and recommendations from other agents, publishers, writers. "Clyde Evans is an attorney and also will review publisher contracts and/or negotiate with them at the rate of $75 per hour for review (usual total fee $75 to $150) and $125 per hour for negotiating with publisher. Initial consultation—no charge."

EXECUTIVE EXCELLENCE (IV), 1 East Center, Suite 303, Provo UT 84606. (801)375-4060. Fax: (801)377-5960. President: Ken Shelton. Agent: Trent Price. Estab. 1984. Represents 35-50 clients. Specializes in nonfiction trade books/management and personal development—books with a special focus such as ethics in business, managerial effectiveness, organizational productivity. Currently handles: 100% nonfiction. Member agents: Ken Shelton (president, editor); Trent Price (literary agent, acquisitions and sales); Jennifer Day (assistant agent and editor).
Handles: Nonfiction books, magazine articles, some foreign and multimedia rights. Considers these nonfiction areas: business; religious/inspirational; self-help/personal improvement.
Recent Sales: *Wave 3* (Prima).
Terms: Agent receives 15% commission on domestic sales. 75% of business is derived from commissions on ms sales; 10% from reading and review fees; 15% from assisted self-publishing services.
Fees: "We charge a $2 per page ($150 minimum) critical reading and review fee. $500 taken from initial advance to cover expenses (phone, mail, travel, etc.)"

Writer's Conferences: ABA (Chicago).

*FRIEDA FISHBEIN LTD. (II), 2556 Hubbard St., Brooklyn NY 11235-6223. (212)247-4398. Contact: Janice Fishbein. Estab. 1928. Represents 32 clients. 50% of clients are new/previously unpublished writers. Currently handles: 10% nonfiction books; 5% young adult; 60% novels; 10% movie scripts; 10% stage plays; 5% TV scripts. Member agents: Heidi Carlson (literary and contemporary); Douglas Michael (play and screenplay scripts).
Handles: Nonfiction books, young adult books, novels. Considers these nonfiction areas: animals; biography/autobiography; cooking/food/nutrition; current affairs; juvenile nonfiction; military/war; nature/environment; self-help/personal improvement; true crime/investigative; women's issues/women's studies. Considers these fiction areas: action/adventure; contemporary issues; detective/police/crime; family saga; fantasy; feminist; historical; humor/satire; mainstream; mystery/suspense; romance (contemporary, historical, regency); science fiction; thriller/espionage; young adult. Query letter a must before sending ms or fees. Reports in 2-3 weeks on queries; 4-6 weeks on mss accepted for evaluation.
Also Handles: Movie scripts, TV scripts ("not geared to a series"), stage plays.
Recent Sales: *Ghost in The Machine*, by David Gilman (play and screenplay).
Terms: Agent receives 10% commission on domestic sales; 15% on foreign sales. Offers written contract, binding for 30 days, cancellable by either party, except for properties being marketed or already sold.
Fees: Charges $80 reading fee up to 50,000 words, $1 per 1,000 words thereafter for new authors; $80 for plays, TV, screenplays. Criticism service included in reading fee. Offers "an overall critique. Sometimes specific staff readers may refer to associates for no charge for additional readings if warranted." 60% of business is derived from commissions on ms sales; 40% is derived from reading fees or criticism services. Payment of criticism fee does not ensure representation.
Tips: Obtains new clients through recommendations from others. "*Always* submit a query letter first with an SASE. Manuscripts should be done in large type, double-spaced and one and one-half-inch margins, clean copy and edited for typos, etc."

*FLANNERY, WHITE AND STONE/THE WRITERS ADVOCATE (II), 1675 Larimer St., 4th Floor, Denver CO 80202. (303)592-1233. Fax: (303)534-0577. Contact: Robin Barrett. Estab. 1987. Represents 45 clients. 20% of clients are new/previously unpublished writers. Specializes in mainstream and literary fiction, unique nonfiction, business and medical books. Currently handles: 40% nonfiction books; 25% juvenile books; 40% fiction. Member agents: Kendall Bohannon (mainstream and literary fiction, juvenile); Constance Solowiej (mainstream and literary fiction, nonfiction, business); Robert FitzGerald (business, medical).
Handles: Nonfiction books, history; juvenile books; novels; short story collections. Considers these nonfiction areas: business; child guidance/parenting; current affairs; ethnic/cultural interests; gay/lesbian issues; government/politics/law; health/medicine; history; juvenile nonfiction; money/finance/economics; music/dance/theater/film; nature/environment; New Age/metaphysics; photography; psychology; religious/inspirational; self-help/personal improvement; sociology; sports; women's issues/women's studies. Considers these fiction areas: action/adventure; contemporary issues; ethnic; experimental; family saga; feminist; gay; historical; humor/satire; juvenile; lesbian; literary; mainstream; mystery/suspense; picture book; psychic/supernatural; regional; romance (contemporary, historical); science fiction; thriller/espionage; young adult. Send outline/proposal plus 2 sample chapters. Reports in 1 month on queries; 2 months on mss.
Recent Sales: *The Kind of Light That Shines on Texas*, by Reginald McKnight (Little, Brown & Co.); *Confessions of a Healer*, by Dr. O.T. Bonnett (MacMurray Beck Publishers).
Terms: Agent receives 15% on domestic sales; 20% on foreign sales. Offers written contract.
Fees: "Due to the overwhelming number of manuscripts we receive, we now charge a reading and analysis fee for new and unpublished writers. The fee includes a three to five page overall evaluation report. Charges for photocopying unless author provides copies." 90% of business is derived from commissions; 10% from critiques. Payment of reading fee does not ensure representation.
Writers' Conferences: Aspen Writers' Conference (Aspen CO).
Tips: "Make your nonfiction proposals professional and publisher-ready; let your fiction speak for itself."

An asterisk indicates those agents who only charge fees to new or previously unpublished writers or to writers only under certain conditions.

*JOAN FOLLENDORE LITERARY AGENCY (II), 298 Country Club Dr., San Luis Obispo CA 93401-8921. (805)545-9297. Fax: (805)545-9297. Contact: Joan Follendore, Kevin Menton, William Brown. Estab. 1988. Member of Book Publicists of Southern California; ABA. Represents 60 clients. 50% of clients are new/previously unpublished writers. Currently handles: 55% nonfiction books; 12% scholarly books; 20% juvenile books; 10% novels; 1% poetry books; 2% short story collections. Member agents: Joan Follendore (adult nonfiction); Kevin Menton (children's books); William Brown (art and architecture).

Handles: Nonfiction books, textbooks, scholarly books, religious books, juvenile books, novels, picture books, poetry, short story collections. No scripts for stage or screen. Considers these nonfiction areas: agriculture/horticulture; animals; art/architecture/design; biography/autobiography; business; child guidance/parenting; crafts/hobbies; current affairs; education; ethnic/cultural interests; government/politics/law; health/medicine; history; how-to; humor; interior design/decorating; juvenile nonfiction; language/literature/criticism; military/war; money/finance/economics; nature/environment; New Age/metaphysics; popular culture; psychology; religious/inspirational; science/technology; self-help/personal improvement; sociology; true crime/investigative; women's issues/women's studies. Considers all fiction areas. Query first. Reports in 1 week on queries.

Recent Sales: *Point of Power: A Relationship With Your Soul,* by Kay Snow-Davis (Element Books).

Terms: Agent receives 15% on domestic sales; 20% on foreign sales. Offers written contract.

Fees: "No fee to authors who've been published in the prior few years by a major house. Other authors are charged a reading fee and our editing service is offered. For nonfiction, we completely edit the proposal/outline and sample chapter; for fiction and children's, we need the entire manuscript. Editing includes book formats, questions, comments, suggestions for expansion, cutting and pasting, etc." Also offers other services: proofreading, rewriting, proposal development, authors' public relations, etc. 65% of business is derived from commissions on ms sales; 35% is derived from reading or editing fees. Payment of fees does not ensure representation unless "revisions meet our standards."

Writer's Conferences: ABA (Chicago).

Tips: Obtains new clients through recommendations from others and personal contacts at literary functions. "Study and make your query as perfect and professional as you possibly can."

FORTHWRITE LITERARY AGENCY (II), 3579 E. Foothill Blvd., Suite 327, Pasadena CA 91107. Phone/fax: (818)798-0793. E-mail: dfde10a (Prodigy). Contact: Wendy L. Zhorne. Estab. 1989. Member of WNBA. Represents 50 clients. 25% of clients are new/previously unpublished writers. Specializes in nonfiction, fiction, juvenile. Currently handles: 40% nonfiction books; 18% juvenile books; 40% novels; 2% scripts. Member agent: Roy Carlisle (academic, religious and psychology books).

Handles: Considers commercial nonfiction in these areas: self-help and how-to on psychology, pop psychology, health, alternative health, business, child care/parenting, theology, religion, inspirational, spirituality, home maintenance and management, cooking, crafts, interior design, art, biography, writing, film, consumer reference, ecology, coffee table and art books, current affairs, women's studies, economics and history. Considers these adult fiction areas: historical fiction; also literary, romantic suspense, religious, mainstream, mystery/suspense/thriller, metaphysical. "Exemplary fiction from new or established authors." Query. Reports in 3-4 weeks on queries; 4-6 weeks on ms. "No unsolicited manuscripts!"

Recent Sales: *The Official Guide to North American Flea Markets,* by Jim Goodridge (Bob Adams, Inc.); *The All New How-to Guides,* (juvenile series) by Trevor Romain; *Nature Crafts for Children* (Baker House); *Women of Faith,* by David Collins (Crossway).

Also Handles: TV scripts (episodic drama, sitcom). Considers scripts for existing TV shows. "We have sold many things to Star Trek, Voyager and Deep Space Nine. We also occasionally sell the film rights to books we handle." Considers scripts for features, TV and cable, and pilots for sitcoms. All genres *except* horror, and "B-movie science fiction."

Recent Sales: "Deep Space Nine" and "Voyager" by Mark Gehred O'Connell (Paramount Studios); "The Trevor Romain Show," by Trevor Romain (Hollywood & Vine Productions).

Terms: Agent receives 15% on domestic sales; 20% on foreign sales. Offers written contract, which is binding for 1 year.

Fees: Charges reading/critique fee "for all materials requested, unless writer has previous serious credits related to topic (same field/genre); $25 for juvenile under 5,000 words. In extreme circumstances we will line critique an exemplary manuscript to aid in improvement so we can represent the writer (fewer than three manuscripts/year). Our reading fee includes an overview of major strengths/weaknesses, such as dialogue, plot, flow, characterization for fiction; structure, subject organization, readability, for nonfiction and the 'why' of acceptance or rejection by us."

Writers' Conferences: Attends ABA, CBA, Frankfurt Booksellers' Convention, many regional conferences and regularly lectures at local colleges and universities on finding an agent or how to write nonfiction.

Tips: Obtains new clients through referrals, recommendations by editors and producers, chambers of commerce, satisfied authors, advertising, conferences etc. "Please check your material, including query and cover letter, for spelling and typing errors before sending. If you are worried whether your material will arrive, send a postcard to return to you dated; don't search area codes for agent's home number; always send a SASE with queries. Never tell an agent, 'My grandmother loved it.' Know your subject, genre and competition."

FRAN LITERARY AGENCY (I, II), 7235 Split Creek, San Antonio TX 78238-3627. (210)684-1659. Contact: Fran Rathmann. Estab. 1993. Signatory of WGA, ASCAP. Represents 22 clients. 55% of clients are new/previously unpublished writers. "Very interested in Star Trek novels/screenplays." Currently handles: 15% nonfiction books; 10% juvenile books; 30% novels; 5% novellas; 5% poetry books; 15% movie scripts; 20% TV scripts.

Handles: Nonfiction books, novels. Considers these nonfiction areas: agriculture/horticulture; animals; biography/autobiography; business; child guidance/parenting; cooking/food/nutrition; crafts/hobbies; ethnic/cultural interests; health/medicine; history; how-to; humor; interior design/decorating; juvenile nonfiction; military/war; nature/environment; religious/inspirational; self-help/personal improvement. Considers these fiction areas: action/adventure; cartoon/comic; contemporary issues; detective/police/crime; fantasy; historical; horror; humor/satire; juvenile; mainstream; mystery/suspense; picture book; regional; romance (contemporary, historical); science fiction; thriller/espionage; westerns/frontier; young adult. Send outline plus 3 sample chapters. For picture books and poetry send entire ms. Reports in 2 weeks on queries; 2 months on mss.

Recent Sales: *101 Ways to Raise a Good Kid*, by Albert Santos (Globe); *Of Myths and Men*, by Louise Felix (Pocket Books); *Endlight*, by Skylan Kent (TOR).

Also Handles: Movie scripts (feature film, documentary, animation), TV scripts (TV mow, episodic drama). Considers these script subject areas: action/adventure; cartoon/animation; comedy; contemporary issues; detective/police/crime; family saga; historical; horror; humor; juvenile; mainstream; mystery/suspense; romantic comedy and drama; science fiction; thriller; westerns/frontier. Send entire ms.

Recent Sales: *The Life of St. Andrew*, by Henry Sauveneot (Davis Entertainment); *Leatherbreeches*, by Patt Nelson (Davis Entertainment).

Terms: Agent receives 15% commission on domestic sales; 20% on foreign sales. Needs "letter of authorization," usually binding for 6 months.

Fees: Charges $25 processing fee, nonrefundable. Offers criticism service. 80% of business is derived from commissions on mss sales; 20% from criticism services. Payment of fee does not ensure representation.

Writers' Conferences: SAWG, San Antonio (Spring).

Tips: Obtains clients through recommendations, listing in telephone book. "Please send SASE or Box!"

GELLES-COLE LITERARY ENTERPRISES (II), 12 Turner Rd., Pearl River NY 10965. (914)735-1913. President: Sandi Gelles-Cole. Estab. 1983. Represents 50 clients. 25% of clients are new/unpublished writers. "We concentrate on published and unpublished, but we try to avoid writers who seem stuck in mid-list." Specializes in commercial fiction and nonfiction. Currently handles: 50% nonfiction books; 50% novels.

Handles: Nonfiction books, novels. "We're looking for more nonfiction—fiction has to be complete to submit—publishers buying fewer unfinished novels." Does not read unsolicited mss. Reports in 3 weeks.

Terms: Agent receives 15% commission on domestic and dramatic sales; 20% on foreign sales.

Fees: Charges $100 reading fee for proposal; $150/ms under 250 pages; $250/ms over 250 pages. "Our reading fee is for evaluation. Writer receives total evaluation, what is right, what is wrong, is book 'playing' to market, general advice on how to fix." Charges writers for overseas calls, overnight mail, messenger. 5% of income derived from fees charged to writers. 50% of income derived from sales of writer's work; 45% of income derived from editorial service.

THE GISLASON AGENCY (II), 219 Main St. SE, Suite 506, Minneapolis MN 55414-2160. (612)331-8033. Fax: (612)331-8115. Attorney/Agent: Barbara J. Gislason. Estab. 1992. Member of Minnesota State Bar Association, Art & Entertainment Law Section, MIPLA Copyright Committee, The Loft, Midwest Fiction Writers, UMBA. 70% of clients are new/previously unpublished writers. Specializes in fiction and nonfiction. Currently handles: 30% nonfiction books; 70% novels. Member agents: Dara Moskowitz, Teri Russek.

Handles: Nonfiction books, novels. Considers these nonfiction areas: how-to; law; self-help/ personal improvement; true crime/investigative. Considers these fiction areas: fantasy; mystery/ suspense; romance (contemporary, gothic, historical, regency); science fiction; law-related. Query with outline plus 3 sample chapters. Reports in 1 month on queries, 2 months on mss.
Terms: Agent receives 15% commission on domestic sales; 20% on foreign sales. Offers written contract, binding for 1 year with option to renew.
Fees: Client pays for all submission costs.
Writer's Conferences: Midwest Fiction Writers; ABA.
Tips: Obtains half of new clients through recommendations from others and half from *Guide to Literary Agents* and *Literary Market Place.* "Cover letter should be well written and include a detailed synopsis of the work, the first three chapters and author information. If the work was written with a specific publisher in mind, this should be communicated. In addition to owning an agency, Ms. Gislason practices law in the area of Art and Entertainment and has a broad spectrum of industry contacts."

GLADDEN UNLIMITED (II), P.O. Box 7912, San Diego CA 92167. (619)224-5051. Agent Contact: Carolan Gladden. Estab. 1987. Represents 15 clients. 90% of clients are new/previously unpublished writers. Currently handles: 40% nonfiction; 60% novels.
Handles: Novels, nonfiction. Considers these nonfiction areas: celebrity biography; business; how-to; self-help; true crime/investigative. Considers these fiction areas: action/adventure; detective/police/crime; ethnic; glitz; horror; mainstream; thriller. "No romance or children's." Query with synopsis. Reports in two weeks on queries; two months on mss.
Recent Sales: Two nonfiction titles.
Terms: Agent receives 15% commission on domestic sales; 20% on foreign sales.
Fees: Does not charge a reading fee. Criticism service: $100 (manuscript to 400 pages.) $200 (over 400 pages.) for diagnostic marketability evaluation. "Offers six to eight pages of specific recommendations to turn the project into a saleable commodity. Also includes a copy of handy guide 'Be a Successful Writer.' Dedicated to helping new authors achieve publication."

LUCIANNE S. GOLDBERG LITERARY AGENTS, INC. (II), Suite 6-A, 255 W. 84th St., New York NY 10024. (212)799-1260. Editorial Director: Jonah Goldberg. Estab. 1974. Represents 65 clients. 10% of clients are new/unpublished writers. "Any author we decide to represent must have a good idea, a good presentation of that idea and writing skill to compete with the market. Representation depends solely on the execution of the work whether writer is published or unpublished." Specializes in nonfiction works, "but will review a limited number of novels." Currently handles: 75% nonfiction books; 25% novels. Member agents: Cyril Hiltebrand (editorial); Jane Moseley (editorial).
Handles: Nonfiction books, novels. Query with outline. Reports in 2 weeks on queries; 3 weeks on mss. "If our agency does not respond within 1 month to your request to become a client, you may submit requests elsewhere."
Recent Sales: *Death Row Women*, by Tom Kuncl (Simon & Schuster); *The Immigrants*, by Dylan Ross (HarperCollins).
Terms: Agent receives 15% commission on domestic sales; 25% on dramatic and foreign sales.
Fees: Charges reading fee on unsolicited mss: $150/full-length ms. Criticism service included in reading fee. "Our critiques run three or four pages, single-spaced. They deal with the overall evaluation of the work. Three agents within the organization read and then confer. Marketing advice is included." Payment of fee does not ensure the agency will represent a writer. Charges for phone expenses, cable fees, photocopying and messenger service after the work is sold. 80% of income derived from commission on ms sales.

*ANDREW HAMILTON'S LITERARY AGENCY (II), P.O. Box 604118, Cleveland OH 44104-0118. (216)881-1032. Contact: Andrew Hamilton. Estab. 1991. Represents 15 clients. 60% of clients are new/previously unpublished writers. Currently handles: 50% nonfiction books; 7% scholarly books; 3% juvenile books; 40% novels. Member agent: Andrew Hamilton (music, business, self-help, how-to, sports).
Handles: Nonfiction books, juvenile books, novels, novellas. Considers these nonfiction areas: animals; biography/autobiography; business; child guidance/parenting; cooking/food/nutrition; current affairs; ethnic/cultural interests; government/politics/law; health/medicine; history; juvenile nonfiction; money/finance/economics; music/dance/theater/film; psychology; religious/inspirational; self-help/personal improvement; sociology; sports; true crime/investigative; women's

Check the Subject Index to find the agents who are interested in your nonfiction or fiction subject area.

issues/women's studies; minority concerns; pop music. Considers these fiction areas: action/ adventure; cartoon/comic; confessional; contemporary issues; detective/police/crime; erotica; ethnic; family saga; humor/satire; juvenile; mystery/suspense; psychic/supernatural; religious/ inspiration; romance (contemporary); sports; thriller/espionage; westerns/frontier; young adult. Send entire ms. Reports in 1 week on queries; 3 weeks on mss.
Terms: Agent receives 15% commission on domestic sales; 20% on foreign sales. Offers written contract.
Fees: "Reading fees are for new authors and are nonrefundable. My reading fee is $50 for 60,000 words or less and $100 for manuscripts over 60,000 words. I charge a one time marketing fee of $200 for manuscripts." 70% of business derived from commissions on ms sales; 30% from reading fees or criticism services.
Tips: Obtains new clients through recommendations, solicitation and writing seminars. "Be patient: the wheels turn slowly in the publishing world."

THE HARDY AGENCY (II), 3020 Bridgeway, Suite 204, Sausalito CA 94965. (415)380-9985. Contact: Anne Sheldon, Michael Vidor. Estab. 1990. Represents 10 clients. 75% of clients are new/ previously unpublished writers. Specializes in literary fiction with some nonfiction. Currently handles: 20% nonfiction books; 80% novels. Member agents: Anne Sheldon (literary fiction); Michael Vidor (media, marketing and PR).
Handles: Nonfiction books, novels. Considers these nonfiction areas: biography/autobiography; current affairs; government/politics/law; health/medicine; New Age/metaphysics. Considers these fiction areas: contemporary issues; literary. Send outline plus 5 sample chapters. Reports in 1 month on queries and mss.
Terms: Agent receives 15% commission on domestic sales; 20% on foreign sales. Offers written contract, binding for 1 year. Charges for postage, copying. Book editing available ($25 per hour). 85% of business is derived from commissions on mss; 15% from editing fees.
Tips: Obtains new clients from recommendations. Welcomes new authors.

*GIL HAYES & ASSOC. (III), P.O. Box 63333, Memphis TN 38163. Contact: Gil Hayes. Estab. 1992. Signatory of WGA. Represents 10 clients. 10% of clients are new/previously unpublished writers. Specializes in serious scripts and literary fiction. Currently handles: 20% nonfiction books; 20% fiction; 60% movie scripts. Member agent: Gil Hayes.
• See the expanded listing for this agency in Script Agents.

HEACOCK LITERARY AGENCY, INC. (II), 1523 Sixth St., Suite #14, Santa Monica CA 90401-2514. (310)393-6227. Fax: (310)451-8524. Contact: Jim or Rosalie Heacock. Estab. 1978. Member of AAR, ATA, SCBWI; signatory of WGA. Represents 60 clients. 30% of clients are new/ previously unpublished writers. Currently handles: 85% nonfiction books; 5% juvenile books; 5% novels; 5% movie scripts. Member agents: Jim Heacock (business expertise, parenting, psychology, sports, diet, health, nutrition); Rosalie Heacock (psychology, philosophy, women's studies, alternative health, new technology, futurism, new idea books, art and artists).
Handles: Adult nonfiction books, juvenile books. Considers these nonfiction areas: anthropology; art/architecture/design; biography (contemporary celebrity); business; child guidance/parenting; cooking/food/nutrition; crafts/hobbies; current affairs; education; ethnic/cultural interests; gay/lesbian issues; government/politics; health/medicine (including alternative health); history; how-to; humor; juvenile nonfiction (no beginners); language/literature/criticism; military/war; money/finance/economics; music/dance/theater/film; nature/environment; New Age/ metaphysics; popular culture; psychology; religious/inspirational; science/technology; self-help/ personal improvement; sociology; sports; true crime; women's issues/women's studies. Considers limited selection of top children's book authors; no beginners. Query with sample chapters. Reports in 2 weeks on queries; 2 months on mss.
Recent Sales: *Think Yourself Rich,* by E. Joseph Cossman and William Cohen, Ph.D. (Simon & Schuster); *Tangle Tales,* by Don and Audrey Wood (Harcourt Brace); *Life Song,* by William Schul, Ph.D. (Stillpoint Publishers).
Also Handles: Movie scripts (feature film, documentary, animation), TV scripts (TV mow). Prefers submissions by Writers Guild members. Considers these script subject areas: action/ adventure; contemporary issues; detective/police/crime; family saga; feminist; horror; humor; mainstream; mystery/suspense; psychic/supernatural; sports; thriller.
Recent Sales: *The Name of The Game Is Death,* by Dan J. Marlowe (Hugh Gross Productions); *Never Live Twice,* by Dan J. Marlowe (Nicki Marvin Productions, Inc.).
Terms: Agent receives 15% commission on domestic sales; 25% on foreign sales, "if foreign agent used; if sold directly, 15%." Offers written contract, binding for 1 year.
Fees: Does not charge a reading or evaluation fee. "We provide consultant services to authors who do their own marketing and only need assistance in negotiating their contracts. Charge is $125/hour and no commission charges (5% of our business). Charges for actual expense for

telephone, postage, packing, photocopying. We provide copies of each publisher submission letter and the publisher's response." 95% of business is derived from commission on ms sales.
Writers' Conferences: Attends Santa Barbara City College Annual Writer's Workshop; Pasadena City College Writer's Forum; UCLA Symposiums on Writing Nonfiction Books, Society of Children's Book Writers and Illustrators.
Tips: Obtains new clients through "referrals from present clients and industry sources as well as mail queries. Take time to write an informative query letter expressing your book idea, the market for it, your qualifications to write the book, the 'hook' that would make a potential reader buy the book. Always enclose SASE, compare your book to others on similar subjects and show how it is original."

*ALICE HILTON LITERARY AGENCY (II), 13131 Welby Way, North Hollywood CA 91606. (818)982-2546. Fax: (818)765-8207. Estab. 1986. Eager to work with new/unpublished writers. "Interested in any quality material, although agent's personal taste runs in the genre of 'Cheers.' 'L.A. Law,' 'American Playhouse,' 'Masterpiece Theatre' and Woody Allen vintage humor."
Handles: Nonfiction, fiction, juvenile. Considers these fiction areas: action/adventure; confessional; contemporary issues; detective/police/crime; erotica; ethnic; fantasy; historical; horror; humor/satire; juvenile; literary; mainstream; mystery/suspense; picture book; psychic/supernatural; romance (contemporary, gothic, historical, regency); science fiction; sports; thriller/espionage; westerns/frontier; young adult.
Also Handles: Movie scripts (feature film, documentary), TV scripts (TV mow, sitcom). Considers all script subject areas.
Terms: Agent receives 10% commission. Brochure available with SASE. Preliminary phone call appreciated.
Fees: Charges evaluation fee of $2.50/1,000 words. Charges for phone, postage and photocopy expenses.
Recent Sales: *Madame President*, by Donald Metz (New Saga Press); *Todo Crudo: All Raw Foods for Health and Longevity*, by Boris Isaacson (Tomorrow Now Press).

‡THE EDDY HOWARD AGENCY, % 37 Bernard St., Eatontown NJ 07724-1906. (908)542-3525. Contact: Eddy Howard Pevovar, N.D., M.S., Ph.D. Estab. 1986. Signatory of WGA. Represents 110 clients. 16% of clients are new/previously unpublished writers. Specializes in film, sitcom and literary. Currently handles: 5% nonfiction books; 5% scholarly books; 2% textbooks; 5% juvenile books; 5% novels; 2% novellas; 25% movie scripts; 30% TV scripts; 10% stage plays; 5% short story collections; 1% syndicated material; 5% other. Member agents: Eddy Howard Pevovar, N.D., M.S., Ph.D. (agency executive); Francine Gail (director of comedy development).
 • See the expanded listing for this agency in Script Agents.

*YVONNE TRUDEAU HUBBS AGENCY (II), 32371 Alipaz, #101, San Juan Capistrano CA 92675-4147. (714)496-1970. Contact: Yvonne Hubbs. Estab. 1983; temporarily closed 1990, reopened 1993. Member of RWA. Represents 20 clients. 10% of clients are new/previously unpublished writers. Member agents: Thomas D. Hubbs, journalist (radio broadcasting/public relations); Yvonne Hubbs, agent, lecturer, writer.
Handles: Nonfiction books, novels. Considers these nonfiction areas: current affairs; history; women's issues/women's studies. Considers these fiction areas: action/adventure; contemporary issues; erotica; family saga; fantasy; feminist; glitz; historical; mainstream; mystery/suspense; psychic/supernatural; romance (contemporary, gothic, historical, regency); science fiction; thriller/espionage. Query with outline/proposal plus 1 sample chapter. Reports in 2 weeks on queries, 1 month on mss.
Terms: Agent receives 15% commission on domestic sales; 20% on foreign sales. Offers written contract, binding for 1 year, but can be cancelled with 30 days notice by both parties.
Fees: Charges $50 reading fee to new writers only; refundable if client is sold within 1 year. Criticism service included in reading fee. "I personally write the critiques after reviewing the manuscript." Charges for travel expenses (if approved), photocopying, telegraph/fax expenses, overseas phone calls. 60% of business is derived from commissions on ms sales; 40% derived from reading fees or criticism services. Payment of criticism fee does not ensure representation.
Writer's Conferences: RWA (Hawaii); Romantic Times (Texas).
Tips: Obtains new clients through recommendations, conferences. "Be professional in your query letter. Always SASE with a query."

INDEPENDENT PUBLISHING AGENCY (I), P.O. Box 176, Southport CT 06490-0176. (203)268-4878. Contact: Henry Berry. Estab. 1990. Represents 25 clients. 30% of clients are new/previously unpublished writers. Especially interested in topical nonfiction (historical, political, social topics) and literary fiction. Currently handles: 50% nonfiction books; 10% juvenile books; 20% novels; 20% short story collections.

Handles: Nonfiction books, juvenile books, novels, short story collections. Considers these non-fiction areas: anthropology/archaeology; art/architecture/design; biography/autobiography; business; child guidance/parenting; cooking/food/nutrition; crafts/hobbies; current affairs; ethnic/cultural interests; government/politics/law; history; juvenile nonfiction; language/literature/criticism; military/war; money/finance/economics; music/dance/theater/film; nature/environment; photography; popular culture; psychology; religious; science/technology; self-help/personal improvement; sociology; sports; true crime/investigative; women's issues/women's studies. Considers these fiction areas: action/adventure; cartoon/comic; confessional; contemporary issues; crime; erotica; ethnic; experimental; fantasy; feminist; historical; humor/satire; juvenile; literary; mainstream; mystery/suspense; picture book; psychic/supernatural; thriller/espionage; young adult. Send synopsis/outline plus 2 sample chapters. Reports in 2 weeks on queries; 4-6 weeks on mss.
Terms: Agent receives 15% commission on domestic sales; 20% on foreign sales. Offers "agreement that spells out author-agent relationship."
Fees: Does not charge reading fee. Offers criticism service if requested. Charges average $1/page, with $50 minimum for poetry and stories; $100 minimum for novels and nonfiction. Written critique averages 3 pages—includes critique of the material, suggestions on how to make it marketable and advice on marketing it. Charges for postage, photocopying and UPS mailing, legal fees (if necessary). All expenses over $25 cleared with client. 90% of business is derived from commissions on ms sales; 10% derived from criticism services.
Tips: Usually obtains new clients through referrals from clients, notices in writer's publications. Looks for "proposal or chapters professionally presented, with clarification of the distinctiveness of the project and grasp of intended readership."

CAROLYN JENKS AGENCY (II), 205 Walden St., Cambridge MA 02140-3507. Phone/fax: (617)876-6927. Contact: Carolyn Jenks. Estab. 1966. Signatory of WGA. 50% of clients are new/previously unpublished writers. Currently handles: 15% nonfiction books; 40% novels; 20% movie scripts; 10% stage plays; 15% TV scripts.
Handles: Nonfiction books, juvenile books, novels. Considers these nonfiction areas: animals; anthropology/archaeology; biography/autobiography; business; computers/electronics; current affairs; education; ethnic/cultural interests; gay/lesbian issues; government/politics/law; health/medicine; history; how-to; humor; inspirational; juvenile nonfiction; nature/environment; New Age/metaphysics; popular culture; psychology; science/technology; self-help/personal improvement; sociology; sports; theater/film; true crime/investigative; women's issues/women's studies. Considers these fiction areas: action/adventure; cartoon/comic; contemporary issues; detective/police/crime; ethnic; family saga; fantasy; feminist; gay; glitz; historical; horror; humor/satire; juvenile; lesbian; literary; mystery/suspense; regional; romance (contemporary, historical); science fiction; sports; thriller/espionage; westerns/frontier; young adult. Query. Reports in 2 weeks on queries; 4-6 weeks on mss.
Also Handles: Movie scripts (feature film, documentary), TV scripts (TV mow, episodic drama), stage plays. Considers these script subject areas: action/adventure; comedy; contemporary issues; detective/police/crime; family saga; historical; humor; juvenile; mainstream; mystery/suspense; romantic comedy and drama; science fiction; thriller; westerns/frontier.
Terms: Agent receives 15% commission on domestic sales; 10% on film and TV. Offers written contract.
Fees: Charges reading fee to non-WGA members: 1-100 pages $60; 100-350 pages $100; screenplay $60. WGA members exempted.
Tips: Query first in writing with SASE.

‡*JLM LITERARY AGENTS (III), 5901 Warner Ave., Suite 92, Huntington Beach CA 92649. (714)547-4870. Fax: (714)840-5660. Contact: Judy Semler. Estab. 1985. Represents 25 clients. 5% of clients are new/previously unpublished writers. Agency is "generalist with an affinity for high-quality, spiritual self-help psychology and mystery/suspense." Currently handles: 90% nonfiction books; 10% novels.
Handles: Nonfiction books, novels. Considers these nonfiction areas: biography/autobiography; business (popular); current affairs; music/dance/theater/film; nature/environment; popular culture; psychology; religious/inspirational; self-help/personal improvement; sociology; true crime/investigative; women's issues/women's studies. Considers these fiction areas: glitz; mystery/suspense; psychic/supernatural; contemporary romance. Send an outline with 2 sample chapters for nonfiction, query with 3 chapters for fiction—except for mystery/suspense, send entire ms. No faxed submissions. Reports in 1 month on queries; 8-10 weeks on mss.
Recent Sales: *The Breast Cancer Companion*, by Kathy LaTour (Morrow/Avon); *Diversity Survival Guide*, by Gardenswartz and Rowe (Irwin).
Terms: Agent receives 15% commission on domestic sales; 10% on foreign sales plus 15% to subagent. Offers written contract, binding for 1 year, with 30-day escape clause.

Fees: Does not charge a reading fee. Does not do critiques, but will refer to freelancers. Charges $150 marketing fee for unpublished authors or to authors changing genres. Charges for routine office expenses associated with the marketing. 100% of business is derived from commissions on ms sales.
Tips: "Most of my clients are referred to me by other clients or editors. If you want to be successful, learn all you can about proper submission and invest in the equipment or service to make your project *look* dazzling. Computers are available to everyone and the competition looks good. You must at least match that to even get noticed."

LARRY KALTMAN LITERARY AGENCY (II), 1301 S. Scott St., Arlington VA 22204-4656. (703)920-3771. Contact: Larry Kaltman. Estab. 1984. Represents 15 clients. 75% of clients are new/previously unpublished writers. Currently handles: 10% nonfiction books; 75% novels; 10% novellas; 5% short story collections.
Handles: Nonfiction books, novels, novellas, short story collections. Considers these nonfiction areas: health/medicine; science/technology; self-help/personal improvement; sports. Considers these fiction areas: action/adventure; confessional; contemporary issues; detective/police/crime; erotica; ethnic; family saga; feminist; gay; glitz; historical; humor/satire; lesbian; literary; mainstream; mystery/suspense; regional; romance (contemporary); sports; thriller/espionage; westerns/frontier; young adult. Query. Reports in 1 week on queries; 2 weeks on mss.
Recent Sales: *A Year of Favor*, by Julia MacDonnell (Morrow); *A Well-Behaved Little Boy*, by Tom Smith (STARbooks Press); *Pickleball Practitioners*, by Larry Kaltman (The Washington Post).
Terms: Agent receives 15% commission on domestic sales; 20% on foreign sales. Offers written contract, binding for 1 year.
Fees: Charges reading fee "for all unsolicited manuscripts; for up to 300 pages, the fee is $250. For each additional page the charge is 50¢/page. The criticism and reading services are indistinguishable. Author receives an approximately 1,500-word report commenting on writing quality, structure and organization and estimate of marketability. I write all critiques." Charges for postage, mailing envelopes and long-distance phone calls.
Writers' Conferences: Attends Washington Independent Writers Spring Conference.
Tips: Obtains new clients through query letters, solicitation. "Plots, synopses and outlines have very little effect. A sample of the writing is the most significant factor. I also sponsor the Washington Prize for Fiction, an annual competition for unpublished works." Awards: $3,000 (1st prize), $2,000 (2nd prize), $1,000 (3rd prize).

*J. KELLOCK & ASSOCIATES LTD. (II), 11017 80th Ave., Edmonton, Alberta T6G 0R2 Canada. (403)433-0274. Contact: Joanne Kellock. Estab. 1981. Member of Writer's Guild of Alberta. Represents 50 clients. 10% of clients are new/previously unpublished writers. "I do very well with all works for children but do not specialize as such." Currently handles: 30% nonfiction books; 1% scholarly books; 50% juvenile books; 19% novels.
Handles: Nonfiction, juvenile, novels. Considers these nonfiction areas: animals; anthropology/archaeology; art/architecture/design; biography/autobiography; business; child guidance/parenting; cooking/food/nutrition; current affairs; government/politics/law; health/medicine; history; juvenile nonfiction; language/literature/criticism; money/finance/economics; music/dance/theater/film; nature/environment; New Age/metaphysics; self-help/personal improvement; sports; true crime/investigative; women's issues/women's studies. Considers these fiction areas: action/adventure; contemporary issues; detective/police/crime; ethnic; experimental; family saga; fantasy; feminist; glitz; historical; horror; humor/satire; juvenile; literary; mainstream; mystery/suspense; picture book; romance; science fiction; sports; thriller/espionage; westerns/frontier; young adult. Query with outline plus 3 sample chapters. Reports in 8-10 weeks on queries; 4-5 months on mss.
Recent Sales: *Egg Hunting for Koko*, by Tololwa Mollel (Lodestar/Dutton, US; Lester Publishing, Canada); *Anansi's Feast*, by Tololwa Mollel (Clarion Books); *Sisters of the Dark Moon*, by Frank Pesando (NAL).
Terms: Agent receives 15% commission on domestic sales (English language); 20% on foreign sales. Offers written contract, binding for 2 years.
Fees: Charges $150 reading fee. "Fee under no circumstances is refundable. *New writers only are charged.*" $140 (US) to read 3 chapters plus brief synopsis of any work; $100 for children's picture book material. "If style is working with subject, the balance is read free of charge. Criticism is also provided for the fee. If style is not working with the subject, I explain why not; if talent is obvious, I explain how to make the manuscript work. I either do critiques myself or my reader does them. Critiques concern themselves with use of language, theme, plotting—all the usual. Return postage is always required. I cannot mail to the US with US postage, so always enclose a SAE, plus either IRCs or cash. Canadian postage is more expensive, so double the amount for either international or cash. I do not return on-spec long-distance calls, if the writer

chooses to telephone, please request that I return the call collect. However, a query letter is much more appropriate." 70% of business is derived from commissions on ms sales; 30% is derived from reading fees or criticism service. Payment of criticism fee does not ensure representation.

Tips: Obtains new clients through recommendations from others, solicitations. "Do not send first drafts. Always double space. Very brief outlines and synopsis are more likely to be read first. For the picture book writer, the toughest sale to make in the business, please study the market before putting pen to paper. All works written for children must fit into the proper age groups regarding length of story, vocabulary level. For writers of the genre novel, read hundreds of books in the genre you've chosen to write, first. In other words, know your competition. Follow the rules of the genre exactly. For writers of science fiction/fantasy and the mystery, it is important a new writer has many more than one such book in him/her. Publishers are not willing today to buy single books in most areas of genre. Publishers who buy science fiction/fantasy usually want a two/three book deal at the beginning."

*NATASHA KERN LITERARY AGENCY (II), P.O. Box 2908, Portland OR 97208-2908. (503)297-6190. Contact: Natasha Kern. Estab. 1986. Member of AAR, RWA, MWA, SinC. Specializes in literary and commercial fiction and nonfiction.

Handles: Nonfiction books, novels. Considers these nonfiction areas: agriculture/horticulture; animals; anthropology/archaeology; art/architecture/design; biography/autobiography; business; child guidance/parenting; cooking/food/nutrition; current affairs; education; ethnic/cultural interests; gay/lesbian issues; health/medicine; how-to; language/literature/criticism; money/finance/economics; nature/environment; New Age/metaphysics; popular; psychology; science/technology; self-help/personal improvement; true crime/investigative; women's issues/women's studies; women's spirituality. Considers these fiction areas: contemporary issues; detective/police/crime; ethnic; family saga; feminist; historical; mainstream; mystery/suspense; romance (contemporary, gothic, historical, regency, futuristic); thriller/espionage; westerns/frontier. "Send a detailed, one-page query with a SASE, including the submission history, writing credits and information about how complete the project is. If requested, for fiction send a two to three page synopsis, in addition to the first three chapters, for nonfiction, submit a proposal consisting of an outline, two chapters, SASE, and a note describing market and how project is different or better than similar works. Also send a blurb about the author and information about the length of the manuscript. For category fiction, a five- to ten-page synopsis should be sent with the chapters." Reports in 1-2 weeks on queries.

Recent Sales: *Black Cross*, by Greg Iles (Dutton); *Oprah Winfrey*, by George Mair (Carol); *Liberty Blue*, by Robin Hatcher (Harper); *Enchant The Heavens*, by Kathleen Morgan (Kensington); *Direct Descendant*, by Charles Wilson (St. Martin's); *Serpents in the Manger*, by Harris and Milam (Barricade).

Terms: Agent receives 15% commission on domestic sales; 20% on foreign sales.

Fees: Charges $45 reading fee for unpublished authors. "When your work is sold, your fee will be credited to your account. Please do not send fee unless requested."

Writers' Conference: Attends RWA National Conference (Hawaii); Santa Barbara Writer's Conference; Golden Triangle Writer's Conference.

LAW OFFICES OF ROBERT L. FENTON PC (II), 31800 Northwestern Hwy., #390, Farmington Hills MI 48334. (810)855-8780. Fax: (810)855-3302. Contact: Robert L. Fenton. Estab. 1960. Signatory of SAG. Represents 40 clients. 25% of clients are new/previously unpublished writers. Currently handles: 25% nonfiction books; 10% scholarly books; 10% textbooks; 10% juvenile books; 35% novels; 2½% poetry books; 2½% short story collections; 5% movie scripts. Member agents: Robert L. Fenton; Julia Fenton.

Handles: Nonfiction books, novels, short story collections, syndicated material, movie scripts, TV scripts. Considers these nonfiction areas: biography/autobiography; business; child guidance/parenting; computers/electronics; current affairs; government/politics/law; health/medicine; military/war; money/finance/economics; music/dance/theater/film; religious/inspirational; science/technology; self-help/personal improvement; sports; true crime/investigative; women's issues/women's studies. Considers these fiction areas: action/adventure; contemporary issues; detective/police/crime; ethnic; glitz; historical; humor/satire; mainstream; mystery/suspense; romance;

Agents ranked I-IV are actively seeking new clients. Those ranked V or those who prefer not to be listed have been included to inform you they are not currently looking for new clients.

science fiction; sports; thriller/espionage; westerns/frontier. Send 3-4 sample chapters (approximately 75 pages). Reports in 2 weeks on queries.
Recent Sales: *Black Tie Only*, by Julia Fenton (Contemporary Books); *Clash of Eagles*, by Leo Rutman (Fawcett); *Blue Orchids*, by Julia Fenton (Berkley).
Terms: Agent receives 15% on domestic sales. Offers written contract, binding for 1 year.
Fees: Charges a reading fee. "To waive reading fee, author must have been published at least 3 times by a mainline New York publishing house." Criticism service: $350. Charges for office expenses, postage, photocopying, etc. 75% of business is derived from commissions on ms sales; 25% derived from reading fees or criticism service. Payment of a criticism fee does not ensure representation.
Tips: Obtains new clients through recommendations from others, individual inquiry.

L. HARRY LEE LITERARY AGENCY (II), Box #203, Rocky Point NY 11778-0203. (516)744-1188. Contact: L. Harry Lee. Estab. 1979. Signatory of WGA; member of Dramatists Guild. Represents 285 clients. 65% of clients are new/previously unpublished writers. Specializes in movie scripts. "Comedy is our strength, both features and sitcoms, also movie of the week, science fiction, novels and TV." Currently handles: 30% novels; 50% movie scripts; 5% stage plays; 15% TV scripts.
 • See the expanded listing for this agency in Script Agents.

‡LEE SHORE AGENCY (II), 440 Friday Rd., The Sterling Building, Pittsburgh PA 15209-2114. (412)821-6099. Fax: (412)821-6211. Owner: Cynthia Sterling. Contact: Patrick Freeman. Estab. 1988. Represents 175 clients. 50% of clients are new/previously published writers. "Presently we are actively seeking scholarly and textbooks." Currently handles: 40% nonfiction books; 3% scholarly books; 3% textbooks; 2% juvenile books; 50% novels; 1% movie scripts; 1% short story collections. Member agents: Megan Davidson, Patrick Freeman, Cynthia Sterling.
 • At press time it was learned that this agency has been recommending subsidy publishing contracts to clients.
Handles: Nonfiction books, scholarly books, textbooks, juvenile books, novels. Considers these nonfiction areas: anthropology/archaeology; biography/autobiography; business; child guidance/parenting; education; government/politics/law; health/medicine; history; how-to; military/war; money/finance/economics; music/dance/theater/film; nature/environment; New Age/metaphysical; psychology; religous/inspirational; science/technology; self-help/personal improvement; sociology; sports; true crime/investigative; women's issues/women's studies. Considers these fiction areas: action/adventure; contemporary issues; detective/police/crime; ethnic; family saga; fantasy; historical; horror; juvenile; literary; mainstream; psychic/supernatural; religious/inspirational; romance (contemporary, gothic, historical, regency); science fiction; sports; thriller/espionage; westerns/frontier; young adult. Query. Reports in 3-5 days on queries; 1 month on mss.
Recent Sales: *How to Make and Distribute Your Own Horror Movie*, by John Russo (Zinn Publishing Group); *Loving Enemies*, by Dr. Lynn Hawker (Barclay House); *Adult Survivors*, by Dr. F. Cruz and Laura Essen (Jason Aronson Inc.).
Terms: Agent receives 15% commission on domestic sales; 15% on dramatic sales; 20% on foreign sales. Offers written contract.
Fees: Charges reading fee. Charges for out-of-pocket expenses. "Client is billed within one month of incurred expense; has one month to pay. Client is notified in advance of expenditures." 10% of business is derived from reading or criticism fees.
Writer's Conferences: Poets Society (Greece).

JAMES LEVINE COMMUNICATIONS, INC. (II), 330 Seventh Ave., 14th Floor, New York NY 10001. (212)268-4846. Fax: (212)465-8637. Estab. 1989. Represents 65 clients. 33⅓% of clients are new/previously unpublished writers. Specializes in business, psychology, parenting, health/medicine, narrative nonfiction. Currently handles: 75% nonfiction books; 20% juvenile books; 5% novels.
Handles: Nonfiction books, juvenile books, novels. Considers these nonfiction areas: animals; art/architecture/design; biography/autobiography; business; child guidance/parenting; computers/electronics; cooking/food/nutrition; gardening; gay/lesbian issues; health/medicine; juvenile nonfiction; money/finance/economics; nature/environment; New Age/metaphysics; psychology; religious/inspirational; science/technology; self-help/personal improvement; sociology; sports; women's issues/women's studies. Considers these fiction areas: contemporary issues; juvenile; literary; mainstream; young adult. Send outline/proposal plus 1 sample chapter. Reports in 2 weeks on queries; 1 month on mss.
Recent Sales: *Undercurrents: A Therapist Recovering with Her Depression*, by Martha Manning (Harper San Francisco); *Marguerite Kelly's Family Almanac*, by Marguerite Kelly (Fireside); *The Beer Lover's Bible*, by Robert Klein (Workman); *Why Parents Disagree*, by Ron Tapfel Ph.D. with Roberta Israeloff (William Morrow).

Terms: Agent receives 15% commission on domestic sales; 20% on foreign sales. Offers written contract; length of time varies per project.

Fees: Does not charge reading fee. Provides editorial development services; fee depends upon the project. Charges for out-of-pocket expenses—telephone, fax, postage and photocopying—directly connected to the project. 90% of business is derived from commissions on ms sales; 10% derived from editorial development services. Payment of an editorial development fee ensures representation.

Writers' Conferences: ASJA Annual Conference in New York City (May '95).

Tips: Obtains new clients through client referrals. "We work closely with clients on editorial development and promotion. We work to place our clients as magazine columnists and have created columnists for *McCall's* and *Child*. We work with clients to develop their projects across various media—video, software, and audio."

‡LIGHTHOUSE LITERARY AGENCY (V), P.O. Box 1002, Mooresville NC 28115-1002. Phone/fax: (704)892-8045. Contact: Sandra Kangas. Estab. 1988. Also P.O. Box 2105, Winter Park FL 32790. (407)339-9130. Contact: Tonia Kangas. Member of WIF, Authors Guild, ABA. Represents 50 clients. 54% of clients are new/previously unpublished writers. Specializes in fiction and nonfiction juvenile and adult books. Currently handles: 50% nonfiction books; 10% juvenile books; 30% novels; 10% short story collections.

Handles: Nonfiction, novels. Considers these nonfiction areas: agriculture/horticulture; animals; anthropology/archaeology; art/architecture/design; biography/autobiography; business; child guidance/parenting; computers/electronics; cooking/food/nutrition; crafts/hobbies; current affairs; ethnic/cultural interest; health/medicine; history; interior design/decorating; juvenile nonfiction; military/war; money/finance/economics; music/dance/theater/film; nature/environment; photography; psychology; self-help/personal improvement; sports; women's issues/women's studies. Considers these fiction areas: action/adventure; cartoon/comic; contemporary issues; detective/police/crime; ethnic; experimental; family saga; feminist; historical; humor/satire; juvenile; literary; mainstream; mystery/suspense; picture book; regional; science fiction; sports; thriller/espionage; westerns/frontier; young adult. Query with outline plus 3 or more sample chapters for nonfiction or entire ms for fiction. Reports in 2 weeks on queries; 2 months on mss.

Terms: Agent receives 15% commission on domestic sales; 20% on foreign sales. Offers written contract.

Fees: Charges $60 reading fee. "Waived for recent/trade published authors. Fee is applied toward marketing expenses if author is accepted as client. Criticism service: $1/ms page, minimum $200. Longer works may be discounted. Critiques are done by writers who have been published in the field they are asked to judge. Charges marketing fee for normal marketing expenses such as phone, postage, domestic fax." 82% of business is derived from commissions on ms sales; 18% derived from reading fees or criticism services. Payment of criticism fee does not ensure representation. "If author rewrites the work, we agree to read it again at no charge, no guarantee."

Tips: Obtains new clients through professional organizations, recommendations from clients and editors. "Send a short query or cover letter with brief description of the project. Mention qualifications and experience. Say what made you decide to write it, why there's a need for it, where your book will fit in the marketplace. Always enclose a stamped return mailer. Even if the work is accepted, we might have to return it for changes."

THE LITERARY BRIDGE (I, II), P.O. Box 10593, Sedona AZ 86339. Contact: Genero Capshaw. Estab. 1992. Member of RGV Writers Guild, Prescott Writer's Assoc. Represents 25-30 clients. 50% of clients are new/previously unpublished writers. "We specialize in helping authors turn a good idea and good writing into a marketable manuscript." Currently handles: 60% nonfiction books; 40% novels. Member agents: Genero Capshaw, M. Shephard, T. Tallman.

Handles: Nonfiction books, novels, how-to, self-help. Considers these nonfiction areas: animals; anthropology; business; health/medicine; history; money/finance/economics; nature/environment; psychology; self-help/personal improvement; sports; true crime; women's issues/women's studies. Considers these fiction areas: action/adventure; contemporary issues; detective/police/crime; fantasy; feminist; historical; mainstream; mystery/suspense; romance (contemporary, historical); science fiction; sports; thriller; westerns/frontier. Query with 3 sample chapters. Reports in 1-2 weeks on queries; 4-6 weeks on mss.

Terms: Agent receives 10-15% commission on domestic sales; 15-20% on foreign sales; 20% on dramatic sales. Offers written contract, binding for 1 year. "The handling fee includes phone, photocopying and postage and is refunded upon the sale of the manuscript by this agency." 95% of business is derived from commissions on manuscript sales.

Tips: Obtains new clients through solicitation and conferences. "We bridge the gap between writers who know their genre or category and publishers who want quality work."

‡*LITERARY GROUP WEST (I), 300 W. Shaw, Suite 453, Clovis CA 93612. (209)297-9409. Fax: (209)225-5606. Contact: Ray Johnson. Estab. 1993. Represents 2 clients. 50% of clients are new/ previously unpublished writers. Specializes in novels. Currently handles: 20% nonfiction books; 70% novels; 10% novellas. Member agents: B.N. Johnson Ph.D. (English literature).
Handles: Nonfiction books, novels. Considers these nonfiction areas: current affairs; ethnic/ cultural interests; military/war; true crime/investigative. Considers these fiction areas: action/ adventure; detective/police/crime; historical; mainstream; thriller/espionage. Query. Reports in 1 week on queries; 1 months on mss.
Recent Sales: *Invitro Madonna*, by Beverly White (European-Czech).
Terms: Agent receives 20% commission on domestic sales; 25% on foreign sales. Offers written contract.
Fees: Charges expense fees to unpublished authors. Deducts expenses from sales of published authors.
Writers' Conferences: Fresno County Writers Conf. (Fresno, CA, July).
Tips: Obtains new clients through recommendation. "Query first with strong letter. Please send SASE with query letter."

*TONI LOPOPOLO LITERARY AGENCY (II), P.O. Box 1484-A, Manhattan Beach CA 90266-8484. (310)546-6690. Fax: (310)546-2930. Contact: Toni Lopopolo. Estab. 1990. Member of Sisters in Crime. Represents 40 clients. 85% of clients are new/previously unpublished writers. Specializes in true crime. Currently handles: 75% nonfiction books; 10% scholarly books; 15% novels. Member agent: Toni Lopopolo (mysteries, self-help/how-to).
Handles: Nonfiction books, novels. Considers these nonfiction areas: animals; anthropology/ archaeology; art/architecture/design; biography/autobiography; business; child guidance/parenting; cooking/food/nutrition; ethnic/cultural interests; health/medicine; history; how-to; language/ literature/criticism; money/finance/economics; nature/environment; New Age/metaphysics; popular culture; psychology; self-help/personal improvement; true crime/investigative; women's issues/women's studies. Considers these fiction areas: contemporary issues; detective/police/ crime; erotica; ethnic; family saga; feminist; glitz; historical; literary; mainstream; mystery/suspense; psychic/supernatural; westerns/frontier. Query. Reports in 1 month on queries; 6 weeks on mss, "unless mail is overwhelming!!"
Recent Sales: *Lifebank*, by Harold Olgin, M.D.; *Breeds Apart: Matching Breed Characteristics of Dogs to Lifestyles of Owners*, by Nancy Baer and Steve Duno (Berkley).
Terms: Agent receives 15% commission on domestic sales; 10-15% on foreign sales. Offers written contract, binding for 2 years.
Fees: Charges reading and written evaluation fee "for *unrecommended*, first novelists only. Will work with the promising; entire fee refunded upon sale of novel." Offers criticism service: fee depends on length and genre of novel. Charges marketing fee to cover phone, fax, postage and photocopying only. 95% of business is derived from commissions on ms sales; 5% is derived from reading fees or criticism services. Payment of criticism fee does not ensure representation.
Writers' Conferences: San Diego State University (San Diego, January 1995); California State University (Long Beach CA, September); Mystery Writers (Phoenix AZ, February 1995).
Tips: Obtains new clients through recommendations from clients, lectures, workshops, conferences, publishers.

M.H. INTERNATIONAL LITERARY AGENCY (II), 706 S. Superior St., Albion MI 49224. (517)629-4919. Contact: Mellie Hanke. Estab. 1992. Represents 15 clients. 75% of clients are new/previously unpublished writers. Specializes in historical novels. Currently handles: 100% novels. Member agents: Jeff Anderson (detective/police/crime); Martha Kelly (historical/mystery); Costas Papadopoulos (suspense; espionage); Nikki Stogas (confession); Marisa Handaris (foreign language ms reviewer, Greek); Mellie Hanke (Spanish); Erin Jones Morgart (French).
Handles: Novels. Considers these fiction areas: confession; detective/police/crime; historical; mystery. "We also handle Greek and French manuscripts in the above categories, plus classics. No westerns." Send all material to the attention of Mellie Hanke. Reports in 6 weeks on mss.
Terms: Agent receives 10% commission on domestic sales; 15% on foreign sales.
Fees: Charges reading fee and general office expenses. Offers criticism service, translations from above foreign languages into English, editing, evaluation and typing of mss.
Tips: "We provide translation from Greek and French into English, editing and proofreading."

VIRGINIA C. MCKINLEY, LITERARY AGENCY (I, II), 1830 Roosevelt Ave., #101, Racine WI 53406. (414)637-9590. Contact: Virginia C. McKinley. Estab. 1992. 100% of clients are new/ previously unpublished writers. Currently handles: 30% nonfiction books; 20% juvenile books; 40% novels; 10% poetry books. Member agent: Virginia C. McKinley (religious books, biography/autobiography, fiction).

Handles: Nonfiction books, juvenile books, novels, short story collections, poetry books, movie scripts, stage plays, TV scripts. Considers these nonfiction areas: animals; biography/autobiography; business; child guidance/parenting; ethnic/cultural interests; health/medicine; juvenile nonfiction; military/war; money/finance/economics; music/dance/theater/film; nature/environment; psychology; religious/inspirational; self-help/personal improvement; sociology; sports; women's issues/women's studies. Considers these fiction areas: action/adventure; contemporary issues; detective/police/crime; ethnic; family saga; fantasy; feminist; humor/satire; juvenile; literary; mystery/suspense; religous/inspiration; romance (historical); westerns/frontier. Query with entire ms or 3 sample chapters. Reports in 1 month.
Terms: Agent receives 15% commission on domestic sales; 20% on foreign sales. Offers written contract.
Fees: Criticism service: $125 for 3-page critique. Reports within 2 months. Charges marketing fee—$100 per year for authors under contract, photocopying ms, postage, phone, any unusual expenses. 95% of business is derived from commissions on ms sales; 5% is derived from criticism services. Payment of criticism fee does not ensure representation.
Tips: Obtains new clients through solicitation. "No multiple submissions. We feel a dynamic relationship between author and agent is essential. SASE must be included with ms or 3 chapters; also query. Will work with writer to develop his full potential."

MARCH MEDIA INC., 1114 Oman Dr., Brentwood TN 37027. (615)377-1146. Fax: (615)373-1705. Contact: Etta Wilson. Estab. 1989. Represents 20 clients. Specializes in juvenile authors and illustrators. Currently handles: 30% nonfiction books; 70% juvenile books.
Handles: Considers juvenile nonfiction and fiction and adult gift books. Send entire ms with SASE. Reports in 1 month on ms.
Terms: Agent receives 12% commission on domestic sales, "depends on whether they are author or author/illustrator." Offers a written contract, binding for 5 years.
Fees: Does not charge a reading fee. Criticism service: $30/hour.
Tips: Obtains new clients through contacts from having been editor. "Our agency is helpful in two ways: specific knowledge about publisher's current needs; and reviews and negotiates contract."

THE DENISE MARCIL LITERARY AGENCY (II), 685 West End Ave., New York NY 10025. (212)932-3110. Contact: Denise Marcil. Estab. 1977. Member of AAR. Represents 70 clients. 40% of clients are new/previously unpublished authors. Specializes in women's commercial fiction, how-to, self-help and business books, popular reference. Currently handles: 30% nonfiction books; 70% novels.
• See Denise Marcil's article, *On the Merits: The Case for Reading Fees*, in this edition.
Handles: Nonfiction books, novels. Considers these nonfiction areas: business; child guidance/ parenting; nutrition; health/medicine; how-to; inspirational; interior design/decorating; money/ finance/economics; New Age/metaphysics; psychology; self-help/personal improvement; women's issues/women's studies. Considers these fiction areas: feminist; mystery/suspense; romance (contemporary, historical, regency). Query with SASE *only!* Reports in 2-3 weeks on queries; "we do not read unsolicited manuscripts."
Recent Sales: *Black Gold*, by Anita Richmond Bunkley (Dutton); *Children Who Say No When You Want Them to Say Yes*, by Dr. James Wendell (Macmillan); *Hot Texas Nights*, by Mary Lynn Baxter (Warner Books).
Terms: Agent receives 15% commission on domestic sales; 20% on foreign sales. Offers written contract, binding for 2 years.
Fees: Charges $45 reading fee for 3 chapters and outline "that we request only." Charges $100/year for postage, photocopying, long-distance calls, etc. 99.9% of business is derived from commissions on ms sales; .1% is derived from reading fees and criticism.
Writers' Conferences: University of Texas Conference at Dallas (September 1995); Golden Triangle (Beaumont, TX, October); Pacific Northwest Writers Conference.
Tips: Obtains new clients through recommendations from other authors and "35% of my list is from query letters! Only send a one-page query letter. I read them all and ask for plenty of material; I find many of my clients this way. *Always* send a SASE."

*THE EVAN MARSHALL AGENCY (III), 22 S. Park St., Suite 216, Montclair NJ 07042-2744. (201)744-1661. Fax: (201)744-6312. Contact: Evan Marshall. Estab. 1987. Member of AAR, RWA. Currently handles: 48% nonfiction books; 48% novels; 2% movie scripts; 2% TV scripts.
• See Evan Marshall's article, *An Agent's Day*, in the 1992 edition of the *Guide*.
Handles: Nonfiction books, novels. Considers these nonfiction areas: animals; biography/autobiography; business; child guidance/parenting; cooking/food/nutrition; crafts/hobbies; current affairs; government/politics/law; health/medicine; history; how-to; humor; interior design/decorating; language/literature/criticism; military/war; money/finance/economics; music/dance/theater/

film; nature/environment; New Age/metaphysics; psychology; religious/inspirational; science/ technology; self-help/personal improvement; true crime/investigative; women's issues/women's studies. Considers these fiction areas: action/adventure; contemporary issues; detective/police/ crime; erotica; ethnic; family saga; glitz; historical; horror; humor/satire; literary; mainstream; mystery/suspense; psychic/supernatural; religious/inspirational; romance (contemporary, gothic, historical, regency); science fiction; thriller/espionage; westerns/frontier. Query. Reports in 1 week on queries; 2 months on mss.

Recent Sales: *The Apothecary Rose,* by Candace M. Robb (St. Martin's); *People Will Talk,* by Lucianne Goldberg (Pocket Books); *Presumption,* by Julia Barrett (M. Evans).

Also Handles: Movie scripts (feature film), TV scripts (TV mow, episodic drama, sitcom). Considers these script subject areas: action/adventure; comedy; contemporary issues; detective/ police/crime; erotica; ethnic; family saga; fantasy; glitz; historical; horror; humor; mainstream; mystery/suspense; psychic/supernatural; religious/inspirational; romantic comedy and drama; science fiction; sports; teen; thriller; western/frontier.

Terms: Agent receives 15% on domestic sales; 20% on foreign sales. Offers written contract.

Fees: Charges a fee to consider for representation material by *writers who have not sold a book or script.* "Send SASE for fee schedule. There is no fee if referred by a client or an editor or if you are already published in the genre of your submission."

Tips: Obtains many new clients through referrals from clients and editors.

*MEWS BOOKS LTD., 20 Bluewater Hill, Westport CT 06880. (203)227-1836. Fax: (203)227-1144. Contact: Sidney B. Kramer. Estab. 1972. Represents 35 clients. Prefers to work with published/established authors; works with small number of new/unpublished authors "producing professional work." Specializes in juvenile (pre-school through young adult), cookery, self-help, adult nonfiction and fiction, technical and medical and electronic publishing. Currently handles: 20% nonfiction books; 10% novels; 20% juvenile books; 40% electronic; 10% miscellaneous. Member agent: Fran Pollak (assistant).

Handles: Nonfiction books, novels, juvenile books, character merchandising and video use of illustrated published books. Query with precis, outline, character description, a few pages of sample writing and author's bio.

Recent Sales: *Dr. Susan Love's Breast Book,* by Susan M. Love, MD, with Karen Lindsey (Addison-Wesley); *It Works for Us!,* by Tom McMahon (Pocket Books/S&S).

Terms: Agent receives 15% commission on domestic sales; 20% on foreign sales.

Fees: Does not charge a reading fee. "If material is accepted, agency asks for $350 circulation fee (4-5 publishers), which will be applied against commissions (waived for published authors)." Charges for photocopying, postage expenses, telephone calls and other direct costs.

Tips: "Principle agent is an attorney and former publisher. Offers consultation service through which writers can get advice on a contract or on publishing problems."

‡MID-AMERICA LITERARY AGENCY (I), Rt. 3, Box 1310, Troup TX 75789. (903)842-3788. Contact: Dale Martin. Estab. 1994. Novels only—no nonfiction. Specializes in science fiction, horror, action adventure. Currently handles: 100% novels.

Handles: Novels. Considers these fiction areas: action/adventure; historical; horror; mainstream; romance (contemporary, historical); science fiction; sports; thriller/espionage; westerns/ frontier. Query with outline/proposal, no phone calls please. Reports in 2 weeks on queries; 1 month on mss.

Terms: Agent receives 10% commission on domestic sales; 20% on foreign sales.

Fees: Charges $50 reading fee. "If manuscript is rejected, will provide a written critique." Charges for "bare-bones" expenses (photocopying, etc.)

Tips: Obtains new clients through query letters. "Brand new agency. Run by published author who had his own share of 'horror' stories trying to get published. I think there are a lot of good stories out there by new and exciting authors who are having a hard time seeing their work in print. I'd like to help, but send your best work neatly typed with SASE."

‡MONTGOMERY LITERARY AGENCY (II), P.O. Box 8822, Silver Spring MD 20907-8822. (301)230-1807. Contact: M.E. Olsen. Estab. 1987. Signatory of WGA. Represents 50 clients. 25% of clients are new/previously unpublished writers. Equal interest in scripts (films and TV mainly) and books. Currently handles: 8% nonfiction books; 2% scholarly books; 2% textbooks;

 An asterisk indicates those agents who only charge fees to new or previously unpublished writers or to writers only under certain conditions.

2% poetry; 5% juvenile books; 25% novels; 30% movie scripts; 20% TV scripts; 1% short story collections; 2% syndicated material; 2% comics for varied marketing).
● See the expanded listing for this agency in Script Agents.

*DAVID H. MORGAN LITERARY AGENCY, INC. (II), P.O. Box 14810, Richmond VA 23221. (804)672-2740. Contact: David H. Morgan. Estab. 1987. Represents 25-35 clients. Currently handles: 60% nonfiction books; 40% novels.
Handles: Nonfiction books, novels. Considers all categories, ages middle-reader through adult. No children's illustrated books. No Harlequin or Silhouette romances; all other romances accepted. Query with SASE. Reports in 1 week on queries.
Recent Sales: *The Love Your Heart Guide for the 1990s*, by Lee Belshin (Contemporary); *Prophecies & Predictions: Everyone's Guide to the Coming Changes*, by Moira Timms (Ballantine).
Terms: Agent receives 15% commission on domestic sales; 20% on foreign sales. Offers written contract.
Fees: Charges a fee to evaluate works by unpublished authors. Fee refunded if ms accepted by agency. "Please query for details." Client must provide photocopies of mss. 95% of business is derived from commissions on ms sales; 5% is derived from reading or criticism fees.
Tips: Obtains new clients through recommendations from others, workshops and advertisements.

*BK NELSON LITERARY AGENCY & LECTURE BUREAU (II, III), 84 Woodland Rd., Pleasantville NY 10570-1322. (914)741-1322. Fax: (914)741-1324. Contact: Bonita Nelson, John Benson or Erv Rosenfeld. Estab. 1980. Member of NACA, Author's Guild, NAFE, ABA. Represents 62 clients. 40% of clients are new/previously unpublished writers. Specializes in business, self-help, how-to, novels, biographies. Currently handles: 40% nonfiction books; 5% CD-ROM/electronic products; 40% novels; 5% movie scripts; 5% TV scripts; 5% stage plays. Member agents: Bonita Nelson (business books); John Benson (Director of Lecture Bureau); Erv Rosenfeld (novels and TV scripts); Dave Donnelly (videos).
Handles: Nonfiction books, CD ROM/electronic products, scholarly books, novels. Considers these nonfiction areas: agriculture; animals; anthropology/archaeology; art/architecture/design; biography/autobiography; business; child guidance/parenting; computers/electronics; cooking/food/nutrition; crafts/hobbies; current affairs; education; ethnic/cultural interests; government/politics/law; health/medicine; history; how-to; language/literature/criticism; military/war; money/finance/economics; music/dance/theater/film; nature/environment; popular culture; psychology; religious/inspirational; science/technology; self-help/personal improvement; sociology; sports; true crime/investigative; women's issues/women's studies. Considers these fiction areas: action/adventure; cartoon/comic; contemporary issues; detective/police/crime; family saga; fantasy; feminist; glitz; historical; horror; literary; mainstream; mystery/suspense; psychic/supernatural; romance (contemporary, historical); science fiction; sports; thriller/espionage; westerns/frontier. Query. Reports in 1 week on queries; 2-3 weeks on ms.
Recent Sales: *Woman Language, Woman Power*, by D.R. Mindell (Paramount); *Ads That Sell*, by Robert W. Bly (Paramount); *Where No One Has Gone: Star Trek Trivia*, by Robert W. Bly (HarperCollins); *Quick Tips For Business Writers*, by Gary Blake, Ph.D. (McGraw-Hill).
Also Handles: Movie scripts (feature film, documentary, animation), TV scripts (TV mow, episodic drama, sitcom), stage plays. Considers these script subject areas: action/adventure; family saga; fantasy; historical; horror; mainstream; psychic/supernatural; romantic comedy and drama; thriller; westerns/frontier.
Terms: Agent receives 15% on domestic sales; 10% on foreign sales. Offers written contract, exclusive for 8-12 months.
Fees: Charges $325 reading fee for *new clients' material only*. "It is not refundable. We usually charge for the first reading only. The reason for charging in addition to time/expense is to determine if the writer is saleable and thus a potential client."
Tips: Obtains new clients through referrals and reputation with editors. "We handle the business aspect of the literary and lecture fields. We handle careers as well as individual book projects. If the author has the ability to write and we are harmonious, success is certain to follow with us handling the selling/business."

NEW WRITING AGENCY (I, II), Box 1812, Amherst NY 14226-7812. Contact: Richard Lynch. Estab. 1991. Presently seeking new clients. 90% of clients are new/previously unpublished writers. Specializes in "nurturing and representation of new writers." Currently handles: 20% nonfiction books; 60% novels; 5% novellas; 5% poetry books; 5% short story collections; 5% other. Member agents: Richard Lynch (literary, short story, poetry); Sam Meade (science fiction, western, action/adventure); Mason Deitz (nonfiction); Rita Howard (romance).
Handles: Nonfiction books, scholarly books, novels, novellas, short story collections, poetry books, movie scripts, stage plays. Considers these nonfiction areas: animals, anthropology/ar-

chaeology; art/architecture/design; biography/autobiography; business; child guidance/parenting; computers/electronics; cooking/food/nutrition; crafts/hobbies; current affairs; history; how-to; humor; military/war; music/dance/theater/film; nature/environment; New Age/metaphysics; photography; popular culture; psychology; religious/inspirational; science/technology; self-help/personal improvement; sociology; sports; true crime/investigative. Considers these fiction areas: action/adventure; confessional; contemporary issues; detective/police/crime; erotica; ethnic; experimental; family saga; fantasy; historical; horror; humor/satire; literary; mainstream; mystery/suspense; psychic/supernatural; romance (contemporary, gothic, historical, regency); science fiction; sports, thriller/espionage; westerns/frontier. Reports in 1 week on queries; 2-3 weeks on mss. Send SASE.

Terms: Agent receives 12.5% commission on domestic sales; 17.5% on foreign sales and sub-agents. Offers written contract, binding for 1 year (options).

Fees: Charges "$35 for unsolicited manuscripts seeking representation (rejections include one to two page critique). Developmental editing or reading critique fee is $1/page (four to eight page single-spaced critique addresses content, form, writing problems and successes and offers suggestions). Line editing fee is based on a sample edit. Workshops by mail available, developed individually to meet the needs of participants. Submissions for all services are considered for representation. Active marketing fees limited by agreement with author." Payment of criticism fee does not ensure representation.

Tips: "We often obtain clients from workshop or reading/critiquing service as we work to achieve proper standards in the writing. We accept only exceptional work for representation, but are willing to work with those who can take our criticism and use it in improving a text. Criticism is based on the market, and our replies to writers reflect marketability."

*NORTHEAST LITERARY AGENCY (II), 69 Broadway, Concord NH 03301-2736. (603)225-9162. Contact: Dale Harrington. Estab. 1973. Represents 15 clients. 50% of clients are new/previously unpublished writers. Specializes in popular fiction and nonfiction, children's picture books. Currently handles: 75% nonfiction books; 25% novels. Member agents: Victor A. Levine (fiction, mainstream, serious nonfiction); Dale Harrington (genre fiction and how-to nonfiction); Don Emmons (scholarly nonfiction).

Handles: Novels, nonfiction books, juvenile books, short story collections, poetry books, movie and TV scripts. Considers all nonfiction subjects, especially biography/autobiography; business; history; how-to; humor; music/dance/theater/film; science/technology; true crime/investigative. Considers all fiction especially cartoon/comic; detective/police/crime; humor/satire; mystery/suspense, picture book; science fiction; thriller/espionage. Query. Reports in 5 days on queries; 10 days on mss.

Recent Sales: *Surefire Way to Better Spelling*, by Robert Dixon (St, Martin's); *Making Words Stand Still*, by Donald Lyman (Houghton-Mifflin).

Terms: Agent receives 15% commission on domestic sales; 25% on foreign sales. Offers written contract, cancellable on 3-months' notice.

Fees: Charges a reading fee to unpublished writers, "refundable following a sale." Criticism service: costs depend on type of criticism and whether conducted by mail or in a seminar or workshop setting. Charges for extraordinary expenses, such as express mail, long-distance phone calls, extensive photocopying but not for marketing or ordinary office expenses."

Writers' Conferences: Underwrites Wells Writers' Workshop, which meets twice yearly in Wells, Maine.

Tips: Obtains new clients through classes, workshops, conferences, advertising in *Writer's Digest*, referrals. "Please be very specific about writing background, published credits and current project(s)." Always include SASE.

*NORTHWEST LITERARY SERVICES (II), 9-2845 Bellendean Rd. RR1, Shawnigan Lake, British Columbia V0R 2W0 Canada. (604)743-8236. Contact: Brent Laughren. Estab. 1986. Represents 20 clients. 75% of clients are new/previously unpublished writers. Specializes in working with new writers. Currently handles: 25% nonfiction books; 10% juvenile books; 60% novels; 5% short story collections. Member agent: Jennifer Chapman (juvenile books). Send juvenile queries etc. to Jennifer Chapman 2840 West Sixth Ave., Vancouver, British Columbia U6K 1X1 Canada.

Handles: Nonfiction books, juvenile books, novels, movie scripts, stage plays, TV scripts. Considers these nonfiction areas: agriculture/horticulture; animals; art/architecture/design; biography/autobiography; child guidance/parenting; cooking/food/nutrition; crafts/hobbies; ethnic/cultural interests; gay/lesbian issues; health/medicine; history; how-to; humor; juvenile nonfiction; language/literature/criticism; music/dance/theater/film; nature/environment; New Age/metaphysics; photography; popular culture; psychology; religious/inspirational; self-help/personal improvement; sports; translations; true crime/investigative; women's issues/women's studies. Considers these fiction areas: action/adventure; confessional; contemporary issues; detective/police/crime; erotica; ethnic; experimental; family saga; fantasy; feminist; historical; humor/

satire; juvenile; literary; mainstream; mystery/suspense; picture book; psychic/supernatural; regional; romance; science fiction; sports; thriller/espionage; westerns/frontier; young adult. Query with outline/proposal. Reports in 1 month on queries; 2 months on mss.

Terms: Agent receives 15% on domestic sales; 20% on foreign sales. Offers written contract.

Fees: Charges reading fee for unpublished authors. Children's picture books $50; fiction/nonfiction synopsis and first 3 chapters $75. Reading fee includes short evaluation. Criticism service: $100 for book outline and sample chapters up to 20,000 words. Charges 75¢-$1/page for copyediting and content editing; $1/page for proofreading; $10-20/page for research. "Other related editorial services available at negotiated rates. Critiques are two to three page overall evaluations, with suggestions. All fees, if charged, are authorized by the writer in advance." 75% of business is derived from commissions on ms sales; 25% is derived from reading fees or criticism service. Payment of criticism fee does not ensure representation.

Tips: Obtains new clients through recommendations. "Northwest Literary Services is particularly interested in the development and marketing of new and unpublished writers. We are also interested in literary fiction."

*OCEANIC PRESS (II), Seaview Business Park, 1030 Calle Cordillera, Unit #106, San Clemente CA 92673. (714)498-7227. Contact: Janis Hawkridge. Estab. 1956. Represents 35 clients. 15% of clients are new/previously unpublished writers. Specializes in celebrity interviews. Currently handles: 20% nonfiction books; 20% novels; 60% syndicated material. Member agents: Katherine Singer (child development, family relations). Janis Hawkridge (nonfiction editor); Peter Carbone (editor); Harvey Simonsen (subscriptions).

Handles: Nonfiction books, novels, syndicated material, biographies. Considers these nonfiction areas: biography/autobiography; business; cartoon books; child guidance/parenting; computers/electronics; health/medicine; how-to; juvenile nonfiction; money/finance/economics; music/dance/theater/film; New Age/metaphysics; psychology; science/technology; self-help/personal improvement; sports; true crime/investigative; women's issues/women's studies; movies. Considers these fiction areas: contemporary issues; detective/police/crime; erotica; experimental; family saga; fantasy; glitz; horror; mainstream; mystery/suspense; picture book; psychic/supernatural; romance (contemporary, gothic, regency); science fiction; sports; thriller/espionage; westerns/frontier; young adult. Send outline/proposal and list of published work. Reports in 1 month on queries; 6 weeks on mss.

Writer's Conference: ABA, International Book Fair in Frankfurt, Germany; International Book Fair in Tokyo, Japan; also New Delhi, India and London Book Fairs.

Recent Sales: *God's Pharmay*, by Marian Treben (Diana); *Solve a Crime*, by C. Gordon (Dover).

Terms: Agent receives 15% commission on domestic sales; 20% on foreign sales; "50% syndication only if wanted." Offers written contract, binding for 1 year.

Fees: Charges $350 reading fee to new writers only. Criticism service included in reading fee and done by professional readers. 98% of business is derived from commissions on ms sales; 2% is derived from reading fees or criticism service. Payment of criticism fee ensures representation, if marketable.

Tips: Obtains new clients through recommendations. "Do good writing and good research. Study the market."

*OCEANIC PRESS SERVICE, Seaview Business Park, 1030 Calle Cordillera, Unit #106, San Clemente CA 92672. (714)498-7227. Fax: (714)498-2162. Manager: Helen J. Lee. Estab. 1940. Represents 100 clients. Prefers to work with published/established authors; will work with a small number of new/unpublished authors. Specializes in selling features of worldwide interest; romance books, mysteries, biographies, nonfiction of timeless subjects, reprints of out-of-print titles. Currently handles: 20% nonfiction books; 30% novels; 10% juvenile books; 40% syndicated material.

Handles: Magazine articles, nonfiction books, novels, juvenile books, syndicated material. Will read—at no charge—unsolicited queries and outlines. Reports in 2 weeks on queries.

Recent Sales: *400 Crosswords* (Landoll); *60 Second Shiatzu*, by Eva Shaw (Heyne and 6 foreign publishers).

Terms: Agent receives 15% commission on domestic sales; 20% on foreign sales.

Fees: Charges $350/350 pages reading fee for unpublished writers. Reading fee includes detailed critique. "We have authors who published many books of their own to do the reading and give a very thorough critique." 2% of income derived from reading fees.

*ANDREA OLESHA AGENCY (I, II), P.O. Box 243, Wood Village OR 97060-0243. (503)667-9039. Contact: Andrea Olesha. Estab. 1992. Member of Willamette Writer's. Represents 2 clients. 100% of clients are new/previously unpublished writers. Specializes in nonfiction. Currently handles: 50% nonfiction books; 50% fiction.

Handles: Nonfiction books, juvenile books, novels. Considers these nonfiction areas: cooking/food/nutrition; ethnic/cultural interests; gay/lesbian issues; interior design/decorating; language/literature/criticism; music/dance/theater/film; nature/environment; self-help/personal improvement; women's issues/women's studies. Considers these fiction areas: action/adventure; contemporary issues; ethnic; experimental; family saga; fantasy; feminist; gay; glitz; humor/satire; juvenile; lesbian; literary; mainstream; mystery/suspense; psychic/supernatural; regional; religious/inspiration; science fiction; young adult. Query with sample chapters. Reports in 2 months on queries; 1 month on mss. "I do not return any material without an SASE."
Terms: Agent receives 10% commission on domestic sales; 15% on foreign sales. Offers written contract, binding for 1 year.
Fees: Charges reading fee "to new authors, refundable upon sale." Charges for postage.
Writers' Conferences: Willamette Writers Conference (Portland, OR, August).
Tips: Obtains new clients through advertising and listings in literary circles. "We have the contacts."

‡PACIFIC LITERARY SERVICES, (I, II), 1220 Club Court, Richmund CA 94803. (510)222-6555. Contact: Victor West. Estab. 1993. Represents 4 clients. 100% of clients are new/previously unpublished writers. Specializes in science fiction, fantasy, horror, military, historical and genre and general fiction and nonfiction. Currently handles: 25% movie scripts; 25% short story collections; 50% novels.
Handles: Nonfiction books, scholarly books, juvenile books, novels, movie scripts, TV scripts, unusual stories and factual subjects. Open to all nonfiction and fiction subject areas. Query. Send outline and 2-3 sample chapters. Reports in 3-4 weeks on queries; 2-4 months on mss.
Terms: Agent receives 15% commission on domestic sales; 25% on foreign sales. Offers written contract, binding for 4 years.
Fees: Criticism service: book ms up to 100,000 words $200; analysis of screenplay up to 150 pages $100; analysis of treatment, teleplay or sitcom script $60; marketing analysis $30. Critiques done by Victor West and vary from 2-3 pages for book almost ready to submit to 34½ pages for one needing extensive work; average 8-16 pages. Charges for postage only—clients supply copies. 100% of business is derived from reading or criticism fees.
Tips: Recommendations and queries. "The best way to get an agent and make a sale is to write well and be professional in all areas related to the writing business."

*WILLIAM PELL AGENCY (II), 300 E. 40th St., Suite 8D, New York NY 10016. (212)490-2845. Contact: Susan Kelly. Estab. 1990. Represents 6 clients. 95% of clients are new/previously unpublished writers. Member agent: Susan Kelly (fiction).
Handles: Novels. Considers these nonfiction areas: biography/autobiography; photography. Considers these fiction areas: action/adventure; detective/police/crime; humor/satire; thriller/espionage. Query with 2 sample chapters. Reports in 1 month on queries; 3 months on mss.
Recent Sales: *Endangered Beasties*, by Derek Pell (Dover).
Terms: Agent receives 15% commission on domestic sales; 20% on foreign sales. Offers written contract, binding for 1 year.
Fees: Charges $100 reading fee for new writers. 90% of business is derived from commission on ms sales; 10% is derived from reading fees or criticism services. Payment of criticism fees does not ensure representation.

PENMARIN BOOKS (II), P.O. Box 286, 58 Oak Grove Ave., Woodacre CA 94973-0286. (415)488-1628. Fax: (415)488-1123. President: Hal Lockwood. Editorial Director: John Painter. Estab. 1987. Represents 20 clients. 80% of clients are new/unpublished writers. "No previous publication is necessary. We do expect authoritative credentials in terms of history, politics, science and the like." Handles general trade nonfiction and illustrated books, as well as fiction. Member agent: John Painter (general, science, health).
Handles: Nonfiction books, fiction. Nonfiction books, query with outline. For fiction, query with outline and sample chapters. Will read submissions at no charge, but may charge a criticism fee or service charge for work performed after the initial reading. Reports in 2 weeks on queries; 1 month on mss.
Recent Sales: *How to Outsmart the Sun: The Ultimate Guide to Healthy, Young-Looking Skin*, by Michael Martin, M.D.; *Fast & Fabulous Parties*, by Michele Braden; *The Red Witch* and *Wolf in the Sanctuary*, by Georgia Elizabeth Taylor; *Compromised: Bush, Clinton and the CIA*, by Terry Reed.
Terms: Agent receives 15% commission on domestic sales; 15% on dramatic sales; 15% on foreign sales.
Fees: "We normally do not provide extensive criticism as part of our reading but, for a fee, will prepare guidance for editorial development. Charges $200/300 pages. Our editorial director writes critiques. These may be two to ten pages long. They usually include an overall evaluation

and then analysis and recommendations about specific sections, organization or style."

‡*PERKINS' LITERARY AGENCY (II)**, P.O. Box 48, Childs MD 21916. (410)398-2647. Contact: Esther R. Perkins. Estab. 1979. Represents 40 clients. 100% of clients are new/previously unpublished writers. Specializes in contemporary mainstream regency, mystery and suspense fiction. Currently handles: 100% novels.
Handles: Novels. Considers these fiction areas: action/adventure; detective/police/crime; family saga; historical; literary; mainstream; romance (contemporary, historical, regency); western/ frontier. Query with outline/proposal. Reports in 1 week on queries; 3 weeks on mss.
Terms: Agent receives 15% commission on domestic sales; 20% on foreign sales. Offers written contract.
Fees: Charges reading fee: 70-10,000 words $75; 125,000 words $100; 200,000 words $150; for writers not published by a major publisher within past 2 years, refundable if sale made within 1 year. 5% of business derived from reading or criticism fees.
Tips: Obtains new clients through word of mouth.

‡**ARTHUR PINE ASSOCIATES, INC. (III)**, 250 W. 57th St., New York NY 10019. (212)265-7330. Estab. 1966. Represents 100 clients. 25% of clients are new/previously unpublished writers. Specializes in fiction and nonfiction. Currently handles: 75% nonfiction; 25% novels.
Handles: Nonfiction books, novels. Considers these nonfiction areas: business; current affairs; health/medicine; money/finance/economics; psychology; self-help/personal improvement. Considers these fiction areas: action/adventure; detective/police/crime; family saga; literary; mainstream; romance; thriller/espionage. Send outline/proposal. Reports in 3 weeks on queries. "All correspondence must be accompanied by a SASE. Will not read manuscripts before receiving a letter of inquiry."
Recent Sales: *Harry Anderson's Games You Can't Lose*, by Harry Anderson (Pocket Books); *Evil Pranks: The True Story of a Perfect Murder*, by Doris Bacon (Dell); *Sunday Nights at Seven: The Jack Benny Story*, bio by Jack and Joan Benny (Warner).
Terms: Agency receives 15% commission on domestic sales; 25% on foreign sales. Offers written contract, which varies from book to book.
Fees: Charges a reading fee based on word count of ms. Offers criticism service. 98% of business is derived from commissions on ms sales; 2% is derived from reading fees or criticism service. Payment of criticism fee does not ensure representation.
Tips: Obtains new clients through recommendations from others. "Our agency will only look at submissions that have not been submitted to any other agent or publisher simultaneously or at any time whatsoever and must be accompanied by a self-addressed, stamped envelope for return purposes . . . otherwise materials will not be returned."

PMA LITERARY AND FILM MANAGEMENT, INC., Suite 501, 220 W., 19th St., New York NY 10011. (212)929-1222. Fax: (212)206-0238. President: Peter Miller. Member agents: Lory Manrique; Jennifer Robinson (film and fiction); Yuri Skujins (fiction); Anthony Schneider (fiction, nonfiction). Estab. 1975. Represents 80 clients. 50% of clients are new/unpublished writers. Specializes in commercial fiction and nonfiction, thrillers, true crime and "fiction with *real* motion picture and television potential." Currently handles: 50% fiction; 25% nonfiction; 25% screenplays.
Handles: Fiction, nonfiction, film scripts. Considers these nonfiction areas: Considers these nonfiction areas: art/architecture/design; biography/autobiography; business; health/medicine; history; how-to; popular culture; true crime/investigative; women's issues/women's studies. Considers these fiction areas: action/adventure; contemporary issues; detective/police/crime; family saga; historical; horror; literary; mainstream; mystery/suspense; romance (contemporary); thriller/espionage. Query with outline and/or sample chapters. Writer's guidelines for 5 × 8½ SASE with 2 first-class stamps. Reports in 1 week on queries; 2-4 weeks on ms.
Recent Sales: *California Angel*, by Nancy Taylor Rosenberg (Dutton); *Against The Law*, by Michael Eberhardt (Dutton).
Terms: Agent receives 15% commission on domestic sales; 20-25% on foreign sales.
Fees: Does not charge a reading fee. Paid reading evaluation service available upon request. "The evaluation, usually four to seven pages in length, gives a detailed analysis of literary craft and commercial potential as well as further recommendations for improving the work." Charges for photocopying expenses.
Writer's Conferences: Maui Writer's Conference, Santa Fe Writer's Conference.

JULIE POPKIN (II), 15340 Albright St., #204, Pacific Palisades CA 90272. (310)459-2834. Fax: (310)459-4128. Estab. 1989. Represents 26 clients. 40% of clients are new/unpublished writers. Specializes in selling book-length mss including fiction—all genres—and nonfiction. Especially interested in social issues. Currently handles: 50% nonfiction books; 50% novels; some scripts.

Handles: Nonfiction books, novels. Considers these nonfiction areas: art; criticism; feminist; history; politics. Considers these fiction areas: juvenile; literary; mainstream; mystery; romance; science fiction. Reports in 1 month on queries; 2 months on mss.
Recent Sales: *Preteens First Book About Love, Sex and AIDS*, by Dr. Michelle Harrison (American Psychiatric Press); *Two Days in April*, by G.S. Graber (John Wiley); *Glint*, by Joseph Valinetti (St. Martin's).
Terms: Agent receives 15% commission on domestic sales; 10% on dramatic sales; 25% on foreign sales.
Fees: Does not charge a reading fee. Charges $100/year for photocopying, mailing, long distance calls.

‡*THE PORTMAN ORGANIZATION (III), 7337 N. Lincoln Ave., Suite 283, Chicago IL 60076. (312)509-6421. Fax: (708)982-9386. Contact: Ms. Ludmilla Dudin, Julien John Portman. Estab. 1972. Represents 33 clients. 10-15% of clients are new/previously unpublished writers. Currently handles: 50% nonfiction books; 10% movie scripts; 25% novels; 15% TV scripts. Member agents: Julien Portman (Hollywood); Ludmilla Dudin (novels); Paula Chalk (nonfiction); Phyllis Emer (general).
Handles: Nonfiction books, novels, movie scripts, TV scripts. Considers these nonfiction areas: biography/autobiography; current affairs; history; military/war; music/dance/theater/film; sports; true crime/investigative; women's issues/women's studies. Considers these fiction areas: action/adventure; detective/police/crime; family saga; historical; romance (contemporary, historical); science fiction; sports; thriller/espionage; westerns/frontier. Query. Reports in 10 days on queries; 20-30 days on mss.
Recent Sales: *Shadow Over China*, by J. Portman/L. Kipfer (Knightsbridge); *Marketing of the President*, by B. Newman (Morrow Publications); *Profile of a Killer*, by Paul Stemm (Doubleday).
Terms: Agent receives 15% commission on domestic sales; 25% on foreign sales. Offers written contract, binding for 1 year.
Fees: Charges reading fee for new writers only, $150 for 350 pages, $200 for 350- 600 pages. Fees refundable if representation offered. Less than 10% of business is derived from reading fees.
Writers' Conferences: "Rarely do we attend writers conferences, but do attend the yearly show, [ABA] which will be in Chicago for the next three years."
Tips: Obtains clients through referrals, recommendations and from referrals. "We have an excellent track record—we're very careful with solicitation. Reputation in the field of war, due to working with CIA for years. Spent time in Vietnam, and played the role in other areas: Australia, Hong Kong, Thailand, Japan and China. We, also, are involved with TV and motion picture projects. Our agent is William Morris Agency. Two properties are presently optioned. Our office has been successful (modestly) through the years. *Shadow Over China*, a book, is optioned for a major motion picture; 75% in China."

PUDDINGSTONE LITERARY AGENCY (II), Affiliate of SBC Enterprises Inc., 11 Mabro Dr., Denville NJ 07834-9607. (201)366-3622. Contact: Alec Bernard or Eugenia Cohen. Estab. 1972. Represents 25 clients. 80% of clients are new/previously unpublished writers. Currently handles: 10% nonfiction books; 70% novels; 20% movie scripts.
Handles: Nonfiction books, novels, movie scripts. Considers these nonfiction areas: business; how-to; language/literature/criticism; military/war; true crime/investigative. Considers these fiction areas: action/adventure; detective/police/crime; horror; science fiction; thriller/espionage. Query first with SASE including $1 cash processing fee, "which controls the volume and eliminates dilettantism among the submissions." Reports immediately on queries; 1 month on mss "that are requested by us."
Recent Sales: *The Cestus Microbe*, by Saul Morris (Montekin Press).
Terms: Agent receives 10-15% sliding scale (decreasing) on domestic sales; 20% on foreign sales. Offers written contract, binding for 1 year with renewals.
Fees: Reading fee charged for unsolicited mss over 20 pages. Negotiated fees for market analysis available. Charges for photocopying for foreign sales.
Tips: Obtains new clients through referrals and listings.

QCORP LITERARY AGENCY (I), P.O. Box 8, Hillsboro OR 97123-0008. (800)775-6038. Contact: William C. Brown. Estab. 1990. Represents 14 clients. 75% of clients are new/previously unpublished writers. Currently handles: 40% nonfiction books; 60% fiction books. Member agent: William C. Brown.
Handles: Fiction and nonfiction books, including textbooks, scholarly books, novels, novellas, short story collections. Considers all nonfiction areas. Considers all areas of fiction, excluding cartoon/comic books. Query through critique service. Reports in 2 weeks on queries; 2 months on mss.

Recent Sales: *Legal Extortion*, by Jack Atchison (Northwest Publishing).
Terms: Agent receives 10% commission on domestic sales; 20% on foreign sales. Offers written contract, binding for 6 months, automatically renewed unless cancelled by author.
Fees: "No charges are made to agency authors if no sales are procured. If sales are generated, then charges are itemized and collected from proceeds up to a limit of $200, after which all expenses are absorbed by agency." Offers criticism service.
Tips: Obtains new clients through recommendations from others and from critique service. "New authors should use our critique service and its free, no obligation first chapter critique to introduce themselves. Call or write for details. Our critique service is serious business, line by line and comprehensive. Established writers should call or send résumé. We are admittedly new but very attentive and vigorous."

*RAINTREE AGENCY (II), 360 W. 21 St., New York NY 10011. (212)242-2387. Contact: Diane Raintree. Estab. 1977. Represents 6-8 clients. Specializes in novels, film and TV scripts, plays, poetry and children's books.
Handles: Considers all fiction areas and some nonfiction. Phone first.
Terms: Agent receives 10% on domestic sales.
Fees: May charge reading fee. "Amount varies from year to year."

IRENE ROGERS, LITERARY REPRESENTATIVE (III), 9454 Wilshire Blvd., Suite 600, Beverly Hills CA 90212. (213)837-3511 or (310)276-7588. Estab. 1977. Currently represents 10 clients. 10% of clients are new/previously unpublished authors. "We are currently accepting new clients." Currently handles: 50% nonfiction; 50% novels.
Handles: Nonfiction, novels. Considers all nonfiction areas, especially medicine and self-help/personal improvement. Considers all areas of fiction. Query. Responds to queries in 6-8 weeks.
Terms: Agent receives 10% commission on domestic sales; 5% on foreign sales.
Fees: Charges $150 editorial fee, refundable on sale of property.

ROSE AGENCY (I), 2033 Ontario Circle, Ft. Wayne IN 46802-6737. (219)432-5857. Contact: Lynn Clough. Estab. 1993. Currently handles: 25% nonfiction books; 25% juvenile books; 50% novels.
Handles: Nonfiction books, juvenile books, novels. Considers these nonfiction areas: business; child guidance/parenting; crafts/hobbies; education; health/medicine; how-to-humor; juvenile nonfiction; religious/inspirational; self-help/personal improvement. Considers these fiction areas: action/adventure; contemporary issues; family saga; historical; humor/satire; juvenile; mainstream; mystery/suspense; religious/inspiration; romance (contemporary, gothic, historical, regency); thriller/espionage; westerns/frontier; young adult. Query only. No phone calls. Reports in 4-6 weeks on mss.
Terms: Agent receives 15% commission on domestic sales; 20% on foreign sales. Offers written contract, binding for 1 year.
Fees: Does not charge reading fee. Charges $35 handling for complete ms.
Tips: "If you have come this far, you probably have what it takes to be a published author. We find that writers are dreamers driven by some inner compulsion to put words on paper. Just because you aren't published doesn't mean you aren't a writer. We'd like to read your best work."

‡RYDAL (III, IV), P.O. Box 2247, Santa Fe NM 87504. (505)983-1680. Fax: (505)982-9105. Director: Clark Kimball. Estab. 1986. Represents 15 clients. 20% of clients are new/previously published writers. Currently handles: 40% nonfiction books; 10% scholarly books; 10% juvenile books; 40% novels.
Handles: Nonfiction books, novels. Considers these nonfiction areas: anthropology/archaeology; ethnic/cultural interests; nature/environment; photography. Considers these fiction areas: literary; mainstream; regional; westerns/frontier. Send outline and 3 sample chapters. Reports in 3 weeks on mss.
Recent Sales: *En Divina Luz*, by Wallis/Varjabedian (UNM); *Plane Truth*, by Stevens (New Horizon).
Terms: Agent receives 15% commission on domestic sales; 20% on foreign sales. Offers written contract.

Agents who specialize in a specific subject area such as computer books or in handling the work of certain writers such as gay or lesbian writers are ranked IV.

Fees: Charges annual account fee, from $100-400.
Tips: "Obtains new clients through referrals to us by clients, trade connections. Don't try to hype agent—be straight forward and to the point."

SEBASTIAN LITERARY AGENCY (III), 333 Kearny St., Suite 708, San Francisco CA 94108. (415)391-2331. Fax: (415)391-2377. Owner Agent: Laurie Harper. Estab. 1985. Represents approximately 50 clients. Specializes in business, sociology and current affairs. Currently handles: 75% nonfiction books; 25% fiction (novels).
Handles: Nonfiction books, select novels. "No children's or YA." Considers these nonfiction areas: anthropology/archaeology; art/architecture/design; biography; business; child guidance/parenting; computers/electronics; current affairs; ethnic/cultural interests; government/politics/law; health/medicine; history; money/finance/economics; psychology; self-help/personal improvement; sociology; sports; true crime/investigative; women's issues/women's studies. Not actively soliciting new fiction clients at this time. Reports in 3 weeks on queries; 4-6 weeks on mss.
Recent Sales: *Turn Your Business Around* (Prentice Hall) and *A Piece of the Action* (Amacom) by Suzanne Caplan; *Lili*, by Marjorie Edelson (Ballantine—historical novel); *Natural Beauty at Home*, by Janice Cox (Henry Holt).
Terms: Agent receives 15% commission on domestic sales; 20% on foreign sales. Offers written contract.
Fees: Charges a $100 annual administration fee for clients and charges for photocopies of ms for submission to publisher. No reading fees.
Tips: Obtains new clients mostly through "referrals from authors and editors but some at conferences and some from unsolicited queries from around the country."

‡SHOESTRING PRESS (I), Box 1223, Main Post Office, Edmonton, Alberta T5J 2M4 Canada. Contact: Carolyn. Estab. 1991. Represents 5 clients. 40% of clients are new/previously unpublished writers. Currently handles: 30% nonfiction books; 50% scholarly books; 20% novellas.
Handles: Nonfiction books, scholarly books, novels, novellas, poetry books. Considers these nonfiction areas: biography/autobiobraphy; government/politics/law; history; military/war; New Age/metaphysics; religious/inspirational; science/technology. Considers these fiction areas: action/adventure; literary; science fiction; espionage; westerns. Query or send entire ms, outline/proposal. Include Canadian SASE. Reports in 6 months on mss.
Terms: Offer written contract, binding for 2-5 years.
Fees: Fees are "very situational. We get a lot of junk. Charges for postage, photocopying, "but depends on client." 90% of business is derived from commissions on ms sales; 10% is derived from reading fees or criticism services.
Tips: Obtains new business through recommendations from others. "We respond slowly."

*SINGER MEDIA CORPORATION (III), Seaview Business Park, 1030 Calle Cordillera, Unit #106, San Clemente CA 92672. (714)498-7227. Fax: (714)498-2162. Contact: Janis Hawkridge. Estab. 1940. Represents 100+ clients for books, features, cartoons. 15% of clients are new/previously unpublished writers. Specializes in romance, business, self-help, dictionaries, quiz books, cartoons, interviews. Currently handles: 25% nonfiction books; 35% novels; 40% syndicated material. Member agents: Helen J. Lee (general novels); Kurt Singer (business books); Katherine Han (self-help); Peter Carbone (Asia department); Janis Hawkridge (romance books); Kristy Lee (cartoons and comic strips).
Handles: Nonfiction books, syndicated material, business titles, cartoons. Considers these nonfiction areas: biography/autobiography; business; child guidance/parenting; computers/electronics; crafts/hobbies; health/medicine; how-to; money/finance/economics; psychology; self-help/personal improvement; sports; translations; true crime/investigative; women's issues/women's studies; cartoons; dictionaries; juvenile activities; interviews with celebrities. Considers these fiction areas: action/adventure; cartoon/comic; detective/police/crime; erotica; fantasy; glitz; horror; mystery/suspense; picture book; psychic/supernatural; romance (contemporary); science fiction; sports; thriller/espionage; westerns/frontier; teenage romance. Query with writing credits. Reports in 3 weeks on queries; 4-6 weeks on mss.
Recent Sales: *Jade Princess*, by P. Oates (Bridge Books); *The Ultimate Quiz Book*, by Kurt and Jane Singer (H.I.S.).
Terms: Agent receives 15% commission on domestic sales; 20% on foreign sales.
Fees: Charges $350 reading fee "only to unpublished writers. Criticism included in reading fee. Our readers are published authors or ghostwriters." 97% of business is derived from commissions on ms and book sales; 1% is derived from reading fees or criticism service. Payment of criticism fee ensures representation "unless it is not saleable to the commercial market."
Writers' Conferences: Attends Romance Writers of America; ABA (Chicago); Frankfurt Book Fair (Frankfurt); London Book Fair (London).

Tips: "We have been in business for 54 years and are known. If interested in agency representation, books are not written, but rewritten and rewritten. Syndication is done on a worldwide basis, and must be of global interest. Hollywood's winning formula is God/inspiration, sex and action. Try to get reprints of books overseas and in the USA if out of print. We concentrate on licensing published books to foreign book publishers as well as magazines plus regular releases of features, columns cartoons, comic strips to the U.S. and world press."

‡SLC ENTERPRISES, 852 Highland Place, Highland Park IL 60035. (708)432-7553. Contact: Ms. Carole Colin. Estab. 1985. Represents 30 clients. 50% of clients are new/previously unpublished writers. Currently handles: 65% nonfiction books; 5% textbooks; 5% poetry; 5% juvenile books; 20% novels. Member agents: Stephen Cogil (sports).
Handles: Nonfiction books, poetry books, juvenile books, novels, short story collections. Considers these nonfiction areas: biography/autobiography, business, cooking/food/nutrition; current affairs; history; sports; women's issues/women's studies; Holocaust studies. Considers these fiction areas: detective/police/crime; feminist; historical; juvenile; literary; picture book; regional; romance (contemporary, historical); sports; young adult. Query with outline/proposal. Reports in 2 weeks on queries; 1 months on mss.
Recent Sales: *Eyeopeners II*, by Kubrin (Scholastic); *There's Always Time to Die*, by Starkopt (SUNY).
Terms: Agent receives 15% commission on domestic sales. Offers written contract, binding for 9 months.
Fees: Charges $150 reading fee for entire ms; $75-150 for childrens, depending on length and number of stories. Reading fee includes overall critique plus specifics. No line editing for grammar etc. Charges no other fees. 20% of business is derived from reading and criticism fees.
Tips: Recommendations, listings in literary manuals.

MICHAEL STEINBERG LITERARY AGENCY (III), P.O. Box 274, Glencoe IL 60027-0274. (708)835-8881. Contact: Michael Steinberg. Estab. 1980. Represents 27 clients. 5% of clients are new/previously unpublished writers. Specializes in business and general nonfiction, mysteries, science fiction. Currently handles: 75% nonfiction books; 25% novels.
Handles: Nonfiction books, novels. Considers these nonfiction areas: biography; business; computers; law; history; how-to; money/finance/economics; self-help/personal improvement. Considers these fiction areas: action/adventure; contemporary issues; detective/police/crime; erotica; mainstream; mystery/suspense; science fiction; thriller/espionage. Query for guidelines. Reports in 2 weeks on queries; 6 weeks on mss.
Recent Sales: *How to Buy Mutual Funds the Smart Way*, by Stephen Littauer (Dearborn Publishing); *The Complete Day Trader*, by Jake Bernstein (McGraw-Hill).
Terms: Agent receives 15% on domestic sales; 15-20% on foreign sales. Offers written contract, which is binding, "but at will."
Fees: Charges $75 reading fee for outline and chapters 1-3; $200 for a full ms to 100,000 words. Criticism included in reading fee. Charges actual phone and postage, which is billed back quarterly. 95% of business is derived from commissions on ms sales; 5% derived from reading fees or criticism services.
Writer's Conferences: ABA (Chicago).
Tips: Obtains new clients through unsolicited inquiries and referrals from editors and authors. "We do not solicit new clients. Do not send unsolicited material. Write for guidelines and include SASE. Do not send generically addressed, photocopied query letters."

GLORIA STERN AGENCY (II), 1235 Chandler Blvd., #3, North Hollywood CA 91607-1934. Phone/fax: (818)508-6296. Contact: Gloria Stern. Estab. 1984. Member of IWOSC, SCW. Represents 14 clients. 80% of clients are new/unpublished writers. Specializes in consultation, writer's services (ghost writing, editing, critiquing, etc.). Currently handles: 79% fiction; 19% nonfiction books; 8% movie scripts; 2% reality based. Member agent: Gloria Stern (romance, detective, science fiction).
● This agency is not affiliated with the Gloria Stern Literary Agency in Texas.
Handles: Novels, short story collections. Considers these nonfiction areas: biography/autobiography; business; child guidance/parenting; computers/electronics; cooking; current affairs; education; ethnic/cultural interests; gay/lesbian issues; health/medicine; how-to; language/literature/criticism; money/finance/economics; music/dance/theater/film; New Age/metaphysical; popular culture; psychology (pop); self-help/personal improvement; sociology; true crime/investigative; women's issues/women's studies. Considers these fiction areas: action/adventure; contemporary issues; detective/police/crime; erotica; fantasy; feminist; glitz; horror; literary; mainstream; romance (contemporary, gothic, historical, regency); science fiction; thriller/espionage; western/frontier. Query with short bio, credits. Reports in 3-4 weeks on queries; 3-5 weeks on mss.

Also Handles: Movie scripts (feature film, TV mow). Considers these script subject areas: action/adventure; comedy; contemporary issues; detective/police/crime; erotica; ethnic; family saga; fantasy; feminist; glitz; horror; mainstream; mystery/suspense; psychic/supernatural; romance (comedy, drama); science fiction; sports; thriller; westerns/frontier.

Terms: Agent receives 12% commission on domestic sales; 20% on foreign sales. Offers written contract, binding for 1 year.

Fees: Charges reading fee, by project (by arrangement), $35/hour for unpublished writers. Criticism service: $35/hour. Critiques are "detailed analysis of all salient points regarding such elements as structure, style, pace, development, publisher's point of view and suggestions for rewrites if needed." Charges for long-distance, photocopying and postage. 38% of income derived from sales, 29% from reading fees, 26% from correspondence students, 7% from teaching. Payment of criticism fee does not insure representation.

Writer's Conferences: Pasadena Writer's Forum (Spring '94).

Tips: Obtains new clients from book (*Do the Write Thing: Making the Transition to Professional*), classes, lectures, listings, word of mouth. "To a writer interested in representation: Be sure that you have researched your field and are aware of current publishing demands. Writing is the only field in which all the best is readily available to the beginning writer. Network, take classes, persevere and most of all, write, write and rewrite."

‡*MARIANNE STRONG LITERARY AGENCY (III), 65 E. 96th St., New York NY 10128. (212)249-1000. Fax: (212)831-3241. Contact: Marianne Strong. Estab. 1978. Represents 15 clients. 1% of clients are new/previously unpublished writers. Specializes in biographies. Currently handles: 80% nonfiction books; 5% scholarly books; 5% novels; 10% TV scripts. Member agent: Jeanne Toomey (true crime).

Handles: Nonfiction books, novels, TV scripts, syndicated material. Considers these nonfiction areas: art/architecture/design; biography/autobiography; business; child guidance/parenting; cooking/food/nutrition; current affairs; education; health/medicine; history; how-to; interior design/decorating; juvenile nonfiction; military/war; money/finance/economics; religious/inspirational; self-help/personal improvement; true crime; women's issues/women's studies. Considers these fiction areas: action/adventure; contemporary issues; detective/police/crime; family saga; glitz; historical; literary; mainstream; religious/inspirational; romance (contemporary, gothic, historical, regency); thriller/espionage; western/frontier. Send outline plus 3-4 sample chapters. Reports "fairly soon" on queries; 1-2 months on mss.

Terms: Agent receives 15% commission on domestic sales; 15% on foreign sales. Offers written contract, binding for the life of book or play.

Fees: Charges a reading fee for new writers only, "refundable when manuscript sold." Offers criticism service. "Fee to read and service a manuscript to six to eight publishers $350. If using outside freelance writers and editors, entire fee goes to them. Critiques prepared by freelance writers and editors who receive entire fee." Charges for long distance calls for established clients, but not for unpublished writers as their fee covers these out-of-pocket expenses.

Tips: Obtains new clients through recommendations from others. "Submit a totally professional proposal with a story line that elucidates the story from A to Z plus several perfectly typed or word processed chapters. No disks, please. Also include background information on the author, especially literary or journalistic references."

*MARK SULLIVAN ASSOCIATES (II), 521 Fifth Ave., Suite 1700, New York NY 10175. (212)682-5844. Contact: Mark Sullivan. Estab. 1989. 50% of clients are new/previously unpublished writers. Currently handles: 20% nonfiction books; 5% textbooks; 60% novels; 5% poetry books; 10% movie scripts. Specializes in science fiction, women's romance, detective/mystery/spy, but handles all genres. Member agents: Linda Tsai (romance); Jay Milligan (science fiction and nonfiction).

Handles: Nonfiction books, textbooks, scholarly books, novels, novellas, short story collections, poetry books. Considers these nonfiction areas: anthropology/archaeology; biography/autobiography; business; cooking/food/nutrition; crafts/hobbies; current affairs; health/medicine; interior design/decorating; language/literature/criticism; military/war; money/finance/economics; music/dance/theater/film; nature/environment; New Age/metaphysics; photography; psychology; religious/inspirational; science/technology; sports. Considers all fiction areas. Query or send query, outline plus 3 sample chapters. Reports in 2 weeks on queries; 3-4 weeks on mss.

Recent Sales: *Mutual Funds*, by Lyle Allen (Avon).

Terms: Agent receives 10-15% commission on domestic sales; 20% on foreign sales. Offers written contract.

Fees: Charges $95 reading fee for new writers. Critique included in reading fee. Charges for photocopying and long-distance telephone calls. 90% of business is derived from commissions on ms sales; 10% of business is derived from reading fees or criticism services. Payment of fee does not ensure representation.

Tips: Obtains new clients through "advertising, recommendations, conferences. Quality of presentation of query letter, sample chapters and manuscript is important. Completed manuscripts are preferred to works in progress."

DAWSON TAYLOR LITERARY AGENCY (II), 4722 Holly Lake Dr., Lake Worth FL 33463-5372. (407)965-4150. Fax: (407)641-8765. Contact: Dawson Taylor, Attorney at Law. Estab. 1974. Represents 34 clients. 80% of clients are new/previously unpublished writers. Specializes in nonfiction, fiction, sports, military history. Currently handles: 80% nonfiction; 5% scholarly books; 15% novels.
Handles: Nonfiction books, textbooks, scholarly books, novels. Considers all nonfiction areas. Specializes in nonfiction on sports, especially golf. Considers these fiction areas: detective/police/crime; mystery/suspense; thriller/espionage. Query with outline. Reports in 5 days on queries; 10 days on mss.
Recent Sales: *Winning Bowling*, by Earl Anthony (Contemporary Books).
Terms: Agent receives 15% or 20% commission "depending upon editorial help." Offers written contract. Indefinite, but cancellable on 60 days notice by either party.
Fees: "Reading fees are subject to negotiation, usually $100 for normal length manuscript, more for lengthy ones. Reading fee includes critique and sample editing. Criticism service subject to negotiation, from $100. Critiques are on style and content, include editing of manuscript, and are written by myself." 90% of business is derived from commissions on ms sales; 10% is derived from reading fees or criticism services. Payment of reading or criticism fee does not ensure representation.
Tips: Obtains new clients through "recommendations from publishers and authors who are presently in my stable."

TIGER MOON ENTERPRISES (I), 1249 Palm St., #5, San Luis Obispo CA 93401-3142. (805)927-3920. Contact: Terry Kennedy or Mark James Miller. Estab. 1991. Represents 14 clients. 50% of clients are new/previously unpublished writers. "We prefer books written by successful entrepreneurs, teaching their skills to others. Children's books which teach the five human values of love, truth, peace, nonviolence and righteous living also interest us." Currently handles: 40% novels; 20% poetry books; 40% short story collections (10% of these are New Age). Member agents: Terry Kennedy (business, how-to, children's); Mark Miller (fiction, history, investigative research).
Handles: Nonfiction books, scholarly books, juvenile books, novels, novellas, short story collections, poetry books and work that is "spiritually uplifting, life-guiding." Considers these nonfiction areas: cooking; crafts; health/medicine; history; juvenile nonfiction; military/war; money; music; nature; new age; religious; self-help; true crime/investigative. Considers these fiction areas: contemporary issues; family saga; historical; literary; psychic; regional; religious. Query with a 10-page sample and SASE. Reports "immediately" on queries; in 2 weeks on mss.
Recent Sales: *Future Tense*, by Virgil Smith.
Terms: Agent receives 15% commission on domestic sales; 15% on foreign sales. Offers a written contract, duration varies.
Fees: Does not charge a reading fee. Offers criticism service.
Tips: "If you are the type of person who really believes in your work, we are interested in doing business with you. We are not equipped to build up your self esteem as a writer. Believe that what you have written is going to be of genuine interest to many readers, send us a professional package and we'll be attentive to your proposal."

*JEANNE TOOMEY ASSOCIATES (II), 95 Belden St., Falls Village CT 06031. (203)824-0831/5469. Fax: (203)824-5460. Contact: Jeanne Toomey. Estab. 1985. Represents 10 clients. 50% of clients are new/previously unpublished writers. Specializes in "nonfiction; biographies of famous men and women; history with a flair—murder and detection. No children's books, no poetry, no Harlequin-type romances." Currently handles: 45% nonfiction books; 20% novels; 35% movie scripts.
Handles: Nonfiction books, novels, short story collections, movie scripts. Considers these nonfiction areas: agriculture/horticulture; animals; anthropology/archaeology; art/architecture/design; biography/autobiography; government/politics/law; history; interior design/decorating; money/finance/economics; nature/environment; true crime/investigative. Considers these fiction areas: detective/police/crime; psychic/supernatural; thriller/espionage. Send outline plus 3 sample chapters. "Query first, please!" Reports in 1 month.
Recent Sales: *A Woman Named Jackie*, by C. David Heymann (Lyle Stuart); *Llantarnam*, by Muriel Maddox (Sunstone Books).

Terms: Agent receives 15% commission on domestic sales.
Fees: Charges $100 reading fee for unpublished authors; no fee for published authors. "The $100 covers marketing fee, office expenses, postage, photocopying. We absorb those costs in the case of published authors."

A TOTAL ACTING EXPERIENCE, Suite 399, Sept. N.W., 20501 Ventura Blvd., Woodland Hills CA 91364. (818)901-1044. Contact: Dan A. Bellacicco. Estab. 1984. Signatory of WGA, SAG, AFTRA. Represents 30 clients. 50% of clients are new/previously unpublished writers. Specializes in "quality instead of quantity." Currently handles: 5% nonfiction books; 5% juvenile books; 10% novels; 5% novellas; 5% short story collections; 50% movie scripts; 10% TV scripts; 5% stage plays; 5% how-to books and videos.
  • See the expanded listing for this agency in Script Agents.

*VISIONS PRESS (II), P.O. Box 4904, Valley Village CA 91617-0904. (805)285-8174. Contact: Allen Williams Brown. Estab. 1991. Represents 9 clients. 60% of clients are new/previously unpublished writers. "We prefer to support writers who incorporate African-American issues in the storyline. We handle adult romance novels, children's books and consciousness-raising pieces." Currently handles: 50% novels; 50% magazine pieces.
Handles: Novels, magazine pieces. Considers these magazine areas: ethnic/cultural interests; gay/lesbian issues; religious/inspirational; self-help/personal improvement; women's issues/women's studies. Considers these fiction areas: confessional; contemporary issues; erotica; ethnic; gay; lesbian; mainstream; romance (contemporary); young adult. Send outline plus 2 sample chapters and author bio or description of self. Reports in 2 weeks on queries; 1 month on mss.
Recent Sales: "Help for the homebound," by Diana Williams (Los Angeles Times); "African American see O.J. Simpson as family," by Diana Williams (Glendale News Press).
Terms: Agent receives 10% commission on domestic sales; 15% on foreign sales. Offers written contract, specific length of time depends on type of work—novel or magazine piece.
Fees: Charges reading fee. "Reading fees are charged to new writers only. Fee is refunded if agency decides to represent author. Fees are based on length of manuscript ($100 for up to 300 pages; $150 for any length thereafter.)" Offers criticism service. "Same as for the reading fee. Both the reading fee and the criticism fee entitle the author to a critique of his/her work by one of our editors. We are interested in everyone who has a desire to be published . . . to hopefully realize their dream. To that end, we provide very honest and practical advice on what needs to be done to correct a manuscript." Additional fees "will be negotiated with the author on a project by project basis. Often there is a one-time fee charged that covers all office expenses associated with the marketing of a manuscript." 90% of business is derived from commissions on ms sales; 10% is derived from reading fees or criticism services. Payment of criticism fee does not ensure representation.
Writers' Conferences: "We do not usually attend writing conferences. Most of our contacts are made through associations with groups such as NAACP, Rainbow Coalition, Urban League and other such groups that promote consciousness-raising activities by African-Americans. We look for talent among African-American scholars and African-American "common folk" who can usually be found sharing their opinions and visions at an issues-related conference and town hall type meeting."
Tips: Obtains new clients through recommendations from others and through inquiries. "We believe the greatest story ever told has yet to be written! For that reason we encourage every writer to uninhibitedly pursue his/her dream of becoming published. A no from us should simply be viewed as a temporary setback that can be overcome by another attempt to meet our high expectations. Discouraged, frustrated, and demoralized are words we have deleted from our version of the dictionary. An aspiring writer must have the courage to press on and believe in his/her talent."

*THE GERRY B. WALLERSTEIN AGENCY (II), 2315 Powell Ave., Suite 12, Erie PA 16506-1843. (814)833-5511. Fax: (814)833-6260. Contact: Ms. Gerry B. Wallerstein. Estab. 1984. Member of Authors Guild, Inc., ASJA. Represents 40 clients. 25% of clients are new/previously unpublished writers. Specializes in nonfiction books and "personalized help for new novelists." Currently handles: 52% nonfiction books; 2% scholarly books; 2% juvenile books; 35% novels; 2% short story collections; 2% TV scripts; 2% short material. (Note: juvenile books, scripts and short material marketed for *clients only!*)
Handles: Nonfiction books, scholarly trade books, novels, no textbooks. Considers these nonfiction areas for general trade: agriculture/horticulture; animals; anthropology/archaeology; art/architecture/design; biography/autobiography (celebrity only); business; child guidance/parenting; cooking/food/nutrition; crafts/hobbies; current affairs; education; ethnic/cultural interests; gay/lesbian issues; government/politics/law; health/medicine; history; how-to; humor; interior design/decorating; language/literature/criticism; military/war; money/finance/economics; music/

dance/theater/film; nature/environment; photography; popular culture; psychology; science/
technology; self-help/personal improvement; sociology; sports; true crime/investigative; women's
issues/women's studies. Considers these fiction areas: action/adventure; contemporary issues;
detective/police/crime; family saga; fantasy; glitz; historical; horror; humor/satire; literary; mainstream; mystery/suspense; romance (contemporary, historical); thriller/espionage; young adult.
To query, send entire ms for fiction; proposal (including 3 chapters) for nonfiction books. "No
manuscripts are reviewed until writer has received my brochure." Reports in 1 week on queries;
2 months on mss.
Recent Sales: *Surrender The Night*, by Susan P. Teklits (HarperPaperbacks/Monogram); *Thun-
der Along The Mississippi*, by Jack D. Coombe (Brassey's); *Racism of Attitude? The First Step
Toward Liberation*, by James L. Robinson, Ph.D. (Insight Books/Plenum Publishing Corp.).
Terms: Agent receives 15% on domestic sales; 20% on foreign sales. Offers written contract,
which "can be cancelled by either party, with 60 days' notice of termination."
Fees: "To justify my investment of time, effort and expertise in working with newer or beginning
writers, I charge a reading/critique fee based on length of manuscript, for example: $400 for
each manuscript of 105,000-125,000 words." Critique included in reading fee. "Reports are 1-2
pages for proposals and short material; 2-4 pages for full-length mss; done by agent." Charges
clients $20/month postage/telephone fee; and if required, ms photocopying or typing, copyright
fees, cables, attorney fees (if approved by author), travel expense (if approved by author). 50%
of business is derived from commissions on ms sales; 50% is derived from reading fees and
critique services. Payment of criticism fee does not ensure representation.
Writers' Conferences: Westminster College Conference; Midwest Writers' Conference; National Writers' Uplink, Writer's Center at Chautauqua, Midland Writers' Conference.
Tips: Obtains new clients through recommendations; listings in directories; referrals from clients
and publishers/editors. "A query letter that tells me something about the writer and his/her
work is more likely to get a personal response."

JAMES WARREN LITERARY AGENCY (II), 13131 Welby Way, North Hollywood CA 91606.
(818)982-5423. Agent: James Warren. Editor: Michael Hofstein. Estab. 1969. Represents 60
clients. 60% of clients are new/unpublished writers. "We are willing to work with select unpublished writers." Specializes in fiction, history, textbooks, professional books, craft books, how-to
books, self-improvement books, health books and diet books. Currently handles: 40% nonfiction
books; 20% novels; 10% textbooks; 5% juvenile books; 10% movie scripts; 15% TV scripts and
teleplays.
Handles: Juvenile books, historical romance novels. Query with outline. Does not read unsolicited mss. No reply without SASE. Brochure available for SASE. Reports in 1 week on queries;
1 month on mss.
Recent Sales: *Madame President* (New Saga Press); *Witty Words* (Sterling Press).
Also Handles: Movie scripts (especially drama and humor), TV scripts (drama, humor, documentary).
Terms: Agent receives 10% commission on domestic sales; 20% on foreign sales.
Fees: Charges reading fee of $3/1,000 words; refunds reading fee if material sells. 80% of income
derived from commission on ms sales; 20% of income derived from fees. Payment of reading
fee does not ensure representation.

*SANDRA WATT & ASSOCIATES (II), 8033 Sunset Blvd., Suite 4053, Hollywood CA 90046-
2427. (213)851-1021. Contact: Davida South. Estab. 1977. Signatory of WGA. Represents 55
clients. 15% of clients are new/previously unpublished writers. Specializes in scripts: film noir;
family; romantic comedies; books: women's fiction, mystery, commercial nonfiction. Currently
handles: 40% nonfiction books; 35% novels; 25% movie scripts. Member agents: Sandra Watt
(scripts, nonfiction, novels); Davida South (scripts).
Handles: Nonfiction books, novels. Considers these nonfiction areas: agriculture/horticulture;
animals; anthropology/archaeology; art/architecture/design; crafts/hobbies; current affairs; how-
to; humor; language/literature/criticism; nature/environment; New Age/metaphysics; popular
culture; psychology; reference; religious/inspirational; self-help/personal improvement; sports;
true crime/investigative; women's issues/women's studies. Considers these fiction areas: contemporary issues; detective/police/crime; family saga; mainstream; mystery/suspense; regional; reli-
gious/inspirational; thriller/espionage; women's mainstream novels. Query. Reports in 1 week
on queries; 2 months on mss.
Recent Sales: *Earth Angel*, by Laramie Dunaway (Warner); *Renaissance Reader*, by D. Atchity
(HarperCollins); *Love Bite*, by Sherry Gottlieb (Warner).
Also Handles: Movie scripts (feature film), TV scripts (TV mow). Considers these script subject
areas: contemporary issues; detective/police/crime; family saga; psychic/supernatural; religious/
inspirational; romantic comedy and drama.

Recent Sales: *Afraid of the Dark*, by Mick Strawser (Citadel); *Ladies of Parkwood Lane*, by Andy Gross (Citadel); *Northstar*, by Emily Gaydos (David Lancaster).
Terms: Agent receives 15% commission on domestic sales; 25% on foreign sales. Offers written contract, binding for 1 year.
Fees: Does not charge a reading fee. Charges one-time nonrefundable marketing fee of $100 *for unpublished authors*.
Tips: Obtains new clients through recommendations from others, referrals and "from wonderful query letters. Don't forget the SASE!"

WEST COAST LITERARY ASSOCIATES (II), 7960-B Soquel Dr., Suite 151, Aptos CA 95003-3945. (408)685-9548. Contact: Richard Van Der Beets. 1986. Member of Authors League of America, Authors Guild. Represents 60 clients. 75% of clients are new/previously unpublished clients. Currently handles: 20% nonfiction books; 80% novels.
Handles: Nonfiction books, novels. Considers these nonfiction areas: biography/autobiography; current affairs; ethnic/cultural interests; government/politics/law; history; language/literature/criticism; music/dance/theater/film; nature/environment; psychology; true crime/investigative; women's issues/women's studies. Considers these fiction areas: action/adventure; contemporary issues; detective/police/crime; experimental; historical; literary; mainstream; mystery/suspense; regional; romance (contemporary and historical); science fiction; thriller/espionage; westerns/frontier. Query first. Reports in 2 weeks on queries; 1 month on mss.
Terms: Agent receives 10% commission on domestic sales; 20% commission on foreign sales. Offers written contract, binding for 6 months.
Recent Sales: *The Ballad of Rocky Ruiz* (MWA Edgar nominee) and *The Ballad of Gato Guerrero*, by Manuel Ramos (St. Martin's); *Carnival of Saints* (Ballantine) and *A Comedy of Murders* (Carroll & Graf), by George Herman.
Fees: Does not charge a reading fee. Charges a $75-95 marketing and materials fee, depending on genre and length. Fees are refunded in full upon sale of the property.
Writers' Conferences: California Writer's Conference (Asilomar, CA 1995).
Tips: "Query with SASE for submission guidelines before sending material."

WILDSTAR ASSOCIATES (II), 26 Nantucket Place, Scarsdale NY 10583. (914)961-3085. Fax: (914)337-0361. Contact: Cecilia Dos Santos. Estab. 1978. Represents 50 clients. 20% of clients are new/previously unpublished writers. Specializes in women's fiction, romance (historical, contemporary), horror, science fiction, nonfiction, hard science, self-help, parenting, nutrition. Currently handles: 40% nonfiction books; 60% novels. Member agents: Cecilia Dos Santos (crime, romance, nonfiction); Richard Monaco (horror, fantasy, science fiction, nonfiction); Matt Jorgensen (graphics, comics, art).
Handles: Nonfiction books, novels. Considers these nonfiction areas: biography/autobiography; business; child guidance/parenting; cooking/food/nutrition; crafts/hobbies; current affairs; ethnic/cultural interests; gay/lesbian issues; government/politics/law; health/medicine; history; interior design/decorating; language/literature/criticism; military/war; money/finance/economics; music/dance/theater/film; nature/environment; new age/metaphysics; psychology; true crime/investigative; science/technology; self-help/personal improvement; sports; women's issues/women's studies. Considers these fiction areas: action/adventure; detective/police/crime; family saga; fantasy; glitz; historical; horror; literary; mainstream; mystery/suspense; psychic/supernatural; romance; science fiction; thriller/espionage; westerns/frontier. Query. Reports in 2 weeks on queries.
Recent Sales: *Book of the Dead III*, by Skipp/Spector; *Fractals*, by John Briggs (St. Martin's).
Terms: Agent receives 15% commission on domestic sales; 15% on foreign sales, "unless foreign agent is used, then 10% additional." Offers written contract, binding "no less than 1 year."
Fees: Charges $75 reading fee. Offers criticism service.
Writers' Conferences: PEN Writers Conference; World Horror, World Fantasy, ABA.
Tips: Obtains new clients through recommendations from others, at conferences. "Send simple clear queries and return postage."

*STEPHEN WRIGHT AUTHORS' REPRESENTATIVE (III), P.O. Box 1341, FDR Station, New York NY 10150-1341. (212)213-4382. Contact: Stephen Wright. Estab. 1984. Prefers to work with published/established authors. Works with a small number of new/unpublished authors. Member of MWA, signatory of WGA. Currently handles: 20% nonfiction; 60% novels; 10% movie scripts; 10% TV scripts.
Handles: Nonfiction books, novels, young adult and juvenile books, syndicated material. Considers "most if not all" nonfiction and fiction areas. Query first; do *not* send ms. Include SASE with query. Reports in 3 weeks on queries.
Also Handles: Movie scripts (feature films), TV scripts (documentary, episodic drama, TV mow), radio scripts, stage plays. Considers "most if not all" script areas.

Terms: Agent receives 10-15% commission on domestic sales; 10-15% on dramatic sales; 15-20% on foreign sales.

Fees: "When the writer is a beginner or has had no prior sales in the medium for which he or she is writing, we charge a reading criticism fee; does not waive fee when representing the writer. Charges $600/300 pages; or $100/50 pages (double-spaced). We simply do not 'read' a manuscript, but give the writer an in-depth criticism. If we like what we read, we would represent the writer. We tell the writer whether we believe his/her work is marketable. I normally provide the critiques."

WRITE DESIGNS LITERARY AGENCY (I), P.O. Box 191554, Atlanta GA 31119-1554. (404)634-5874. Contact: Judy Strickland. Estab. 1993. Represents 4 clients. 80% of clients are new/previously unpublished writers. Specializes in travel (guidebooks, travelogues, picture books), spy and WWII adventure novels, reference books on consumer and general interest topics. Currently handles: 70% nonfiction books; 30% novels.

Handles: Nonfiction books, novels. Considers these nonfiction areas: art/architecture/design; biography/autobiography; business; computers/electronics; cooking/food/nutrition; crafts/hobbies; health/medicine; history; how-to; humor; military/war; money/finance/economics; nature/environment; photography; popular culture; religious/inspirational; sports; travel; southern topics. Considers these fiction areas: action/adventure; detective/police/crime; historical; literary (Southern writers); mainstream; mystery/suspense; religious/inspiration; thriller/espionage. "Will not accept works with overt sex, profanity. No occult/horror." Query with outline/proposal and SASE for nonfiction; query with 3-5 sample chapters but no more than 50 pages and SASE for fiction. Reports in 4-6 weeks on queries; 1-2 months on mss.

Terms: Agent receives 15% commission on domestic sales; 20% on foreign sales. Offers written contract.

Fees: Does not charge a reading fee. Criticism service: $1 per page. Written critique with suggestions. Charges for excessive postage, telephone calls, "which may be waived, depending on status of book (% of advance, sales, etc.)." 95% of business is derived from commissions on ms sales; 5% from reading or critique fees.

Tips: Obtains new clients from recommendations. "We have wide-ranging tastes, but take a look at what sells before sending us a proposal. Convince us that your work is worth selling. Send concise, clear and well thought out queries and proposals. Prefer experienced writers (magazines, technical work, etc.); send clips with proposals and queries."

THE WRITE THERAPIST (II), (formerly Literary/Business Associates), 2000 N. Ivar, Suite 3, Hollywood CA 90068. (213)465-2630. Contact: Shelley Gross. Estab. 1980. Represents 5 clients. 90% of clients are new/previously unpublished writers. Specializes in contemporary fiction and nonfiction; pop psychology, philosophy, mysticism, Eastern religion, self-help, business, health, commerical novels. "No fantasy or SF." Currently handles: 40% nonfiction; 60% fiction (novels).

Terms: Agent receives 15% commission on domestic sales; 20% on foreign sales.

Fees: Does not charge a reading fee. Charges $95 critique fee for mss up to 300 pages, $10 each additional 50 pages. "Critique fees are 100% refundable if a sale is made." Critique consists of "detailed analysis of manuscript in terms of structure, style, characterizations, etc. and marketing potential, plus free guidesheets for fiction or nonfiction." Charges $75 one-time marketing fee. 50% of business is derived from commission on ms sales; 50% is derived from criticism and editing services. Payment of a criticism fee does not ensure agency representation. Offers editing on potentially publishable mss.

Tips: Obtains new clients through recommendations from others, solicitation, seminars.

*WRITER'S CONSULTING GROUP (II, III), P.O. Box 492, Burbank CA 91503-0492. (818)841-9294. Director: Jim Barmeier. Estab. 1983. Represents 10 clients. "We will work with established and unestablished writers. We welcome unsolicited queries." Currently handles: 40% nonfiction books; 20% novels; 40% movie scripts.

Handles: Nonfiction books, novels. Considers these nonfiction areas: biography/autobiography; business; current affairs; education; health/medicine; money/finance/economics; music/dance/theater/film; popular culture; psychology; science/technology; self-help/personal improvement; true crime/investigative. Considers these fiction areas: action/adventure; contemporary issues; detective police/crime; family saga; feminist; horror; mainstream; mystery/suspense; thriller/espionage. True stories (for which the author has legal rights) about women and families put in crisis situations in which they must make controversial moral decisions; also of men and women overcoming adversities or challenges; true stories of unusual survival and profiles in courage; true stories about women who have overcome major obstacles in their lives; topical true stories out of the news for which the author can obtain the rights; stories about historical women; stories with irony; unusual family stories; off-beat mother-daughter, wife-husband, sister-sister stories; death row or prison stories; true crime (especially if the villain is a female); novels

(women's, mainstream, contemporary thrillers); movie scripts (comedies, love stories, thrillers, women's stories). Query or send proposal. Include SASE. Reports in 1 month on queries; 3 months on mss.
Recent Sales: *Moment to Moment* (Medical Consumers Publishing).
Also Handles: Movie scripts (feature film), TV scripts (TV mow). Considers these script subject areas: action/adventure; comedy; contemporary issues; detective/police/crime; family saga; feminist; horror; humor; mainstream; mystery/suspense; psychic/supernatural; romantic comedy and drama; thriller.
Recent Sales: "Witness Against My Mother" (CBS Movie of the Week).
Terms: "We will explain our terms to clients when they wish to sign. We receive a 10% commission on domestic sales. We also work with other agencies in the sale of stories."
Fees: Sometimes charges reading fee. "Additionally, we offer ghostwriting and editorial services, as well as book publicity services for authors. Mr. Barmeier is a graduate of Stanford University's Master's Degree in Creative Writing Program."
Tips: "We will help an author from concept to final product—if need be, designing the proposal, creating the package, doing rewrites on the manuscript. We are on the lookout for controversial women's stories that can be turned into movies-of-the-week. These usually involve women who take risks, are involved in jeopardy or crisis situations, and have upbeat endings."

Additional Fee-charging Agents

The following fee-charging agencies have indicated they are *primarily* interested in handling the work of scriptwriters. They also handle less than ten to fifteen percent book manuscripts. After reading the listing (you can find the page number in the Listings Index), send them a query to obtain more information on their needs and manuscript submission policies.

Marian Berzon Agency

Fee-charging Agents/'94-'95 changes

The following agencies appeared in past editions of *Guide to Literary Agents* but are absent from the 1995 edition. These agencies failed to respond to our request for an update of their listing, or were left out for the reasons indicated in parentheses following the agency name.

Aardvark Literary Agents (complaints—formerly Charles Neighbors Literary Agency)
Ace Consultants (unable to contact)
Farel T. Alden (unable to contact)
Ashby Literary Agency
The Curtis Bruce Agency (removed by request)
The Dorothy Deering Literary Agency (complaints)
The Film & Fiction Agency (unable to contact)
Glenmark Literary Agency (complaints)
The Hamersfield Agency (unable to contact)

Elizabeth Haynes Ltd. (removed by request for one year)
Keyser Literary Agency
Klausner International Agency
Living Faith Literary Agency (complaints)
Scott Meredith Literary Agency
Greg Merhige-Merdon Marketing/Promo Co. (complaints)
Charles Neighbors Literary Agency (complaints—name change to Aardvark Literary Agents)
New Age World Services
New Writers Literary Project (unable to contact)

Pen & Ink Literary Agency (unable to contact)
Renaissance Literary Agency (complaints)
Rhodes Literary Agency
A Rising Sun Literary Agency (complaints)
Southern Literary Agency
State of the Art Ltd.
TARC Literary Agency (see The Artists' Resource Center, this section)
Bess Wallace Literary Agency (complaints)
The Writer's Advocate (see Flannery White & Stone, this section)
Tom Zelasky Literary Agency (out of business)

Script Agents

The Ins and Outs of Working with Script Agents

by Gary Salt

Cows don't give milk. As anyone raised on a farm knows perfectly well, you have to get up (usually around dawn) and go out and take it from them. Thus is it also within the film and television industry. No one is waiting at the bus depot or the other end of a modem to give you money, a production commitment, options, assignments, credit, development deals, prestige, glory, or studio parking space. Agents can go out and get some of these things for you—some, but not all. Writers have agents because cows don't give milk. Agents level the playing field. They help minimize (but do not eliminate) the odds that are stacked severely against all but a handful of film and television writers.

What does an agent do?

In simple terms, an agent represents someone else's professional interests in return for a commission. Therefore, the least to expect and demand is that the agent is also a professional: full-time, with an office, business hours and, hopefully, a verifiable reputation. The most common functions undertaken every day by agents are those of introducer, negotiator and advisor; and every good agent should be able to do all three all the time.

Agents can either introduce their clients' work or their clients *to* work and usually they do both. They are constantly searching by every possible means for buyers and customers for existing scripts or treatments and much of their time is spent covering a massive field of potential markets. Moreover, these markets can change from month to month in their signals and writing requirements. In all of this, either by personal contact or by phone, the agent is scanning and evaluating when and to whom to submit which scripts. This process is ongoing and never stops. Like the surf, it can be high or low, cold or warm, but always ceaseless. It goes on over weekends, at social events, on "vacation." Agencies may keep office hours, but no agent punches a clock. There are few professional contacts who are not also possible customers for a client's script. With few exceptions, the bulk of

Gary Salt entered the agency business in 1972, and joined Paul Kohner, Inc. in 1976. In 1987 he and his partner purchased the firm and he subsequently became president. Paul Kohner, Inc. is one of the oldest continuously-operated agencies in the country, and is a mid-sized full-service agency representing a range of clients including actors, writers, directors, composers and authors. In addition, the firm conducts a substantial rights business in film and television and represents several major publishers in this market.

an agent's time is spent reading and evaluating material and then organizing and making submissions of that material to the marketplace. Nearly all of the latter business is done over the phone.

But agents can also introduce their clients to the work and this means setting up personal meetings either to have a client pitch a concept in the hope of securing a deal to write it or to have the client audition for an open writing assignment. In television, such meetings are nearly always with the producers or development staff of a production company if the subject is a film, or with the "show-runners" if it's a 30-minute or 60-minute episodic show. Pilots and TV movies that get past the first step will lead to meetings with network development executives, but the agent will not have to organize these once things get rolling. Feature pitch meetings are usually held at production companies or studio offices with development executives responsible for screening new material. Occasionally, a writer will start out meeting with a director and carry on from there.

Where open writing assignments are at stake, expect merciless competition. There are more qualified writers than there are ever jobs available. Writers who get into these meetings will have already been screened by submission of résumés and, where necessary, writing samples appropriate to the assignment in question. Usually, by the time a meeting is set up, the producer basically wants to get a sense of the writer's "take" on the project and there is also an element of checking the writer out personally. Is he or she someone we can deal with? Does he present himself well? Does he listen? Do we want to spend much time and much money working with this person? While highly personalized, these meetings are always limited to creative matters and no deals or negotiations are discussed. The producer will have already ascertained the writer's availability and his or her "quotes" or current price for similar, recent work.

Aside from introducer, an agent is also a professional advisor with a strong vested interest in putting your best work or best foot forward. Resolve early on that when you challenge the marketplace for position you are going to face consequences that include all forms of rejection both personal and professional and in every conceiveable manner from flat-out hardball passes to soft-soap copouts. Regardless of the type of spoon used to convey the castor oil, brace yourself to swallow it quickly and get on with your work. Let the agent deal with the politics of the situation and if there is anything useful to be gleaned from a pass, the agent will convey it. Spec scripts are sometimes returned with comments worth considering in possible rewrites.

If a personal meeting or pitch fails to deliver a deal or a sale, move on at once unless there is some specific shortcoming that can be corrected for future meetings.

An advisor with knowledge of the market

Part of the advisor's function requires an agent to evaluate your material. This area, more than any other, will determine the kind of relationship you have with an agent, because this is where disagreements about your work will first appear. Agents do not *have* to represent or submit anything you deliver to them. In fact, if you have decided to embark on a new script, the person to call *before* typing the first page is your agent. You may thus discover that two studios have been developing "your" script for several months or, worse, that principal photography just wrapped on the same story only with a Doberman pinscher in the lead role. Use your agent as a sounding board before, during and after writing anything you expect him to put on the market. Aside from knowing how to protect your interests in negotiations, the most frequent and valuable service from good representation is knowing the market, thus often saving the writer time and much wasted effort.

If a first consultation does not shut a project down, give the finished product to your agent before you make any other professional submissions. It can be a scratch draft but should be fairly well proofed. The important thing is to get the best evaluation you can from the agent before you decide to go forward. If there is complete disagreement on the quality of the script and your agent refuses to submit it, you might suggest a limited number (four or five) of selected submissions where a pass does the least harm (therefore, not to the head of production) and thereby test the waters. You can agree to rewrite or abandon for now if these submissions turn up generally negative results. If, after all best efforts and good faith discussion are exhausted, the agent still will not go out with your material, start looking for someone else to represent you.

What agents are not

They are not your mother or father, nor your priest or rabbi. They are not your editor, tax consultant or investment counselor. They are not social secretaries, tennis partners or psychiatrists (except where your aberrant behavior threatens continued employment). Agencies are not banks and agents not loan officers. (Yet I have never talked with an agent who has done the job for more than a couple of years who has not, at one time or another, loaned a client money. But you had better be either a longtime client or have a firm deal coming in the door.)

Agents do not guarantee success; they reduce the odds of complete failure. An agent may become a good friend in the long term, but unless he does, agents are not entitled to love, birthday cards, gifts, gratitude, or public acclaim as you nervously clutch your Oscar. What an agent *is* entitled to is your payment of commissions. All of the other things may come in the fullness of time, but what an agent deserves and has a right to expect for services rendered is commission. Regardless of anything else, the relationship is always fundamentally an economic one and therefore completely predictable and dependable.

What about commissions?

One of your main career goals is to pay as much in commissions as possible. That means you are working frequently and making obscenely high fees. Agents are franchised by the Writers Guild of America (WGA) through the Association of Talent Agents (ATA); agents in California are also licensed by the State Labor Commissioner. These bodies set commission rates at no more than 10% for film and television writers. The ATA is a professional group which bargains with various guilds and unions which have jurisdiction over clients and it also supports quality control on its members. ATA and WGA affiliations are good indicators of professional competence and integrity when seeking representation.

Generally when signing agency contracts you will also be asked to sign authorizations which permit the agency to receive your checks. This is a standard practice among all established agencies. By this method the agency knows if *timely* payments have been made; they can deduct commission and send your check wherever you direct. This also permits the agency to verify the correct amounts are being paid and there are no unauthorized deductions or holdbacks taken by the employer.

Seeking representation

Basically, there are two ways to go about finding an agent to represent you or your work. Either you get a third-party reference (you know someone I know and they've read your work and give me a call), or you contact agents cold through query letters. The first way is better, but the second is far more likely, especially for writers just starting out. Unless you have a personal relationship with an agent, cold calls are virtually useless and can do more harm than good; they place you in about the same category of desirability as a strange stockbroker pushing shares of Montana Smelting.

A few words now about query letters:

● They should be typed, readable and to the point.

● Always include your address and phone number.

● If you expect an answer, include sufficient return postage to send back whatever you want back.

● Avoid sending sample pages or "teaser" scenes which, at best, can represent barely 5% of the finished work.

● State clearly and quickly what type of script you have or are writing and a suitable summary of the plot. Use your own judgment as to how much detail you want to disclose.

● *A query letter is not a résumé.* You are trying to induce a complete stranger to read your script, not applying for a job. Therefore, academic credentials, work history, family tree, awards and honors, and special skills and hobbies have no place in a query *unless* something in them bears *directly* on the subject matter of your script. If you are writing about the murder of a game warden in Kenya and you have lived in Africa or count murder among your special skills, then the agent will certainly want to know about it.

● Before you dispatch scads of letters hither and yon, do some decent research about your targets. Know why and to whom you are sending a query. Some agencies and/or agents represent only TV material and don't really deal very much in the feature market and vice-versa. Check the current *Guide to Literary Agents* and other standard reference guides which list agents' preferences and the correct spelling of their names.

● Queries may be sent at any time. Agents may be busier at certain times of the year than others if they deal in episodic television, but as a practical matter there is no easy way for you to figure that out, so don't worry about it. Start making contacts whenever the script is ready to be seen outside your immediate family.

● If you get a pass from an agent or no answer at all, move on to others.

● If you get a request to send in your script, GREAT! You're off the street and into the lobby, even if you aren't yet through the office door.

What to expect when you're represented

Having secured the interest of an agent(s) in your script, what kind of representation can you expect?

First, an agent can represent you and/or your script. What's the difference? For one thing, representing just your script but not you as a client means the agent does not assume the obligation to solicit and procure employment for you as a writer. In the television markets especially, this is always time-consuming and usually a fruitless task unless you present some existing credentials that an agent can work with. By limiting the representation to your script alone the agent can focus time, energy and resources where they will do the most good; he can concentrate on his main goal: to sell the script to the best customer for the best deal (we will come back to this). Some agencies have developed special contracts called "single project" agreements, specifically designed to lock in an individual script or TV treatment as the client rather than the actual writer. Where the sale of a script is the first career step, there are no "career strategies" to worry about yet. With luck and good writing, those headaches will come later.

If the agent wants to represent you *and* your work and you are a new writer to film and television, then he will inevitably use your best available writing as sample scripts to solicit other work on assignment. Thus, a spec script often serves two functions on the market: as submitted material and as a "calling card" which might land the writer unforeseen employment—"We don't want to make what you wrote, but we like the quality of the work so how about considering what we *do* want to make," etc. It is a commonly heard observation in the film business that some writers' best work has earned them a great deal of money and has never been produced.

What makes the best deal best?

Earlier I said the agent's goal was the best deal from the best customer, so let's look at this concept for a minute.

Why not just go after the best deal? The most money? Writers often read and hear about "auctions" and "bidding wars" for new scripts and deals with breathtaking numbers. Yes, these deals do happen every so often, but they are not the usual course of business. Part of useful representation is having skillful and experienced advice about when and with whom to make deals. Agents know who the good buyers are but they should also be able to discern for you the traps you cannot see for yourself—the wannabe producers, the time-wasters, the energy-vampires who never quite come through with the deal or the money; in short, all of the marginal and lightweight players whose tactics in the marketplace can ruin an otherwise solid script. One of the most essential and valuable parts of any agent's job is to protect you from these types. The most money may not be the best deal if it comes from someone who has no real chance or intention of getting your film or television project into production or to distribute it adequately. Some option money trickles into your checking account, but then a year or more goes by and nothing happens. The option lapses after the script has been shopped to death and worn out its welcome everywhere because nobody wants to make it with the knucklehead who is attached to it like a bad rash.

A bad deal is not better than no deal!

That's because a bad deal can kill a script forever but at least with no deal the script remains available and can still seek out a home. Thus, if the agent is on the ball and has really found the best customer, then it won't ever be a bad deal.

Learning to be a good client

There is more to the agent-writer relationship than just sending in material with the attitude of "call me when it sells." Clients can be their own worst enemy, usually when they decide to take on both the jobs of writer *and* agent. To be a client means you are willing to put your livelihood in someone else's hands. If you take your work seriously, take your agent seriously as well. You can learn to be a good writer and you can learn to be a good client. This requires reasonable diligence, fairness, and cooperation in dealing with your agent. Remember that your agent is the prism through which employers see you and your work. In short, if you have a jerk or a clown for an agent, then you can be mistaken for a jerk or a clown. There is simply no foolproof test to guarantee the success of any agency alliance. Like romance, it is the indefinable chemistry and it either works or it doesn't. Nevertheless, here are a few tips on the elusive problem of how to be a client:

- Try to find someone who sees the agency business as a *profession*, not a way station on a career path to being a producer or studio executive. If you ever get a whiff of this sort of thing, get out quick and find someone else. You cannot afford to be represented by someone who has one eye cocked on studio or network office; they will always be willing to satisfy someone other than you and they will always be willing to settle for less.
- The most valuable items an agent can give you are time and judgment, so make the most of both. When in doubt about calling, leave the agent alone. Every ten minutes spent in small talk about smaller issues is ten minutes not spent contacting a possible buyer or setting up a useful meeting. Don't expect or request daily or even weekly briefings on the course of your career. This is the real business world here, not the State Department press room. If there is an agreed program of submissions of material, updates every couple of weeks would be about right.
- If you make any contacts or submissions on your own, notify your agent, especially if you have sent a script on your own. Even better, discuss this upfront. You want to be kept informed and so does your agent. Also, there may be good reasons why you should not submit to or contact a certain party directly at a certain time.
- Find out if there is a preferred time during the business day when you can call.
- Concede the fact that, at least in the early going, the agent's knowledge counts for something and that his job is to set the priorities of what and when to move and to whom. He is making a living doing his job and you may not be.
- For short, informational messages, faxes are best of all. Consider investing in this purchase. Communication can thus be frequent but quick and there is a written record.
- Be as informed about the business as you can be. If you have easy access to the Hollywood trade papers, learn how to read them with sensible skepticism. A good substitute is weekly *Variety* out of New York, which encapsulates most of the previous week's important news from the West Coast's daily edition.

Finally, somewhere around your workspace find a place for these words from Winston Churchill: "Never give up. Never give up. Never, never, never."

Myths, Magic and Misconceptions: The Truth About Agents

by David Dworski

I opened my literary agency in 1984 after 14 years as a freelance writer, story editor and development executive with the idea of becoming the agent I'd wished I'd had when I was a writer. It was not as simple as I expected. In retrospect, I think a lot of it had to do with agendas.

The fact is, writers and agents often have different agendas. While the Big Agenda is usually the same for both at the outset — financial and artistic success — eventually even that may come to mean something different to each of the players. After a whirlwind courtship, the writer and agent waltz blissfully around the Great Dance Floor of Hollywood until, all too often, trouble sets in. Cracks in the ballroom floor widen, the partners stumble, and after a time nobody can hear the music for the grousing. The relationship takes a header, a lot of energy is spent being angry, and the ubiquitous, time-consuming and debilitating Search for a New Agent (and/or client) begins once again.

Writers' myths about agents are many and they are pervasive. Sometimes funny, sometimes sad, sometimes outrageous, they are also sometimes true. But, not always. And that "but" is important, for myths get in the way of one of the most important dialogues that needs to take place between a writer and his agent — a clear and open discussion of both their agendas.

Myths get in the way of this process. They lead to confusion, obfuscation and eventual misery. They muck things up. Badly. I was certainly victimized by my own favorite agent myths during my freelance years. I think every writer is. Maybe you'll recognize these.

Myth: Agent as Nostradamus

"Tell me, what are They *looking for?"*

Agents aren't mind readers, astrologers or fortune tellers. Although they can accurately report what they've seen and heard recently in the trenches (such as specific needs for a given star, or markers out to various producers or directors), and make well-informed guesses about the shape of things to come, they haven't got a crystal ball. Not by a long shot. The truth is, the industry is looking for the same stuff it has always looked for since the beginning: solid ideas and solid writing.

*Literary agent **David Dworski** has worked in the entertainment industry for over 30 years. His seminar for screenwriters "Hollywood: How to Break In from Wherever You Are" is available on two 90-minute audiocassettes from Dworski & Associates. Based on his Pitching Workshop, it teaches you how to sell your scripts, your ideas, and yourself. See the Resources section for more information.*

Don't look to your agent to give you some intelligence report from the future. You're the artist. It's you reacting to life, your aliveness to this time and place, to what you've read, seen and thought which will make your work different . . . and sell. You, the writer, create the future.

Myth: Agent as Merlin

"He made just one phone call and got him/her the job"

Although it may appear the agent (usually someone else's agent) is a stand-in for Merlin, the fact is that every deal that gets signed represents hundreds of long hours spent slaving on other deals that go up in smoke. Indeed, the decision to take on a new writer is a tremendous act of faith on the agent's part, representing an investment of time, money and energy that may not pay off for a long time — if ever.

Myth: A New Agent is Good; A Newer Agent is Better; The Newest Agent is Best

"I don't know what's wrong with my career. Maybe I should get another agent."
Not necessarily. On all counts.

I bought this myth a couple of times as a writer. And it worked . . . for a while. But after the honeymoon was over, I was pretty much back in the same old soup. The same problems afflicted the new relationship, plus a few new ones.

Be honest. Assess your talents. Scrutinize your agenda. Discuss it with your agent. Is a change of representation really necessary? Or have you been expecting your agent to outperform Miracle Max in representing you and selling you without new material, attitudes or ideas?

It's tough to market a talent that doesn't keep renewing itself. In large part, this business is about that which is new. Sure, it's true every writer goes through fallow times which are both organic and necessary. But ask yourself: Have you initiated new work recently, or are you waiting for lightning to strike? Have you been holding up your end of the bargain?

Unless you genuinely believe your agent has neglected his responsibility, unless there's zero communication, I'd hold off in seeking new representation and start talking.

It comes back to agendas. Beyond surviving this season, beyond getting free-lance assignments, moving up to a staff-writing position (and holding on to it), beyond the marketing of the current original scripts or notion for a television movie, what have you and your agent decided on as a workable vision of the future?

A good agent makes you face facts. Indeed, perhaps the single most important thing an agent can do for a writer is to truthfully and informatively advise him on his career. It is also the hardest. And a lot of agents are loath to do it. It's hard work, and time-consuming, analyzing one writer's career when there are 25 other writers on hold, each with his or her own set of problems. But a periodic and serious discussion of where you both are and how you view your future is essential to maintaining a good writer-agent relationship.

Myth: Agent as Bon Vivant

"He's living it up, while I'm doing all the work!"

What's wrong with this myth? It's true, isn't it? Your agent invariably returns your phone calls from his car phone on his way to play tennis.

Be glad, not mad. He's probably working the court. And, most important, he's returning your call!

The truth is the agent and writer are actors in the same circus, but each performs in a different ring. Both performances are equally fraught with anxiety; each a high wire act with no net. Although it may appear to the writer like an easygoing cinch, the agent's life is in fact as bedeviled as his own. Clients come and go. Careers blow hot and cold. Studio heads and production executives change more often than the menu at Spago. Segments of the industry shift like tectonic plates, and the job market slides with them.

Of necessity, agents live in a different world. That's what the writer is paying them for: so *they* don't have to be there, caught up in the business of the business, in the grinding nuts and bolts of the deal.

The writer lives alone in his head, wrestling with ideas and words, putting them down on a blank page, intense and driven. The agent lives in the town, surrounded by other people, culling information and cultivating relationships, intense and driven. I used to think the ten percent commission my agent took was too much. After four years on the other side of the fence, I know differently.

Myth: There is a perfect agent out there for me

It's no myth.

If not a perfect agent, there's at least a damn good one somewhere out there. Could be you already have that agent. A more successful career might just be a question of chucking out a few tired myths, taking stock, and clarifying your agendas.

What an Agent Really Looks For

by Carolyn Hodges

I entered this profession without prior planning, or even desire. After five years of organizing an annual screenwriting conference in Boulder, it became clear that writers in my area desperately needed local representation. Truthfully, I didn't know the first thing about being an agent. Fortunately, one of Los Angeles' most prominent and well respected agents, Stuart Robinson, encouraged me to open an office. Six years later I owe him my deepest thanks for his continuing support and belief in my ability to operate as a "long distance" agent.

An agent's job is selling work she believes in

When I was new to the business, I accepted every screenplay offered; read each and every word; edited and corrected spelling, grammar and typos. Now, I realize this is not my job. If I'm going to *sell* projects, my time must be devoted to selling. Today, I'm unwilling to read six drafts of a screenplay and correct it six different times. This equates to approximately 18 hours of my time, or two full working days. When I receive a professionally-completed screenplay of topical interest, I can devote the same 18 hours to circulating a project in the marketplace.

I will invest time, effort and expense in marketing your material, but you must also invest yourself. Hire an editor to check for errors. Join a writer's support group to work with you through the six drafts. Work with a script doctor. Then, send me the seventh draft. Please respect my position as an agent, and understand that my job is to sell your work. Your job is to write it.

I accept or decline projects described in query letters based on subject matter. If it doesn't interest me, I can't find the artificial enthusiasm to sell it. If I connect, then nothing will stop me. I may not sell your material, but it won't be for lack of trying.

If I turn down your proposal or treatment, don't waste time fretting. Send it to another agent who may be more receptive. Being an agent is subjective. I can't change who or what I am to suit the needs of hundreds of writers. Just because I can't connect with your project doesn't mean it isn't highly valuable to another agent. It only means my background and history disallow my consideration of your project. Find an agent who is on your wavelength.

Creative considerations

Don't write for today's market

I can't tell you what to write. I can suggest potential trends, but it's still up to you to make creative decisions. What's hot and fast at the theaters today could

Carolyn Hodges has optioned projects to various production companies including Spelling Entertainment, Gallo Entertainment and River Road Productions, and has sold to First Take Productions. Many of her clients gain income as "writers for hire" while waiting for their Big Break. "I truly hope to be their catalyst."

be slow as syrup tomorrow. No one can predict the future. The industry can be subjective and rigid, or objective and flexible. In any event, it's always fickle. If action/adventure is a hit, then writers tend to send these types of scripts to me — six months too late. The same is true of any other popular genre of the moment. Writing for the current market is fruitless. Films are in development for months, or years, before production. Word leaks of one studio's project, and others follow suit. Therefore, many similar films appear in a short period of time and writers assume this is the type of material they should produce. It isn't.

Don't write for the current market. Write what is precious and dear to you. Write from intimate knowledge and experience, and create a project based on your feelings and experience.

The story should be yours, but not you

I want your story, but not your autobiography. I do feel that most "first" screenplays are autobiographical and *must* be written. They *must* be gotten out of one's system. But the script should then be placed in a desk drawer, and not submitted. You are always being told to "write what you know." This is excellent advice. Since you know yourself and your history better than anything else, it's natural to believe that's what you should write. It's not, unless you've lived an extraordinary existence. Most of us have valleys and peaks that are momentous to us, our friends and family, but will these events attract a large audience outside of that circle? Write what you know, but frame it outside of your actual experiences. Let your knowledge transcend your ego and lend it to your characters.

Don't go too far afield from your core instincts. It is disheartening to read a screenplay that is devised, contrived and constructed on an "idea" from nowhere. If you haven't lived the character or shared the emotions inherent to a story, it won't ring true. You can't fool the audience. Even an historical project must contain elements of your own personal joy, elation and despair.

Let the reader know what happens . . . and why

Unfortunately, I am unable to care if you were an abused child or severely battered person unless I know your feelings about the events. What interest is there in an uncle, father or sister who scaled Mt. Everest in the nude while under the influence of LSD, unless we know the most private interior thoughts and emotions of the people involved? Please don't convey the sequence of events in a story without allowing the reader into your characters' motivations. I often read screenplays and question "why" the characters are acting their parts. I wonder why anyone cares what they're doing. Let the reader know. I want to smile, laugh, shed tears and cringe with anxiety when reading a screenplay. Do your work correctly and I will respond appropriately. If I experience extreme emotion, then I'll be able to share my belief in your ability with producers, story editors and studio executives.

Writing with emotion and conveying characters' motivation are essential to a good script. Plot should also be of primary concern. Know where your story is going. Start it. Expand and develop it. Stop it. A beginning, middle and end. Make it happen! Don't use characters, scenes or subplots that have nothing to do with moving your story forward. When you introduce a character, use it. If you can't use it, kill it before it reaches the page.

But leave room for the reader's imagination

Please give a reader/viewer credit for the ability to understand your material. It isn't necessary to record every small detail of a character's movement. If a telephone rings, we know the character "rises from his chair, crosses the room and lifts the receiver." On the page it is excess baggage. You are also "directing" your script at that point. When a director reads your script, he will probably see it much differently than presented. If you lay it all out, there isn't room for imagination and interpretation. Your job is to tell the story. Allow other professionals to do their jobs.

Overwriting fills pages with extraneous words. A screenplay isn't a novel; it isn't page after page of black lines. A screenplay is "white" with relatively few lines to a page. Psychologically, the pace of a script is increased if the pages are being turned quickly. Spending two or three minutes reading one page is extremely boring and usually means very little is actually happening. Please, let me fly through the script while being totally absorbed by each priceless word and phrase.

Dialogue is interaction

Writing dialogue is more than an art—it's a gift. You may write a story that's never been told before. The format may be perfect. The length is exact at 115 pages, but your characters speak with encyclopedic formality.

"I'm going to drive to the grocery story to purchase a loaf of bread. I will return as soon as possible."

No! No! No! Consider the following:

"I'm gonna run to the corner and get some bread . . . back in a few minutes."

Listen to yourself. Listen to your friends. How do you relate to each other conversationally? Are there pauses while you search for the correct word? Do you always speak in complete sentences? I don't. If you don't, why should your characters? If they are vital and alive, they must be touched by the frailties and vulnerabilities that give real humans character. This "life" is most evident in characters' actions, but defined and personalized by dialogue. But don't overdo it. Remember that some of life's most powerful statements are accomplished in silence.

Professional presentation invites professional consideration

Rejection of material is blameless and impersonal, but definitely a harsh fact of life in the film industry. Wasting energy on self pity or agent bashing diminishes your creative reserve. Accept rejection and move on. I've had writers beg, intimidate and threaten me to market their material. I'm sorry, but I can't always help. A successful agent must represent clients whose material is professional and marketable. It should go without saying that the client should also be professional and marketable. I feel great sympathy for struggling writers and have always gone far beyond the call of duty to boost a flagging career, but I've also always said that I have to make a lot of people rich before I can make a decent living.

The presentation of your material must be technically correct. Format should be second nature. When you fight with margins, indentations and capitalizations, your artistic efforts will suffer. Creativity shouldn't be impeded by stops and starts. Naturally, the use of a word-processor and a user-friendly screenwriting program is invaluable. I still receive a few typewritten screenplays which are as good as computer-generated projects, but most aren't. A capital investment in your future may be necessary; a screenwriting career can be a costly endeavor. However, compared to a four-year college education, which may yield a similar financial return over a period of time, the cost is small — if you're committed to your art and craft.

Your script should look the part. Use a three-hole punch and cardstock covers, front and back. Brads are OK, but Chicago or Revere screws are better because they're flat headed and cause less damage. I once received a script with very long metal brads which had been cut to fit. The edges were razor sharp and I cut my finger deeply. This sort of presentation does not make a good impression! Comb bindings and other permanent methods are a nuisance when corrected pages must later be inserted. Loose-leaf binders work on the same principal as the three-hole punch, but are unwieldy and do not stack well on shelves.

A small label on the cover with the title and your name is all that's necessary. Inside, the title page should contain the same. Your address and phone number, WGA registration number and dates of different drafts, if included, should be on a separate page.

Submission etiquette

My agency is considered "boutique," which means I do not have a large staff. I ask writers to supply extra copies of screenplays when necessary. I also require that return postage and a large SASE be included with each screenplay for its return. Otherwise, I may choose to recycle your material rather than return it. As a writer you may be submitting to a number of agents before you gain representation. As an agent, I am dealing with dozens of writers at any given moment. Returning screenplays to writers is an expensive proposition. The costs of postage, mailers and labels add up quickly, and I no longer incur this expense. A 10×13 return SASE needs no more than $1.48 postage, book rate.

The same is true of query letters. A business size SASE is expected, not a postcard. If I respond positively to your query letter I will include a Submission Agreement which must be returned with your screenplay. A postcard doesn't allow for inclusion of a letter or other forms. However, a postcard enclosed with your screenplay is fine if you wish to know your script has been received.

I'm always excited to read new material. Although I now request queries by referral only, I will still read short treatments (six pages) from anyone. My problem is finding time to read all that I receive. If you don't mind waiting two to three months for a response to your script, I'll be delighted to accommodate. My agency deals with feature film and television/cable movies exclusively. Television episodics, miniseries, sitcoms and proposals are not viable propositions; these areas are best served by an agent in Los Angeles.

Questions for you

If you were an agent, how would you sell your project? Could you pick up the phone and call Universal, Warner Brothers or Paramount and pitch your story? Do you honestly believe in your work? Are you unwaveringly committed to your writing career? If you don't believe in yourself and your work, neither do I. My goal is to establish and nurture our artist/agent relationship so that we may play a part in creating visual legacies for future generations. It's a lofty goal, but anything's possible.

Pitching a Winner

by J. Michael Straczynski

In many cases, writers prefer the written word because they don't like public speaking. I know several writers who can put together wonderful short stories, but who panic when asked to read those self-same stories.

Writers write. Performers perform. Which is as it should be . . . with one notable exception.

Pitching.

If you have any ambitions whatsoever of working in television, or film, or any related field, *there is absolutely no alternative to learning how to pitch.*

Let me explain by way of example.

Part of my working as story editor for *The Twilight Zone* meant going through the equivalent of a publisher's slush pile—sample and spec scripts from freelance writers, some known to us, some unknown, some with agents and some without. In this case, that meant about 3,000 submissions. These scripts are first read by a staff reader, who sifts through and finds those he believes either 1) are appropriate to the show as they stand, or 2) indicate good writing skills even though the story may not be quite what we're looking for.

These scripts are passed up the line and read again. I should mention now that spec scripts are rarely bought. The script simply demonstrates that you can write for this particular kind of show. Out of those 3,000 scripts, we bought only two over-the-transom submissions.

The well-written scripts convinced us that their authors had what it takes to write for our show, even though their particular story didn't do it for us. Each writer got a telephone call from our production office and was called in to pitch some more stories.

Pitching is not something done only by established writers. On *The Twilight Zone*, we called in brand-new writers as well as established names, out-of-state writers as well as locals. Simply put, *pitching* is plain, old-fashioned storytelling. You work out some ideas, flesh them out, give them a beginning, a middle and an end, and then come in and tell us what you've come up with.

Understand that very specific Writers Guild rules govern speculative writing. No story editor or producer can *ask* you to write something without also agreeing to pay you for it. So the only thing that I, as a story editor, could do is call you, tell you that we're interested, give you some suggestions, tell you what areas we've already covered, and set up a time for you to come in and tell us your stories.

There are disadvantages to the system. The process tends to favor those who are good performers, but who may, down the line, turn out to be less than superb writers. At the same time, it tends to penalize writers who are terrified of public storytelling, or who just aren't as good at it as they'd like. And in some cases,

J. Michael Stracyznski is executive producer of Babylon 5, *currently in its second season. He has been a producer on* Murder She Wrote, *as well as story editor on* The Twilight Zone, *among others. Nominated for WGA, Ace, Gemini and Bram Stoker Awards, he is also the author of* The Complete Book of Scriptwriting, *published by Writer's Digest Books.*

writers find the prospect so daunting that they don't even want to risk it.

A good story editor will always go out of his or her way to make the writer feel comfortable, to create a nonthreatening environment—but under even the best of circumstances the process of pitching is unnerving. Nonetheless, it is necessary, and because it is necessary you must learn how to do it.

The storyteller at work

Let me tell you a story that may dispel some fears.

I was taking a creative writing class at San Diego State University, under Elizabeth Chater. It was a good class, and I learned a lot. But throughout the semester, a cloud hung overhead: To pass the class, I had to read one of my stories aloud at some point during the session.

Nothing else that semester, which included classes in subjects far beyond my intellectual reach, held more terror for me than that one requirement. I put it off, refused to think about it.

Finally, the semester nearly over, I hit on what I thought was the solution. I wrote a very short story, about 10 or 11 pages, *designed* to be read aloud. Short sentences so I wouldn't run out of breath, no alliteration that could lead to a stammer, no hard consonants butting up against one another, a rather funny plot and so on.

I practiced it, over and over. Then the day came, and I went to the front of the room (which was getting strangely warmer by the moment), stood at the lecturn (which seemed the wrong size), and began to read. And the panic set in. And I began to speed up, then falter.

"Louder!" someone called from the back.

My face was hot, the room seemed to tilt, and I felt as if I were watching myself from a distance, watching this poor soul self-destructing in front of an audience of peers. Only gradually did I become aware of Mrs. Chater's voice cutting in and, with as much gentleness and understanding as she could muster, telling me that it was all right and perhaps I could finish the story another time.

I was halfway through the story.

I could not bring myself to go back to class again for two weeks.

It took this event to finally push this little button in my head that says *Find what you're afraid of and do it*. I'd always believed in that, but had been putting off facing this particular fear for as long as possible. Now the moment had come.

Find what you're afraid of and do it. In this case, that was talking in front of people.

So that summer, I signed on to become a peer/orientation counselor for new students. Which meant talking to large groups from eight in the morning until four in the afternoon.

All day.

Every day.

For the entire summer.

That fall, I took the first of many classes in public speaking, diction and dramatics. In all the time since then, speaking at crowded conventions and workshops and seminars and, yes, in pitches, I've never stopped being nervous, at least a little, but the fear no longer rules me.

Pitching in

If the prospect of pitching fills you with alarm, you should start *now* to learn the process if you're serious about working in television or film, because there *is* no alternative. (And even if you're not interested in those two areas, you should do it for no better reason than it makes you nervous, and because it can be used to help your writing in other ways, which I'll get to in a moment.)

When I first had to pitch, I solicited advice from others. Over time, I've added some tricks of my own. These I pass on to you:

• Remember that we—the story editors and producers—are on your side. We want to hear a good story. That's why you were invited. It's not a hostile room.

• Trick yourself with this analogy: Most of the time, people have no problem summarizing a movie they saw last night when friends ask what it was about. There's not as much emotional pressure to get every single detail in—you hit the high points, tell the story and get out. Pretend the story you're pitching was something you saw on TV last night, and use the same approach.

• Confine yourself to about four or five pitches, with a couple of less worked-out quickies in reserve. As a rule, you will have about 45 minutes to make your pitches. Six pitches is about all you can realistically expect to tell with any degree of completeness in that amount of time, and story editors tend to glaze over after more than six stories. (One person came in to pitch at *The Twilight Zone* with 14 stories, a record. To say we were annoyed by the time she left is a massive understatement.)

• Don't over-complicate your pitches. You don't have to describe and follow every single character and delineate every single subplot. In a pitch, we're looking for the broad strokes. If we need more information, we'll ask for it, and it's in your best interests to have an answer in the back of your head, or be able to think fast on your feet.

• Related to this, writers often sense that there's not enough plot when they're just *telling* a story. Hence, we commonly encounter writers with incredibly elaborate, over-worked-out stories. You know you have a problem, for instance, when it takes 25 minutes to tell a story, that in full script form, will run only 22 minutes.

• Write out only spare notes. Three-by-five cards are often more of a hindrance than a help. Your best bet is one sheet of typing paper per story, with the main points written in capital letters so you can read them without having to search, and in as few words as possible. This way you don't accidentally miss a point and have to backtrack (sure and sudden death in most pitches), but you don't end up reading us your story. (Most writers seem to have a harder time doing a good, dramatic reading of a story than just telling the story informally.)

• Practice the pitches with someone else, preferably someone who hasn't seen your notes or the written stories. Is there anything he or she doesn't get, anything that isn't clear? If so, you can be reasonably sure the same question will come up in the pitch. (I would discourage practicing with a tape recorder only because most people are put off by the sound of their own voice. Better to get an audience, if available, with the tape recorder only as a last recourse.)

• Be sure what you're pitching is a *story*, not a springboard. On occasion, writers have come in and pitched just a one-line idea, sort of a *TV Guide* synopsis, trusting that we will fill in the details for them. This almost never works, and nine times out of ten ends up antagonizing everyone.

• Try not to go out of your way to annoy the story editor. I know this sounds like obvious and unnecessary advice, but sometimes people who get nervous get defensive without being aware of it. We had one writer come in who answered every concern we brought up in his pitch by responding, in a sarcastic voice, "Thank you for sharing that." It was only when I left the office and returned with a claw hammer, put it on the couch beside me and said, "Continue," that he got the message.

• If you live out of state, and flying in to pitch would be a financial hardship, ask if you can pitch over the phone. Failing this, you can *volunteer* to write out your premises and mail them in. The producer/story editor cannot in good faith ask you to do this, but if you would prefer to do so for financial reasons, no one is going to stop you.

The same is true if, even with all the practice and the other hints, you still don't feel comfortable with the idea of pitching, and don't want to do it. You *can* volunteer to send in premises—as long as you strictly understand that this is not binding, that the production company in no way obligates itself by reading the premises, and that you're doing so for your own convenience, not at the request of the story editor/producer.

Because of my own background, I try to accommodate writers who just can't find it in themselves to pitch—and there are quite a few. But many other story editors simply won't take the time to do so, and you'll either have to pitch verbally or not at all.

The only thing to fear . . .

One side benefit of pitching, and preparing to pitch, is that the process of verbalizing your story often makes you aware of inadequacies you wouldn't have seen otherwise. I've occasionally had a story in my head that *seems* fine, but once I start to tell someone about it, I begin to realize that *this* part sounds kind of lame, and *that* part doesn't relate to the rest as well as it should. Obviously, such verbalizing isn't for everyone. There are many writers who defuse the dramatic impulse, let the steam out, by talking about their stories.

The bottom line on all this is that pitching—like it or not—is a necessary and vital part of the scriptwriting business, whether you're a novice or an established name. Often it's the *only* way you can make a sale. It profits you nothing to be able to write a dynamite sample of your work, then not be able to capitalize on it because of fear.

And to be perfectly honest with you, it's a skill you should learn even if you *never* intend to go into a pitch session. There is always the book editor you'll meet at a party, who will ask you to describe the novel you're writing and trying to sell . . . or the magazine editor to whom you're trying to sell a hot, last-minute idea that requires a go-ahead *now*, not in three days when the query letter arrives. . . .

Or the writing workshop that requires you to read your work in front of the rest of the class.

There are many kinds of victories. One is conquering an editor or a producer and selling a story. Another is conquering yourself. And sometimes they're the same thing.

Find what you're afraid of, and do it.

Script Agents: Nonfee-charging and Fee-charging

A quick test: What do you need to succeed in Hollywood?
   a) Great scripts.
   b) Insecurity.
   c) Confidence.
   d) A good agent.
   e) All of the above.
If you answered "e," you've got a good start.

A good script takes time. It takes time to write. It takes time to rewrite. It takes time to write the four or five scripts that precede the really great one. The learning curve from one script to the next is tremendous and you'll probably have a drawer full of work before you've got a script with which to approach an agent. Your talent has to show on the page, and the page has to excite people.

Once you have a script that says what you want it to say, that is the best idea you've ever had, expressed in the best way you know, put it aside. And get on with the next "best idea you've ever had." Practice and hone your skills until you are ready to enter the race. The more horses you enter, the better your chances to win, place or show.

You'll need both confidence and insecurity at the same time. Confidence to enter the business at all. There are less than 300 television movies and far fewer big screen movies made each year. For a 22-week season, a half-hour sitcom buys two freelance scripts. Every year, thousands of new graduates of film schools and writing programs enter the market. But talent will out. If you're good, and you persevere, you will find work. Believe in yourself and your talent, because if you don't, no one else will either.

Use your insecurity to spur you and your work on to become better. Accept that, at the beginning, you know little. Then go out and learn. Read all the books you can find on scriptwriting, from format to dramatic structure. Learn the formulas, but don't become formulaic. Observe the rules, but don't be predictable. Absorb what you learn and make it your own.

And finally, you'll need a good agent. In this book we call agents handling screenplays or teleplays script agents, but in true West Coast parlance they are literary agents, since they represent writers as opposed to actors or musicians. Most studios, networks and production companies will return unsolicited manuscripts unopened and unread for legal protection. An agent has the entree to get your script in the office and on the desk of a story analyst or development executive.

The ideal agent understands what a writer writes, is able to explain it to others, and has credibility with individuals who are in a position to make decisions. An agent sends out material, advises what direction a career should take and makes the financial arrangements. And how do you get a good agent? By going back to the beginning—great scripts.

The spec script

There are two sides to an agent's representation of a scriptwriter: finding work on an existing project and selling original scripts. Most writers break in with scripts written on "spec," that is, on speculation without a specific sale in mind. A spec script is a calling card that demonstrates skills and gets your name and abilities before influential people. Movie spec scripts are always original, not for a sequel. Spec scripts for TV are always based on existing TV shows, not for an original concept.

More often than not, a spec script will not be made. An original movie spec can either be optioned or bought outright, with the intention of making a movie, or it can attract rewrite work on a script for an existing project. For TV, on the basis of the spec script a writer can be invited in to pitch five or six ideas to the producers. If an idea is bought, the writer is paid to flesh out the story to an outline. If that is acceptable, the writer can be commissioned to write the script. At that point the inhouse writing staff comes in, and in a lot of cases, rewrites the script. But it's a sale, and the writer receives the residuals every time that episode is shown anywhere in the world. The goal is to sell enough scripts so that you are invited to join the writing staff.

What makes a good spec script? Good writing for a start. Write every single day. Talk to as many people you can find who are different from you. Take an acting class to help you really hear dialogue. Take a directing class to see how movies are put together. Live and experience life.

Learn the correct dramatic structure and internalize those rules. Then throw them away and write intuitively. The three act structure is basic and crucial to any dramatic presentation. Act 1—get your hero up a tree. Act 2—throw rocks at him. Act 3—get him down. Some books will tell you that certain events have to happen by a certain page. What they're describing is not a template, but a rhythm. Good scriptwriting is good storytelling.

Spec scripts for movies

If you're writing for movies, explore the different genres until you find one you feel comfortable writing. Read and study scripts for movies you admire to find out what makes them work. Choose a premise for yourself, not "the market." What is it you care most about? What is it you know the most about? Write it. Know your characters and what they want. Know what the movie is about and build a rising level of tension that sucks the reader in and makes her care about what happens.

For feature films, you'll need two or three spec scripts, and perhaps a few long-form (miniseries, movies of the week or episodics) as well. Your scripts should depict a layered story with well-developed characters who feel real, each interaction presenting another facet of their personalities.

Spec scripts for TV

If you want to write for TV, watch a lot of it. Tape four or five episodes of a show and analyze them. Where do the jokes fall? Where do the beats or plot points come? How is the story laid out? Read scripts of a show to find out what professional writers do that works. (Script City (800)676-2522) and Book City ((800)4-CINEMA) have thousands of movie and TV scripts for sale.)

Your spec script will demonstrate your knowledge of the format and ability to create believable dialogue. Choose a show you like, that has a voice you can speak. Knowing the show is the most important thing you can do, and you should understand the characters as if they are a part of you. Current hot shows for writers include *Northern Exposure, NYPD Blue, Law and Order, Mad About You, Frasier* and *Seinfeld*. Shows that are newer, such as *Friends* may also be good bets. If a show has been on three or more years a lot of story lines have already been done, either on camera or in spec scripts. Your spec should be for today's hits, not yesterday's.

You may have a specific program in mind that you want to write for. Paradoxically, to be considered for that show your agent will submit a spec script for a different show. To protect themselves from lawsuits, producers do not read scripts written for their characters. Pick a show that is similar in tone and theme. A *Home Improvement* for *Dave's World*, for example. The hour-long dramatic shows are more individual in nature. You practically would have had to attend med school to write for *ER*, but *Homicide, Law and Order* and *NYPD Blue* have a number of things in common that would make them good specs for one another. Half-hour shows generally have a writing staff and only occasionally buy freelance scripts. Hour-long shows are more likely to pick up scripts written by freelancers.

In writing a spec script, you're not just writing an episode. You're writing an *Emmy-winning* episode. You'll write for the show as it is—and then better than it ever has been. You are not on staff yet, you have plenty of time. Make this the episode the staff writers wish they had written.

But at the same time, certain conventions must be observed. The regular characters always have the most interesting story line. Involve all the characters in the episode. Don't introduce important new characters.

Selling yourself to the salespeople

Scriptwriting is an art and craft. Marketing your work is salesmanship, and it's a very competitive world. Give yourself an edge. Read the trades, attend seminars, stay on top of the news. Make opportunities for yourself.

But at the same time, your writing side has to always be working, producing pages for the selling side to hawk. First you sell yourself to an agent. Then the agent sells herself to you. If you both feel the relationship is mutually beneficial, the agent starts selling you to others.

All agents are open to third party recommendations, referrals from a person whose opinion is trusted. To that end, you can pursue development people, producers' assistants, anyone who will read your script. Mail room employees at the bigger agencies are agents in training. They're looking out for the next great script that will earn them a raise, approval and a promotion to the next rung.

The most common path, however, is through a query letter. In one page you identify yourself, what your script is about and why you're contacting this particular agent. Show that you've done some research and make the agent inclined to read your script. Find a connection to the agent—from "my mother hit your sister's car in the parking lot at the mall," to "we both attended the same college," to recent sales you know through your reading the agent has made. Give a three or four line synopsis of your screenplay, with some specific plot elements, not just a generic premise. Use comparisons as shorthand. "It's a *Deliverance* meets *Thelma & Louise*" lets the reader into the story quickly, through something she's familiar with already. Be sure to include your name, return address and telephone number in your letter, as well as a SASE. If the response is positive, the agent probably will want to contact you by phone to let you know of her interest, but will need the SASE to send you a release form that must accompany your script.

Your query may not be read by the agent, but by an assistant instead. That's okay. There are few professional secretaries in Hollywood, and the assistants are looking for the material that will earn them the step up they've been working for.

To be taken seriously, your script must be presented as professionally as possible. Few agents have the time to develop talent. A less than professional script will be read only once. If it's not ready to be seen, you may have burned that bridge. Putting the cart before the horse, or the agent before the script, will not get you to where you want to go. Your script should sound right and look right before you look for an agent.

The basics of script presentation are simple. Keep your query letter succinct. Never send a script unless it is requested. Always include a SASE with a query or script. Study the correct format for your type of script. Cole and Haag's *Complete Guide to Standard Script Formats* is a good source for the various formats.

Read everything you can about scriptwriting and the industry. As in all business ventures, you must educate yourself about the market to be successful. There are a vast number of books to read. Samuel French ((213)876-0570) is a good source, as is The Write Stuff ((800)989-8833). *Lew Hunter's Screenwriting 434* and Richard Walter's *Screenwriting* are both highly recommended books on the art of scriptwriting. Newsletters such as *Hollywood Scriptwriter* are good sources of information. Trade publications such as *Premiere, The WGA Journal, Variety* and *The Hollywood Reporter* are invaluable as well. A number of smaller magazines have sprung up in the last few years, including *Screenwrite Now!, Creative Screenwriting* and *New York Screenwriter*. See the Resources section for information.

The Writers Guild of America

Many of the script agents listed in the book are signatories to the Writers Guild of America Artists' Manager Basic Agreement. This means they have paid a membership fee and agreed to abide by a standard code of behavior. Enforcement is uneven, however. Although a signatory can, theoretically, be stripped of its signatory status, this rarely happens. Contact the WGA for more information on specific agencies or to check if an agency is a signatory. Agents who are signatories are not permitted to charge a reading fee to WGA members, but are allowed to do so to nonmembers. They are permitted to charge for critiques and other services, but may not refer you to a particular script doctor.

The WGA also offers a registration service which is available to members and nonmembers alike. It's a good idea to register your script before sending it out. Membership in the WGA is earned through the accumulation of professional credits and carries a number of significant benefits. Write the Guild for more information on script registration as well as membership requirements.

Help with your search

This section contains agents who sell feature film scripts, teleplays and theatrical stage plays. Many of the agencies in the Literary Agents section also handle scripts, but agencies that primarily handle scripts are listed here.

To help you with your search for an agent, we've included a number of special indexes in the back of the book. The Subject Index is divided into sections for fee-charging and nonfee-charging literary agents and script agents. The script agent index is divided into various subject areas specific to scripts, such as mystery, romantic comedy and teen. Some agencies indicated that they were open to all categories. These have been grouped in the subject heading "open." This year we've also indexed the agents according to script types, such as TV movie of the week (mow), sitcom and episodic drama in the Script Agents Format Index.

We've included an Agents Index as well. Often you will read about an agent who is an employee of a larger agency and may not be able to locate her business phone or address. We asked agencies to list the agents on staff, then listed the names in alphabetical order along with the name of the agency they work for. Find the name of the person you would like to contact and then check the agency listing. You will find the page number for the agency's listing in the Listings Index.

A geographic index lists agents state by state for those who are looking for an agent close to home.

Many script agents are also interested in book manuscripts; many literary agents will also consider scripts. Agents who primarily sell books but also handle at least 10 to 15 percent scripts appear among the listings in this section, with the contact information, breakdown of work currently handled and a note to check the full listing in the literary agents section. Those literary agents that sell mostly books and less than 10 to 15 percent scripts appear in Additional Script Agents at the end of this section. Complete listings for these agents appear in the Literary Agents section.

Before contacting any agency, check the listing to make sure it is open to new clients. Those designated (V) are currently not interested in expanding their rosters. Some agents will only accept new clients through referrals. Read the listings carefully.

For more information on approaching script agents in particular, see the various articles at the beginning of this section. For information on agents in general and the specifics of the listings, read *How to Use Your Guide to Literary Agents* and *The Right Agent For You*.

About the listings

The listings in this section differ slightly from those in the literary agent sections. A breakdown of the types of scripts each agency handles is included in the listing. Nonfee-charging and fee-charging agencies are listed together. If an agency is a WGA signatory, we include this information in the listing. As noted above, WGA signatories are not permitted to charge reading fees to members, but may do so to nonmembers. However, most signatories do not charge a reading fee across the board. Many agencies do charge for other services—critiques, consultations, promotion, marketing, etc. Those agencies who charge some type of fee have been indicated with a box (□) symbol by their name. The heading "Recent Sales" is also slightly different. Reflecting the different ways scriptwriters work, we asked for movies optioned or sold and scripting assignments procured for clients. We've found the film industry is very secretive about sales, but you may be able to get a list of clients or other references upon request.

We've ranked the agencies listed in this section according to their openness to submissions. Below is our ranking system:

I Newer agency actively seeking clients.
II Agency seeking both new and established writers.
III Agency prefers to work with established writers, mostly obtains new clients through referrals.
IV Agency handling only certain types of work or work by writers under certain circumstances.

V Agency not currently seeking new clients. We have included mention of agencies rated **V** to let you know they are currently not open to new clients. In addition to those ranked **V**, we have included a few well-known agencies' names who have declined the opportunity to receive full listings at this time. *Unless you have a strong recommendation from someone well respected in the field, our advice is to approach only those agents ranked I-IV.*

‡ABOVE THE LINE AGENCY (III), 9200 Sunset Blvd., #401, Los Angeles CA 90069. (310)859-6115. Contact: Bruce Bartlett. Owner: Rima Bauer Greer. Estab. 1994. Signatory of WGA. Represents 14 clients. 5% of clients are new/previously unpublished writers. Currently handles: 2½% juvenile books; 5% novels; 90% movie scripts; 2½% TV scripts.
• Ms. Greer was with the well-known Writers and Artists Agency for over 10 years before starting her own agency.
Handles: Movie scripts. Query. Reports in 2 weeks on queries.
Recent Sales: *Movie scripts sold*: *Sorceror's Apprentice* (indieprod). *Scripting assignments*: *Dial M for Murder* (A. Kopelson); *Oliver* (Disney); *The Computer Wore Tennis Shoes* (Disney); *Academic Decathlon* (Fox); *Wild Swans* (Disney); *Deep Space 9* (Paramount TV).
Terms: Agent receives 10% commission on domestic sales; 10% on foreign sales. Offers written contract, binding for 2 years.
Tips: Obtains new clients through referrals.

‡□AGAPÉ PRODUCTIONS (III), P.O. Box 147, Flat Rock IN 47234. (812)587-5654. Contact: Mr. Terry D. Porter. Estab. 1990. Member of Indiana Film Commission, signatory of WGA. Represents 35 clients. 30% of clients are new/previously unpublished writers. Specializes in movie scripts, TV scripts, packaging deals. Currently handles: 2% juvenile books; 4% novels; 70% movie scripts; 10% TV scripts; 2% stage plays; 6% syndicated material; 4% animation; 2% poetry.
Handles: Movie scripts (feature film), TV scripts, stage plays. Considers these script subject areas: action/adventure; biography/autobiography; cartoon/comic; family saga; humor/satire; psychic/supernatural; science fiction; self-help/personal improvement; thriller/espionage; true crime/investigative; westerns/frontier. Query. Send outline/proposal. Reports in 2 weeks on queries; 1 month on mss.
Also Handles: Novels, syndicated material, animation/cartoon, poetry books.
Terms: Agent receives 10% commission on domestic sales; 15% on foreign sales. Offers written contract, binding for 1 year.
Fees: Charges reading fee: $15 for MP/TV scripts, $25 for novels. "If we represent, half of fee is returned." Offers criticism service at same rates. "Critiques written by agent and professional readers I employ." Charges $50/quarter for all except photocopying. Will provide binders if necessary.
Writer's Conferences: Hollywood Scriptwriters (Universal Studios, CA, October); Media Focus (NBC Studios, CA, October); WGA Awards (Beverly Hills, CA, March 1995).
Tips: Obtains new clients through solicitation, at conferences. "Mr. Porter has numerous contacts within entertainment industry that allow production companies and film executive (director of development) to review/consider purchasing or optioning material. Publishing company contacts very good."

AGENCY CHICAGO (I), P.O. Box 11200, Chicago IL 60611. Contact: Ernest Santucci. Estab. 1990. Signatory of WGA. Represents 14 clients. 50% of clients are new/previously unpublished writers. Specializes in ghost writing. Currently handles: 40% nonfiction books; 20% scholarly books; 10% novels; 10% movie scripts; 20% TV scripts.
• See the expanded listing for this agency in Literary Agents: Nonfee-charging.

AGENCY FOR THE PERFORMING ARTS (II), 9000 Sunset Blvd., Suite 1200, Los Angeles CA 90069. (310)273-0744. Fax: (310)275-9401. Contact: Stuart M. Miller. Estab. 1962. Signatory of WGA. Represents 50+ clients. Specializes in film and TV scripts.

The double dagger before a listing indicates the listing is new in this edition.

Handles: Movie scripts (feature film), TV scripts (feature film). Considers all nonfiction and fiction areas. Query must include SASE. Reports in 2-3 weeks on queries.
Recent Sales: *Final Design*, by Noreen Gilpatrick (The Don Johnson Co.).
Terms: Agent receives 10% commission on domestic sales. Offers written contract.
Tips: Obtains new clients through recommendations from others.

‡THE AGENCY (III), 1800 Avenue of the Stars, Suite 400, Los Angeles CA 90067-4206. (310)551-3000. Fax: (310)551-1424. Contact: Walter Morgan. Estab. 1984. Signatory of WGA. Represents 300 clients. No new previously unpublished writers. Specializes in TV and motion pictures. Currently handles: 45% movie scripts; 45% TV scripts; 10% syndicated material.
Handles: Movie scripts (feature film, animation), TV scripts (TV mow, miniseries, episodic drama, sitcom, animation). Considers these script subject areas: action/adventure; cartoon/animation; comedy; contemporary issues; detective/police/crime; ethnic; family saga; fantasy; historical; horror; humor; juvenile; mainstream; military/war; mystery/suspense; psychic/supernatural; romantic comedy and drama; science fiction; teen; thriller; westerns/frontier; women's issues.
Query: Reports in 2 weeks.
Terms: Agent receives 10% commission on domestic sales; 10% on foreign sales. Offers written contract, binding for 2 years.
Tips: Obtains new clients through recommendations from others.

ALL-STAR TALENT AGENCY (I), 7834 Alabama Ave., Canoga Park CA 91304-4905. (818)346-4313. Contact: Robert Allred. Estab. 1991. Signatory of WGA. Represents 8 clients. 100% of clients are new/previously unpublished writers. Specializes in film, TV. Currently handles: movie scripts, TV scripts, 4 books.
Handles: Movie scripts (feature film), TV scripts (TV mow, episodic drama, sitcom). Considers these script subject areas: action/adventure; comedy; detective/police/crime; fantasy; historical; horror; humor; juvenile; mainstream; mystery/suspense; psychic/supernatural; romantic comedy and drama; science fiction; sports; thriller; westerns/frontier; "any mainstream film or TV ideas."
Query. Reports in 3 weeks on queries; 2 months on mss.
Also Handles: Novels. Considers these fiction areas: action/adventure; cartoon/comic; contemporary issues; detective/police/crime; family saga; fantasy; historical; humor/satire; mainstream; mystery/suspense; psychic/supernatural; romance (contemporary); science fiction; sports; thriller/espionage; westerns/frontier.
Terms: Agent receives 10% commission on domestic sales; 10% on foreign sales with foreign agent receiving additional 10%. Offers written contract, binding for 1 year. 100% of business derived from commissions on ms.
Tips: Obtains new clients through recommendations and solicitation. "A professional appearance in script format, dark and large type and simple binding go a long way to create good first impressions in this business, as does a professional business manner."

MICHAEL AMATO AGENCY (II), 1650 Broadway, Suite 307, New York NY 10019. (212)247-4456-57. Fax: (212)664-0641. Contact: Susan Tomkins. Estab. 1970. Signatory of WGA, member of SAG, AFTRA. Represents 6 clients. 2% of clients are new/previously unpublished writers. Specializes in TV. Currently handles nonfiction books; stage plays.
Handles: Novels, movie scripts (feature film, documentary, animation), TV scripts (TV mow, miniseries, episodic drama, animation). Considers action/adventure stories only. Query. Reports "within a month" on queries. Does not return scripts.
Tips: Obtains new clients through recommentaions.

☐AMERICAN PLAY CO., INC. (II), 19 W. 44th St., Suite 1204, New York NY 10036. (212)921-0545. Fax: (212)869-4032. President: Sheldon Abend. Estab. 1889. Century Play Co. is subsidiary of American Play Co. Specializes in novels, plays, screenplays and film production.
Handles: Novels, movie scripts (feature film, documentary, TV mow, animation), stage plays. Considers all nonfiction and fiction areas. Send entire ms, "double space each page." Reports as soon as possible on ms.
Terms: Agent receives 15% commission on domestic sales; 15% on foreign sales.
Fees: Call or send letter of inquiry.
Tips: Obtains new clients through referrals, unsolicited submissions by authors. "Writers should write novels first before screenplays. They need to know what's going on behind the camera. Before they write or attempt a play, they need to understand the stage and sets. Novels need strong plots, characters who are fully developed."

MARCIA AMSTERDAM AGENCY (II), 41 W. 82nd St., New York NY 10024-5613. (212)873-4945. Contact: Marcia Amsterdam. Estab. 1970. Signatory of WGA. Currently handles: 5% nonfiction books; 80% novels; 10% movie scripts; 5% TV scripts.

• See the expanded listing for this agency in Literary Agents: Nonfee-charging.

‡APOLLO ENTERTAINMENT (I), 3838 N. Bernard St., 2nd Floor, Chicago IL 60618. (312)267-8126. Contact: Bruce Harrington. Estab. 1993. Signatory of WGA. Represents 5 clients. 20% of clients are new/previously unpublished writers. Specializes in feature screenplays of unordinary topics. Currently handles: 20% nonfiction books; 80% movie scripts; 10% TV scripts.
Handles: Movie scripts, TV scripts. Considers these script subject areas: action/adventure; contemporary issues; detective/police/crime; family saga; fantasy; feminist; gay; glitz; historical; horror; humor; lesbian; mainstream; psychic/supernatural; romance; science fiction; teen; thriller/espionage. Query. Replies in 2 weeks on queries; 1 month on mss.
Also Handles: Nonfiction books. Considers these nonfiction areas: ethnic/cultural interests; gay/lesbian issues; history.
Terms: Agent receives 10% commission on domestic sales. Offers written contract, binding for 6 months, 1 year or for sale only, with 30 day cancellation clause.
Tips: Obtains new clients through WGA listing, cold readings, through known sources. "Be patient, know your craft and be true to your talent."

APPLESEEDS MANAGEMENT (II), 200 E. 30th St., Suite 302, San Bernardino CA 92404. (909)882-1667. For screenplays and teleplays only, send to 1870 N. Vermont, Suite 560, Hollywood CA 90027. Executive Manager: S. James Foiles. Estab. 1988. Signatory of WGA, licensed by state of California. Represents 25 clients. 40% of clients are new/previously unpubilshed writers. "We're not accepting unsolicited screenplays and teleplays at this time." Currently handles: 25% nonfiction books; 40% novels; 20% movie scripts; 15% teleplays (mow).
• See the expanded listing for this agency in Literary Agents: Nonfee-charging.

‡ARIA TALENT (I, II), 1017 W. Washington, Suite 2A, Chicago IL 60607. (312)243-9400. Fax: (312)243-9020. Contact: Claire Simon. Estab. 1993. Signatory of WGA. Represents 5 clients. 50% of clients are new/previously unpublished writers. Specializes in screenplays. Currently handles: 1% novels; 89% movie scripts; 10% stage plays.
Handles: Movie scripts (feature film), TV scripts (TV mow, miniseries, episodic drama, sitcom, soap opera), stage plays. Considers these script subject areas: comedy; contemporary issues; detective/police/crime; ethnic; family saga; humor; juvenile; mystery/suspense; romantic comedy and drama; teen. Query with outline and 2 sample chapters. "Always include SASE!" Reports in 1 months on queries.
Terms: Agent receives 10% commission.
Tips: Obtains new clients through recommendations.

‡THE ARTISTS AGENCY (II,IV), 10000 Santa Monica Blvd., Suite 305, Los Angeles, CA 90035. (310)277-7779. Fax: (310)785-9338. Contact: Merrily Kane. Estab. 1974. Signatory of WGA. Represents 80 clients. 20% of clients are new/previously unpublished writers. Obtains new clients through referrals. Currently handles: 50% movie scripts; 50% TV scripts.
Handles: Movie scripts (feature film), TV scripts (TV mow). Considers these script subject areas: action/adventure; comedy; contemporary issues; detective/police/crime; mystery/suspense; romantic comedy and drama; thriller. Query. Reports in 2 weeks on queries.
Terms: Agent receives 10% commission. Offers written contract, binding for 1-2 years, per WGA.
Tips: Obtains new clients through recommendations from others.

BDP & ASSOCIATES TALENT AGENCY (IV), 10637 Burbank Blvd., North Hollywood CA 91601. (818)506-7615. Fax: (818)506-4983. Vice President, Literary: Samuel W. Gelfman. Estab. 1980. Signatory of WGA, DGA, SAG. "Not seeking clients, but will discuss representation with playwrights and screenwriters referred by mutually known professional acquaintance." Specializes in legitimate theater, theatrical motion pictures and long-form TV (mows and miniseries, not episodic).
Handles: Movie scripts (feature film), long-form TV scripts (TV mow, miniseries), stage plays. Will read samples of writing after referral and conversation.
Also Handles: Represents dramatic subsidiary sales for prose material (nonfiction and fiction) referred by literary agents.
Terms: Agent receives 10-15% commission on domestic sales. Charges for postage, photocopying, any other expenses entailed in sale (legal fees, etc.).
Tips: Obtains new clients through "recommendations from known professionals in the entertainment industry only!"

‡THE BENNETT AGENCY (II, III), 150 S. Barrington Ave., Suite #1, Los Angeles CA 90035. (310)471-2251. Fax: (310)471-2254. Contact: Carole Bennett. Estab. 1984. Signatory of WGA,

DGA. Represents 15 clients. 2% of clients are new/previously unpublished writers. Specializes in TV sitcom. Currently handles: 5% movie scripts; 95% TV scripts. Member agents: Dani Alpert, Carole Bennett (owner).
Handles: Movie scripts, TV scripts. Considers these script subject areas: family saga; humor/satire; mainstream; young adult. Query. Reports in 10 days on queries; 10 days on mss.
Terms: Agent receives 10% commission on domestic sales. Offers written contract.
Tips: Obtains new clients through recommendations from others.

LOIS BERMAN, WRITERS' REPRESENTATIVE (III), 21 W. 26th St., New York NY 10010. (212)684-1835. Contact: Lois Berman or Judy Boals. Estab. 1972. Member of AAR. Represents about 25 clients. Specializes in dramatic writing for stage, film, TV.
Handles: Movie scripts, TV scripts, stage plays. Query first.
Terms: Agent receives 10% commission.
Tips: Obtains new clients through recommendations from others.

☐**THE MARIAN BERZON AGENCY (II)**, 1614 Victory Blvd., #110, Glendale CA 91201. (818)552-2669. Fax: (818)548-1560. Also: 336 E. 17th St., Costa Mesa CA 92627. Contact: Mike Ricciardi or Eric Segucio. Estab. 1979. Signatory of WGA. "We are also a talent agent and signatory of SAG, AFTRA, Equity and AGVA." 80% of clients are new/previously unpublished writers. Specializes in screenplays of all genres, especially comedy (must be honest), family movies and thrillers. Currently handles: 2% juvenile books; 20% novels; 65% movie scripts; 6% stage plays; 12% TV scripts; 5% songs for movies and musical theater (cassettes only). Member agents: Mike Ricciardi (literary/screenplay, comedy, action romantic comedy); Eric Sagucio (comedy sitcom); Jeffrey Cohen (character-driven and drama screenplay, also fantasy-adventure); Mark Amador (dramatic TV and social issue screenplay); Steve Grieger (screwball comedy, sitcoms and farce).
Handles: Movie scripts (feature film, animation), TV scripts (TV mow, sitcom), stage plays. Considers these script subject areas: action/adventure; cartoon/animation; comedy; contemporary issues; family saga; fantasy; gay; historical; humor; juvenile; religious/inspirational; romantic comedy; teen; thrillers; westerns/frontier; screen stories about real people and scripts based on famous comic-strip properties. "No slasher or serial killers!" Query with bio, small photo, cover letter and 1-page summary. SASE. *"Unsolicited scripts will be returned unread C.O.D."* Reports in 1 month or sooner on queries. "We will not answer any query without SASE. *Please* inquiry telephone calls only between the hours of 4:00-6:30 p.m. M-F (Pacific Time). We will send you a release by mail."
Recent Sales: *Mary Christmas*, by Steve Grieger and Tim Irving (A&M Films); *The Funnies*, by Bill Dubay and Frank Richardson (Disney cartoon feature); *User Hostile*, by John E. Stith and John Kennedy (Terence Michael Production); *Angel in the Bullring*, by Kirk Evan (Tricoast Production); *287*, by Jeff Cohen (fantasy-comedy—Horner-Mandell); *Shadows of Mountains*, by Brian Beaty; *Halloween Parade*, by James Ricardo.
Terms: Agent receives 10% commission on domestic sales; 15% on foreign sales (short fiction and plays 15%; advances 15% on novels). Offers written contract and WGA Rider W with agreement. "Never charges a reading fee. We give a detailed and complete breakdown for free. We charge only for postage, fax, long distance and postal insurance directly related to the client for writers who are not established or members of the Guild and only until the writer's first sale. No charges after that." 100% of business derived from commissions on ms sales. "We offer some probationary representations to film students who demonstrate outstanding potential, even before their screenplay is finished."
Tips: Obtains new clients through recommendations from others and known producers. "If you really want to be represented, take note of the old saying 'you never get a second chance to make a first impression.' Be sure your queries intrigue us. Forget your ego. Include a photo and #10 envelope with sufficient postage. Write us a personal cover letter. No computer draft or mimeographed correspondence. Write to us like you really want to be considered. Include short creative bio. Read and absorb *How to Write a Movie in 21 Days*, by Vicki King; *The Writer's Journey*, by Christopher Vogel and Margaret Mehring's *The Screenplay: A Blend of Film Form & Content* before submitting. Comedy screenplays should never be longer than 110 pages, all others genres 114 pages as Robert Towne (*Witness*) puts it "if your screenplay's not finished by page

☐ *An open box indicates script agents who charge fees to writers. WGA signatories are not permitted to charge for reading manuscripts, but may charge for critiques or consultations.*

114—*you're* finished." They must be visual and not dialogue heavy. Save the dialogue for stage play. Structure, character development and narrative drive are the most important elements we look for. Screenplay description must be visually and actually alive. Make certain the opening of your screenplay is a 'grabber.' We believe in the new writer and will even spend time and effort by appointment (in person) in our offices in California. Don't be in love with words when you write a screenplay—think images. Today's big market is 'pg'—feel-good stories with kids, old-fashioned romantic comedies and fantasy. Don't fill the page with words—make your script a comfortable and wonderful read. As Robert Browning once proclaimed, 'less is more!' "

CURTIS BROWN LTD. (II), 10 Astor Place, New York NY 10003-6935. (212)473-5400. Member of AAR; signatory of WGA. Perry Knowlton, chairman & CEO. Peter L. Ginsberg, president. Member agents: Laura J. Blake; Ellen Geiger; Emilie Jacobson, vice president; Virginia Knowlton; Timothy Knowlton, COO (films, screenplays, plays); Chris McKerrow (audio rights); Marilyn Marlow, executive vice president; Jess Taylor (film, screenplays, plays); Maureen Walters. Queries to Laura J. Blake.
   • See the expanded listing for this agency in Literary Agents: Nonfee-charging.

DON BUCHWALD AGENCY (III), 10 E. 44th St., New York NY 10017. (212)867-1070. Contact: Traci Ching Weinstein. Also: 9229 Sunset Blvd., Suite 70, Los Angeles CA 90069. Estab. 1977. Signatory of WGA. Represents 50 literary clients. Talent and literary agency.
Handles: Movie scripts (feature film, documentary, animation), TV scripts (TV mow, miniseries, episodic drama, sitcom, variety show, animation, soap opera), stage play. Query with SASE only.
Tips: Obtains new clients through other authors, agents.

KELVIN C. BULGER AND ASSOCIATES (I), 123 W. Madison, Suite 905, Chicago IL 60602. (312)280-2403. Fax: (312)922-4221. Contact: Kelvin C. Bulger. Estab. 1992. Signatory of WGA. Represents 25 clients. 90% of clients are new/previously unpublished writers. Currently handles: 75% movie scripts; 25% TV scripts.
Handles: Movie scripts (feature film, documentary), TV scripts (TV mow), syndicated material. Considers these script subject areas: action/adventure; cartoon/animation; contemporary issues; ethnic; family saga; historical; humor; religious/inspirational. Query. Reports in 2 weeks on queries; 2 months on mss. "If material is to be returned, writer must enclose SASE."
Recent Sales: *The Playing Field*, (documentary) by Darryl Pitts (CBS).
Terms: Agent receives 10% commission on domestic sales; 10% on foreign sales. Offers written contract, binding from 6 months-1 year.
Tips: Obtains new clients through solicitations and recommendations. "Proofread before submitting to agent. Only replies to letter of inquiries if SASE is enclosed."

☐**THE MARSHALL CAMERON AGENCY (II)**, Rt. 1 Box 125, Lawtey FL 32058. Phone/fax: (904)964-7013. Contact: Margo Prescott. Estab. 1986. Signatory of WGA. Specializes in feature films and TV scripts and true story presentations for MFTS. Currently handles: 80% movie scripts; 20% TV scripts. Member agents: Margo Prescott; Ashton Prescott.
Handles: Movie scripts (feature film), TV scripts (TV mow). No longer represents books. Considers these script subject areas: action/adventure; comedy; contemporary issues; detective/police/crime; drama (contemporary); juvenile; mainstream; mystery/suspense; romantic comedy and drama; thriller/espionage; westerns/frontier. Query. Reports in 1 week on queries; 1-2 months on mss.
Recent Sales: *Rosewood*, by Jim Mooton (Kaye/Bienhak Production).
Terms: Agent receives 10% commission on domestic sales; 20% on foreign sales. Offers written contract, binding for 1 year.
Fees: No reading fee for screenplays. Charges $85 to review all true story material for TV or film ("maybe higher for extensive material"). Offers criticism service, overall criticism, some on line criticism. "We recommend changes, usually 3-10 pages depending on length of the material (on request only)." Charges nominal marketing fee which includes postage, phone, fax, Federal Express. 95% of business is derived from commissions on sales; 15% is derived from reading fees or criticism services. Payment of criticism fee does not ensure representation.
Tips: "Often professionals in film and TV will recommend us to clients. We also actively solicit material. Always enclose SASE with your query."

If you're looking for a particular agent, check the Agents Index to find at which agency the agent works. Then check the listing for that agency in the appropriate section.

MARGARET CANATELLA AGENCY (III), P.O. Box 674, Chalmette LA 70044-0674. (504)279-7493. Fax: (504)277-2561. Contact: Roy Canatella. Estab. 1987. Signatory of WGA. Represents 3 clients. 33⅓% of clients are new/previously unpublished writers. Specializes in screenplays. Currently handles: 90% movie scripts; 10% TV scripts. Member agents: Margaret Canatella (owner); Roy Canatella (talent); Milton Bowser (studio contact person in CA).
Handles: Movie scripts; TV scripts. Query with outline and sample of shooting script format. Reports in 1-2 months on queries.
Terms: Agent receives 10% commission on domestic sales. Offers written contract.
Tips: "Learn how to write a story in proper film script format. Be very visual. Keep dialogue short."

☐**THE CHANDELYN LITERARY AGENCY (II)**, P.O. Box 50162, 7750 Maryland, Clayton MO 63105. Fax: (314)531-2627. President: T. Patrick Miller (Tim). Estab. 1991. Signatory of AFTRA. Represents 30 clients. 50% of clients are new/previously unpublished writers. Currently handles: 10% nonfiction books; 10% juvenile books; 10% novels; 50% movie scripts; 10% stage plays; 10% TV scripts. Member agents: T. Patrick Miller (picture books, novels, plays, screenplays, teleplays), N. Rochelle Collins (children's books).
Handles: Movie scripts (feature film, documentary), TV scripts (TV mow, episodic drama, sitcom, variety show animation), stage plays. Considers these script subjects: action/adventure; cartoon/animation; comedy; contemporary issues; ethnic; family saga; fantasy; historical; juvenile; mainstream; mystery/suspense; religious/inspirational; romantic comedy and drama; science fiction; sports; teen; westerns/frontier. Query with entire ms or outline/proposal and 3 sample chapters. Reports in 4-6 weeks on queries; 4-6 months on mss. Include SASE with all submissions. "Will not report on submissions without SASE. Include release form with scripts."
Recent Sales: *The Popcorn Parade* (Thorn Productions).
Also Handles: Nonfiction books, scholarly books, juvenile books, novels. Considers these nonfiction areas: agriculture/horticulture; animals; anthropology/archaeology; art/architecture/design; biography/autobiography; business; child guidance/parenting; computers; cooking/food/nutrition; crafts/hobbies; current affairs; education; ethnic/cultural interests; government/politics; health/medicine; history; how-to; humor; interior design/decorating; juvenile nonfiction; language/literature/criticism; military/war; money/finance/economics; music/dance/theater/film; nature/environment; photography; popular culture; psychology; religious/inspirational; science/technology; self-help/personal improvement; sociology; sports; translations; women's issues/women's studies. Considers these fiction areas: action/adventure; cartoon/comic; confessional; contemporary issues; detective/police/crime; ethnic; experimental; family saga; fantasy; historical; humor/satire; juvenile; literary; mainstream; mystery/suspense; picture book; religious/inspiration; romance (contemporary, historical); science fiction; sports; thriller/espionage; westerns/frontier; young adult.
Recent Sales: *The Good Agent*, by Sterling Perkins (Jordan Enterprises Publishing Co.); *The Private Albert Einstein*, by Peter Bucley and Albert Weakland (celebrity biography).
Terms: Agent receives 10% commission on domestic sales; 20% on foreign sales (using subagent). Offers written contract and WGA Rider W; binding for 3 months-1 year.
Fees: Criticism service: $25-50 for ms under 100 pages; ($1/page line edit). "We provide writers with a written critique of their work. We charge writers for postage, photocopying and there is a $150 initial marketing fee." Travel fee after contract is offered to client from producer/publisher-deductible from agents commission. Editorial and marketing services provided by Tim Patrick Miller (subsidiary/agency) or non-WGA clients script consultant Judith Culp Associates). 50% of business is derived from commissions on ms sales; 50% derived from services. Payment of fees does not ensure representation. $25-50 mss criticism fees do not apply to WGA signatories/members.
Tips: Obtains new clients through recommendations from editors, publishers and clients. "Professional or enthusiastic new/unpublished writers must be inspired and determined to work with their agents by contributing their time, to promote their published works to build their writing career."

CINEMA TALENT INTERNATIONAL (II), 8033 Sunset Blvd., Suite 808, West Hollywood CA 90046. (213)656-1937. Contact: George Kriton and George N. Rumanes. Estab. 1976. Represents approximately 23 clients. 3% of clients are new/previously unpublished writers. Currently handles: 1% nonfiction books; 1% novels; 95% movie scripts; 3% TV scripts. Member agents: George Kriton, George N. Rumanes.
Handles: Movie scripts, TV scripts. Query with outline/proposal plus 2 sample chapters. Reports in 4-5 weeks on queries; 4-5 weeks on ms.
Terms: Agent receives 10% on domestic sales; 20% on foreign sales. Offers written contract, binding for 2 years.
Tips: Obtains new clients through recommendations from others.

CIRCLE OF CONFUSION LTD. (II), 666 Fifth Ave., Suite 303, New York NY 10103. (212)969-0653. Fax: (718)997-0512. Contact: Rajeev K. Agarwal, Lawrence Mattis. Estab. 1990. Signatory of WGA. Represents 70 clients. 70% of clients are new/previously unpublished writers. Specializes in screenplays for film and TV. Currently handles: 15% novels; 5% novellas; 80% movie scripts. Member agents: Rajeev Agarwal, Lawrence Mattis, Annmarie Negretti, Jasmine Lam.
Handles: Movie scripts (feature film). Considers all script subject areas. Send entire ms. Reports in 1 week on queries; 6 weeks on mss.
Recent Sales: *Movie/TV mow scripts optioned*: *Assassins* and *Matrix*, by Wachowski/Wachowski (Warner Bros.); *Conversations in Public Places*, by Travers (Elwes/Morrissey). *Movie/TV mow scripts in development*: *Reptile Man*, by Schill (Shoreline); *Weekend Dad* and *Mel's Baby*, by John Lynn (Laurel). *Scripting assignments*: available upon request.
Also Handles: Nonfiction books, novels, novellas, short story collections. Considers these nonfiction areas: anthropology/archaeology; biography/autobiography; business; current affairs; gay/lesbian issues; government/politics/law; health/medicine; history; humor; juvenile nonfiction; military/war; New Age/metaphysics; popular culture; sports; true crime/investigative; women's issues/women's studies. Considers all fiction areas.
Terms: Agent receives 10% commission on domestic sales; 10% on foreign sales. Offers written contract, binding for 1 year.
Recent Sales: *Fourth Mansion*, by Cozad (Movicorp).
Tips: Obtains new clients through queries, recommendations and writing contests. "We pitch books, scripts, short stories and plays for film/TV."

CLIENT FIRST—A/K/A LEO P. HAFFEY AGENCY (II), P.O. Box 795, White House TN 37188. (615)325-4780. Contact: Charlene Adams. Estab. 1990. Signatory of WGA. Represents 21 clients. 70% of clients are new/previously unpublished writers. Specializes in movie scripts. Currently handles: 5% novels; 95% movie scripts. Member agent: Leo P. Haffey Jr. (attorney/agent to the motion picture industry).
Handles: Novels, novellas, short story collections, movie scripts. Considers these script subject areas: action/adventure; cartoon/comic; contemporary issues; detective/police/crime; family saga; historical; humor/satire; mystery/suspense; romance (contemporary, historical); science fiction; sports; thriller/espionage; westerns/frontier. Query. Reports in 1 week on queries; 2 months on mss.
Terms: Offers written contract, binding for a negotiable length of time.
Tips: Obtains new clients through referrals. "The motion picture business is a numbers game like any other. The more you write the better your chances of success."

☐COAST TO COAST TALENT AND LITERARY (II), 4942 Vineland Ave., Suite 200, North Hollywood CA 91601. (818)762-6278. Fax: (818)762-7049. Estab. 1986. Signatory of WGA. Represents 20 clients. 35% of clients are new/previously unpublished writers. Specializes in "true stories and true crime books that can be packaged into movies/scripts." Currently handles: 25% nonfiction books; 50% movie scripts; 25% TV scripts.
Handles: Movie scripts (feature film, documentary, animation), TV scripts (TV mow, miniseries, episodic drama, sitcom, variety show, animation, soap opera), syndicated material, true stories, humor books. Considers these script subject areas: action/adventure; detective/police/crime; erotica; humor/satire; literary; mystery/suspense; psychic/supernatural; romance; thriller/espionage; true crime. Query. Reports in 2 months on queries; 6 months on mss.
Recent Sales: "Deep Space 9," by Hilary Rader (Paramount); *Tales from the Cryptkeeper*, by Larry Black (Donner/Nelvana); *The Melinda Mason Story*, movie of the week (Alexander/Enright); *Veronica's Room*, by Brad Mendelson (original screenplay based on Ira Levin play) (Hemdale Entertainment).
Also Handles: Nonfiction books, novels, humor books. Considers these nonfiction areas: music/dance/theater/film; New Age/metaphysics; self-help/personal improvement; true crime/investigative; women's issues/women's studies; mystery.
Terms: Agent receives 10% commission on domestic sales; 15% on foreign sales. Offers written contract, binding for 1 year.
Fees: Does not charge a reading fee. Criticism service: for mss only, not screenplays.
Tips: Obtains new clients through recommendations, query letter. "Be concise in what you're looking for. Don't go on and on in your query letter, get to the point."

‡COMMUNICATIONS AND ENTERTAINMENT, INC. (III), 5902 Mount Eagle Dr., #903, Alexandria VA 22303-2518. (703)329-3796. Fax: (301)589-2222. Contact: James L. Bearden. Estab. 1989. Signatory of WGA. Represents 10 clients. 50% of clients are new/previously unpublished writers. Specializes in TV, film and print media. Currently handles: 5% juvenile books; 40% movie scripts; 10% novels; 40% TV scripts. Member agents: James Bearden (TV/film); Roslyn Ray (literary).

Starting a Career with an *Ace* in the Hole

When Jack Bernstein moved to Los Angeles from Florida, he wanted a career as a professional writer. Agent Michael Douroux of Douroux & Co. got him there. The route involved a number of TV series and feature films, including a huge hit movie.

Bernstein came to Douroux with several original screenplays he'd written, referred by a development executive he'd come to know. "I looked at his work, and could see he had talent. I said, 'Let's go to work. We can take this property and get you launched in series work, but I also think there's a movie here or a series of movies.' The script had a franchise character, a very unusual private eye. It was a piece where the case was secondary to the character—it's all about seeing the character in action. To make a long story short, the piece was called *Ace Ventura   Pet Detective* and became a very successful movie."

Douroux started showing the script around. "A lot of people saw the potential of it, but just couldn't get their heads around the idea of a pet detective." It took about three years of shepherding the screenplay from one producer to another, but finally Morgan Creek Productions expressed an interest.

Douroux received a call from David Nicksay, a development executive who had seen the script while he was working at Paramount. When Nicksay moved to Morgan Creek as its new president of production, he called Douroux to ask what had happened to the *Ace Ventura* screenplay. "It's a matter of finding the right person who sees it and says, 'I understand this. I see that it could be a success, and I know how to do it.' Morgan Creek was that place.

"It was in development at Morgan Creek for another three or four years, which is typical for the features business, but in the meantime, that screenplay launched Jack's career as a writer in both TV and features."

Douroux parlayed *Ace Ventura* into a number of scripting assignments for his client. "For a TV series, it was a matter of showing the original screenplay to producers on shows where the sensibility of the characters, situations and material were similar to what he'd created for himself in his script. Certain pieces have a lot of translation. You read the sample of work, you can clearly see that the writer can make a contribution to a particular show. *Ace* had that kind of translation to a number of shows out there."

Bernstein started writing for a show called *Sonny Spoon* for NBC. He went from that show to another, *Top of the Hill*, a political comedy set in Washington. He worked on *Black Jack Savage* and *Broken Badges* for Stephen J. Cannell Productions and NBC, as well as a pilot for Aaron Spelling. Bernstein also wrote for *Rachel Gunn, R.N.*, a half-hour comedy for Columbia TV and CBS, and *Danger Theatre* for FBC and Universal. Another of Jack's feature scripts, *Rock U.*, is in active development at New Line Cinema.

"Most recently Jack has been the supervising producer on *Fortune Hunter*, created by Columbia for the Fox Network. He's also writing a two-hour pilot based on the Captain Marvel comic books for Harvey Shephard, Warner Brothers and CBS. He has a blossoming career."

Douroux says he looks for clients with a diversity of creative talent, who are interested in developing those talents in more than one area. Versatility, combined with creativity, can take a writer as far as he wants to go.

Handles: Novels, movie scripts, TV scripts. Considers these nonfiction areas: history; music/dance/theater/film. Considers these fiction areas: action/adventure; cartoon/comic; contemporary issues; fantasy; historical; science fiction; thriller/espionage. Query with outline/proposal or send entire ms. Reports in 1 months on queries; 3 months on mss.
Terms: Agent receives 10% commission on domestic sales; 5% on foreign sales. Offers written contract, varies with project.
Tips: Obtains new clients through referrals and recommendations. "Be patient."

THE COPPAGE COMPANY (III), 11501 Chandler Blvd., North Hollywood CA 91601. (818)980-1106. Fax: (818)509-1474. Contact: Judy Coppage. Estab. 1984. Signatory of WGA, DGA, SAG. Represents 25 clients. Specializes in "literary novels; writers who do other jobs, i.e., producing, directing, acting."
Handles: Novels, novellas, movie scripts (feature films), TV scripts (episodic drama, sitcoms), stage plays. Considers all script subject areas.
Terms: Agent receives 10% commission on domestic sales; 10% on foreign sales. Offers written contract, binding for 2 years.
Tips: Obtains new clients through recommendation only.

DOUROUX & CO. (II), 445 S. Beverly Dr., Suite 310, Beverly Hills CA 90212-4401. (310)552-0900. Fax: (310)552-0920. Contact: Michael E. Douroux. Estab. 1985. Signatory of WGA, member of DGA. 20% of clients are new/previously unpublished writers. Currently handles: 50% movie scripts; 50% TV scripts. Member agents: Michael E. Douroux (chairman/CEO); Tara T. Thiesmeyer (assistant).
Handles: Movie scripts (feature film), TV scripts (TV mow, episodic drama, sitcom, animation). Considers these script subject areas: action/adventure; comedy; detective/police/crime; family saga; fantasy; historical; humor/satire; mainstream; mystery/suspense; romantic comedy and drama; science fiction; thriller/espionage; westerns/frontier. Query. Reports in 1 week on queries; 3 weeks on mss.
Terms: Agent receives 10% commission. Offers written contract, binding for 2 years. Charges for photocopying only.

DRAGON LITERARY, INC. (II), P.O. Box 16290, Salt Lake City UT 84116-0290. Contact: Theron Wood. Estab. 1991. Signatory of WGA. 100% of clients are new/previously unpublished writers. Currently handles: 10% novels; 70% movie scripts; 20% TV scripts. Member agent: Bruce D. Richardson, president.
Handles: Novels, movie scripts, TV scripts. Open to all nonfiction areas on a case-by-case basis. Open to all fiction areas on a case-by-case basis. "We'll look at anything; if it's too entertaining to put down, it'll get a good read." Send detailed synopsis with reference to writer's guide. Reports in approximately 1 week on queries, 3 months on mss.
Terms: Agent receives 10% commission on domestic sales; 10% on foreign sales (depending on circumstances). Offers written contract, binding for 1 year; 90-day "no sale" clause. Free critique with review. "Reader (agent) writes critique during review with respect to: development/format, page by page issues, premise, characterization, dialogue, story, overall effect and climax."
Tips: "Approximately 300 submissions per year. Don't be overanxious or annoying; we're all busy and being overbearing won't help. Writing exceptional material is the best way to find an agent."

‡DRAMATIC PUBLISHING (IV), 311 Washington, Woodstock IL 60098. (815)338-7170. Fax: (815)338-8981. Contact: Sara Clark. Estab. 1885. Specializes in stage plays, musicals and instructional books about theater. Currently handles: 2% textbooks; 98% stage plays.
Handles: Stage plays. Reports in 2 weeks on queries; 14-18 weeks on mss.

☐**DYKEMAN ASSOCIATES INC. (III),** 4115 Rawlins, Dallas TX 65219. (214)528-2991. Fax: (214)528-0241. Contact: Alice Dykeman. Estab. 1988. 20% of clients are new/previously unpublished writers. Currently handles: 20% novels; 20% business and other; 60% TV scripts.
Handles: Movie scripts, TV scripts. Considers these script subject areas: action/adventure; biography/autobiography; business; contemporary issues; detective/police/crime; fantasy; money/finance/economics; mystery/suspense; religious/inspirational. science fiction; thriller/espionage. Query with outline/proposal or outline plus 3 sample chapters. Reports in 1 week on queries; 1 month on mss.
Also Handles: Novels, short story collections.
Terms: Agent receives 15% commission on domestic and foreign sales. Offers written contract.
Fees: Charges $250 reading fee. Criticism service included in reading fee. Critiques are written by readers and reviewed by Alice Dykeman. Charges for postage, copies, long distance phone calls. Payment of criticism fee does not ensure representation.
Tips: Obtains new clients through listings in directories and word of mouth.

☐**EARTH TRACKS AGENCY (I, II),** 4809 Ave. N, Suite 286, Brooklyn NY 11234. Contact: David Krinsky. Estab. 1990. Signatory of WGA. Represents 5 clients. 50% of clients are new/previously unpublished writers. Specializes in "movie and TV script sales of original material." Currently handles: 20% novels; 60% movie scripts; 20% TV scripts. Member agent: David Krinsky (movie scripts).
Handles: Movie scripts (feature film), TV scripts (TV mow, sitcom). Considers these script subject areas: action/adventure; comedy; contemporary issues; detective/police/crime; erotica; ethnic; experimental; horror; humor; mainstream; teen; thriller/espionage. Query with SASE. Reports in 4-6 weeks on queries; 6-8 weeks on mss (only if requested).
Terms: Agent receives 10-12% commission on domestic sales; 10-12% on foreign sales. Offers written contract, binding for 6-24 months.
Fees: "No fee for TV or movie scriptwriters. For books I charge $100 a book, nonrefundable. Criticism service: $25 per manuscript submitted. I personally write the critiques. Critiques not provided on scripts. An author *must* provide *proper* postage (SASE) if author wants material returned. If no SASE enclosed, material is not returned." 90% of business is derived from commissions on ms sales; 10% is derived from reading fees or criticism service. Payment of criticism fee does not ensure representation.
Tips: Obtains new clients through recommendations and letters of solicitations by mail. "Send a one-page letter describing the material the writer wishes the agency to represent. Do *not* send anything other than query letter with SASE. Unsolicited scripts will not be returned. Do not 'hype' the material—just explain exactly what you are selling. If it is a play, do not state 'screenplay.' If it is a movie script, do not state 'manuscript,' as that implies a book. Be specific, give description (summary) of material."

‡**EPSTEIN-WYCKOFF-LA MANNA AND ASSOCIATES (II),** 280 S. Beverly Dr., #400, Beverly Hills CA 90212-3904. (310)278-7222. Fax: (310)278-4640. Contact: Karin Wakefield. Estab. 1993. Signatory of WGA. Represents 20 clients. Specializes in features, TV, books and stage plays. Currently handles: 1% nonfiction books; 1% novels; 80% movie scripts; 25% TV scripts; 2% stage plays.
Handles: Movie scripts (feature film), TV scripts (TV mow, miniseries, episodic drama, sitcom, animation, soap opera), stage plays. Considers these script subject areas: action/adventure; comedy; contemporary issues; detective/police/crime; erotica; family saga; feminist; gay; historical; humor; juvenile; lesbian; mainstream; mystery/suspense; romantic comedy and drama; teen; thriller. Query with SASE. Reports in 1 week on queries; 1 month on mss, if solicited.
Terms: Agent receives 15% commission on domestic sales of books, 10% on domestic sales of scripts; 20% on foreign. Offers written contract, binding for 1 year. Charges for photocopying.
Writers' Conferences: ABA.
Tips: Obtains new clients through recommendations, queries.

MARY EVANS INC. (II), 242 E. Fifth St., New York NY 10003. (212)979-0880. Fax: (212)979-5344. Contact: Mary Evans. Estab. 1994. Member of AAR. Represents 25 clients. 8% of clients are new/previously unpublished writers. Specializes in upmarket, literary, commercial fiction and nonfiction. Currently handles: 30% nonfiction books; 60% novels; 5% movie scripts; 5% short story collections.
• See the expanded listing for this agency in Literary Agents: Nonfee-charging.

☐**F.L.A.I.R. or FIRST LITERARY ARTISTS INTERNATIONAL REPRESENTATIVES (II, IV)**, P.O. Box 666, Coram NY 11727-0666. Contact: Jacqulin Chambers. Estab. 1991. Represents 15 clients. Specializes in sitcoms, screenplays, mows. Member agents: Ruth Schulman, Jacqulin Chambers.
Handles: Movie scripts (feature film), TV scripts (TV mow, sitcom). Considers these script subject areas: action/adventure; animals; archaeology; child guidance/parenting; comedy; contemporary issues; detective/police/crime; erotica; family saga; fantasy; film; health/medicine; humor/satire; inspirational; juvenile; mainstream; money/finance/economics; mystery/suspense; nature/environment; psychology; psychic/supernatural; romantic comedy and drama; teen; true crime/investigative; women's issues. Query with synopsis. Reports in 2 weeks on queries; 6 months on mss.
Recent Sales: *Movie/TV mow optioned*: *Body of the Crime*, by Danny Brockner (Lock-n-Load Productions); *in development*: *Witness to Murder*, by Bill Johnston (Stuart Benjamin Productions).
Terms: Agent receives 10% commission on domestic sales; 10% on foreign sales. Offers written contract, binding for 1 year.
Fees: Criticism service: screenplays $150; sitcoms $100. "I give a complete listing of what can be improved within their script, as well as suggested changes. I have compiled an at-home workshop for screen and sitcom writers: screenwriters $25; sitcom writers $15." Charges marketing fee, office expenses, postage, photocopying and phone calls. 70% of business is derived from commissions on ms sales; 30% from reading fees or criticism service. Payment of criticism fee does not ensure representation.
Tips: "Become a member of the Writer's Digest Book Club and you will learn a lot. Learning the format for screenplays and sitcoms is essential. Register all your work with either the copyright office or the WGA. You must send a query letter and synopsis of your script with a SASE. Please do not call."

FLORENCE FEILER LITERARY AGENCY (III), 1524 Sunset Plaza Dr., Los Angeles CA 90069. (213)652-6920. Fax: (213)652-0945. Associate: Joyce Boorn. Estab. 1976. Member of PEN American Center, Women in Film, California Writers Club, MWA. Represents 40 clients. None are unpublished writers. "Quality is the criterion." Specializes in fiction, nonfiction, screenplays, TV. No short stories.
Handles: Movie scripts (feature film), TV scripts (TV mow, episodic drama), stage plays. Considers these script subject areas: detective/police/crime; family saga; gay; historical; juvenile; lesbian; mystery/suspense; romantic comedy and drama; thriller. Query with outline only. Reports in 2 weeks on queries. "We will not accept simultaneous queries to other agents."
Recent Sales: *A Lantern In Her Hand*, by Bess Streeter Aldrich (Kraft-General Foods); *Cheers For Miss Bishop*, by Bess Streeter Aldrich (Scripps Howard); *The Caryatids* and *The Angelic Avengers*, by Isak Dinesen (Kenneth Madsen).
Also Handles: Nonfiction books, novels, juvenile books. Considers these nonfiction areas: art/architecture/design; cooking/food/nutrition; crafts/hobbies; education; gay/lesbian issues; health/medicine; history; how-to; juvenile nonfiction; military/war; photography; psychology; religious/inspirational; self-help/personal improvement; true crime/investigative; women's issues/women's studies. Consider these fiction areas: contemporary issues; detective/police/crime; family saga; gay; historical; juvenile; lesbian; literary; mainstream; mystery/suspense; religious/inspirational; romance (contemporary, gothic, historical, regency); young adult.
Recent Sales: *Time's Fool*, by Patricia Veryan (St. Martin's); *Passion's Bitter Brew*, by Barbara Jones (Harlequin); *Shadows & Whispers*, by Collin McDonald (Penguin).
Terms: Agent receives 10% commission on domestic sales; 10% on dramatic sales; 20% on foreign sales.

☐**FRIEDA FISHBEIN LTD. (II)**, 2556 Hubbard St., Brooklyn NY 11235-6223. (212)247-4398. Contact: Janice Fishbein. Estab. 1928. Represents 32 clients. 50% of clients are new/previously unpublished writers. Currently handles: 10% nonfiction books; 5% young adult; 60% novels; 10% movie scripts; 10% stage plays; 5% TV scripts. Member agents: Heidi Carlson (contemporary and literary); Douglas Michael (play and screenplay scripts).
  ● See the expanded listing for this agency in Literary Agents: Fee-charging.

The publishing field is constantly changing! If you're still using this book and it is 1996 or later, buy the newest edition of Guide to Literary Agents *at your favorite bookstore or order directly from Writer's Digest Books.*

‡**B.R. FLEURY AGENCY (I, II)**, 1228 E. Colonial Dr., Orlando FL 32803. (407)896-4976. Contact: Blanche or Margaret. Estab. 1994. Signatory of WGA. Currently handles: 50% books; 50% scripts. Considers these nonfiction areas: agriculture/horticulture; animals; anthropology/archaeology; art/architecture/design; biography/autobiography; business; child guidance/parenting; computers/electronics; cooking/food/nutrition; crafts/hobbies; current affairs; education; ethnic/cultural interests; government/politics/law; health/medicine; how-to; humor; interior design/decorating; juvenile; language/literature; military/war; money/finance/economics; music/dance/theater/film; nature/environment; New Age/metaphysics; photography; popular cultural; psychology; science/technology; self-help/personal improvement; sociology; sports; translations; true crime/investigative; women's issues/women's studies. Considers these fiction areas: action; cartoon/comic; contemporary issues; detective/police/crime; ethnic; experimental; family saga; fantasy; glitz; historical; horror; humor/satire; juvenile; literary; mainstream; myster/suspense; picture book; psychic/supernatural; regional; romance (contemporary, gothic, historical, regency); science fiction; sports; thriller/espionage; westerns/frontier; young adult. Call or make personal contact.
Terms: Agent receives 10% commission on domestic sales; 10% on foreign sales on scripts. On books, agent receives 10-15% commission on domestic sales; 20-25% commission on foreign sales. Offers written contract, binding as per contract.
Fees: Charges for business expenses directly related to work represented.
Tips: Obtains new clients through referrals and listings. "Be creative."

☐**FRAN LITERARY AGENCY (I, II)**, 7235 Split Creek, San Antonio TX 78238-3627. (210)684-1569. Contact: Fran Rathman. Estab. 1993. Signatory of WGA, ASCAP. Represents 22 clients. 55% of clients are new/previously unpublished writers. "Very interested in Star Trek novels/screenplays." Currently handles: 15% nonfiction books; 10% juvenile books; 30% novels; 5% novellas; 5% poetry books; 15% movie scripts; 20% TV scripts.
• See the expanded listing for this agency in Literary Agents: Fee-charging.

ROBERT A. FREEDMAN DRAMATIC AGENCY, INC. (II, III), 1501 Broadway, Suite 2310, New York NY 10036. (212)840-5760. President: Robert A. Freedman. Vice President: Selma Luttinger. Estab. 1928. Member of AAR, signatory of WGA. Prefers to work with established authors; works with a small number of new authors. Specializes in plays, movie scripts and TV scripts.
• Robert Freedman is the current Vice President of the dramatic division of AAR.
Handles: Movie scripts, TV scripts, stage plays. Query. Does not read unsolicited mss. Usually reports in 2 weeks on queries; 3 months on mss.
Terms: Agent receives 10% on dramatic sales; "and, as is customary, 20% on amateur rights." Charges for photocopying mss.
Recent Sales: "We will speak directly with any prospective client concerning sales that are relevant to his/her specific script."

SAMUEL FRENCH, INC. (II, III), 45 W. 25th St., New York NY 10010-2751. (212)206-8990. Fax: (212)206-1429. Editors: William Talbot and Lawrence Harbison. Estab. 1830. Member of AAR. Represents plays which it publishes for production rights. Member agents: Pam Newton, Jim Merrilat, Henry Wallengren.
Handles: Stage plays (theatrical stage play, variety show). Considers these script subject areas: comedy; contemporary issues; detective/police/crime; ethnic; experimental; fantasy; horror; mystery/suspense; religious/inspirational; thriller. Query or send entire ms. Replies "immediately" on queries; decision in 2-8 months regarding publication. "Enclose SASE."
Terms: Agent usually receives 10% professional production royalties; 20% amateur production royalties.

THE GARDNER AGENCY (IV), 4952 New Ross Ave., Richmond VA 23228-6335. (804)747-1871. Fax: (804)649-0475. Contact: Charles G. Meyst. Estab. 1981. Signatory of WGA. 85% of clients are new/previously unpublished writers. Currently handles: 50% movie scripts, 50% TV scripts.
Handles: Movie scripts (feature film, documentary), TV scripts (TV mow, miniseries, episodic drama). Considers these script subject areas: action/adventure; comedy; contemporary issues; detective/police/crime; erotica; experimental; fantasy; feminist; glitz; historical; horror; humor/satire; mainstream; mystery/suspense; psychic/supernatural; romantic comedy and drama; science fiction; teen; thriller/espionage; western/frontier. Send outline/proposal. Does not accept unsolicited mss. Reports in 2 months on queries.
Terms: Agent receives 10% commission on domestic sales; 10% on foreign sales. Offers written contract. Charges for unusual expenses.

Tips: Obtains new clients through recommendations from others.

☐**THE GARY-PAUL AGENCY (II),** 84 Canaan Court, #17, Stratford CT 06497-4538. (203)336-0257. Fax: (203)336-0257. Contact: Gary Maynard or Chris Conway. Estab. 1989. Represents 78 clients. Specializes in client representation and ms/product marketing. Most clients are freelance writers/designers/producers. Member agents: Gary Maynard, Christopher Conway, Miguel Valenti, Paul Caravatt.
Handles: Movie scripts, TV scripts, educational and technical publications, films/videos, products. Consider all script subject areas. Query with letter of introduction. Reports in 10 days on requested submissions.
Terms: Agent receives 10% commission on mss and products.
Fees: No charge for client representation. Charges $300-800 for ms marketing, $2,000-6,000 for film/video and product marketing. "All promotional and marketing costs are the responsibility of the client."
Writers' Conferences: NBC Writers' Workshop (Burbank, CA), Script Festival (Los Angeles, CA), Yale University Writers' Workshop, Media Art Center Writers' Workshop (New Haven, CT), Fairfield University "Industry Profile Symposium" (Fairfield, CT).
Tips: "There is no such thing as a dull story, just dull story telling. Give us a call."

‡**RICHARD GAUTHREAUX—A LITERARY AGENCY (II),** 729 Frisella St., Gretna LA 70056. (504)362-6019. Contact: Jay Richards. Estab. 1985. Signatory of WGA. Represents 6 clients. 75% of clients are new/previously unpublished writers. Currently handles: 45% novels; 25% movie scripts; 20% TV scripts; 5% stage plays; 5% short story.
Handles: Movie scripts, novels, TV scripts, stage plays. Considers these nonfiction areas: sports; true crime/investigative. Considers these fiction areas: horror; thriller/espionage. Query. Reports in 2 weeks on queries; 2 months on mss.
Terms: Agent receives 10% commission on domestic sales; 15% on foreign sales. Offers written contract, binding for 6 months.
Tips: Obtains new listings through guild listing, local referrals.

GEDDES AGENCY (IV), 1201 Greenacre Ave., Los Angeles CA 90046. (213)878-1155. Fax: (213)878-1150. Contact: Ann Geddes. Estab. 1983 in L.A., 1967 in Chicago. Signatory of WGA, SAG, AFTRA. Represents 10 clients. 100% of clients are new/previously unpublished writers. "We are mainly representing actors—writers are more 'on the side.'" Currently handles: 100% movie scripts.
Handles: Movie scripts. Query with synopsis. Reports in 2 months on mss only if interested.
Terms: Agent receives 10% commission on domestic sales. Offers written contract, binding for 1 year. Charges for "handling and postage for a script to be returned—otherwise it is recycled."
Tips: Obtains new clients through recommendations from others and through mailed-in synopses. "Send in query—say how many scripts available for representation. Send synopsis of each one. Mention something about yourself."

‡**THE LAYA GELFF AGENCY (IV),** 16133 Ventura Blvd., Suite 700, Encino CA 91436. (818)713-2610. Estab. 1985. Signatory of WGA. Represents many clients. No new/previously unpublished writers. Specializes in TV and film scripts; WGA members only. Currently handles: 50% movie scripts; 50% TV scripts.
Handles: Movie scripts, TV scripts. Query. Reports in 2 weeks on queries; 1 month on mss.
Terms: Agent receives 10% commission on domestic sales; 10% on foreign sales. Offers standard WGA contract.
Tips: Obtains new clients through recommendations from others.

THE GERSH AGENCY (II, III), 232 N. Canon Dr., Beverly Hills CA 90210. (310)274-6611. Contact: Ron Bernstein. Estab. 1962. Less than 10% of clients are new/previously unpublished writers. Special interests: "mainstream—convertible to film and television."
Handles: Movie scripts (feature film, animation), TV scripts (TV mow, miniseries, sitcom). Considers all script subject areas. Send query letter with SASE, a brief synopsis and brief personal background. Does not accept any unsolicited material.
Recent Sales: Film rights to *Shot in the Heart,* by Mikal Gilmore; *Pigs in Heaven,* by Barbara Kingsolver.
Terms: Agent receives 10% commission on domestic sales. "We strictly deal in *published* manuscripts in terms of potential film or television sales, on a strictly 10% commission—sometimes split with a New York literary agency or various top agencies."

‡**GOLD/MARSHAK & ASSOCIATES (II),** 3500 W. Olive Ave., Suite 1400, Burbank CA 91505. (818)972-4300. Fax: (818)955-6411. Contact: Ms. Evan Corday; Mr. Jeff Melnick. Estab. 1993.

Signatory of WGA. Represents 34 literary clients. 40% of clients are new/previously unpublished writers. Currently handles: 40% movie scripts; 30% TV scripts; 20% stage plays; 10% syndicated material. Member agents: Ms. Evan Corday (TV series/mows); Mr. Jeff Melnick (mows/features).

Handles: Movie scripts (feature film), TV scripts (TV mows, miniseries, episodic drama, sitcom, soap opera), stage play, syndicated material. Considers these script subject areas: action/adventure; comedy; contemporary issues; detective/police/crime/family saga; ethnic; family saga; feminist; gay; humor; lesbian; mainstream; mystery/suspense; psychic/supernatural; romantic comedy and drama; science fiction; sports; thriller/espionage; women's issues. Query with outline/proposal. Reports in 1 week on queries; 1 month on mss.

Terms: Agent receives 10% commission on domestic sales; 10% on foreign sales.

Tips: Obtains new clients through recommendations from others, solicitation and at conferences.

‡MICHELLE GORDON & ASSOCIATES (III), 260 S. Beverly Dr., Suite 308, Beverly Hills CA 90212. (310)246-9930. Contact: Michelle Gordon. Estab. 1993. Signatory of WGA. Represents 4 clients. None are new/previously unpublished writers. Currently handles: 100% movie scripts.

Handles: Movie scripts. Considers these script subject areas: biography/autobiography; contemporary issues; detective/police/crime; feminist; government/politics/law; psychology; true crime/investigative; women's issues/women's studies. Query. Reports in 2 weeks on queries.

Terms: Agent receives 10% commission on domestic sales; 10% on foreign sales. Offers written contract, binding for 1 year.

Tips: Obtains new clients through recommendations and solicitation.

GRAHAM AGENCY (II), 311 W. 43rd St., New York NY 10036. (212)489-7730. Owner: Earl Graham. Estab. 1971. Represents 40 clients. 30% of clients are new/unproduced writers. Specializes in playwrights and screenwriters only. "We're interested in commercial material of quality." Currently handles: 20% movie scripts, 80% stage plays.

Handles: Stage plays, movie scripts. No one-acts, no material for children. "We consider on the basis of the letters of inquiry." Writers *must* query before sending any material for consideration. Reports 3 months on queries; 6 weeks on mss.

Terms: Agent receives 10% commission. No written contract.

Tips: Obtains new clients through queries and referrals. "Contact appropriate agents, not all of them. Write a concise, intelligent letter giving the gist of what you are offering."

‡THE SUSAN GURMAN AGENCY (IV), #4B, 865 West End Ave., New York NY 10025. (212)864-5243. Fax: (212)864-5055. Estab. 1993. Signatory of WGA. Represents 5 clients. 100% of clients are new/previously unpublished writers. Specializes in referred screenwriters and playwrights. Currently handles: 80% movie scripts; 20% stage plays.

Handles: Movie scripts, stage plays. Referral only. Reports in 2 weeks on queries; 2 months on mss.

Terms: Agent receives 10% commission on domestic sales; 10% on foreign sales.

Tips: Obtains new clients through referral only.

‡REECE HALSEY AGENCY (II, III), 8733 Sunset Blvd., Suites 101, 102, Los Angeles CA 90069. (310)652-2409. Fax: (310)652-7595. Contact: Dorris Halsey (#101), Kimberley Cameron (#102). Estab. 1957. Signatory of WGA. Represents 30 clients. 20% of clients are new/previously unpublished writers. Specializes in mostly books and excellent writing. Currently handles: 10% nonfiction books; 60% novels; 30% movie scripts. Member agents: Dorris Halsey, Kimberley Cameron.

• See the expanded listing for this agency in Literary Agents: Nonfee-charging.

‡THE HANSON AGENCY (II, IV), P.O. Box 1335, Southampton NY 11969. (516)287-2525. Fax: (516)287-2582. Contact Ralph Schiano or Leslie Jennemann. Estab. 1992. Signatory of WGA. Represents 46 clients. 80% of clients are new/previously unpublished writers. Specializes in science fiction, horror, fantasy. Currently handles: 5% nonfiction books; 10% juvenile books; 60% novels; 20% movie scripts; 5% short story collections.

• See the expanded listing for this agency in Literary Agents: Nonfee-charging.

☐GIL HAYES & ASSOC. (III), P.O. Box 63333, Memphis TN 38163. (901)685-0116. Contact: Gil Hayes. Estab. 1992. Signatory of WGA. Represents 10 clients. 40% of clients are new/previously

 The double dagger before a listing indicates the listing is new in this edition.

unpublished writers. Specializes in serious scripts and literary fiction. Currently handles: 20% nonfiction books; 20% fiction; 60% movie scripts. Member agent: Gil Hayes.

Handles: Movie scripts. Considers these script subject areas: biography/autobiography; comedy; current affairs; family saga; mainstream; mystery/suspense. Query with outline/proposal. Reports in 1-3 months on queries, 3-6 months on mss.

Also Handles: Nonfiction, novels. Considers these nonfiction areas: biography/autobiography; current affairs; health/medicine; language/literature/criticism; military/war; sports; women's issues/women's studies. Considers these fiction areas: feminist; historical; humor/satire; literary; mainstream; mystery/suspense; regional; Hispanic fiction in English. Query with outline/proposal and first chapter.

Terms: Agent receives 10% commission on domestic sales; 15-20% on foreign sales. Offers written contract, length of time varies, normally 2 years.

Fees: Criticism service: $50 for script, $100 if requesting written notes in advance. "Gil Hayes writes and reviews all critiques. Some major input from writers I already represent if area is appropriate. Writers must provide bound copies, usually five to ten at a time if I represent them. I pay postage, handling, express mail to studios, producers, etc." 90% of business is derived from commission on ms sales; 10% is derived from reading fees or criticism services. Payment of criticism fee does not ensure representation.

Tips: Obtains new clients through "recommendations from others—contacts at tape and film commission offices around the nation. Always register with WGA or copyright material before sending to anyone."

☐**HEACOCK LITERARY AGENCY, INC. (II),** 1523 Sixth St., Suite #14, Santa Monica CA 90401-2514. (310)393-6227. Fax: (310)451-8524. Contact: Jim or Rosalie Heacock. Estab. 1978. Member of AAR, ATA, SCBWI, signatory of WGA. Represents 60 clients. 30% of clients are new/previously unpublished writers. Currently handles: 85% nonfiction books; 5% juvenile books; 5% novels; 5% movie scripts. Member agents: Jim Heacock (business expertise, parenting, psychology, sports, diet, health, nutrition); Rosalie Heacock (psychology, philosophy, women's studies, alternative health, new technology, futurism, new idea books art and artists).
  • See the expanded listing for this agency in Literary Agents: Fee-charging.

GARY L. HEGLER LITERARY AGENCY (III), P.O. Box 890101, Houston TX 77289-0101. (713)333-0173. Contact: Gary L. Hegler or Nikki Cane. Estab. 1985. Signatory of WGA. 10% of clients are new/previously unpublished writers. Specializes in young adult, nonfiction and adult westerns. Currently handles: 50% nonfiction books; 30% juvenile books; 5% novels; 5% movie scripts; 10% TV scripts.
  • See the expanded listing for this agency in Literary Agents: Nonfee-charging.

☐**ALICE HILTON LITERARY AGENCY (II),** 13131 Welby Way, North Hollywood CA 91606. (818)982-2546. Fax: (818)765-8207. Estab. 1986. Eager to work with new/unpublished writers. "Interested in any quality material, although agent's personal taste runs in the genre of 'Cheers,' 'L.A. Law,' 'American Playhouse,' 'Masterpiece Theatre' and Woody Allen vintage humor."
  • See the expanded listing for this agency in the Literary Agents: Fee-charging.

CAROLYN HODGES AGENCY (III), 1980 Glenwood Dr., Boulder CO 80304-2329. (303)443-4636. Contact: Carolyn Hodges. Estab. 1989. Signatory of WGA. Represents 12 clients. 90% of clients are new/previously unpublished writers. Represents only screenwriters for film and TV mows. Currently handles: 80% movie scripts; 20% TV scripts.
  • See Carolyn Hodges's article, *What an Agent Really Looks For*, in this edition of the *Guide.*

Handles: Movie scripts (feature film), TV scripts (TV mow). Considers these script subject areas: action/adventure; contemporary issues; detective/police/crime; ethnic; experimental; fantasy; feminist; gay; glitz; historical; juvenile; lesbian; literary; mainstream; mystery/suspense; psychic/supernatural; regional; romance (contemporary, historical); science fiction; thriller/espionage. Query with 1 page synopsis. Reports in 1 week on queries; 4-6 weeks on mss.

Terms: Agent receives 10% on domestic sales; foreign sales "depend on each individual negotiation." Offers written contract, standard WGA. No charge for criticism. "I always try to offer concrete feedback, even when rejecting a piece of material. I do request that writers supply me with copies of their screenplays. I pay all other expenses."

Recent Sales: *Movie optioned*: Goodbye, Yellow Brick Road. *Movie in development*: So This Could Be Christmas. *Scripting assignment*: Adrift (rewrite).

Writers' Conferences: Director and founder of Writers In The Rockies Film Screenwriting Conference (Boulder CO, August).

Tips: Obtains new clients via WGA Agency list or by referral. "Become proficient at your craft. Attend all workshops accessible to you. READ all the books applicable to your area of interest.

READ as many 'produced' screenplays as possible. Live a full, vital and rewarding life so your writing will have something to say. Get involved in a writer's support group. Network with other writers. Receive 'critiques' from your peers and consider merit of suggestions. Don't be afraid to re-examine your perspective."

‡**BARBARA HOGENSON AGENCY (III)**, 2472 Broadway, Suite 255, New York NY 10025. (212)580-3293. Estab. 1995. Signatory of WGA. Represents 25 clients. 10% of clients are new/previously unpublished writers. Currently handles: 30% nonfiction books; 10% novels; 30% movie scripts; 30% stage plays.
 • Ms. Hogenson was with the prestigious Lucy Kroll Agency for ten years before starting her own agency.
Handles: Nonfiction books, novels, movie scripts, TV scripts. Considers these nonfiction areas: biography/autobiography; history; how-to; humor; interior design/decorating; language/literature/criticism; music/dance/theater/film; popular culture; true crime/investigative. Open to all fiction areas; "Just good ideas and good writing." Query. Reports in 2 weeks on queries; 4-6 weeks on mss.
Terms: Agent receives 10% on film and TV sales; 15% commission on domestic sales of books; 20% on foreign sales of books. Offers written contract, binding for 2 years with 90 day cancellation clause. 100% of business derived from commissions on sales.
Tips: Obtains new clients strictly by referral.

☐**THE EDDY HOWARD AGENCY (III)**, % 37 Bernard St., Eatontown NJ 07724-1906. (908)542-3525. Contact: Eddy Howard Pevovar, N.D., M.S., Ph.D. Estab. 1986. Signatory of WGA. Represents 110 clients. 16% of clients are new/previously unpublished writers. Specializes in film, sitcom and literary. Currently handles: 5% nonfiction books; 5% scholarly books; 2% textbooks; 5% juvenile books; 5% novels; 2% novellas; 25% movie scripts; 30% TV scripts; 10% stage plays; 5% short story collections; 1% syndicated material; 5% other. Member agents: Eddy Howard Pevovar, N.D., M.S., Ph.D. (agency executive); Francine Gail (director of comedy development).
Handles: Movie scripts (feature film, documentary, animation), TV scripts (TV mows, miniseries, episodic drama, sitcom, variety show, animation, soap opera, educational), stage plays. Considers these script subject areas: action/adventure; cartoon/animation; comedy; erotica; experimental; family saga; fantasy; historical; humor; juvenile; mainstream; mystery/suspense; psychic/supernatural; religious/inspirational; romantic comedy; science fiction; sports; teen; thriller; western/frontier.
Also Handles: Nonfiction books, scholarly books, textbooks, juvenile books, novels, novellas. Considers these areas: agriculture/horticulture; animals; anthropology/archaeology; cooking/food/nutrition; crafts/hobbies; education; health/medicine; humor; juvenile nonfiction; music/dance/theater/film; nature/environment; New Age/metaphysics; photography; psychology; science/technology; self-help/personal improvement; sports; translations; women's issues/women's studies. Considers these fiction areas: cartoon/comic; erotica; experimental; fantasy; humor/satire; juvenile; literary; mainstream; picture book; psychic/supernatural; regional; young adult. Query with outline and proposal—include phone number. Reports in 3-5 days on queries; 30-60 days on mss.
Terms: Agent receives 10% commission on domestic sales; 15% on foreign sales. Offers written contract.
Fees: No fees. Offers criticism service: corrective—style, grammar, punctuation, spelling, format. Technical critical evaluation with fee (saleability, timeliness, accuracy).
Writers' Conferences: Instructor—Writers Workshops at Brookdale College; Community Education Division.
Tips: Obtains new clients through recommendations from others. "I was rejected 12 times before I ever had my first book published and I was rejected 34 times before my first magazine article was published. Stick to what you believe in . . . Don't give up! Never give up! Take constructive criticism for whatever its worth and keep yourself focused. Each rejection a beginner receives is one step closer to the grand finale—acceptance. It's sometimes good to get your manuscript peer reviewed. This is one way to obtain objective analysis of your work, and see what others think about it. Remember, if it weren't for new writers . . . there'd be *no* writers."

‡**HUDSON AGENCY (I, IV)**, 3 Travis Lane, Montrose NY 10548. (914)737-1475. Fax: (914)737-1475. Contact: Susan or Pat Giordano. Estab. 1994. Signatory of WGA. Represents 12 clients. 80% of clients are new/previously unpublished writers. Specializes in feature film and TV only. Currently handles: 50% movie scripts; 50% TV scripts. Member agents: Sue Giordano, Pat Giordano.
Handles: Movie scripts (feature film, documentary), TV scripts (TV mow, miniseries). Considers these script subject areas: action/adventure; comedy; contemporary issues; detective/police/

crime; ethnic; family saga; fantasy; historical; humor/satire; juvenile; mainstream; mystery/suspense; romantic comedy and drama; science fiction; sports; teen; thriller/espionage; westerns/frontier. Send outline and sample pages. Reports in 1 week on queries; 3 weeks on mss.

Terms: Agent receives 15% commission on domestic sales; 15% on foreign sales. Offers criticism service. "Free, if we think the script is workable. Critiques done by paid story analysts. Writer receives a critique on story structure, plot development, character development and dialogue, etc. Writer supplies all the necessary scripts; if that is not practical we have copies made for $5 a copy."

Tips: Obtains new clients through recommendations from others and listing on WGA agency list. "Yes, we may be small, but we work very hard for our clients. Any script we are representing gets excellent exposure to producers. Our network is over 50 contacts in the business and growing rapidly. We are GOOD salespeople. Ultimately it all depends on the quality of the writing and the market for the subject matter."

INTERNATIONAL CREATIVE MANAGEMENT (III), 8942 Wilshire Blvd., Beverly Hills CA 90211. (310)550-4000. Fax: (310)550-4108. East Coast office: 40 W. 57th St., New York NY 10019. (212)556-5600. Signatory of WGA, member of AAR. Member agents: *TV:* Scott Arnovitz; Tricia Davey; Bill Douglass; Ariel Emanuel; David Greenblatt; Bob Gumer; Paul Haas; Nancy Josephson; Steve Sanford; Jeanne Williams. *Movies:* Diane Cairns; Barbara Dreyfus; Richard Feidman; Ken Kamins; Steve Rabineau; Elizabeth Rieger; Jeff Robinov; Jim Rosen; Tom Strickler; Irene Webb; David Wirtschafter.

INTERNATIONAL LEONARDS CORP. (II), 3612 N. Washington Blvd., Indianapolis IN 46205-3534. (317)926-7566. Contact: David Leonards. Estab. 1972. Signatory of WGA. Currently handles: 50% movie scripts; 50% TV scripts.

Handles: Movie scripts (feature film, animation), TV scripts (TV mow, sitcom, variety show). Considers these script subject areas: action/adventure; cartoon/animation; contemporary issues; detective/police/crime; horror; humor; mystery/suspense; romantic comedy; science fiction; sports; thriller. Query. Reports in 1 month on queries; 6 months on mss.

Terms: Agent receives 10% commission on domestic sales; 10% on foreign sales. Offers written contract, "WGA standard," which "varies."

Tips: Obtains new clients through recommendations and queries.

□**CAROLYN JENKS AGENCY,** 205 Walden St., Cambridge MA 02140-3507. Phone/fax: (617)876-6927. Contact: Carolyn Jenks. Estab. 1966. 50% of clients are new/previously unpublished writers. Currently handles: 15% nonfiction books; 40% novels; 20% movie scripts; 10% stage plays; 15% TV scripts.

    ● See the expanded listing for this agency in Literary Agents: Fee-charging.

‡**JNG ENTERTAINMENT (I, II),** P.O. Box 1142, New York NY 10028. (212)535-0864. Contact: Peter Vasapolli. Estab. 1993. Signatory of WGA. Represents 2 clients. Specializes in "just good material! Please include a SASE with each letter or inquiry for a response."

Handles: Movie scripts. Considers all script subject areas. Query with outline/proposal. Reports in 1-2 weeks "if they include SASE (a must)."

Terms: Agent receives 10% commission on domestic sales. Offers written contract, binding for 6-12 months. No fees. "If we like the material we tell him/her and if we want to represent it — we will. If not, we'll read it and if we pass on it — we tell the writer why!" Offers criticism service, critiques done by "myself (the owner) and wife (who's a producer)."

Tips: "We're listed with The Writer's Guild (East) in New York as an agency that will read material from new writers. When sending any material, please include a SASE with all material. Make sure your material looks great — not good, but great. Typed, organized material not written is crucial. Agents like to read organized material. Presentation makes a great impression. If any material looks good, with SASE enclosed, I'll get around to reading it. But, if I have material that's sloppy and has no SASE I may or may not read it. All we ask for is a small bit of professionalism from new writers."

‡**LESLIE KALLEN AGENCY (III),** 15303 Ventura Blvd., Sherman Oaks CA 91401. (818)906-2785. Fax: (818)906-8931. Contact: Tracy Moore. Estab. 1988. Signatory of WGA, DGA. Specializes in feature films and mows.

Handles: Movie scripts (feature film), TV scripts (TV mow). Query. "No phone inquiries for representation."

Terms: Agent receives 10% commission on domestic sales.

Tips: "Write a two to three page query that makes an agent excited to read the material."

CHARLENE KAY AGENCY, 901 Beaudry St., Suite 6, St. Jean/Richelieu, Quebec J3A 1C6 Canada. (514)348-5296. Director of Development: Louise Meyers. Estab. 1992. Signatory of WGA; member of BMI. 100% of clients are new/previously unpublished writers. Specializes in teleplays and screenplays. Currently handles: 50% TV scripts; 50% movie scripts.
Handles: Movie scripts (feature film), TV scripts (TV mow). Considers these script subject areas: action/adventure, biography/autobiography; family saga. "Real-life stories and biographical movies or something unique: a story that is out of the ordinary something we don't see too often. A *well-written* and *well-constructed* script." Query with outline/proposal by mail only. Reports in 1 month on queries with SASE (or IRC outside Canada). Reports in 8-10 weeks on mss.
Recent Sales: "TV and motion picture scripts are being considered by Gimbel Adelson Prods (multimedia) and Warner Bros. at the present time."
Terms: Agent receives 10% commission on domestic sales; 10% on foreign sales. Offers written contract, binding for 1 year. Returns Canadian scripts if SASE provided; does not return scripts from US.
Tips: "My agency is listed on the WGA lists and query letters arrive by the dozens every week. I don't even have to advertise in any magazine. As my present clients understand, success comes with patience. A sale rarely happens overnight, especially when you are dealing with totally unknown writers. Many top agencies don't want to deal with unsolicited materials because they know how hard it is to make someone unknown known to the industry. I like the challenge of breaking down doors for new talents: they are the giants of tomorrow!"

THE JOYCE KETAY AGENCY, 1501 Broadway, Suite 1910, New York NY 10036. (212)354-6825. Fax: (212)354-6732. Contact: Joyce Ketay, Carl Mulert. Member of AAR. Member agents: Joyce Ketay, Carl Mulert, Tania Farrell (associate, film scripts).
Handles: Movie scripts (feature film), TV scripts (TV mow, episodic drama, sitcom). Considers these script subject areas: action/adventure; comedy; contemporary issues; detective/police/crime; ethnic; experimental; family saga; fantasy; feminist; gay; glitz; historical; humor; juvenile; lesbian; mainstream; mystery/suspense; psychic/supernatural; romantic comedy and drama; thriller; westerns/frontier. Playwrights and screenwriters only. No novels.
Recent Sales: *Angels in America*, by Tony Kushner (Robert Altman and Avenue Pictures).

KICK ENTERTAINMENT (I), 1934 E. 123rd St., Cleveland OH 44106. Phone/fax: (216)795-2515. Contact: Sam Klein. Estab. 1992. Signatory of WGA. Represents 8 clients. 100% of clients are new/previously unpublished writers. Currently handles: 100% movie scripts. Member agent: Geno Trunzo (director-creative affairs).
Handles: Movie scripts (feature film). Considers these script subject areas: action/adventure; comedy; detective/police/crime; family saga; fantasy; horror; humor; mainstream; military/war; mystery/suspense; psychic/supernatural; romantic comedy and drama; science fiction; thriller/espionage; true crime/investigative; westerns/frontier. Query. Reports in 2 weeks on queries; 6-8 weeks on mss.
Terms: Agent receives 10% commission on domestic sales; 10% on foreign sales. Offers written contract, binding for 2 years.
Tips: "Always send a query letter first, and enclose a SASE. We now presently represent clients in six states."

‡□TYLER KJAR AGENCY (II), 10643 Riverside Dr., Toluca Lake CA 91602. (818)760-6326. Fax: (818)760-0642. Contact: Tyler Kjar. Estab. 1974. Signatory of WGA. Represents 11 clients. 10% of clients are new/previously unpublished writers. "Seeking youth-oriented screenplays with positive emphasis on personal exchange; no guns or drugs." Currently handles: 50% movie scripts; 50% TV scripts.
Handles: Movie scripts (feature film), TV scripts (TV mow, miniseries, sitcom), stage plays. Considers these script subject areas: action/adventure; family saga; horror; romantic comedy and drama; science fiction; teen; American period pieces (nonwestern); children/8+ with positive roles (no drugs, blood, guns, relating in today's society). Query; do not send outline or script. Reports in 2 weeks on queries; 6 weeks on mss.
Recent Sales: *Movie scripts optioned/sold: Baby on Board*, by Gary Eggers (Lantana Films); *Hollywood Storage*, by Gardner Compton; *Scripting assignment: Empty Nest.*
Fees: Charges reading fee. Criticism service: $100. Critiques done by Tyler Kjar.
Tips: Obtains new clients from recommendations. "Most scripts are poorly written, with incorrect format, too much description, subject matter usually borrowed from films they have seen. Must follow established format."

PAUL KOHNER, INC. (IV), 9169 Sunset Blvd., West Hollywood CA 90069. (310)550-1060. Contact: Gary Salt. Estab. 1938. Member of ATA, signatory of WGA. Represents 150 clients. 10%

of clients are new/previously unpublished writers. Specializes in film and TV rights sales and representation of film and TV writers.

● See Gary Salt's article, *The Ins and Outs of Script Agents*, in this edition of the *Guide*.

Handles: Nonfiction books, movie scripts (feature film, documentary, animation), TV scripts (TV mow, miniseries, episodic drama, sitcom, variety show, animation, soap opera), stage plays. Considers these script subject areas: action/adventure; comedy; detective/police/crime; ethnic; family saga; feminist; historical; humor; mainstream; mystery/suspense; romantic comedy and drama. Query with SASE. Reports in 2 weeks on queries.

Recent Sales: Has sold scripts to 20th Century Fox, Warner's, Disney.

Terms: Agent receives 10% commission on domestic sales; 10% on foreign sales. Offers written contract, binding for 1-3 years. "We charge for copying manuscripts or scripts for submission unless a sufficient quantitiy is supplied by the author. All unsolicited material is automatically returned unread."

LUCY KROLL AGENCY (II, III), 390 W. End Ave., New York NY 1024. (212)877-0627. Fax: (212)769-2832. Member of AAR, signatory of WGA. Represents 60 clients. 5% of clients are new/unpublished writers. Specializes in nonfiction, screenplays, plays. Currently handles: 45% nonfiction books; 15% novels; 15% movie scripts; 25% stage plays.

● See the expanded listing for this agency in Literary Agents: Nonfee-charging.

☐L. HARRY LEE LITERARY AGENCY (II), Box #203, Rocky Point NY 11778-0203. (516)744-1188. Contact: L. Harry Lee. Estab. 1979. Signatory of WGA, member of Dramatists Guild. Represents 285 clients. 65% of clients are new/previously unpublished writers. Specializes in movie scripts. "Comedy is our strength, both features and sitcoms, also movie of the week, science fiction, novels and TV. We have developed two sitcoms of our own." Currently handles: 30% novels; 50% movie scripts; 5% stage plays; 15% TV scripts. Member agents: Mary Lee Gaylor (episodic TV, feature films); Charles Rothery (feature films, sitcoms, movie of the week); Katie Polk (features, mini-series, children's TV); Patti Roenbeck (science fiction, fantasy, romance, historical romance); Frank Killeen (action, war stories, American historical, westerns); Hollister Barr (mainstream, feature films, romantic comedies); Ed Van Bomel (sitcoms, movie of the week, mysteries, adventure stories); Colin James (horror, Viet Nam, war stories); Judith Faria (all romance, fantasy, mainstream); Charis Biggis (plays, historical novels, westerns, action/suspense/thriller films); Stacy Parker (love stories, socially significant stories/films, time travel science fiction); Jane Breoge (sitcoms, after-school specials, mini-series, episodic TV); Cami Callirgos (mainstream/contemporary/humor, mystery/suspense); Vito Brenna (action/adventure, romantic comedy, feature films, horror); Anastassia Evereaux (feature films, romantic comedies).

Handles: Movie scripts (feature film), TV scripts (TV mow, episodic drama, sitcom) stage plays. Considers these script subject areas: action/adventure; comedy; contemporary issues; detective/police/crime; family saga; fantasy; feel good family stories; foreign intrigue; historical; humor; mainstream; mystery/suspense; psychic/supernatural; reality shows; romantic drama (futuristic, contemporary, historical); science fiction; sports; thriller; westerns/frontier; zany comedies. Query "with a short writing or background résumé of the writer. A SASE is a must. No dot matrix, we don't read them." Reports in "return mail" on queries; 3-4 weeks on mss. "We notify the writer when to expect a reply."

Recent Sales: *Movie/TV mow optioned/sold*: *Snake-Check*, by James E. Colaneri (Panache/Warner Bros.); *Tia*, by J.E. Colaneri/Anastassia Evereaux (Panache/Warner Bros.). *Outta Australia*, by Anastassi Evereaux (Panache/Warner Bros.); *Star-Light*, by Anastassia Evereaux (Universal/Lighthorse); *Scripting assignments*: Bob Schau, untitled (Paramount); Patti Roenbeck, "Dangerous Illusions"; James G. Kingston, "The Competition Was Murder" (Diane Sokolow).

Also Handles: Novels. Considers these fiction areas: action/adventure; detective/police/crime; erotica; family saga; fantasy; historical; horror; humor/satire; literary; mainstream; mystery/suspense; romance (contemporary, gothic, historical, regency); science fiction; sports; thriller/espionage; westerns/frontier; young adult.

Terms: Agent receives 10% on movie/TV scripts and plays; 15% commission on domestic sales; 20% on foreign sales. Offers written contract "by the manuscript which can be broken by mutual consent; the length is as long as the copyright runs."

Fees: Does not charge a reading fee. Criticism service: $195 for screenplays; $150 for movie of the week; $95 for TV sitcom; $195 for a mini-series; $1 per page for one-act plays."All of the agents and readers write the carefully thought-out critiques, three-page checklist, two to four pages of notes, and a manuscript that is written on, plus tip sheets and notes that may prove helpful. It's a thorough service, for which we have received the highest praise." Charges for postage, handling, photocopying per submission, "not a general fee." 90% of business is derived from commissions on ms sales. 10% is derived from criticism services. Payment of a criticism fee does not ensure representation.

Tips: Obtains new clients through recommendations, "but mostly queries. If interested in agency representation, write a good story with interesting characters and that's hard to do. Learn your form and format. Take courses, workshops. Read *Writer's Digest*; it's your best source of great information."

LEGACIES (I), 501 Woodstock Circle, Perico Bay, Bradenton FL 34209. Phone/fax: (813)792-9159. Executive Director: Mary Ann Amato. Estab. 1993. Signatory of WGA, member of Florida Motion Picture & Television Association, Board of Talent Agents, Dept. of Professional Regulations License No. TA 0000404. 50% of clients are new/previously unpublished writers. Specializes in screenplays. Currently handles: 10% nonfiction books; 80% movie scripts; 10% stage plays.
Handles: Movie scripts (feature film), TV scripts (TV mow, sitcom), stage plays. Considers these script subject areas: contemporary issues; ethnic; family saga; feminist; historical; humor/satire. Query, then send entire ms. Enclose SASE. Reports in 2 weeks on queries; 4-6 weeks on mss.
Recent Sales: *Journey from the Jacarandas*, by Patricia A. Friedberg (Eva Monley, producer of *A Far Away Place*).
Terms: Agent receives 15% commission on domestic sales; 20% on foreign sales (WGA percentages on member sales). Offers written contract.
Tips: Speaker at the Florida Motion Picture and TV Association conference.

‡LENHOFF/ROBINSON TALENT AND LITERARY AGENCY, INC. (III), 1728 S. La Cienega Blvd., 2nd Floor, Los Angeles CA 90035. (310)558-4700. Fax: (310)558-4440. Contact: Lloyd Robinson. Estab. 1992. Signatory of WGA, franchised by DGA/SAG. Represents 120 clients. 10% of screenwriting clients are new/previously unpublished writers; all are WGA members. We represent screenwriters, playwrights, novelists and producers, directors. Currently handles: 15% novels; 40% movie scripts; 40% TV scripts; 5% stage plays. Member agents: Charles Lenhoff; Lloyd Robinson; Dan Pasternack.
Handles: Movie scripts (feature film, documentary), TV scripts (TV mow, miniseries, episodic drama, variety show), stage play, CD-ROM. Considers these script subject areas: action/adventure; cartoon/animation; comedy; contemporary issues; detective/police/crime; erotica; ethnic; experimental; family saga; fantasy; mainstream; mystery/suspense; psychic/supernatural; religious/inspirational; romantic comedy and drama; science fiction; sports; teen; thriller; western/frontier. Send outline/proposal, synopsis or log line.
Recent Sales: *Movie scripts optioned/sold*: *Return of Philo T. McGiffen*, by David Poyer; *Silent Partners*, by Burt Prelutsky (Finnegan-Pinchuk); *Scripting assignments*: "Burke's Law," Stanley Ralph Ross (Spelling & CBS). "We sell or place most of our writers for staff positions in TV and movies. Scripts are sold to individual producing companies and studios."
Terms: Agent receives 10% commission on domestic sales; 10% on foreign sales. Offers written contract, binding for 2 years minimum. Charges for photocopying/messenger when required.
Tips: Obtains new clients only through referral. "We are a talent agency specializing in the copyright business. Fifty percent of our clients generate copyright—screenwriters, playwrights and novelists. Fifty percent of our clients service copyright—producers, directors and cinematographers. We represent only produced, published and/or WGA writers who are eligible for staff TV positions as well as novelists and playwrights whose works may be adapted for film on television."

‡LINDSTROM LITERARY GROUP (I), 871 N. Greenbrier St., Arlington VA 22205. (703)522-4730. Fax: (703)527-7624. Contact: Kristin Lindstrom. Estab. 1994. Represents 22 clients. 75% of clients are new/previously unpublished writers. Currently handles: 50% nonfiction books; 30% novels; 10% movie scripts; 10% TV scripts.
• See the expanded listing for this agency in Literary Agents: Nonfee-charging.

LYCEUM CREATIVE PROPERTIES (I, II) P.O. Box 12370, San Antonio TX 78212. (210)732-0200. President: Guy Robim Custer. Estab. 1992. Signatory of WGA. Represents 25 clients. 50% of clients are new/previously unpublished writers. Currently handles: 20% nonfiction books; 5% scholarly books; 40% novels; 25% movie scripts; 5% stage plays; 5% TV scripts. Member agents: Guy Robin Custer (novels, nonfiction, some screenplays); Dave Roy (novels, screenplays, stage plays); Geoff Osborne (nonfiction, screenplays, stage plays).
• See expanded listing for this agency in Literary Agents: Nonfee-charging.

MANUS & ASSOCIATES LITERARY AGENCY (II), 417 E. 57th St., Suite 5-D, New York NY 10022. (212)644-8020. Fax: (212)644-3374. Contact: Janet Wilkins Manus. Also: 430 Cowper St., Palo Alto CA 94301. (415)617-4556. Fax: (415)617-4546. Contact: Jillian Manus. Estab. 1985. Member of AAR. Represents 60 clients. 15% of clients are new/previously unpublished writers.

Specializes in quality fiction, mysteries, thrillers, true crime, health, pop psychology. Currently handles: 60% nonfiction books; 10% juvenile books; 20% novels; 10% film rights, TV and feature films.

• See the expanded listing for this agency in Literary Agents: Nonfee-charging.

‡MARBEA AGENCY (II, IV), 1946 NE 149th St., North Miami FL 33181. (305)949-0615. Fax: (305)949-6104. Contact: Martin Lewis. Estab. 1970. Signatory of WGA. Represents 6 clients. 100% of clients are new/previously unpublished writers. Specializes in screenplays of various genres. Currently handles 100% movie scripts. Member agents: Phillip Jennings (action/adventure films).
Handles: Movie scripts (feature film). Considers all script subject areas. Query. Reports in 2 weeks.
Terms: Agent receives 10% commission on domestic sales; 10% on foreign sales. Offers written contract, binding for 2 years. Charges for expenses.
Tips: Obtains new clients through WGA list and referrals. "Be polite; write well."

‡□MONTGOMERY LITERARY AGENCY (II), P.O. Box 8822, Silver Spring MD 20907-8822. (301)230-1807. Contact: M.E. Olsen. Estab. 1987. Signatory of WGA. 25% of clients are new/previously unpublished writers. Equal interest in scripts (films and TV mainly) and books. Currently handles: 8% nonfiction books; 2% scholarly books; 2% textbooks; 2% poetry; 5% juvenile books; 25% novels; 30% movie scripts; 20% TV scripts; 1% stage plays; 1% short story collections; 2% syndicated material; 2% other (comics for varied marketing).
Handles: Movie scripts (feature film), TV scripts, stage plays. Considers these script subject areas: action/adventure; comedy; contemporary issues; detective/police/crime; family saga; glitz; mystery/suspense; romantic comedy and drama; science fiction; sports; thriller; western/frontier.
Also Handles: Nonfiction books, scholarly books, textbooks, poetry books, juvenile books, novels, novellas, short story collections, syndicated material, essay article collections. Considers these nonfiction areas: agriculture/horticulture; animals; anthropology/archaeology; art/architecture/design; biography/autobiography; business; child guidance/parenting; computers/electronics; cooking/food/nutrition; crafts/hobbies; current affairs; education; ethnic/cultural interests; government/politics/law; health/medicine; history; how-to;humor; juvenile nonfiction; language/literature/criticism; military/war; money/finance/economics; music/dance/theater/film; nature/environment; New Age/metaphysics; photography; popular culture; psychology; science/technology; self-help/personal improvement; sociology; sports; true crime/investigative. Considers these fiction areas: action/adventure; cartoon/comic; contemporary issues; detective/police/crime; ethnic; experimental; family saga; fantasy; glitz; historical; horror; humor/satire; juvenile; literary; mainstream; picture book; psychic/supernatural; regional; romance (contemporary, gothic, historical, regency); science fiction; sports; thriller/espionage; westerns/frontier; young adult; New Age. Send entire ms or script. Reports in 1-2 weeks on queries; 4-6 weeks on mss.
Terms: Agent receives 10% on scripts; 15% commission on domestic sales; 15% on foreign sales. Offers written contract, binding for 2 years with 30 day cancellation clause.
Fees: Editorial service: $350.

MONTGOMERY-WEST LITERARY AGENCY (IV), 7450 Butler Hills Dr., Salt Lake City UT 84121. Contact: Carole Western. Estab. 1989. Signatory of WGA. Represents 30 clients. 80% of clients are new/previously unpublished writers. Specializes in movie and TV scripts. Currently handles: 10% novels; 90% movie scripts. Member agents: Carole Western (movie and TV scripts); Nancy Gummery (novel, consultant and editor).
Handles: Movie scripts (feature film), TV scripts (TV mow). Considers these script subject areas: action/adventure; comedy; detective/police/crime; family saga; feminist; glitz; juvenile family; mainstream; mystery/suspense; romantic comedy and drama; science fiction; teen; thriller/espionage. Query with outline and first act (approximately 26 pages) and SAE. Reports in 6-8 weeks on queries; 8-10 weeks on mss.
Recent Sales: *Spaceless*, by Jeff Vintar (Laurel).
Terms: Agent receives 10% commission on movie scripts; 15% on foreign sales; 15% on networking sales with other agencies. Charges for telephone, postage and consultations.
Writers' Conferences: Attends 3 workshops a year; WGA West Conference.
Tips: "Send in only the finest product you can and keep synopses and treatments brief and to the point. Have patience and be aware of the enormous competition in the writing field."

 The double dagger before a listing indicates the listing is new in this edition.

‡**BRIAN KEITH MOODY MANAGEMENT (I, II)**, GPO Box 7996, New York NY 10116-7996. (212)969-8537. Contact: J. Cooperman. Estab. 1992 as publisher; 1994 as agent. Signatory of WGA. Represents 3 clients. 33% of clients are new/previously unpublished writers. Specializes in African-American stage, TV and screenwriters. "We consider writers of all races though." Currently handles: 90% movie scripts; 5% TV scripts; 5% stage plays.
   • Mr. Moody publishes *The Directory of African American Stage, Television and Screenwriters*, containing credits, awards, available scripts and contact info on 250 Black writers. *Black Dramatist Magazine*, a quarterly magazine featuring interviews with Black professional stage, TV and film writers, premiered in February 1995.
Handles: Movie scripts (feature film), TV scripts (TV mow, episodic drama, sitcom), stage plays. Considers these script subject areas: action/adventure; comedy; contemporary issues; detective/police/crime; ethnic; family saga; fantasy; feminist; gay; glitz; historical; horror; humor; juvenile; lesbian; mainstream; mystery/suspense; psychic/supernatural; religious/inspirational; romantic comedy and drama; science fiction; sports; teen; thriller. Query with 1 page synopsis and SASE. Reports in 10 days.
Terms: Agent receives 10% commission on domestic sales; 15% on foreign sales. Offers written contract, binding for 2 years (WGA rules). Offers criticism service "free for scripts we intend to market. I simply call a writer and we talk about it. If this agency believes in a project, it is more than happy to finance its marketing."
Tips: Usually finds new clients through their directory, recommendations and solicitations. "Learn how to write a good, catchy pitch letter, then have a script ready that is written in the correct format, if the format is not right, it won't get read—even if we did ask for it. Don't worry about 'the market' so much. Write the story you have to write. The worst that will happen is you'll have a great writing sample."

‡**DEE MURA ENTERPRISES, INC. (II)**, 269 West Shore Dr., Massapequa NY 11758-8225. (516)795-1616. Fax: (516)795-8797. E-mail: samurai5@netcom.com. Contact: Dee Mura. Estab. 1987. Signatory of WGA. 50% of clients are new/previously published writers. "We work on everything, but are especially interested in true life stories, true crime and women's stories and issues." Currently handles: 20% nonfiction books; 15% scholarly books; 15% juvenile books; 20% novels; 15% movie scripts; 15% TV scripts.
   • See the expanded listing for this agency in Literary Agents: Nonfee-charging.

OTITIS MEDIA (II), 1926 DuPont Ave. S., Minneapolis MN 55403. (612)377-4918. Fax: (612)377-3096. Contact: Richard Boylan or Hannibal Harris. Signatory of WGA. Currently handles: novels; movie scripts; stage plays; TV scripts. Member agents: B.R. Boylan (novels, nonfiction, screenplays, stage plays); Hannibal Harris (queries, evaluation of proposals, books) Greg Boylan (screenplays, TV scripts); Ingrid DiLeonardo (script and ms evaluation, story development).
Handles: Movie scripts (feature film), TV scripts (TV mow), stage plays. Considers these script subject areas: action/adventure; comedy; historical; humor; mystery/suspense; romantic comedy and drama; thriller. Send proposal.
Also Handles: Nonfiction books, novels. Considers these nonfiction areas: anthropology/archaeology; biography/autobiography; health/medicine; history; humor; military/war; music/dance/theater/film; photography; true crime/investigative. Considers these fiction areas: action/adventure; historical; humor/satire; mainstream; mystery/suspense; thriller/espionage.
Terms: Agent receives 15% on domestic sales; negotiable on foreign sales. Offers written contract. "We prefer that the writer supply whatever additional copies we request."
Tips: "Seminars or classes in creative writing alone are insufficient to attract our attention. You should be constantly writing and rewriting before you submit your first work. Correct format, spelling and grammar are essential. We shall respond quickly to a query letter containing a one page outline, a list of your writing credits, and the opening ten pages of only *one* work at a time . . . plus an SASE. (No SASE means we do not return anything.) Please, in your query letter, try not to be cute, clever, or hardsell. Save us all the time of having to read about what your relatives, friends, teachers, paid 'editors' or gurus think about your story. Nor do we need a pitch about who will want this book or movie, spend money for it and how much it will earn for writer, editor/producer, and agent. You should, in a few short paragraphs, be able to summarize the work to the point where we'll ask for more. You also should indicate your own survey of the market to see what other similar works are available and then demonstrate why yours is better. We are appalled to receive works whose cover page is dated and who indicate that this is a first draft. No producer or editor is likely to read a first draft of anything. Please don't call us the day we receive your manuscript, asking us how much we like it. In fact, please don't call us. We'll contact you if we want more."

DOROTHY PALMER (III), 235 W. 56 St., New York NY 10019. Phone/fax: (212)765-4280. Estab. 1990. Signatory of WGA. Represents 12 clients. 90% of clients are new/previously unpublished

writers. Specializes in screenplays, TV. Currently handles: 70% movie scripts, 30% TV scripts.
Handles: Movie scripts (feature film), TV scripts (TV mow, episodic drama, sitcom, soap opera).
Considers these script subject areas: cooking/food/nutrition; current affairs; detective/police/
crime; family saga; health/medicine; humor/satire; mainstream; mystery/suspense; romantic
comedy; romantic drama; thriller/espionage; true crime/investigative; women's issues/women's
studies. Send entire ms with outline/proposal.
Recent Sales: "Startek," by Manuel Garcia (Paramount).
Terms: Agent receives 10% commission on domestic sales; 10% on foreign sales. Offers written
contract, binding for 1 year.
Tips: Obtains new clients through recommendations from others. "Do *not* telephone. When I
find a script that interests me, I call the writer. Calls to me are a turn-off because it cuts into
my reading time."

PANDA TALENT (II), 3721 Hoen Ave., Santa Rosa CA 95405. (707)576-0711. Fax: (707)544-2765.
Contact: Audrey Grace. Estab. 1977. Signatory of WGA, SAG, AFTRA, Equity. Represents 10
clients. 80% of clients are new/previously unpublished writers. Currently handles: 5% novels;
40% TV scripts; 50% movie scripts; 5% stage plays. Member agents: Steven Grace (science
fiction/war/action); Vicki Lima (mysterious/romance); Cleo West (western/true stories).
Handles: Movie scripts (feature film), TV scripts (TV mow, episodic drama, sitcom), stage
plays. Handles these script subject areas: action/adventure; animals; comedy; detective/police/
crime; ethnic; family saga; humor/satire; juvenile; military/war; mystery/suspense; psychology;
romantic comedy and drama; science fiction; sports; true crime/investigative; westerns/frontier.
Query with treatment. Reports in 3 weeks on queries; 2 months on mss. Must include SASE.
Terms: Agent receives 10% commission on domestic sales; 10% on foreign sales.

PANETTIERE & CO. (I, II), 1841 N. Fuller Ave., Los Angeles CA 90046. (213)876-5984. Fax:
(213)876-5076. Contact: Vincent Panettiere. Estab. 1992. Signatory of WGA, DGA. Represents
40 clients. 40% of clients are new/previously unpublished writers. Currently handles: 80% movie
scripts; 20% TV scripts.
Handles: Movie scripts (feature film, animation), TV scripts (TV mow, miniseries, episodic
drama, sitcom, animation), stage play. Considers comedy scripts. Query. Reports in 1 month.
Terms: Agent receives 10% commission. Offers written contract, binding for 1 year. "We bill
client for copies of scripts that are distributed."
Tips: Obtains new clients through recommendations from others and solicitation.

☐**PMA LITERARY AND FILM MANAGEMENT, INC.**, 220 W., 19th St., Suite 501, New York
NY 10011. (212)929-1222. Fax: (212)206-0238. President: Peter Miller. Member agents: Lory
Manrique; Jennifer Robinson (film and fiction); Yuri Skuins (fiction); Anthony Schneider (fic-
tion, nonfiction). Estab. 1975. Represents 80 clients. 50% of clients are new/unpublished writers.
Specializes in commercial fiction and nonfiction, thrillers, true crime and "fiction with *real*
motion picture and television potential." Currently handles: 50% fiction; 25% nonfiction; 25%
screenplays.
   • See the expanded listing for this agency in Literary Agents: Fee-charging.

‡**REDWOOD EMPIRE AGENCY (II)**, P.O. Box 1946, Guerneville CA 95446. (707)869-1146. Contact: Jim Sorrells or Rodney Shull. Estab. 1992. Represents 6 clients. 90% of clients are new/
previously unpublished writers. Specializes in screenplays, big screen or TV. Currently handles:
100% movie scripts.
Handles: Movie scripts (feature film, TV mow). Considers these script subject areas: contemporary issues; erotica; family saga; fantasy; feminist; gay; historical; humor/satire; juvenile; lesbian;
romance (contemporary). Query with 1 page synopsis. Reports in 1 week on queries; 1 month
on mss.
Terms: Agent receives 10% commission on domestic sales; 10% on foreign sales. Offers criticism
service: structure, characterization, dialogue, format style. No fee. "Writer must supply copies
of script as needed. We ship and handle."
Tips: Obtains new clients through word of mouth, letter in *Hollywood Scriptwriter*. "Most interested in ordinary people confronting real-life situations."

STEPHANIE ROGERS AND ASSOCIATES (III), 3575 Cahuenga Blvd. West, 2nd Floor, Los
Angeles CA 90068. (213)851-5155. Owner: Stephanie Rogers. Estab. 1980. Signatory of WGA.
Represents 40 clients. 20% of clients are new/unproduced writers. Prefers that the writer has
been produced (movies or TV), his/her properties optioned or has references. Prefers to work
with published/established authors. Currently handles: 10% novels; 50% movie scripts; 40% TV
scripts.

Handles: Movie scripts (feature film), TV scripts (TV mow). Considers these script subject areas: action/adventure; dramas (contemporary); romantic comedies; suspense/thrillers. Must be professional in presentation and not over 125 pages. Query. Does not read unsolicited mss. SASE required.

Also Handles: Novels (only wishes to see those that have been published and can translate to screen).

Terms: Agent receives 10% commission on domestic sales; 10% on dramatic sales; 20% on foreign sales. Charges for phone, photocopying and messenger expenses.

Tips: "When writing a query letter, you should give a short bio of your background, a thumbnail sketch (no more than a paragraph) of the material you are looking to market and an explanation of how or where (books, classes or workshops) you studied screenwriting." Include SASE for response.

‡VICTORIA SANDERS LITERARY AGENCY (II), 241 Avenue of the Americas, New York NY 10014. (212)633-8811. Fax: (212)633-0525. Contact: Victoria Sanders and/or Diane Dickensheid. Estab. 1993. Member of AAR, signatory of WGA. Represents 25 clients. 50% of clients are new/previously unpublished writers. currently handles: 50% nonfiction books; 30% novels; 10% movie scripts; 10% short story.
  • See the expanded listing for this agency in Literary Agents: Nonfee-charging.

JACK SCAGNETTI TALENT & LITERARY AGENCY (III), 5118 Vineland Ave., #102, North Hollywood CA 91601. (818)762-3871. Contact: Jack Scagnetti. Estab. 1974. Signatory of WGA, member of Academy of Television Arts and Sciences. Represents 40 clients. 50% of clients are new/previously unpublished writers. Specializes in film books with many photographs. Currently handles: 10% nonfiction books; 80% movie scripts; 10% TV scripts. Member agents: Jack Scagnetti (nonfiction and screenplays) and staff of 6 freelance readers/analysts.

Handles: Movie scripts (feature film), TV scripts (TV mow, episodic drama). Considers these script subject areas: action/adventure; comedy; detective/police/crime; family saga; historical; horror; mainstream; mystery/suspense; romantic comedy and drama; sports; thriller; westerns/frontier. Query with outline/proposal. Reports in 1 month on queries; 6-8 weeks on mss.

Also Handles: Nonfiction. Considers these nonfiction areas: biography/autobiography; current affairs; how-to; military/war; music/dance/theater/film; sports; true crime/investigative. Considers these fiction areas: action/adventure; contemporary issues; detective/police/crime; family saga; historical; mainstream; mystery/suspense; picture book; romance (contemporary); sports; thriller/espionage; westerns/frontier.

Recent Sales: *Sight Unseen*, by Barbara Wanbaugh (Leucadia Films).

Terms: Agent receives 10% commission on domestic sales; 15% on foreign sales. Offers written contract, binding for 6 months-1 year. Charges for postage and photocopies.

Tips: Obtains new clients through "referrals by others and query letters sent to us. Write a good synopsis, short and to the point and include marketing data for the book."

SUSAN SCHULMAN, A LITERARY AGENCY (III), 454 W. 44th St., New York NY 10036-5205. (212)713-1633/4/5. Fax: (212)586-8830. President: Susan Schulman. Estab. 1979. Member of AAR, Dramatists Guild, Women's Media Group. 10-15% of clients are new/unpublished writers. Prefers to work with published/established authors; works with a small number of new/unpublished authors. Currently handles: 70% nonfiction books; 20% novels; 10% stage plays. Member agents: Jake Holder (submissions); Holly Frederick (foreign rights).
  • See the expanded listing for this agency in Literary Agents: Nonfee-charging.

‡KEN SHERMAN & ASSOCIATES, 9507 Santa Monica Blvd. Beverly Hills CA 90210. (310)273-3840. Fax: (310)271-3875. Contact: Ken Sherman. Estab. 1989. Member of DGA, BAFTA, PEN Int'l, signatory of WGA. Represents 30 clients. 10% of clients are new/previously unpublished writers. Specializes in good writers for films, TV, books and rights to books for films and TV. Currently handles: nonfiction books, scholarly books, juvenile books, novels, movie scripts, TV scripts.

Handles: Nonfiction, novels, movie scripts, TV scripts. Considers all nonfiction and fiction areas. Contact by referral only. Reports in 1 month on mss.

Recent Sales: *Fifth Sacred Thing*, by Starhawk (Bantam); *Questions From Dad*, by Dwight Twilly (Tuttle).

Terms: Agent receives 15% commission on domestic sales. Offers written contract. Charges for office expenses, postage, photocopying, negotiable expenses.

Writer's Conferences: Maui, Squaw Valley, Santa Barbara.

Tips: Obtains new clients through recommendations from others.

☐**SILVER SCREEN PLACEMENTS (II)**, 602 65th St., Downers Grove IL 60516. (708)963-2124. Fax: (708)963-1998. Contact: William Levin. Estab. 1991. Signatory of WGA. Represents 6 clients. 100% of clients are new/previously unpublished writers. Currently handles: 5% juvenile books; 5% novels; 80% movie scripts; 10% TV scripts.
Handles: Movie scripts (feature film), TV scripts. Considers these script subject areas: action/adventure; cartoon/comic; contemporary issues; detective/police/crime; family saga; fantasy; historical; humor/satire; juvenile; mainstream; mystery/suspense; science fiction; thriller/espionage; young adult. Query with outline/proposal and SASE. Reports in 1 week on queries, 6 weeks on mss.
Also Handles: Juvenile books, novels. Considers these nonfiction areas: education; juvenile nonfiction; language/literature/criticism. Consider these fiction areas: action/adventure; cartoon/comic; contemporary issues; detective/police/crime; family saga; fantasy; historical; humor/satire; juvenile; mainstream; mystery/suspense; science fiction; thriller/espionage; young adult.
Terms: Agent receives 10% commission on domestic sales; 15% on foreign sales. Offers written contract, binding for 2-4 years.
Fees: Criticism service: $185 per script or ms. Critiques written by William Levin, and are 4-5 pages plus partial editing of work.
Tips: Obtains new clients through "recommendations from other parties, as well as being listed with WGA and *Guide to Literary Agents*."

‡**SISTER MANIA PRODUCTIONS, INC. (III, V)**, 916 Penn St., Brackenridge PA 15014. (412)226-2964. Fax: (412)339-8526. Contact: Literary Department. Estab. 1988. Signatory of WGA. Represents 5 clients. 20% of clients are new/previously unpublished writers. "We also package, develop and produce." Currently handles: 80% movie scripts; 10% TV scripts; 10% syndicated material.
Handles: Movie scripts (feature film), TV scripts, syndicated material. Considers these script subject areas: action/adventure; detective/police/crime; experimental; family saga; horror; humor/satire; language/literature/criticism; money/finance/economics; romance; thriller/espionage; true crime/investigative. Query. Reports up to 1 month on queries; 1-2 months on mss.
Terms: Offers written contract. Offers criticism service, no fees for clients.
Tips: Usually obtains new clients through "very creative query with project creative and executive appeal in maintaining integrity through quality products."

CAMILLE SORICE AGENCY (II), 16661 Ventura Blvd., #400, Encino CA 91436-1925. (818)995-1775. Contact: Camille Sorice. Estab. 1988. Signatory of WGA.
Handles: Movie scripts (feature film); TV scripts (TV mow). Considers these script subject areas: action/adventure; comedy; detective/police/crime; family saga; historical; mystery/suspense; romantic comedy and drama; westerns/frontier. Send query letters. Reports in 6 weeks on mss.
Tips: "No calls. Query letters accepted."

STANTON & ASSOCIATES INTERNATIONAL LITERARY AGENCY (II), 4413 Clemson Dr., Garland TX 75042. (214)276-5427. Fax: (214)348-6900. Contact: Henry Stanton, Harry Preston. Estab. 1990. Signatory of WGA. Represents 36 clients. 90% of clients are new screenwriters. Specializes in screenplays only. Currently handles: 50% movie scripts; 50% TV scripts.
Handles: Movie scripts (feature film), TV scripts (TV mow). Query. Reports in 1 week on queries; 1 month on screenplays (review).
Recent Sales: *Crossing the Line* (LaMoth Productions); *Splintered Image* (Hearst Entertainment); *Belle and Her Boys* (Bob Banner Associates); *The Body Shop* and *Sisters Revenge* (Esquivel Entertainment).
Terms: Agent receives 15% commission on domestic sales. Offers written contract, binding for 2 years on individual screenplays. Returns scripts with reader's comments.
Tips: Obtains new clients through WGA listing, *Hollywood Scriptwriter*, word of mouth (in Dallas). "We have writers available to edit or ghostwrite screenplays. Fees vary dependent on the writer. All writers should always please enclose a SASE with any queries."

‡☐**STAR LITERARY SERVICE (II)**, 1540 N. Louis, Tucson AZ 85712. (602)326-4146. Contact: Marilyn Caponegri. Estab. 1990. Signatory of WGA. Represents 9 clients. 80% of clients are new/previously unpublished writers. Currently handles: 100% movie scripts.
Handles: Movie scripts (feature film). Considers these script subject areas: action/adventure; biography/autobiography; detective/police/crime; mystery; psychic/supernatural; romance; thriller/espionage. Query. Reports in 2 weeks on queries; 6 weeks on mss.
Terms: Agent receives 10% commission on domestic sales. Offers written contract, binding for 2 years.

Fees: Criticism service: $100 for a maximum of 150 pages. Agent writes critiques that "point out problems in dialogue, plotting and character development and determines the overall marketability of the project."
Tips: Obtains new clients through queries. "Stick with popular genres such as mystery, comedy, romance."

H.N. SWANSON INC. (III), 8523 Sunset Blvd., Los Angeles CA 90069. President: Thomas J. Shanks. Estab. 1934. Contact: Anna Courtney. Signatory of WGA. Represents over 100 clients. 10% of clients are new/previously unpublished writers. Currently handles: 60% novels; 40% movie and TV scripts. Member agents: Steven Fisher, Gail Barrick, Tim Anderson, Larry Kennar.
  • This agency was recently acquired by Joel Gotler and Renaissance: A Literary and Talent Agency. H.N. Swanson is recognized as the first Hollywood literary agency, and Mr. Gotler started his agenting career under H.N. Swanson. The new company will be called Renaissance – H.N. Swanson.
Handles: Movie scripts (feature film); TV scripts (TV mow, episodic drama, sitcom and animation). Considers these script subject areas: action/adventure; cartoon/animation; comedy; contemporary issues; detective/police/crime; erotica; ethnic; experimental; family saga; fantasy; feminist; gay; historical; horror; humor; juvenile; lesbian; mainstream; mystery/suspense; psychic/supernatural; romantic comedy and drama; science fiction; sports; teen; thriller; westerns/frontier. Query. Reports within 3-4 weeks on queries must be accompanied by SASE.
Recent Sales: *Two By Two*, By David Golden/Jay Rosen (Byegam-Baer); *In Contempt*, by Ken Nolan (Weintraub Entertainment).
Also Handles: Novels, novellas. Considers these fiction areas: action/adventure; confessional; contemporary issues; detective/police/crime; erotica; ethnic; experimental; family saga; fantasy; feminist; gay; glitz; historical; horror; humor/satire; juvenile; lesbian; literary; mainstream; mystery/suspense; psychic/supernatural; regional; romance (contemporary, gothic, historical, regency); science fiction; sports; thriller/espionage; westerns/frontier; young adult.
Recent Sales: *Chicken Little Was Right*, by Jean Ruryk (Golden Quill/Prod.); *A Crack in Forever*, by Jeannie Brewer (Simon & Schuster).
Terms: Agent receives 10% commission on domestic sales; 15% for domestic book sales; 20% for foreign book sales. Offers written contract.

‡TALENT SOURCE, 237 Dayton St., P.O. Box 14120, Savannah GA 31416. (912)232-9390. Fax: (912)232-8213. Contact: Michael L. Shortt. Estab. 1991. Signatory of WGA. 35% of clients are new/previously unpublished writers. Currently handles: 50% movie scripts; 50% TV scripts.
Handles: Movie scripts (feature film), TV scripts. Send outline with character breakdown. Reports in 4-6 weeks on queries.
Terms: Agent receives 10% commission on domestic sales; 15% on foreign sales. Offers written contract.
Tips: Obtains new clients through word of mouth.

THE TANTLEFF OFFICE (II), 375 Greenwich St., Suite 700, New York NY 10013. (212)941-3939. President: Jack Tantleff. Estab. 1986. Signatory of WGA, member of AAR. Specializes in TV, theater, film, fiction and nonfiction. Currently handles: 15% movie scripts; 70% stage plays; 15% TV scripts. Member agents: John Santoianni (theater); Jill Bock (TV and film); Anthony Gardner (fiction, nonfiction books); Alan Willig (talent); Jay Kane (talent).
Handles: Movie scripts, TV scripts, stage plays. Query with outline.
Also Handles: Nonfiction books, fiction.
Terms: Agent receives 10% commission on domestic sales; 10% on dramatic sales; 10% on foreign sales: 15% on book sales.

‡TAURO BROTHERS MANAGEMENT (II), 1541 Ocean Ave., #200, Santa Monica CA 90401. (310)458-1505. Fax: (310)393-7777. Contact: Chris Maggiore, Robert Tauro. Estab. 1992. Represents 2 clients. None are new/previously unpublished writers. Currently handles: 75% movie scripts; 25% TV scripts.

For explanation of symbols, see the Key to Symbols and Abbreviations. For translation of an organization's acronym, see the Table of Acronyms. For unfamiliar words, check the Glossary.

Handles: Movie scripts, TV scripts. Considers these script subject areas: action/adventure; cartoon/comic; contemporary issues; current affairs; detective/police/crime; erotica; ethnic; gay; historical; horror; humor/satire; juvenile; lesbian; military/war; photography; religious/inspirational; romance; sports; thriller/espionage; true crime/investigative. Send entire ms. Reports in 10 days.

Terms: Agent receives 10% commission on domestic sales; 10% on foreign sales.

Tips: Obtains new clients through recommendations.

☐**A TOTAL ACTING EXPERIENCE (II),** Dept. N.W., 20501 Ventura Blvd., Suite 399, Woodland Hills CA 91364. (818)340-9249. Contact: Dan A. Bellacicco. Estab. 1984. Signatory of WGA, SAG, AFTRA. Represents 30 clients. 50% of clients are new/previously unpublished writers. Specializes in "quality instead of quantity." Currently handles: 5% nonfiction books; 5% juvenile books; 10% novels; 5% novellas; 5% short story collections; 50% movie scripts; 5% stage plays; 10% TV scripts; 5% how-to books and videos.

Handles: Movie scripts (feature film, documentary), TV scripts (TV mow, episodic drama, sitcom, variety show, soap opera, animation); stage plays; syndicated material, how-to books, videos. "No heavy drugs." Considers these script subject areas: action/adventure; cartoon/animation; comedy; contemporary issues; detective/police/crime; erotica; ethnic; experimental; family saga; fantasy; historical; horror; humor; juvenile; mainstream; mystery/suspense; psychic/supernatural; religious/inspirational; romantic comedy and drama; science fiction; sports; teen; thriller; westerns/frontier. Query with outline plus 3 sample chapters. Reports in 3 months on mss. "We will respond *only* if interested, material will *not* be returned."

Also Handles: Nonfiction books, textbooks, juvenile books, novels, novellas, short story collections, poetry books. Considers these nonfiction areas: animals; art/architecture/design; biography/autobiography; business; child guidance/parenting; computers/electronics; cooking/food/nutrition; crafts/hobbies; current affairs; education; ethnic/cultural interests; government/politics/law; health/medicine; history; how-to; humor; juvenile nonfiction; language/literature/criticism; military/war; money/finance/economics; music/dance/theater/film; nature/environment; New Age/metaphysics; photography; popular culture; psychology; religious/inspirational; science/technology; self-help/personal improvement; sociology; sports; translations; true crime/investigative; women's issues/women's studies; "any well-written work!" Considers these fiction areas: action/adventure; cartoon/comic; confessional; contemporary issues; detective/police/crime; erotica; ethnic; experimental; family saga; fantasy; glitz; historical; horror; humor/satire; juvenile; literary; mainstream; mystery/suspense; picture book; psychic/supernatural; regional; religious/inspirational; romance (contemporary, gothic, historical, regency); science fiction; sports; thriller/espionage; westerns/frontier; young adult.

Terms: Agent receives 10% on domestic sales; 10% on foreign sales. Offers written contract, binding for 2 years or more.

Fees: Offers criticism service (for our clients only at no charge.) 60% of business is derived from commission on ms sales.

Tips: Obtains new clients through mail and conferences. "We seek new sincere, quality writers for long-term relationships. We would love to see film, television, and stage material that remains relevant and provocative 20 years from today; dialogue that is fresh and unpredictable; story, and characters that are enlightening, humorous, witty, creative, inspiring, and, most of all, entertaining. Please keep in mind quality not quantity. Your character must be well delineated and fully developed with high contrast. Respond only if you apprecieate our old fashioned agency nurturing, strong guidance, and in return: your honesty, loyalty and a quality commitment."

THE TURTLE AGENCY (III), 12456 Ventura Blvd., Studio City CA 91604. (818)506-6898. Fax: (818)506-1723. Contact: Cindy Turtle, Beth Bohn. Estab. 1985. Signatory of WGA, member of SAG, AFTRA. Represents 45 clients. Specializes in network TV, features, interactive. Currently handles: 5% novels; 25% movie scripts; 70% TV scripts.

Handles: Movie scripts (feature film), TV scripts (TV mow). Considers these script subject areas: action/adventure; detective/police/crime; erotica; fantasy; historical; mainstream; mystery/suspense; psychic/supernatural; romance; science fiction; thriller/espionage; westerns/frontier; young adult. Query. Reports in 2 weeks on queries; 1 month on mss. "If writer would like material returned, enclose SASE."

Terms: Agent receives 10% commission on domestic sales. Offers written contract, binding for 2 years.

Tips: Obtains new clients through recommendations, usually — on *rare* occassions through query letters.

ERIKA WAIN AGENCY (II), 1418 N. Highland, #102, Hollywood CA 90028. (213)460-4224. Contact: Erika Wain. Estab. 1979. Signatory of WGA, SAG-AFTRA, member of Authors Guild.

50% of clients are new/previously unpublished writers. Currently handles: 5% juvenile books; 80% movie scripts; 15% TV scripts.
Handles: Movie scripts (feature film, documentary, animation), TV scripts (TV mow, miniseries, animation). Considers these script subject areas: action/adventure; animals; detective/police/crime; family saga; fantasy; feminist; humor/satire; military/war; mystery/suspense; science/technology; science fiction; thriller/espionage; true crime/investigative; women's issues. Query. Reports immediately if interested on queries and ms.
Also Handles: Juvenile books.
Terms: Agent receives 10% commission on domestic sales. Offers written contract.
Tips: Obtains new clients through recommendation from others, solicitation.

‡**WARDEN, WHITE & KANE, INC. (IV),** 8444 Wilshire Blvd., 4th Floor, Beverly Hills CA 90211. Estab. 1990. Signatory of WGA. Represents 100 clients. 10% of clients are new/previously unpublished writers. Specializes in film and TV. Currently handles: 100% movie scripts. Member agents: David Warden, Steve White, Michael Kane.
Handles: Movie scripts (feature film). Only by referral. Reports in 2 months on queries.
Recent Sales: *Mango,* by Miles Millar (New Line); *Bullet Proof,* by Phoebe Dorin and Christian Stoianovich (Universal). "Also sold *Sleepless in Seattle* and represents author of *Batman.*"
Terms: Agent receives 10% commission on domestic sales; 10% on foreign sales. Offers written contract, binding for 2 years. Charges for photocopying.
Tips: Obtains new clients only through referrals.

☐**SANDRA WATT & ASSOCIATES (II),** 8033 Sunset Blvd., Suite 4053, Hollywood CA 90046. (213)653-2339. Contact: Davida South. Estab. 1977. Signatory of WGA. Represents 55 clients. 15% of clients are new/previously unpublished writers. Specializes in scripts: film noir; family; romantic comedies; books, women's fiction, mystery, commercial nonfiction. Currently handles: 40% nonfiction books; 35% novels; 25% movie scripts. Member agents: Sandra Watt (scripts, nonfiction, novels); Davida South (scripts).
• See the expanded listing for this agency in Literary Agents: Fee-charging.

‡☐**PEREGRINE WHITTLESEY AGENCY (II),** 345 E. 80th St., New York NY 10021. (212)737-0153. Contact: Peregrine Whittlesey. Estab. 1986. Signatory of WGA. Represents 25 English and American clients. 60% of clients are new/previously unpublished writers. Specializes in plays and screenplays; original playwrights who write for screen and TV. Currently handles: 10% movie scripts; 90% stage plays.
Handles: Movie scripts (feature film); stage plays. Query first with SASE. Reports in 1 month.
Recent Sales: *The Song of Jacob Zulu,* by Tug Yourgrau (The Shubert Organization); projects to ABC, Showtime, CBS; plays placed in US and England.
Terms: Agent receives 10% commission on domestic sales; 10% on foreign sales. Offers written contract, binding for 2 years.
Fees: Criticism service: $100. "Critiques are usually 3-4 pages, single-spaced, written by Peregrine Whittlesey." 5% of business is derived from criticism fees.
Tips: Obtains new clients through recommendations from recognized source.

‡**WILE ENTERPRISES, INC. (III),** 2730 Wilshire Blvd., Suite 500, Santa Monica CA 90403. (310)828-9768. Fax: (310)988-3336. Contact: (Mr.) Shelly Wile. Estab. 1989. Signatory of WGA. Represents 28 clients. 15% of clients are new/previously unpublished writers. "I handle film and TV writers only for services. For rights, I handle film and TV rights to books for publication literary agents." Currently handles: 50% movie scripts; 50% TV scripts.
Handles: Movie scripts (feature film), TV scripts. Only by referral.
Terms: Agent receives 10% commission on domestic sales; 20% on foreign sales. Offers written contract, binding for 2 years. "If I photocopy scripts or screenplays, I send them to a local photocopy service and pass the charge along to the client, at cost."
Tips: Referrals from recognized people in the motion picture or television industry.

☐**JULIUS WINDERMERE AGENCY (I, II),** P.O. Box 1901, Independence MO 64055. (816)252-7276. Contact: Mr. Prince. Estab. 1993. Represents 2 clients. Signatory of WGA. 100% of clients are new/previously unpublished writers. Currently handles: 50% movie screenplays; 40% telescripts; 10% manuscripts.
Handles: Movie scripts (feature film), TV scripts (TV mow, animation). Considers these script subject areas: action/adventure; cartoon/animation; comedy; detective/police/crime; family saga; mainstream; mystery/suspense; romantic drama; thriller; young adult. "Sorry, Agency will not review horror or science fiction, period." Reports in 8-12 weeks on mss.
Terms: Agent receives 10% commission on domestic sales; 10% on foreign sales. Offers written contract, binding for 1 year with 3 month cancellation clause (standard contract used by all

signatory agencies in WGA). "Clients who have signed must supply agency with clean, crisp copies of manuscript for submissions." Synopsis required with scripts.

Fees: Charges evaluation fee: $75 for screenplay/telescript. $100 for manuscript. "Payment must be enclosed with all submissions, made payable to Mr. Prince. Fee is nonrefundable."

Tips: Obtains new clients through recommendation, solicitation. "Submissions must accompany a self-addressed stamped envelope."

ANN WRIGHT REPRESENTATIVES (II), 136 E. 56th St., 9J, New York NY 10022-3619. (212)832-0110. Fax: (212)750-9686. Head of Literary Department: Dan Wright. Estab. 1961. Signatory of WGA. Represents 50 clients. 50% of clients are new/unpublished writers. Prefers to work with published/established authors; works with a small number of new/unpublished authors. "Eager to work with published/established authors; works with a small number of new/unpublished authors. "Eager to work with any author with material that we can effectively market in the motion picture business worldwide." Specializes in "book or screenplays with strong motion picture potential." Currently handles: 40% novels; 40% movie scripts; 20% TV scripts.

Handles: Movie scripts (feature film), TV scripts (TV mow, episodic drama, sitcom). Considers these script subject areas: action/adventure; comedy; detective/police/crime; gay; historical; horror; humor; lesbian; mainstream; mystery/suspense; psychic/supernatural; romantic comedy and drama; sports; thriller; westerns/frontier. Query with outline and SASE. Does not read unsolicited mss. Reports in 3 weeks on queries; 2-3 months on mss. "All work must be sent with a SASE to ensure its return."

Recent Sales: *Movie/TV mow scripts optioned/sold: Men of Means. Movie/TV mow scripts in development: Sing Soft, Sing Loud; Baubles.*

Also Handles: Novels. Considers these fiction areas: action/adventure; detective/police/crime; family saga; fantasy; feminist; gay; historical; horror; humor/satire; lesbian; literary; mainstream; mystery/suspense; romance (contemporary, historical, regency); sports; thriller/espionage; westerns/frontier; young adult.

Terms: Agent receives 10% commission on domestic sales; 10% on dramatic sales; 15-20% on foreign sales; 20% on packaging. Offers written contract, binding for 2 years. critiques only works of signed clients. Charges for photocopying expenses.

Tips: "Send a letter with SASE. Something about the work, something about the writer."

WRITERS & ARTISTS (III), 19 W. 44th St., Suite 1000, New York NY 10036. (212)391-1112. Fax: (212)398-9877. Contact: Scott Hudson, William Craver or Peter Hagen. Estab. 1970. Member of AAR, signatory of WGA. Represents 100 clients. West Coast location: Suite 900, 924 Westwood Blvd., Los Angeles CA 90024. (310)824-6300. Fax: (310)824-6343.

Handles: Movie scripts (feature film), TV scripts (TV mow, miniseries, episodic drama), stage plays. Considers all script subject areas. Query with brief description of project, bio and SASE. Reports in 2-4 weeks on queries only when accompanied by SASE. No unsolicited mss accepted.

Recent Sales: *M Butterfly,* David Henry Hwang (Tony Award play for 1989).

Terms: Agent receives 10% commission on domestic sales; varies on foreign sales. Offers written contract (required).

☐**WRITER'S CONSULTING GROUP (II, III)** P.O. Box 492, Burbank CA 91503-0492. (818)841-9294. Director: Jim Barmeier. Estab. 1983. Represents 10 clients. "We will work with established and unestablished writers. We welcome unsolicited queries." Currently handles: 40% nonfiction books; 20% novels; 40% movie scripts.

● See the expanded listing for this agency in Literary Agents: Fee-charging.

Additional Script Agents

The following agencies have indicated that they are *primarily* interested in handling book manuscripts, but also handle less than ten to fifteen percent scripts. After reading the listing (you can find the page number in the Listings Index), send them a query to obtain more information on their needs and manuscript submission policies.

The Abacus Group
The Joan Brandt Agency
Pema Browne, Ltd.
Bruce Cook Agency
The Lois de la Haba Agency Inc.
Diamond Literary Agency, Inc.
Emerald Literary Agency, Inc.

Farber Literary Agency Inc.
ForthWrite Literary Agency
Jay Garon-Brooke Assoc. Inc.
Goldfarb & Graybill, Attorneys at Law
Lew Grimes Literary Agency
The Charlotte Gusay Literary Agency

Lawrence Jordan Literary Agency
Law Offices of Robert L. Fenton PC
Lazear Agency Inc.
Literary and Creative Artists Agency
Elaine Markson Literary

The Evan Marshall Agency
William Morris Agency
Henry Morrison, Inc.
BK Nelson Literary Agency & Lecture Bureau
Northwest Literary Services
Fifi Oscard Agency, Inc.
Julie Popkin

Puddingstone Literary Agency
Irene Rogers, Literary Representative
Russell-Simenauer Literary Agency Inc.
Gloria Stern Agency, (CA)
Marianne Strong Literary Agency

Mary Jack Wald Associates, Inc.
Wallace Literary Agency, Inc.
James Warren Literary Agency
Gary S. Wohl Literary Agency
Stephen Wright Authors' Representatives
Writer's Consulting Group

Script Agents/'94-'95 changes

The following agencies appeared in the last (1994) edition of *Guide to Literary Agents* but are absent from the 1995 edition. These agencies failed to respond to our request for an update of their listings, or were left out for the reasons indicated in parentheses following the agency name.

Allied Artists
The Mary Beal Management Co. (unable to contact)
Bethel Agency
Comedy Ink
Cyberstorm! (out of business)
Diamond Literary (CAN) (unable to contact)

Diskant & Associates (out of business)
Michael Imison Playwrights Ltd.
Helen Merrill Ltd. (deleted by request)
Scribe Associates (unable to contact)

Lee Sobel Management Associates (unable to contact)
Ellen Lively Steele & Associates (removed for one year by request)
The Talent Bank Agency (unable to contact)

Resources

Professional Organizations

Organizations for agents

ASSOCIATION OF AUTHORS' REPRESENTATIVES (AAR), 3rd Floor, 10 Astor Place, New York NY 10003. A list of member agents is available for $5 and SAE with 52 cents for postage.

Organizations for writers

The following professional organizations publish newsletters and hold conferences and meetings in which they often share information on agents.

AMERICAN SOCIETY OF JOURNALISTS & AUTHORS, 1501 Broadway, Suite 302, New York NY 10036. (212)997-0947.

THE AUTHORS GUILD INC., 330 W. 42nd St., New York NY 10036. (212)563-5904.

THE AUTHORS LEAGUE OF AMERICA, INC., 330 W. 42nd St., New York NY 10036. (212)564-8350.

CANADIAN AUTHORS ASSOCIATION, 275 Slater St., #500, Ottawa, Ontario K1P 5H9 Canada. (613)233-2846.

COUNCIL OF WRITERS ORGANIZATIONS, % Michigan Living, 1 Auto Club Dr., Dearborn MI 48126. (313)336-1211.

THE DRAMATISTS GUILD, 234 W. 44th St., 11th Floor, New York NY 10036. (212)398-9366.

HORROR WRITERS OF AMERICA, V. Aalko, Executive Secretary, 5336 Reef Way, Oxnard CA 93035. (805)985-2320.

INTERNATIONAL ASSOCIATION OF CRIME WRITERS INC., North American Branch, JAF Box 1500, New York NY 10016. (212)757-3915.

THE INTERNATIONAL WOMEN'S WRITING GUILD, P.O. Box 810, Gracie Station, New York NY 10016. (212)737-7536. Provides a literary agent list to members and holds "Meet the Agents and Editors" in April and October.

MYSTERY WRITERS OF AMERICA (MWA), 17 E. 47th St., 6th Floor, New York NY 10017.

NATIONAL LEAGUE OF AMERICAN PEN WOMEN, 1300 17th St. NW, Washington DC 20036.

NATIONAL WRITERS ASSOCIATION, 1450 S. Havana, Suite 424, Aurora CO 80012. (303)751-7844. In addition to agent referrals, also operates an agency for members.

NATIONAL WRITERS UNION, 873 Broadway, Suite 203, New York NY 10003-1209. (212)254-0279. A trade union, this organization has an agent data base available to members.

PEN AMERICAN CENTER, 568 Broadway, New York NY 10012. (212)334-1660.

POETS & WRITERS, 72 Spring St., New York NY 10012. (212)226-3586. Operates an information line, taking calls from 11-3 EST Monday through Friday.

ROMANCE WRITERS OF AMERICA, 13700 Veterans Memorial Dr., #315, Houston TX 77014. Publishes an annual agent list for members for $10.

SCIENCE FICTION AND FANTASY WRITERS OF AMERICA, 5 Winding Brook Dr., #1B, Guilderland NY 12084.

SOCIETY OF CHILDREN'S BOOK WRITERS & ILLUSTRATORS, 22736 Van Owen St., #106, West Hills CA 91307. Provides a literary agents list to members.

VOLUNTEER LAWYERS FOR THE ARTS, 1 E. 53rd St., 6th Floor, New York NY 10022. (212)319-2787.

WASHINGTON INDEPENDENT WRITERS, 733 15th St. Room 220, NW, Washington DC 20005.

WESTERN WRITERS OF AMERICA, 2800 N. Campbell, El Paso TX 79902-2522.

WOMEN IN COMMUNICATIONS, INC., 2101 Wilson Blvd., Suite 417, Arlington VA 22201.

WRITERS GUILD OF ALBERTA, 10523-100 Ave., Edmonton, Alberta T5J 0A8 Canada. (403)426-5892.

WRITERS GUILD OF AMERICA-EAST, 555 W. 57th St., New York NY 10019. (212)767-7800. Provides list of WGA signatory agents for $1.29.

WRITERS GUILD OF AMERICA-WEST, 8955 Beverly Blvd., West Hollywood CA 90048. (213)550-1000. Provides a list of WGA signatory agents for $2 and SASE sent to Agency Department.

Recommended Books & Publications

ADVENTURES IN THE SCREEN TRADE, by *William Goldman, published by Warner Books, 666 Fifth Ave., New York NY 10103. An insider's view of screenwriting and the entertainment business.*

THE ART OF DRAMATIC WRITING, by *Lajos Egri, published by Touchstone, a division of Simon & Schuster, 1230 Avenue of the Americas, New York, NY 10020.*

BEYOND THE BESTSELLER: A LITERARY AGENT TAKES YOU INSIDE PUBLISHING, by *Richard Curtis, published by NAL, 375 Hudson St., New York NY 10014. The "inside story" on publishing by a New York agent.*

BUSINESS & LEGAL FORMS FOR AUTHORS AND SELF-PUBLISHERS, by *Tad Crawford, published by Allworth Press, c/o Writer's Digest Books, 1507 Dana Ave., Cincinnati OH 45207. Forms for all types of agreements and contracts needed in the publishing business.*

CHILDREN'S WRITER'S & ILLUSTRATOR'S MARKET, edited by *Christine Martin, published by Writer's Digest Books, 1507 Dana Ave., Cincinnati OH 45207. Annual market directory for children's writers and illustrators. Includes information on writing and art business.*

THE COMPLETE GUIDE TO STANDARD SCRIPT FORMAT (Parts 1 and 2), by *Hillis Cole and Judith Haag, published by CMC Publishing, 11642 Otsego St., N. Hollywood CA 91601. Standard script formats and other information for scriptwriters.*

THE COPYRIGHT HANDBOOK: How to Protect and Use Written Works, by *Stephen Fishman, published by Nolo Press, 950 Parker St., Berkeley CA 94710.*

THE CRAFT OF THE SCREENWRITER, by *John Brady, published by Simon & Schuster, 1230 Avenue of the Americas, New York NY 10020.*

CREATIVE SCREENWRITING, published by the *Creative Screenwriters Group, 518 Ninth St., NE, Suite 308, Washington D.C. 20002. Quarterly journal publishing critical, theoretical, historical and practical essays on all aspects of writing for the screen. Also publishes a quarterly newsletter.*

DAILY VARIETY, *5700 Wilshire Blvd., Los Angeles CA 90036. Publication featuring information on the entertainment business, trade oriented.*

DRAMATISTS SOURCEBOOK, edited by *Angela E. Mitchell and Gilliam Richards, published by Theatre Communications Group, Inc., 355 Lexington Ave., New York NY 10017. Directory listing opportunities for playwrights. Includes agents.*

THE DRAMATIST'S TOOLKIT, by *Jeffrey Sweet, published by Heinemann, 361 Hanover St., Portsmouth NH 03801-3912. Guide to the craft of dramatic writing.*

EDITOR & PUBLISHER, *The Editor & Publisher Co., Inc., 11 W. 19th St., New York NY 10011. Weekly magazine covering latest developments in journalism and newspaper production.*

ESSENTIAL SOFTWARE FOR WRITERS, by *Hy Bender, published by Writer's Digest Books, 1507 Dana Ave., Cincinnati OH 45207. Examines software suited for book writers, screenwriters and playwrights.*

FOUR SCREENPLAYS, by *Syd Field, published by Dell, 1540 Broadway, New York NY 10036. A frame-by-frame look at four movies and why they work.*

FROM SCRIPT TO SCREEN, by *Linda Seger and Edward Jay Whetmore, published by Henry Holt & Co., Inc. 115 W. 18th St., New York NY 10011.*

FUNNY BUSINESS, by *Sol Saks, published by Lone Eagle Publishing Co., 2337 Roscomare Rd., Suite 9, Los Angeles CA 90077-1851. How to write comedy and sell it.*

GETTING YOUR SCRIPT THROUGH THE HOLLYWOOD MAZE, by *Linda Stuart, published by Acrobat Books, P.O. Box 870, Venice CA 90294. An insider's guide to writing and marketing movie scripts.*

THE GUIDE TO WRITERS CONFERENCES, published by *ShawGuides, Suite 1406, Biltmore Way, Coral Gables FL 33134. Directory of writers' conferences.*

HOLLYWOOD AGENTS & MANAGERS DIRECTORY, published by *Hollywood Creative Directory, 3000 Olympic Blvd., Suite 2413, Santa Monica CA 90404. Triannual directory of agents and managers.*

HOLLYWOOD CREATIVE DIRECTORY, published by *Hollywood Creative Directory, 3000 Olympic Blvd., Suite 2413, Santa Monica CA 90404. Triannual directory of producers, studios, TV and cable networks, and companies with studio deals, listing addresses, phones, produced credits and staff members.*

THE HOLLYWOOD JOB-HUNTER'S SURVIVAL GUIDE, by *Hugh Taylor, published by Lone Eagle Publishing, 2337 Roscomare Rd., Suite 9, Los Angeles CA 90077-1851. Finding, getting and keeping entry-level jobs in Hollywood.*

HOLLYWOOD REPORTER, *Billboard Publications, Inc., 6715 Sunset Blvd., Hollywood CA 90028. Publication covering news and information on the entertainment industry. Includes information on scriptwriters and sales of scripts.*

HOLLYWOOD SCRIPTWRITER, *#385, 1626 N. Wilcox, Hollywood CA 90028. Newsletter featuring information for scriptwriters. Includes an annual agents issue.*

HOW TO BE YOUR OWN LITERARY AGENT, *by Richard Curtis, published by Houghton Mifflin Company, 2 Park St., Boston MA 02108. An insider's guide to contract negotiations, deal-making and the business of publishing.*

HOW TO BREAK IN FROM WHEREVER YOU ARE, *audiotape, by David Dworski, published by Dworski & Associates, 821 Nowita Place, Venice CA 90291. (310)823-5181. $29, including shipping and handling. "The Pitching Workshop" teaches you how to sell your scripts, your ideas, and yourself. "Your Creative Career" gives break-in shortcuts to accelerate your writing life.*

HOW TO FIND AND WORK WITH A LITERARY AGENT *audiotape, by Anita Diamant, published by Writer's AudioShop, 204 E. 35th St., Austin TX 78705. A comprehensive look at the author/agent relationship from a respected agent with over 30 years' experience.*

HOW TO MAKE IT IN HOLLYWOOD, *by Linda Buzzell, published by Harper Perennial, 10 E. 53rd St., New York NY 10022. Opportunities in Hollywood for a wide variety of areas, including writing.*

HOW TO PITCH & SELL YOUR TV SCRIPT, *by David Silver, published by Writer's Digest Books, 1507 Dana Ave., Cincinnati OH 45207. Information on marketing your television scripts. Includes information on working with script agents.*

HOW TO SELL YOUR IDEA TO HOLLYWOOD, *by Robert Kosberg with Mim Eichler, published by Harper-Collins, 10 E. 53rd St., New York NY 10022. How to create and develop your own unique movie ideas and sell them to studios.*

HOW TO SELL YOUR SCREENPLAY, *by Carl Sautter, published by New Chapter Press, 381 Park Ave., S., Suite 1122, New York NY 10016. How Hollywood works.*

HOW TO WRITE A BOOK PROPOSAL, *by Michael Larsen, published by Writer's Digest Books, 1507 Dana Ave., Cincinnati OH 45207. How to put together a professional-quality book proposal package.*

HOW TO WRITE IRRESISTIBLE QUERY LETTERS, *by Lisa Collier Cool, published by Writer's Digest Books, 1507 Dana Ave., Cincinnati OH 45207. How to write professional, effective queries.*

LEW HUNTER'S SCREENWRITING 434, *by Lew Hunter, published by Perigee Books, a division of Berkley, 200 Madison Ave,. New York NY 10016. Hunter, chairman of UCLA's Screenwriting Department, outlines the graduate workshop on writing for the movies.*

THE INSIDER'S GUIDE TO BOOK EDITORS, PUBLISHERS & LITERARY AGENTS, *by Jeff Herman, published by Prima Communications, Box 1260, Rocklin CA 95677-1260. An inside look at the publishing industry. Includes information on agents.*

LITERARY AGENTS: A WRITER'S GUIDE, *by Adam Begley, published by Poets & Writer's, 72 Spring St., New York NY 10012. Directory of literary agents with articles on working with agents.*

LITERARY MARKET PLACE (LMP), *R.R. Bowker Company, 121 Chanlon Road, New Providence NJ 07974. Book publishing industry directory. In addition to publishing companies, includes a list of literary agents and a list of art representatives.*

MAKING A GOOD SCRIPT GREAT, *by Dr. Linda Seger, published by Samuel French Trade, 7623 Sunset Blvd., Hollywood CA 90046. Information on improving your script.*

MANUSCRIPT SUBMISSION, *by Scott Edelstein, published by Writer's Digest Books, 1507 Dana Ave., Cincinnati OH 45207. How to prepare submissions for publishers and agents.*

THE NEW SCREENWRITER LOOKS AT THE NEW SCREENWRITER, *by William Froug, published by Silman-James Press, 1181 Angelo Dr., Beverly Hills, CA 90210. A second volume of interviews with Hollywood screenwriters discussing their craft.*

NEW YORK SCREENWRITER, *published by the New York Screenwriter, 548 8th Ave., Suite 401, New York NY 10018. Newsletter published ten times a year featuring interviews and articles of interest to screenwriters, from software reviews to agency profiles. Annual guide to products and services.*

NOVEL & SHORT STORY WRITER'S MARKET, *edited by Robin Gee, published by Writer's Digest Books, 1507 Dana Ave., Cincinnati OH 45207. Annual market directory for fiction writers. Includes information on the writing business, organizations and conferences for fiction writers.*

POETS AND WRITERS, *72 Spring St., New York NY 10012. Magazine for writers. Includes interviews and articles of interest to poets and literary writers. Poets and Writers also publishes several books and directories for writers.*

PREMIERE MAGAZINE, *published by K-III Magazines, 2 Park Ave., New York NY 10016. Monthly magazine covering current news on feature films and the personalities involved.*

PROFESSIONAL WRITER'S GUIDE, *revised and expanded edition, edited by Donald Bower and James Lee Young, National Writers Press, Suite 424, 1450 S. Havana, Aurora CO 80012. The basics of starting and building a writing career.*

PUBLISHERS WEEKLY, *249 W. 17th St., New York NY 10011. Weekly magazine covering industry trends and news in the book publishing industry. Contains announcements of new agencies.*

ROSS REPORTS, *published by Television Index, Inc. 40-29 27th St., Long Island City, NY 11101. Monthly booklet listing opportunities for actors, writers, technicians and TV personnel in New York.*

SCREENWRITE NOW!, *published by Forum, P.O. Box 7, Long Green Pike, Baldwin MD 21013-0007. Quarterly magazine with articles and interviews on writing and marketing screenplays.*

THE SCREENWRITER LOOKS AT THE SCREENWRITER, *by William Froug, published by Silman-James Press, 1191 Angelo Dr., Beverly Hills, CA 90210. Twelve screenwriters discuss their craft.*

THE SCREENWRITER'S WORKBOOK, *by Syd Field, published by Dell, 1540 Broadway, New York NY 10036. Exercises and step-by step instruction in creating a successful screenplay.*

SCREENWRITING TRICKS OF THE TRADE, *by William Froug, published by Silman James Press, 1181 Angelo Dr., Beverly Hills CA 90210. A guide to writing and selling scripts.*

SCREENWRITING, *by Richard Walter, published by Plume, an imprint of Penguin USA, 375 Hudson St.,*

New York NY 10014. The Chairman of Department of Film and Television at UCLA shows how to write a script that sells.

THE SCRIPT IS FINISHED, NOW WHAT DO I DO?, *by K. Callan, published by Sweden Press, Box 1612, Studio City CA 91614. Numerous interviews with agents on issues such as query letters, meetings, agent/ author relationships and what to expect, as well as agency listings.*

SELLING YOUR SCREENPLAY, *by Cynthia Whitcomb, published by Crown, 201 E. 50th St., New York NY 10022. A guide to screenwriting, with information on agents, producers, spec scripts and what to expect.*

SUCCESSFUL SCRIPTWRITING, *by Jurgen Wolff and Kerry Cox, published by Writer's Digest Books, 1507 Dana Ave., Cincinnati OH 45207. Includes information on the movie and television business, as well as tips on marketing and selling scripts.*

THEATRE DIRECTORY, *Theatre Communications Group, Inc., 355 Lexington Ave., New York NY 10017. Directory listing theaters in the U.S.*

TOP SECRETS: SCREENWRITING, *by Jurgen Wolff & Kerry Cox, published by Lone Eagle Publishing, 2337 Roscomare Rd., Suite 9, Los Angeles CA 90077-1851. Interviews with top screenwriters and commentary on their work, with advice and guidance to aspiring screenwriters.*

THE TV SCRIPTWRITER'S HANDBOOK, *by Alfred Brenner, published by Writer's Digest Books, 1507 Dana Ave., Cincinnati OH 45207. Includes all aspects of writing for television including marketing scripts.*

WORKING IN HOLLYWOOD, *by Alexandra Brouwer and Thomas Lee Wright, published by Avon, 1350 Avenue of the Americas, New York NY 10019. Insiders discuss what they do and how they got there.*

THE WRITER, *120 Boylston St., Boston MA 02116. Magazine for writers. Includes articles on technique and writing issues.*

THE WRITER'S BOOK OF CHECKLISTS, *by Scott Edelstein, published by Writer's Digest Books, 1507 Dana Ave., Cincinnati OH 45207. Checklists on topics of concern to writers, from legal matters to qualities of a good agent.*

WRITER'S DIGEST, *1507 Dana Ave., Cincinnati OH 45207. Monthly magazine for writers. Includes technique, lifestyle, business and market information.*

THE WRITER'S DIGEST GUIDE TO MANUSCRIPT FORMATS, *by Dian Dincin Buchman and Seli Groves, published by Writer's Digest Books, 1507 Dana Ave., Cincinnati OH 45207. Models for all types of manuscript formats including query and cover letters to editors, publishers and agents.*

WRITER'S ESSENTIAL DESK REFERENCE, *edited by Glenda Tennant Neff, published by Writer's Digest Books, 1507 Dana Ave., Cincinnati OH 45207. Reference guide for writers including business, tax and legal information for both U.S. and Canadian writers.*

A WRITER'S GUIDE TO CONTRACT NEGOTIATIONS, *by Richard Balkin, published by Writer's Digest Books, 1507 Dana Ave., Cincinnati OH 45207. Written by an agent, this is an insider's view of book contract negotiations.*

WRITERS GUILD OF AMERICA, *Membership Directory, published by the Writers Guild of America, 8955 Beverly Blvd., West Hollywood CA 90048. Member writers of WGA east and west, including list of signatory agencies.*

THE WRITER'S LEGAL COMPANION, *by Brad Bunnin and Peter Beren, published by Addison Wesley, Jacob Way, Reading MA 01867. Legal guide for writers. Bunnin is a publishing-industry lawyer.*

WRITER'S MARKET, *edited by Mark Garvey, published by Writer's Digest Books, 1507 Dana Ave., Cincinnati OH 45207. Annual market directory for writers and scriptwriters. Includes information on the writing business.*

WRITING SCREENPLAYS THAT SELL, *by Michael Hauge, published by HarperCollins, 10 E. 53rd St., New York NY 10022.*

Bookstores and Catalogs

BOOK CITY, *Dept. 101, 308 N. San Fernando Blvd., Burbank CA 91502. (800)4-CINEMA. Offers hundreds of movie and TV scripts and books on screenwriting. Catalog $2.50.*

SAMUEL FRENCH THEATRE & FILM BOOKSHOPS, *7623 Sunset Blvd., Hollywood CA 90046. (213)876-0570. Books on film, screenwriting, and making movies, as well as scripts for TV and movies.*

SCRIPT CITY, *8033 Sunset Blvd., Suite 1500, Hollywood CA 90046. (800)676-2522. Offers hundreds of movie and TV scripts, books on writing and screenwriting, as well as movie paraphenalia. Catalog $2.*

THE WRITE STUFF, *21115 Devonshire St., #182, Chatsworth CA 91311. (800)989-8833. Discount catalog of books, audiotapes and computer software for writers of all genres.*

Glossary

Above the line. A budgetary term for movies and TV. The line refers to money budgeted for creative talent, such as actors, writers, directors and producers.

Advance. Money that a publisher pays a writer prior to publication of a book, usually paid in installments, such as one-half upon signing the contract; one-half upon delivery of the complete, satisfactory manuscript. An advance is paid against the royalty money to be earned by the book. Agents take their percentage off the top of the advance as well as from the royalties earned.

Auction. Publishers sometimes bid for the acquisition of a book manuscript with excellent sales prospects. The bids are for the amount of the author's advance, guaranteed dollar amounts, advertising and promotional expenses, royalty percentage, etc.

Backlist. Those books still in print from previous years' publication.

Backstory. The history of what has happened before the action in your script takes place, affecting a character's current behavior.

Beat. Major plot points of a story.

Below the line. A budgetary term for movies and TV, referring to production costs, including production manager, cinematographer, editor and crew members such as gaffers, grips, set designers, make-up etc.

Bible. The collected background information on all characters and storylines of all existing episodes, as well as projections of future plots.

Bio. Brief (usually one page) background information about an artist, writer or photographer. Includes work and educational experience.

Boilerplate. A standardized publishing contract. "Our standard contract" usually means the boilerplate without any changes. Most authors and agents make many changes on the boilerplate before accepting the contract.

Business-size envelope. Also known as a #10 envelope.

Castable. A script with attractive roles for known actors.

Category fiction. A term used to include all various types of fiction. See *genre*.

Client. When referring to a literary or script agent "client" is used to mean the writer whose work the agent is handling.

Clips. Writing samples, usually from newspapers or magazines, of your published work.

Commercial novel. A novel designed to appeal to a broad audience. It often falls into a category or genre such as western, romance, mystery, science fiction and horror. See also *genre*.

Concept. A statement that summarizes a screenplay or teleplay—before the treatment is written.

Contributor's copies. Copies of the author's book sent to the author. The number of contributor's copies is often negotiated in the publishing contract.

Copyediting. Editing of a manuscript for writing style, grammar, punctuation and factual accuracy. Some agents offer this service.

Cover letter. A brief descriptive letter sent with a manuscript submitted to an agent or publisher.

Coverage. A brief synopsis and analysis of a script, provided by a reader to a buyer considering purchasing the work.

Critiquing service. A service offered by some agents in which writers pay a fee for comments on the saleability or other qualities of their manuscript. Sometimes the critique includes suggestions on how to improve the work. Fees vary, as do the quality of the critiques.

D person. Development person. Includes readers and story editors through creative executives who work in development and acquisition of properties for TV and movies.

Development. The process where writers present ideas to producers overseeing the developing script through various stages to finished product.

Division. An unincorporated branch of a company.

Docudrama. A fictional film rendition of recent newsmaking events or people.

Editing service. A service offered by some agents in which writers pay a fee—either lump sum or per-page—to have their manuscript edited. The quality and extent of the editing varies from agency to agency.

Elements. Actors, directors and producers attached to a project to make an attractive package. Writers are rarely elements.

El-hi. Elementary to high school. A term used to indicate reading or interest level.

Episodic drama. Hour-long continuing TV show, often shown at 10 o'clock.

Evaluation fees. Fees an agent may charge to evaluate material. The extent and quality of this evaluation varies, but comments usually concern the saleability of the manuscript.

Exclusive. Offering a manuscript, usually for a set period of time, to just one agent and guaranteeing that agent is the only one looking at the manuscript.

Floor bid. If a publisher is very interested in a manuscript he may offer to enter a floor bid when the book goes to auction. The publisher sits out of the auction, but agrees to take the book by topping the highest bid by an agreed-upon percentage (usually 10 percent).

Foreign rights agent. An agent who handles selling the rights to a country other than that of the first book agent. Usually an additional percentage (about 5 percent) will be added on to the first book agent's commission to cover the foreign rights agent.

Genre. Refers to either a general classification of writing such as a novel, poem or short story or to the categories within those classifications, such as problem novels or sonnets. Genre fiction is a term that covers various types of commercial novels such as mystery, romance, western, science fiction or horror.

Ghosting or ghost writing. When a writer puts into literary form the words, ideas or knowledge of another person under that person's name it is called ghostwriting. Some agents offer this service. Others will pair ghostwriters with celebrities or experts.

Green light. To give the go-ahead to a movie or TV project.

Half-hour. A 30-minute TV show, also known as a sitcom.

High concept. A story idea easily expressed in a quick, one-line description.

Imprint. The name applied to a publisher's specific line of books (e.g., Lisa Drew, an imprint of Simon & Schuster).

IRC. International Reply Coupons; purchased at a post office to enclose with material sent outside your country to cover the cost of return postage. The recipient can turn in the coupons for stamps in their own country.

Log line. A one-line description of a plot as it might appear in *TV Guide*.

Long-form TV. Movies of the week or miniseries.

Mainstream fiction. Fiction on subjects or trends that transcend popular novel categories such as mystery or romance. Using conventional methods, this kind of fiction tells stories about people and their conflicts.

Marketing fee. Fee charged by some agents to cover marketing expenses. It may be used to cover postage, telephone calls, faxes, photocopying or any other expense incurred in marketing a manuscript.

Mass market paperbacks. Softcover book, usually around 4 × 7, on a popular subject directed at a general audience and sold in groceries and drugstores as well as bookstores.

MFTS. Made for TV series. A series developed for television also known as episodics.

Middle reader. The general classification of books written for readers 9-11 years old.

Midlist. Those titles on a publisher's list expected to have limited sales. Midlist books are mainstream, not literary, scholarly or genre, and are usually written by new or relatively unknown writers.

Miniseries. A limited dramatic series written for television, often based on a popular novel.

MOW. Movie of the week. A movie script written especially for television, usually seven acts with time for commercial breaks. Topics are often contemporary, sometimes controversial, fictional accounts. Also known as a made-for-TV-movie.

Net receipts. One method of royalty payment based on the amount of money a book publisher receives on the sale of the book after the booksellers' discounts, special sales discounts and returned copies.

Novelization. A novel created from the script of a popular movie, usually called a movie "tie-in" and published in paperback.

Novella. A short novel or long short story, usually 7,000 to 15,000 words. Also,called a novelette.

Option clause. A contract clause giving a publisher the right to publish an author's next book.

Outline. A summary of a book's contents in 5 to 15 double-spaced pages; often in the form of chapter headings with a descriptive sentence or two under each one to show the scope of the book. A screenplay's or teleplay's outline is a scene-by-scene narrative description of the story (10-15 pages for a ½-hour teleplay; 15-25 pages for 1-hour; 25-40 pages for 90 minutes and 40-60 pages for a 2-hour feature film or teleplay).

Over-the-transom. Slang for the path of an unsolicited manuscript into the slush pile.

Packaging. The process of putting elements together, increasing the chances of a project being made.

Picture book. A type of book aimed at the preschool to 8-year-old that tells the story primarily or entirely with artwork. Agents and reps interested in selling to publishers of these books often handle both artists and writers.

Pitch. The process where a writer meets with a producer and briefly outlines ideas that could be developed if the writer is hired to write a script for the project.

Proofreading. Close reading and correction of a manuscript's typographical errors. A few agents offer this service for a fee.

Property. Books or scripts forming the basis for a movie or TV project.

Proposal. An offer to an editor or publisher to write a specific work, usually a package consisting of an outline and sample chapters.

Prospectus. A preliminary, written description of a book, usually one page in length.

Query. A letter written to an agent or a potential market, to elicit interest in a writer's work.

Reader. A person employed by an agent or buyer to go through the slush pile of scripts and select those worth considering.

Release. A statement that your idea is original, has never been sold to anyone else and that you are selling negotiated rights to the idea upon payment.

Remainders. Leftover copies of an out-of-print or slow-selling book, which can be purchased from the publisher at a reduced rate. Depending on the author's contract, a reduced royalty or no royalty is paid on remaindered books.

Reporting time. The time it takes the agent to get back to you on your query or submission.

Royalties. A percentage of the retail price paid to the author for each copy of the book that is sold. Agents take their percentage from the royalties earned as well as from the advance.

SASE. Self-addressed, stamped envelope. This or a self-addressed, stamped postcard should be included with all correspondence.

Scholarly books. Books written for an academic or research audience. These are usually heavily researched, technical and often contain terms used only within a specific field.

Screenplay. Script for a film intended to be shown in movie theaters.

Script. Broad term covering teleplay, screenplay or stage play. Sometimes used as a shortened version of the word "manuscript" when referring to books.

Show runner. A TV writer-producer with responsibility over an entire TV series.

Simultaneous submission. Sending the same manuscript to several agents or publishers at the same time. Simultaneous query letters are common, but simultaneous submissions are unacceptable to many agents or publishers.

Sitcom. Situation comedy. Episodic comedy script for a television series. Term comes from the characters dealing with various situations with humorous results.

Slush pile. A stack of unsolicited submissions in the office of an editor, agent or publisher.

Spec script. A script written on speculation without expectation of a sale.

Standard commission. The commission an agent earns on the sales of a manuscript or script. For literary agents, this commission percentage (usually between 10 and 20 percent) is taken from the advance and royalties paid to the writer. For script agents, the commission is taken from script sales; if handling plays, agents take a percentage from the box office proceeds.

Story analyst. See reader.

Storyboards. Series of panels which illustrates a progressive sequence or graphics and story copy for a TV commercial, film or filmstrip.

Subagent. An agent who handles certain subsidiary rights. This agent usually works in conjunction with the agent who has handled the book rights and the percentage paid the book agent is increased to cover paying the subagent.

Subsidiary. An incorporated branch of a company or conglomerate (e.g. Alfred Knopf, Inc., is a subsidiary of Random House, Inc.)

Subsidiary rights. All rights other than book publishing rights included in a book publishing contract, such as paperback rights, bookclub rights, movie rights. Part of an agent's job is to negotiate those rights and advise you on which to sell and which to keep.

Synopsis. A brief summary of a story, novel or play. As a part of a book proposal, it is a comprehensive summary condensed in a page or page and a half, single-spaced. See also *outline*.

Tearsheet. Published samples of your work, usually pages torn from a magazine.

Textbook. Book used in a classroom on the elementary, high school or college level.

Trade book. Either a hard cover or soft cover book; subject matter frequently concerns a special interest for a general audience; sold mainly in bookstores.

Trade paperback. A softbound volume, usually around 5 × 8, published and designed for the general public, available mainly in bookstores.

Treatment. Synopsis of a television or film script (40-60 pages for a 2-hour feature film or teleplay).

Turnaround. When a script has been in development but not made in the time allotted, it can be put back on the market. Scripts in turnaround can be very desireable to other buyers since some of the problems have already been worked out by previous development personnel.

Unsolicited manuscript. An unrequested manuscript sent to an editor, agent or publisher.

Young adult. The general classification of books written for readers age 12-18.

Young reader. Books written for readers 5-8 years old, where artwork only supports the text.

Table of Acronyms

The organizations and their acronyms listed below are frequently referred to in the listings and are widely used in the industries of agenting and writing.

AAP	American Association of Publishers
AAR	Association of Author's Representatives (1991 merger of ILAA and SAR)
ABA	American Booksellers Association
ABWA	Associated Business Writers of America
AEB	Association of Editorial Businesses
AFTRA	American Federation of TV and Radio Artists
AGVA	American Guild of Variety Artists
AMWA	American Medical Writer's Association
ASJA	American Society of Journalists and Authors
ATA	Association of Talent Agents
AWA	Aviation/Space Writers Association
CAA	Canadian Authors Association
DGA	Director's Guild of America
GWAA	Garden Writers Association of America
HWA	Horror Writers of America
IACP	International Association of Culinary Professionals
ILAA	Independent Literary Agents Association (see AAR)
MWA	Mystery Writers of America, Inc.
NASW	National Association of Science Writers
NLAPW	National League of American Pen Women
NWA	National Writers Association
OWAA	Outdoor Writers Association of America, Inc.
RWA	Romance Writers of America
SAG	Screen Actor's Guild
SAR	Society of Authors' Representatives (see AAR)
SATW	Society of American Travel Writers
SCBWI	Society of Children's Book Writers & Illustrators
SFWA	Science Fiction and Fantasy Writers of America
WGA	Writers Guild of America
WIA	Women in the Arts Foundation, Inc.
WIF	Women in Film
WICI	Women in Communications, Inc.
WIW	Washington Independent Writers
WNBA	Women's National Book Association
WRW	Washington Romance Writers (chapter of RWA)
WWA	Western Writers of America

Indexes

Subject Index

The subject index is divided into nonfiction and fiction subject categories for each section — Nonfee-charging Literary Agents, Fee-charging Literary Agents and Script Agents. To find an agent interested in the type of manuscript you've written, see the appropriate sections under subject headings that best describe your work. Check the Listings Index for the page number of the agent's listing. Agents who are open to most fiction or nonfiction subjects appear in the "Open" heading.

Nonfee-charging literary agents/Fiction

Action/adventure. Acton, Leone, Hanson & Jaffe; Adler & Robin Books; Allan Agency, Lee; Allen, Literary Agency, James; Allen Literary Agency, Linda; Amsterdam Agency, Marcia; Baldi Literary Agency, Malaga; Beekman Literary Agency; Behar Literary Agency, Josh; Bova Literary Agency, Barbara; Brandt & Brandt Literary Agents; Carvainis Agency, Maria; Castiglia Literary Agency, Julie; Circle of Confusion; Ciske Literary Agency, Francine; Curtis Assoc., Richard; Diamant, Writer's Workshop, Anita; Diamond Literary Agency; Doyen Literary Services; Ducas, Robert; Dupree/Miller and Assoc. Literary; Dystel Literary Management, Jane; Elmo Agency , Ann; Emerald Literary Agency; Esquire Literary Productions; Farber Literary Agency; Flannery Literary; Garon-Brooke Assoc., Jay; Goldfarb & Graybill, Attorneys at Law; Green, Literary Agent, Randall Elisha; Greenburger Assoc., Sanford J.; Gusay Literary Agency, Charlotte; Halsey Agency, Reece; Hanson Agency; Hawkins & Assoc., John; Hegler Literary Agency, Gary L.; Hendin Literary, David; Herner Rights Agency, Susan; Kidde, Hoyt & Picard; Klinger, Harvey; Lampack Agency, Peter; Lantz-Joy Harris Literary Agency, Robert; Larsen/Elizabeth Pomada Literary Agents, Michael; Lasher Agency, Maureen; Lincoln Literary Agency, Ray; Lindstrom Literary Group; Literary Group; Love Literary Agency, Nancy; Lyceum Creative Properties; McBride Literary Agency, Margret; Madsen Agency, Robert; Mainhardt Agency, Ricia; Manus & Assoc. Literary Agency ; Morrison, Henry; Mura Enterprises, Dee; Naggar Literary Agency, Jean V.; Nazor Literary Agency, Karen; Norma-Lewis Agency; Otitis Media; Otte Co.; Parks Agency, Richard; Pelter, Rodney; Perkins Assoc., L.; Picard Literary Agent, Alison J.; Pocono Literary Agency; Potomac Literary Agency; Printed Tree; Quicksilver Books-Literary Agents; Rees Literary Agency, Helen; Renaissance: A Literary/Talent Agency; Rock Literary Agency; Sanders Literary Agency, Victoria; Schmidt Literary Agency, Harold; Seymour Agency; Siegel Literary Agency, Bobbe; Sierra Literary Agency; Swanson, H.N.; Wald Assoc., Mary Jack; Weiner Literary Agency, Cherry; Westchester Literary Agency; Wreschner, Authors' Representative, Ruth; Wright Representatives, Ann; Zeckendorf Assoc., Susan

Cartoon/comic. Axelrod Agency; Baldi Literary Agency, Malaga; Beekman Literary Agency; Circle of Confusion; Dupree/Miller and Assoc. Literary; Gusay Literary Agency, Charlotte; Hawkins & Assoc., John; Hendin Literary, David; Lantz-Joy Harris Literary Agency, Robert; Levant & Wales, Literary Agency; Literary Group; Lyceum Creative Properties; Mainhardt Agency, Ricia; Nazor Literary Agency, Karen; Pelter, Rodney; Picard Literary Agent, Alison J.; Rock Literary Agency; Van der Leun & Assoc.

Confessional. Circle of Confusion; Gusay Literary Agency, Charlotte; Lantz-Joy Harris Literary Agency, Robert; Manus & Assoc. Literary Agency; March Tenth; Pelter, Rodney; Rock Literary Agency; Swanson, H.N.

Contemporary issues. Acton, Leone, Hanson & Jaffe; Adler & Robin Books; Agents for Medical and Mental Health Professionals; Allen Literary Agency, Linda; Baldi Literary Agency, Malaga; Bartczak Assoc., Gene; Beekman Literary Agency; Blassingame Spectrum Corp.; Boates Literary Agency, Reid; Bova Literary Agency, Barbara; Brandt Agency, Joan; Brandt & Brandt Literary Agents; Brown Assoc., Marie; Cantrell-Colas, Literary Agency; Castiglia Literary Agency, Julie; Circle of Confusion; de la Haba Agency, Lois; Diamant, Writer's Workshop, Anita; Diamond Literary Agency; Dijkstra Literary Agency, Sandra;. Doyen Literary Services; Ducas, Robert; Dupree/Miller and Assoc. Literary; Dystel Literary Management, Jane; Elmo Agency, Ann; Emerald Literary Agency; Esquire Literary Productions; Farber Literary Agency; Feiler Literary Agency, Florence; Flaherty, Literary Agent, Joyce A.; Flannery Literary; Garon-Brooke Assoc., Jay; Goldfarb & Graybill; Gordon Agency, Charlotte; Green, Literary Agent, Randall Elisha; Greenburger Assoc., Sanford J.; Gusay Literary Agency, Charlotte; Halsey Agency, Reece; Hanson Agency; Hawkins & Assoc., John; Hendin Literary, David; Herner Rights Agency, Susan; Kidde, Hoyt & Picard; Kouts, Literary Agent, Barbara S.; Kroll Literary Agency, Edite; Lampack Agency, Peter; Lantz-Joy Harris Literary

Agency, Robert; Larsen/Elizabeth Pomada Literary Agents, Michael; Lasher Agency, Maureen; Lincoln Literary Agency, Ray; Lindstrom Literary Group; Literary Group; Love Literary Agency, Nancy; Lyceum Creative Properties; McGrath, Helen; Mainhardt Agency, Ricia; Manus & Assoc. Literary Agency; Markowitz Literary Agency, Barbara; Marmur Assoc., Mildred; Miller Assoc., Roberta D.; Multimedia Product Development; Mura Enterprises, Dee; Naggar Literary Agency, Jean V.; Nazor Literary Agency, Karen; Norma-Lewis Agency; Novak III Literary Representation, Edward A.; Otte Co.; Parks Agency, Richard; Pelter, Rodney; Picard Literary Agent, Alison J.; Potomac Literary Agency, ; Printed Tree; Pryor, Roberta; Publishing Services; Quicksilver Books-Literary Agents; Raymond, Literary Agent, Charlotte Cecil; Rees Literary Agency, Helen; Rock Literary Agency; Rose Literary Agency; Russell-Simenauer Literary Agency; Sanders Literary Agency, Victoria; Schmidt Literary Agency, Harold; Schulman, A Literary Agency, Susan; Schwartz Agency, Laurens R.; Seligman, Literary Agent, Lynn; Shepard Agency; Siegel Literary Agency, Bobbe; Singer Literary Agency, Evelyn; Spitzer Literary Agency, Philip G.; Stauffer Assoc., Nancy; Stepping Stone; Stern Literary Agency (TX), Gloria; Swanson, H.N.; Van der Leun & Assoc.; Wald Assoc., Mary Jack; Watkins Loomis Agency; Wecksler-Incomco; Weiner Literary Agency, Cherry; Weingel-Fidel Agency; Westchester Literary Agency; Wieser & Wieser; Witherspoon & Assoc.; Wreschner, Authors' Representative, Ruth; Zeckendorf Assoc., Susan; Ziegler Literary Agency, George

Detective/police/crime. Acton, Leone, Hanson & Jaffe; Adler & Robin Books ; Allan Agency, Lee; Allen, Literary Agency, James; Allen Literary Agency, Linda; Amsterdam Agency, Marcia; Authors' Literary Agency; Axelrod Agency; Baldi Literary Agency, Malaga; Beekman Literary Agency; Behar Literary Agency, Josh; Boates Literary Agency, Reid; Bova Literary Agency, Barbara; Brandt Agency, Joan; Brandt & Brandt Literary Agents; Bykofsky Assoc., Sheree; Cantrell-Colas, Literary Agency; Carvainis Agency, Maria; Castiglia Literary Agency, Julie; Circle of Confusion; Cohen, Literary Agency, Ruth; Collin Literary Agent, Frances; Curtis Assoc., Richard; de la Haba Agency, Lois; Diamant, Writer's Workshop, Anita; Diamond Literary Agency (CO); Dijkstra Literary Agency, Sandra; Doyen Literary Services, ; Ducas, Robert; Dupree/Miller and Assoc. Literary; Dystel Literary Management, Jane; Ellenberg Literary Agency, Ethan; Elmo Agency, Ann; Emerald Literary Agency; Esquire Literary Productions; Farber Literary Agency; Feiler Literary Agency, Florence; Flaherty, Literary Agent, Joyce A.; Garon-Brooke Assoc., Jay; Goddard, Connie: Book Development; Goldfarb & Graybill; Green, Literary Agent, Randall Elisha; Greenburger Assoc., Sanford J.; Gusay Literary Agency, Charlotte; Halsey Agency, Reece; Hawkins & Assoc., John; Hegler Literary Agency, Gary L.; Hendin Literary, David; Herner Rights Agency, Susan; Hull House Literary Agency; Img-Julian Bach Literary Agency; J de S Assoc.; Kidde, Hoyt & Picard; Klinger, Harvey; Lampack Agency, Peter; Lantz-Joy Harris Literary Agency, Robert; Larsen/Elizabeth Pomada Literary Agents, Michael; Lasher Agency, Maureen; Lincoln Literary Agency, Ray; Lindstrom Literary Group; Literary Group; Love Literary Agency, Nancy; Lyceum Creative Properties; Maass Literary Agency, Donald; McBride Literary Agency, Margret; McGrath, Helen; Mainhardt Agency, Ricia; Manus & Assoc. Literary Agency; Markowitz Literary Agency, Barbara; Marmur Assoc., Mildred; Miller Assoc., Roberta D.; Morhaim Literary Agency, Howard; Morrison, Henry; Multimedia Product Development; Mura Enterprises, Dee; Naggar Literary Agency, Jean V.; Norma-Lewis Agency; Novak III Literary Representation, Edward A.; Otte Co.; Parks Agency, Richard; Pelter, Rodney; Perkins Assoc., L.; Picard Literary Agent, Alison J.; Potomac Literary Agency; Protter Literary Agent, Susan Ann; Pryor, Roberta; Rees Literary Agency, Helen; Renaissance: A Literary/Talent Agency; Rock Literary Agency; Rubenstein Literary Agency, Pesha; Russell-Simenauer Literary Agency ; Schlessinger Agency, Blanche; Schmidt Literary Agency, Harold; Schulman, A Literary Agency, Susan; Seligman, Literary Agent, Lynn; Seymour Agency; Siegel Literary Agency, Bobbe; Sierra Literary Agency; Singer Literary Agency, Evelyn; Spitzer Literary Agency, Philip G.; Steele & Co., Lyle; Stern Literary Agency (TX), Gloria; Wald Assoc., Mary Jack; Wallace Literary Agency; Watkins Loomis Agency; Weiner Literary Agency, Cherry; Weingel-Fidel Agency; Westchester Literary Agency; Wieser & Wieser; Witherspoon & Assoc.; Wreschner, Authors' Representative, Ruth; Wright Representatives, Ann; Zeckendorf Assoc., Susan

Erotica. Acton, Leone, Hanson & Jaffe; Agency Chicago; Baldi Literary Agency, Malaga; Beekman Literary Agency; Brandt & Brandt Literary Agents; Circle of Confusion; de la Haba Agency, Lois; Gusay Literary Agency, Charlotte; Lantz-Joy Harris Literary Agency, Robert; Love Literary Agency, Nancy; Lyceum Creative Properties; Mainhardt Agency, Ricia; Nazor Literary Agency, Karen; Pelter, Rodney; Picard Literary Agent, Alison J.; Rock Literary Agency; Swanson, H.N.

Ethnic. Acton, Leone, Hanson & Jaffe; Allen Literary Agency, Linda; Altshuler Literary Agency, Miriam; Baldi Literary Agency, Malaga; Beekman Literary Agency; Brandt & Brandt Literary Agents ; Brown Assoc., Marie; Cantrell-Colas, Literary Agency; Castiglia Literary Agency, Julie; Circle of Confusion; Cohen, Literary Agency, Ruth; Collin Literary Agent, Frances; Crown International Literature and Arts Agency, Bonnie R.; de la Haba Agency, Lois; Dijkstra Literary Agency, Sandra; Doyen Literary Services; Dupree/Miller and Assoc. Literary; Dystel Literary Management, Jane; Elmo Agency, Ann; Eth Literary Representation, Felicia; Flannery Literary; Goldfarb & Graybill; Greenburger Assoc., Sanford J.; Gusay Literary Agency, Charlotte; Halsey Agency, Reece; Hanson Agency; Hawkins & Assoc., John; Herner Rights Agency, Susan; Kidde, Hoyt & Picard; Lantz-Joy Harris Literary Agency, Robert; Larsen/Elizabeth Pomada Literary Agents, Michael; Levant & Wales, Literary Agency; Lichtman, Trister, Singer & Ross; Lincoln Literary Agency, Ray; Lindstrom Literary Group; Literary Group; Love Literary Agency, Nancy; Lyceum Creative Properties; McBride Literary Agency, Margret; Mainhardt Agency, Ricia; Manus & Assoc. Literary Agency; March Tenth; Markowitz Literary Agency, Barbara; Multimedia Product Development; Mura Enterprises, Dee; Naggar Literary Agency, Jean V.; Nazor Literary Agency, Karen; Nine Muses and Apollo; Parks Agency, Richard; Pelter, Rodney; Perkins Assoc., L.; Picard Literary Agent, Alison J.; Potomac Literary Agency;

Publishing Services; Raymond, Literary Agent, Charlotte Cecil; Renaissance: A Literary/Talent Agency; Rock Literary Agency; Rose Literary Agency; Rubenstein Literary Agency, Pesha; Schmidt Literary Agency, Harold; Seligman, Literary Agent, Lynn; Seymour Agency; Siegel Literary Agency, Bobbe; Singer Literary Agency, Evelyn; Spieler, F. Joseph; Stepping Stone; Stern Literary Agency (TX), Gloria; Van der Leun & Assoc.; Wald Assoc., Mary Jack; Watkins Loomis Agency; Witherspoon & Assoc.; Wreschner, Authors' Representative, Ruth; Zeckendorf Assoc., Susan

Experimental. Agency Chicago; Baldi Literary Agency, Malaga; Brandt & Brandt Literary Agents; Cantrell-Colas, Literary Agency; Circle of Confusion; de la Haba Agency , Lois; Diamant, Writer's Workshop, Anita; Doyen Literary Services; Dupree/Miller and Assoc. Literary; Flannery Literary; Gusay Literary Agency, Charlotte; Hanson Agency; Hawkins & Assoc., John; Lantz-Joy Harris Literary Agency, Robert; Larsen/Elizabeth Pomada Literary Agents, Michael; Levant & Wales, Literary Agency; Lyceum Creative Properties; Mura Enterprises, Dee; Pelter, Rodney; Potomac Literary Agency; Rock Literary Agency; Stern Literary Agency (TX), Gloria; Swanson, H.N.; Wald Assoc., Mary Jack

Family saga. Acton, Leone, Hanson & Jaffe; Allen, Literary Agency, James; Axelrod Agency; Beekman Literary Agency; Boates Literary Agency, Reid; Brandt & Brandt Literary Agents ; Brown Assoc., Marie; Cantrell-Colas, Literary Agency; Carvainis Agency, Maria; Castiglia Literary Agency, Julie; Circle of Confusion; Cohen, Literary Agency, Ruth; Collin Literary Agent, Frances; Crown Int'l Literature and Arts Agency, Bonnie R.; Curtis Assoc., Richard; Diamant, Writer's Workshop, Anita; Diamond Literary Agency (CO); Dijkstra Literary Agency, Sandra; Doyen Literary Services; Ducas, Robert; Dupree/Miller and Assoc. Literary; Dystel Literary Management, Jane; Ellenberg Literary Agency, Ethan; Elmo Agency, Ann; Esquire Literary Productions; Feiler Literary Agency, Florence; Flaherty, Literary Agent, Joyce A.; Flannery Literary; Garon-Brooke Assoc., Jay; Gordon Agency, Charlotte; Green, Literary Agent, Randall Elisha; Greenburger Assoc., Sanford J.; Gusay Literary Agency, Charlotte; Halsey Agency, Reece; Hawkins & Assoc., John; Herner Rights Agency, Susan; Klinger, Harvey; Kouts, Literary Agent, Barbara S.; Lampack Agency, Peter; Lantz-Joy Harris Literary Agency , Robert; Larsen/Elizabeth Pomada Literary Agents, Michael; Lasher Agency, Maureen; Lincoln Literary Agency, Ray; Lindstrom Literary Group; Literary Group; Maass Literary Agency, Donald; McGrath, Helen; Mainhardt Agency, Ricia; Manus & Assoc. Literary Agency; March Tenth; Marmur Assoc., Mildred; Morhaim Literary Agency, Howard; Morrison, Henry; Mura Enterprises, Dee; Naggar Literary Agency, Jean V.; Norma-Lewis Agency; Parks Agency, Richard; Pelter, Rodney; Picard Literary Agent, Alison J.; Pocono Literary Agency; Potomac Literary Agency; Printed Tree; Rees Literary Agency, Helen; Renaissance: A Literary/Talent Agency; Rock Literary Agency; Russell-Simenauer Literary Agency ; Sanders Literary Agency, Victoria; Schmidt Literary Agency, Harold; Shepard Agency; Siegel Literary Agency, Bobbe; Spieler, F. Joseph; Steele & Co., Lyle; Swanson , H.N.; Wald Assoc., Mary Jack; Weiner Literary Agency, Cherry; Westchester Literary Agency; Wieser & Wieser; Witherspoon & Assoc.; Wreschner, Authors' Representative, Ruth; Wright Representatives, Ann; Zeckendorf Assoc., Susan; Ziegler Literary Agency, George

Fantasy. Allan Agency, Lee; Allen, Literary Agency, James; Allen Literary Agency, Linda; Behar Literary Agency, Josh; Butler, Art and Literary Agent, Jane; Carvainis Agency, Maria; Circle of Confusion; Collin Literary Agent, Frances; Curtis Assoc., Richard; de la Haba Agency, Lois; Doyen Literary Services; Dupree/Miller and Assoc. Literary; Ellenberg Literary Agency, Ethan; Emerald Literary Agency; Garon-Brooke Assoc., Jay; Gusay Literary Agency, Charlotte; Hanson Agency; Herner Rights Agency, Susan; Larsen/Elizabeth Pomada Literary Agents, Michael; Lincoln Literary Agency, Ray; Lindstrom Literary Group; Literary Group; Lyceum Creative Properties; Maass Literary Agency, Donald; Mainhardt Agency, Ricia; Naggar Literary Agency, Jean V.; Pelter, Rodney; Renaissance: A Literary/Talent Agency; Rock Literary Agency; Schwartz Agency, Laurens R.; Seligman, Literary Agent, Lynn; Siegel Literary Agency, Bobbe; Smith, Literary Agent, Valerie; Swanson, H.N.; Wald Assoc., Mary Jack; Weiner Literary Agency, Cherry; Wright Representatives, Ann

Feminist. Acton, Leone, Hanson & Jaffe; Allen Literary Agency, Linda; Altshuler Literary Agency, Miriam; Baldi Literary Agency, Malaga; Bartczak Assoc., Gene; Beekman Literary Agency; Brandt & Brandt Literary Agents ; Brown Assoc., Marie; Cantrell-Colas, Literary Agency; Castiglia Literary Agency, Julie; Circle of Confusion ; Curtis Assoc., Richard; de la Haba Agency, Lois; Diamant, Writer's Workshop, Anita; Diamond Literary Agency; Dijkstra Literary Agency, Sandra; Dupree/Miller and Assoc. Literary; Eth Literary Representation, Felicia; Flaherty, Literary Agent, Joyce A.; Goldfarb & Graybill; Gordon Agency, Charlotte; Gusay Literary Agency, Charlotte; Hanson Agency; Hawkins & Assoc., John; Hendin Literary, David; Herner Rights Agency, Susan; Kidde, Hoyt & Picard; Kouts, Literary Agent, Barbara S.; Kroll Literary Agency, Edite; Lantz-Joy Harris Literary Agency, Robert; Larsen/Elizabeth Pomada Literary Agents, Michael; Lasher Agency, Maureen; Levant & Wales, Literary Agency; Lichtman, Trister, Singer & Ross; Lincoln Literary Agency, Ray; Literary Group; Lyceum Creative Properties; Mainhardt Agency, Ricia; Manus & Assoc. Literary Agency; Marmur Assoc., Mildred; Naggar Literary Agency, Jean V.; Nazor Literary Agency, Karen; Parks Agency, Richard; Pelter, Rodney; Picard Literary Agent, Alison J.; Potomac Literary Agency; Publishing Services; Rees Literary Agency, Helen; Rock Literary Agency; Rose Literary Agency; Russell-Simenauer Literary Agency ; Sanders Literary Agency, Victoria; Schmidt Literary Agency, Harold; Seligman, Literary Agent, Lynn; Siegel Literary Agency, Bobbe; Sierra Literary Agency; Singer Literary Agency , Evelyn; Spieler, F. Joseph; Stern Literary Agency (TX), Gloria; Swanson , H.N.; Wald Assoc., Mary Jack; Watkins Loomis Agency; Witherspoon & Assoc.; Wright Representatives, Ann

Gay. Allen Literary Agency, Linda; Altshuler Literary Agency, Miriam; Brandt & Brandt Literary Agents;

Brown Assoc., Marie; Castiglia Literary Agency, Julie; Circle of Confusion; de la Haba Agency, Lois; Diamant, Writer's Workshop, Anita; Dupree/Miller and Assoc. Literary; Dystel Literary Management, Jane; Eth Literary Representation, Felicia; Feiler Literary Agency, Florence; Garon-Brooke Assoc., Jay; Goldfarb & Graybill; Gordon Agency, Charlotte; Greenburger Assoc., Sanford J.; Gusay Literary Agency, Charlotte; Hanson Agency; Hawkins & Assoc., John; Hendin Literary, David; Kidde, Hoyt & Picard; Lantz-Joy Harris Literary Agency, Robert; Larsen/Elizabeth Pomada Literary Agents, Michael; Levant & Wales, Literary Agency; Lichtman, Trister, Singer & Ross; Lincoln Literary Agency, Ray; Literary Group; Love Literary Agency, Nancy; Lyceum Creative Properties; Mura Enterprises, Dee; Naggar Literary Agency, Jean V.; Parks Agency, Richard; Perkins Assoc., L.; Picard Literary Agent, Alison J.; Potomac Literary Agency; Raymond, Literary Agent, Charlotte Cecil; Rock Literary Agency; Rose Literary Agency; Russell-Simenauer Literary Agency ; Sanders Literary Agency, Victoria; Seligman, Literary Agent, Lynn; Spieler, F. Joseph; Steele & Co., Lyle; Swanson, H.N.; Wald Assoc., Mary Jack; Watkins Loomis Agency, ; Westchester Literary Agency; Witherspoon & Assoc.; Wreschner, Authors' Representative, Ruth; Wright Representatives, Ann; Ziegler Literary Agency, George

Glitz. Acton, Leone, Hanson & Jaffe; Allan Agency, Lee; Allen, Literary Agency, James; Allen Literary Agency, Linda; Amsterdam Agency, Marcia; Axelrod Agency; Beekman Literary Agency; Bova Literary Agency, Barbara; Bykofsky Assoc., Sheree; Carvainis Agency, Maria; Castiglia Literary Agency, Julie; Circle of Confusion; de la Haba Agency, Lois; Diamond Literary Agency; Doyen Literary Services; Dupree/Miller and Assoc. Literary; Elmo Agency, Ann; Garon-Brooke Assoc., Jay; Goldfarb & Graybill; Greenburger Assoc., Sanford J.; Gusay Literary Agency, Charlotte; Hanson Agency; Hawkins & Assoc., John; Hendin Literary, David; Herner Rights Agency, Susan; Kidde, Hoyt & Picard; Klinger, Harvey; Lampack Agency, Peter; Lantz-Joy Harris Literary Agency, Robert; Larsen/Elizabeth Pomada Literary Agents, Michael; Lindstrom Literary Group; Love Literary Agency, Nancy; Mainhardt Agency, Ricia; March Tenth; Morhaim Literary Agency, Howard; Multimedia Product Development; Mura Enterprises, Dee; Naggar Literary Agency, Jean V.; Parks Agency, Richard; Pelter, Rodney; Picard Literary Agent, Alison J.; Quicksilver Books-Literary Agents; Rees Literary Agency, Helen; Rock Literary Agency; Rubenstein Literary Agency, Pesha; Russell-Simenauer Literary Agency; Schlessinger Agency, Blanche; Schmidt Literary Agency, Harold; Seymour Agency; Siegel Literary Agency, Bobbe; Swanson, H.N.; Teal Literary Agency, Patricia; Wald Assoc., Mary Jack; Weiner Literary Agency, Cherry; Witherspoon & Assoc.; Wreschner, Authors' Representative, Ruth; Zeckendorf Assoc., Susan

Historical. Acton, Leone, Hanson & Jaffe; Adler & Robin Books; Allan Agency, Lee; Allen, Literary Agency, James; Amsterdam Agency, Marcia; Axelrod Agency; Baldi Literary Agency, Malaga; Beekman Literary Agency; Blassingame Spectrum Corp.; Brandt & Brandt Literary Agents ; Brown Assoc., Marie; Brown Literary Agency, Andrea; Butler, Art and Literary Agent, Jane; Cantrell-Colas, Literary Agency; Carvainis Agency, Maria; Circle of Confusion; Cohen, Literary Agency, Ruth; Collin Literary Agent, Frances; Crown Int'l Literature and Arts Agency, Bonnie R.; Curtis Assoc., Richard; Davie Literary Agency, Elaine; de la Haba Agency, Lois; Diamant, Writer's Workshop, Anita; Diamond Literary Agency; Doyen Literary Services; Dupree/Miller and Assoc. Literary; Ellenberg Literary Agency, Ethan; Elmo Agency, Ann; Farber Literary Agency ; Feiler Literary Agency, Florence; Flaherty, Literary Agent, Joyce A.; Flannery Literary; Garon-Brooke Assoc., Jay; Goddard, Connie: Book Development; Goldfarb & Graybill; Greenburger Assoc., Sanford J.; Gusay Literary Agency, Charlotte; Halsey Agency, Reece; Hanson Agency; Hawkins & Assoc., John; Hendin Literary, David; Herner Rights Agency, Susan; J de S Assoc.; Kidde, Hoyt & Picard; Kouts, Literary Agent, Barbara S.; Lampack Agency, Peter; Lantz-Joy Harris Literary Agency , Robert; Larsen/Elizabeth Pomada Literary Agents, Michael; Lasher Agency, Maureen; Lincoln Literary Agency, Ray; Lindstrom Literary Group; Literary Group; Lyceum Creative Properties; Maass Literary Agency, Donald; McBride Literary Agency, Margret; Mainhardt Agency, Ricia; March Tenth; Morhaim Literary Agency, Howard; Multimedia Product Development; Mura Enterprises, Dee; Naggar Literary Agency, Jean V.; Norma-Lewis Agency; Novak III Literary Representation, Edward A.; Otitis Media; Otte Co.; Parks Agency, Richard; Pelter, Rodney; Picard Literary Agent, Alison J.; Pocono Literary Agency; Potomac Literary Agency; Protter Literary Agent, Susan Ann; Pryor, Roberta; Publishing Services; Rees Literary Agency, Helen; Renaissance: A Literary/Talent Agency; Rock Literary Agency; Rubenstein Literary Agency, Pesha; Russell-Simenauer Literary Agency ; Schulman, A Literary Agency, Susan; Seligman, Literary Agent, Lynn; Seymour Agency; Shepard Agency; Siegel Literary Agency, Bobbe; Singer Literary Agency, Evelyn; Steele & Co., Lyle; Swanson, H.N.; Van der Leun & Assoc.; Wald Assoc., Mary Jack; Wecksler-Incomco; Weiner Literary Agency, Cherry; Westchester Literary Agency; Wieser & Wieser; Witherspoon & Assoc.; Wreschner, Authors' Representative, Ruth; Wright Representatives, Ann; Zeckendorf Assoc., Susan; Ziegler Literary Agency, George

Humor. Agency Chicago; Ajlouny Agency, Joseph S.; Amsterdam Agency, Marcia; Baldi Literary Agency, Malaga; Bartczak Assoc., Gene; Brandt & Brandt Literary Agents ; Brown Assoc., Marie; Cantrell-Colas, Literary Agency; Carvainis Agency, Maria; Crown Int'l Literature and Arts Agency, Bonnie R.; de la Haba Agency, Lois; Doyen Literary Services; Dupree/Miller and Assoc. Literary; Ellenberg Literary Agency, Ethan; Farber Literary Agency; Flannery Literary; Green, Literary Agent, Randall Elisha; Greenburger Assoc., Sanford J.; Gusay Literary Agency, Charlotte; Hanson Agency; Hawkins & Assoc., John; Kidde, Hoyt & Picard; Lampack Agency, Peter; Lantz-Joy Harris Literary Agency, Robert; Larsen/Elizabeth Pomada Literary Agents, Michael; Lincoln Literary Agency, Ray; Literary Group; Lyceum Creative Properties; Madsen Agency, Robert; Mainhardt Agency, Ricia; March Tenth; Markowitz Literary Agency, Barbara; Miller Assoc., Roberta D.; Nine Muses and Apollo; Norma-Lewis Agency; Otitis Media; Pelter, Rodney; Picard Literary Agent, Alison J.; Potomac Literary Agency; Rees Literary Agency, Helen; Renaissance: A

Literary/Talent Agency; Rock Literary Agency; Rose Literary Agency; Russell-Simenauer Literary Agency ; Seligman, Literary Agent, Lynn; Seymour Agency; Shepard Agency; Spieler, F. Joseph; Swanson, H.N.; Wald Assoc., Mary Jack; Witherspoon & Assoc.; Wohl Literary Agency, Gary S.

Juvenile. Allan Agency, Lee; Allen Literary Agency, Linda; Bartczak Assoc., Gene; Brown Assoc., Marie; Brown Literary Agency, Andrea; Butler, Art and Literary Agent, Jane; Cantrell-Colas, Literary Agency; Carvainis Agency, Maria; Circle of Confusion; Cohen, Literary Agency, Ruth; de la Haba Agency, Lois; Diamant, Writer's Workshop, Anita; Doyen Literary Services; Elek Assoc., Peter; Ellenberg Literary Agency, Ethan; Elmo Agency, Ann; Farber Literary Agency; Feiler Literary Agency, Florence; Flannery Literary; Gordon Agency, Charlotte; Gotham Art & Literary Agency; Greenburger Assoc., Sanford J.; Gusay Literary Agency, Charlotte; Hanson Agency; Hawkins & Assoc., John; Hegler Literary Agency, Gary L.; J de S Assoc.; Kirchoff/Wohlberg, Authors' Representation Division; Kouts, Literary Agent, Barbara S.; Lincoln Literary Agency, Ray; Lyceum Creative Properties; Maccoby Literary Agency, Gina; Mainhardt Agency, Ricia; Markowitz Literary Agency, Barbara; Marmur Assoc. , Mildred; Multimedia Product Development; Mura Enterprises, Dee; Naggar Literary Agency, Jean V.; Norma-Lewis Agency; Picard Literary Agent, Alison J.; Pocono Literary Agency; Printed Tree; Pryor, Roberta; Rubenstein Literary Agency, Pesha; Swanson, H.N.; Wald Assoc., Mary Jack; Wasserman Literary Agency; Wecksler-Incomco; Westchester Literary Agency; Wreschner, Authors' Representative, Ruth

Lesbian. Allen Literary Agency, Linda; Baldi Literary Agency, Malaga; Brandt & Brandt Literary Agents; Circle of Confusion; Dupree/Miller and Assoc. Literary; Dystel Literary Management, Jane; Eth Literary Representation, Felicia; Feiler Literary Agency, Florence; Gordon Agency, Charlotte; Greenburger Assoc., Sanford J.; Gusay Literary Agency, Charlotte; Hawkins & Assoc., John; Hendin Literary, David; Kidde, Hoyt & Picard; Lantz-Joy Harris Literary Agency, Robert; Larsen/Elizabeth Pomada Literary Agents, Michael; Levant & Wales, Literary Agency; Lincoln Literary Agency, Ray; Literary Group; Lyceum Creative Properties; Mura Enterprises, Dee; Naggar Literary Agency, Jean V.; Parks Agency, Richard; Pelter, Rodney; Perkins Assoc., L.; Picard Literary Agent, Alison J.; Potomac Literary Agency; Raymond, Literary Agent, Charlotte Cecil; Rock Literary Agency; Russell-Simenauer Literary Agency ; Sanders Literary Agency, Victoria; Schmidt Literary Agency, Harold; Schulman, A Literary Agency, Susan; Seligman, Literary Agent, Lynn; Spieler, F. Joseph; Steele & Co., Lyle; Swanson, H.N.; Westchester Literary Agency; Witherspoon & Assoc.; Wreschner, Authors' Representative, Ruth; Wright Representatives, Ann; Ziegler Literary Agency, George

Literary. Acton, Leone, Hanson & Jaffe; Adler & Robin Books; Agents for Medical and Mental Health Professionals; Allan Agency, Lee; Allen Literary Agency, Linda; Altshuler Literary Agency, Miriam; Authors' Literary Agency; Axelrod Agency; Baldi Literary Agency, Malaga; Beekman Literary Agency; Behar Literary Agency, Josh; Blassingame Spectrum Corp.; Borchardt, Georges; Brandt Agency, Joan; Brandt & Brandt Literary Agents; Brown Assoc., Marie; Brown Limited, Curtis; Bykofsky Assoc., Sheree; Cantrell-Colas, Literary Agency; Carvainis Agency, Maria; Castiglia Literary Agency, Julie; Circle of Confusion; Cohen, Literary Agency, Ruth; Collin Literary Agent, Frances; Congdon Assoc., Don; Cornfield Literary Agency, Robert; Crown Int'l Literature and Arts Agency, Bonnie R.; Darhansoff & Verrill Literary Agents; de la Haba Agency, Lois; Diamant, Writer's Workshop, Anita; Dijkstra Literary Agency, Sandra; Doyen Literary Services; Ducas, Robert; Dupree/Miller and Assoc. Literary; Dystel Literary Management, Jane; Ellenberg Literary Agency, Ethan; Ellison, Nicholas; Elmo Agency, Ann; Emerald Literary Agency; Eth Literary Representation, Felicia; Feiler Literary Agency, Florence; Flaherty, Literary Agent, Joyce A.; Flaming Star Literary Enterprises; Flannery Literary; Garon-Brooke Assoc., Jay; Goldfarb & Graybill; Gordon Agency, Charlotte; Gotham Art & Literary Agency; Green, Literary Agent, Randall Elisha; Greenburger Assoc., Sanford J.; Gregory Assoc., Maia; Gusay Literary Agency, Charlotte; Halsey Agency, Reece; Hanson Agency; Hawkins & Assoc., John; Hendin Literary, David; Herner Rights Agency, Susan; Hill Assoc., Frederick; Hull House Literary Agency; IMG-Julian Bach Literary Agency; J de S Assoc.; Kidde, Hoyt & Picard; Klinger, Harvey; Kouts, Literary Agent, Barbara S.; Kroll Literary Agency, Edite; Lampack Agency, Peter; Lantz-Joy Harris Literary Agency, Robert; Larsen/Elizabeth Pomada Literary Agents, Michael; Lasher Agency, Maureen; Levant & Wales, Literary Agency; Levine Literary Agency, Ellen; Lichtman, Trister, Singer & Ross; Lincoln Literary Agency, Ray; Lindstrom Literary Group; Love Literary Agency, Nancy; Lyceum Creative Properties; Maass Literary Agency, Donald; McBride Literary Agency, Margret; Maccoby Literary Agency, Gina; McGrath, Helen; Mainhardt Agency, Ricia; Mann Agency, Carol; March Tenth; Markson Literary Agency, Elaine; Marmur Assoc., Mildred; Miller Assoc., Roberta D.; Multimedia Product Development; Mura Enterprises, Dee; Naggar Literary Agency, Jean V.; Nazor Literary Agency, Karen; Nine Muses and Apollo; Novak III Literary Representation, Edward A.; Otte Co.; Parks Agency, Richard; Paton Literary Agency, Kathi J.; Pelter, Rodney; Perkins Assoc., L.; Potomac Literary Agency; Pryor, Roberta; Publishing Services; Quicksilver Books-Literary Agents; Raymond, Literary Agent, Charlotte Cecil; Rees Literary Agency, Helen; Renaissance: A Literary/Talent Agency; Rock Literary Agency; Rose Literary Agency; Russell-Simenauer Literary Agency; Sanders Literary Agency, Victoria; Sandum & Assoc.; Schmidt Literary Agency, Harold; Schulman, A Literary Agency, Susan; Schwartz Agency, Laurens R.; Seligman, Literary Agent, Lynn; Shepard Agency; Siegel Literary Agency, Bobbe; Singer Literary Agency, Evelyn; Smith, Literary Agent, Valerie; Spieler, F. Joseph; Spieler Literary Agency, Gretchen; Spitzer Literary Agency, Philip G.; Stauffer Assoc., Nancy; Steele & Co., Lyle; Stepping Stone; Stern Literary Agency (TX), Gloria; Swanson, H.N.; Van der Leun & Assoc.; Wald Assoc., Mary Jack; Wallace Literary Agency; Watkins Loomis Agency; Wecksler-Incomco; Weingel-Fidel Agency; Westchester Literary Agency; Wieser & Wieser; Witherspoon & Assoc.; Wreschner, Authors' Representative, Ruth; Wright Representatives, Ann; Writers' Productions; Writers' Representatives; Zeckendorf Assoc., Susan; Ziegler Literary Agency, George

Mainstream. Acton, Leone, Hanson & Jaffe; Adler & Robin Books; Allan Agency, Lee; Allen, Literary Agency, James; Allen Literary Agency, Linda; Altshuler Literary Agency, Miriam; Amsterdam Agency, Marcia; Authors' Literary Agency; Axelrod Agency; Baldi Literary Agency, Malaga; Bartczak Assoc., Gene; Beekman Literary Agency; Blassingame Spectrum Corp.; Boates Literary Agency, Reid; Bova Literary Agency, Barbara; Brandt Agency, Joan; Brandt & Brandt Literary Agents; Brown Assoc., Marie; Bykofsky Assoc., Sheree; Cantrell-Colas, Literary Agency; Carvainis Agency, Maria; Castiglia Literary Agency, Julie; Circle of Confusion; Cleaver, Diane; Cohen, Literary Agency, Ruth; Collin Literary Agent, Frances; Columbia Literary Assoc.; Curtis Assoc., Richard; de la Haba Agency, Lois; Diamant, Writer's Workshop, Anita; Diamond Literary Agency (CO); Dijkstra Literary Agency, Sandra; Doyen Literary Services; Ducas, Robert; Dupree/Miller and Assoc. Literary; Dystel Literary Management, Jane; Ellenberg Literary Agency, Ethan; Ellison, Nicholas; Elmo Agency, Ann; Emerald Literary Agency; Esquire Literary Productions; Eth Literary Representation, Felicia; Farber Literary Agency; Feiler Literary Agency, Florence; Flaherty, Literary Agent, Joyce A.; Flannery Literary; Garon-Brooke Assoc., Jay; Goddard, Connie: Book Development; Goldfarb & Graybill; Gotham Art & Literary Agency; Green, Literary Agent, Randall Elisha; Greenburger Assoc., Sanford J.; Gusay Literary Agency, Charlotte; Halsey Agency, Reece; Hawkins & Assoc., John; Hegler Literary Agency, Gary L.; Hendin Literary, David; Herner Rights Agency, Susan; Hill Assoc., Frederick; Hull House Literary Agency; IMG-Julian Bach Literary Agency; International Publisher Assoc.; J de S Assoc.; Kidde, Hoyt & Picard; Klinger, Harvey; Kouts, Literary Agent, Barbara S.; Kroll Literary Agency, Edite; Lampack Agency, Peter; Lantz-Joy Harris Literary Agency, Robert; Larsen/Elizabeth Pomada Literary Agents, Michael; Lasher Agency, Maureen; Lincoln Literary Agency, Ray; Lindstrom Literary Group; Lipkind Agency, Wendy; Love Literary Agency, Nancy; Lowenstein Assoc.; Lyceum Creative Properties; Maass Literary Agency, Donald; McBride Literary Agency, Margret; Maccoby Literary Agency, Gina; McGrath, Helen; Mainhardt Agency, Ricia; Manus & Assoc. Literary Agency; March Tenth; Markowitz Literary Agency, Barbara; Markson Literary Agency, Elaine; Marmur Assoc., Mildred; Miller Assoc., Roberta D.; Morhaim Literary Agency, Howard; Multimedia Product Development; Mura Enterprises, Dee; Naggar Literary Agency, Jean V.; Nine Muses and Apollo; Norma-Lewis Agency; Novak III Literary Representation, Edward A.; Otitis Media; Otte Co.; Parks Agency, Richard; Paton Literary Agency, Kathi J.; Pelter, Rodney; Perkins Assoc., L.; Picard Literary Agent, Alison J.; Potomac Literary Agency; Printed Tree; Pryor, Roberta; Publishing Services; Quicksilver Books-Literary Agents; Raymond, Literary Agent, Charlotte Cecil; Rees Literary Agency, Helen; Renaissance: A Literary/Talent Agency; Rock Literary Agency; Rubenstein Literary Agency, Pesha; Russell-Simenauer Literary Agency ; Sandum & Assoc.; Schlessinger Agency, Blanche; Schmidt Literary Agency, Harold; Schulman, A Literary Agency, Susan; Schwartz Agency, Laurens R.; Seligman, Literary Agent, Lynn; Seymour Agency; Siegel Literary Agency, Bobbe; Sierra Literary Agency; Singer Literary Agency, Evelyn; Smith, Literary Agent, Valerie; Spieler, F. Joseph; Spitzer Literary Agency, Philip G.; Stauffer Assoc., Nancy; Stepping Stone; Sterling Lord Literistic; Stern Literary Agency (TX); Gloria; Swanson, H.N.; Teal Literary Agency, Patricia; Van der Leun & Assoc.; Wald Assoc., Mary Jack; Wallace Literary Agency; Ware Literary Agency, John A.; Watkins Loomis Agency; Wecksler-Incomco; Weiner Literary Agency, Cherry; Weingel-Fidel Agency; Westchester Literary Agency; Wieser & Wieser; Witherspoon & Assoc.; Wreschner, Authors' Representative, Ruth; Wright Representatives, Ann; Zeckendorf Assoc., Susan; Ziegler Literary Agency, George

Mystery. Acton, Leone, Hanson & Jaffe; Adler & Robin Books; Agents for Medical and Mental Health Professionals; Allan Agency, Lee; Allen, Literary Agency, James; Allen Literary Agency, Linda; Amsterdam Agency, Marcia; Authors' Literary Agency; Axelrod Agency; Baldi Literary Agency, Malaga; Blassingame Spectrum Corp.; Boates Literary Agency, Reid; Bova Literary Agency, Barbara; Brandt Agency, Joan; Brandt & Brandt Literary Agents; Brown Assoc., Marie; Brown Limited, Curtis; Butler, Art and Literary Agent, Jane; Bykofsky Assoc., Sheree; Cantrell-Colas, Literary Agency; Carvainis Agency, Maria; Castiglia Literary Agency, Julie; Circle of Confusion; Ciske Literary Agency, Francine; Cleaver, Diane; Cohen, Literary Agency, Ruth; Collin Literary Agent, Frances; Columbia Literary Assoc.; Curtis Assoc., Richard; Davie Literary Agency, Elaine; de la Haba Agency, Lois; Diamant, Writer's Workshop, Anita; Diamond Literary Agency (CO); Dijkstra Literary Agency, Sandra; Doyen Literary Services; Ducas, Robert; Dupree/Miller and Assoc. Literary; Ellenberg Literary Agency, Ethan; Elmo Agency, Ann; Emerald Literary Agency; Esquire Literary Productions; Farber Literary Agency; Feiler Literary Agency, Florence; Flaherty, Literary Agent, Joyce A.; Flannery Literary; Garon-Brooke Assoc., Jay; Goddard, Connie: Book Development; Goldfarb & Graybill; Gordon Agency, Charlotte; Greenburger Assoc., Sanford J.; Gusay Literary Agency, Charlotte; Halsey Agency, Reece; Hawkins & Assoc., John; Hegler Literary Agency, Gary L.; Herner Rights Agency, Susan; Hull House Literary Agency; J de S Assoc.; Kidde, Hoyt & Picard; Klinger, Harvey; Kouts, Literary Agent, Barbara S.; Kroll Literary Agency, Edite; Lampack Agency, Peter; Lantz-Joy Harris Literary Agency, Robert; Larsen/Elizabeth Pomada Literary Agents, Michael; Levine Literary Agency, Ellen; Lincoln Literary Agency, Ray; Lipkind Agency, Wendy; Literary Group; Love Literary Agency, Nancy; Lyceum Creative Properties; Maass Literary Agency, Donald; McBride Literary Agency, Margret; Maccoby Literary Agency, Gina; McGrath, Helen; Madsen Agency, Robert; Manus & Assoc. Literary Agency; March Tenth; Markowitz Literary Agency, Barbara; Marmur Assoc., Mildred; Morhaim Literary Agency, Howard; Multimedia Product Development; Mura Enterprises, Dee; Naggar Literary Agency, Jean V.; Norma-Lewis Agency; Novak III Literary Representation, Edward A.; Otitis Media; Otte Co.; Parks Agency, Richard; Pelter, Rodney; Perkins Assoc., L.; Picard Literary Agent, Alison J.; Protter Literary Agent, Susan Ann; Pryor, Roberta; Quicksilver Books-Literary Agents; Rees Literary Agency, Helen; Renaissance: A Literary/Talent Agency; Rock Literary Agency; Rubenstein Literary Agency, Pesha; Russell-Simenauer Literary Agency; Schlessinger Agency, Blanche; Schmidt Literary Agency, Harold; Schulman, A Literary Agency, Susan; Seligman, Literary Agent,

Lynn; Seymour Agency; Siegel Literary Agency, Bobbe; Singer Literary Agency, Evelyn; Spitzer Literary Agency, Philip G.; Steele & Co., Lyle; Stepping Stone; Stern Literary Agency (TX), Gloria; Swanson, H.N.; Teal Literary Agency, Patricia; Wald Assoc., Mary Jack; Wallace Literary Agency; Ware Literary Agency, John A.; Watkins Loomis Agency; Weiner Literary Agency, Cherry; Weingel-Fidel Agency; Westchester Literary Agency; Wieser & Wieser; Witherspoon & Assoc.; Wreschner, Authors' Representative, Ruth; Wright Representatives, Ann; Zeckendorf Assoc., Susan

Open to all fiction. Barrett Books, Loretta; Brown, Curtis; Buck Agency, Howard; Bykofsky Assoc., Sheree; Circle of Confusion; Cohen Literary Agency, Hy; Congdon Assoc., Don; Evans, Mary; Gantz Zahler Literary Agency, Karen; Goodman Assoc.; Hamilburg Agency, Mitchell J.; Hoffman Literary Agency, Berenice; Lazear Agency; Maccampbell, Donald; Madsen Agency, Robert; Martell Agency; Ober Assoc., Harold; Writers House

Picture book. Axelrod Agency; Brown Assoc., Marie; Brown Literary Agency, Andrea; Castiglia Literary Agency, Julie; Circle of Confusion; Cohen, Literary Agency, Ruth; Doyen Literary Services; Dupree/Miller and Assoc. Literary; Elek Assoc., Peter; Ellenberg Literary Agency, Ethan; Flannery Literary; Greenburger Assoc., Sanford J.; Gusay Literary Agency, Charlotte; Hanson Agency; Hawkins & Assoc., John; Kouts, Literary Agent, Barbara S.; Kroll Literary Agency, Edite; Lantz-Joy Harris Literary Agency , Robert; Lyceum Creative Properties; Mainhardt Agency, Ricia; Multimedia Product Development; Naggar Literary Agency, Jean V.; Norma-Lewis Agency; Picard Literary Agent, Alison J.; Pocono Literary Agency; Pryor, Roberta; Rubenstein Literary Agency, Pesha; Wald Assoc., Mary Jack; Wecksler-Incomco

Regional. Allen Literary Agency, Linda; Baldi Literary Agency, Malaga; Beekman Literary Agency; Bova Literary Agency, Barbara; Brandt & Brandt Literary Agents; Brown Assoc., Marie; Castiglia Literary Agency, Julie; Circle of Confusion; Collin Literary Agent, Frances; Elmo Agency, Ann; Green, Literary Agent, Randall Elisha; Greenburger Assoc., Sanford J.; Gusay Literary Agency, Charlotte; Hawkins & Assoc., John; Hegler Literary Agency, Gary L.; Kidde, Hoyt & Picard; Lantz-Joy Harris Literary Agency, Robert; Lincoln Literary Agency, Ray; March Tenth; Mura Enterprises, Dee; Naggar Literary Agency, Jean V.; Nazor Literary Agency, Karen; Pelter, Rodney; Raymond, Literary Agent, Charlotte Cecil; Rock Literary Agency; Shepard Agency; Singer Literary Agency, Evelyn; Swanson, H.N.; Westchester Literary Agency

Religious/inspirational. Brandenburgh & Assoc. Literary Agency; Circle of Confusion; Ciske Literary Agency, Francine; de la Haba Agency, Lois; Diamant, Writer's Workshop, Anita; Dupree/Miller and Assoc. Literary; Emerald Literary Agency; Feiler Literary Agency, Florence; Gusay Literary Agency, Charlotte; Hawkins & Assoc., John; Lantz-Joy Harris Literary Agency, Robert; Larsen/Elizabeth Pomada Literary Agents, Michael; Multimedia Product Development; Pelter, Rodney; Picard Literary Agent, Alison J.; Printed Tree; Rock Literary Agency; Seymour Agency; Westchester Literary Agency

Romance. Acton, Leone, Hanson & Jaffe; Adler & Robin Books; Allan Agency, Lee; Allen, Literary Agency, James; Allen Literary Agency, Linda; Amsterdam Agency, Marcia; Axelrod Agency; Beekman Literary Agency; Behar Literary Agency, Josh; Bova Literary Agency, Barbara; Brandt & Brandt Literary Agents; Brown Literary Agency, Andrea; Carvainis Agency, Maria; Castiglia Literary Agency, Julie; Circle of Confusion; Ciske Literary Agency, Francine; Cohen, Literary Agency, Ruth; Collin Literary Agent, Frances; Columbia Literary Assoc.; Curtis Assoc., Richard; Davie Literary Agency, Elaine; Diamant, Writer's Workshop, Anita; Diamond Literary Agency (CO); Doyen Literary Services; Dupree/Miller and Assoc. Literary; Ellenberg Literary Agency, Ethan; Elmo Agency, Ann; Emerald Literary Agency; Farber Literary Agency; Feiler Literary Agency, Florence; Flaherty, Literary Agent, Joyce A.; Fogelman Literary Agency; Garon-Brooke Assoc., Jay; Gordon Agency, Charlotte; Green, Literary Agent, Randall Elisha; Halsey Agency, Reece; Hanson Agency; Hegler Literary Agency, Gary L.; Herner Rights Agency, Susan; Kidde, Hoyt & Picard; Klinger, Harvey; Kouts, Literary Agent, Barbara S.; Lantz-Joy Harris Literary Agency, Robert; Larsen/Elizabeth Pomada Literary Agents, Michael; Lincoln Literary Agency, Ray; Literary Group; Lowenstein Assoc.; Lyceum Creative Properties; McGrath, Helen; Mainhardt Agency, Ricia; Morhaim Literary Agency, Howard; Multimedia Product Development; Mura Enterprises, Dee; Norma-Lewis Agency; Novak III Literary Representation, Edward A.; Parks Agency, Richard; Picard Literary Agent, Alison J.; Pocono Literary Agency; Rock Literary Agency; Rubenstein Literary Agency, Pesha; Russell-Simenauer Literary Agency; Seymour Agency; Siegel Literary Agency, Bobbe; Swanson, H.N.; Teal Literary Agency, Patricia; Wald Assoc., Mary Jack; Weiner Literary Agency, Cherry; Westchester Literary Agency; Witherspoon & Assoc.; Wreschner, Authors' Representative, Ruth; Wright Representatives, Ann

Science fiction. Adler & Robin Books; Agents for Medical and Mental Health Professionals; Allan Agency, Lee; Allen, Literary Agency, James; Amsterdam Agency, Marcia; Behar Literary Agency, Josh; Blassingame Spectrum Corp.; Bova Literary Agency, Barbara; Brandt & Brandt Literary Agents; Brown Assoc., Marie; Brown Literary Agency, Andrea; Butler, Art and Literary Agent, Jane; Cantrell-Colas, Literary Agency; Circle of Confusion; Collin Literary Agent, Frances; Curtis Assoc., Richard; Doyen Literary Services; Dupree/Miller and Assoc. Literary; Ellenberg Literary Agency, Ethan; Emerald Literary Agency; Garon-Brooke Assoc., Jay; Halsey Agency, Reece; Hanson Agency; Hawkins & Assoc., John; Herner Rights Agency, Susan; Kidd, Literary Agent, Virginia; Lincoln Literary Agency, Ray; Lindstrom Literary Group; Literary Group; Lyceum Creative Properties; Maass Literary Agency, Donald; McGrath, Helen; Madsen Agency, Robert; Mainhardt Agency, Ricia; Mura Enterprises, Dee; Naggar Literary Agency, Jean V.; Pocono Literary Agency; Printed Tree; Protter Literary Agent, Susan Ann; Rees Literary Agency, Helen; Renaissance: A Literary/Talent Agency; Rock Literary Agency; Russell-Simenauer Literary Agency; Schmidt Literary Agency, Harold; Siegel Literary Agency, Bobbe; Smith, Literary Agent, Valerie; Swanson, H.N.; Wald Assoc., Mary Jack; Weiner Literary Agency, Cherry

Sports. Acton, Leone, Hanson & Jaffe; Brandt & Brandt Literary Agents; Circle of Confusion; Ducas, Robert; Dupree/Miller and Assoc. Literary; Flannery Literary; Greenburger Assoc., Sanford J.; Gusay Literary Agency, Charlotte; Hawkins & Assoc., John; Lantz-Joy Harris Literary Agency, Robert; Lasher Agency, Maureen; Lincoln Literary Agency, Ray; Literary Group; McGrath, Helen; Mainhardt Agency, Ricia; Markowitz Literary Agency, Barbara; Multimedia Product Development; Mura Enterprises, Dee; Novak III Literary Representation, Edward A.; Pelter, Rodney; Picard Literary Agent, Alison J.; Pocono Literary Agency; Potomac Literary Agency; Rock Literary Agency; Shepard Agency; Spitzer Literary Agency, Philip G.; Swanson, H.N.; Wald Assoc., Mary Jack; Ware Literary Agency, John A.; Wright Representatives, Ann

Thriller/espionage. Acton, Leone, Hanson & Jaffe; Adler & Robin Books; Allan Agency, Lee; Allen Literary Agency, Linda; Amsterdam Agency, Marcia; Authors' Literary Agency; Axelrod Agency; Baldi Literary Agency, Malaga; Behar Literary Agency, Josh; Boates Literary Agency, Reid; Bova Literary Agency, Barbara; Brandt Agency, Joan; Brandt & Brandt Literary Agents; Cantrell-Colas, Literary Agency; Carvainis Agency, Maria; Circle of Confusion; Ciske Literary Agency, Francine; Cleaver, Diane; Columbia Literary Assoc.; Curtis Assoc., Richard; Darhansoff & Verrill Literary Agents; Diamant, Writer's Workshop, Anita; Diamond Literary Agency (CO); Dijkstra Literary Agency, Sandra; Doyen Literary Services; Ducas, Robert; Dupree/Miller and Assoc. Literary; Dystel Literary Management, Jane; Ellenberg Literary Agency, Ethan; Elmo Agency, Ann; Esquire Literary Productions; Eth Literary Representation, Felicia; Farber Literary Agency; Flaherty, Literary Agent, Joyce A.; Goddard, Connie: Book Development; Goldfarb & Graybill; Green, Literary Agent, Randall Elisha; Greenburger Assoc., Sanford J.; Gusay Literary Agency, Charlotte; Halsey Agency, Reece; Hawkins & Assoc., John; Hendin Literary, David; Herner Rights Agency, Susan; Kidde, Hoyt & Picard; Klinger, Harvey; Lampack Agency, Peter; Lantz-Joy Harris Literary Agency, Robert; Lasher Agency, Maureen; Levine Literary Agency, Ellen; Lincoln Literary Agency, Ray; Lindstrom Literary Group; Literary Group; Love Literary Agency, Nancy; Lyceum Creative Properties; Maass Literary Agency, Donald; McBride Literary Agency, Margret; Maccoby Literary Agency, Gina; McGrath, Helen; Mainhardt Agency, Ricia; Manus & Assoc. Literary Agency; March Tenth; Markowitz Literary Agency, Barbara; Marmur Assoc., Mildred; Morhaim Literary Agency, Howard; Multimedia Product Development; Mura Enterprises, Dee; Naggar Literary Agency, Jean V.; Norma-Lewis Agency; Novak III Literary Representation, Edward A.; Otitis Media; Parks Agency, Richard; Pelter, Rodney; Perkins Assoc., L.; Picard Literary Agent, Alison J.; Pocono Literary Agency; Potomac Literary Agency; Printed Tree; Protter Literary Agent, Susan Ann; Rees Literary Agency, Helen; Renaissance: A Literary/Talent Agency; Rock Literary Agency; Rose Literary Agency; Russell-Simenauer Literary Agency ; Sanders Literary Agency, Victoria; Schmidt Literary Agency, Harold; Shepard Agency; Siegel Literary Agency, Bobbe; Singer Literary Agency, Evelyn; Spitzer Literary Agency, Philip G.; Steele & Co., Lyle; Stepping Stone; Stern Literary Agency (TX), Gloria; Swanson, H.N.; Wald Assoc., Mary Jack; Weiner Literary Agency, Cherry; Westchester Literary Agency; Wieser & Wieser; Witherspoon & Assoc.; Wreschner, Authors' Representative, Ruth; Wright Representatives, Ann; Zeckendorf Assoc., Susan

Westerns/frontier. Agency Chicago; Allan Agency, Lee; Amsterdam Agency, Marcia; Beekman Literary Agency; Brandt & Brandt Literary Agents; Carvainis Agency, Maria; Circle of Confusion; Ciske Literary Agency, Francine; Curtis Assoc., Richard; Davie Literary Agency, Elaine; Diamant, Writer's Workshop, Anita; Doyen Literary Services; Dupree/Miller and Assoc. Literary; Ellenberg Literary Agency, Ethan; Flaherty, Literary Agent, Joyce A.; Flannery Literary; Gusay Literary Agency, Charlotte; Hawkins & Assoc., John; Hegler Literary Agency, Gary L.; Hendin Literary, David; J de S Assoc.; Lindstrom Literary Group; Literary Group; Lyceum Creative Properties; McBride Literary Agency, Margret; McGrath, Helen; Madsen Agency, Robert; Mainhardt Agency, Ricia; Multimedia Product Development; Mura Enterprises, Dee; Norma-Lewis Agency; Parks Agency, Richard; Pelter, Rodney; Picard Literary Agent, Alison J.; Pocono Literary Agency; Potomac Literary Agency; Rock Literary Agency; Schmidt Literary Agency, Harold; Seymour Agency; Swanson, H.N.; Wald Assoc., Mary Jack; Weiner Literary Agency, Cherry; Westchester Literary Agency; Wright Representatives, Ann

Young adult. Allan Agency, Lee; Allen, Literary Agency, James; Allen Literary Agency, Linda; Amsterdam Agency, Marcia; Bartczak Assoc., Gene; Brandt & Brandt Literary Agents; Brown Literary Agency, Andrea; Butler, Art and Literary Agent, Jane; Cantrell-Colas, Literary Agency; Carvainis Agency, Maria; Casselman Literary Agent, Martha; Circle of Confusion; Ciske Literary Agency, Francine; Cohen, Literary Agency, Ruth; de la Haba Agency, Lois; Diamant, Writer's Workshop, Anita; Doyen Literary Services; Ellenberg Literary Agency, Ethan; Elmo Agency, Ann; Farber Literary Agency ; Feiler Literary Agency, Florence; Flannery Literary; Gordon Agency, Charlotte; Gusay Literary Agency, Charlotte; Hanson Agency, ; Hegler Literary Agency, Gary L.; J de S Assoc. ; Kirchoff/Wohlberg, Authors' Rep. Div.; Kouts, Literary Agent, Barbara S.; Lantz-Joy Harris Literary Agency, Robert; Lincoln Literary Agency, Ray; Literary Group; Maccoby Literary Agency, Gina; Mainhardt Agency, Ricia; Markowitz Literary Agency, Barbara; Marmur Assoc., Mildred; Miller Assoc., Roberta D.; Mura Enterprises, Dee; Norma-Lewis Agency; Parks Agency, Richard; Picard Literary Agent, Alison J.; Pocono Literary Agency; Printed Tree; Pryor, Roberta; Raymond, Literary Agent, Charlotte Cecil; Schulman, A Literary Agency, Susan; Smith, Literary Agent, Valerie; Swanson, H.N.; Wald Assoc., Mary Jack; Wasserman Literary Agency, Harriet; Watkins Loomis Agency; Westchester Literary Agency; Wreschner, Authors' Representative, Ruth; Wright Representatives, Ann

Multimedia. Curtis Assoc., Richard; Elek Assoc., Peter; Kellock Co.; Larsen/Elizabeth Pomada Literary

Agents, Michael; Lazear Agency; Multimedia Product Development; Nine Muses and Apollo; Renaissance: A Literary/Talent Agency; Writers House; Writers' Productions

Nonfee-charging literary agents/Nonfiction

Agriculture/horticulture. Baldi Literary Agency, Malaga; Brandt & Brandt Literary Agents; Casselman Literary Agent, Martha; de la Haba Agency, Lois; Doyen Literary Services; Ellison, Nicholas; Gartenberg, Literary Agent, Max; Goddard, Connie: Book Development; Green, Literary Agent, Randall Elisha; Hawkins & Assoc., John; Hendin Literary, David; Levant & Wales, Literary Agency; Lincoln Literary Agency, Ray; Mainhardt Agency, Ricia; Multimedia Product Development; Mura Enterprises, Dee; Parks Agency, Richard; Shepard Agency; Urstadt Writers and Artists Agency, Susan P.; Ware Literary Agency, John A.

Animals. Acton, Leone, Hanson & Jaffe; Baldi Literary Agency, Malaga; Balkin Agency; Bartczak Assoc., Gene; Beekman Literary Agency; Boates Literary Agency, Reid; Brandt & Brandt Literary Agents; Breitman, Patti; Brown Literary Agency, Andrea; Castiglia Literary Agency, Julie; Cornfield Literary Agency, Robert; de la Haba Agency, Lois; Diamant, Writer's Workshop, Anita; Doyen Literary Services; Ducas, Robert; Dystel Literary Management, Jane; Ellison, Nicholas; Eth Literary Representation, Felicia; Flaherty, Literary Agent, Joyce A.; Gartenberg, Literary Agent, Max; Goddard, Connie: Book Development; Hawkins & Assoc., John; Hegler Literary Agency, Gary L.; Hendin Literary, David; Lasher Agency, Maureen; Levant & Wales, Literary Agency; Lincoln Literary Agency, Ray; Lindstrom Literary Group; Literary Group; Love Literary Agency, Nancy; Mainhardt Agency, Ricia; Multimedia Product Development; Mura Enterprises, Dee; Nine Muses and Apollo; Parks Agency, Richard; Picard Literary Agent, Alison J.; Pryor, Roberta; Russell-Simenauer Literary Agency; Shepard Agency; Stauffer Assoc., Nancy; Stepping Stone; Teal Literary Agency, Patricia; Urstadt Writers and Artists Agency, Susan P.; Writers House; Ziegler Literary Agency, George

Anthropology. Allen Literary Agency, Linda; Baldi Literary Agency, Malaga; Balkin Agency; Beekman Literary Agency; Boates Literary Agency, Reid; Borchardt, Georges; Brandt & Brandt Literary Agents ; Brown Literary Agency, Andrea; Cantrell-Colas, Literary Agency; Casselman Literary Agent, Martha; Castiglia Literary Agency, Julie; Circle of Confusion; Collin Literary Agent, Frances; Coover Agency, Doe; Cornfield Literary Agency, Robert; Darhansoff & Verrill Literary Agents; de la Haba Agency, Lois; Dijkstra Literary Agency, Sandra; Doyen Literary Services; Dystel Literary Management, Jane; Educational Design Services; Elek Assoc., Peter; Ellison, Nicholas; Elmo Agency, Ann; Eth Literary Representation, Felicia; Goddard, Connie: Book Development; Gordon Agency, Charlotte; Hawkins & Assoc., John; Hendin Literary, David; Herner Rights Agency, Susan; Hochmann Books, John L.; Hull House Literary Agency; IMG-Julian Bach Literary Agency; James Peter Assoc.; Kellock Co.; Ketz Agency, Louise B.; Lampack Agency, Peter; Larsen/Elizabeth Pomada Literary Agents, Michael; Lasher Agency, Maureen; Levant & Wales, Literary Agency; Levine Literary Agency, Ellen; Lichtman, Trister, Singer & Ross; Lincoln Literary Agency, Ray; Literary Group; Lyceum Creative Properties; Mainhardt Agency, Ricia; Mann Agency, Carol; Manus & Assoc. Literary Agency; Morrison, Henry; Multimedia Product Development; Mura Enterprises, Dee; Otitis Media; Otte Co.; Parks Agency, Richard; Picard Literary Agent, Alison J.; Pryor, Roberta; Quicksilver Books-Literary Agents; Rose Literary Agency; Schmidt Literary Agency, Harold; Schulman, A Literary Agency, Susan; Seligman, Literary Agent, Lynn; Siegel Literary Agency, Bobbe; Singer Literary Agency, Evelyn; Steele & Co., Lyle; Stepping Stone; Stern Literary Agency (TX), Gloria; Urstadt Writers and Artists Agency, Susan P.; Wallace Literary Agency; Ware Literary Agency, John A.; Waterside Productions; Weingel-Fidel Agency; Witherspoon & Assoc.; Ziegler Literary Agency, George

Art/architecture/design. Agency Chicago; Allen Literary Agency, Linda; Axelrod Agency; Baldi Literary Agency, Malaga; Beekman Literary Agency; Boates Literary Agency, Reid; Brandt & Brandt Literary Agents; Brown Assoc., Marie; Brown Literary Agency, Andrea; Cantrell-Colas, Literary Agency; Castiglia Literary Agency, Julie; Cornfield Literary Agency, Robert; de la Haba Agency, Lois; Diamant, Writer's Workshop, Anita; Doyen Literary Services; Ellison, Nicholas; Elmo Agency, Ann; Emerald Literary Agency; Feiler Literary Agency, Florence; Gartenberg, Literary Agent, Max; Goddard, Connie: Book Development; Gregory Assoc., Maia; Hawkins & Assoc., John; Henderson Literary Representation; Hendin Literary, David; Hochmann Books, John L.; Hull House Literary Agency; James Peter Assoc.; Kellock Co.; Kidde, Hoyt & Picard; Lampack Agency, Peter; Larsen/Elizabeth Pomada Literary Agents, Michael; Lasher Agency, Maureen; Levant & Wales, Literary Agency ; Lincoln Literary Agency, Ray; Lyceum Creative Properties; Mann Agency, Carol; Miller Assoc., Roberta D.; Morhaim Literary Agency, Howard; Nathan, Ruth; Norma-Lewis Agency; Novak III Literary Representation, Edward A.; Parks Agency, Richard; Perkins Assoc., L.; Picard Literary Agent, Alison J.; Pryor, Roberta; Rose Literary Agency; Schmidt Literary Agency, Harold; Seligman, Literary Agent, Lynn; Seymour Agency; Spieler Literary Agency, Gretchen; Stepping Stone; Stern Literary Agency (TX), Gloria; Urstadt Writers and Artists Agency, Susan P.; Van Der Leun & Assoc.; Waterside Productions; Watkins Loomis Agency; Wecksler-Incomco; Weingel-Fidel Agency; Writers House; Zeckendorf Assoc., Susan

Biography/autobiography. Acton, Leone, Hanson & Jaffe; Adler & Robin Books; Ajlouny Agency, Joseph S.; Allen Literary Agency, Linda; Altshuler Literary Agency, Miriam; Andrews & Assoc., Bart; Baldi Literary Agency, Malaga; Balkin Agency; Bartczak Assoc., Gene; Beekman Literary Agency; Behar Literary Agency, Josh; Boates Literary Agency, Reid; Borchardt, Georges; Brandt & Brandt Literary Agents; Brown Assoc., Marie; Brown Literary Agency, Andrea; Bykofsky Assoc., Sheree; Cantrell-Colas, Literary Agency; Carvainis Agency, Maria; Casselman Literary Agent, Martha; Castiglia Literary Agency, Julie; Circle of Confusion; Clausen Assoc., Connie; Collin Literary Agent, Frances; Coover Agency, Doe;

Cornfield Literary Agency, Robert; Crawford Literary Agency; Curtis Assoc., Richard; Darhansoff & Verrill Literary Agents; de la Haba Agency, Lois; Diamant, Writer's Workshop, Anita; Dijkstra Literary Agency, Sandra; Doyen Literary Services; Ducas, Robert; Dystel Literary Management, Jane; Ellenberg Literary Agency, Ethan; Elmo Agency, Ann; Emerald Literary Agency; Eth Literary Representation, Felicia; Flaherty, Literary Agent, Joyce A.; Fogelman Literary Agency; Garon-Brooke Assoc., Jay; Gartenberg, Literary Agent, Max; Goddard, Connie: Book Development; Green, Literary Agent, Randall Elisha; Halsey Agency, Reece; Hawkins & Assoc., John; Hegler Literary Agency, Gary L.; Henderson Literary Representation; Hendin Literary, David; Herner Rights Agency, Susan; Hill Assoc., Frederick; Hochmann Books, John L.; Holub & Assoc.; Hull House Literary Agency; IMG-Julian Bach Literary Agency; J de S Assoc.; James Peter Assoc.; Jordan Literary Agency, Lawrence; Kellock Co.; Ketz Agency, Louise B.; Kidde, Hoyt & Picard; Klinger, Harvey; Kouts, Literary Agent, Barbara S.; Lampack Agency, Peter; Larsen/Elizabeth Pomada Literary Agents, Michael; Lasher Agency, Maureen; Levant & Wales, Literary Agency; Levine Literary Agency, Ellen; Lichtman, Trister, Singer & Ross; Lincoln Literary Agency, Ray; Lindstrom Literary Group; Lipkind Agency, Wendy; Literary Group; Love Literary Agency, Nancy; Lyceum Creative Properties; McBride Literary Agency, Margret; McCauley, Gerard; Maccoby Literary Agency, Gina; McGrath, Helen; Mainhardt Agency, Ricia; Mann Agency, Carol; Manus & Assoc. Literary Agency; March Tenth; Markowitz Literary Agency, Barbara; Marmur Assoc., Mildred; Miller Assoc., Roberta D.; Morhaim Literary Agency, Howard; Morrison, Henry; Multimedia Product Development; Mura Enterprises, Dee; Naggar Literary Agency, Jean V.; Nathan, Ruth; Nazor Literary Agency, Karen; New England Publishing Assoc.; Nine Muses and Apollo; Norma-Lewis Agency; Novak III Literary Representation, Edward A.; Nugent Literary; Otitis Media; Otte Co.; Parks Agency, Richard; Picard Literary Agent, Alison J.; Potomac Literary Agency; Protter Literary Agent, Susan Ann; Pryor, Roberta; Publishing Services; Quicksilver Books-Literary Agents; Raymond, Literary Agent, Charlotte Cecil; Rees Literary Agency, Helen; Renaissance: A Literary/Talent Agency; Rose Literary Agency; Russell-Simenauer Literary Agency; Sanders Literary Agency, Victoria; Schlessinger Agency, Blanche; Schmidt Literary Agency, Harold; Schulman, A Literary Agency, Susan; Seligman, Literary Agent, Lynn; Shepard Agency; Siegel Literary Agency, Bobbe; Singer Literary Agency, Evelyn; Spieler, F. Joseph; Spitzer Literary Agency, Philip G.; Stauffer Assoc., Nancy; Steele & Co., Lyle; Stepping Stone; Stern Literary Agency (TX), Gloria; TCA; Teal Literary Agency, Patricia; 2M Communications; Urstadt Writers and Artists Agency, Susan P.; Wald Assoc., Mary Jack; Wallace Literary Agency; Ware Literary Agency, John A.; Waterside Productions; Watkins Loomis Agency; Wecksler-Incomco; Weingel-Fidel Agency; Westchester Literary Agency; Witherspoon & Assoc.; Wreschner, Authors' Representative, Ruth; Wright Representatives, Ann; Writers House; Zeckendorf Assoc., Susan; Ziegler Literary Agency, George

Business. Acton, Leone, Hanson & Jaffe; Adler & Robin Books; Agents for Medical and Mental Health Professionals; Allen Literary Agency, Linda; Axelrod Agency; Baldi Literary Agency, Malaga; Beekman Literary Agency; Behar Literary Agency, Josh; Boates Literary Agency, Reid; Brandt & Brandt Literary Agents; Breitman, Patti; Brown Assoc., Marie; Bykofsky Assoc., Sheree; Carvainis Agency, Maria; Castiglia Literary Agency, Julie; Clausen Assoc., Connie; Collin Literary Agent, Frances; Coover Agency, Doe; Crawford Literary Agency; Curtis Assoc., Richard; de la Haba Agency, Lois; Diamant, Writer's Workshop, Anita; Diamond Literary Agency (CO); Dijkstra Literary Agency, Sandra; Doyen Literary Services; Ducas, Robert; Dystel Literary Management, Jane; Educational Design Services; Ellenberg Literary Agency, Ethan; Ellison, Nicholas; Elmo Agency, Ann; Emerald Literary Agency; Eth Literary Representation, Felicia; Fogelman Literary Agency; Goddard, Connie: Book Development; Gordon Agency, Charlotte; Green, Literary Agent, Randall Elisha; Hawkins & Assoc., John; Henderson Literary Representation; Hendin Literary, David; Herman Agency, Jeff; Herner Rights Agency, Susan; Hull House Literary Agency; IMG-Julian Bach Literary Agency; J de S Assoc.; James Peter Assoc.; Jordan Literary Agency, Lawrence; Kellock Co.; Ketz Agency, Louise B.; Kouts, Literary Agent, Barbara S.; Lampack Agency, Peter; Larsen/Elizabeth Pomada Literary Agents, Michael; Lasher Agency, Maureen; Levant & Wales, Literary Agency; Lichtman, Trister, Singer & Ross; Lincoln Literary Agency, Ray; Lindstrom Literary Group; Literary and Creative Artists Agency; Literary Group; Lyceum Creative Properties; McBride Literary Agency, Margret; McGrath, Helen; Mainhardt Agency, Ricia; Mann Agency, Carol; Manus & Assoc. Literary Agency; Marmur Assoc., Mildred; Multimedia Product Development; Mura Enterprises, Dee; Naggar Literary Agency, Jean V.; Nazor Literary Agency, Karen; New England Publishing Assoc.; Nine Muses and Apollo; Novak III Literary Representation, Edward A.; Otte Co.; Parks Agency, Richard; Paton Literary Agency, Kathi J.; Picard Literary Agent, Alison J.; Potomac Literary Agency; Printed Tree; Quicksilver Books-Literary Agents; Rees Literary Agency, Helen; Rock Literary Agency; Rose Literary Agency; Russell-Simenauer Literary Agency; Schmidt Literary Agency, Harold; Schulman, A Literary Agency, Susan; Seligman, Literary Agent, Lynn; Shepard Agency; Singer Literary Agency, Evelyn; Spieler, F. Joseph; Spitzer Literary Agency, Philip G.; Stauffer Assoc., Nancy; Steele & Co., Lyle; Stepping Stone; Stern Literary Agency (TX), Gloria; TCA; Urstadt Writers and Artists Agency, Susan P.; Ware Literary Agency, John A.; Waterside Productions; Wecksler-Incomco; Westchester Literary Agency; Wieser & Wieser; Witherspoon & Assoc.; Wohl Literary Agency, Gary S.; Wreschner, Authors' Representative, Ruth; Writers House; Zeckendorf Assoc., Susan

Child guidance/parenting. Acton, Leone, Hanson & Jaffe; Adler & Robin Books; Agents for Medical and Mental Health Professionals; Allan Agency, Lee; Allen Literary Agency, Linda; Beekman Literary Agency; Boates Literary Agency, Reid; Brandt & Brandt Literary Agents; Breitman, Patti; Brown Assoc., Marie; Bykofsky Assoc., Sheree; Cantrell-Colas, Literary Agency; Castiglia Literary Agency, Julie; Coover Agency, Doe; Crawford Literary Agency; Curtis Assoc., Richard; Diamant, Writer's Workshop, Anita; Dijkstra Literary Agency, Sandra; Doyen Literary Services; Dystel Literary Management, Jane; Educational Design Services; Elek Assoc., Peter; Ellenberg Literary Agency, Ethan; Ellison, Nicholas; Elmo

Agency, Ann; Emerald Literary Agency; Eth Literary Representation, Felicia; Farber Literary Agency; Flaherty, Literary Agent, Joyce A.; Flannery Literary; Fogelman Literary Agency; Garon-Brooke Assoc., Jay; Gartenberg, Literary Agent, Max; Goddard, Connie: Book Development; Hawkins & Assoc., John; Henderson Literary Representation; Hendin Literary, David; Herner Rights Agency, Susan; James Peter Assoc.; Kellock Co.; Kouts, Literary Agent, Barbara S.; Larsen/Elizabeth Pomada Literary Agents, Michael; Lasher Agency, Maureen; Levant & Wales, Literary Agency; Lincoln Literary Agency, Ray; Literary Group; Love Literary Agency, Nancy; Lyceum Creative Properties; McBride Literary Agency, Margret; Mainhardt Agency, Ricia; Mann Agency, Carol; Manus & Assoc. Literary Agency; Morhaim Literary Agency, Howard; Multimedia Product Development; Mura Enterprises, Dee; Naggar Literary Agency, Jean V.; New England Publishing Assoc.; Norma-Lewis Agency; Novak III Literary Representation, Edward A.; Parks Agency, Richard; Picard Literary Agent, Alison J.; Printed Tree; Protter Literary Agent, Susan Ann; Publishing Services; Quicksilver Books-Literary Agents; Rose Literary Agency; Rubenstein Literary Agency, Pesha; Russell-Simenauer Literary Agency; Schulman, A Literary Agency, Susan; Seligman, Literary Agent, Lynn; Shepard Agency; Siegel Literary Agency, Bobbe; Singer Literary Agency, Evelyn; Spieler, F. Joseph; Spieler Literary Agency, Gretchen; Steele & Co., Lyle; Stepping Stone; Stern Literary Agency (TX), Gloria; Teal Literary Agency, Patricia; 2M Communications; Urstadt Writers and Artists Agency, Susan P.; Ware Literary Agency, John A.; Waterside Productions; Westchester Literary Agency; Wreschner, Authors' Representative, Ruth; Writers House; Zeckendorf Assoc., Susan

Computers/electronics. Adler & Robin Books; Allen Literary Agency, Linda; Axelrod Agency; Baldi Literary Agency, Malaga; Beekman Literary Agency; Doyen Literary Services; Ellison, Nicholas; Elmo Agency, Ann; Emerald Literary Agency; Goddard, Connie: Book Development; Henderson Literary Representation; Herman Agency, Jeff; Jordan Literary Agency, Lawrence; Lindstrom Literary Group; Lyceum Creative Properties; Moore Literary Agency; Mura Enterprises, Dee; Nazor Literary Agency, Karen; Picard Literary Agent, Alison J.; Shepard Agency; Singer Literary Agency, Evelyn; Waterside Productions

Cooking/food/nutrition. Adler & Robin Books; Agents for Medical and Mental Health Professionals; Ajlouny Agency, Joseph S.; Allan Agency, Lee; Baldi Literary Agency, Malaga; Beekman Literary Agency; Brandt & Brandt Literary Agents; Breitman, Patti; Brown Assoc., Marie; Bykofsky Assoc., Sheree; Cantrell-Colas, Literary Agency; Casselman Literary Agent, Martha; Castiglia Literary Agency, Julie; Ciske Literary Agency, Francine; Clausen Assoc., Connie; Columbia Literary Assoc.; Coover Agency, Doe; Cornfield Literary Agency, Robert; Crawford Literary Agency; de la Haba Agency, Lois; Diamant, Writer's Workshop, Anita; Dijkstra Literary Agency, Sandra; Doyen Literary Services; Dystel Literary Management, Jane; Ellenberg Literary Agency, Ethan; Ellison, Nicholas; Elmo Agency, Ann; Farber Literary Agency; Feiler Literary Agency, Florence; Fogelman Literary Agency; Goddard, Connie: Book Development; Hawkins & Assoc., John; Henderson Literary Representation; Hendin Literary, David; Herner Rights Agency, Susan; Hochmann Books, John L.; IMG-Julian Bach Literary Agency; Kellock Co.; Klinger, Harvey; Larsen/Elizabeth Pomada Literary Agents, Michael; Lasher Agency, Maureen; Lichtman, Trister, Singer & Ross; Lincoln Literary Agency, Ray; Lindstrom Literary Group; Literary and Creative Artists Agency; Love Literary Agency, Nancy; Lyceum Creative Properties, ; McBride Literary Agency, Margret; Mainhardt Agency, Ricia; Marmur Assoc., Mildred; Multimedia Product Development; Naggar Literary Agency, Jean V.; Nazor Literary Agency, Karen; Norma-Lewis Agency, ; Parks Agency, Richard; Picard Literary Agent, Alison J.; Printed Tree; Publishing Services; Quicksilver Books-Literary Agents; Rose Literary Agency; Russell-Simenauer Literary Agency ; Schlessinger Agency, Blanche; Seligman, Literary Agent, Lynn; Shepard Agency; Siegel Literary Agency, Bobbe; Spieler Literary Agency, Gretchen; Steele & Co., Lyle; Stepping Stone; Stern Literary Agency (TX), Gloria; TCA; Urstadt Writers and Artists Agency, Susan P.; Watkins Loomis Agency; Wieser & Wieser; Wohl Literary Agency, Gary S.; Writers House; Ziegler Literary Agency, George

Crafts/hobbies. Beekman Literary Agency; Brandt & Brandt Literary Agents; Diamant, Writer's Workshop, Anita; Doyen Literary Services; Ellison, Nicholas; Elmo Agency, Ann; Feiler Literary Agency, Florence; Flaherty, Literary Agent, Joyce A.; Goddard, Connie: Book Development; Hawkins & Assoc., John; Kellock Company; Larsen/Elizabeth Pomada Literary Agents, Michael; Lincoln Literary Agency, Ray; Literary Group, ; Mainhardt Agency, Ricia; Multimedia Product Development; Norma-Lewis Agency; Parks Agency, Richard; Picard Literary Agent, Alison J.; Printed Tree; Shepard Agency; Spieler Literary Agency, Gretchen; Urstadt Writers and Artists Agency, Susan P.; Wohl Literary Agency, Gary S.; Wreschner, Authors' Representative, Ruth; Ziegler Literary Agency, George

Current affairs. Acton, Leone, Hanson & Jaffe; Adler & Robin Books; Altshuler Literary Agency, Miriam; Baldi Literary Agency, Malaga; Balkin Agency; Beekman Literary Agency; Boates Literary Agency, Reid; Borchardt , Georges; Brandt & Brandt Literary Agents; Brown Literary Agency, Andrea; Bykofsky Assoc., Sheree; Cantrell-Colas, Literary Agency; Carvainis Agency, Maria; Castiglia Literary Agency, Julie; Circle of Confusion; Clausen Assoc., Connie; Darhansoff & Verrill Literary Agents; de la Haba Agency, Lois; Diamant, Writer's Workshop, Anita; Dijkstra Literary Agency, Sandra; Doyen Literary Services, ; Ducas, Robert; Dystel Literary Management, Jane; Educational Design Services; Ellenberg Literary Agency, Ethan; Ellison, Nicholas; Elmo Agency , Ann; Emerald Literary Agency; Eth Literary Representation, Felicia; Flaming Star Literary Enterprises; Fogelman Literary Agency; Gartenberg, Literary Agent, Max; Goddard, Connie: Book Development; Green, Literary Agent, Randall Elisha; Halsey Agency, Reece; Hawkins & Assoc., John; Henderson Literary Representation; Hendin Literary, David; Herner Rights Agency, Susan; Hill Assoc., Frederick; Hochmann Books, John L.; Hull House Literary Agency; IMG-Julian Bach Literary Agency; J de S Assoc.; James Peter Assoc.; Kellock Co.; Ketz Agency, Louise B.; Kidde, Hoyt & Picard; Kouts, Literary Agent, Barbara S.; Kroll Literary Agency, Edite; Lampack Agency, Peter; Larsen/Elizabeth

Government/politics/law. Acton, Leone, Hanson & Jaffe; Adler & Robin Books; Allen Literary Agency, Linda; Axelrod Agency; Baldi Literary Agency, Malaga; Beekman Literary Agency; Black Literary Agency, David; Boates Literary Agency, Reid; Brandt & Brandt Literary Agents; Cantrell-Colas, Literary Agency; Carvainis Agency, Maria; Circle of Confusion; de la Haba Agency, Lois; Diamant, Writer's Workshop, Anita; Dijkstra Literary Agency, Sandra; Doyen Literary Services; Ducas, Robert; Dystel Literary Management, Jane; Educational Design Services; Ellison, Nicholas; Emerald Literary Agency; Eth Literary Representation, Felicia; Flaming Star Literary Enterprises; Fogelman Literary Agency; Goddard, Connie: Book Development; Green, Literary Agent, Randall Elisha; Hawkins & Assoc., John; Henderson Literary Representation; Hendin Literary, David; Herman Agency, Jeff; Herner Rights Agency, Susan; Hill Assoc., Frederick; Hochmann Books, John L.; Hull House Literary Agency; IMG-Julian Bach Literary Agency; J de S Assoc.; James Peter Assoc.; Kellock Co.; Kidde, Hoyt & Picard; Lampack Agency, Peter; Larsen/Elizabeth Pomada Literary Agents, Michael; Lasher Agency, Maureen; Lichtman, Trister, Singer & Ross; Lincoln Literary Agency, Ray; Lindstrom Literary Group; Literary and Creative Artists Agency; Literary Group; Love Literary Agency, Nancy; Lyceum Creative Properties; McBride Literary Agency, Margret; Madsen Agency, Robert; Mainhardt Agency, Ricia; Mann Agency, Carol; Marmur Assoc. , Mildred; Morrison, Henry; Mura Enterprises, Dee; Naggar Literary Agency, Jean V.; Nazor Literary Agency, Karen; New England Publishing Assoc.; Nine Muses and Apollo; Norma-Lewis Agency, ; Novak III Literary Representation, Edward A.; Otte Co.; Parks Agency, Richard; Picard Literary Agent, Alison J.; Pryor, Roberta; Rees Literary Agency, Helen; Rose Literary Agency; Sanders Literary Agency, Victoria; Schmidt Literary Agency, Harold; Schulman, A Literary Agency, Susan; Seligman, Literary Agent, Lynn; Shepard Agency; Sierra Literary Agency; Singer Literary Agency, Evelyn; Snell Literary Agency, Michael; Spieler, F. Joseph; Spitzer Literary Agency, Philip G.; Steele & Co., Lyle; Stepping Stone; Stern Literary Agency (TX), Gloria; Ware Literary Agency, John A.; Westchester Literary Agency; Witherspoon & Assoc.; Wreschner, Authors' Representative, Ruth

Health/medicine. Adler & Robin Books; Agency Chicago; Agents for Medical and Mental Health Professionals; Ajlouny Agency, Joseph S.; Allan Agency, Lee; Axelrod Agency; Baldi Literary Agency, Malaga; Balkin Agency; Beekman Literary Agency; Boates Literary Agency, Reid; Bova Literary Agency, Barbara; Brandt & Brandt Literary Agents; Breitman, Patti; Brown Literary Agency, Andrea; Bykofsky Assoc., Sheree; Cantrell-Colas, Literary Agency; Carvainis Agency, Maria; Casselman Literary Agent, Martha; Castiglia Literary Agency, Julie; Circle of Confusion; Clausen Assoc., Connie; Collin Literary Agent, Frances; Columbia Literary Assoc.; Coover Agency, Doe; Darhansoff & Verrill Literary Agents; de la Haba Agency, Lois; Diamant, Writer's Workshop, Anita; Dijkstra Literary Agency, Sandra; Doyen Literary Services; Ducas, Robert; Dystel Literary Management, Jane; Ellenberg Literary Agency, Ethan; Ellison, Nicholas; Elmo Agency, Ann; Eth Literary Representation, Felicia; Feiler Literary Agency, Florence; Flaherty, Literary Agent, Joyce A.; Flaming Star Literary Enterprises; Garon-Brooke Assoc. , Jay; Gartenberg, Literary Agent, Max; Goddard, Connie: Book Development; Gordon Agency, Charlotte; Hawkins & Assoc., John; Hegler Literary Agency, Gary L.; Henderson Literary Representation; Hendin Literary, David; Herman Agency, Jeff; Herner Rights Agency, Susan; Hochmann Books, John L.; J de S Assoc.; James Peter Assoc.; Jordan Literary Agency, Lawrence; Kellock Co.; Klinger, Harvey; Kouts, Literary Agent, Barbara S.; Lampack Agency, Peter; Larsen/Elizabeth Pomada Literary Agents, Michael; Lasher Agency, Maureen; Levant & Wales, Literary Agency; Levine Literary Agency, Ellen; Lincoln Literary Agency, Ray; Lindstrom Literary Group; Lipkind Agency, Wendy; Literary and Creative Artists Agency; Literary Group; Love Literary Agency, Nancy; Lowenstein Assoc.; McBride Literary Agency, Margret; McGrath, Helen; Mainhardt Agency, Ricia; Mann Agency, Carol; Manus & Assoc. Literary Agency; March Tenth; Marmur Assoc., Mildred; Multimedia Product Development; Mura Enterprises, Dee; Naggar Literary Agency, Jean V.; New England Publishing Assoc.; Nine Muses and Apollo; Norma-Lewis Agency; Novak III Literary Representation, Edward A.; Nugent Literary; Otitis Media; Otte Co.; Parks Agency, Richard; Picard Literary Agent, Alison J.; Protter Literary Agent, Susan Ann; Publishing Services; Quicksilver Books-Literary Agents; Rees Literary Agency, Helen; Rose Literary Agency; Russell-Simenauer Literary Agency; Schlessinger Agency, Blanche; Schmidt Literary Agency, Harold; Schulman, A Literary Agency, Susan; Seligman, Literary Agent, Lynn; Shepard Agency; Siegel Literary Agency, Bobbe; Singer Literary Agency, Evelyn; Snell Literary Agency, Michael; Spitzer Literary Agency, Philip G.; Steele & Co., Lyle; Stepping Stone; Stern Literary Agency (TX), Gloria; Teal Literary Agency, Patricia; 2M Communications; Urstadt Writers and Artists Agency, Susan P.; Ware Literary Agency, John A.; Waterside Productions; Westchester Literary Agency; Wieser & Wieser; Witherspoon & Assoc.; Wreschner, Authors' Representative, Ruth; Writers House; Zeckendorf Assoc., Susan; Ziegler Literary Agency, George

History. Acton, Leone, Hanson & Jaffe; Adler & Robin Books; Ajlouny Agency, Joseph S.; Allen, Literary Agency, James; Allen Literary Agency, Linda; Altshuler Literary Agency, Miriam; Apollo Entertainment; Axelrod Agency; Baldi Literary Agency, Malaga; Balkin Agency; Beekman Literary Agency; Boates Literary Agency, Reid; Borchardt, Georges; Brandt & Brandt Literary Agents; Brown Assoc., Marie; Brown, Curtis; Brown Literary Agency, Andrea; Bykofsky Assoc., Sheree; Cantrell-Colas, Literary Agency; Carvainis Agency, Maria; Castiglia Literary Agency, Julie; Circle of Confusion; Collin Literary Agent, Frances; Coover Agency, Doe; Cornfield Literary Agency, Robert; Curtis Assoc., Richard; Darhansoff & Verrill Literary Agents; de la Haba Agency, Lois; Diamant, Writer's Workshop, Anita; Dijkstra Literary Agency, Sandra; Doyen Literary Services; Ducas, Robert; Dystel Literary Management, Jane; Educational Design Services; Ellenberg Literary Agency, Ethan; Ellison, Nicholas; Elmo Agency, Ann; Eth Literary Representation, Felicia; Feiler Literary Agency, Florence; Flaherty, Literary Agent, Joyce A.; Garon-Brooke Assoc., Jay; Gartenberg, Literary Agent, Max; Goddard, Connie: Book Development; Gordon Agency, Charlotte; Green,

Literary Agent, Randall Elisha; Gregory Assoc., Maia; Halsey Agency, Reece; Hawkins & Assoc., John; Henderson Literary Representation; Hendin Literary, David; Herman Agency, Jeff; Herner Rights Agency, Susan; Hochmann Books, John L.; Hull House Literary Agency; IMG-Julian Bach Literary Agency; J de S Assoc.; James Peter Assoc.; Kellock Co.; Ketz Agency, Louise B.; Kidde, Hoyt & Picard; Kouts, Literary Agent, Barbara S.; Lampack Agency, Peter; Larsen/Elizabeth Pomada Literary Agents, Michael; Lasher Agency, Maureen; Lincoln Literary Agency, Ray; Lindstrom Literary Group; Lipkind Agency, Wendy; Literary Group; Love Literary Agency, Nancy; Lyceum Creative Properties; McBride Literary Agency, Margret; McCauley, Gerard; McGrath, Helen; Madsen Agency, Robert; Mainhardt Agency, Ricia; Mann Agency, Carol; March Tenth; Marmur Assoc., Mildred; Morrison, Henry; Mura Enterprises, Dee; Naggar Literary Agency, Jean V.; Nazor Literary Agency, Karen; New England Publishing Assoc.; Nine Muses and Apollo; Norma-Lewis Agency, ; Novak III Literary Representation, Edward A.; Otitis Media; Otte Co.; Parks Agency, Richard; Picard Literary Agent, Alison J.; Pocono Literary Agency; Potomac Literary Agency; Pryor, Roberta; Quicksilver Books-Literary Agents; Raymond, Literary Agent, Charlotte Cecil; Rees Literary Agency, Helen; Renaissance: A Literary/Talent Agency; Rock Literary Agency; Rose Literary Agency; Russell-Simenauer Literary Agency; Sanders Literary Agency, Victoria; Schmidt Literary Agency, Harold; Schulman, A Literary Agency, Susan; Seligman, Literary Agent, Lynn; Shepard Agency; Siegel Literary Agency, Bobbe; Spieler, F. Joseph; Spieler Literary Agency, Gretchen; Spitzer Literary Agency, Philip G.; Steele & Co., Lyle; Stepping Stone; Stern Literary Agency (TX), Gloria; TCA; Urstadt Writers and Artists Agency, Susan P.; Van Der Leun & Assoc.; Wald Assoc., Mary Jack; Wallace Literary Agency; Ware Literary Agency, John A.; Watkins Loomis Agency; Wecksler-Incomco; Westchester Literary Agency; Wieser & Wieser; Witherspoon & Assoc.; Wreschner, Authors' Representative, Ruth; Writers House; Zeckendorf Assoc., Susan; Ziegler Literary Agency, George

Horror. Allan Agency, Lee; Allen, Literary Agency, James; Allen Literary Agency, Linda; Amsterdam Agency, Marcia; Beekman Literary Agency; Butler, Art and Literary Agent, Jane; Circle of Confusion; Curtis Assoc., Richard; Doyen Literary Services, ; Dupree/Miller and Assoc. Literary; Hanson Agency; Hendin Literary, David; Herner Rights Agency, Susan; Klinger, Harvey; Lampack Agency, Peter; Larsen/Elizabeth Pomada Literary Agents, Michael; Lindstrom Literary Group; Literary Group; Maass Literary Agency, Donald; Mainhardt Agency, Ricia; March Tenth; Multimedia Product Development; Norma-Lewis Agency; Otte Co.; Parks Agency, Richard; Perkins Assoc., L.; Picard Literary Agent, Alison J.; Pocono Literary Agency; Printed Tree; Rubenstein Literary Agency, Pesha; Schmidt Literary Agency, Harold; Seligman, Literary Agent, Lynn; Seymour Agency, ; Siegel Literary Agency, Bobbe; Steele & Co., Lyle; Swanson, H.N.; Wreschner, Authors' Representative, Ruth; Ziegler Literary Agency, George

How to. Adler & Robin Books ; Authors' Literary Agency; Bartczak Assoc., Gene; Beekman Literary Agency; Bova Literary Agency, Barbara; Breitman, Patti; Brown, Curtis; Brown Literary Agency, Andrea; Bykofsky Assoc., Sheree; Crawford Literary Agency; Doyen Literary Services; Elmo Agency, Ann; Emerald Literary Agency; Feiler Literary Agency, Florence; Flaherty, Literary Agent, Joyce A.; Green, Literary Agent, Randall Elisha; Henderson Literary Representation; Hendin Literary, David; Herner Rights Agency, Susan; Kellock Company; Larsen/Elizabeth Pomada Literary Agents, Michael; Lasher Agency, Maureen; Lindstrom Literary Group; Literary Group; Love Literary Agency, Nancy; McBride Literary Agency, Margret; Mainhardt Agency, Ricia; Manus & Assoc. Literary Agency; Multimedia Product Development; Mura Enterprises, Dee; Nazor Literary Agency, Karen; Parks Agency, Richard; Picard Literary Agent, Alison J.; Pocono Literary Agency; Printed Tree; Quicksilver Books-Literary Agents; Russell-Simenauer Literary Agency; Schlessinger Agency, Blanche; Schulman, A Literary Agency, Susan; Seligman, Literary Agent, Lynn; Sierra Literary Agency; Singer Literary Agency, Evelyn; Stern Literary Agency (TX), Gloria; Teal Literary Agency, Patricia; Urstadt Writers and Artists Agency, Susan P.; Westchester Literary Agency; Wreschner, Authors' Representative, Ruth

Humor. Acton, Leone, Hanson & Jaffe; Beekman Literary Agency; Brown, Curtis; Brown Literary Agency, Andrea; Bykofsky Assoc., Sheree; Circle of Confusion; Doyen Literary Services; Dystel Literary Management, Jane; Henderson Literary Representation; Hendin Literary, David; Lampack Agency, Peter; Larsen/Elizabeth Pomada Literary Agents, Michael; Lichtman, Trister, Singer & Ross; Lindstrom Literary Group; Literary Group; Mainhardt Agency, Ricia; March Tenth; Multimedia Product Development; Mura Enterprises, Dee; Otitis Media; Parks Agency, Richard; Picard Literary Agent, Alison J.; Russell-Simenauer Literary Agency; Sanders Literary Agency, Victoria; Seligman, Literary Agent, Lynn; Westchester Literary Agency

Interior design/decorating. Baldi Literary Agency, Malaga; Brandt & Brandt Literary Agents; Castiglia Literary Agency, Julie; Doyen Literary Services; Ellison, Nicholas; Goddard, Connie: Book Development; Hawkins & Assoc., John; Henderson Literary Representation; Kellock Co.; Larsen/Elizabeth Pomada Literary Agents, Michael; Lincoln Literary Agency, Ray; Mainhardt Agency, Ricia; Mann Agency, Carol; Naggar Literary Agency, Jean V.; Picard Literary Agent, Alison J.; Pocono Literary Agency; Pryor, Roberta; Seligman, Literary Agent, Lynn; Shepard Agency; Spieler Literary Agency, Gretchen; Stepping Stone; Urstadt Writers and Artists Agency, Susan P.; Writers House

Juvenile nonfiction. Allen Literary Agency, Linda; Bartczak Assoc., Gene; Brandt & Brandt Literary Agents; Brown Assoc., Marie; Brown Literary Agency, Andrea; Cantrell-Colas, Literary Agency; Castiglia Literary Agency, Julie; Circle of Confusion; Cohen, Literary Agency, Ruth; de la Haba Agency, Lois; Diamant, Writer's Workshop, Anita; Doyen Literary Services; Educational Design Services; Elek Assoc., Peter; Ellenberg Literary Agency, Ethan; Elmo Agency, Ann; Emerald Literary Agency; Feiler Literary Agency, Florence; Flannery Literary; Gordon Agency, Charlotte; Hawkins & Assoc., John; Hegler Literary Agency,

Gary L.; Henderson Literary Representation; Kellock Co.; Kirchoff/Wohlberg, Authors' Rep. Div.; Kouts, Literary Agent, Barbara S.; Lincoln Literary Agency, Ray; Literary Group; Lyceum Creative Properties; Maccoby Literary Agency, Gina; Mainhardt Agency, Ricia; Markowitz Literary Agency, Barbara; Marmur Assoc., Mildred; Morrison, Henry; Multimedia Product Development; Mura Enterprises, Dee; Naggar Literary Agency, Jean V.; Norma-Lewis Agency; Picard Literary Agent, Alison J.; Pocono Literary Agency; Printed Tree; Pryor, Roberta; Raymond, Literary Agent, Charlotte Cecil; Rubenstein Literary Agency, Pesha; Schulman, A Literary Agency, Susan; Seymour Agency; Shepard Agency; Siegel Literary Agency, Bobbe; Singer Literary Agency, Evelyn; Urstadt Writers and Artists Agency, Susan P.; Wald Assoc., Mary Jack; Wasserman Literary Agency, Harriet; Westchester Literary Agency; Wreschner, Authors' Representative, Ruth; Writers House

Language/literature/criticism. Ajlouny Agency, Joseph S.; Baldi Literary Agency, Malaga; Balkin Agency; Beekman Literary Agency; Boates Literary Agency, Reid; Brandt & Brandt Literary Agents; Cantrell-Colas, Literary Agency; Castiglia Literary Agency, Julie; Coover Agency, Doe; Cornfield Literary Agency, Robert; Darhansoff & Verrill Literary Agents; Dijkstra Literary Agency, Sandra; Educational Design Services; Ellison, Nicholas; Emerald Literary Agency; Goddard, Connie: Book Development; Green, Literary Agent, Randall Elisha; Gregory Assoc., Maia; Halsey Agency, Reece; Hawkins & Assoc., John; Hendin Literary, David; Herner Rights Agency, Susan; Hill Assoc., Frederick; IMG-Julian Bach Literary Agency; James Peter Assoc.; Kidde, Hoyt & Picard; Larsen/Elizabeth Pomada Literary Agents, Michael; Levant & Wales, Literary Agency; Lincoln Literary Agency, Ray; Literary Group; Lyceum Creative Properties; March Tenth; Miller Assoc., Roberta D.; New England Publishing Assoc.; Nine Muses and Apollo; Otte Co.; Parks Agency, Richard; Picard Literary Agent, Alison J.; Potomac Literary Agency; Quicksilver Books-Literary Agents; Rose Literary Agency; Russell-Simenauer Literary Agency; Sanders Literary Agency, Victoria; Schmidt Literary Agency, Harold; Seligman, Literary Agent, Lynn; Shepard Agency; Siegel Literary Agency, Bobbe; Spieler Literary Agency, Gretchen; Spitzer Literary Agency, Philip G.; Stern Literary Agency (TX), Gloria; Wald Assoc., Mary Jack; Wallace Literary Agency; Ware Literary Agency, John A.; Westchester Literary Agency

Military/war. Acton, Leone, Hanson & Jaffe; Baldi Literary Agency, Malaga; Brandt & Brandt Literary Agents; Cantrell-Colas, Literary Agency; Carvainis Agency, Maria; Circle of Confusion; Curtis Assoc., Richard; Dijkstra Literary Agency, Sandra; Doyen Literary Services; Ducas, Robert; Dystel Literary Management, Jane; Educational Design Services; Ellison, Nicholas; Feiler Literary Agency, Florence; Flaherty, Literary Agent, Joyce A.; Garon-Brooke Assoc., Jay; Gartenberg, Literary Agent, Max; Goddard, Connie: Book Development; Hawkins & Assoc., John; Hegler Literary Agency, Gary L.; Hendin Literary, David; Hochmann Books, John L.; Hull House Literary Agency; Img-Julian Bach Literary Agency; J de S Assoc.; James Peter Assoc.; Kellock Co.; Ketz Agency, Louise B.; Literary Group; McCauley, Gerard; McGrath, Helen; Madsen Agency, Robert; Mura Enterprises, Dee; New England Publishing Assoc.; Novak III Literary Representation, Edward A.; Otitis Media; Otte Co.; Parks Agency, Richard; Picard Literary Agent, Alison J.; Potomac Literary Agency; Printed Tree; Pryor, Roberta; Rose Literary Agency; Schmidt Literary Agency, Harold; Schulman, A Literary Agency, Susan; Spitzer Literary Agency, Philip G.; Urstadt Writers and Artists Agency, Susan P.; Wald Assoc., Mary Jack; Wallace Literary Agency; Ware Literary Agency, John A.; Writers House

Money/finance/economics. Acton, Leone, Hanson & Jaffe; Adler & Robin Books; Axelrod Agency; Baldi Literary Agency, Malaga; Beekman Literary Agency; Behar Literary Agency, Josh; Bova Literary Agency, Barbara; Brandt & Brandt Literary Agents; Brown Assoc., Marie; Cantrell-Colas, Literary Agency; Carvainis Agency, Maria; Clausen Assoc., Connie; Coover Agency, Doe; Curtis Assoc., Richard; de la Haba Agency, Lois; Diamant, Writer's Workshop, Anita; Diamond Literary Agency (CO); Dijkstra Literary Agency, Sandra; Doyen Literary Services; Ducas, Robert; Dystel Literary Management, Jane; Educational Design Services, ; Ellison, Nicholas; Elmo Agency, Ann; Emerald Literary Agency; Fogelman Literary Agency; Gartenberg, Literary Agent, Max; Goddard, Connie: Book Development; Gordon Agency, Charlotte; Hawkins & Assoc., John; Hegler Literary Agency, Gary L.; Henderson Literary Representation; Hendin Literary, David; Hull House Literary Agency; James Peter Assoc.; Kellock Co.; Ketz Agency, Louise B.; Lampack Agency, Peter; Larsen/Elizabeth Pomada Literary Agents, Michael; Lichtman, Trister, Singer & Ross; Lincoln Literary Agency, Ray; Lindstrom Literary Group; Literary Group; McBride Literary Agency, Margret; Mainhardt Agency, Ricia; Mann Agency, Carol; Marmur Assoc. , Mildred; Multimedia Product Development; Mura Enterprises, Dee; Naggar Literary Agency, Jean V.; New England Publishing Assoc.; Nine Muses and Apollo; Novak III Literary Representation, Edward A.; Otte Co.; Parks Agency, Richard; Picard Literary Agent, Alison J.; Potomac Literary Agency; Rees Literary Agency, Helen; Rose Literary Agency; Russell-Simenauer Literary Agency; Schmidt Literary Agency, Harold; Schulman, A Literary Agency, Susan; Seligman, Literary Agent, Lynn; Shepard Agency; Singer Literary Agency, Evelyn; Spieler, F. Joseph; Steele & Co., Lyle; Stern Literary Agency (TX), Gloria; TCA; Urstadt Writers and Artists Agency, Susan P.; Waterside Productions; Wieser & Wieser; Witherspoon & Assoc.; Wreschner, Authors' Representative, Ruth; Writers House

Music/dance/theater/film. Acton, Leone, Hanson & Jaffe; Allan Agency, Lee; Allen Literary Agency, Linda; Andrews & Assoc., Bart; Axelrod Agency; Baldi Literary Agency, Malaga; Balkin Agency; Beekman Literary Agency; Brandt & Brandt Literary Agents; Brown Assoc., Marie; Bykofsky Assoc., Sheree; Casselman Literary Agent, Martha; Castiglia Literary Agency, Julie; Clausen Assoc., Connie; Cornfield Literary Agency, Robert; Curtis Assoc., Richard; de la Haba Agency, Lois; Doyen Literary Services; Ellison, Nicholas; Elmo Agency, Ann; Emerald Literary Agency; Farber Literary Agency ; Garon-Brooke Assoc., Jay; Gartenberg, Literary Agent, Max; Goddard, Connie: Book Development; Gregory Assoc., Maia; Hawkins &

Literary Agency, Linda; Beekman Literary Agency; Brown, Curtis; Brown Literary Agency, Andrea; Bykofsky Assoc., Sheree; Circle of Confusion; Doyen Literary Services; Dystel Literary Management, Jane; Elek Assoc., Peter; Elmo Agency, Ann; Emerald Literary Agency; Eth Literary Representation, Felicia; Flaherty, Literary Agent, Joyce A.; Fogelman Literary Agency; Halsey Agency, Reece; Henderson Literary Representation; Hendin Literary, David; Herner Rights Agency, Susan; James Peter Assoc.; Kellock Co.; Kidde, Hoyt & Picard; Lampack Agency, Peter; Larsen/Elizabeth Pomada Literary Agents, Michael; Lasher Agency, Maureen; Levine Literary Agency, Ellen; Lindstrom Literary Group; Literary Group; Love Literary Agency, Nancy; McBride Literary Agency, Margret; Mainhardt Agency, Ricia; Manus & Assoc. Literary Agency; March Tenth; Markowitz Literary Agency, Barbara; Morhaim Literary Agency, Howard; Multimedia Product Development; Nazor Literary Agency, Karen; Norma-Lewis Agency; Parks Agency, Richard; Perkins Assoc., L.; Picard Literary Agent, Alison J.; Pryor, Roberta; Publishing Services; Quicksilver Books-Literary Agents; Russell-Simenauer Literary Agency ; Sanders Literary Agency, Victoria; Schulman, A Literary Agency, Susan; Seligman, Literary Agent, Lynn; Spitzer Literary Agency, Philip G.; Stauffer Assoc., Nancy; Urstadt Writers and Artists Agency, Susan P.; Ware Literary Agency, John A.; Watkins Loomis Agency; Westchester Literary Agency; Wreschner, Authors' Representative, Ruth

Psychic/supernatural. Allan Agency, Lee; Allen Literary Agency, Linda; Beekman Literary Agency; Behar Literary Agency, Josh; Brandt & Brandt Literary Agents ; Cantrell-Colas, Literary Agency; Circle of Confusion ; Collin Literary Agent, Frances; Diamant, Writer's Workshop, Anita; Doyen Literary Services, ; Dupree/Miller and Assoc. Literary; Elmo Agency , Ann; Emerald Literary Agency; Flaherty, Literary Agent, Joyce A.; Greenburger Assoc., Sanford J.; Gusay Literary Agency, Charlotte; Hanson Agency, ; Hawkins & Assoc., John; Lantz-Joy Harris Literary Agency, Robert; Larsen/Elizabeth Pomada Literary Agents, Michael; Lincoln Literary Agency, Ray; Literary Group, ; Lyceum Creative Properties, ; Maass Literary Agency, Donald; McGrath, Helen; Mainhardt Agency, Ricia; Mura Enterprises, Dee; Naggar Literary Agency, Jean V.; Parks Agency, Richard; Pelter, Rodney; Perkins Assoc., L.; Picard Literary Agent, Alison J.; Rock Literary Agency; Rubenstein Literary Agency, Pesha; Russell-Simenauer Literary Agency ; Schmidt Literary Agency, Harold; Siegel Literary Agency, Bobbe; Steele & Co., Lyle; Swanson, H.N.; Wald Assoc., Mary Jack; Weiner Literary Agency, Cherry; Ziegler Literary Agency, George

Psychology. Acton, Leone, Hanson & Jaffe; Agents for Medical and Mental Health Professionals; Allen Literary Agency, Linda; Altshuler Literary Agency, Miriam; Baldi Literary Agency, Malaga; Beekman Literary Agency; Boates Literary Agency, Reid; Brandenburgh & Assoc. Literary Agency; Brandt & Brandt Literary Agents; Brown Assoc., Marie; Bykofsky Assoc., Sheree; Cantrell-Colas, Literary Agency; Carvainis Agency, Maria; Castiglia Literary Agency, Julie; Clausen Assoc., Connie; Coover Agency, Doe; Diamant, Writer's Workshop, Anita; Diamond Literary Agency (CO); Dijkstra Literary Agency, Sandra; Doyen Literary Services; Dystel Literary Management, Jane; Ellenberg Literary Agency, Ethan; Ellison, Nicholas; Elmo Agency, Ann; Emerald Literary Agency; Eth Literary Representation, Felicia; Farber Literary Agency; Feiler Literary Agency, Florence; Flaherty, Literary Agent, Joyce A.; Garon-Brooke Assoc., Jay; Gartenberg, Literary Agent, Max; Goddard, Connie: Book Development; Gordon Agency, Charlotte; Green, Literary Agent, Randall Elisha; Hawkins & Assoc., John; Hegler Literary Agency, Gary L.; Henderson Literary Representation; Hendin Literary, David; Herman Agency, Jeff; Herner Rights Agency, Susan; IMG-Julian Bach Literary Agency; James Peter Assoc.; Kellock Co.; Kidde, Hoyt & Picard; Klinger, Harvey; Kouts, Literary Agent, Barbara S.; Larsen/Elizabeth Pomada Literary Agents, Michael; Lasher Agency, Maureen; Levant & Wales, Literary Agency; Levine Literary Agency, Ellen; Lichtman, Trister, Singer & Ross; Lincoln Literary Agency, Ray; Lindstrom Literary Group; Literary Group; Love Literary Agency, Nancy; Lyceum Creative Properties; McBride Literary Agency, Margret; McGrath, Helen; Mainhardt Agency, Ricia; Mann Agency, Carol; Manus & Assoc. Literary Agency; Morhaim Literary Agency, Howard; Naggar Literary Agency, Jean V.; New England Publishing Assoc.; Nine Muses and Apollo; Parks Agency, Richard; Paton Literary Agency, Kathi J.; Picard Literary Agent, Alison J.; Potomac Literary Agency; Protter Literary Agent, Susan Ann; Quicksilver Books-Literary Agents; Raymond, Literary Agent, Charlotte Cecil; Rose Literary Agency; Russell-Simenauer Literary Agency; Sanders Literary Agency, Victoria; Schmidt Literary Agency, Harold; Schulman, A Literary Agency, Susan; Seligman, Literary Agent, Lynn; Shepard Agency; Siegel Literary Agency, Bobbe; Singer Literary Agency, Evelyn; Snell Literary Agency, Michael; Spieler Literary Agency, Gretchen; Spitzer Literary Agency, Philip G.; Steele & Co., Lyle; Stepping Stone; Stern Literary Agency (TX), Gloria; Teal Literary Agency, Patricia; Ware Literary Agency, John A.; Waterside Productions; Weingel-Fidel Agency; Westchester Literary Agency; Wieser & Wieser; Wreschner, Authors' Representative, Ruth; Writers House; Zeckendorf Assoc., Susan

Religious/inspirational. Acton, Leone, Hanson & Jaffe; Adler & Robin Books; Beekman Literary Agency; Brandenburgh & Assoc. Literary Agency; Brown Assoc., Marie; Bykofsky Assoc., Sheree; Castiglia Literary Agency, Julie; Ciske Literary Agency, Francine; Coover Agency, Doe; de la Haba Agency, Lois; Diamant, Writer's Workshop, Anita; Donlan, Thomas C.; Dystel Literary Management, Jane; Ellenberg Literary Agency, Ethan; Ellison, Nicholas; Emerald Literary Agency; Feiler Literary Agency, Florence; Goddard, Connie: Book Development; Green, Literary Agent, Randall Elisha; Hegler Literary Agency, Gary L.; Henderson Literary Representation; Hendin Literary, David; Herner Rights Agency, Susan; Holub & Assoc.; Jordan Literary Agency, Lawrence; Kellock Co.; Larsen/Elizabeth Pomada Literary Agents, Michael; Lichtman, Trister, Singer & Ross; Literary Group; McBride Literary Agency, Margret; Marmur Assoc., Mildred; Multimedia Product Development; Naggar Literary Agency, Jean V.; Picard Literary Agent, Alison J.; Printed Tree; Quicksilver Books-Literary Agents; Russell-Simenauer Literary Agency; Schulman, A Literary Agency, Susan; Seymour Agency; Shepard Agency; Singer Literary Agency, Evelyn; Stepping Stone; Westchester Literary Agency; Wreschner, Authors' Representative, Ruth; Ziegler Literary Agency, George

Science/technology. Acton, Leone, Hanson & Jaffe; Adler & Robin Books; Agents for Medical and Mental Health Professionals; Allan Agency, Lee; Axelrod Agency; Baldi Literary Agency, Malaga; Balkin Agency; Beekman Literary Agency; Boates Literary Agency, Reid; Bova Literary Agency, Barbara; Brandt & Brandt Literary Agents; Brown Literary Agency, Andrea; Cantrell-Colas, Literary Agency; Carvainis Agency, Maria; Castiglia Literary Agency, Julie; Coover Agency, Doe; Curtis Assoc., Richard; Darhansoff & Verrill Literary Agents; Diamant, Writer's Workshop, Anita; Dijkstra Literary Agency, Sandra; Doyen Literary Services; Ducas, Robert; Dystel Literary Management, Jane; Educational Design Services; Elek Assoc., Peter; Ellenberg Literary Agency, Ethan; Ellison, Nicholas; Eth Literary Representation, Felicia; Flaming Star Literary Enterprises; Gartenberg, Literary Agent, Max; Goddard, Connie: Book Development; Hawkins & Assoc., John; Hegler Literary Agency, Gary L.; Henderson Literary Representation; Hendin Literary, David; Herner Rights Agency, Susan; Jordan Literary Agency, Lawrence; Ketz Agency, Louise B.; Klinger, Harvey; Larsen/Elizabeth Pomada Literary Agents, Michael; Lasher Agency, Maureen; Levant & Wales, Literary Agency; Levine Literary Agency, Ellen; Lichtman, Trister, Singer & Ross; Lincoln Literary Agency, Ray; Lindstrom Literary Group; Lipkind Agency, Wendy; Literary Group; Love Literary Agency, Nancy; Lowenstein Assoc.; McBride Literary Agency, Margret; Madsen Agency, Robert; Mainhardt Agency, Ricia; Marmur Assoc. , Mildred; Multimedia Product Development; Mura Enterprises, Dee; Nazor Literary Agency, Karen; New England Publishing Assoc.; Nine Muses and Apollo; Novak III Literary Representation, Edward A.; Parks Agency, Richard; Picard Literary Agent, Alison J.; Potomac Literary Agency; Protter Literary Agent, Susan Ann; Quicksilver Books-Literary Agents; Rose Literary Agency; Schmidt Literary Agency, Harold; Seligman, Literary Agent, Lynn; Singer Literary Agency, Evelyn; Snell Literary Agency, Michael; Steele & Co., Lyle; Stern Literary Agency (TX), Gloria; Wallace Literary Agency; Ware Literary Agency, John A.; Weingel-Fidel Agency; Witherspoon & Assoc.; Wreschner, Authors' Representative, Ruth; Writers House; Zeckendorf Assoc., Susan

Self-help/personal improvement. Acton, Leone, Hanson & Jaffe; Adler & Robin Books; Agents for Medical and Mental Health Professionals; Ajlouny Agency, Joseph S.; Allan Agency, Lee; Authors' Literary Agency; Baldi Literary Agency, Malaga; Bartczak Assoc., Gene; Beekman Literary Agency; Behar Literary Agency, Josh; Boates Literary Agency, Reid; Bova Literary Agency, Barbara; Brandt & Brandt Literary Agents; Breitman, Patti; Brown Assoc., Marie; Bykofsky Assoc., Sheree; Cantrell-Colas, Literary Agency; Castiglia Literary Agency, Julie; Ciske Literary Agency, Francine; Clausen Assoc., Connie; Columbia Literary Assoc.; Curtis Assoc., Richard; Davie Literary Agency, Elaine; de la Haba Agency, Lois; Diamant, Writer's Workshop, Anita; Diamond Literary Agency (CO); Dijkstra Literary Agency, Sandra; Doyen Literary Services; Ellenberg Literary Agency, Ethan; Elmo Agency, Ann; Emerald Literary Agency; Feiler Literary Agency, Florence; Flaherty, Literary Agent, Joyce A.; Flaming Star Literary Enterprises; Fogelman Literary Agency; Garon-Brooke Assoc., Jay; Gartenberg, Literary Agent, Max; Goddard, Connie: Book Development; Hawkins & Assoc., John; Hegler Literary Agency, Gary L.; Henderson Literary Representation; Hendin Literary, David; Herman Agency, Jeff; Herner Rights Agency, Susan; Holub & Assoc.; IMG-Julian Bach Literary Agency; J de S Assoc.; James Peter Assoc., ; Jordan Literary Agency, Lawrence; Kellock Co.; Kidde, Hoyt & Picard; Klinger, , Harvey; Kouts, Literary Agent, Barbara S.; Larsen/Elizabeth Pomada Literary Agents, Michael; Lasher Agency, Maureen; Levant & Wales, Literary Agency; Lichtman, Trister, Singer & Ross; Lincoln Literary Agency, Ray; Lindstrom Literary Group; Literary and Creative Artists Agency; Literary Group; Love Literary Agency, Nancy; McBride Literary Agency, Margret; McGrath, Helen; Madsen Agency, Robert; Mainhardt Agency, Ricia; Mann Agency, Carol; Manus & Assoc. Literary Agency; Morhaim Literary Agency, Howard; Multimedia Product Development; Mura Enterprises, Dee; Naggar Literary Agency, Jean V.; New England Publishing Assoc.; Nine Muses and Apollo; Norma-Lewis Agency; Novak III Literary Representation, Edward A.; Parks Agency, Richard; Picard Literary Agent, Alison J.; Potomac Literary Agency; Printed Tree; Publishing Services; Quicksilver Books-Literary Agents; Rees Literary Agency, Helen; Rose Literary Agency; Russell-Simenauer Literary Agency; Schlessinger Agency, Blanche; Schmidt Literary Agency, Harold; Schulman, A Literary Agency, Susan; Seligman, Literary Agent, Lynn; Shepard Agency; Siegel Literary Agency, Bobbe; Sierra Literary Agency; Singer Literary Agency , Evelyn; Spieler Literary Agency, Gretchen; Stauffer Assoc., Nancy; Steele & Co. Lyle; Stepping Stone; Stern Literary Agency (TX), Gloria; Teal Literary Agency, Patricia; 2M Communications; Urstadt Writers and Artists Agency, Susan P.; Weiner Literary Agency, Cherry; Westchester Literary Agency; Witherspoon & Assoc.; Wreschner, Authors' Representative, Ruth; Writers House; Ziegler Literary Agency, George

Sociology. Agents for Medical and Mental Health Professionals; Ajlouny Agency, Joseph S.; Allen Literary Agency, Linda; Baldi Literary Agency, Malaga; Balkin Agency; Brandt & Brandt Literary Agents; Brown Assoc., Marie; Brown Literary Agency, Andrea; Cantrell-Colas, Literary Agency; Castiglia Literary Agency, Julie; Coover Agency, Doe; Dijkstra Literary Agency, Sandra; Doyen Literary Services; Educational Design Services; Ellison , Nicholas; Emerald Literary Agency; Eth Literary Representation, Felicia; Flaherty, Literary Agent, Joyce A.; Goddard, Connie: Book Development; Gordon Agency, Charlotte; Hawkins & Assoc., John; Henderson Literary Representation; Hendin Literary, David; Herner Rights Agency, Susan; Hochmann Books, John L.; Hull House Literary Agency; J de S Assoc.; Kellock Co.; Kidde, Hoyt & Picard; Larsen/Elizabeth Pomada Literary Agents, Michael; Lasher Agency, Maureen; Lichtman, Trister, Singer & Ross; Lincoln Literary Agency, Ray; Lindstrom Literary Group; Lipkind Agency, Wendy; Literary Group; Love Literary Agency, Nancy; Lyceum Creative Properties; McBride Literary Agency, Margret; Mainhardt Agency, Ricia; Mann Agency, Carol; Multimedia Product Development; Mura Enterprises, Dee; Naggar

Literary Agency, Jean V.; Nazor Literary Agency, Karen; New England Publishing Assoc.; Otte Co.; Parks Agency, Richard; Paton Literary Agency, Kathi J.; Picard Literary Agent, Alison J.; Pryor, Roberta; Quicksilver Books-Literary Agents; Raymond, Literary Agent, Charlotte Cecil; Rees Literary Agency, Helen; Rose Literary Agency; Russell-Simenauer Literary Agency; Schmidt Literary Agency, Harold; Schulman, A Literary Agency, Susan; Seligman, Literary Agent, Lynn; Shepard Agency; Spieler, F. Joseph; Spitzer Literary Agency, Philip G.; Stauffer Assoc., Nancy; Steele & Co., Lyle; Stern Literary Agency (TX), Gloria; Wald Assoc., Mary Jack; Waterside Productions, ; Weiner Literary Agency, Cherry; Weingel-Fidel Agency; Westchester Literary Agency; Zeckendorf Assoc., Susan

Sports. Acton, Leone, Hanson & Jaffe; Agency Chicago; Agents for Medical and Mental Health Professionals; Allan Agency, Lee; Beekman Literary Agency; Black Literary Agency, David; Boates Literary Agency, Reid; Brandt & Brandt Literary Agents; Brown Literary Agency, Andrea; Castiglia Literary Agency, Julie; Circle of Confusion; Curtis Assoc., Richard; Diamant, Writer's Workshop, Anita; Dijkstra Literary Agency, Sandra; Doyen Literary Services; Ducas, Robert; Emerald Literary Agency; Flaming Star Literary Enterprises; Gartenberg, Literary Agent, Max; Goddard, Connie: Book Development; Hawkins & Assoc., John; Henderson Literary Representation; Hendin Literary, David; IMG-Julian Bach Literary Agency; J de S Assoc.; Jordan Literary Agency, Lawrence; Kellock Co.; Ketz Agency, Louise B.; Klinger, Harvey; Larsen/Elizabeth Pomada Literary Agents, Michael; Lasher Agency, Maureen; Levant & Wales, Literary Agency; Lichtman, Trister, Singer & Ross; Lincoln Literary Agency, Ray; Literary Group; McBride Literary Agency, Margret; McCauley, Gerard; McGrath, Helen; Mainhardt Agency, Ricia; Markowitz Literary Agency, Barbara; Marmur Assoc., Mildred; Mura Enterprises, Dee; Nazor Literary Agency, Karen; Novak III Literary Representation, Edward A.; Picard Literary Agent, Alison J.; Pocono Literary Agency; Potomac Literary Agency; Quicksilver Books-Literary Agents; Rose Literary Agency; Russell-Simenauer Literary Agency ; Shepard Agency; Siegel Literary Agency, Bobbe; Spitzer Literary Agency, Philip G.; Steele & Co., Lyle; Stern Literary Agency (TX), Gloria; Urstadt Writers and Artists Agency, Susan P.; Wald Assoc., Mary Jack; Ware Literary Agency, John A.; Waterside Productions; Westchester Literary Agency; Wohl Literary Agency, Gary S.

Translations. Balkin Agency; Crown Int'l Literature and Arts Agency, Bonnie R.; Donlan, Thomas C.; Ellison , Nicholas; Goddard, Connie: Book Development; J de S Assoc.; Lyceum Creative Properties; Picard Literary Agent, Alison J.; Raymond, Literary Agent, Charlotte Cecil; Sanders Literary Agency, Victoria; Schmidt Literary Agency, Harold; Schulman, A Literary Agency, Susan; Seligman, Literary Agent, Lynn; Stauffer Assoc., Nancy; Wald Assoc., Mary Jack; Westchester Literary Agency; Wieser & Wieser

True crime/investigative. Acton, Leone, Hanson & Jaffe; Adler & Robin Books; Agency Chicago; Allan Agency, Lee; Allen, Literary Agency, James; Allen Literary Agency, Linda; Authors' Literary Agency; Baldi Literary Agency, Malaga; Balkin Agency; Beekman Literary Agency; Boates Literary Agency, Reid; Bova Literary Agency, Barbara; Brandt & Brandt Literary Agents ; Bykofsky Assoc., Sheree; Cantrell-Colas, Literary Agency; Carvainis Agency, Maria; Circle of Confusion; Ciske Literary Agency, Francine; Clausen Assoc., Connie; Cohen, Literary Agency, Ruth; Collin Literary Agent, Frances; Coover Agency, Doe; Crawford Literary Agency; Curtis Assoc., Richard; Davie Literary Agency, Elaine; Diamant, Writer's Workshop, Anita; Dijkstra Literary Agency, Sandra; Doyen Literary Services; Ducas, Robert; Dystel Literary Management, Jane; Elek Assoc., Peter; Ellenberg Literary Agency, Ethan; Ellison , Nicholas; Elmo Agency, Ann; Emerald Literary Agency; Eth Literary Representation, Felicia; Feiler Literary Agency, Florence; Flaherty, Literary Agent, Joyce A.; Fogelman Literary Agency; Garon-Brooke Assoc., Jay; Gartenberg, Literary Agent, Max; Goddard, Connie: Book Development; Green, Literary Agent, Randall Elisha; Halsey Agency, Reece; Hawkins & Assoc., John; Hegler Literary Agency, Gary L.; Henderson Literary Representation; Hendin Literary, David; Herner Rights Agency, Susan; Hull House Literary Agency; IMG-Julian Bach Literary Agency; Ketz Agency, Louise B.; Klinger, Harvey; Lampack Agency, Peter; Larsen/Elizabeth Pomada Literary Agents, Michael; Lasher Agency, Maureen; Lichtman, Trister, Singer & Ross; Lindstrom Literary Group; Literary Group; Love Literary Agency, Nancy; McBride Literary Agency, Margret; Madsen Agency, Robert; Mainhardt Agency, Ricia; Mann Agency, Carol; Manus & Assoc. Literary Agency; March Tenth; Marmur Assoc., Mildred; Morhaim Literary Agency, Howard; Multimedia Product Development; Mura Enterprises, Dee; Naggar Literary Agency, Jean V.; Nathan, Ruth; New England Publishing Assoc.; Nine Muses and Apollo; Norma-Lewis Agency; Novak III Literary Representation, Edward A.; Nugent Literary; Otitis Media; Otte Co.; Parks Agency, Richard; Picard Literary Agent, Alison J.; Potomac Literary Agency; Pryor, Roberta; Quicksilver Books-Literary Agents; Rees Literary Agency, Helen; Renaissance: A Literary/Talent Agency; Rose Literary Agency; Russell-Simenauer Literary Agency; Schlessinger Agency, Blanche; Schmidt Literary Agency, Harold; Schulman, A Literary Agency, Susan; Seligman, Literary Agent, Lynn; Siegel Literary Agency, Bobbe; Spitzer Literary Agency, Philip G.; Steele & Co., Lyle; Stepping Stone; Stern Literary Agency (TX), Gloria; TCA; Teal Literary Agency, Patricia; Wald Assoc., Mary Jack; Wallace Literary Agency; Ware Literary Agency, John A.; Waterside Productions; Watkins Loomis Agency; Westchester Literary Agency; Wieser & Wieser; Witherspoon & Assoc.; Wreschner, Authors' Representative, Ruth; Wright Representatives, Ann; Writers House; Zeckendorf Assoc., Susan

Women's issues/women's studies. Acton, Leone, Hanson & Jaffe; Adler & Robin Books; Allen Literary Agency, Linda; Altshuler Literary Agency, Miriam; Authors' Literary Agency; Baldi Literary Agency, Malaga; Bartczak Assoc., Gene; Beekman Literary Agency; Behar Literary Agency, Josh; Boates Literary Agency, Reid; Borchardt, Georges; Bova Literary Agency, Barbara; Brandt & Brandt Literary Agents; Brown Assoc., Marie; Bykofsky Assoc., Sheree; Cantrell-Colas, Literary Agency; Carvainis Agency, Maria; Casselman Literary Agent, Martha; Castiglia Literary Agency, Julie; Circle of Confusion; Ciske Literary Agency, Francine; Clausen Assoc., Connie; Cohen, Literary Agency, Ruth; Coover Agency, Doe; Crawford Literary Agency; Crown Int'l Literature and Arts Agency, Bonnie R.; Davie Literary Agency, Elaine; de la Haba Agency Lois; Diamant, Writer's Workshop, Anita; Dijkstra Literary Agency, Sandra; Doyen Literary Services; Dystel Literary Management, Jane; Educational Design Services; Ellison, Nicholas; Elmo Agency, Ann; Emerald Literary Agency; Eth Literary Representation, Felicia; Feiler Literary Agency, Florence; Flaherty, Literary Agent, Joyce A.; Fogelman Literary Agency; Gartenberg, Literary Agent, Max; Goddard, Connie: Book Development; Gordon Agency, Charlotte; Halsey Agency, Reece; Hawkins & Assoc., John; Henderson Literary Representation; Hendin Literary, David; Herner Rights Agency, Susan; Hill Assoc., Frederick; IMG-Julian Bach Literary Agency; Kellock Co.; Kidde, Hoyt & Picard; Klinger, Harvey; Kouts, Literary Agent, Barbara S.; Kroll Literary Agency, Edite; Lampack Agency, Peter; Larsen/Elizabeth Pomada Literary Agents, Michael; Lasher Agency, Maureen; Levant & Wales, Literary Agency; Levine Literary Agency, Ellen; Lincoln Literary Agency, Ray; Lindstrom Literary Group; Literary Group; Love Literary Agency, Nancy; McBride Literary Agency, Margret; Maccoby Literary Agency, Gina; McGrath, Helen; Mainhardt Agency, Ricia; Mann Agency, Carol; Manus & Assoc. Literary Agency; Markowitz Literary Agency, Barbara; Marmur Assoc., Mildred; Morhaim Literary Agency, Howard; Multimedia Product Development; Mura Enterprises, Dee; Naggar Literary Agency, Jean V.; Nazor Literary Agency, Karen; New England Publishing Assoc.; Nine Muses and Apollo; Norma-Lewis Agency; Novak III Literary Representation, Edward A.; Parks Agency, Richard; Paton Literary Agency, Kathi J.; Picard Literary Agent, Alison J.; Printed Tree; Pryor, Roberta; Publishing Services; Quicksilver Books-Literary Agents; Raymond, Literary Agent, Charlotte Cecil; Rees Literary Agency, Helen; Rose Literary Agency; Russell-Simenauer Literary Agency; Sanders Literary Agency, Victoria; Schmidt Literary Agency, Harold; Schulman, A Literary Agency, Susan; Seligman, Literary Agent, Lynn; Shepard Agency; Siegel Literary Agency, Bobbe; Sierra Literary Agency; Singer Literary Agency , Evelyn; Snell Literary Agency, Michael; Spieler, F. Joseph; Spieler Literary Agency, Gretchen; Stepping Stone; Stern Literary Agency (TX), Gloria; TCA; Teal Literary Agency, Patricia; 2M Communications; Urstadt Writers and Artists Agency, Susan P.; Waterside Productions; Watkins Loomis Agency; Weingel-Fidel Agency; Westchester Literary Agency; Witherspoon & Assoc.; Wreschner, Authors' Representative, Ruth; Writers House; Zeckendorf Assoc., Susan

Fee-charging literary agents/Fiction

Action/adventure. A & R Burke; Abacus Group; Acacia House Publishing Services; Ahearn Agency; Anthony Agency, Joseph; Argonaut Literary Agency; Author Aid Assoc.; Author Author Literary Agency; Authors' Marketing Services; Berzon Agency, Marian; Brinke Literary Agency; Browne, Pema; Catalog Literary Agency; Chandelyn Literary Agency; Collier Assoc.; Cook Agency, Bruce; Dorese Agency; Eden Literary Agency; Fishbein, Frieda; Flannery White and Stone; ForthWrite Literary Agency; Fran Literary Agency; Gladden Unlimited; Hamilton's Literary Agency, Andrew; Hilton Literary Agency, Alice; Hubbs Agency, Yvonne Trudeau; Independent Publishing Agency; Jenks Agency, Carolyn; Kaltman Literary Agency, Larry; Kellock & Assoc., J.; Kern Literary Agency, Natasha; Law Offices of Robert L. Fenton PC; Lee Literary Agency, L. Harry; Lee Shore Agency; Lighthouse Literary Agency; Literary Bridge; Literary Group West; McKinley, Literary Agency, Virginia C.; Marshall Agency, Evan; Mid-America Literary Agency; Montgomery Literary Agency; Nelson Literary Agency & Lecture Bureau, BK; New Writing Agency; Northwest Literary Services; Olesha Agency, Andrea; Pell Agency, William; Penmarin Books; Perkins' Literary Agency; Pine Assoc., Arthur; PMA Literary and Film Management; Portman Organization; Puddingstone Literary Agency; QCorp Literary Agency; Rose Agency; Shoestring Press; Singer Media; Steinberg Literary Agency, Michael; Stern Agency (CA), Gloria; Strong Literary Agency, Marianne; Wallerstein Agency, Gerry B.; West Coast Literary Assoc.; Wildstar Assoc.; Write Designs Literary Agency; Writer's Consulting Group; Puddingstone Literary Agency

Cartoon/comic. Authors' Marketing Services; Chandelyn Literary Agency; Colby: Literary Agency; Cook Agency, Bruce; Eden Literary Agency; Fran Literary Agency; Hamilton's Literary Agency, Andrew; Howard Agency, Eddy; Independent Publishing Agency; Jenks Agency, Carolyn; Lighthouse Literary Agency; Montgomery Literary Agency; Nelson Literary Agency & Lecture Bureau, BK; Northeast Literary Agency; Singer Media

Confessional. Ackerman Literary Services; Anthony Agency, Joseph; Argonaut Literary Agency; Author Aid Assoc.; Chandelyn Literary Agency; Eden Literary Agency; Hamilton's Literary Agency, Andrew; Hilton Literary Agency, Alice; Independent Publishing Agency; Kaltman Literary Agency, Larry; New Writing Agency; Northwest Literary Services; QCorp Literary Agency; Visions Press

Contemporary issues. A & R Burke; Abacus Group; Ahearn Agency; Argonaut Literary Agency; Author Aid Assoc.; Author Author Literary Agency; Berzon Agency, Marian; Browne, Pema; Chandelyn Literary Agency; Connor Literary Agency; Dorese Agency; Fishbein, Frieda; Flannery White and Stone; Fran Literary Agency; Hamilton's Literary Agency, Andrew; Hardy Agency; Heacock Literary Agency; HHilton Literary Agency, Alice; Hubbs Agency, Yvonne Trudeau; Independent Publishing Agency; Jenks Agency, Carolyn; Kaltman Literary Agency, Larry; Kellock & Assoc., J.; Kern Literary Agency, Natasha; Law Offices of Robert L. Fenton PC; Lee Shore Agency; Levine Communications, James; Lighthouse Literary Agency; Literary Bridge; Lopopolo Literary Agency, Toni; McKinley, Literary Agency, Virginia C.; Marshall Agency, Evan; Montgomery Literary Agency; Nelson Literary Agency & Lecture Bureau, BK; New Writing Agency; Northwest Literary Services; Oceanic Press; Olesha Agency, Andrea; Penmarin Books; PMA Literary and

Film Management; QCorp Literary Agency; Rose Agency; Steinberg Literary Agency, Michael; Stern Agency (CA), Gloria; Strong Literary Agency, Marianne; Tiger Moon Enterprises; Visions Press; Wallerstein Agency, Gerry B.; West Coast Literary Assoc.; Writer's Consulting Group

Detective/police/crime. A & R Burke; Abacus Group; Acacia House Publishing Services; Ackerman Literary Services; Ahearn Agency; Anthony Agency, Joseph; Argonaut Literary Agency; Author Aid Assoc.; Author Author Literary Agency; Authors' Marketing Services; Brinke Literary Agency; Browne, Pema; Chandelyn Literary Agency; Clark Literary Agency, SJ; Colby: Literary Agency; Collier Assoc.; Connor Literary Agency; Dorese Agency; Eden Literary Agency; Fishbein, Frieda; Fran Literary Agency; Gladden Unlimited; Hamilton's Literary Agency, Andrew; Hilton Literary Agency, Alice; Independent Publishing Agency; Jenks Agency, Carolyn; Kaltman Literary Agency, Larry; Kellock & Assoc., J.; Kern Literary Agency, Natasha; Law Offices of Robert L. Fenton PC; Lee Literary Agency, L. Harry; Lee Shore Agency; Lighthouse Literary Agency; Literary Bridge; Literary Group West; Lopopolo Literary Agency, Toni; M.H. International Literary Agency; McKinley, Literary Agency, Virginia C.; Marshall Agency, Evan; Montgomery Literary Agency; Nelson Literary Agency & Lecture Bureau, BK; New Writing Agency; Northeast Literary Agency; Northwest Literary Services; Oceanic Press; Pell Agency, William; Penmarin Books; Perkins' Literary Agency; Pine Assoc., Arthur; PMA Literary and Film Management; Portman Organization; Puddingstone Literary Agency; QCorp Literary Agency; Singer Media; SLC Enterprises; Steinberg Literary Agency, Michael; Stern Agency (CA), Gloria; Strong Literary Agency, Marianne; Taylor Literary Agency, Dawson; Toomey Assoc., Jeanne; Wallerstein Agency, Gerry B.; Watt & Assoc., Sandra; West Coast Literary Assoc.; Wildstar Assoc.; Write Designs Literary Agency; Writer's Consulting Group

Erotica. Abacus Group; Anthony Agency, Joseph; Author Aid Assoc.; Author Author Literary Agency; Eastwind Writers; Hamilton's Literary Agency, Andrew; Hilton Literary Agency, Alice; Howard Agency, Eddy; Hubbs Agency, Yvonne Trudeau; Independent Publishing Agency; Kaltman Literary Agency, Larry; Lee Literary Agency, L. Harry; Lopopolo Literary Agency, Toni; Marshall Agency, Evan; New Writing Agency; Northwest Literary Services; Oceanic Press; QCorp Literary Agency; Singer Media; Steinberg Literary Agency, Michael; Stern Agency (CA), Gloria; Visions Press

Ethnic. A & R Burke; Ahearn Agency; Author Aid Assoc.; Backman, Elizabeth H.; Browne, Pema; Chandelyn Literary Agency; Connor Literary Agency; Dorese Agency; Eastwind Writers; Flannery White and Stone; Gladden Unlimited; Hamilton's Literary Agency, Andrew; Hilton Literary Agency, Alice; Independent Publishing Agency; Jenks Agency, Carolyn; Kaltman Literary Agency, Larry; Kellock & Assoc., J.; Kern Literary Agency, Natasha; Law Offices of Robert L. Fenton PC; Lee Shore Agency; Lighthouse Literary Agency; Lopopolo Literary Agency, Toni; McKinley, Literary Agency, Virginia C.; Marshall Agency, Evan; Montgomery Literary Agency; New Writing Agency; Northwest Literary Services; Olesha Agency, Andrea; Penmarin Books; QCorp Literary Agency; Visions Press

Experimental. Author Aid Assoc.; Author Author Literary Agency; Chandelyn Literary Agency; Connor Literary Agency; Eden Literary Agency; Flannery White and Stone; Howard Agency, Eddy; Independent Publishing Agency; Kellock & Assoc., J.; Lighthouse Literary Agency; Montgomery Literary Agency; New Writing Agency; Northwest Literary Services; Oceanic Press; Olesha Agency, Andrea; Penmarin Books; QCorp Literary Agency; West Coast Literary Assoc.

Family saga. A & R Burke; Abacus Group; Ahearn Agency; Author Aid Assoc.; Author Author Literary Agency; Authors' Marketing Services; Berzon Agency, Marian; Catalog Literary Agency; Chandelyn Literary Agency; Connor Literary Agency; Cook Agency, Bruce; Dorese Agency; Fishbein, Frieda; Flannery White and Stone; ForthWrite Literary Agency; Hamilton's Literary Agency, Andrew; Hubbs Agency, Yvonne Trudeau; Jenks Agency, Carolyn; Kaltman Literary Agency, Larry; Kellock & Assoc., J.; Kern Literary Agency, Natasha; Lee Literary Agency, L. Harry; Lee Shore Agency; Lighthouse Literary Agency; Lopopolo Literary Agency, Toni; McKinley, Literary Agency, Virginia C.; Marcil Literary Agency, Denise; Marshall Agency, Evan; Montgomery Literary Agency; Nelson Literary Agency & Lecture Bureau, BK; New Writing Agency; Northwest Literary Services; Oceanic Press; Olesha Agency, Andrea; Perkins' Literary Agency; Pine Assoc., Inc, Arthur; PMA Literary and Film Management, Inc.; Portman Organization; QCorp Literary Agency; Rose Agency; Strong Literary Agency, Marianne; Tiger Moon Enterprises; Wallerstein Agency, Gerry B.; Writer's Consulting Group

Fantasy. A & R Burke; Abacus Group; Ahearn Agency; Anthony Agency, Joseph; Author Aid Assoc.; Author Author Literary Agency; Authors' Marketing Services Ltd.; Backman, Elizabeth H.; Berzon Agency, Marian; Brinke Literary Agency; Chandelyn Literary Agency; Collier Assoc.; Cook Agency, Bruce; Eden Literary Agency; Fishbein Ltd., Frieda; Fran Literary Agency; Gislason Agency; Hilton Literary Agency, Alice; Howard Agency, Eddy; Hubbs Agency, Yvonne Trudeau; Independent Publishing Agency; Jenks Agency, Carolyn; Kellock & Assoc., J.; Lee Literary Agency, L. Harry; Lee Shore Agency; Literary Bridge; McKinley, Literary Agency, Virginia C.; Montgomery Literary Agency; Nelson Literary Agency & Lecture Bureau, BK; New Writing Agency; Northwest Literary Services; Oceanic Press; Olesha Agency, Andrea; QCorp Literary Agency; Singer Media; Stern Agency (CA), Gloria; Wildstar Assoc.

Feminist. A & R Burke; Ahearn Agency; Author Author Literary Agency; Browne, Pema; Dorese Agency; Fishbein, Frieda; Flannery White and Stone; Gislason Agency; Hayes & Assoc., Gil; Hubbs Agency, Yvonne Trudeau; Independent Publishing Agency; Jenks Agency, Carolyn; Kaltman Literary Agency, Larry; Kellock & Assoc., J.; Kern Literary Agency, Natasha; Lighthouse Literary Agency; Literary Bridge; Lopopolo Literary Agency, Toni; McKinley, Literary Agency, Virginia C.; Marcil Literary Agency, Denise; Nelson

ment; Popkin, Julie; QCorp Literary Agency; Rydal; Shoestring Press; SLC Enterprises; Stern Agency (CA), Gloria; Strong Literary Agency, Marianne; Tiger Moon Enterprises; Wallerstein Agency, Gerry B.; West Coast Literary Assoc.; Wildstar Assoc.; Write Designs Literary Agency

Mainstream. A & R Burke; Abacus Group; Acacia House Publishing Services; Ahearn Agency; Author Aid Assoc.; Authors' Marketing Services; Berzon Agency, Marian; Browne, Pema; Catalog Literary Agency; Chandelyn Literary Agency; Collier Assoc.; Daley, Aleta M.; Dorese Agency; Fishbein, Frieda; Flannery White and Stone; ForthWrite Literary Agency; Fran Literary Agency; Gladden Unlimited; Hayes & Assoc., Gil; Hilton Literary Agency, Alice; Howard Agency, Eddy; Hubbs Agency, Yvonne Trudeau; Independent Publishing Agency; Kaltman Literary Agency, Larry; Kellock & Assoc., J.; Kern Literary Agency, Natasha; Law Offices of Robert L. Fenton PC; Lee Literary Agency, L. Harry; Lee Shore Agency; Levine Communications, James; Lighthouse Literary Agency; Literary Bridge; Literary Group West; Lopopolo Literary Agency, Toni; Marshall Agency, Evan; Mid-America Literary Agency; Montgomery Literary Agency; Nelson Literary Agency & Lecture Bureau, BK; New Writing Agency; Northwest Literary Services; Oceanic Press; Olesha Agency, Andrea; Penmarin Books; Perkins' Literary Agency; Pine Assoc., Arthur; PMA Literary and Film Management; Popkin, Julie; QCorp Literary Agency; Rose Agency; Rydal; Steinberg Literary Agency, Michael; Stern Agency (CA), Gloria; Strong Literary Agency, Marianne; Visions Press; Wallerstein Agency, Gerry B.; Watt & Assoc., Sandra; West Coast Literary Assoc.; Wildstar Assoc.; Write Designs Literary Agency; Writer's Consulting Group

Mystery/suspense. A & R Burke; Acacia House Publishing Services; Ackerman Literary Services; Ahearn Agency; Anthony Agency, Joseph; Argonaut Literary Agency; Author Aid Assoc.; Author Author Literary Agency; Authors' Marketing Services; Backman, Elizabeth H.; Berzon Agency, Marian; Brinke Literary Agency; Browne, Pema; Chandelyn Literary Agency; Clark Literary Agency, SJ; Colby: Literary Agency; Collier Assoc.; Connor Literary Agency; Cook Agency, Bruce; Daley, Aleta M.; Dorese Agency; Eastwind Writers; Eden Literary Agency; Fishbein, Frieda; Flannery White and Stone; ForthWrite Literary Agency; Fran Literary Agency; Gislason Agency; Hamilton's Literary Agency, Andrew; Hayes & Assoc., Gil; Hilton Literary Agency, Alice; Hubbs Agency, Yvonne Trudeau; Independent Publishing Agency; Jenks Agency, Carolyn; JLM Literary Agents; Kaltman Literary Agency, Larry; Kellock & Assoc., J.; Kern Literary Agency, Natasha; Law Offices of Robert L. Fenton PC; Lee Literary Agency, L. Harry; Lighthouse Literary Agency; Literary Bridge; Lopopolo Literary Agency, Toni; M.H. International Literary Agency; McKinley, Literary Agency, Virginia C.; Marcil Literary Agency, Denise; Marshall Agency, Evan; Nelson Literary Agency & Lecture Bureau, BK; New Writing Agency; Northeast Literary Agency; Northwest Literary Services; Oceanic Press; Oceanic Press Service; Olesha Agency, Andrea; Penmarin Books; PMA Literary and Film Management; Popkin, Julie; QCorp Literary Agency; Rose Agency; Singer Media; Steinberg Literary Agency, Michael; Taylor Literary Agency, Dawson; Wallerstein Agency, Gerry B.; Watt & Assoc., Sandra; West Coast Literary Assoc.; Wildstar Assoc.; Write Designs Literary Agency; Writer's Consulting Group

Open to all fiction. Bernstein Literary Agency, Meredith; Brinke Literary Agency; Evans & Assoc.; Follendore Literary Agency, Joan; Morgan Literary Agency, David H.; Northeast Literary Agency; Pacific Literary Services; Raintree Agency; Sullivan Assoc., Mark; Total Acting Experience

Picture book. A & R Burke; Alp Arts; Author Aid Assoc.; Author Author Literary Agency; Browne, Pema; Chandelyn Literary Agency; Clark Literary Agency, SJ; Eastwind Writers; Eden Literary Agency; Flannery White and Stone; ForthWrite Literary Agency; Fran Literary Agency; Hilton Literary Agency, Alice; Howard Agency, Eddy; Independent Publishing Agency; Kellock & Assoc., J.; Lighthouse Literary Agency; Montgomery Literary Agency; Northeast Literary Agency; Northwest Literary Services; Oceanic Press; QCorp Literary Agency; Singer Media; SLC Enterprises

Psychic/supernatural. Abacus Group; Ackerman Literary Services; Ahearn Agency; Anthony Agency, Joseph; Author Aid Assoc.; Author Author Literary Agency; Authors' Marketing Services; Brinke Literary Agency; Browne, Pema; Chandelyn Literary Agency; Clark Literary Agency, SJ; Dorese Agency; Flannery White and Stone; Hamilton's Literary Agency, Andrew; Heacock Literary Agency; Hilton Literary Agency, Alice; Howard Agency, Eddy; Hubbs Agency, Yvonne Trudeau; Independent Publishing Agency; JLM Literary Agents; Lee Shore Agency; Lopopolo Literary Agency, Toni; Marshall Agency, Evan; Montgomery Literary Agency; Nelson Literary Agency & Lecture Bureau, BK; New Writing Agency; Northwest Literary Services; Oceanic Press; Olesha Agency, Andrea; QCorp Literary Agency; Singer Media; Tiger Moon Enterprises; Toomey Assoc., Jeanne; Wildstar Assoc.

Regional. Ahearn Agency; Author Aid Assoc.; Author Author Literary Agency; Backman, Elizabeth H.; Chandelyn Literary Agency; Cook Agency, Bruce; Dorese Agency; Flannery White and Stone; Fran Literary Agency; Hayes & Assoc., Gil; Howard Agency, Eddy; Jenks Agency, Carolyn; Kaltman Literary Agency, Larry; Lighthouse Literary Agency; Montgomery Literary Agency; Northwest Literary Services; Olesha Agency, Andrea; QCorp Literary Agency; Rydal; SLC Enterprises; Tiger Moon Enterprises; West Coast Literary Assoc.

Religious/inspiration. Abacus Group; Author Aid Assoc.; Berzon Agency, Marian; Brinke Literary Agency; Browne, Pema; Chandelyn Literary Agency; Cook Agency, Bruce; Hamilton's Literary Agency, Andrew; Lee Shore Agency; McKinley, Literary Agency, Virginia C.; Marshall Agency, Evan; Olesha Agency, Andrea; QCorp Literary Agency; Rose Agency; Shoestring Press; Strong Literary Agency, Marianne; Tiger Moon Enterprises; Write Designs Literary Agency

Romance. A & R Burke; Abacus Group; Acacia House Publishing Services; Ackerman Literary Services;

Ahearn Agency; Anthony Agency, Joseph; Author Aid Assoc.; Author Author Literary Agency; Authors' Marketing Services; Berzon Agency, Marian; Browne, Pema; Catalog Literary Agency; Chandelyn Literary Agency; Collier Assoc.; Eastwind Writers; Eden Literary Agency; Fishbein Ltd., Frieda; Flannery White and Stone; ForthWrite Literary Agency; Gislason Agency; Hamilton's Literary Agency, Andrew; Hilton Literary Agency, Alice; Hubbs Agency, Yvonne Trudeau; Jenks Agency, Carolyn; JLM Literary Agents; Kaltman Literary Agency, Larry; Kellock & Assoc., J.; Kern Literary Agency, Natasha; Law Offices of Robert L. Fenton PC; Lee Literary Agency, L. Harry; Lee Shore Agency; Literary Bridge; M.H. International Literary Agency; McKinley, Literary Agency, Virginia C.; Marcil Literary Agency, Denise; Marshall Agency, Evan; Mid-America Literary Agency; Montgomery Literary Agency; Nelson Literary Agency & Lecture Bureau, BK; New Writing Agency; Northwest Literary Services; Oceanic Press; Oceanic Press Service; Perkins' Literary Agency; Pine Assoc., Arthur; PMA Literary and Film Management; Popkin, Julie; Portman Organization; QCorp Literary Agency; Rose Agency; Singer Media; SLC Enterprises; Strong Literary Agency, Marianne; Visions Press; Wallerstein Agency, Gerry B.; Warren Literary Agency, James; West Coast Literary Assoc.; Wildstar Assoc.

Science fiction. A & R Burke; Abacus Group; Ahearn Agency; Anthony Agency, Joseph; Author Aid Assoc.; Author Author Literary Agency; Authors' Marketing Services; Backman, Elizabeth H.; Brinke Literary Agency; Browne, Pema; Catalog Literary Agency; Chandelyn Literary Agency; Collier Assoc.; Cook Agency, Bruce; Daley, Aleta M.; Eastwind Writers; Eden Literary Agency; Fishbein, Frieda; Flannery White and Stone; Fran Literary Agency; Gislason Agency; Hilton Literary Agency, Alice; Hubbs Agency, Yvonne Trudeau; Jenks Agency, Carolyn; Kellock & Assoc., J.; Law Offices of Robert L. Fenton PC; Lee Literary Agency, L. Harry; Lee Shore Agency; Lighthouse Literary Agency; Literary Bridge; Marshall Agency, Evan; Mid-America Literary Agency; Montgomery Literary Agency; Nelson Literary Agency & Lecture Bureau, BK; New Writing Agency; Northeast Literary Agency; Northwest Literary Services; Oceanic Press; Olesha Agency, Andrea; Popkin, Julie; Portman Organization; Puddingstone Literary Agency; QCorp Literary Agency; Shoestring Press; Singer Media; Steinberg Literary Agency, Michael; Stern Agency (CA), Gloria; West Coast Literary Assoc.; Wildstar Assoc.

Sports. A & R Burke; Abacus Group; Argonaut Literary Agency; Author Aid Assoc.; Author Author Literary Agency; Backman, Elizabeth H.; Chandelyn Literary Agency; Colby: Literary Agency; Dorese Agency; Hamilton's Literary Agency, Andrew; Hilton Literary Agency, Alice; Jenks Agency, Carolyn; Kaltman Literary Agency, Larry; Kellock & Assoc., J.; Law Offices of Robert L. Fenton PC; Lee Literary Agency, L. Harry; Lee Shore Agency; Lighthouse Literary Agency; Literary Bridge; Mid-America Literary Agency; Montgomery Literary Agency; Nelson Literary Agency & Lecture Bureau, BK; New Writing Agency; Northwest Literary Services; Oceanic Press; Portman Organization; QCorp Literary Agency; Singer Media; SLC Enterprises

Thriller/espionage. A & R Burke; Abacus Group; Acacia House Publishing Services; Ahearn Agency; Anthony Agency, Joseph; Argonaut Literary Agency; Author Aid Assoc.; Author Author Literary Agency; Authors' Marketing Services; Backman, Elizabeth H.; Berzon Agency, Marian; Brinke Literary Agency; Browne, Pema; Catalog Literary Agency; Chandelyn Literary Agency; Clark Literary Agency, SJ; Colby: Literary Agency; Collier Assoc.; Connor Literary Agency; Cook Agency, Bruce; Fishbein, Frieda; Flannery White and Stone; Fran Literary Agency; Gladden Unlimited; Hamilton's Literary Agency, Andrew; Hilton Literary Agency, Alice; Hubbs Agency, Yvonne Trudeau; Independent Publishing Agency; Jenks Agency, Carolyn; Kaltman Literary Agency, Larry; Kellock & Assoc., J.; Kern Literary Agency, Natasha; Law Offices of Robert L. Fenton PC; Lee Literary Agency, L. Harry; Lee Shore Agency; Lighthouse Literary Agency; Literary Bridge; Literary Group West; M.H. International Literary Agency; Marshall Agency, Evan; Mid-America Literary Agency; Montgomery Literary Agency; Nelson Literary Agency & Lecture Bureau, BK; New Writing Agency; Northeast Literary Agency; Northwest Literary Services; Oceanic Press; Pell Agency, William; Penmarin Books; Pine Assoc., Arthur; PMA Literary and Film Management; Portman Organization; Puddingstone Literary Agency; QCorp Literary Agency; Rose Agency; Shoestring Press; Singer Media; Steinberg Literary Agency, Michael; Stern Agency (CA), Gloria; Strong Literary Agency, Marianne; Taylor Literary Agency, Dawson; Toomey Assoc., Jeanne; Wallerstein Agency, Gerry B.; Watt & Assoc., Sandra; West Coast Literary Assoc.; Wildstar Assoc.; Write Designs Literary Agency; Writer's Consulting Group

Westerns/frontier. Abacus Group; Ahearn Agency; Argonaut Literary Agency; Author Aid Assoc.; Author Author Literary Agency; Browne, Pema; Chandelyn Literary Agency; Colby: Literary Agency; Collier Assoc.; Eastwind Writers; Eden Literary Agency; Flannery White and Stone; Fran Literary Agency; Hamilton's Literary Agency, Andrew; Hilton Literary Agency, Alice; Jenks Agency, Carolyn; Kaltman Literary Agency, Larry; Kellock & Assoc., J.; Kern Literary Agency, Natasha; Law Offices of Robert L. Fenton PC; Lee Literary Agency, L. Harry; Lee Shore Agency; Lighthouse Literary Agency; Literary Bridge; Lopopolo Literary Agency, Toni; McKinley, Literary Agency, Virginia C.; Marshall Agency, Evan; Mid-America Literary Agency; Montgomery Literary Agency; Nelson Literary Agency & Lecture Bureau, BK; New Writing Agency; Northwest Literary Services; Oceanic Press; Perkins' Literary Agency; Portman Organization; QCorp Literary Agency; Rose Agency; Rydal; Shoestring Press; Singer Media; Stern Agency (CA), Gloria; Strong Literary Agency, Marianne; Wallerstein Agency, Gerry B.; West Coast Literary Assoc.; Wildstar Assoc.

Young adult. A & R Burke; Ahearn Agency; Alp Arts; Anthony Agency, Joseph; Author Aid Assoc.; Author Author Literary Agency; Berzon Agency, Marian; Browne, Pema; Chandelyn Literary Agency; Clark Literary Agency, SJ; Cook Agency, Bruce; Dorese Agency; Eastwind Writers; Eden Literary Agency; Fishbein, Frieda; Flannery White and Stone; ForthWrite Literary Agency; Fran Literary Agency; Hamilton's Literary Agency, Andrew; Hilton Literary Agency, Alice; Howard Agency, Eddy; Independent Publishing Agency; Jenks Agency, Carolyn; Kaltman Literary Agency, Larry; Kellock & Assoc., J.; Kern Literary Agency, Natasha; Lee Literary Agency, L. Harry; Lee Shore Agency; Levine Communications, James; Lighthouse Literary Agency; Montgomery Literary Agency; Northwest Literary Services; Oceanic Press; Olesha Agency, Andrea; QCorp Literary Agency; Rose Agency; Singer Media; SLC Enterprises; Visions Press; Wallerstein Agency, Gerry B.

Multimedia. Howard Agency, Eddy; Jenks Agency, Carolyn; Marcil Literary Agency, Denise; Marshall Agency, Evan; Nelson Literary Agency & Lecture Bureau, BK; Oceanic Press

Fee-charging literary agents/Nonfiction

Agriculture/horticulture. Catalog Literary Agency; Chandelyn Literary Agency; Eden Literary Agency; Follendore Literary Agency, Joan; ForthWrite Literary Agency; Fran Literary Agency; Howard Agency, Eddy; Kern Literary Agency, Natasha; Levine Communications, James; Lighthouse Literary Agency; Montgomery Literary Agency; Nelson Literary Agency & Lecture Bureau, BK; Northwest Literary Services; Toomey Assoc., Jeanne; Wallerstein Agency, Gerry B.

Animals. Abacus Group; Acacia House Publishing Services; Ahearn Agency; Author Aid Assoc.; Brinke Literary Agency; Catalog Literary Agency; Chandelyn Literary Agency; Eden Literary Agency; Fishbein, Frieda; Follendore Literary Agency, Joan; ForthWrite Literary Agency; Fran Literary Agency; Hamilton's Literary Agency, Andrew; Howard Agency, Eddy; Jenks Agency, Carolyn; Kellock & Assoc., J.; Kern Literary Agency, Natasha; Levine Communications, James; Lighthouse Literary Agency; Literary Bridge; Lopopolo Literary Agency, Toni; McKinley, Literary Agency, Virginia C.; Marshall Agency, Evan; Montgomery Literary Agency; Nelson Literary Agency & Lecture Bureau, BK; New Writing Agency; Northwest Literary Services; Penmarin Books; Toomey Assoc., Jeanne; Total Acting Experience; Wallerstein Agency, Gerry B.; Watt & Assoc., Sandra

Anthropology. Abacus Group; Author Aid Assoc.; Author Author Literary Agency; Brinke Literary Agency; Browne, Pema; Catalog Literary Agency; Chandelyn Literary Agency; ForthWrite Literary Agency; Heacock Literary Agency; Howard Agency, Eddy; Independent Publishing Agency; Jenks Agency, Carolyn; Kellock & Assoc., J.; Kern Literary Agency, Natasha; Lee Shore Agency; Lighthouse Literary Agency; Lopopolo Literary Agency, Toni; Montgomery Literary Agency; Nelson Literary Agency & Lecture Bureau, BK; New Writing Agency; Penmarin Books; Rydal; Sebastian Literary Agency; Sullivan Assoc., Mark; Toomey Assoc., Jeanne; Total Acting Experience; Wallerstein Agency, Gerry B.; Watt & Assoc., Sandra

Art/architecture/design. A & R Burke; Abacus Group; Browne, Pema; Chandelyn Literary Agency; Dorese Agency; Follendore Literary Agency, Joan; ForthWrite Literary Agency; Heacock Literary Agency; Independent Publishing Agency; Kellock & Assoc., J.; Kern Literary Agency, Natasha; Levine Communications, James; Lighthouse Literary Agency; Lopopolo Literary Agency, Toni; Marshall Agency, Evan; Montgomery Literary Agency; Nelson Literary Agency & Lecture Bureau, BK; New Writing Agency; Northwest Literary Services; Penmarin Books; PMA Literary and Film Management; Popkin, Julie; Sebastian Literary Agency; Strong Literary Agency, Marianne; Toomey Assoc., Jeanne; Total Acting Experience; Wallerstein Agency, Gerry B.; Write Designs Literary Agency

Biography/autobiography. A & R Burke; Abacus Group; Acacia House Publishing Services; Ahearn Agency; Argonaut Literary Agency; Author Aid Assoc.; Author Author Literary Agency; Authors' Marketing Services; Backman, Elizabeth H.; Brinke Literary Agency; Browne, Pema; Chandelyn Literary Agency; Collier Assoc.; Cook Agency, Bruce; Daley, Aleta M.; Dorese Agency; Eastwind Writers; Fishbein, Frieda; Follendore Literary Agency, Joan; ForthWrite Literary Agency; Fran Literary Agency; Gladden Unlimited; Hamilton's Literary Agency, Andrew; Hardy Agency; Hayes & Assoc., Gil; Heacock Literary Agency; Independent Publishing Agency; Jenks Agency, Carolyn; JLM Literary Agents; Kellock & Assoc., J.; Kern Literary Agency, Natasha; Law Offices of Robert L. Fenton PC; Lee Shore Agency; Levine Communications, James; Lighthouse Literary Agency; Lopopolo Literary Agency, Toni; McKinley, Literary Agency, Virginia C.; Marshall Agency, Evan; Montgomery Literary Agency; Nelson Literary Agency & Lecture Bureau, BK; New Writing Agency; Northeast Literary Agency; Northwest Literary Services; Oceanic Press; Oceanic Press Service; Pell Agency, William; Penmarin Books; PMA Literary and Film Management; Portman Organization; Sebastian Literary Agency; Shoestring Press; Singer Media; SLC Enterprises; Steinberg Literary Agency, Michael; Stern Agency (CA), Gloria; Strong Literary Agency, Marianne; Sullivan Assoc., Mark; Toomey Assoc., Jeanne; Total Acting Experience; Wallerstein Agency, Gerry B.; West Coast Literary Assoc.; Wildstar Assoc.; Write Designs Literary Agency; Writer's Consulting Group

Business. A & R Burke; Abacus Group; Ahearn Agency; Author Author Literary Agency; Authors' Marketing Services; Backman, Elizabeth H.; Browne, Pema; Catalog Literary Agency; Chandelyn Literary Agency; Collier Assoc.; Connor Literary Agency; Cook Agency, Bruce; Dorese Agency; Eden Literary Agency; Executive Excellence; Flannery White and Stone; Follendore Literary Agency, Joan; ForthWrite Literary Agency; Fran Literary Agency; Gladden Unlimited; Hamilton's Literary Agency, Andrew; Heacock Literary Agency; Independent Publishing Agency; Jenks Agency, Carolyn; JLM Literary Agents; Kellock & Assoc., J.; Kern Literary Agency, Natasha; Law Offices of Robert L. Fenton PC; Lee Shore Agency; Levine Communications, James; Lighthouse Literary Agency; Literary Bridge; Lopopolo Literary Agency, Toni;

McKinley, Literary Agency, Virginia C.; Marcil Literary Agency, Denise; Marshall Agency, Evan; Montgomery Literary Agency; Nelson Literary Agency & Lecture Bureau, BK; New Writing Agency; Northeast Literary Agency; Oceanic Press; Penmarin Books; Pine Assoc., Arthur; PMA Literary and Film Management; Rose Agency; Sebastian Literary Agency; Singer Media; SLC Enterprises; Steinberg Literary Agency, Michael; Stern Agency (CA), Gloria; Strong Literary Agency, Marianne; Sullivan Assoc., Mark; Total Acting Experience; Wallerstein Agency, Gerry B.; Wildstar Assoc.; Write Designs Literary Agency; The Write Therapist; Writer's Consulting Group

Child guidance/parenting. Ahearn Agency; Author Author Literary Agency; Authors' Marketing Services; Backman, Elizabeth H.; Brinke Literary Agency; Browne, Pema; Catalog Literary Agency; Chandelyn Literary Agency; Connor Literary Agency; Cook Agency, Bruce; Dorese Agency; Flannery White and Stone; Follendore Literary Agency, Joan; ForthWrite Literary Agency; Fran Literary Agency; Hamilton's Literary Agency, Andrew; Heacock Literary Agency; Independent Publishing Agency; Kellock & Assoc., J.; Kern Literary Agency, Natasha; Law Offices of Robert L. Fenton PC; Lee Shore Agency; Levine Communications, James; Lighthouse Literary Agency; Lopopolo Literary Agency, Toni; McKinley, Literary Agency, Virginia C.; Marcil Literary Agency, Denise; Marshall Agency, Evan; Montgomery Literary Agency; Nelson Literary Agency & Lecture Bureau, BK; New Writing Agency; Northwest Literary Services; Oceanic Press; Penmarin Books; Rose Agency; Sebastian Literary Agency; Singer Media; Stern Agency (CA), Gloria; Strong Literary Agency, Marianne; Total Acting Experience; Wallerstein Agency, Gerry B.; Wildstar Assoc.

Computers/electronics. A & R Burke; Catalog Literary Agency; Chandelyn Literary Agency; Collier Assoc.; Eden Literary Agency; Jenks Agency, Carolyn; Law Offices of Robert L. Fenton PC; Levine Communications, James; Lighthouse Literary Agency; Montgomery Literary Agency; Nelson Literary Agency & Lecture Bureau, BK; New Writing Agency; Oceanic Press; Sebastian Literary Agency; Singer Media; Steinberg Literary Agency, Michael; Stern Agency (CA), Gloria; Total Acting Experience; Write Designs Literary Agency

Cooking/food/nutrition. Abacus Group; Acacia House Publishing Services; Author Author Literary Agency; Authors' Marketing Services; Backman, Elizabeth H.; Browne, Pema; Catalog Literary Agency; Chandelyn Literary Agency; Collier Assoc.; Connor Literary Agency; Cook Agency, Bruce; Dorese Agency; Eden Literary Agency; Fishbein, Frieda; ForthWrite Literary Agency; Fran Literary Agency; Hamilton's Literary Agency, Andrew; Heacock Literary Agency; Howard Agency, Eddy; Independent Publishing Agency; Jenks Agency, Carolyn; Kellock & Assoc., J.; Kern Literary Agency, Natasha; Levine Communications, James; Lighthouse Literary Agency; Lopopolo Literary Agency, Toni; Marcil Literary Agency, Denise; Marshall Agency, Evan; Montgomery Literary Agency; Nelson Literary Agency & Lecture Bureau, BK; New Writing Agency; Northwest Literary Services; Olesha Agency, Andrea; Penmarin Books; SLC Enterprises; Stern Agency (CA), Gloria; Strong Literary Agency, Marianne; Sullivan Assoc., Mark; Tiger Moon Enterprises; Total Acting Experience; Wallerstein Agency, Gerry B.; Wildstar Assoc.; Write Designs Literary Agency

Crafts/hobbies. Acacia House Publishing Services; Ackerman Literary Services; Author Author Literary Agency; Backman, Elizabeth H.; Catalog Literary Agency; Chandelyn Literary Agency; Collier Assoc.; Connor Literary Agency; Dorese Agency; Eden Literary Agency; Follendore Literary Agency, Joan; ForthWrite Literary Agency; Fran Literary Agency; Heacock Literary Agency; Howard Agency, Eddy; Independent Publishing Agency; Lighthouse Literary Agency; Marshall Agency, Evan; Montgomery Literary Agency; Nelson Literary Agency & Lecture Bureau, BK; New Writing Agency; Northwest Literary Services; Penmarin Books; Rose Agency; Singer Media; Sullivan Assoc., Mark; Tiger Moon Enterprises; Total Acting Experience; Wallerstein Agency, Gerry B.; Wildstar Assoc.; Write Designs Literary Agency

Current affairs. A & R Burke; Abacus Group; Acacia House Publishing Services; Ahearn Agency; Argonaut Literary Agency; Author Aid Assoc.; Authors' Marketing Services; Backman, Elizabeth H.; Browne, Pema; Catalog Literary Agency; Chandelyn Literary Agency; Connor Literary Agency; Dorese Agency Ltd.; Eden Literary Agency; Fishbein, Frieda; Flannery White and Stone; Follendore Literary Agency, Joan; Hamilton's Literary Agency, Andrew; Hardy Agency; Hayes & Assoc., Gil; Hubbs Agency, Yvonne Trudeau; Independent Publishing Agency; Jenks Agency, Carolyn; JLM Literary Agents; Kellock & Assoc., J.; Kern Literary Agency, Natasha; Law Offices of Robert L. Fenton PC; Lighthouse Literary Agency; Literary Group West; Marshall Agency, Evan; Montgomery Literary Agency; Nelson Literary Agency & Lecture Bureau, BK; New Writing Agency; Penmarin Books; Pine Assoc., Arthur; Portman Organization; Sebastian Literary Agency; SLC Enterprises; Stern Agency (CA), Gloria; Strong Literary Agency, Marianne; Sullivan Assoc., Mark; Total Acting Experience; Wallerstein Agency, Gerry B.; West Coast Literary Assoc.; Wildstar Assoc.; Writer's Consulting Group

Education. Abacus Group; Author Author Literary Agency; Authors' Marketing Services; Browne, Pema; Catalog Literary Agency; Chandelyn Literary Agency; Follendore Literary Agency, Joan; Heacock Literary Agency; Howard Agency, Eddy; Jenks Agency, Carolyn; Kern Literary Agency, Natasha; Lee Shore Agency; Montgomery Literary Agency; Nelson Literary Agency & Lecture Bureau, BK; Rose Agency; Stern Agency (CA), Gloria; Strong Literary Agency, Marianne; Total Acting Experience; Wallerstein Agency, Gerry B.; Writer's Consulting Group

Ethnic/cultural interests. Abacus Group; Ahearn Agency; Author Aid Assoc.; Author Author Literary Agency; Backman, Elizabeth H.; Browne, Pema; Catalog Literary Agency; Chandelyn Literary Agency; Connor Literary Agency; Daley, Aleta M.; Eastwind Writers; Flannery White and Stone; Follendore

Literary Agency, Joan; Fran Literary Agency; Hamilton's Literary Agency, Andrew; Heacock Literary Agency; Independent Publishing Agency; Jenks Agency, Carolyn; Kern Literary Agency, Natasha; Lighthouse Literary Agency; Literary Group West; Lopopolo Literary Agency, Toni; McKinley, Literary Agency, Virginia C.; Montgomery Literary Agency; Nelson Literary Agency & Lecture Bureau, BK; Northwest Literary Services; Olesha Agency, Andrea; Rydal; Sebastian Literary Agency; Stern Agency (CA), Gloria; Total Acting Experience; Visions Press; Wallerstein Agency, Gerry B.; West Coast Literary Assoc.; Wildstar Assoc.

Gay/lesbian issues. Ahearn Agency; Author Author Literary Agency; Browne, Pema; Dorese Agency; Flannery White and Stone; Heacock Literary Agency; Jenks Agency, Carolyn; Kern Literary Agency, Natasha; Levine Communications, James; Northwest Literary Services; Olesha Agency, Andrea; Stern Agency (CA), Gloria; Visions Press; Wallerstein Agency, Gerry B.; Wildstar Assoc.

Government/politics/law. A & R Burke; Abacus Group; Author Author Literary Agency; Backman, Elizabeth H.; Browne, Pema; Catalog Literary Agency; Chandelyn Literary Agency; Connor Literary Agency; Dorese Agency Ltd.; Eden Literary Agency; Flannery White and Stone; Follendore Literary Agency, Joan; Gislason Agency; Hamilton's Literary Agency, Andrew; Hardy Agency; Heacock Literary Agency; Independent Publishing Agency; Jenks Agency, Carolyn; Kellock & Assoc., J.; Law Offices of Robert L. Fenton PC; Lee Shore Agency; Marshall Agency, Evan; Montgomery Literary Agency; Nelson Literary Agency & Lecture Bureau, BK; Penmarin Books; Popkin, Julie; Sebastian Literary Agency; Shoestring Press; Toomey Assoc., Jeanne; Total Acting Experience; Wallerstein Agency, Gerry B.; West Coast Literary Assoc.; Wildstar Assoc.

Health/medicine. Abacus Group; Acacia House Publishing Services; Ahearn Agency; Anthony Agency, Joseph; Author Aid Assoc.; Author Author Literary Agency; Authors' Marketing Services; Backman, Elizabeth H.; Browne, Pema; Catalog Literary Agency; Chandelyn Literary Agency; Connor Literary Agency; Cook Agency, Bruce; Dorese Agency; Flannery White and Stone; Follendore Literary Agency, Joan; Forth-Write Literary Agency; Fran Literary Agency; Hamilton's Literary Agency, Andrew; Hardy Agency; Hayes & Assoc., Gil; Heacock Literary Agency; Howard Agency, Eddy; Jenks Agency, Carolyn; Kaltman Literary Agency, Larry; Kellock & Assoc., J.; Kern Literary Agency, Natasha; Law Offices of Robert L. Fenton PC; Lee Shore Agency; Levine Communications, James; Lighthouse Literary Agency; Literary Bridge; Lopopolo Literary Agency, Toni; McKinley, Literary Agency, Virginia C.; Marcil Literary Agency, Denise; Marshall Agency, Evan; Montgomery Literary Agency; Nelson Literary Agency & Lecture Bureau, BK; Northwest Literary Services; Oceanic Press; Penmarin Books; Pine Assoc., Arthur; PMA Literary and Film Management; Raintree Agency; Rogers, Literary Representative, Irene; Rose Agency; Sebastian Literary Agency; Singer Media; Stern Agency (CA), Gloria; Strong Literary Agency, Marianne; Sullivan Assoc., Mark; Tiger Moon Enterprises; Total Acting Experience; Wallerstein Agency, Gerry B.; Wildstar Assoc.; Write Designs Literary Agency; Write Therapist; Writer's Consulting Group

History. A & R Burke; Abacus Group; Ahearn Agency; Argonaut Literary Agency; Author Aid Assoc.; Author Author Literary Agency; Authors' Marketing Services; Backman, Elizabeth H.; Brinke Literary Agency; Chandelyn Literary Agency; Collier Assoc.; Cook Agency, Bruce; Dorese Agency; Eden Literary Agency; Flannery White and Stone; Follendore Literary Agency, Joan; ForthWrite Literary Agency; Fran Literary Agency; Hamilton's Literary Agency, Andrew; Heacock Literary Agency; Hubbs Agency, Yvonne Trudeau; Independent Publishing Agency; Jenks Agency, Carolyn; Kellock & Assoc., J.; Lee Literary Agency, L. Harry; Lee Shore Agency; Lighthouse Literary Agency; Literary Bridge; Lopopolo Literary Agency, Toni; Marshall Agency, Evan; Montgomery Literary Agency; Nelson Literary Agency & Lecture Bureau, BK; New Writing Agency; Northeast Literary Agency; Northwest Literary Services; Penmarin Books; PMA Literary and Film Management; Popkin, Julie; Portman Organization; Sebastian Literary Agency; Shoestring Press; SLC Enterprises; Steinberg Literary Agency, Michael; Strong Literary Agency, Marianne; Tiger Moon Enterprises; Toomey Assoc., Jeanne; Total Acting Experience; Wallerstein Agency, Gerry B.; West Coast Literary Assoc.; Wildstar Assoc.; Write Designs Literary Agency

How to. Abacus Group; Author Aid Assoc.; Author Author Literary Agency; Authors' Marketing Services; Brinke Literary Agency; Browne, Pema; Catalog Literary Agency; Chandelyn Literary Agency; Collier Assoc.; Connor Literary Agency; Eden Literary Agency; Follendore Literary Agency, Joan; Fran Literary Agency; Gislason Agency; Heacock Literary Agency; Jenks Agency, Carolyn; Kern Literary Agency, Natasha; Lee Shore Agency; Lopopolo Literary Agency, Toni; Marcil Literary Agency, Denise; Marshall Agency, Evan; Montgomery Literary Agency; Nelson Literary Agency & Lecture Bureau, BK; New Writing Agency; Northeast Literary Agency; Northwest Literary Services; Oceanic Press; Penmarin Books; PMA Literary and Film Management; Puddingstone Literary Agency; Rose Agency; Singer Media; Steinberg Literary Agency, Michael; Stern Agency (CA), Gloria; Strong Literary Agency, Marianne; Total Acting Experience; Wallerstein Agency, Gerry B.; Write Designs Literary Agency

Humor. Abacus Group; Author Aid Assoc.; Author Author Literary Agency; Chandelyn Literary Agency; Coast To Coast Talent and Literary; Connor Literary Agency; Eden Literary Agency; Follendore Literary Agency, Joan; Fran Literary Agency; Heacock Literary Agency; Howard Agency, Eddy; Jenks Agency, Carolyn; Marshall Agency, Evan; Montgomery Literary Agency; New Writing Agency; Northeast Literary Agency; Northwest Literary Services; Rose Agency; Total Acting Experience; Wallerstein Agency, Gerry B.; Write Designs Literary Agency

Interior design/decorating. Author Author Literary Agency; Backman, Elizabeth H.; Chandelyn Literary Agency; Connor Literary Agency; Dorese Agency; Follendore Literary Agency, Joan; ForthWrite

Literary Agency; Fran Literary Agency; Lighthouse Literary Agency; Marcil Literary Agency, Denise; Marshall Agency, Evan; Olesha Agency, Andrea; Strong Literary Agency, Marianne; Sullivan Assoc., Mark; Toomey Assoc., Jeanne; Total Acting Experience; Wallerstein Agency, Gerry B.; Wildstar Assoc.

Juvenile nonfiction. A & R Burke; Ahearn Agency; Alp Arts; Author Aid Assoc.; Author Author Literary Agency; Browne, Pema; Catalog Literary Agency; Chandelyn Literary Agency; Cook Agency, Bruce; Eden Literary Agency; Fishbein, Frieda; Flannery White and Stone; Follendore Literary Agency, Joan; ForthWrite Literary Agency; Fran Literary Agency; Hamilton's Literary Agency, Andrew; Heacock Literary Agency; Howard Agency, Eddy; Independent Publishing Agency; Jenks Agency, Carolyn; Kellock & Assoc., J.; Levine Communications, James; Lighthouse Literary Agency; McKinley, Literary Agency, Virginia C.; March Media; Montgomery Literary Agency; Northwest Literary Services; Oceanic Press; Rose Agency; Singer Media; Strong Literary Agency, Marianne; Tiger Moon Enterprises; Total Acting Experience

Language/literature/criticism. A & R Burke; Abacus Group; Acacia House Publishing Services; Author Aid Assoc.; Author Author Literary Agency; Chandelyn Literary Agency; Connor Literary Agency; Cook Agency, Bruce; Dorese Agency; Eden Literary Agency; Follendore Literary Agency, Joan; Hayes & Assoc., Gil; Heacock Literary Agency; Independent Publishing Agency; Kellock & Assoc., J.; Kern Literary Agency, Natasha; Lopopolo Literary Agency, Toni; Marshall Agency, Evan; Montgomery Literary Agency; Nelson Literary Agency & Lecture Bureau, BK; Northwest Literary Services; Olesha Agency, Andrea; Popkin, Julie; Puddingstone Literary Agency; Stern Agency (CA), Gloria; Sullivan Assoc., Mark; Total Acting Experience; Wallerstein Agency, Gerry B.; West Coast Literary Assoc.; Wildstar Assoc.

Military/war. A & R Burke; Abacus Group; Acacia House Publishing Services; Anthony Agency, Joseph; Argonaut Literary Agency; Author Aid Assoc.; Author Author Literary Agency; Authors' Marketing Services; Browne, Pema; Catalog Literary Agency; Chandelyn Literary Agency; Dorese Agency; Eden Literary Agency; Fishbein, Frieda; Follendore Literary Agency, Joan; Fran Literary Agency; Hayes & Assoc., Gil; Heacock Literary Agency; Independent Publishing Agency; Law Offices of Robert L. Fenton PC; Lee Literary Agency, L. Harry; Lee Shore Agency; Lighthouse Literary Agency; Literary Group West; McKinley, Literary Agency, Virginia C.; Marshall Agency, Evan; Montgomery Literary Agency; Nelson Literary Agency & Lecture Bureau, BK; New Writing Agency; Portman Organization; Puddingstone Literary Agency; Shoestring Press; Strong Literary Agency, Marianne; Sullivan Assoc., Mark; Taylor Literary Agency, Dawson; Tiger Moon Enterprises; Total Acting Experience; Wallerstein Agency, Gerry B.; Wildstar Assoc.; Write Designs Literary Agency

Money/finance/economics. A & R Burke; Argonaut Literary Agency; Author Author Literary Agency; Authors' Marketing Services; Browne, Pema; Catalog Literary Agency; Chandelyn Literary Agency; Connor Literary Agency; Dorese Agency; Eden Literary Agency; Flannery White and Stone; Follendore Literary Agency, Joan; ForthWrite Literary Agency; Hamilton's Literary Agency, Andrew; Heacock Literary Agency; Independent Publishing Agency; JLM Literary Agents; Kellock & Assoc., J.; Kern Literary Agency, Natasha; Law Offices of Robert L. Fenton PC; Lee Shore Agency; Levine Communications, James; Lighthouse Literary Agency; Literary Bridge; Lopopolo Literary Agency, Toni; McKinley, Literary Agency, Virginia C.; Marcil Literary Agency, Denise; Marshall Agency, Evan; Montgomery Literary Agency; Nelson Literary Agency & Lecture Bureau, BK; Oceanic Press; Penmarin Books; Pine Assoc., Arthur; Sebastian Literary Agency; Singer Media; Steinberg Literary Agency, Michael; Stern Agency (CA), Gloria; Strong Literary Agency, Marianne; Sullivan Assoc., Mark; Tiger Moon Enterprises; Toomey Assoc., Jeanne; Total Acting Experience; Wallerstein Agency, Gerry B.; Wildstar Assoc.; Write Designs Literary Agency; Writer's Consulting Group

Music/dance/theater/film. A & R Burke; Abacus Group; Acacia House Publishing Services; Ahearn Agency; Author Aid Assoc.; Backman, Elizabeth H.; Chandelyn Literary Agency; Coast To Coast Talent and Literary; Cook Agency, Bruce; Dorese Agency; Eden Literary Agency; Flannery White and Stone; ForthWrite Literary Agency; Hamilton's Literary Agency, Andrew; Heacock Literary Agency; Howard Agency, Eddy; Independent Publishing Agency; Jenks Agency, Carolyn; JLM Literary Agents; Kellock & Assoc., J.; Law Offices of Robert L. Fenton PC; Lee Shore Agency; Lighthouse Literary Agency; McKinley, Literary Agency, Virginia C.; Marcil Literary Agency, Denise; Marshall Agency, Evan; Montgomery Literary Agency; Nelson Literary Agency & Lecture Bureau, BK; New Writing Agency; Northeast Literary Agency; Northwest Literary Services; Oceanic Press; Olesha Agency, Andrea; Portman Organization; Stern Agency (CA), Gloria; Sullivan Assoc., Mark; Tiger Moon Enterprises; Total Acting Experience; Wallerstein Agency, Gerry B.; West Coast Literary Assoc.; Wildstar Assoc.; Writer's Consulting Group

Nature/environment. Abacus Group; Acacia House Publishing Services; Author Aid Assoc.; Author Author Literary Agency; Authors' Marketing Services; Browne, Pema; Catalog Literary Agency; Chandelyn Literary Agency; Cook Agency, Bruce; Eastwind Writers; Eden Literary Agency; Fishbein, Frieda; Flannery White and Stone; Follendore Literary Agency, Joan; ForthWrite Literary Agency; Fran Literary Agency; Heacock Literary Agency; Howard Agency, Eddy; Independent Publishing Agency; Jenks Agency, Carolyn; JLM Literary Agents; Kellock & Assoc., J.; Kern Literary Agency, Natasha; Lee Shore Agency; Levine Communications, James; Lighthouse Literary Agency; Literary Bridge; Lopopolo Literary Agency, Toni; McKinley, Literary Agency, Virginia C.; Marshall Agency, Evan; Montgomery Literary Agency; Nelson Literary Agency & Lecture Bureau, BK; New Writing Agency; Northwest Literary Services; Olesha Agency, Andrea; Penmarin Books; Raintree Agency; Rydal; Sullivan Assoc., Mark; Tiger Moon Enterprises; Toomey Assoc., Jeanne; Total Acting Experience; Wallerstein Agency, Gerry B.; West Coast Literary Assoc.; Wildstar Assoc.; Write Designs Literary Agency

New Age/metaphysics. Author Aid Assoc.; Author Author Literary Agency; Brinke Literary Agency; Browne, Pema; Clark Literary Agency, SJ; Coast To Coast Talent and Literary; Dorese Agency; Flannery White and Stone; Follendore Literary Agency, Joan; Hardy Agency; Heacock Literary Agency; Howard Agency, Eddy; Jenks Agency, Carolyn; Kellock & Assoc., J.; Kern Literary Agency, Natasha; Lee Shore Agency; Levine Communications, James; Lopopolo Literary Agency, Toni; Marcil Literary Agency, Denise; Marshall Agency, Evan; Montgomery Literary Agency; New Writing Agency; Northwest Literary Services; Oceanic Press; Shoestring Press; Sullivan Assoc., Mark; Tiger Moon Enterprises; Total Acting Experience; Watt & Assoc., Sandra; Wildstar Assoc.

Open to all nonfiction. Authors And Artists Resource Center/Tarc Literary Agency; Bernstein Literary Agency, Meredith; Evans & Assoc.; Morgan Literary Agency, David H.; Northeast Literary Agency; Pacific Literary Services; QCorp Literary Agency; Rogers, Literary Representative, Irene; Wallerstein Agency, Gerry B.

Photography. Author Author Literary Agency; Backman, Elizabeth H.; Catalog Literary Agency; Chandelyn Literary Agency; Connor Literary Agency; Dorese Agency; Eden Literary Agency; Flannery White and Stone; ForthWrite Literary Agency; Howard Agency, Eddy; Independent Publishing Agency; Lighthouse Literary Agency; Montgomery Literary Agency; New Writing Agency; Northwest Literary Services; Pell Agency, William; Rydal; Sullivan Assoc., Mark; Total Acting Experience; Wallerstein Agency, Gerry B.; Write Designs Literary Agency

Popular culture. Acacia House Publishing Services; Ahearn Agency; Author Aid Assoc.; Author Author Literary Agency; Authors' Marketing Services; Browne, Pema; Catalog Literary Agency; Connor Literary Agency; Follendore Literary Agency, Joan; Heacock Literary Agency; Independent Publishing Agency; Jenks Agency, Carolyn; JLM Literary Agents; Kern Literary Agency, Natasha; Lopopolo Literary Agency, Toni; Montgomery Literary Agency; Nelson Literary Agency & Lecture Bureau, BK; New Writing Agency; Northwest Literary Services; Penmarin Books; PMA Literary and Film Management; Stern Agency (CA), Gloria; Total Acting Experience; Wallerstein Agency, Gerry B.; Write Designs Literary Agency; Writer's Consulting Group

Psychology. A & R Burke; Abacus Group; Acacia House Publishing Services; Anthony Agency, Joseph; Author Aid Assoc.; Author Author Literary Agency; Authors' Marketing Services; Backman, Elizabeth H.; Browne, Pema; Catalog Literary Agency; Chandelyn Literary Agency; Cook Agency, Bruce; Dorese Agency; Flannery White and Stone; Follendore Literary Agency, Joan; ForthWrite Literary Agency; Hamilton's Literary Agency, Andrew; Heacock Literary Agency; Howard Agency, Eddy; Independent Publishing Agency; Jenks Agency, Carolyn; JLM Literary Agents; Kern Literary Agency, Natasha; Lee Shore Agency; Levine Communications, James; Lighthouse Literary Agency; Literary Bridge; Lopopolo Literary Agency, Toni; McKinley, Literary Agency, Virginia C.; Marcil Literary Agency, Denise; Marshall Agency, Evan; Montgomery Literary Agency; Nelson Literary Agency & Lecture Bureau, BK; New Writing Agency; Northwest Literary Services; Oceanic Press; Penmarin Books; Pine Assoc., Arthur; Sebastian Literary Agency; Singer Media; Steinberg Literary Agency, Michael; Stern Agency (CA), Gloria; Sullivan Assoc., Mark; Total Acting Experience; Wallerstein Agency, Gerry B.; West Coast Literary Assoc.; Wildstar Assoc.; Write Therapist; Writer's Consulting Group

Religious/inspirational. Abacus Group; Author Aid Assoc.; Backman, Elizabeth H.; Browne, Pema; Chandelyn Literary Agency; Cook Agency, Bruce; Executive Excellence; Flannery White and Stone; Follendore Literary Agency, Joan; ForthWrite Literary Agency; Fran Literary Agency; Hamilton's Literary Agency, Andrew; Heacock Literary Agency; Independent Publishing Agency; Jenks Agency, Carolyn; JLM Literary Agents; Law Offices of Robert L. Fenton PC; Lee Shore Agency; Levine Communications, James; McKinley, Literary Agency, Virginia C.; Marcil Literary Agency, Denise; Marshall Agency, Evan; Nelson Literary Agency & Lecture Bureau, BK; New Writing Agency; Northwest Literary Services; Rose Agency; Shoestring Press; Strong Literary Agency, Marianne; Sullivan Assoc., Mark; Tiger Moon Enterprises; Total Acting Experience; Visions Press; Write Designs Literary Agency; Write Therapist

Science/technology. A & R Burke; Abacus Group; Anthony Agency, Joseph; Author Aid Assoc.; Authors' Marketing Services; Backman, Elizabeth H.; Browne, Pema; Catalog Literary Agency; Chandelyn Literary Agency; Eden Literary Agency; Follendore Literary Agency, Joan; ForthWrite Literary Agency; Howard Agency, Eddy; Independent Publishing Agency; Jenks Agency, Carolyn; Kaltman Literary Agency, Larry; Kern Literary Agency, Natasha; Law Offices of Robert L. Fenton PC; Lee Shore Agency; Levine Communications, James; Marshall Agency, Evan; Montgomery Literary Agency; Nelson Literary Agency & Lecture Bureau, BK; New Writing Agency; Northeast Literary Agency; Oceanic Press; Penmarin Books; Shoestring Press; Sullivan Assoc., Mark; Total Acting Experience; Wallerstein Agency, Gerry B.; Wildstar Assoc.; Writer's Consulting Group

Self-help/personal improvement. A & R Burke; Ahearn Agency; Anthony Agency, Joseph; Author Aid Assoc.; Author Author Literary Agency; Authors' Marketing Services; Backman, Elizabeth H.; Brinke Literary Agency; Browne, Pema; Catalog Literary Agency; Chandelyn Literary Agency; Coast To Coast Talent and Literary; Collier Assoc.; Connor Literary Agency; Cook Agency, Bruce; Dorese Agency Ltd.; Executive Excellence; Fishbein, Frieda; Flannery White and Stone; Follendore Literary Agency, Joan; ForthWrite Literary Agency; Fran Literary Agency; Gislason Agency; Gladden Unlimited; Hamilton's Literary Agency, Andrew; Howard Agency, Eddy; Independent Publishing Agency; Jenks Agency, Carolyn; JLM Literary Agents; Kaltman Literary Agency, Larry; Kellock & Assoc., J.; Kern Literary Agency, Natasha; Law

Offices of Robert L. Fenton PC; Lee Shore Agency; Levine Communications, James; Lighthouse Literary Agency; Literary Bridge; Lopopolo Literary Agency, Toni; McKinley, Literary Agency, Virginia C.; Marcil Literary Agency, Denise; Marshall Agency, Evan; Montgomery Literary Agency; Nelson Literary Agency & Lecture Bureau, BK; New Writing Agency; Northwest Literary Services; Oceanic Press; Olesha Agency, Andrea; Penmarin Books; Pine Assoc., Arthur; Rogers, Literary Representative, Irene; Rose Agency; Sebastian Literary Agency; Singer Media Corp.; Steinberg Literary Agency, Michael; Stern Agency (CA), Gloria; Strong Literary Agency, Marianne; Tiger Moon Enterprises; Total Acting Experience; Visions Press; Wallerstein Agency, Gerry B.; Watt & Assoc., Sandra; Wildstar Assoc.; The Write Therapist; Writer's Consulting Group

Sociology. A & R Burke; Abacus Group; Author Aid Assoc.; Author Author Literary Agency; Brinke Literary Agency; Catalog Literary Agency; Chandelyn Literary Agency; Cook Agency, Bruce; Dorese Agency; Flannery White and Stone; Follendore Literary Agency, Joan; ForthWrite Literary Agency; Hamilton's Literary Agency, Andrew; Heacock Literary Agency; Independent Publishing Agency; Jenks Agency, Carolyn; JLM Literary Agents; Lee Shore Agency; Levine Communications, James; McKinley, Literary Agency, Virginia C.; Montgomery Literary Agency; Nelson Literary Agency & Lecture Bureau, BK; New Writing Agency; Penmarin Books; Raintree Agency; Sebastian Literary Agency; Stern Agency (CA), Gloria; Total Acting Experience; Wallerstein Agency, Gerry B.

Sports. A & R Burke; Abacus Group; Argonaut Literary Agency; Author Aid Assoc.; Author Author Literary Agency; Authors' Marketing Services; Backman, Elizabeth H.; Browne, Pema; Catalog Literary Agency; Chandelyn Literary Agency; Connor Literary Agency; Dorese Agency; Eden Literary Agency; Flannery White and Stone; Hamilton's Literary Agency, Andrew; Hayes & Assoc., Gil; Heacock Literary Agency; Howard Agency, Eddy; Independent Publishing Agency; Jenks Agency, Carolyn; Kaltman Literary Agency, Larry; Kellock & Assoc., J.; Law Offices of Robert L. Fenton PC; Lee Shore Agency; Levine Communications, James; Lighthouse Literary Agency; Literary Bridge; McKinley, Literary Agency, Virginia C.; Montgomery Literary Agency; Nelson Literary Agency & Lecture Bureau, BK; New Writing Agency; Northwest Literary Services; Oceanic Press; Penmarin Books; Portman Organization; Singer Media; SLC Enterprises; Sullivan Assoc., Mark; Taylor Literary Agency, Dawson; Total Acting Experience; Wallerstein Agency, Gerry B.; Watt & Assoc., Sandra; Wildstar Assoc.; Write Designs Literary Agency

Translations. Author Aid Assoc.; Chandelyn Literary Agency; Eastwind Writers; Eden Literary Agency; Howard Agency, Eddy; M.H. International Literary Agency; Northwest Literary Services; Singer Media Corp.; Total Acting Experience; Write Designs Literary Agency

True crime/investigative. A & R Burke; Abacus Group; Ackerman Literary Services; Ahearn Agency; Anthony Agency, Joseph; Argonaut Literary Agency; Author Aid Assoc.; Author Author Literary Agency; Authors' Marketing Services; Browne, Pema; Clark Literary Agency, SJ; Coast To Coast Talent and Literary; Collier Assoc.; Connor Literary Agency; Dorese Agency; Eden Literary Agency; Fishbein, Frieda; Follendore Literary Agency, Joan; Gislason Agency; Gladden Unlimited; Hamilton's Literary Agency, Andrew; Heacock Literary Agency; Independent Publishing Agency; Jenks Agency, Carolyn; JLM Literary Agents; Kellock & Assoc., J.; Kern Literary Agency, Natasha; Law Offices of Robert L. Fenton PC; Lee Shore Agency; Literary Bridge; Literary Group West; Lopopolo Literary Agency, Toni; Marcil Literary Agency, Denise; Marshall Agency, Evan; Montgomery Literary Agency; Nelson Literary Agency & Lecture Bureau, BK; New Writing Agency; Northeast Literary Agency; Northwest Literary Services; Oceanic Press; Penmarin Books; PMA Literary and Film Management; Portman Organization; Puddingstone Literary Agency; Sebastian Literary Agency; Singer Media; Stern Agency (CA), Gloria; Strong Literary Agency, Marianne; Tiger Moon Enterprises; Toomey Assoc., Jeanne; Total Acting Experience; Wallerstein Agency, Gerry B.; Watt & Assoc., Sandra; West Coast Literary Assoc.; Writer's Consulting Group

Women's issues/women's studies. A & R Burke; Ahearn Agency; Author Aid Assoc.; Author Author Literary Agency; Backman, Elizabeth H.; Browne, Pema; Catalog Literary Agency; Chandelyn Literary Agency; Coast To Coast Talent and Literary; Collier Assoc.; Connor Literary Agency; Daley, Aleta M.; Dorese Agency; Eden Literary Agency; Fishbein, Frieda; Flannery White and Stone; Follendore Literary Agency, Joan; ForthWrite Literary Agency; Hamilton's Literary Agency, Andrew; Hayes & Assoc., Gil; Heacock Literary Agency; Howard Agency, Eddy; Hubbs Agency, Yvonne Trudeau; Independent Publishing Agency; Jenks Agency, Carolyn; JLM Literary Agents; Kellock & Assoc., J.; Kern Literary Agency, Natasha; Law Offices of Robert L. Fenton PC; Lee Shore Agency; Levine Communications, James; Lighthouse Literary Agency; Literary Bridge; Lopopolo Literary Agency, Toni; McKinley, Literary Agency, Virginia C.; Marcil Literary Agency, Denise; Marshall Agency, Evan; Nelson Literary Agency & Lecture Bureau, BK; Northwest Literary Services; Oceanic Press; Olesha Agency, Andrea; PMA Literary and Film Management; Portman Organization; Raintree Agency; Sebastian Literary Agency; Singer Media; SLC Enterprises; Stern Agency (CA), Gloria; Strong Literary Agency, Marianne; Total Acting Experience; Visions Press; Wallerstein Agency, Gerry B.; Watt & Assoc., Sandra; West Coast Literary Assoc.; Wildstar Assoc.

Script agents/Fiction and Nonfiction

Action/adventure. Agape Productions; Agency, The; All-Star Talent Agency; Berzon Agency, Marian; Brown, Curtis; Bulger and Assoc., Kelvin C.; Cameron Agency, Marshall; Chandelyn Literary Agency; Circle of Confusion; Client First — A/K/A Leo P. Haffey Agency; Coast to Coast Talent and Literary; Douroux

& Co.; Dykeman Assoc.; Earth Tracks Agency; Epstein-Wyckoff-La Manna and Assoc.; F.L.A.I.R.; Fleury Agency, B.R.; Fran Literary Agency; Gardner Agency; Gold/Marshak & Assoc.; Heacock Literary Agency; Hodges Agency, Carolyn; Howard Agency, Eddy; Hudson Agency; International Leonards; Jenks Agency, Carolyn; Kay Agency, Charlene; Ketay Agency, Joyce; Kjar Agency, Tyler; Kohner, Paul; Lee Literary Agency, L. Harry; Lindstrom Literary Group; Montgomery Literary Agency; Montgomery-West Literary Agency; Moody Management, Brian Keith; Mura Enterprises, Dee; Otitis Media; Panda Talent; Rogers and Assoc., Stephanie; Scagnetti Talent & Literary Agency, Jack; Silver Screen Placements; Sister Mania Productions; Sorice Agency, Camille; Star Literary Service; Swanson, H.N.; Tauro Brothers Management; Total Acting Experience; Turtle Agency; Wain Agency, Erika; Windermere Agency, Julius; Wright Representatives, Ann; Writer's Consulting Group

Biography/autobiography. Agape Productions; Dykeman Assoc.; Fleury Agency, B.R.; Gordon & Assoc., Michelle; Hayes & Assoc., Gil; Hogenson Agency, Barbara; Star Literary Service

Cartoon/comic. Agape Productions; Agency, The; Berzon Agency, Marian; Bulger and Assoc., Kelvin C.; Chandelyn Literary Agency; Circle of Confusion; Client First—A/K/A Leo P. Haffey Agency; Fleury Agency, B.R.; Fran Literary Agency; Howard Agency, Eddy; International Leonards; Mura Enterprises, Dee; Silver Screen Placements; Swanson, H.N.; Tauro Brothers Management; Total Acting Experience; Windermere Agency, Julius

Comedy. Agency, The; All-Star Talent Agency; Aria Talent; Berzon Agency, Marian; Brown, Curtis; Cameron Agency, Marshall; Chandelyn Literary Agency; Circle of Confusion; Douroux & Co.; Earth Tracks Agency; Epstein-Wyckoff-La Manna and Assoc.; F.L.A.I.R.; International Representatives; Fran Literary Agency; French, Samuel; Gardner Agency; Gold/Marshak & Assoc.; Hayes & Assoc., Gil; Howard Agency, Eddy; Hudson Agency; International Leonards; Jenks Agency, Carolyn; Ketay Agency, Joyce; Kick Entertainment; Kohner, Paul; Lee Literary Agency, L. Harry; Lindstrom Literary Group; Montgomery Literary Agency; Montgomery-West Literary Agency; Moody Management, Brian Keith; Mura Enterprises, Dee; Otitis Media; Panda Talent; Scagnetti Talent & Literary Agency, Jack; Sorice Agency, Camille; Swanson, H.N.; Total Acting Experience; Windermere Agency, Julius; Wright Representatives, Ann; Writer's Consulting Group

Contemporary issues. Fleury Agency, B.R.; Agency, The; Aria Talent; Berzon Agency, Marian; Bulger and Assoc., Kelvin C.; Cameron Agency, Marshall; Chandelyn Literary Agency; Circle of Confusion; Client First—A/K/A Leo P. Haffey Agency; Dykeman Assoc.; Earth Tracks Agency; Epstein-Wyckoff-La Manna and Assoc.; F.L.A.I.R.; Fleury Agency, B.R.; Fran Literary Agency; French, Samuel; Gardner Agency; Gold/Marshak & Assoc.; Gordon & Assoc., Michelle; Hayes & Assoc., Gil; Heacock Literary Agency; Hodges Agency, Carolyn; Hudson Agency; International Leonards Corp.; Jenks Agency, Carolyn; Ketay Agency, Joyce; Lee Literary Agency, L. Harry; Legacies; Montgomery Literary Agency; Moody Management, Brian Keith; Mura Enterprises, Dee; Palmer, Dorothy; Redwood Empire Agency; Rogers and Assoc., Stephanie; Silver Screen Placements; Swanson, H.N.; Tauro Brothers Management; Total Acting Experience; Watt & Assoc., Sandra; Writer's Consulting Group

Detective/police/crime. Agency, The; All-Star Talent Agency; Aria Talent; Brown, Curtis; Cameron Agency, Marshall; Circle of Confusion; Client First—A/K/A Leo P. Haffey Agency; Coast to Coast Talent and Literary; Douroux & Co.; Dykeman Assoc.; Earth Tracks Agency; Epstein-Wyckoff-La Manna and Assoc.; F.L.A.I.R.; Feiler Literary Agency, Florence; Fleury Agency, B.R.; Fran Literary Agency; French, Samuel; Gardner Agency; Gold/Marshak & Assoc.; Gordon & Assoc., Michelle; Heacock Literary Agency; Hodges Agency, Carolyn; Hudson Agency; International Leonards; Ketay Agency, Joyce; Kohner, Paul; Lee Literary Agency, L. Harry; Lindstrom Literary Group; Montgomery Literary Agency; Montgomery-West Literary Agency; Moody Management, Brian Keith; Mura Enterprises, Dee; Palmer, Dorothy; Panda Talent; Scagnetti Talent & Literary Agency, Jack; Silver Screen Placements; Sister Mania Productions; Sorice Agency, Camille; Star Literary Service; Swanson, H.N.; Tauro Brothers Management; Total Acting Experience; Turtle Agency; Wain Agency, Erika; Watt & Assoc., Sandra; Windermere Agency, Julius; Wright Representatives, Ann; Writer's Consulting Group

Erotica. Circle of Confusion Ltd.; Coast to Coast Talent and Literary; Earth Tracks Agency; Epstein-Wyckoff-La Manna and Assoc.; F.L.A.I.R.; Gardner Agency; Gold/Marshak & Assoc.; Howard Agency, Eddy; Redwood Empire Agency; Swanson, H.N.; Tauro Brothers Management; Total Acting Experience; Turtle Agency

Ethnic. Agency, The; Aria Talent; Brown, Curtis; Bulger and Assoc., Kelvin C.; Chandelyn Literary Agency; Circle of Confusion; Earth Tracks Agency; Fleury Agency, B.R.; French, Samuel; Gold/Marshak & Assoc.; Hodges Agency, Carolyn; Hudson Agency; Ketay Agency, Joyce; Kohner, Paul; Legacies; Lindstrom Literary Group; Moody Management, Brian Keith; Panda Talent; Swanson, H.N.; Tauro Brothers Management; Total Acting Experience

Experimental. Circle of Confusion; Earth Tracks Agency; Fleury Agency, B.R.; French, Samuel; Gardner Agency; Hodges Agency, Carolyn; Howard Agency, Eddy; Ketay Agency, Joyce; Sister Mania Productions; Swanson, H.N.; Total Acting Experience

Family saga. Agape Productions; Agency, The; Aria Talent; Bennett Agency; Berzon Agency, Marian; Bulger and Assoc., Kelvin C.; Chandelyn Literary Agency; Circle of Confusion; Client First—A/K/A Leo P. Haffey Agency; Douroux & Co.; Epstein-Wyckoff-La Manna and Assoc.; F.L.A.I.R.; Feiler Literary Agency,

Marshall; Chandelyn Literary Agency; Circle of Confusion; Douroux & Co.; Earth Tracks Agency; Epstein-Wyckoff-La Manna and Assoc.; F.L.A.I.R.; Fleury Agency, B.R.; Fran Literary Agency; Gardner Agency; Hayes & Assoc., Gil; Heacock Literary Agency; Hodges Agency, Carolyn; Howard Agency, Eddy; Jenks Agency, Carolyn; Ketay Agency, Joyce; Kick Entertainment; Kohner, Paul; Lee Literary Agency, L. Harry; Lindstrom Literary Group; Montgomery-West Literary Agency; Moody Management, Brian Keith; Mura Enterprises, Dee; Palmer, Dorothy; Scagnetti Talent & Literary Agency, Jack; Silver Screen Placements; Swanson, H.N.; Total Acting Experience; Turtle Agency; Windermere Agency, Julius; Wright Representatives, Ann; Writer's Consulting Group

Military/war. Agency, The; Kohner, Paul; Panda Talent; Tauro Brothers; Wain Agency, Erika

Mystery/suspense. Agency, The; All-Star Talent Agency; Aria Talent; Brown, Curtis; Cameron Agency, Marshall; Chandelyn Literary Agency; Circle of Confusion; Client First—A/K/A Leo P. Haffey Agency; Coast to Coast Talent and Literary; Douroux & Co.; Dykeman Assoc.; Epstein-Wyckoff-La Manna and Assoc.; F.L.A.I.R.; Feiler Literary Agency, Florence; Fleury Agency, B.R.; Fran Literary Agency; French, Samuel; Gardner Agency; Gold/Marshak & Assoc.; Hayes & Assoc., Gil; Heacock Literary Agency; Hodges Agency, Carolyn; Howard Agency, Eddy; Hudson Agency; International Leonards; Jenks Agency, Carolyn; Ketay Agency, Joyce; Kohner, Paul; Lee Literary Agency, L. Harry; Lindstrom Literary Group; Montgomery Literary Agency; Montgomery-West Literary Agency; Moody Management, Brian Keith; Mura Enterprises, Dee; Otitis Media; Palmer, Dorothy; Panda Talent; Scagnetti Talent & Literary Agency, Jack; Silver Screen Placements; Sorice Agency, Camille; Star Literary Service; Swanson, H.N.; Total Acting Experience; Turtle Agency; Wain Agency, Erika; Windermere Agency, Julius; Wright Representatives, Ann; Writer's Consulting Group

Open to all fiction. Agency for the Performing Arts; American Play Co.; Circle of Confusion; Coppage Co.; Dragon Literary; Gary-Paul Agency; Gersh Agency; Hilton Literary Agency, Alice; Hogenson Agency, Barbara; JNG Entertainment; Marbea Agency; Sherman & Assoc., Ken; Writers & Artists

Open to all nonfiction. Agency for the Performing Arts; American Play Co.; Dragon Literary; JNG Entertainment; Marbea Agency; Sherman & Assoc., Ken

Psychic/supernatural. Agape Productions; Agency, The; All-Star Talent Agency; Brown, Curtis; Circle of Confusion; Coast to Coast Talent and Literary; F.L.A.I.R.; Fleury Agency, B.R.; Gardner Agency; Gold/Marshak & Assoc.; Heacock Literary Agency; Hodges Agency, Carolyn; Howard Agency, Eddy; Ketay Agency, Joyce; Lee Literary Agency, L. Harry; Moody Management, Brian Keith; Mura Enterprises, Dee; Swanson, H.N.; Total Acting Experience; Turtle Agency; Watt & Assoc., Sandra; Wright Representatives, Ann; Writer's Consulting Group

Regional. Bulger and Assoc., Kelvin C.; Circle of Confusion; Hodges Agency, Carolyn

Religious/inspiration. Agency, The; Berzon Agency, Marian; Chandelyn Literary Agency; Dykeman Assoc.; French, Samuel; Howard Agency, Eddy; Moody Management, Brian Keith; Mura Enterprises, Dee; Swanson, H.N.; Tauro Brothers Management; Total Acting Experience; Watt & Assoc., Sandra

Romance. Client First—A/K/A Leo P. Haffey Agency; Coast to Coast Talent and Literary; Fleury Agency, B.R.; Hodges Agency, Carolyn; Kay Agency, Charlene; Lee Literary Agency, L. Harry; Montgomery-West Literary Agency; Palmer, Dorothy; Redwood Empire Agency; Sister Mania Productions; Swanson, H.N.; Tauro Brothers Management; Turtle Agency

Romantic comedy. Agency, The; All-Star Talent Agency; Aria Talent; Berzon Agency, Marian; Brown, Curtis; Cameron Agency, Marshall; Chandelyn Literary Agency; Circle of Confusion; Douroux & Co.; Epstein-Wyckoff-La Manna and Assoc.; F.L.A.I.R.; Feiler Literary Agency, Florence; Fran Literary Agency; Gardner Agency; Gold/Marshak & Assoc.; Howard Agency, Eddy; Hudson Agency; International Leonards; Jenks Agency, Carolyn; Ketay Agency, Joyce; Kick Entertainment; Kjar Agency, Tyler; Kohner, Paul; Lindstrom Literary Group; Montgomery Literary Agency; Montgomery-West Literary Agency; Moody Management, Brian Keith; Mura Enterprises, Dee; Otitis Media; Palmer, Dorothy; Panda Talent; Rogers and Assoc., Stephanie; Scagnetti Talent & Literary Agency, Jack; Sorice Agency, Camille; Total Acting Experience; Watt & Assoc., Sandra; Watt & Assoc., Sandra; Wright Representatives, Ann; Writer's Consulting Group

Romantic drama. Agency, The; All-Star Talent Agency; Aria Talent; Brown, Curtis; Cameron Agency, Marshall; Chandelyn Literary Agency; Circle of Confusion; Douroux & Co.; Epstein-Wyckoff-La Manna and Assoc.; F.L.A.I.R.; Feiler Literary Agency, Florence; Fran Literary Agency; Gardner Agency; Gold/Marshak & Assoc.; Hudson Agency; Jenks Agency, Carolyn; Ketay Agency, Joyce; Kick Entertainment; Kjar Agency, Tyler; Kohner, Paul; Lee Literary Agency, L. Harry; Lindstrom Literary Group; Montgomery Literary Agency; Montgomery-West Literary Agency; Moody Management, Brian Keith; Mura Enterprises, Dee; Otitis Media; Palmer, Dorothy; Panda Talent; Scagnetti Talent & Literary Agency, Jack; Sorice Agency, Camille; Total Acting Experience; Watt & Assoc., Sandra; Windermere Agency, Julius; Wright Representatives, Ann; Writer's Consulting Group

Science fiction. Agape Productions; Agency The; All-Star Talent Agency; Chandelyn Literary Agency; Circle of Confusion; Client First—A/K/A Leo P. Haffey Agency; Douroux & Co.; Dykeman Assoc.; Fleury Agency, B.R.; Fran Literary Agency; Gardner Agency; Gold/Marshak & Assoc.; Hodges Agency, Carolyn; Howard Agency, Eddy; Hudson Agency; International Leonards; Jenks Agency, Carolyn; Kjar Agency,

Tyler; Lee Literary Agency, L. Harry; Montgomery Literary Agency; Montgomery-West Literary Agency; Moody Management, Brian Keith; Mura Enterprises, Dee; Panda Talent; Silver Screen Placements; Swanson, H.N.; Turtle Agency; Wain Agency, Erika

Sports. All-Star Talent Agency; Chandelyn Literary Agency; Circle of Confusion; Client First—A/K/A Leo P. Haffey Agency; Fleury Agency, B.R.; Gold/Marshak & Assoc.; Heacock Literary Agency; Howard Agency, Eddy; Hudson Agency; International Leonards; Lee Literary Agency, L. Harry; Montgomery Literary Agency; Moody Management, Brian Keith; Mura Enterprises, Dee; Scagnetti Talent & Literary Agency, Jack; Swanson, H.N.; Total Acting Experience; Wright Representatives, Ann

Teen. Agency, The; Aria Talent; Berzon Agency, Marian; Chandelyn Literary Agency; Circle of Confusion; Earth Tracks Agency; Epstein-Wyckoff-La Manna and Assoc.; F.L.A.I.R.; Gardner Agency; Howard Agency, Eddy; Hudson Agency; Kjar Agency, Tyler; Montgomery-West Literary Agency; Moody Management, Brian Keith; Mura Enterprises, Dee; Swanson, H.N.; Total Acting Experience

Thriller/espionage. Agape Productions; Agency, The; All-Star Talent Agency; Berzon Agency, Marian; Brown, Curtis; Cameron Agency, Marshall; Circle of Confusion; Client First—A/K/A Leo P. Haffey Agency; Coast to Coast Talent and Literary; Douroux & Co.; Dykeman Associates; Earth Tracks Agency; Epstein-Wyckoff-La Manna and Assoc.; F.L.A.I.R.; Feiler Literary Agency, Florence; Fleury Agency, B.R.; Fran Literary Agency; French, Samuel; Gardner Agency; Gold/Marshak & Assoc.; Heacock Literary Agency; Hodges Agency, Carolyn; Howard Agency, Eddy; Hudson Agency; International Leonards; Jenks Agency, Carolyn; Kay Agency, Charlene; Ketay Agency, Joyce; Lee Literary Agency, L. Harry; Lindstrom Literary Group; Montgomery Literary Agency; Montgomery-West Literary Agency; Moody Management, Brian Keith; Mura Enterprises, Dee; Otitis Media; Palmer, Dorothy; Rogers and Assoc., Stephanie; Scagnetti Talent & Literary Agency, Jack; Silver Screen Placements; Sister Mania Productions; Star Literary Service; Swanson, H.N.; Tauro Brothers Management; Total Acting Experience; Turtle Agency; Wain Agency, Erika; Windermere Agency, Julius; Wright Representatives, Ann; Writer's Consulting Group

True crime/investigative. Agape Productions; F.L.A.I.R; Fleury Agency, B.R.; Gordon & Assoc., Michelle; Hogenson Agency, Barbara; Kohner, Paul; Palmer, Dorothy; Panda Talent; Sister Mania Productions; Tauro Brothers; Wain Agency, Erika

Westerns/frontier. Agape Productions; Agency, The; All-Star Talent Agency; Berzon Agency, Marian; Brown, Curtis; Cameron Agency, Marshall; Chandelyn Literary Agency; Circle of Confusion; Client First—A/K/A Leo P. Haffey Agency; Douroux & Co.; Fleury Agency, B.R.; Fran Literary Agency; Gardner Agency; Howard Agency, Eddy; Hudson Agency; Jenks Agency, Carolyn; Ketay Agency, Joyce; Lee Literary Agency, L. Harry; Montgomery Literary Agency; Mura Enterprises, Dee; Panda Talent; Scagnetti Talent & Literary Agency, Jack; Sorice Agency, Camille; Swanson, H.N.; Total Acting Experience; Turtle Agency; Wright Representatives, Ann

Women's issues. Agency, The; F.L.A.I.R.; Fleury Agency, B.R.; Gold/Marshak & Assoc.; Gordon & Assoc., Michelle; Palmer, Dorothy; Wain Agency, Erika

Young adult. Bennett Agency; Fleury, B.R.; Silver Screen Placements; Turtle Agency

Multimedia. Agency, The; Circle of Confusion; Howard Agency, Eddy; International Leonards; Jenks Agency, Carolyn; Montgomery Literary Agency; Total Acting Experience; Turtle Agency

Packaging agents. Agency for the Performing Arts; Agency, The; Artists Agency, The; Berzon Agency, Marian; International Creative Management; Ketay Agency, Joyce; Kohner, Paul; Palmer, Dorothy; Panda Talent; Swanson, H.N.

Script agents/Format Index

Animation. Above The Line Agency; Agency, The; American Play Co.; Berzon Agency, Marian; Buchwald Agency, Don; Chandelyn Literary Agency; Coast to Coast Talent and Literary; Douroux & Co.; Epstein-Wyckoff-La Manna and Assoc.; Fran Literary Agency; Gersh Agency; Heacock Literary Agency; Howard Agency, Eddy; International Leonards; Kohner, Paul; Mura Enterprises, Dee; Panettiere & Co.; Swanson, H.N.; Total Acting Experience; Wain Agency, Erika; Windermere Agency, Julius

Documentary. American Play Co.; Buchwald Agency, Don; Bulger And Assoc., Kelvin C.; Chandelyn Literary Agency; Coast to Coast Talent and Literary; Fran Literary Agency; Gardner Agency; Heacock Literary Agency; Hilton Literary Agency, Alice; Howard Agency, Eddy; Hudson Agency; Jenks Agency, Carolyn; Kohner, Paul; Mura Enterprises, Dee; Total Acting Experience; Wain Agency, Erika

Episodic drama. Agency, The; All-Star Talent Agency; Aria Talent; Buchwald Agency, Don; Chandelyn Literary Agency; Coast to Coast Talent and Literary; Coppage Co.; Douroux & Co.; Epstein-Wyckoff-La Manna and Assoc.; Feiler Literary Agency, Florence; Fran Literary Agency; Gardner Agency; Gold/Marshak & Assoc.; Howard Agency, Eddy; Jenks Agency, Carolyn; Ketay Agency, Joyce; Kohner, Paul; Lee Literary Agency, L. Harry; Moody Management, Brian Keith; Mura Enterprises, Dee; Palmer, Dorothy; Panda Talent; Panettiere & Co.; Scagnetti Talent & Literary Agency, Jack; Swanson, H.N.; Total Acting Experience; Turtle Agency; Wright Representatives, Ann; Writers & Artists

Feature film. Above The Line Agency; Agape Productions; Agency, The; Agency for the Performing

Arts; All-Star Talent Agency; American Play Co.; Aria Talent; BDP & Assoc. Talent Agency ; Berzon Agency, Marian; Buchwald Agency, Don; Bulger And Assoc., Kelvin C.; Cameron Agency, Marshall; Chandelyn Literary Agency; Circle of Confusion; Coast to Coast Talent and Literary; Coppage Co.; Douroux & Co.; Earth Tracks Agency; Epstein-Wyckoff-La Manna and Assoc.; Feiler Literary Agency, Florence; Fishbein, Frieda; Fran Literary Agency; Gardner Agency; Gersh Agency; Gold/Marshak & Assoc.; Gordon & Assoc., Michelle; Graham Agency; Gurman Agency, Susan; Halsey Agency, Reece; Hayes & Assoc., Gil; Heacock Literary Agency; Hilton Literary Agency, Alice; Hodges Agency, Carolyn; Howard Agency, Eddy; Hudson Agency; International Leonards; Jenks Agency, Carolyn; JNG Entertainment; Kallen Agency, Leslie; Kay Agency, Charlene; Ketay Agency, Joyce; Kick Entertainment; Kjar Agency, Tyler; Kohner, Paul; Lee Literary Agency, L. Harry; Legacies; Lindstrom Literary Group; Marbea Agency; Montgomery Literary Agency; Montgomery-West Literary Agency; Mura Enterprises, Dee; Otitis Media; Palmer, Dorothy; Panda Talent; Panettiere & Co.; Redwood Empire Agency; Rogers and Assoc., Stephanie; Scagnetti Talent & Literary Agency, Jack; Sister Mania Productions; Sorice Agency, Camille; Stanton & Assoc. Int'l Literary Agency; Swanson, H.N.; Talent Source; Total Acting Experience; Turtle Agency; Wain Agency, Erika; Warden, White & Kane; Watt & Assoc., Sandra; Whittlesey Agency, Peregrine; Wile Enterprises; Windermere Agency, Julius; Wright Representatives, Ann; Writers & Artists; Writer's Consulting Group

Movie of the week. Above The Line Agency; Agency, The; All-Star Talent Agency; American Play Co.; Aria Talent; BDP & Assoc. Talent Agency ; Berzon Agency, Marian; Buchwald Agency, Don; Bulger and Assoc., Kelvin C.; Cameron Agency, Marshall; Chandelyn Literary Agency; Coast to Coast Talent and Literary; Douroux & Co.; Earth Tracks Agency; Epstein-Wyckoff-La Manna and Assoc.; Feiler Literary Agency, Florence; Fishbein, Frieda; Fran Literary Agency; Gardner Agency; Gersh Agency; Gold/Marshak & Assoc.; Heacock Literary Agency; Hilton Literary Agency, Alice; Hodges Agency, Carolyn; Howard Agency, Eddy; Hudson Agency; International Leonards; Jenks Agency, Carolyn; Kallen Agency, Leslie; Kay Agency, Charlene; Ketay Agency, Joyce; Kjar Agency, Tyler; Kohner, Paul; Lee Literary Agency, L. Harry; Legacies; Lindstrom Literary Group; Montgomery-West Literary Agency; Moody Management, Brian Keith; Mura Enterprises, Dee; Otitis Media; Palmer, Dorothy; Panda Talent; Panettiere & Co.; Redwood Empire Agency; Rogers and Assoc., Stephanie; Scagnetti Talent & Literary Agency, Jack; Sorice Agency, Camille; Stanton & Assoc. Int'l Literary Agency; Swanson, H.N.; Total Acting Experience; Turtle Agency; Wain Agency, Erika; Watt & Assoc., Sandra; Windermere Agency, Julius; Wright Representatives, Ann; Writers & Artists; Writer's Consulting Group

Sitcom. Agency, The; Agency for the Performing Arts; All-Star Talent Agency; Aria Talent; Berzon Agency, Marian; Buchwald Agency, Don; Chandelyn Literary Agency; Coast to Coast Talent and Literary; Coppage Company; Douroux & Co.; Earth Tracks Agency; Epstein-Wyckoff-La Manna and Assoc.; Gersh Agency; Gold/Marshak & Assoc.; Hilton Literary Agency, Alice; Howard Agency, Eddy; International Leonards; Ketay Agency, Joyce; Kjar Agency, Tyler; Kohner, Paul; Lee Literary Agency, L. Harry; Legacies; Moody Management, Brian Keith; Mura Enterprises, Dee; Palmer, Dorothy; Panda Talent; Panettiere & Co.; Swanson, H.N.; Total Acting Experience; Turtle Agency; Wright Representatives, Ann

Soap opera. Aria Talent; Buchwald Agency, Don; Coast to Coast Talent and Literary; Epstein-Wyckoff-La Manna and Assoc.; Gold/Marshak & Assoc.; Howard Agency, Eddy; Kohner, Paul; Mura Enterprises, Dee; Palmer, Dorothy; Total Acting Experience

Stage play. Agape Productions; American Play Co.; Aria Talent; BDP & Assoc. Talent Agency ; Berzon Agency, Marian; Buchwald Agency, Don; Chandelyn Literary Agency; Dramatic Publishing; Epstein-Wyckoff-La Manna and Assoc.; Feiler Literary Agency, Florence; Fishbein, Frieda; French, Samuel; Gold/Marshak & Assoc.; Graham Agency; Gurman Agency, Susan; Howard Agency, Eddy; Jenks Agency, Carolyn; Ketay Agency, Joyce; Kjar Agency, Tyler; Kohner, Paul; Lee Literary Agency, L. Harry; Legacies; Montgomery Literary Agency; Moody Management, Brian Keith; Otitis Media; Panda Talent; Panettiere & Co.; Total Acting Experience; Whittlesey Agency, Peregrine; Writers & Artists

Variety show. Buchwald Agency, Don; Chandelyn Literary Agency; Coast to Coast Talent and Literary; French, Samuel; Howard Agency, Eddy; International Leonards; Kohner, Paul; Mura Enterprises, Dee; Total Acting Experience

Geographic Index

Nonfee-charging

California
Agents for Medical and Mental Health Professionals
Allen Literary Agency, Linda
Andrews & Assoc., Bart
Appleseeds Management
Brandenburgh & Assoc.
Breitman, Patti
Brown Agency, Andrea
Casselman, Martha
Castiglia Literary Agency, Julie
Cohen, Literary Agency, Ruth
Diamond Literary Agency
Dijkstra, Sandra
Emerald Literary Agency
Esquire Literary Productions
Eth, Felicia
Feiler, Florence
Fleming Agency, Peter
Gusay, Charlotte
Halsey Agency, Reece
Hamilburg Agency, Mitchell J.
Hill Assoc., Frederick
Larsen/Elizabeth Pomada, Michael
Lasher Agency, Maureen
McBride, Margret
McGrath, Helen
Madsen Agency, Robert
Manus & Assoc.
Markowitz, Barbara
Nazor Literary Agency, Karen
Renaissance: A Literary/Talent Agency
Sierra Literary Agency
Spieler, Gretchen
Swanson, H.N.
Teal Literary Agency, Patricia
Waterside Productions

Colorado
Diamond Literary Agency

Connecticut
Holub & Assoc.
J de S Assoc.
New England Publishing Assoc.
Urstadt Writers and Artists Agency, Susan P.
Van der Leun & Assoc.
Writers' Productions

District of Columbia
Adler & Robin Books
Goldfarb & Graybill
Lichtman, Trister, Singer & Ross
Literary and Creative Artists

Florida
Bova Literary Agency, Barbara
Fleury Agency, B.R.
International Publisher Assoc.
Nugent Literary
Westchester Literary Agency

Georgia
Brandt Agency, Joan

Illinois
Agency Chicago
Apollo Entertainment
Goddard, Connie
Multimedia Product Development

Indiana
Printed Tree

Iowa
Doyen Literary Services

Kentucky
Green, Randall Elisha

Louisiana
Gautreaux, Richard

Maine
Kroll Literary Agency, Edite

Maryland
Columbia Literary Assoc.
Potomac Literary Agency

Massachusetts
Axelrod Agency
Balkin Agency
Coover Agency, Doe
McClellan Assoc., Anita D.
McDonough, Richard P.
Moore Literary Agency
Otte Company
Picard, Alison J.
Raymond, Charlotte Cecil
Rees Literary Agency, Helen
Riverside Literary Agency
Snell Literary Agency, Michael
Stauffer Assoc., Nancy

Michigan
Ajlouny Agency, Joseph S.

Minnesota
Lazear Agency Inc.
Otitis Media

Missouri
Flaherty, Literary Agent, Joyce

New Hampshire
Crawford Literary Agency

New Jersey
Boates Literary Agency, Reid
Henderson Literary
James Peter Assoc.
March Tenth
Russell-Simenauer Agency
Seligman, Literary Agent, Lynn
Weiner Literary Agency, Cherry

New York
Acton, Leone, Hanson & Jaffe
Altshuler, Miriam
Amsterdam Agency, Marcia
Baldi Literary Agency, Malaga
Barber Agency, Virginia
Barrett Books, Loretta
Bartczak Assoc. Inc.
Beekman Literary Agency
Behar Literary Agency, Josh
Black Literary Agency, David
Blassingame Spectrum Corp.
Borchardt, Georges
Brandt & Brandt
Brown Assoc., Marie
Brown, Curtis
Buck Agency, Howard
Bykofsky Assoc., Sheree
Cantrell-Colas
Carvainis Agency, Maria
Circle of Confusion
Clausen Assoc., Connie
Cleaver, Diane
Cohen Literary Agency, Hy
Congdon Assoc., Don
Cornfield, Robert
Crown Int'l Literature and Arts Agency, Bonnie R.
Curtis Assoc., Richard
Darhansoff & Verrill
Davie Literary Agency, Elaine
de la Haba Agency, Lois
Diamant, Anita
Dolger Agency, Jonathan
Donadio and Ashworth
Donlan, Thomas C.
Ducas, Robert
Dystel, Jane
Educational Design Services

Elek Assoc., Peter
Ellenberg, Ethan
Ellison, Nicholas
Elmo Agency, Ann
Evans, Mary
Farber Literary Agency
Flaming Star Literary Enter-
  prises
Flannery Literary
Garon-Brooke Assoc., Jay
Gartenberg, Max
Goodman Assoc.
Gordon Agency, Charlotte
Gotham Art & Literary Agency
Greenburger Assoc., Sanford J.
Gregory Assoc., Maia
Grimes Literary Agency, Lew
Hanson Agency
Hawkins & Assoc., John
Hendin Literary, David
Herman Agency, Jeff
Herner Rights Agency, Susan
Hochmann Books, John L.
Hoffman, Berenice
Hogenson Agency, Barbara
Hull House Literary Agency
IMG-Julian Bach
Int'l Creative Management
Jet Literary Assoc.
Jordan, Lawrence
Karpfinger Agency
Kellock Co.
Ketz Agency, Louise B.
Kidde, Hoyt & Picard
Kirchoff/Wohlberg, Authors'
  Representation Division
Klinger, Harvey
Kouts, Literary Agent, Barbara
Kroll Agency, Lucy
Lampack Agency, Peter
Lantz-Joy Harris, Robert
Lescher & Lescher
Levine Literary Agency, Ellen
Lewis, Robert
Lipkind Agency, Wendy
Literary Group
Lord Literistic, Sterling
Love Literary Agency, Nancy
Lowenstein Assoc.
Maass Literary Agency, Donald

Maccampbell , Donald
McCauley, Gerard
Maccoby, Gina
Mainhardt Agency, Ricia
Mann Agency, Carol
Manus & Assoc.
Markson, Elaine
Marmur Assoc. , Mildred
Martell Agency
Miller Assoc., Roberta D.
Morhaim, Howard
Morris Agency, William
Morrison, Henry
Mura Enterprises, Dee
Naggar Literary Agency, Jean
Nathan, Ruth
Nine Muses and Apollo
Nolan Literary Agency, Betsy
Norma-Lewis Agency
Ober Assoc., Harold
Oscard Agency, Fifi
Parks Agency, Richard
Paton Literary Agency, Kathi J.
Pelter, Rodney
Perkins Assoc., L.
Priest Literary Agency, Aaron
Protter, Susan Ann
Pryor, Roberta
Publishing Services
Quicksilver Books
Robbins Office
Rose Literary Agency
Rosenthal, Jean
Rotrosen Agency, Jane
Rubenstein, Pesha
Sanders, Victoria
Sandum & Assoc.
Schmidt, Harold
Schulman, Susan
Schwartz Agency, Laurens R.
Seymour Agency
Sheedy, Charlotte
Shepard Agency
Siegel Literary Agency, Bobbe
Singer Literary Agency, Evelyn
Smith, Literary Agent, Valerie
Sommer, Elyse
Spieler, F. Joseph
Spitzer Literary Agency, Philip
Steele & Co., Lyle
Stepping Stone
TCA

2M Communications
Wald Assoc., Mary Jack
Wallace Literary Agency
Ware, John A.
Wasserman, Harriet
Watkins Loomis Agency
Wecksler-Incomco
Weingel-Fidel Agency
Weyr Agency, Rhoda
Wieser & Wieser
Witherspoon & Assoc.
Wohl Literary Agency, Gary S.
Wreschner, Ruth
Wright Representatives, Ann
Writers House
Writers' Representatives
Zahler Agency, Karen Gantz
Zeckendorf Assoc., Susan
Ziegler, George

Pennsylvania
Allen, Literary Agency, James
Butler, Jane
Collin Literary Agent, Frances
Kidd, Literary Agent, Virginia
Lincoln Literary Agency, Ray
Novak III, Edward A.
Pocono Literary Agency
Schlessinger Agency, Blanche

Rhode Island
Rock Literary Agency

Texas
Authors' Literary Agency
Dupree/Miller and Assoc.
Fogelman Literary Agency
Hegler Literary Agency, Gary
Lyceum Creative Properties
Stern, Gloria

Virginia
Lindstrom Literary Group

Washington
Levant & Wales

Wisconsin
Allan Agency, Lee
Ciske, Francine

Fee-charging

Arizona
Authors And Artists Resource
  Center/Tarc
Literary Bridge

California
Abacus Group
Berzon Agency, Marian
Brinke Literary Agency
Clark Literary Agency, SJ

Coast To Coast Talent and Lit-
  erary
Colby: Literary Agency
Dorese Agency Ltd.
Eastwind Writers
Follendore, Joan
ForthWrite Literary Agency
Gladden Unlimited
Hardy Agency
Heacock Literary Agency
Hilton Literary Agency, Alice

Hubbs, Yvonne Trudeau
JLM Literary Agents
Literary Group West
Lopopolo, Toni
Oceanic Press
Oceanic Press Service
Pacific Literary Services
Penmarin Books
Popkin, Julie
Rogers, Irene
Sebastian Literary Agency

Singer Media Corp.
Stern Agency, Gloria
Tiger Moon Enterprises
Total Acting Experience
Visions Press
Warren Literary Agency, James
Watt & Assoc., Sandra
West Coast Literary Assoc.
The Write Therapist
Writer's Consulting Group

Colorado
Alp Arts
Eden Literary Agency
Flannery White and Stone

Connecticut
Independent Publishing
Agency
Mews Books Ltd.
Toomey Assoc., Jeanne

Florida
A & R Burke Corp.
Argonaut Literary Agency
Collier Assoc.
Taylor, Dawson

Georgia
Ackerman Literary Services
Write Designs Literary Agency

Illinois
Portman Organization
SLC Enterprises
Steinberg, Michael

Indiana
Rose Agency

Louisiana
Ahearn Agency

Maryland
Montgomery Literary Agency
Perkins' Literary Agency

Massachusetts
Jenks Agency, Carolyn

Michigan
Law Offices of Robert L. Fenton PC
M.H. Int'l Literary Agency

Minnesota
Cook Agency, Bruce
Gislason Agency

Missouri
Chandelyn Literary Agency

New Hampshire
Northeast Literary Agency

New Jersey
Anthony Agency, Joseph
Howard Agency, Eddy
Marshall Agency, Evan
Puddingstone Literary Agency

New Mexico
Rydal

New York
Author Aid Assoc.
Backman, Elizabeth H.
Bernstein, Meredith
Browne, Pema
Connor Literary Agency
Daley, Aleta M.
Fishbein Ltd., Frieda
Gelles-Cole Literary Enterprises
Goldberg, Lucianne S.
Lee Literary Agency, L. Harry
Levine Communications, James
Marcil Literary Agency, Denise
Nelson Literary Agency & Lecture Bureau, BK
New Writing Agency
Pell Agency, William
Pine Assoc., Arthur
PMA Literary and Film Management, Inc.
Raintree Agency
Strong, Marianne
Sullivan Assoc., Mark
Wildstar Assoc.

Wright Authors' Representative, Stephen

North Carolina
Lighthouse Literary Agency

Ohio
Evans & Assoc.
Hamilton's Literary Agency, Andrew

Oregon
Kern Literary Agency, Natasha
Olesha Agency, Andrea
QCorp Literary Agency

Pennsylvania
Lee Shore Agency
Wallerstein Agency, Gerry B.

Tennessee
Hayes & Assoc., Gil
March Media

Texas
Chadd-Stevens
Fran Literary Agency
Mid-America Literary Agency

Utah
Executive Excellence

Virginia
Kaltman, Larry
Morgan, Inc., David H.

Washington
Catalog Literary Agency

Wisconsin
McKinley, Virginia C.

Canada
Acacia House Publishing Services Ltd.
Author Author Literary Agency
Authors' Marketing Services Ltd.
Kellock & Assoc., J.
Northwest Literary Services
Shoestring Press

Script agents

Arizona
Star Literary Service

California
Above The Line Agency
Agency for the Performing Arts Agency, The
All-Star Talent Agency
Appleseeds Management
Artists Agency, The
BDP & Assoc. Talent Agency
Bennett Agency
Berzon Agency, Marian

Cinema Talent International
Coast to Coast
Coppage Company
Douroux & Co.
Epstein-Wyckoff-La Manna
Feiler, Florence
Geddes Agency
Gelff Agency, Laya
Gersh Agency
Gold/Marshak & Assoc.
Gordon & Assoc., Michelle
Halsey Agency, Reece
Heacock Literary Agency

Hilton Literary Agency, Alice
Int'l Creative Management
Kallen Agency, Leslie
Kjar Agency, Tyler
Kohner, Paul
Lenhoff/Robinson
Manus & Assoc.
Panda Talent
Panettiere & Co.
Redwood Empire Agency
Rogers and Assoc., Stephanie
Scagnetti Talent & Literary Agency, Jack

Sherman & Assoc., Ken
Sorice Agency, Camille
Swanson, H.N.
Tauro Brothers Management
Total Acting Experience
Turtle Agency
Wain Agency, Erika
Warden, White & Kane
Watt & Assoc., Sandra
Whittlesey Agency, Peregrine
Wile Enterprises
Writer's Consulting Group

Colorado
Hodges Agency, Carolyn

Connecticut
Gary-Paul Agency

Florida
Cameron Agency, Marshall
Fleury Agency, B.R.
Legacies
Marbea Agency

Georgia
Talent Source

Illinois
Agency Chicago
Apollo Entertainment
Aria Talent
Bulger and Assoc., Kelvin C.
Dramatic Publishing
Silver Screen Placements

Indiana
Agape Productions
International Leonards Corp.

Louisiana
Canatella Agency, Margaret

Gauthreaux, Richard

Maryland
Montgomery Literary Agency

Massachusetts
Jenks Agency, Carolyn

Minnesota
Otitis Media

Missouri
Chandelyn Literary Agency
Windermere Agency, Julius

New Jersey
Howard Agency, Eddy

New York
Amato Agency, Michael
American Play Co.
Amsterdam Agency, Marcia
Berman, Lois
Brown Ltd., Curtis
Buchwald Agency, Don
Circle of Confusion Ltd.
Earth Tracks Agency
Evans, Mary
F.L.A.I.R.
Fishbein Ltd., Frieda
Freedman Dramatic Agency,
    Robert A.
French, Samuel
Graham Agency
Gurman Agency, Susan
Hanson Agency, The
Hogenson Agency, Barbara
Hudson Agency
JNG Entertainment
Ketay Agency, Joyce
Kroll Agency
Lee Literary Agency, L. Harry

Manus & Assoc.
Moody, Brian Keith
Mura Enterprises, Dee
Palmer, Dorothy
PMA Literary and Film Man-
    agement
Sanders, Victoria
Schulman, Susan
Tantleff Office
Wright Representatives, Ann
Writers & Artists

Ohio
Kick Entertainment

Pennsylvania
Sister Mania Productions

Tennessee
Client First—A/K/A Leo P.
    Haffey Agency
Hayes & Assoc., Gil

Texas
Dykeman Assoc.
Fran Literary Agency
Hegler Literary Agency, Gary
Lyceum Creative Properties
Stanton & Assoc.

Utah
Dragon Literary
Montgomery-West

Virginia
Communications and Enter-
    tainment
Gardner Agency
Lindstrom Literary Group

Canada
Kay Agency, Charlene

Agents Index

This index of agent names was created to help you locate agents you may have read or heard about even when you do not know which agency they work for. Agent names are listed with their agencies' names. Check the Listing Index for the page number of the agency.

A

Abend, Sheldon (American Play Co.)

Abrahams, John (Writers House)

Ackerman, Sharon (Ackerman Literary Services)

Acton, Edward J. (Acton, Leone, Hanson & Jaffe)

Adams, Charlene (Client First-A/K/A Leo P. Haffey Agency)

Adams, Deborah (The Jeff Herman Agency)

Adler, Bill Jr. (Adler & Robin Books)

Agarwal, Rajeev K. (Circle of Confusion)

Ahearn, Pamela G. (The Ahearn Agency)

Ajlouny, Joe (The Joseph S. Ajlouny Agency)

Allen, James (James Allen, Literary Agency)

Allen, Linda (Linda Allen Literary Agency)

Allred, Robert (All-Star Talent Agency)

Alperen, Julie (Kirchoff/Wohlberg)

Alpert, Dani (The Bennett Agency)

Altshuler, Miriam (Miriam Altshuler Literary Agency)

Amador, Mark (The Marian Berzon Agency)

Amato, Mary Ann (Legacies)

Amato, Michael (Michael Amato Agency)

Amparan, Joann (Wecksler-Incomco)

Amsterdam, Marcia (Marcia Amsterdam Agency)

Anderson, Jeff (M.H. Int'l Literary Agency)

Anderson, Tim (H.N. Swanson)

Andrews, Bart (Bart Andrews & Assoc.)

Anthony, Joseph (Joseph Anthony Agency)

Aragi, Nicole (Watkins Loomis Agency)

Armenta, Judith (Martha Casselman Literary Agent)

Arnovitz, Scott (Int'l Creative Management-CA)

Axelrod, Steven (The Axelrod Agency)

B

B.R. Boylan, Richard (Otitis Media)

Bach, Julian (IMG-Julian Bach Literary Agency)

Backman, Elizabeth H. (Elizabeth H. Backman)

Baldi, Malaga (Malaga Baldi Literary Agency)

Balkin, Richard (Balkin Agency)

Bankoff, Lisa (Int'l Creative Management-NY)

Barber, Virginia (Virginia Barber Literary Agency)

Barmeier, Jim (Writer's Consulting Group)

Barr, Mary (Sierra Literary Agency)

Barrett, Loretta (Loretta Barrett Books)

Barrett, Robin (Flannery, White and Stone/The Writers Advocate)

Barrick, Gail (H.N. Swanson)

Bartczak, Gene (Gene Bartczak Assoc.)

Barvin, Jude (The Brinke Literary Agency)

Basserman, Andrea (Watkins Loomis Agency)

Bearden, James (Communications and Entertainment)

Behar, Josh (Josh Behar Literary Agency)

Bellacicco, Dan A. (A Total Acting Experience)

Bennett, Carole (The Bennett Agency)

Benson, John (B.K. Nelson Literary Agency & Lecture Bureau)

Berkower, Amy (Writers House)

Berman, Lois (Lois Berman, Writers' Representative)

Bernard, Alec (Puddingstone Literary Agency)

Bernstein, Meredith (Meredith Bernstein Literary Agency)

Bernstein, Ron (The Gersh Agency)

Berry, Henry (Independent Publishing Agency)

Black, David (David Black Literary Agency)

Blackett, Donna (Andrea Brown Literary Agency)

Blake, Laura J. (Curtis Brown)

Blankson, Joanna (Marie Brown Assoc.)

Blanton, Sandra (Peter Lampack Agency)

Blick, Carolyn Hopwood (Pocono Literary Agency)

Boals, Judy (Lois Berman, Writers' Representative)

Boates, Reid (Reid Boates Literary Agency)

Bock, Jill (The Tantleff Office)

Bohannon, Kendall (Flannery, White and Stone/The Writers Advocate)

Bohn, Beth (The Turtle Agency)

Boorn, Joyce (Florence Feiler Literary Agency)

Borchardt, Anne (Georges Borchardt)

Borchardt, Georges (Georges Borchardt)

Bova, Barbara (The Barbara Bova Literary Agency)

Bowser, Milton (Margaret Canatella Agency)

Boylan, Greg (Otitis Media)

Brandenburgh, Don (Brandenburgh & Assoc. Literary Agency)

Brandt, Carl (Brandt & Brandt Literary Agents)

Brandt, Joan (The Joan Brandt Agency)

Breed, Leslie (Lichtman, Trister, Singer & Ross)

Breitman, Patti (Patti Breitman)

Brophy, Philippa (Sterling Lord Literistic)

Brown, Allen Williams (Visions Press)

Brown, Andrea (Andrea Brown Literary Agency)

Brown, Deborah T. (Peter Lampack Agency)

Brown, Laini (Marie Brown Assoc.)

Brown, Marie (Marie Brown Assoc.)

Brown, William (Joan Follendore Literary Agency)

Brown, William C. (QCorp Literary Agency)

Browne, Jane Jordan (Multimedia Product Development)

Browne, Pema (Pema Browne)

Browne, Perry (Pema Browne)

Buchwald, Don (Don Buchwald Agency)

Buck, Howard (Howard Buck Agency)

Bulger, Kelvin C. (Kelvin C. Bulger and Assoc.)

Burke, Anna Mae (A & R Burke Corporation)

Burke, Janet (Alison J. Picard Literary Agent)

Burke, Robert (A & R Burke Corporation)

Busboom, Bok (Authors' Marketing Services)

Butler, Jane (Jane Butler, Art and Literary Agent)

Bykofsky, Sheree (Sheree Bykofsky Assoc.)

C

Cairns, Diane (Int'l Creative Management-CA)

Calhoun, Chris (Sterling Lord Literistic)

Cameron, Kimberly (Reece Halsey Agency)

Campise, Jim (Authors' Literary Agency)

Canatella, Margaret (Margaret Canatella Agency)

Canatella, Roy (Margaret Canatella Agency)

Cane, Nikki (Gary L. Hegler Literary Agency)

Caponegri, Marilyn (Star Literary Service)

Capshaw, Genero (The Literary Bridge)

Caravatt, Paul (The Gary-Paul Agency)

Carbone, Peter (Oceanic Press)

Carbone, Peter (Singer Media Corporation)

Carlisle, Roy (Forthwrite Literary Agency)

Carlson, Heidi (Frieda Fishbein)

Carroll, Ashley (Dupree/Miller and Assoc.)

Carvainis, Maria (Maria Carvainis Agency)

Cashman, Ann (The Maureen Lasher Agency)

Cass, Dennis (Lazear Agency)

Casselman, Martha (Martha Casselman Literary Agent)

Castiglia, Julie (Julie Castiglia Literary Agency)

Cavanaugh, Elizabeth (Meredith Bernstein Literary Agency)

Cavanaugh, Teresa (Jean V. Naggar Literary Agency)

Ceriale, Jodi (Ackerman Literary Services)

Chalfant, David (TCA)

Chalk, Paula (The Portman Organization)

Chambers, Jacqulin (F.L.A.I.R.)

Chapman, Jennifer (Northwest Literary Services)

Cheney, Elyse (Connie Clausen Assoc.)

Choron, Sandra (March Tenth)

Chu, Lynn (Writers' Representatives)

Ciske, Francine (Francine Ciske Literary Agency)

Clark, Sara (Dramatic Publishing)

Clark, Sue (SJ Clark Literary Agency)

Clausen, Connie (Connie Clausen Assoc.)

Cleaver, Diane (Diane Cleaver)

Cleaver, Diane (Sanford J. Greenburger Assoc.)

Clough, Lynn (Rose Agency)

Coffey, Nancy (Jay Garon-Brooke Assoc.)

Cogil, Stephen (SLC Enterprises)

Cohen, Eugenia (Puddingstone Literary Agency)

Cohen, Hy (Hy Cohen Literary Agency)

Cohen, Jeffrey (The Marian Berzon Agency)

Cohen, Roberta (Richard Curtis Assoc.)

Cohen, Ruth (Ruth Cohen Literary Agency)

Cohen, Susan (Writers House)

Cohen, Susan Lee (Riverside Literary Agency)

Coker, Deborah Connor (Connor Literary Agency)

Colas, Maryanne C. (Cantrell-Colas, Literary Agency)

Colby, Pat (Colby: Literary Agency)

Colby, Richard (Colby: Literary Agency)

Collier, Dianna (Collier Assoc.)

Collier, Oscar (Collier Assoc.)

Collin, Frances (Frances Collin Literary Agent)

Collins, N. Rochelle (The Chandelyn Literary Agency)

Congdon, Don (Don Congdon Assoc.)

Congdon, Michael (Don Congdon Assoc.)

Connor, Marlene K. (Connor Literary Agency)

Conway, Christopher (The Gary-Paul Agency)

Coover, Doe (The Doe Coover Agency)

Coppage, Judy (The Coppage Company)

Corday, (Ms.) Evan (Gold/Marshak & Assoc.)

Cornfield, Robert (Robert Cornfield Literary Agency)

Courtney, Anna (H.N. Swanson)

Craver, William (Writers & Artists)

Crawford, Susan (Crawford Literary Agency)

Cronin, Mari (Ann Elmo Agency)

Crown, Bonnie R. (Bonnie R. Crown Int'l Literature and Arts Agency)

Curtis, Richard (Richard Curtis Assoc.)

Custer, Guy Robin (Lyceum Creative Properties)

D

Dahl, Kristine (Int'l Creative Management-NY)

Daley, Aleta M. (Aleta M. Daley/Maximilian Becker)

Dalton, Pat (Diamond Literary Agency)

Darhansoff, Liz (Darhansoff & Verrill Literary Agents)

Davey, Tricia (Int'l Creative Management-CA)

David, Elaine (Elaine Davie Literary Agency)

Davidson, Megan (Lee Shore Agency)

Dawson, G. Terry (The Abacus Group)

Day, Jennifer (Executive Excellence)

de la Haba, Lois (The Lois de la Haba Agency)

de Rogatis, Joseph (Int'l Publisher Assoc.)

de Spoelberch, Jacques (J de S Assoc.)

Deitz, Mason (New Writing Agency)

DeLeonardo, Ingrid (Otitis Media)

Diamant, Anita (Anita Diamant, The Writer's Workshop)

Gores, Martha R. (The Authors and Artists Resource Center/TARC Literary Agency)
Gotler, Joel (Renaissance: A Literary/Talent Agency)
Grace, Audrey (Panda Talent)
Grace, Steven (Panda Talent)
Graham, Earl (Graham Agency)
Graybill, Nina (Goldfarb & Graybill)
Greco, Gerardo (Peter Elek Assoc.)
Greenblatt, David (Int'l Creative Management-CA)
Greene, Randall Elisha (Randall Elisha Greene, Literary Agent)
Gregory, Maia (Maia Gregory Assoc.)
Grieger, Steve (The Marian Berzon Agency)
Griffith, Valerie (Levant & Wales, Literary Agency)
Grimes, Lew (Lew Grimes Literary Agency)
Gross, Shelley (The Write Therapist)
Grossman, Elizabeth (Sterling Lord Literistic)
Gumer, Bob (Int'l Creative Management-CA)
Gummery, Nancy (Montgomery-West Literary Agency)
Gurman, Susan (The Susan Gurman Agency)
Gusay, Charlotte (The Charlotte Gusay Literary Agency)

H
Haas, Paul (Int'l Creative Management-CA)
Haffey Jr., Leo P. (Client First-A/K/A Leo P. Haffey Agency)
Hagen, Peter (Writers & Artists)
Halsey, Dorris (Reece Halsey Agency)
Hamilburg, Mitchell J. (The Mitchell J. Hamilburg Agency)
Hamilton, Andrew (Andrew Hamilton's Literary Agency)
Hamlin, Faith (Sanford J. Greenburger Assoc.)
Han, Katherine (Singer Media Corporation)
Handaris, Marisa (M.H. Int'l Literary Agency)
Hanke, Mellie (M.H. Int'l Literary Agency)
Hanna, Frances (Acacia House Publishing Services)
Hanson, Inge (Acton, Leone, Hanson & Jaffe)

Harbison, Lawrence (Samuel French)
Harper, Laurie (Sebastian Literary Agency)
Harriet, Ph.D., Sydney Harriet (Agents Inc. for Medical and Mental Health Professionals)
Harrington, Bruce (Apollo Entertainment)
Harrington, Dale (Northeast Literary Agency)
Harris, Hannibal (Otitis Media)
Harris, Joy (The Robert Lantz-Joy Harris Literary Agency)
Harris, Sloan (Int'l Creative Management-NY)
Hartley, Glen (Writers' Representatives)
Hawkins, John (John Hawkins & Assoc.)
Hawkridge, Janis (Oceanic Press)
Hawkridge, Janis (Singer Media Corporation)
Hayes, Gil (Gil Hayes & Assoc.)
Hayes, Linda (Columbia Literary Assoc.)
Heacock, Jim (Heacock Literary Agency)
Heacock, Rosalie (Heacock Literary Agency)
Hegler, Gary L. (Gary L. Hegler Literary Agency)
Heifetz, Merrillee (Writers House)
Henderson, Rita Elizabeth (Henderson Literary Representation)
Hendin, David (David Hendin Literary)
Hengen, Jennifer (Sterling Lord Literistic)
Henshaw, Richard (Richard Curtis Assoc.)
Herman, Jeff (The Jeff Herman Agency)
Hill, Frederick (Frederick Hill Assoc.)
Hiltebrand, Cyril (Lucianne S. Goldberg Literary Agents)
Hilton, Alice (Alice Hilton Literary Agency)
Hochman, Gail (Brandt & Brandt Literary Agents)
Hochmann, John L. (John L. Hochmann Books)
Hodges, Carolyn, (Carolyn Hodges Agency)
Hoffman, Berenice (Berenice Hoffman Literary Agency)
Hoffman, Larry (Authors' Marketing Services)
Hofstein, Michael (James Warren Literary Agency)
Hogenson, Barbara (Barbara Hogenson Agency)

Holder, Jake (Susan Schulman, A Literary Agency)
Holman, Sheri (Aaron M. Priest Literary Agency)
Holtje, Bert (James Peter Assoc.)
Holub, William (Holub & Assoc.)
Hoskins, Christine (Ackerman Literary Services)
Hotchkiss, Jody (Sterling Lord Literistic)
Houghton, Henry O. (Gerard McCauley)
Howard, Rita (New Writing Agency)
Howle, Vanessa (Coast to Coast Talent and Literary)
Hubbs, Yvonne Trudeau (Yvonne Trudeau Hubbs Agency)
Hudson, Scott (Writers & Artists)
Hull, David Stewart (Hull House Literary Agency)

J
Jackson, Jennifer (Donald Maass Literary Agency)
Jacobs, Elaine (Westchester Literary Agency)
Jacobson, Emilie (Curtis Brown)
Jaffe, Mark (Acton, Leone, Hanson & Jaffe)
Jeffers, Medved (Westchester Literary Agency)
Jenks, Carolyn (Carolyn Jenks Agency)
Jennemann, Leslie (The Hanson Agency)
Jennings, Phillip (Marbea Agency)
Jensen, Kathryn (Columbia Literary Assoc.)
Jill, Jodi (Eden Literary Agency)
Johnson, B.N. (Literary Group West)
Johnson, Doris (Helen McGrath)
Johnson, Ray (Literary Group West)
Jordan, Lawrence (Lawrence Jordan Literary Agency)
Jordan, Lee F. (Chadd-Stevens Literary Agency)
Jorgensen, Matt (Wildstar Assoc.)
Josephson, Nancy (Int'l Creative Management-CA)

K
Kallen, Leslie (Leslie Kallen Agency)
Kaltman, Larry (Larry Kaltman Literary Agency)
Kamins, Ken (Int'l Creative Management-CA)

McGrath, Helen (Helen Mc-
Grath)

McKerrow, Chris (Curtis
Brown)

Mackey, Elizabeth (The Robbins Office)

McKinley, Virginia C. (Virginia
C. McKinley, Literary
Agency)

Madsen, Robert (Robert Madsen Agency)

Maerov, Michelle (The Beekman Literary Agency)

Maggiore, Chris (Tauro Brothers Management)

Mainhardt, Ricia (Ricia
Mainhardt Agency)

Maley, Margot (Waterside Productions)

Mann, Carol (Carol Mann
Agency)

Manrique, Lory (PMA Literary
and Film Management)

Manus, Janet Wilkens (Manus
& Assoc. Literary Agency)

Manus, Jillian (Manus &
Assoc. Literary Agency)

Marcil, Denise (The Denise
Marcil Literary Agency)

Marketta, Debbie (Peter Elek
Assoc.)

Markowitz, Barbara (Barbara
Markowitz Literary
Agency)

Markson, Elaine (Elaine Markson Literary Agency)

Marlow, Marilyn (Curtis
Brown)

Marmur, Mildred (Mildred
Marmur Assoc.)

Marshall, Evan (The Evan
Marshall Agency)

Martell, Alice Fried (The Martell Agency)

Martin, Dale (Mid-America
Literary Agency)

Matson, Peter (Sterling Lord
Literistic)

Matthias, Lee (Lee Allan
Agency)

Mattis, Lawrence (Circle of
Confusion)

Mauno, Chris (Authors' Literary Agency)

Maynard, Gary (The Gary-Paul
Agency)

Mazmamian, Joan (Helen Rees
Literary Agency)

Meade, Sam (New Writing
Agency)

Melnick, Jeff (Gold/Marshak &
Assoc.)

Menton, Kevin (Joan Follendore Literary Agency)

Merrilat, Jim (Samuel French)

Meth, David L. (Writers' Productions)

Meyers, Louise (Charlene Kay
Agency)

Meyst, Charles G. (The Gardner Agency)

Michael, Douglas (Frieda Fishbein)

Miller, Jan (Dupree/Miller and
Assoc.)

Miller, Kathryn (Sandra Dijkstra Literary Agency)

Miller, Mark James (Tiger
Moon Enterprises)

Miller, Peter (PMA Literary
and Film Management)

Miller, Roberta D. (Roberta D.
Miller Assoc.)

Miller, Stuart M. (Agency for
the Performing Arts)

Miller, T. Patrick (Tim) (The
Chandelyn Literary
Agency)

Milligan, Jay (Mark Sullivan
Assoc.)

Mohyde, Colleen (The Doe
Coover Agency)

Monaco, Richard (Wildstar
Assoc.)

Moody, Brian Keith (Brian
Keith Moody Managment)

Moore, Claudette (Morre Literary Agency)

Moore, Tracy (Leslie Kallen
Agency)

Moran, Maureen (Donald
MacCampbell)

Morel, Madeleine (2M Com-
munications)

Morgan, David H. (David H.
Morgan Literary Agency)

Morgan, Walter (The Agency)

Morgart, Erin Jones (M.H. Int'l
Literary Agency)

Morhaim, Howard (Howard
Morhaim Literary Agency)

Morris, Gary (Loretta Barrett
Books)

Morrison, Henry (Henry Morrison)

Mortimer, Lydia (Hull House
Literary Agency)

Moseley, Jane (Lucianne S.
Goldberg Literary Agents)

Moskowitz, Dara (The Gislason Agency)

Mulert, Carl (The Joyce Ketay
Agency)

Mullen, Allison (Howard Morhaim Literary Agency)

Mura, Dee (Dee Mura Enterprises)

N

Nadell, Bonnie (Frederick Hill
Assoc.)

Naggar, Jean V. (Jean V. Naggar Literary Agency)

Nathan, Ruth (Ruth Nathan)

Nazor, Karen (Karen Nazor
Literary Agency)

Negretti, Annmarie (Circle of
Confusion)

Nellis, Muriel (Literary and
Creative Artists Agency)

Nelson, Bonita (B.K. Nelson
Literary Agency & Lecture
Bureau)

Nevins, Allan (Renaissance: A
Literary/Talent Agency)

Newberg, Esther (Int'l Creative
Management-NY)

Newton, Pam (Samuel French)

Newton, Paula (Authors' Marketing Services)

Nolan, Betsy (The Betsy Nolan
Literary Agency)

Novak, Ed (Edward A. Novak
III Literary Representa-
tion)

Nugent, Ray (Nugent Literary)

O

Olesha, Andrea (Andrea
Olesha Agency)

Olsen, Kay (Dupree/Miller and
Assoc.)

Olsen, M.E. (Montgomery Literary Agency)

Olson, Neil (Donadio and Ashworth)

Orrmont, Arthur (Author Aid
Assoc.)

Osborne, Geoff (Lyceum Creative Properties)

Oscard, Fifi (Fifi Oscard
Agency)

Otte, Jane H. (The Otte Co.)

Otte, L. David (The Otte Co.)

P

Painter, John (Penmarin
Books)

Palmer, Dorothy (Dorothy
Palmer)

Panettiere, Vincent (Panettiere
& Co.)

Pantel, Elena (The Joseph S.
Ajlouny Agency)

Papadopoulos, Costas (M.H.
Int'l Literary Agency)

Parks, Richard (The Richard
Parks Agency)

Pasternak, Dan (Lenhoff/Rob-
inson Talent and Literary
Agency)

Paton, Kathi J. (Kathi J. Paton
Literary Agency)

Pell, William (William Pell
Agency)

Pelter, Rodney (Rodney
Pelter)

Pereira, Cheryl (Emerald Literary Agency)

Perkins, Esther R. (Perkins'
Literary Agency)

Perkins, Lori (L. Perkins
Assoc.)

Perkins, M. (Acton, Leone,
Hanson & Jaffe)

Pevovar, Ph.D. Eddy Howard
(The Eddy Howard Agency)

Assoc.)

Sher, Danis (Mary Jack Wald Assoc.)

Sherman, Ken (Ken Sherman & Assoc.)

Shortt, Michael L. (Talent Source)

Shull, Rodney (Redwood Empire)

Siegel, Bobbe (Bobbe Siegel Literary Agency)

Silverstein, Bob (Quicksilver Books-Literary Agents)

Simenauer, Jacqueline (Russell-Simenauer Literary Agency)

Simon, Claire (Aria Talent)

Simonsen, Harvey (Oceanic Press)

Singer, Evelyn (Evelyn Singer Literary Agency)

Singer, Katherine (Oceanic Press)

Singer, Kurt (Singer Media Corporation)

Skujins, Yuri (PMA Literary and Film Management)

Smith, Claire (Harold Ober Assoc.)

Smith, Dick (Authors' Literary Agency)

Smith, Patricia (Michael Snell Literary Agency)

Smith, Valerie (Valerie Smith, Literary Agent)

Snell, Michael (Michael Snell Literary Agency)

Solowiej, Constance (Flannery, White and Stone/The Writers Advocate)

Sommer, Elyse (Elyse Sommer)

Sorice, Camille (Camille Sorice Agency)

Sorrells, Jim (Redwood Empire)

South, Davida (Sandra Watt & Assoc.)

Spieler, Gretchen (Gretchen Spieler Literary Agency)

Spieler, Joe (F. Joseph Spieler)

Spitzer, Philip G. (Philip G. Spitzer Literary Agency)

Stanton, Henry (Stanton & Assoc. Int'l Literary Agency)

Stauffer, Nancy (Nancy Stauffer Assoc.)

Steele, Lyle (Lyle Steele & Co.)

Steinberg, Michael (Michael Steinberg Literary Agency)

Sterling, Cynthia (Lee Shore Agency)

Stern, Gloria (Gloria Stern Agency—CA)

Stern, Gloria (Gloria Stern Literary Agency—TX)

Stogas, Nikki (M.H. Int'l Literary Agency)

Stone, Ivy Fischer (Fifi Oscard

Agency)

Storey, Douglas (The Catalog Literary Agency)

Strickland, Judy (Write Designs Literary Agency)

Strickler, Tom (Int'l Creative Management-CA)

Strong, Marianne (Marianne Strong Literary Agency)

Sullivan, Mark (Mark Sullivan Assoc.)

Suter, Anne Elisabeth (Gotham Art & Literary Agency)

Swayne, Lisa (Adler & Robin Books)

T

Talbot, William (Samuel French)

Tallman, T. (The Literary Bridge)

Tantleff, Jack (The Tantleff Office)

Tauro, Robert (Tauro Brothers Management)

Taylor, Dawson (Dawson Taylor Literary Agency)

Taylor, Jess (Curtis Brown)

Teal, Patricia (Patricia Teal Literary Agency)

Thiesmeyer, Tara T. (Douroux & Co.)

Thomas, Geri (Elaine Markson Literary Agency)

Thornton, John (F. Joseph Spieler)

Tomins, Susan (Michael Amato Agency)

Toomey, Jeanne (Jeanne Toomey Assoc.)

Toomey, Jeanne (Marianne Strong Literary Agency)

Torrago, Ann (IMG-Julian Bach Literary Agency)

Travis, Susan (Margret McBride Literary Agency)

Trunzo, Geno (Kick Entertainment)

Trupin, James (Jet Literary Assoc.)

Tsai, Linda (Mark Sullivan Assoc.)

Turtle, Cindy (The Turtle Agency)

U

Urban, Amanda (Int'l Creative Management-NY)

Urstadt, Susan P. (Susan P. Urstadt Writers and Artists Agency)

V

Valenti, Miguel (The Gary-Paul Agency)

Vallely, Janis C. (Flaming Star Literary Enterprises)

Vallely, Joseph B. (Flaming

Star Literary Enterprises)

Van Der Beets, Richard (West Coast Literary Assoc.)

Van der Leun, Patricia (Van der Leun & Assoc.)

Van Nguyen, Kim (Robert Madsen Agency)

Vance, Lisa Erbach (Aaron M. Priest Literary Agency)

Vasapolli, Peter (JNG Entertainment)

Verrill, Charles (Darhansoff & Verrill Literary Agents)

Vesel, Beth (Sanford J. Greenburger Assoc.)

Vesneske, Jr., Ed (Nine Muses and Apollo)

Vidor, Michael (The Hardy Agency)

Vines, Jimmy (The Literary Group)

Vrooman, Eric (Lazear Agency)

W

Wade, Ginger (F. Joseph Spieler)

Wagner, Matt (Waterside Productions)

Wain, Erika (Erika Wain Agency)

Wainwright, Jessica (The Literary Group)

Wakefield, Karin (Epstein-Wykoff-La Manna & Assoc.)

Wald, Mary Jack (Mary Jack Wald Assoc.)

Wales, Elizabeth (Levant & Wales, Literary Agency)

Wallace, Lois (Wallace Literary Agency)

Wallace, Thomas C. (Wallace Literary Agency)

Wallengren, Henry (Samuel French)

Wallerstein, Gerry B. (The Gerry B. Wallerstein Agency)

Walters, Maureen (Curtis Brown)

Warden, David (Warden, White & Kane)

Ware, John (John A. Ware Literary Agency)

Warren, James (James Warren Literary Agency)

Wasserman, Harriet (Harriet Wasserman Literary Agency)

Watt, Sandra (Sandra Watt & Assoc.)

Webb, Irene (Int'l Creative Management-CA)

Wecksler, Sally (Wecksler-Incomco)

Weimann, Frank (The Literary Group)

Weiner, Cherry (Cherry Weiner Literary Agency)

Listing Index

More Great Books
to Help You Get Published!